NBC Handbook of Pronunciation

NBC
Handbook of
PRONUNCIATION

FOURTH EDITION, REVISED

Revised and updated by
Eugene Ehrlich and Raymond Hand, Jr.

Introduction by Edwin Newman

 HarperPerennial
A Division of HarperCollins*Publishers*

First HarperPerennial edition published 1991.

Designer: C. Linda Dingler

Library of Congress Cataloging-in-Publication Data

Ehrlich, Eugene H.
    NBC handbook of pronunciation.—4th ed. rev. / revised and updated by Eugene Ehrlich and Raymond Hand, Jr.
        p.   cm.
    ISBN 0-06-096574-6
    1. English language—Pronunciation—Handbooks, manuals, etc.   2. Television broadcasting—Handbooks, manuals, etc.   3. Americanisms—Handbooks, manuals, etc.   I. Hand, Raymond.   II. Title.   III. Title: N.B.C. handbook of pronunciation.
PE1137.E52   1991
421'.54—dc20   90-55604

91 92 93 94 95 AG/MB 10 9 8 7 6 5 4 3 2 1

Contents

Preface to the Fourth Edition

More than forty years have passed since initial publication of the *NBC Handbook of Pronunciation,* compiled originally by James F. Bender, who also prepared the second edition. Thomas Lee Crowell, Jr., prepared the third edition, which appeared after his untimely death more than twenty years ago.

All through these many years, the *NBC Handbook* has served as the standard reference work on pronunciation in General American speech. In preparing this new edition, the editors have striven to maintain the quality of the earlier editions and, in the tradition of the editors who preceded them, have once again expanded the scope of the volume. As a result, the total number of entries now exceeds 21,000 commonly used words and proper names as well as perennially difficult names from history and the arts.

One significant departure from the third edition is the modified pronunciation scheme employed. Because modern readers may lack thorough understanding of the International Phonetic Alphabet, the fourth edition offers a readily understandable respelling system to indicate pronunciation. In addition, the fourth edition supplies indications of secondary stresses as well as primary stresses within words. Needless to say, many proper names included in past editions are no longer in current use, so they have been removed to make room for names of greater value for today's speakers. Finally, pronunciations preferred in the past but no longer commonly heard have been replaced.

Despite the many changes made in the work of the previous editors, the *NBC Handbook* still adheres to the fundamental principle that guided the earlier efforts: to record "the pronunciations used by educated persons in the greater part of the United States, rather than to insist upon arbitrary standards of pronunciation unrelated to those commonly heard." True to this principle, the editors of the Fourth Edition supply American pronunciations of foreign names that have gained widespread use in our country. Where foreign names have not yet been Americanized, the pronunciations that are given approximate the pronunciations heard in the countries in which the names originate. Again in adherence to the practices of the earlier editors, the present editors supply a single pronunciation for each entry rather than a bewildering variety of acceptable pronunciations. This reflects the belief held by all the editors of the *NBC Handbook* that those who consult the book want assistance in pronunciation rather than justification for a particular pronunciation.

The editors wish to acknowledge the help of four United Nations interpreters in pronouncing certain proper names: Hossam Fakhr, Mikhail Farafonov, Judit Foldenyi, and Jacqueline Mitchell. For assistance in pronouncing African proper names, we acknowledge the assistance of the following consular officials: Janvière Baziyaka, Vlok Delport, Pholile Legwaila, Sam Nutakor, Mintsa Zue Ondo, Sulaiman Masamba Sisé, and Richard Waiguchu. We especially wish to thank Hayden Carruth for his assistance in making possible the computerization of this book.

Eugene Ehrlich
Raymond Hand, Jr.

September 1984
Pleasantville, New York

Introduction

This book might have been called *Pronunciation Can Be Fun*. That sort of title has often been used, of course. Almost everything but auto-da-fé has been described as fun for the sake of a book title. The fact is, nonetheless, that pronouncing words correctly can be fun. There is nothing snobbish or elitist about it, any more than there is in doing anything else correctly. Perhaps another word also applies. There is satisfaction to be had from correct pronunciation, particularly when one comes upon an unfamiliar word or name, sets out on uncharted seas, and makes it! It's an exhilarating feeling.

As a broadcaster for three and a half decades, I may have a special view of this. An obligation does rest on people in my position to speak correctly, not only in matters of grammar and usage, but in pronunciation, as well. So it is that NBC has a pronunciation handbook, honored in the breach rather than in the observance though it may sometimes be.

Not that I mean to suggest that my own record in such matters is spotless. It took a letter from an annoyed listener to turn me from saying AN tī to the preferred AN tee. Another listener objected to my saying depot with a short *e*. That, he wrote, was a pronunciation often used by Americans who had spent time in Europe. In the United States, he wrote, we say DEE poh.

I remember, too, doing the evening news one night and for some reason saying LEE mə (as in Lima, Peru, where at that time I had never been) rather than LĪ mə (as in Lima, Ohio, where I had also never been) when indeed it was Lima, Ohio, that was, thanks to a devastating storm, in the news.

Mentioning anti, depot, and Lima does not mean that my on-the-air transgressions were limited to these. Another I remember was not on the air and probably could not have been: the place involved, a town in Scotland named Kirkcudbright, is not in the news very often. One day, in the NBC London office, an employee showed it to me on a map as the place where she had been born.

"Ah, Kirkcudbright," said I, taking the name at face value.

From the hoots of laughter that followed eventually emerged kər KOO bree.

It was a lesson of sorts, like learning that Natchitoches, Louisiana, is pronounced, roughly, NAK ə TOSH; that Biloxi, Mississippi, is bə LUK see; that Schaghticoke, New York, which the alert may find eighteen miles north of Albany, is SKAT ə KOHK; that Houston Street in New York City might elude, or annoy, a Texan as HOW stən Street; and that it is not uncommon for people born in that Wisconsin city to make it, roughly, MWAW kee.

There is, of course, no harm in asking how something is pronounced, or in looking it up. That is why books of this kind exist. That is why *this* book, which is as authoritative as we could make it, exists. It is intended to be useful not only to people who make their living as I do. It is for anybody who speaks in public, habitually, occasionally, or once in a great while. We want it to help the person, for example, who finds that he or she must deliver a book review to a local literary club, or the mother or father with something to say at the PTA meeting. In fact, it is for anyone who engages in conversation, or even in interior monologues. There is no reason to be wrong just because you're talking to yourself.

This handbook is not highbrow, but it is designed to promote correctness. Does correctness matter in this day and age? As much as ever, it seems to me, for correctness does more than add precision, which is desirable in itself; it helps us to understand and get along with one another. Much in our time is not easy to comprehend in the best of circumstances; mispronunciation only makes things harder. Besides, where is the sense of accomplishment in saying, "dimunition" when the word is "diminution"? Or in writing "diffuse" when "defuse" is required? Correct pronunciation would rule that out. When a leading American newspaper tried to show that Congressional salaries were too low, it said that some members of the House and Senate lived in "gentile poverty," which is very different from what was intended, "genteel poverty." Knowing the pronunciation of "gentile" would have ruled that mistake out. Nor is an expatriate a former patriot. Again, correct pronunciation would have precluded that error. When mistakes are *not* made, I am not, as a television correspondent put it, "jubulant." Correct pronunciation would have spared us that.

But, someone may say, dictionaries also provide pronunciations. Why not use them? Indeed they do provide pronunciations. This book, however, uses a simpler guide to pronunciation than dictionaries do. Moreover, it specializes in pronunciation and focuses on words frequently mispronounced. A major part of the list of words pronounced—greatly expanded since the last edition—is the names and places that are in the news and likely to stay there, names and places that pop up on the air, in your newspaper, in conversation. These pronunciations are for anybody who thinks that being correct about these things is worthwhile.

This is the first new edition of the *NBC Handbook of Pronunciation* since 1964. That is much too long an interval. The earlier editions came out much more rapidly: between 1945 and 1964, there were three of them. Since 1964—though we are not quite in another world—a great deal has happened. With its influence on the language, its spawning of new words, the computer very nearly alone makes an updated edition necessary.

Moreover, twenty years, in educational terms, is—from the beginning of primary school through graduation from college—more than a generation. As for names in the news, some of them come and go quickly—who now remembers Joaquin Balaguer, Antonin Novotny, Phoumi Nosavan, Duncan Sandys, Anthony Celebrezze?—while others show remarkable durability. Andrei Gromyko has been prominent, even unavoidable, since 1943; Habib Bourguiba became newsworthy (from our point of view) in 1954; Joseph Mobutu, now Mobutu Sese Seko, in 1960; Sophia

Loren, in the early 1950s. But twenty years is a long time in news. The cast of characters has substantially changed. The *Handbook* should change as well.

Mistakes in pronunciation stay in the mind of a broadcaster. Clearly, they do not equally oppress people in other lines of work, nor should they. Yet, even for those others, or most of them, mispronunciation is unfortunate. For one thing, it embarrasses people who hear it and wonder whether to offer a correction. For another, it is hardly a recommendation, since it suggests not knowledge but rather its absence. I heard a well-known broadcaster (not on NBC) speak of Michelangelo's *Pietà* which he pronounced PEE ah TAH when, of course, Pieta (pronounced PEE ay TAH) is correct. Not the end of the world, granted. Still, how revealing it was, what evidence, in a single word, of pretended knowledge—and of pretension.

Failure to pronounce something correctly must, it seems to me, impair the confidence of others in the mispronouncer. At any rate, it does for those who know that there was a mispronunciation. It always shakes me when I hear someone who has to deal with nuclear energy, still more with nuclear weapons, say "nucular." This mistake has been with us since August 1945, when the nuclear age may be said to have begun (and, unfortunately, the nucular age, as well).

Nuclear/nucular is a special case. The word, correctly pronounced, somehow is too much for a fair part of the population, and education and experience seem to have nothing to do with it. President Eisenhower, for one, could not get it right. Neither could President Carter (though he, a former officer aboard nuclear-powered submarines, made it NOO kee ər). As this introduction was being written, Walter Mondale was busily engaged in his campaign for the 1984 Democratic presidential nomination and saying "nucular," which makes one wonder how other and lesser members of the Carter administration found it tactful to pronounce the word during Cabinet meetings. In any case, thirty-four years should be enough to establish that nuclear has only one *u*, and that an *e* has willfully worked its way into it.

In March 1983, Secretary of State George Shultz, testifying before a Congressional committee, referred to the Caribbean

island of Grenada as grə NAH də. Others in high positions, in-
cluding one of the stars of the "intelligence community" and
many broadcasters, were still making that mistake even after
Grenada was invaded months later. It was not reassuring.

In the same way, if a television anchorman (not on NBC) puts
the accent on the wrong syllable when naming an Italian politi-
cian who has been on the scene for at least thirty years, one
suspects that his knowledge of world affairs is thin, and his
interest even more so. This is also the case when a grandly titled
"diplomatic correspondent" (let's forget about the network affi-
liation at this point) goes wrong on the name of a Swedish prime
minister who has been prominent for fifteen years. If another
news anchor takes the accepted English pronunciation of the
Italian city Padua, a pronunciation associated with *The Taming
of the Shrew* and *Kiss Me, Kate,* and tries to make it sound
Italian when the Italian (Padova) is spelled and pronounced
differently, one can only be sad over the lack of knowledge and
curiosity thus displayed.

I admit that if an anchorman turns assembly into a four-
syllable word—ə SEM bə lee—I do not conclude that he is igno-
rant of what the United Nations General Assembly is and what
it does. Nevertheless, it is unpleasant to listen to him, and there
ought to be some pleasure in listening to the language being
spoken.

Am I arguing, then, that broadcasters ought to be careful
about pronunciation so that they can fool the public? In a way,
yes. Broadcasters do it in their own interest. But a broadcaster
also has an obligation. He—or she—is a teacher of sorts. The
obligation of newspeople is not only to give the news accu-
rately; it is also to say it correctly. Others are listening, so we
presume. They should not be misled.

Should you be ashamed of yourself if you mispronounce
something? Sometimes it can be so disconcerting that you can't
help being ashamed. But we are not suggesting sackcloth and
ashes, or seclusion. We do recommend making fewer mistakes.
This handbook can help. The rules are not ironclad. No punish-
ment, condign (in which the last syllable, taking paradigm as a
paradigm, comes out dine rather than din) or otherwise, will be
visited upon those who err or otherwise do not conform. My

late colleague, Frank McGee, on coming to the word "sit," made it what sounded to me more like "set." No doubt this was Frank's Oklahoma upbringing asserting itself. I said "sit," but hearing "set" never bothered me, and I suppose this must have been true in reverse with Frank. For my part, it was pleasant to hear the *i* turned into an *e*. It was a reminder of how large and varied a country this is, and how important, and often attractive, its regional differences are.

It is not the purpose of a pronunciation guidebook to blot out such differences. One's instinctive reaction on hearing the Cairo in Illinois pronounced KAIR oh is that it is ridiculous; likewise when Bogota, transported from Colombia to New Jersey, is stressed on the second syllable rather than the third. But that feeling wears off. Differences of that kind make life more interesting. Nor could they be blotted out, even if we foolishly wanted to do that. It is also true, of course, that these differences should not be artificially induced. They ought to be natural, not affected. A handbook gives the correct pronunciation, or to put it more exactly, the preferred pronunciation. But no handbook will make New Yorkers say New Orleans the way the locals do, and vice versa. One hears a good deal about the homogenization of America, but southern speech remains (in its numerous variations) southern, and New England speech New England, and so on. The pronunciation scheme employed in the text of the *NBC Handbook* takes regional distinctions into account, as you will see when you begin to use the book. The flavor given the vowel sounds in English varies from region to region, and the pronunciation scheme recognizes this inalienable right.

Not long ago, the telephone rang in my hotel room in Dallas. It was the limousine service entrusted by my hosts with the task of getting me to the airport next morning. The name of the company was Regal but the notable Texas accent at the other end of the line made it RAY gal, and it took me some time to catch on. Still, it was delightful, because the Raygal was authentic.

It is not easy to know why some departures from the norm, or the preferred, are more readily tolerated than others. Euphony may have something to do with it. "Raygal" for Regal I found charming. On the other hand, I went through half my life saying AHR inj (which I now consider not delightful) when I referred to a well-known citrus fruit. It wasn't until a Californian took pity on me (it was in Greece, as it happened, where we were working for the Marshall Plan) or perhaps couldn't stand it any longer, that I learned that the fruit was an OR inj. After all, I didn't say "ahr" for "or," did I? This incident had a side benefit: I stopped saying Flahrida.

Nor is it easy to know why some departures from the preferred are thought to drum up business. Apparently it grows out of the belief that a colloquial, down-to-earth pronunciation will endear the product or service advertised to the masses. This accounts for the popularity of "gonna" in television commercials, as in "You're gonna like us," which was used by an airline, and "Bet you're gonna want one," which was used by an automobile manufacturer. Honesty compels me to add that NBC, pronunciation handbook or no pronunciation handbook, used "You're gonna like it a lot" as an advertising slogan in 1975. It was NBC's program schedule that people were gonna like a lot.

A variation on this is the dropped *g* at the end of *ing* words, so that an airline proclaims that it is "doin' what we do best," the makers of a mint to freshen the breath turn nothing into nothin', and a shampoo, so its creators believe, will capture a larger share of the market if it is recommended for bouncin' and behavin' hair, bouncing and behaving evidently being thought to suggest a stuffy attitude.

It seems to me that if "gonna" is thought to lead people to throw themselves frenziedly onto the product advertised, then "omina" cannot be far behind. "Omina" is a pronunciation, heard most often in New York, of "I'm going to," or as some might put it, "I'm gonna." You will hear people say, "Omina catch the next train," or "Omina have dinner out tonight." This is not the same usage as "Omina hurry" (I'm in a hurry), and it is certainly not the same pronunciation as the "Ah" that some Southerners find in "I."

Foreign names pose a particular problem, which is the reason why names of persons and places are given so much attention in this book. I remember—another mistake comes back to me now—that as the newscaster on the "Today" show in 1961 I stumbled so often over the name of the president of the Philippines that I began to regret not having contributed to his opponent's campaign fund. And there was Nikita Khrushchev, now long gone and largely forgotten, who used to give news broadcasters a particularly difficult time. How far should we have gone in trying to approximate the Russian pronunciation, especially the opening Khr, which sounded something like a clearing of the throat? For that matter, will we ever know if Krushchev's successor pronounced his name Brezhnev or Brezhnyev? And was the last letter pronounced *v, ff,* or something in between?

One answer, not entirely satisfactory but still an answer, is that tradition also has a place in these affairs, tradition and usage. Consider the Fontainebleau Hotel in Miami Beach. The former Paris correspondent for NBC News arrives determined to give it the full treatment, French all the way, and not to yield to the benighted who say Fountainblue. But no taxi drivers use the French pronunciation. Why should they? None of their customers do. Nobody at the hotel calls it anything but Fountainblue. Neither do the correspondent's colleagues. "If they want to call it Fountainblue," he snarls, "why don't they spell it that way?" Eventually he subsides. Fontainebleau seems affected. Fountainblue it is.

In other words, some things are simply because they are, not necessarily because they should be. This book is, therefore, a guide not only to what is preferred; it is a guide also to what is feasible, what is done. Perfect consistency does not exist in these matters. Least of all does it exist in a tongue that draws on as many sources as English does, and has so great a variety of speakers.

What we are saying, valued reader, is that if you follow the guidelines laid down in this book, you will be all right; you'll get along; you won't make a fool of yourself. You may even sound comfortably, but not oppressively, learned.

Now a few words of explanation. There are approximately 21,000 words in this book. How were they chosen? They were chosen according to standards established in earlier editions of this book, which means that they are:

1. Words, especially proper names, most frequently used by broadcasters.
2. Common words often mispronounced.
3. Words from history and the arts that have proved to be difficult to pronounce over the years.

Some of these words have more than one acceptable pronunciation. In each case, we have chosen only one, not to be pedantic but for the sake of simplicity. As for the method of indicating what the pronunciation should be, simplicity, in the sense of ease of understanding, is again what we have tried for. Earlier editions of the *NBC Handbook of Pronunciation* contained two ways of noting pronunciation, the International Phonetic Alphabet and respelling. The IPA is clearer and more universally understood than the diacritical markings used to indicate pronunciation in dictionaries, but it was, nonetheless, largely ignored by those who used the *Handbook*. It was the respelling on which readers leaned.

For that reason, we are using only the respelling method in this edition. Doing so saves time, saves space, and rules out confusion. Broadly speaking, the pronunciation we recommend is that of General American Speech, that which is acceptable to, and used by, the great mass of competent Americans who use the language well—you, we trust, among them.

EDWIN NEWMAN
January 1984

Guide to Pronunciation

With few exceptions, the *NBC Handbook of Pronunciation* employs letters of the English alphabet to make the sounds required to pronounce the entries in the word list. The exceptions are the schwa (ə) and the barred *i*.

The schwa, which is used in the International Phonetic Alphabet, indicates the indistinct vowel sound in the first syllable of *ago* and in the second syllables of *taken, stencil, salmon,* and *circus.*

The barred *i* is used to indicate the vowel sound in such words as *die, high, my, quite,* the *y* in *analyze,* the *i* in *terrorize,* and other words containing the long i sound.

Stressed syllables are printed in capital letters. Boldfaced capital letters indicate a primary stress. Thus, *venture* is pronounced **VEN** chər. Smaller boldfaced capital letters indicate a secondary stress. Thus, *Pennsylvania* is pronounced **PEN** səl **VAY** nyə, and *aviary* is pronounced **AY** vee **ER** ee.

Pronunciations of foreign words and names given in the *NBC Handbook* are only approximations. It is difficult to represent all the sounds found in Russian, French, Spanish, and other languages whose words and names are in frequent use in the United States. In addition, most Americans who have not studied foreign languages find it almost impossible to make some of the sounds essential in pronouncing words and names from those languages. The Russian *r* and German *ch* are but two of many examples. In this handbook, therefore, no attempt is made to reproduce such sounds faithfully. Instead, the pronunciations given are those of educated American speakers with no special competence in foreign languages.

There is a single exception. A great number of French words that have made their way into the American vocabulary require a pronunciation of *n* that is quite unlike our own, and the special *n* sound is called to the reader's attention in pronunciations where it occurs. If readers of the *NBC Handbook* are unfamiliar with this sound, they are best advised to consult someone who speaks French. Through repeated demonstrations plus trial, error, and correction, this difficult sound can be mastered. The presence of a French final *n,* as it is called here, indicates that the vowel sound before the *n* is made with the nasal passages open, as in the French words *garçon* and *vin,* rather than with the nasal passages closed, as in the English words *fan* and *tone.*

A final note on foreign pronunciations: in certain Oriental languages no syllable is stressed more than any other. For this reason the reader will often encounter polysyllabic Oriental words and names pronounced without stress of any syllable. In pronunciations of other Oriental terms, stresses are shown. This is because the latter group comprises words and names that have been spoken by Americans for so long that stresses are normally used by most educated persons. Thus, *Tokyo* is pronounced **TOH** kee **OH**, while *Nakasone* is nah kah soh ne.

Abbreviations Used in This Book

a	adjective
adv	adverb
fem	feminine
masc	masculine
n	noun
pl	plural
sing	singular
US	United States
USSR	Union of Soviet Socialist Republics

Pronunciation Key

ə *as in* ago, taken, stencil, salmon, circus
a *as in* apt, sap
ah *as in* calm, father
ahr *as in* ark, dark, harm
air *as in* care, pair
aw *as in* all, saw
ay *as in* ail, say, tame
b *as in* bob, box, nab
ch *as in* chest, church, preach
d *as in* dud, dug, sad
e *as in* bet, egg
ee *as in* easy, me
eer *as in* beer, ear, tier
f *as in* far, fluff, thief
g *as in* gave, grog, hag
h *as in* half, he
i *as in* is, quick
ī *as in* my, tie
j *as in* jump, judge, magic
k *as in* cuff, kluck
l *as in* left, lull
m *as in* come, merry, mom
n *as in* now, nun, span
French final n *as in* garçon, vin
ng *as in* hang, sing, singer
o *as in* hot, on, sock

oh *as in* clone, coat, oat
oi *as in* boy, toil
oo *as in* soon, too
oor *as in* cure, poor, tour
or *as in* for, tore, warn
ow *as in* cow, ouch
p *as in* put, pop, wrap
r *as in* hear, rap, rare
s *as in* sap, spice, twice
sh *as in* hush, sheep, shush
t *as in* pat, tip, toot
th *as in* bath, fourth, thin
th *as in* bathe, father, this
u *as in* supper, up
ur *as in* first, her, spur
uu *as in* book, foot, full
v *as in* live, valve, very
w *as in* quiet, west
y *as in* yard, you
z *as in* hazy, please, zip
zh *as in* leisure, pleasure

A

Aachen	**AH** kən
Aalborg	**AWL** bawrg
Aalsmeer	**AHLS** mer
Aalten	**AHL** tən
aardvark	**AHRD** vahrk
Aaron	**AIR** ən
Abaco	**AB** ə koh
abacus	**AB** ə kəs
Abada, Abdelouahab	ah **BAH** dah, ahb doo lah **HAHB**
abalone	ab ə **LOH** nee
abattoir	**AB** ə twahr
Abaya, Hernando	ah **BĪ** ah, air **NAHN** doh
Abbas	ah **BAHS**
abbé	a **BAY**
Abdalla, Abdel-Rahman	ahb **DAH** lah, **AHB** del **RAH** mən
Abdallah	ahb **DAH** lah
Abdelghani, Mohamed Ben Ahmed	**AHB** dool **HAH** nee, moh **HAH** med bən **AH** med
Abdnor	**ABD** nər
abdomen	**AB** də mən
abdominal	ab **DOM** ə nəl
Abdulah, Frank Owen	ahb **DOO** lah
Abednego	ə **BED** nə goh
Abelard	**AB** ə lahrd
Abello	ah **BE** yaw
Abercrombie, Abercromby	**AB** ər krom bee
Aberdeen (Scotland)	ab ər **DEEN**
Aberdeen (US)	**AB** ər deen
aberrant	ə **BER** ənt
aberration	ab ə **RAY** shən
Aberystwyth	ab ə **RIST** with
abeyance	ə **BAY** əns
abhor	ab **HOR**
abhorrent	ab **HOR** ənt
Abidin, Tan Sri Zainal	ah bee **DIN**, tahn sree **ZĪ** nahl
Abidjan	ab i **JAHN**
Abigail	**AB** ə gayl
Abilene (Syria)	**AB** ə lee nee
Abilene (US)	**AB** ə leen

Abimelech	ə BIM ə LEK
Abinoam	ə BIN oh əm
Abitibi	AB ə TIB ee
abject	AB jekt
ablation	ab LAY shən
ablative absolute	AB lə tiv AB sə loot
ablution	ə BLOO shən
aboriginal	AB ə RIJ ə nəl
aborigine	AB ə RIJ ə nee
aborigines	AB ə RIJ ə neez
abort	ə BORT
abortive	ə BOR tiv
Abou ben Adhem	AH boo ben AH dem
Aboul-Nasr, Mahmoud	ah BOOL NAH zər, mah MOOD
Abourezk	AB ər ESK
abracadabra	AB rə kə DAB rə
Abraham	AY brə HAM
Abram	AY brəm
abrasion	ə BRAY zhən
abrogate	AB rə gayt
Abruzzi	ah BROOT tsee
abscess	AB ses
abscissa	ab SIS ə
abscond	ab SKOND
absent (a)	AB sənt
absent (v)	ab SENT
absentee	AB sən TEE
absinthe	AB sinth
absolute	AB sə LOOT
absolutely	AB sə LOOT lee
absolve	ab ZOLV
absorb	ab SORB
abstemious	ab STEE mee əs
abstract (a, n)	AB strakt
abstract (v)	ab STRAKT
abstruse	ab STROOS
absurd	ab SURD
absurdity	ab SUR də tee
Abu Dhabi	AH boo DAH bee
Abulhassan, Mohammad A.	ah BOOL HAH sahn, moh HAHM ahd
abuse (n)	ə BYOOS
abuse (v)	ə BYOOZ

ə ago, a at, ah calm, ahr dark, air care, aw saw, ay say, ch church
e bet, ee me, eer beer, hw what, i is, ī my, n French final n vin,

abusive	ə **BYOO** siv
Abydos (Egypt)	ə **BĪ** dos
abyss	ə **BIS**
Abyssinia	AB ə **SIN** ee ə
acacia	ə **KAY** shə
academe	AK ə **DEEM**
academician	ə KAD ə **MISH** ən
académie (French)	a ka day **MEE**
academy	ə **KAD** ə mee
Acadia	ə **KAY** dee ə
acanthus	ə **KAN** thəs
a cappella	AH kə **PEL** ə
a capriccio	AH kah **PREET** chòh
Acapulco	AK ə **PUUL** koh
accelerando	ak SEL ə **RAHN** doh
accelerate	ak **SEL** ə RAYT
accelerator	ak **SEL** ə RAY tər
accelerometer	ak SEL ə **ROM** ə tər
accent	**AK** sent
accept	ak **SEPT**
acceptable	ak **SEP** tə bəl
acceptance	ak **SEP** təns
access	**AK** ses
accessory	ak **SES** ə ree
acclamation	AK lə **MAY** shən
acclimate	**AK** lə MAYT
acclimation	AK lə **MAY** shən
acclimatization	ə KLĪ mə tə **ZAY** shən
acclimatize	ə **KLĪ** mə TĪz
accolade	**AK** ə LAYD
accompaniment	ə **KUM** pə nee mənt
accompanist	ə **KUM** pə nəst
accomplish	ə **KOM** plish
accouchement	ə **KOOSH** mahnt
accoucheur	a koo **SHUR**
accoutre	ə **KOO** tər
accoutrement	ə **KOO** tər mənt
Accra	ə **KRAH**
accredit	ə **KRED** ət
accrue	ə **KROO**
Aceldama	ə **SEL** də mə
acerb	ə **SURB**
acerbate	**AS** ər BAYT

---

o on, oh oat, oi boy, oo soon, oor poor, or for, ow cow, sh shush,
th thin, *th* this, u up, ur spur, uu book, *zh* pleasure

acerbity	ə SUR bi tee
acetanilide	AS ə TAN ə LĪD
acetate	AS ə TAYT
acetic	ə SEE tik
acetylene	ə SET i lən
Achaea	ə KEE ə
Achaean	ə KEE ən
Achaia	ə KAY ə
Achenbach	AH kən bahk
Acheron	AK ə RON
Achilles	ə KIL eez
Achitophel	ə KIT ə FEL
achromatic	AK rə MAT ik
acidity	ə SID ə tee
acidosis	AS ə DOH səs
acidulous	ə SIJ ə ləs
acinus	AS ə nəs
acme	AK mee
acne	AK nee
acolyte	AK ə LĪT
aconite	AK ə NĪT
acorn	AY korn
Acosta	ah KAW stah
acoustics	ə KOO stiks
acquaintance	ə KWAYN təns
acquiesce	AK wee ES
acquisitive	ə KWIZ ə tiv
acrid	AK rid
acrimonious	AK rə MOH nee əs
acrimony	AK rə MOH nee
acromegaly	AK rə MEG ə lee
acronym	AK rə nim
acropolis	ə KROP ə ləs
across	ə KRAWS
acrostic	ə KRAW stik
acrylic	ə KRIL ik
Actaeon	ak TEE ən
actual	AK choo əl
actually	AK choo ə lee
actuary	AK choo ER ee
acuity	ə KYOO ə tee
acumen	ə KYOO mən
acupuncture	AK yə PUNGK chər

ə ago, a at, ah calm, ahr dark, air care, aw saw, ay say, ch church
e bet, ee me, eer beer, hw what, i is, ī my, *n* French final n vin,

acute	ə KYOOT
Ada	AY də
adage	AD ij
adagio	ə DAH joh
Adah	AY də
adamant	AD ə mənt
adamantine	AD ə MAN tən
Adamec, Ladislav	AH də mets, LAH dyə slahv
Adan, Ahmed Mohamed	ah DAHN, AH med moh HAHM ed
adapt	ə DAPT
Addabbo	ə DAH boh
addenda	ə DEN də
addendum	ə DEN dəm
addict (n)	AD ikt
addict (v)	ə DIKT
Addis Ababa	AD əs AB ə bə
Addison	AD ə sən
additive	AD ə tiv
addle	AD əl
address (n)	AD res
address (v)	ə DRES
adduce	ə DOOS
Adelaide	AD ə LAYD
Adelphi	ə DEL fī
Aden	AH dən
Adenauer, Konrad	AD now ər, KON rad
adenoid	AD ə NOID
adenoma	AD ə NOH mə
adenosine	ə DEN ə SEEN
adept (a)	ə DEPT
adept (n)	AD ept
adequate	AD ə kwət
à deux	a DUU
adherence	ad HEER əns
adherent	ad HEER ənt
adhesion	ad HEE zhən
adhesive	ad HEE siv
ad hoc	ad HOK
ad hominem	ad HOM ə nəm
adiabatic	AYD ee ə BAT ik
adieu	ə DYUU
adieux	ə DYUUZ

o on, oh oat, oi boy, oo soon, oor poor, or for, ow cow, sh shush,
th thin, *th* this, u up, ur spur, uu book, *zh* pleasure

Adige	**AH** dee je
ad infinitum	ad **IN** fə **NĪ** təm
ad interim	ad **IN** tə rəm
adios	**AD** ee **OHS**
adipose	**AD** ə **POHS**
adiposity	**AD** ə **POS** ə tee
adjacent	ə **JAY** sənt
adjective	**AJ** ik tiv
adjoin	ə **JOIN**
adjourn	ə **JURN**
adjudicate	ə **JOO** di **KAYT**
adjunct	**AJ** ungkt
adjure	ə **JOOR**
adjutant	**AJ** ə tənt
ad libitum	ad **LIB** ə təm
admirable	**AD** mə rə bəl
admiralty, A-	**AD** mə rəl tee
admittance	ad **MIT** əns
admonish	ad **MON** ish
ad nauseam	ad **NAW** zee əm
adobe	ə **DOH** bee
adolescence	**AD** ə **LES** əns
Adolfo	ə **DOL** foh
Adonais	**AD** ə **NAY** is
Adonijah	**AD** ə **NĪ** jə
Adonis	ə **DON** əs
adorable	ə **DOR** ə bəl
adoration	**AD** ə **RAY** shən
Adoula, Cyrille	ah **DOO** lə, see **RIL**
adrenal	ə **DREEN** əl
adrenalin	ə **DREN** ə lən
adrenocorticotrophic	ə **DREE** noh **KOR** tə koh **TROH** fik
adrenocorticotropic	ə **DREE** noh **KOR** tə koh **TROP** ik
Adriatic	**AY** dree **AT** ik
adroit	ə **DROIT**
adulatory	**AJ** ə lə **TOHR** ee
Adullam	ə **DUL** əm
adult	ə **DULT**
Adum, Mohamet Ali	**AH** doom, moh **HAHM** et **AH** lee
adumbrate	a **DUM** brayt
ad valorem	ad və **LOHR** əm
advantage	ad **VAN** tij
advantageous	**AD** vən **TAY** jəs

ə ago, a at, ah calm, ahr dark, air care, aw saw, ay say, ch church
e bet, ee me, eer beer, hw what, i is, ī my, *n* French final n vin,

advent	**AD** vent
adversary	**AD** vər **SER** ee
adverse	ad **VURS**
advertise	**AD** vər **TĪZ**
advertisement	**AD** vər **TĪZ** mənt
advertiser	**AD** vər **TĪZ** ər
advice (n)	ad **VĪS**
advise (v)	ad **VĪZ**
advocacy	**AD** və kə see
advocate (n)	**AD** və kət
advocate (v)	**AD** və **KAYT**
Adzhubei, Alexei	ahd *zh*ə **BAY**, ah **LEK** see
Aegean	i **JEE** ən
aegis	**EE** jis
Aegisthus	i **JIS** thəs
Aeneas	i **NEE** əs
Aeneid	i **NEE** id
Aeolian	ee **OH** lee ən
Aeolus	**EE** ə ləs
aeon	**EE** ən
aerate	**AIR** ayt
aerial	**AIR** ee əl
aerie	**AIR** ee
aeronautics	**AIR** ə **NAW** tik
Aeschines	**ES** kə **NEEZ**
Aeschylus	**ES** kə ləs
Aesculapius	**ES** kyə **LAY** pee əs
Aesop	**EE** səp
aesthete	**ES** theet
aesthetic	es **THET** ik
aestivate	**ES** tə **VAYT**
Aetna	**ET** nə
affair	ə **FAIR**
affaire	a **FAIR**
afferent	**AF** ər ənt
affirm	ə **FURM**
affirmation	**AF** ər **MAY** shən
affix (n)	**AF** iks
affix (v)	ə **FIKS**
affluence	**AF** loo əns
affluent	**AF** loo ənt
affront	ə **FRUNT**
afghan, A-	**AF** gan

o on, oh oat, oi boy, oo soon, oor poor, or for, ow cow, sh shush,
th thin, *th* this, u up, ur spur, uu book, *zh* pleasure

Afghanistan	af GAN i STAN
aficionado	ə FISH yə NAH doh
a fortiori	ay FOHR shee OHR ee
Africa	AF ri kə
Afrikaans	AF ri KAHNS
Afrikaner	AF ri KAH nər
Agag	AY gag
again	ə GEN
against	ə GENST
Aga Khan	ah gə KAHN
Agamemnon	AG ə MEM non
agape (love)	ah GAH pay
agape (wide open)	ə GAYP
agar, A-	AH gər
Agassiz	AG ə see
agate	AG ət
agave	ə GAH vee
Agca, Mehmet Ali	AHR jah, ME met ah LEE (AHR *R* barely pronounced)
Agee	AY jee
agenda	ə JEN də
ageratum	AJ ə RAY təm
aggrandize	ə GRAN dīz
aggrandizement	ə GRAN dəz mənt
aggravate	AG rə VAYT
aggregate (a, n)	AG rə gət
aggregate (v)	AG rə GAYT
aggressor	ə GRES ər
aghast	ə GAST
agile	AJ əl
agility	ə JIL ə tee
Agincourt	AJ ən KORT
agitato	AJ ə TAH toh
Agnelli	ahn YEL ee
Agnew, Spiro	AG nyoo, SPIR oh
Agnon, Samuel	AG non
agnostic	ag NOS tik
Agnus Dei	AG nəs DEE ī
Ago, Roberto	AH goh, roh BAIR toh
agoraphobia	AG ə rə FOH bee ə
Agrado	ah GRAH doh
agrarian	ə GRAIR ee ən
agronomist	ə GRON ə məst

ə ago, a at, ah calm, ahr dark, air care, aw saw, ay say, ch church
e bet, ee me, eer beer, hw what, i is, ī my, *n* French final n vin,

Agronsky	ə GRON skee
Agt, Andreas van	AHKT, ahn DRAY ahs vahn
ague	AY gyoo
Aguecheek	AY gyoo cheek
Aguilar	AH gi LAHR
Aguinaldo	AH gi NAHL doh
Aguirre de Carcer,	ah GEE ray day KAHR ser, NOO
Nuño	nyoh
Ahab	AY hab
Ahasuerus	ə HAZ yoo EER əs
Ahaz	AY haz
Ahithophel	ə HITH ə FEL
Ahmed	AH med
aide	ayd
aide-de-camp	AYD də KAMP
aide-mémoire	AYD mem WAHR
aiguillette	AY ġwi LET
Aiken	AY kən
aileron	AY lə RON
ailurophobia	ī LUUR ə FOH bee ə
Aimée, Anouk	e MAY, ah NUUK
Ainsworth	AYNZ wurth
aisle	īl
Aisne	ayn
Aix-la-Chapelle	AYKS lah shah PEL
Ajaccio	ah YAHT chaw
Ajax	AY jaks
Akaka, Daniel K.	ah KAH kah
Akeley	AYK lee
Akihito	ah kee hee toh
akimbo	ə KIM boh
akin	ə KIN
Akuete, Ebenezer	AH koo AY tay, EB ə NEE zər
akvavit	AHK vah VEET
Akyab	ak YAB
Alabama	AL ə BAM ə
alabaster	AL ə BAS tər
à la carte	AL ə KAHRT
alacrity	ə LAK rə tee
Aladdin	ə LAD ən
Al-Ali, Salah Omar	əl ah LEE, sah LAH oh MAHR
Al-Ameri, Abdelkader	ahl ah MAH ree, AHB dool KAH dər
Braik	bə RĪ eek

---

o on, oh oat, oi boy, oo soon, oor poor, or for, ow cow, sh shush,
th thin, *th* this, u up, ur spur, uu book, *zh* pleasure

Alamo	AL ə MOH
à la mode	AL ə MOHD
Aland	AH lənd
Alaric	AL ər ik
alas	ə LAS
Al-Ashtal, Abdalla Saleh	ahl AHSH al, AHB də lah SAH lay
Alaska	ə LAS kə
al-Assad, Hafez	əl AS sad, HAH fəth
Alataz, Alex	ahl ah tahz, ah leks
albacore	AL bə KOHR
Alban	AWL bən
Albania	al BAY nee ə
Albany	AWL bə nee
albatross	AL bə TRAWS
albedo	al BEE doh
Albee	AWL bee
albeit	awl BEE it
Albemarle	AL bə MAHRL
Albéniz, Isaac	ahl VE neeth, EE sah AHK
Alberghetti	al bər GE tee
Albergue, Pablo Mauricio	ahl BAIR gay, PAHB loh mow REES ee oh
Alberich	AHL bər ik
Alberoni	AHL be RAW nee
Albert (French)	al BAIR
Alberta	al BUR tə
Alberti	ahl BER tee
Albertina	AL bər TEE nə
Albertinelli	AHL bair ti NEL ee
Albigenses	AL bə JEN seez
Albigensian	AL bə JEN see ən
albinism	AL bə niz əm
albino	al BĪ noh
Albion	AL bee ən
Albornoz, Miguel	ahl bor NAWS, mee GAYL
Albrecht	AHL brekt
Albricht	AWL brikt
album	AL bəm
albumen	al BYOO mən
Albuquerque	AL bə KUR kee
alcalde	al KAL dee
alcántara, A-	ahl KAHN tah rah

ə ago, a at, ah calm, ahr dark, air care, aw saw, ay say, ch church
e bet, ee me, eer beer, hw what, i is, ī my, n French final n vin,

Alcatraz	AL kə TRAZ
alcazar, A-	AL kə ZAHR
Alceste	al SEST
Alcestis	al SES təs
alchemist	AL kə məst
alchemy	AL kə mee
Alcibiades	AL sə BĪ ə DEEZ
Alcinoüs	al SIN oh əs
Alcmene	alk MEE nee
Alcoa	al KOH ə
Alcott	AWL kət
alcove	AL kohv
Aldebaran	al DEB ər ən
aldehyde	AL də HĪD
al dente	al DEN tay
alder	AWL dər
Alderney	AWL dər nee
Aldershot	AWL dər SHOT
Aldine	AWL dīn
Aldrich	AWL drich
aldrin, A-	AWL drən
Aleichem, Sholem	ə LAY kəm, SHUU ləm
Aleixandre, Vicente	ah layk SAHN dray, bee SEN tay
Alemán, Miguel	AH le MAHN, mee GEL
aleph	AH ləf
alert	ə LURT
Al-Eryani, Mohamad	ahl ee YAH nee, moh HAHM ahd
Aleut	ə LOOT
Aleutian	ə LOO shən
Alexander	AL ig ZAN dər
Alexandria	AL ig ZAN dree ə
Alexis	ə LEK sis
Alfaro	ahl FAH roh
Al Fatah	ahl fah TAH
Alfonsin, Raúl	AHL fawn SEEN, rah OOL
Alfonso	al FON soh
Alfreda	al FREE də
Alfredo	ahl FRAY doh
alfresco	al FRES koh
Alfvén, Hannes	ahl VEE ən, HAH nes
alga	AL gə
algae	AL jee
algebraic	AL jə BRAY ik

o on, oh oat, oi boy, oo soon, oor poor, or for, ow cow, sh shush,
th thin, *th* this, u up, ur spur, uu book, *zh* pleasure

Alger	**AL** jər
Algeria	al **JEER** ee ə
Algerian	al **JEER** ee ən
Algernon	**AL** jər nən
Algol	**AL** gol
Algonquin	al **GONG** kwən
algorithm	**AL** gə *RITH* əm
Algren	**AWL** grən
Alhambra	al **HAM** brə
al-Hassani, Ali Nasser Mohammed	ahl **HAH** sah nee, **AH** lee **NAH** zər moh **HAHM** ed
Alhegelan, Faisal	ahl **HAHG** layn, **FĪ** sahl
Ali	**AH** lee
Ali, Muhammad	ah **LEE**, mə **HAHM** əd
alias	**AY** lee əs
aliases	**AY** lee əs əz
Ali Baba	**AH** lee **BAH** bah
alibi	**AL** ə **BĪ**
alidade	**AL** ə **DAYD**
alien	**AYL** yən
alienate	**AYL** yə **NAYT**
alienation	**AYL** yə **NAY** shən
Alighieri	**AH** lee **GYAY** ree
alignment	ə **LĪN** mənt
alimentary	**AL** ə **MEN** tə ree
alimony	**AL** ə **MOH** nee
Alison	**AL** ə sən
Alitalia	ah li **TAHL** yə
alkali	**AL** kə **LĪ**
alkaline	**AL** kə **LĪN**
alkaloid	**AL** kə **LOID**
al-Kasim, Marwan	ahl **KAH** sem, mahr **WAHN**
al-Kassem, Abdel-Raouf	el **KAH** sim, **AHB** duul rah **OOF**
al Khalifa, Emir Isa ibn Salman	ahl kah **LEE** fah, ay **MEER** ee **SAH** ee **BEN SAHL** mən
al Khalifa, Khalifa ibn Salman	ahl kah **LEE** fah, kah **LEE** fah ee **BEN SAHL** mən
alkyd	**AL** kəd
alla breve	**AH** lə **BREV** ay
Allagany, Gaafar	ahl **LAH** jah nee, **ZHAH** fər
Allah	**AL** ə
allargando	**AH** lahr **GAHN** doh

ə ago, a at, ah calm, ahr dark, air care, aw saw, ay say, ch church
e bet, ee me, eer beer, hw what, i is, ī my, *n* French final n vin,

allege	ə LEJ
alleged	ə LEJD
allegedly	ə LEJ əd lee
Alleghany	AL ə GAY nee
Allegheny	AL ə GAY nee
allegiance	ə LEE jəns
allegory	AL ə GOR ee
allegretto	AL ə GRET oh
allegro	ə LEG roh
allele	ə LEEL
alleluia	AL ə LOO yə
allemande	AL ə MAND
Allende Gossens	ah YEN de GAW sens
allergic	ə LUR jik
allergy	AL ər jee
Allers, Franz	AH lərs, FRAHNZ
alleviate	ə LEE vee AYT
alliance	ə LĪ əns
allied (a)	AL īd
allied (v)	ə LĪD
allies (pl of *ally*)	AL īz
alliteration	ə LIT ə RAY shən
alliterative	ə LIT ə rə tiv
allium	AL ee əm
allocate	AL ə KAYT
allomorph	AL ə MORF
allopathic	AL ə PATH ik
allopathy	ə LOP ə thee
allophone	AL ə FOHN
alloy (n)	AL oi
alloy (v)	ə LOI
allspice	AWL spīs
allude	ə LOOD
allure	ə LOOR
allusion	ə LOO zhən
allusive	ə LOO siv
alluvial	ə LOO vee əl
ally (n)	AL ī
ally (v)	ə LĪ
Allyev, Geidar	ah LEE yef, GĪ dahr
Allyson	A li sən
al-Maktum, Rashid ibn Said	ahl mahk TOOM, rah SHEED ee BEN sah EED

---

o on, oh oat, oi boy, oo soon, oor poor, or for, ow cow, sh shush,
th thin, *th* this, u up, ur spur, uu book, *zh* pleasure

alma mater	AL mə MAH tər
almanac	AWL mə NAK
almandine	AL mən DEEN
Alma-Tadema	AL mə TAD ə mə
Almaviva	ahl mah VEE vah
Al-Mokarrab, Ahmed	ahl MOH kə rahb, AH med
almond	AH mənd
almoner	AL mə nər
alms	ahmz
al-Nahayan, Zaid ibn Sultan	ahl nah HĪ yən, SAH eed IB ən sool TAHN
aloe	AL oh
aloes	AL ohz
aloha	ə LOH hah
Alonzo	ə LON zoh
aloof	ə LOOF
alopecia	AL ə PEE shee ə
Aloysius	AL oh ISH əs
alpaca	al PAK ə
alpenhorn	AL pən HORN
alpenstock	AL pən STOK
alpha	AL fə
alphanumeric	AL fə noo MER ik
alpine, A-	AL pīn
Alpinist	AL pə nist
Alpujarras, Alpuxaras	AL puu HAHR əs
Al-Qasimi, Fahim Sultan	ahl HAH sheem, FAH heem sool TAHN
Al-Sabah, Saud Nasir	ahl SHAH bah, sah OOD nah SHEER
Al-Sabbagh, Hussein	ahl SHAH bah, hoo SHAYN
Alsace	al SAS
alsatian	al SAY shən
Altaic	al TAY ik
Altair	al TAH ər
Altamira	AL tə MEER ə
altar	AWL tər
altazimuth	al TAZ ə məth
alter	AWL tər
altercation	AWL tər KAY shən
alter ego	AWL tər EE goh
alternate (a, n)	AWL tər nət
alternate (v)	AWL tər NAYT
alternately	AWL tər nət lee

ə ago, a at, ah calm, ahr dark, air care, aw saw, ay say, ch church
e bet, ee me, eer beer, hw what, i is, ī my, n French final n vin,

alternation	AWL tər NAY shən
alternative	awl TUR nə tiv
althaea	al THEE ə
al-Thani, Khalifa ibn Hamad	ahl TAH nee, kah LEE fə IB ən HAH məd
Althing	AHL thing
altimeter	al TIM ə tər
altitude	AL tə TOOD
alto	AL toh
Alto Adige	AHL toh AH dee je
Altrocchi	ahl TRAW ki
altruism	AL troo IZ əm
alum	AL əm
aluminium (British)	AL yə MIN ee əm
aluminum	ə LOO mə nəm
alumna (fem sing)	ə LUM nə
alumnae (fem pl)	ə LUM nee
alumni (masc pl)	ə LUM nī
alumnus (masc sing)	ə LUM nəs
Alvarado	AHL vah RAH doh
alveolar	al VEE ə lər
al-Wazzan, Shafiq	ahl wah ZEN, shah FEEK
alyssum	ə LIS əm
Alzheimer's disease	AHLTS HĪ mərz
amàbile	ah MAH bee le
Amadeus	AH mah DAY uus
Amadis	AM ə dis
Amado	ah MAH doh
Amalek	AM ə LEK
Amalekite	AM ə LEK īt
Amalfi	ə MAHL fee
amalgam	ə MAL gəm
amalgamate (v)	ə MAL gə MAYT
Amalthea	AM əl THEE ə
amandine	AH mən DEEN
amanuensis	ə MAN yoo EN səs
Amany, René	ah MAH nee, rə NAY
amaranth	AM ə RANTH
amaranthine	AM ə RAN thən
Amarillo	AM ə RIL oh
amaryllis, A-	AM ə RIL əs
amass	ə MAS
amateur	AM ə chuur

---

o on, oh oat, oi boy, oo soon, oor poor, or for, ow cow, sh shush,
th thin, *th* this, u up, ur spur, uu book, *zh* pleasure

amateurish	AM ə CHUUR ish
Amati	ah MAH tee
Amato	ə MAH toh
amatory	AM ə TOR ee
Amaya	ə MĪ ə
Amaye, Shiro	ah mah ye, shee roh
amazon, A-	AM ə ZON
ambassador	am BAS ə dər
ambassadorial	am BAS ə DOR ee əl
ambergris	AM bər GRIS
ambidexterity	AM bi dek STER i tee
ambidextrous	AM bi DEK strəs
ambience	AM bee əns
ambient	AM bee ənt
ambiguity	AM bə GYOO ə tee
ambiguous	am BIG yoo əs
ambivalence	am BIV ə ləns
amblyopia	AM blee OH pee ə
Amboina	am BOI nə
Amboise	ahm BWAHZ
Ambon	AHM bawn
Ambrose	AM brohz
ambrosia	am BROH zhə
ambulance	AM byə ləns
ambulatory	AM byə lə TOR ee
ambuscade	AM bə SKAYD
ambush	AM buush
Amega, Atsu-Koffi	ah MAY gə, ah CHOO koh FEE
Amelia	ə MEEL yə
ameliorate	ə MEEL yə RAYT
ameliorative	ə MEEL yə RAY tiv
amen (singing)	AH MEN
amen (speaking)	AY MEN
amenable	ə MEE nə bəl
amend	ə MEND
amendment	ə MEND mənt
Amenhotep	AH mən HOH tep
amenity	ə MEN ə tee
amenorrhea	ay MEN ə REE ə
ament (flower spike)	AM ənt
ament (mentally deficient person)	AY ment
Americana	ə MER ə KAN ə

ə ago, a at, ah calm, ahr dark, air care, aw saw, ay say, ch church
e bet, ee me, eer beer, hw what, i is, ī my, n French final n vin,

Americanism	ə MER ə kə NIZ əm
Americanize	ə MER ə kə NĪZ
Amerind	AM ə rind
Amerindian	AM ə RIN dee ən
amethyst	AM ə thəst
Amharic	am HAR ik
Amherst	AM ərst
amiability	AY mee ə BIL ə tee
amiable	AY mee ə bəl
amicability	AM i kə BIL ə tee
amicable	AM i kə bəl
amicus curiae	ə MEE kəs KYUUR ee ī
Amiens	AM ee ənz
amiga	ə MEE gə
amigo	ə MEE goh
Amin, Idi	ah MEEN, EE dee
amine	ə MEEN
amino	ə MEE noh
amir	ə MEER
Amish	AH mish
amiss	ə MIS
amity, A-	AM ə tee
Amman	AH mahn
Ammon	AM ən
ammonia	ə MOHN yə
ammoniac	ə MOH nee AK
ammonium	ə MOH nee əm
amnesia	am NEE *zh*ə
amnesty	AM nə stee
amniocentesis	AM nee oh sen TEE səs
amnion	AM nee on
amniotic	AM nee OT ik
amoeba	ə MEE bə
amok	ə MUK
amoral	ay MOR əl
Amorite	AM ə RĪT
amoroso	AH mə ROH soh
amorous	AM ə rəs
amorphous	ə MOR fəs
amortization	AM ər tə ZAY shən
amortize	AM ər TĪZ
Amory	AY mə ree
Amos	AY məs

---

o on, oh oat, oi boy, oo soon, oor poor, or for, ow cow, sh shush,
th thin, *th* this, u up, ur spur, uu book, *zh* pleasure

amour	ə MOOR
Amoy	ah MOI
amperage	AM pə rij
ampere	AM peer
ampersand	AM pər SAND
amphetamine	am FET ə MEEN
amphibian	am FIB ee ən
amphibious	am FIB ee əs
Amphion	am FĪ ən
amphitheater	AM fə THEE ə tər
Amphitrite	AM fə TRĪ tee
Amphitryon	am FĪ tree ən
amphora	AM fə rə
amplifier	AM plə FĪ ər
amplify	AM plə FĪ
amplitude	AM plə TOOD
ampoule	AM pool
ampule	AM pyool
Amritsar	əm RIT sər
Amsterdam	AM stər DAM
Amtorg	AM tawrg
amuck	ə MUK
amulet	AM yə lət
Amundsen	AH mənd sən
Amur	ah MUUR
amusement	ə MYOOZ mənt
Amy	AY mee
Amytal	AM ə TAWL
Anabaptism	AN ə BAP tiz əm
Anabaptist	AN ə BAP təst
anabasis	ə NAB ə səs
anachronism	ə NAK rə NIZ əm
anaconda, A-	AN ə KON də
Anacreon	ə NAK ree ən
anaerobic	AN ə ROH bik
anagram	AN ə GRAM
anal	AY nəl
analgesia	AN əl JEE zee ə
analgesic	AN əl JEE zik
analog	AN ə LAWG
analogous	ə NAL ə gəs
analogy	ə NAL ə jee
analyses	ə NAL ə SEEZ

ə ago, a at, ah calm, ahr dark, air care, aw saw, ay say, ch church
e bet, ee me, eer beer, hw what, i is, ī my, *n* French final n vin,

analysis	ə NAL ə səs
analyst	AN ə ləst
analytic	AN ə LIT ik
analyze	AN ə LĪZ
Ananias	AN ə NĪ əs
anapest	AN ə PEST
anarchism	AN ər KIZ əm
anarchist	AN ər kəst
anarchy	AN ər kee
Anasazi	AH nə SAH zee
Anastasia	AN ə STAY zhə
Anastasius	AN ə STAY shəs
anastigmatic	AN as tig MAT ik
anathema	ə NATH ə mə
Anatole	AN ə TOHL
Anatolia	AN ə TOH lee ə
anatomical	AN ə TOM i kəl
anatomist	ə NAT ə məst
anatomy	ə NAT ə mee
Anaxagoras	AN ak SAG ər əs
ancestor	AN ses tər
ancestral	an SES trəl
ancestry	AN ses tree
anchorite	ANG kə RĪT
anchovy	AN choh vee
ancien régime	ahn SYAN ray ZHEEM (SYAN French final *n*)
ancillary	AN sə LER ee
Ancona	ahn KAW nah
Andalusia	AN də LOO zhə
Andaman	AN də mən
andante	ahn DAHN tay
andantino	AHN dahn TEE noh
Andean	an DEE ən
Andes	AN deez
andiron	AND ī ərn
Andorra	an DOR ə
Andover	AN DOH vər
Andrade	ahn DRAH day
Andrassy	ahn DRAHSH ee
André	AHN dray
Andrea del Sarto	ahn DRAY ah del SAHR toh
Andreev	ahn DRE yəf

o on, oh oat, oi boy, oo soon, oor poor, or for, ow cow, sh shush,
th thin, *th* this, u up, ur spur, uu book, *zh* pleasure

Andreotti, Giulio	AHN dre AW tee, JOOL yoh
Andreyev	ahn DRE yəf
Andrić, Ivo	AHN drich, EE vaw
Androcles	AN drə KLEEZ
Androclus	AN drə kləs
androgen	AN drə jən
androgynous	an DROJ ə nəs
android	AN droid
Andromache	an DROM ə KEE
Andromeda	an DROM ə də
Andronicus	AN drə NĪ kəs
Andronicus	an DRON ik əs
(Shakespeare)	
Andropov, Yuri	ahn DRAW pəf, YOO ri
Andvari, Andwari	AHN dwah ree
anecdotal	AN ik DOH təl
anecdote	AN ik DOHT
anecdotist	AN ik DOH təst
anemia	ə NEE mee ə
anemic	ə NEE mik
anemometer	AN ə MOM ə tər
anemone	ə NEM ə NEE
anent	ə NENT
anesthesia	AN əs THEE zhə
anesthesiologist	AN əs THEE zee OL ə jist
anesthesiology	AN əs THEE zee OL ə jee
anesthetic	AN əs THET ik
anesthetist	ə NES thə təst
aneurysm	AN yə RIZ əm
anew	ə NOO
angel	AYN jəl
Angel (Spanish)	AHN hel
Angela	AN jə lə
Angelica	an JEL i kə
Angelico	ahn JAI li koh
Angell	AYN jəl
Angelus, a-	AN jə ləs
Angevin	AN jə vən
angina pectoris	an JĪ nə PEK tə rəs
angiosperm	AN jee ə SPURM
Angkor Wat	ANG kohr WAHT
angle	ANG gəl
angler	ANG glər

Anglican	ANG gli kən
Anglicanism	ANG gli kə NIZ əm
Anglophile	ANG glə FĪL
Anglophobe	ANG glə FOHB
Anglo-Saxon	ANG gloh SAK sən
Angola	ang GOH lə
Angora	ang GOR ə
angostura	ANG gə STOOR ə
angry	ANG gree
angst	ahngst
angstrom, A-	ANG strəm
Anguilla	ang GWIL ə
anguish	ANG gwish
angular	ANG gyə lər
Angus	ANG gəs
Anhalt	AHN hahlt
Anhui	ahn hwee
Anhwei	ahn hway
aniline	AN ə lən
animadversion	AN ə mad VUR zhən
animal	AN ə məl
animalcule	AN ə MAL kyool
animate (a)	AN ə mət
animate (v)	AN ə MAYT
animism	AN ə MIZ əm
animosity	AN ə MOS ə tee
animus	AN ə məs
anion	AN Ī ən
anionic	AN ī ON ik
anise	AN əs
aniseikonia	AN ī sī KOH nee ə
anisette	AN ə SET
anisotropic	an Ī sə TROP ik
Anita	ə NEE tə
Anjou	AHN joo
Ankara	ANG kə rə
ankh	angk
ankle	ANG kəl
Anna	AN ə
annalist	AN ə ləst
annals	AN əlz
Annapolis	ə NAP ə ləs
anneal	ə NEEL

---

o on, oh oat, oi boy, oo soon, oor poor, or for, ow cow, sh shush,
th thin, *th* this, u up, ur spur, uu book, *zh* pleasure

annelid	AN ə lid
annex (n)	AN eks
annex (v)	ə NEKS
annnexation	AN ek SAY shən
annihilate	ə NĪ ə LAYT
annihilation	ə NĪ ə LAY shən
anniversary	AN ə VUR sə ree
anno Domini	AN oh DOM ə NEE
annotate	AN oh TAYT
annotation	AN oh TAY shən
annotator	AN oh TAY tər
annual	AN yoo əl
annuity	ə NOO ə tee
annul	ə NUL
annular	AN yə lər
annunciation	ə NUN see AY shən
Annunzio, Gabriele d'	dahn NOON tsyaw, GAH bree E le
annus mirabilis	AH nəs mi RAH bə ləs
anode	AN ohd
anodize	AN ə DĪZ
anodyne	AN ə DĪN
anoint	ə NOINT
anomalous	ə NOM ə ləs
anomaly	ə NOM ə lee
anonymous	ə NON ə məs
anorectic	AN ə REK tik
anorexia nervosa	AN ə REK see ə nər VOH sə
Anouilh, Jean	ah NOO yə, ZHAHN
anoxia	an OK see ə
Anschluss	AHN shluus
Ansermet	ahn ser MAY
answerable	AN sə rə bəl
antacid	ant AS əd
antagonism	an TAG ə NIZ əm
Antananarivo	AN tə NAN ə REE voh
antarctic, A-	ant AHRK tik
Antarctica	ant AHRK ti kə
Antares	an TAIR eez
ante	AN tee
antebellum	AN ti BEL əm
antecedence	AN tə SEED əns
antecedent	AN tə SEE dənt
antechamber	AN ti CHAYM bər

ə ago, a at, ah calm, ahr dark, air care, aw saw, ay say, ch church
e bet, ee me, eer beer, hw what, i is, ī my, n French final n vin,

antedate	AN ti DAYT
antediluvian	AN ti də LOO vee ən
antelope	AN tə LOHP
ante meridiem	AN ti mə RID ee əm
antenna	an TEN ə
antennae	an TEN ee
antepenult	AN ti PEE nult
antepenultimate	AN ti pi NUL tə mət
anterior	an TEER ee ər
anteroom	AN ti ROOM
Antheil	AN tīl
anthelion	ant HEE lee ən
anthem	AN thəm
anthill	ANT hil
anthology	an THOL ə jee
Anthony	AN thə nee
anthracite	AN thrə SĪT
anthrax	AN thraks
anthropoid	AN thrə POID
anthropologist	AN thrə POL ə jəst
anthropology	AN thrə POL ə jee
anthropomorphism	AN thrə pə MOR fiz əm
anthropophagi	AN thrə POF ə JĪ
antiaircraft	AN tee AIR KRAFT
Antibes	ahn TEEB
antibiotic	AN ti bī OT ik
antibody	AN ti BOD ee
antic	AN tik
antichrist, A-	AN ti KRĪST
anticipate	an TIS ə PAYT
anticipation	an TIS ə PAY shən
anticipatory	an TIS ə pə TOR ee
anticlimax	AN ti KLĪ maks
anticline	AN ti KLĪN
Anticosti	ANT ə KAW stee
antidote	AN ti DOHT
Antietam	an TEE təm
antigen	AN ti jən
Antigone	an TIG ə NEE
antigravity	AN ti GRAV ə tee
Antigua	an TEE gə
antihero	AN ti HEER oh
antihistamine	AN ti HIS tə MEEN

o on, oh oat, oi boy, oo soon, oor poor, or for, ow cow, sh shush,
th thin, *th* this, u up, ur spur, uu book, *zh* pleasure

antiknock	AN ti NOK
Antillean	an TIL ee ən
Antilles	an TIL eez
antimacassar	AN ti mə KAS ər
antimatter	AN ti MAT ər
antimony	AN tə MOH nee
antinomy	an TIN ə mee
Antioch	AN tee OK
antiparticle	AN ti PAHR ti kəl
antipasto	AN ti PAH stoh
antipathy	an TIP ə thee
antipersonnel	AN ti PUR sə NEL
antiphon	AN tə FON
antiphony	an TIF ə nee
antipodal	an TIP ə dəl
antipodean	an TIP ə DEE ən
antipodes	an TIP ə DEEZ
antipope	AN ti POHP
antiquarian	AN tə KWAIR ee ən
antiquated	AN tə KWAY təd
antique	an TEEK
antiquity	an TIK wə tee
antirrhinum	AN tə RĪ nəm
anti-Semitic	AN ti sə MIT ik
anti-Semitism	AN ti SEM ə TIZ əm
antiseptic	AN tə SEP tik
antisocial	AN ti SOH shəl
antistrophe	an TIS trə fee
antithesis	an TITH ə səs
antithetic	AN tə THET ik
antitoxin	AN ti TOK sən
antitrust	AN ti TRUST
antivivisectionist	AN ti VIV ə SEK shə nəst
antler	ANT lər
Antoinette (US)	AN twə NET
Antoinette (French)	ahn twah NET
Antonescu	AN tə NES koo
Antonov, Sergei	ahn TAW nawv, seer GAY
Antony	AN tə nee
antonym	AN tə nim
antrum	AN trəm
Antwerp	AN twurp
anxiety	ang ZĪ ə tee

ə ago, a at, ah calm, ahr dark, air care, aw saw, ay say, ch church
e bet, ee me, eer beer, hw what, i is, ī my, *n* French final n vin,

anxious	**ANGK** shəs
anybody	**EN** ee **BOD** ee
Anzac	**AN** zak
aorta	ay **OR** tə
aoudad	**AH** uu **DAD**
apace	ə **PAYS**
Apache	ə **PACH** ee
apache (French)	a **PASH**
Apalachicola	**AP** ə **LACH** ə **KOH** lə
Aparri	ah **PAHR** ee
apartheid	ə **PAHR** tayt
apathetic	**AP** ə **THET** ik
apathy	**AP** ə thee
Apel	**AH** pəl
Apennines	**AP** ə **NĪNZ**
apéritif	ə **PER** ə **TEEF**
aperture	**AP** ər chər
apex	**AY** peks
aphasia	ə **FAY** *zh*ə
aphasic	ə **FAY** zik
aphelion	ə **FEE** lee ən
aphid	**AY** fəd
aphonia	ay **FOH** nee ə
aphorism	**AF** ə **RIZ** əm
aphoristic	**AF** ə **RIS** tik
Aphrodite	**AF** rə **DĪ** tee
Apia	ah **PEE** ah
apian	**AY** pee ən
apiary	**AY** pee **ER** ee
apiculture	**AY** pə **KUL** chər
apiece	ə **PEES**
apish	**AY** pish
aplomb	ə **PLOM**
apnea	**AP** nee ə
apocalypse, A-	ə **POK** ə **LIPS**
apocalyptic	ə **POK** ə **LIP** tik
apocope	ə **POK** ə pee
apocrypha, A-	ə **POK** rə fə
apocryphal, A-	ə **POK** rə fəl
apogee	**AP** ə **JEE**
apolitical	**AY** pə **LIT** i kəl
Apollinaire	ə **POL** ə **NAIR**
Apollinaris	a **POL** i **NAIR** is

o on, oh oat, oi boy, oo soon, oor poor, or for, ow cow, sh shush,
th thin, *th* this, u up, ur spur, uu book, *zh* pleasure

Apollo	ə POL oh
Apollyon	ə POL yən
apologetic	ə POL ə JET ik
apologia	AP ə LOH jee ə
apoplectic	AP ə PLEK tik
apoplexy	AP ə PLEK see
apostasy	ə POS tə SEE
apostate	ə POS tayt
apostatize	ə POS tə TĪZ
a posteriori	AH poh STI ree OH ree
apostle, A-	ə POS əl
apostolic	AP ə STOL ik
apothegm, apothem	AP ə them
apotheosis	ə POTH ee OH səs
Appalachian	AP ə LAY chee ən
appall	ə PAWL
Appaloosa	AP ə LOO sə
apparat	AH pə RAHT
apparatchik	AH pə RAHT chik
apparatus	AP ə RAT əs
apparel	ə PAR əl
apparent	ə PAR ənt
apparition	AP ə RISH ən
appeal	ə PEEL
appease	ə PEEZ
appellant	ə PEL ənt
appellate	ə PEL ət
appendage	ə PEN dij
appendectomy	AP ən DEK tə mee
appendices	ə PEN də SEEZ
appendicitis	ə PEN də SĪ təs
appendix	ə PEN diks
apperception	AP ər SEP shən
appertain	AP ər TAYN
appetite	AP ə TĪT
appetizer	AP ə TĪ zər
Appian	AP ee ən
applause	ə PLAWZ
applicable	AP lə kə bəl
applicant	AP lə kənt
application	AP lə KAY shən
applicator	AP lə KAY tər
appliqué	AP lə KAY

ə ago, a at, ah calm, ahr dark, air care, aw saw, ay say, ch church
e bet, ee me, eer beer, hw what, i is, ī my, *n* French final n vin,

appoggiatura	ə POJ ə TUUR ə
appointee	ə poin TEE
Appomattox	AP ə MAT əks
apportionment	ə POR shən mənt
apposite	AP ə zət
apposition	AP ə ZISH ən
appositive	ə POZ ə tiv
appraisal	ə PRAY zəl
appreciable	ə PREE shə bəl
appreciate	ə PREE shee AYT
appreciation	ə PREE shee AY shən
appreciative	ə PREE shə tiv
apprentice	ə PREN təs
apprise	ə PRĪZ
approbation	AP rə BAY shən
appropriate (a)	ə PROH pree ət
appropriate (v)	ə PROH pree AYT
approval	ə PROO vəl
approximate (a)	ə PROK sə mət
approximate (v)	ə PROK sə MAYT
appurtenance	ə PUR tə nəns
apricot	AP rə KOT
April	AY prəl
a priori	AH pree OH ree
à propos	AP rə POH
apse	aps
aptitude	AP tə rOOD
Apuleius	AP yə LEE əs
Apulia	ə PYOOL yə
Aqaba	AH kah BAH
aqua	AK wə
aquamarine	AK wə mə REEN
aquanaut	AK wə NAWT
aquarium	ə KWAIR ee əm
Aquarius	ə KWAIR ee əs
aquatic	ə KWAHT ik
aquatint	AK wə TINT
aquavit	AH kwə VEET
aqua vitae	AK wə VĪ tee
aqueduct	AK wə DUKT
aqueous	AY kwee əs
aquifer	AK wə fər
Aquila	AK wə lə

o on, oh oat, oi boy, oo soon, oor poor, or for, ow cow, sh shush,
th thin, *th* this, u up, ur spur, uu book, *zh* pleasure

aquilegia	AK wə LEE jee ə
aquiline	AK wə LĪN
Aquinas	ə KWĪ nəs
Aquino, Benigno	ah KEEN oh, bə NEEN yoh
Aquino, Corazon	ah KEEN oh, KAW rah ZAWN
arabesque	AR ə BESK
Arabia	ə RAY bee ə
Arabic	AR ə bik
arable	AR ə bəl
Araby	AR ə bee
Arafat, Yasir	AHR ə FAHT, YAH sər
Aramaic	AR ə MAY ik
Aranha	ah RAH nyah
Arapaho	ə RAP ə HOH
Ararat	AR ə RAT
Arawak	AR ə WAHK
Arawakan	AR ə WAH kən
arbiter	AHR bə tər
arbitrage	AHR bə TRAHZH
arbitrament	ahr BI trə mənt
arbitrary	AHR bə TRER ee
arbitrate	AHR bə TRAYT
arbitration	AHR bə TRAY shən
arbitrator	AHR bə TRAY tər
arbor	AHR bər
arboreal	ahr BOR ee əl
arboretum	AHR bə REE təm
arbor vitae	AHR bər VĪ tee
arbutus	ahr BYOO təs
Arc, Jeanne d'	dark, zhahn
arcade	ahr KAYD
Arcadia	ahr KAY dee ə
Arcady	AHR kə dee
arcane	ahr KAYN
arcanum	ahr KAY nəm
Arc de Triomphe	ark də tree AWNF
Arce, José	AHR say, hoh SAY
arch	ahrch
archaeologist	AHR kee OL ə jəst
archaeology	AHR kee OL ə jee
archaic	ahr KAY ik
archaism	AHR kee IZ əm
archangel	AHRK AYN jəl

ə ago, a at, ah calm, ahr dark, air care, aw saw, ay say, ch church
e bet, ee me, eer beer, hw what, i is, ī my, n French final n vin,

archbishop	AHRCH BISH əp
archdiocese	AHRCH DĪ ə səs
archenemy	ahrch EN ə mee
archeologist	AHR kee OL ə jəst
archeology	AHR kee OL ə jee
archer, A-	AHR chər
archetype	AHR ki TĪP
archfiend	AHRCH FEEND
archiepiscopal	AHR kee ə PIS kə pəl
archimandrite	AHR kə MAN drīt
Archimedean	AHR kə MEE dee ən
Archimedes	AHR kə MEE deez
arching	AHR ching
archipelago	AHR kə PEL ə GOH
Archipenko	AHR kə PENG koh
architect	AHR kə TEKT
architectonic	AHR kə tek TON ik
architecture	AHR kə TEK chər
architrave	AHR kə TRAYV
archive	AHR kīv
archivist	AHR kə vəst
archly	AHRCH lee
archon	AHR kon
Arciniegas, Germán	ahr see NYE gahs, hair MAHN
arctic, A-	AHRK tik
Arcturus	ahrk TUUR əs
Ardennes	ahr DEN
ardent	AHR dənt
Arditi	ahr DEE tee
ardor	AHR dər
arduous	AHR joo əs
Arecibo	AR ə SEE boh
Arens, Moshe	AHR ənz, MOH she
Arensky	ə REN skee
Areopagus	AR ee OP ə gəs
Arethusa	AR ə THOO zə
Arévalo	ah RE vah law
Arezzo	ə RET soh
Argana	ahr GAH nah
argent	AHR jənt
Argentina	AHR jen TEE nə
argentine, A-	AHR jən teen
Argive	AHR jīv

o on, oh oat, oi boy, oo soon, oor poor, or for, ow cow, sh shush,
th thin, *th* this, u up, ur spur, uu book, *zh* pleasure

argon	AHR gon
Argonaut	AHR gə NAWT
Argonne	AHR gon
argosy	AHR gə see
argot	AHR goh
argue	AHR gyoo
argument	AHR gyə mənt
argumentative	AHR gyə MEN tə tiv
Argus	AHR gəs
argyle	AHR gīl
Argyll	ahr GĪL
aria	AHR ee ə
Ariadne	AR ee AD nee
Arian	AIR ee ən
Arias	AH ryahs
arid	AR əd
aridity	ə RID ə tee
Ariel, a-	AIR ee əl
Aries	AIR eez
Aristarchus	AR ə STAHR kəs
Aristides	AR ə STĪ deez
aristocracy	AR ə STOK rə see
aristocrat	ə RIS tə KRAT
Aristophanes	AR ə STOF ə NEEZ
Aristotelian	AR ə stə TEEL yən
Aristotle	AR ə STOT əl
arithmetic (a)	AR ith MET ik
arithmetic (n)	ə RITH mə tik
arrivederci	AHR ree ve DER chee
Arizona	AR ə ZOH nə
Arkansan	ahr KAN zən
Arkansas	AHR kən SAW
armada	ahr MAH də
armadillo	AHR mə DIL oh
Armageddon	AHR mə GED ən
armament	AHR mə mənt
Armas	AHR mahs
armature	AHR mə chər
Armenia	ahr MEE nee ə
armistice	AHR mə stəs
armor, A-	AHR mər
armory	AHR mə ree
Arnhem	AHRN hem

ə ago, a at, ah calm, ahr dark, air care, aw saw, ay say, ch church
e bet, ee me, eer beer, hw what, i is, ī my, *n* French final n vin,

arnica	AHR ni kə
Arnold	AHR nəld
aroma	ə ROH mə
aromatic	AR ə MAT ik
arouse	ə ROWZ
Arp	ahrp
arpeggio	ahr PEJ ee OH
arraign	ə RAYN
arrangement	ə RAYNJ mənt
arrant	AR ənt
arras, A-	AR əs
Arrau, Claudio	ahr RAH oo, KLOW dyaw
array	ə RAY
arrears	ə REERZ
arrière pensée	AR ee AIR pahn SAY
arrival	ə RĪ vəl
arriviste	AR ee VEEST
arrogance	AR ə gəns
arrogant	AR ə gənt
arrogate	AR ə GAYT
arrondissement	a rawn dees MAHN (MAHN French final *n*)
arroyo	ə ROI oh
arroz con pollo	ah RAWTH kawn PAW lyaw
arsenal	AHR sə nəl
arsenic (n)	AHR sə nik
arsenic (a)	ahr SEN ik
arson	AHR sən
Artaxerxes	AHR tə ZURK seez
Artemis	AHR tə məs
arterial	ahr TEER ee əl
arteriosclerosis	ahr TEER ee oh sklə ROH səs
artery	AHR tə ree
artesian	ahr TEE *zh*ən
arthritis	ahr THRĪ təs
arthropod	AHR thrə POD
Arthurian	ahr THUUR ee ən
artichoke	AHR tə CHOHK
articulate (a)	ahr TIK yə lit
articulate (v)	ahr TIK yə LAYT
artifice	AHR tə fəs
artificer	ahr TIF ə sər
artificial	AHR tə FISH əl
artillery	ahr TIL ə ree

o on, oh oat, oi boy, oo soon, oor poor, or for, ow cow, sh shush,
th thin, *th* this, u up, ur spur, uu book, *zh* pleasure

artisan	**AHR** tə zən
artist	**AHR** təst
artiste	ahr **TEEST**
artistic	ahr **TIS** tik
artistry	**AHR** tə stree
Art Nouveau	**AHR** noo **VOH**
Artzybasheff	**AHR** tsi **BAH** shef
Artzybashev	**AHR** tsi **BAH** shef
Aruba	ah **ROO** bah
Arundel (England)	**AR** ən dəl
Arundel (Maryland)	ə **RUN** dəl
aryan, A-	**AIR** ee ən
Asa	**AY** sə
Asad	ə **SAHD**
asafetida	**AS** ə **FET** ə də
Asahi	ah sah hee
Asakai, Koichiro	ah sah kī, koh ee chee roh
Asaph	**A** səf
asbestos	as **BES** təs
asbestosis	**AS BES TOH** səs
Ascanius	a **SKAY** nee əs
ascend	ə **SEND**
ascendancy	ə **SEN** dən see
ascension	ə **SEN** shən
ascent	ə **SENT**
ascertain	**AS** ər **TAYN**
ascetic	ə **SET** ik
Asch, Sholem	**ASH, SHOH** ləm
Ascham	**AS** kəm
Asclepius	ə **SKLEE** pee əs
ascorbic	ə **SKOR** bik
ascot, A-	**AS** kət
ascribe	ə **SKRĪB**
aseptic	ay **SEP** tik
Ásgeirsson, Asgeir	**AHS** gair sən, **AHS** gair
ashamed	ə **SHAYMD**
Ashanti	ə **SHAN** tee
Ashdod	**ASH** dod
Ashe	ash
ashen	**ASH** ən
Asher	**ASH** ər
Ashkenazi	**AHSH** kə **NAH** zee
Ashkenazim	**AHSH** kə **NAH** zəm

ə ago, a at, ah calm, ahr dark, air care, aw saw, ay say, ch church
e bet, ee me, eer beer, hw what, i is, ī my, n French final n vin,

Ashland	**ASH** lənd
ashore	ə **SHOR**
ashram	**AHSH** rəm
Ashtoreth	**ASH** tə **RETH**
Ashur	**AH** shuur
Asia	**AY** *zh*ə
Asiatic	**AY** *zh*ee **AT** ik
aside	ə **SĪD**
Asimov	**AZ** ə mof
asinine	**AS** ə **NĪN**
askance	ə **SKANS**
Askelon	**A** skə lahn
askew	ə **SKYOO**
aslant	ə **SLANT**
Asmara	ahs **MAHR** ə
asocial	ay **SOH** shəl
asparagus	ə **SPAR** ə gəs
Aspasia	a **SPAY** *zh*ə
aspect	**AS** pekt
aspen	**AS** pən
asperity	ə **SPER** ə tee
aspersion	ə **SPUR** *zh*ən
asphalt	**AS** fawlt
asphodel	**AS** fə **DEL**
asphyxia	as **FIK** see ə
asphyxiate	as **FIK** see **AYT**
asphyxiation	as **FIK** see **AY** shən
aspic	**AS** pik
aspidistra, A-	**AS** pə **DIS** trə
aspirant	ə **SPĪR** ənt
aspirate (a, n)	**AS** pə rət
aspirate (v)	**AS** pə **RAYT**
aspiration	**AS** pə **RAY** shən
aspire	ə **SPĪR**
aspirin	**AS** pə rən
Asquith	**AS** kwith
as-Sabah, Jabir al-Ahmad al-Jabir	ahsh **SHAH** bah, jah **BEER** ahl **AH** mahd ahl jah **BEER**
as-Sabah, Saad al-Adbullah al-Salim	ahsh **SHAH** bah, sah **EED** ahl **AHB** doo lah ahl sah **LEEM**
Assad, Hafez al-	**AS** sad, **HAH** fə*th*
assail	ə **SAYL**
assailant	ə **SAY** lənt

---

o on, oh oat, oi boy, oo soon, oor poor, or for, ow cow, sh shush,
th thin, *th* this, u up, ur spur, uu book, *zh* pleasure

Assam	as SAM
Assamese	AS ə MEEZ
assassin	ə SAS ən
assassinate	ə SAS ə NAYT
assassination	ə SAS ə NAY shən
assault	ə SAWLT
assay (n)	AS ay
assay (v)	ə SAY
assemblage	ə SEM blij
assembly	ə SEM blee
assent	ə SENT
assert	ə SURT
assertion	ə SUR shən
asset	AS et
asseverate	ə SEV ə RAYT
assiduous	ə SIJ oo əs
assign	ə SĪN
assignable	ə SĪ nə bəl
assignation	AS ig NAY shən
assignee	ə sī NEE
assimilable	ə SIM ə lə bəl
assimilate	ə SIM ə LAYT
assimilation	ə SIM ə LAY shən
Assisi	ə SEE see
assize	ə SĪZ
associate (a, n)	ə SOH see ət
associate (v)	ə SOH see AYT
association	ə SOH see AY shən
associative	ə SOH see AY tiv
assonance	AS ə nəns
assuage	ə SWAYJ
assume	ə SOOM
assumption	ə SUMP shən
assurance	ə SHOOR əns
assure	ə SHOOR
Assyrian	ə SIR ee ən
Assyriology	ə SIR ee OL ə jee
astatine	AS tə TEEN
aster	AS tər
asterisk	AS tə RISK
astern	ə STURN
asteroid	AS tə ROID
asthenia	as THEE nee ə

ə ago, a at, ah calm, ahr dark, air care, aw saw, ay say, ch church
e bet, ee me, eer beer, hw what, i is, ī my, n French final n vin,

asthenic	as THEN ik
asthma	AZ mə
asthmatic	az MAT ik
astigmatic	AS tig MAT ik
astigmatism	ə STIG mə TIZ əm
astir	ə STUR
Astor	AS tər
astound	ə STOWND
Astraea	a STREE ə
astrakhan	AS trə KAN
Astrakhan (USSR)	AHS trah KAHN
astral	AS trəl
astray	ə STRAY
astride	ə STRĪD
astringent	ə STRIN jənt
astrodome	AS trə DOHM
astrolabe	AS trə LAYB
astrologer	as TROL ə jər
astrological	AS trə LOJ i kəl
astrology	ə STROL ə jee
astronaut	AS trə NAWT
astronautics	AS trə NAWT iks
astrophysics	AS trə FIZ iks
Asturias	ahs TOOR yahs
astute	ə STOOT
Asunción	AH suun see AWN
asunder	ə SUN dər
Aswan, Assuan	AS wahn
asylum	ə SĪ ləm
asymmetric	AY sə ME trik
asymmetry	ay SIM ə tree
asymptote	AS əm TOHT
Atahualpa	AH tah WAHL pah
Atalanta	AT ə LAN tə
Ataturk, Kemal	AT ə TURK, ke MAHL
atavism	AT ə VIZ əm
ataxia	ə TAK see ə
Ate	AY tee
atelier	AT əl YAY
a tempo	ah TEM poh
Athanasian	ATH ə NAY zhən
atheism	AY thee IZ əm
atheist	AY thee əst

---

o on, oh oat, oi boy, oo soon, oor poor, or for, ow cow, sh shush,
th thin, *th* this, u up, ur spur, uu book, *zh* pleasure

Athena	ə THEE nə
athenaeum, A-	ATH ə NEE əm
Athenian	ə THEE nee ən
Athens	ATH ənz
atherosclerosis	ATH ə roh sklə ROH səs
athirst	ə THURST
athwart	ə THWORT
Atiyeh, Victor	ə TEE ə
Atlanta	at LAN tə
atlantean, A-	AT lan TEE ən
Atlantic	at LAN tik
Atlantis	at LAN təs
atlas, A-	AT ləs
atmosphere	AT məs FEER
atmospheric	AT məs FER ik
atoll	AT awl
atomic	ə TOM ik
atomizer	AT ə MĪ zər
atonal	ay TOH nəl
atonality	AY toh NAL ə tee
atone	ə TOHN
atonement	ə TOHN mənt
atonic	ay TON ik
atony	AT ən ee
Atreus	AY tree əs
atrium	AY tree əm
atrocious	ə TROH shəs
atrocity	ə TROS ə tee
atrophy	AT rə fee
atropine, A-	AT rə PEEN
attach	ə TACH
attaché	AT ə SHAY
attachment	ə TACH mənt
attacked	ə TAKT
attain	ə TAYN
attainable	ə TAY nə bəl
attainment	ə TAYN mənt
attar	AT ər
attempt	ə TEMPT
attendance	ə TEN dəns
attention	ə TEN shən
attentive	ə TEN tiv
attenuate (a)	ə TEN yoo ət

ə ago, a at, ah calm, ahr dark, air care, aw saw, ay say, ch church
e bet, ee me, eer beer, hw what, i is, ī my, *n* French final n vin,

attenuate (v)	ə TEN yoo AYT
attenuation	ə TEN yoo AY shən
attic, A-	AT ik
Attica	AT ə kə
atticism, A-	AT ə SIZ əm
Attila	ə TIL ə
attire	ə TĪR
attitude	AT ə TOOD
attitudinize	AT ə TOO di NĪZ
attorney	ə TUR nee
attribute (n)	A trə BYOOT
attribute (v)	ə TRIB yoot
attribution	A trə BYOO shən
attributive	ə TRIB yə tiv
attrition	ə TRISH ən
Attu	A too
Attucks, Crispus	AT əks, KRIS pəs
attune	ə TOON
Atuona	AHT ə WOH nə
atypical	ay TIP i kəl
auberge	oh BAIRZH
Aubrey	AW bree
auburn, A-	AW bərn
Aubusson	OH bə SAWN (SAWN French final *n*)
Auchincloss	AW kən KLAWS
Auchinleck	AW kən LEK
Auckland	AWK lənd
au courant	oh koo RAHN (RAHN French final *n*)
audacious	aw DAY shəs
audacity	aw DAS ə tee
Auden	AWD ən
audible	AW də bəl
audience	AW dee əns
audio	AW dee OH
audiology	AW dee OL ə jee
audiophile	AW dee ə FĪL
audit	AW dət
audition	aw DISH ən
auditor	AW də tər
auditorium	AW də TOR ee əm
Audubon	AW də BON
Auer	OW ər
au fait	oh FAY

---

o on, oh oat, oi boy, oo soon, oor poor, or for, ow cow, sh shush,
th thin, *th* this, u up, ur spur, uu book, zh pleasure

au fond	oh FAWN (FAWN French final *n*)
auf Wiedersehen	owf VEE dər ZAY ən
Augean	aw JEE ən
auger	AW gər
aught	awt
augment	awg MENT
au gratin	oh GRAH tən
augur	AW gər
augury	AW gyə ree
August	AW gəst
august	aw GUST
Augustan	aw GUS tən
Auguste, Carlet	oh GUUST, kahr LAY
Augustine	AW gə STEEN
Augustus	aw GUS təs
au jus	oh *ZHOO*
auk	awk
au lait	oh LAY
auld lang syne	AWLD lang ZĪN
au naturel	oh na tyə REL
aunt	ant
auntie	AN tee
au pair	oh PAIR
aura	OR ə
aural	OR əl
aureole	OR ee OHL
aureomycin	OR ee oh MĪ sən
au revoir	oh rə VWAHR
auricular	aw RIK yə lər
auriferous	aw RIF ə rəs
Auriga	aw RĪ gə
Auriol	OR ee OHL
aurora, A-	aw ROR ə
Auschwitz	OWSH vits
auscultation	AW skəl TAY shən
Ausgleich	OWS glīk
auspice	AW spəs
auspices	AW spə səz
auspicious	aw SPISH əs
Auster	AW stər
austere	aw STEER
austerity	aw STER ə tee
Austerlitz	AW stər lits

ə ago, a at, ah calm, ahr dark, air care, aw saw, ay say, ch church
e bet, ee me, eer beer, hw what, i is, ī my, *n* French final n vin,

Australasia	AW strə LAY zhə
Australasian	AW strə LAY zhən
Australia	aw STRAYL yə
Australian	aw STRAYL yən
Australopithecus	aw STRAY loh PITH ə kəs
Austria	AW stree ə
autarchic	aw TAHR kik
autarchist	AW tahr kəst
autarchy	AW tahr kee
authentic	aw THEN tik
authenticate	aw THEN ti KAYT
authenticity	AW then TIS ə tee
author	AW thər
authoritarian	ə THOR ə TAIR ee ən
authoritative	ə THOR ə TAY tiv
authority	ə THOR ə tee
authorization	AW thə rə ZAY shən
authorize	AW thə RĪZ
autism	AW tiz əm
autistic	aw TIS tik
autobahn	AW toh BAHN
autobiographical	AW toh BĪ ə GRAF i kəl
autobiography	AW toh bī OG rə fee
autochthonous	aw TOK thə nəs
autoclave	AW toh KLAYV
autocracy	aw TOK rə see
autocrat	AW tə KRAT
auto-da-fé	AW toh də FAY
autogiro	AW toh JĪ roh
autoharp	AW toh HAHRP
autoimmune	AW toh i MYOON
Automat	AW tə MAT
automate	AW tə MAYT
automatic	AW tə MAT ik
automation	AW tə MAY shən
automatism	aw TOM ə TIZ əm
automaton	aw TOM ə tən
autonomous	aw TON ə məs
autonomy	aw TON ə mee
autopilot	AW toh PĪ lət
autopsy	AW top see
autosuggestion	AW toh səg JES chən
autumn	AW təm

---

o on, oh oat, oi boy, oo soon, oor poor, or for, ow cow, sh shush,
th thin, *th* this, u up, ur spur, uu book, *zh* pleasure

autumnal	aw TUM nəl
auxiliary	awg ZIL yə ree
avail	ə VAYL
availability	ə VAY lə BIL ə tee
available	ə VAY lə bəl
avalanche	AV ə LANCH
Avalon	AV ə LON
avant-garde	A vahn GAHRD
avarice	AV ə rəs
avaricious	AV ə RISH əs
avast	ə VAST
avatar	AV ə tahr
ave, A-	AH vay
Ave Maria	AH vay mə REE ə
avenge	ə VENJ
avenue	AV ən YOO
aver	ə VUR
averse	ə VURS
aversion	ə VUR zhən
avert	ə VURT
avian	AY vee ən
aviary	AY vee ER ee
aviator	AY vee AY tər
aviatrix	AY vee AY triks
avid	AV əd
avidity	ə VID ə tee
Avignon	a vee NYAWN (NYAWN French final n)
Ávila	AH vee LAH
avionics	AY vee ON iks
avitaminosis	ay vī tə mə NOH səs
avocado	AV ə KAH doh
avocation	AV ə KAY shən
avoidance	ə VOID əns
avoirdupois	AV ər də POIZ
Avon	AY vən
avow	ə VOW
avowal	ə VOW əl
Avril, Prosper	ahv REEL, proh SPAIR
avuncular	ə VUNG kyə lər
Awaji	ə WAHJ ee
aweigh	ə WAY
awesome	AW səm
awful	AW fəl

ə ago, a at, ah calm, ahr dark, air care, aw saw, ay say, ch church
e bet, ee me, eer beer, hw what, i is, ī my, n French final n vin,

awfully	AW fə lee
awhile	ə HWĪL
awkward	AWK wərd
Awolowo, Obafemi	a woh LAW waw, aw BAH fe mee
awry	ə RĪ
ax	aks
axe	aks
axel	AK səl
axes (pl of *ax*)	AK səz
axes (pl of *axis*)	AK seez
axial	AK see əl
axiom	AK see əm
axiomatic	AK see ə MAT ik
axis	AK səs
axle	AK səl
Axminster	AKS MIN stər
axon	AKS on
ayatollah	AH yə TOH lə
Ayling	AY ling
Ayr	air
Ayres	airz
Ayrshire	AIR sheer
Azad	ah ZAHD
azalea, A-	ə ZAYL yə
Azcona Hoyo, José	ahs COH nə OY oh, hoh SAY
Azerbaijan	AH zər bī JAHN
Azikwe, Nnamdi	a zee kee WE, nahm DEE
Azim, Ejaz	ah ZEEM, ay JAHZ
azimuth	AZ ə məth
Aziz, Tariq	ah ZEEZ, TAW rik
Azores	AY zorz
Azov	ah ZAWF
Azraai, Zain	AHS rah ee, zayn
Aztec	AZ tek
Aztecan	AZ te kən
Azuma, Tokuho	ahd zoo MAH, toh kuu HOH
azure	*AZH* ər

---

o on, oh oat, oi boy, oo soon, oor poor, or for, ow cow, sh shush,
th thin, *th* this, u up, ur spur, uu book, *zh* pleasure

B

baa	bah
Baal	**BAY** əl
Baalim	**BAY** ə ləm
Baal Shem-Tov	bahl shem tohv
Baba	**BAH** bah
baba au rhum	**BAH** bə oh **RUM**
babbitt, B-	**BAB** ət
babbittry, B-	**BAB** ə tree
babble	**BAB** əl
babel, B-	**BAY** bəl
Babel, Isaac	**BAH** bel, i **SAHK**
Babism	**BAHB** iz əm
Babist	**BAHB** əst
Babite	**BAH** bīt
babka	**BAHB** kə
baboo, B-	**BAH** boo
baboon	ba **BOON**
babu, B-	**BAH** boo
babushka	bə **BUUSH** kə
Babylon	**BAB** ə lən
Babylonia	BAB ə **LOH** nee ə
Bacall	bə **KAWL**
baccalaureate	BAK ə **LOR** ee ət
baccarat	**BAH** kə RAH
Bacchae	**BAK** ee
bacchanal	BAK ə **NAL**
bacchanalia, B-	BAK ə **NAYL** yə
bacchanalian, B-	BAK ə **NAY** lee ən
bacchant	**BAK** ənt
Bacchus	**BAK** əs
Bach	bahk
Bache	baysh
bachelor	**BACH** ə lər
bacilli	bə **SIL** ī
bacillus	bə **SIL** əs
backache	**BAK** ayk
backgammon	**BAK** GAM ən
backstage	**BAK** stayj

ə ago, a at, ah calm, ahr dark, air care, aw saw, ay say, ch church
e bet, ee me, eer beer, hw what, i is, ī my, *n* French final n vin,

Baconian	bay **KOH** nee ən
bacteria	bak **TEER** ee ə
bacteriology	bak **TEER** ee **OL** ə jee
bacteriophage	bak **TEER** ee ə **FAYJ**
bacterium	bak **TEER** ee əm
Bactrian	**BAK** tree ə
bade	bad
Baden (Germany)	**BAHD** ən
Baden (US)	**BAYD** ən
Baden-Powell	**BAYD** ən **POH** əl
badger	**BAJ** ər
badinage	**BAD** ə **NAHZ***H*
badlands, B-	**BAD** **LANDZ**
badminton	**BAD** min tən
baedeker, B-	**BAY** də kər
Baez	bī **EZ**
Baffin	**BAF** ən
bagasse	bə **GAS**
bagatelle	**BAG** ə **TEL**
Bagaya	bah **GAH** yah
Bagaza	bah **GAH** zah
Bagdad	**BAG** dad
Bagehot	**BAJ** ət
bagel	**BAY** gəl
baggage	**BAG** ij
baggy	**BAG** ee
Baghdad	**BAG** dad
bagnio	**BAHN** yoh
Bagnold, Enid	**BAG** nohld, **EE** nid
bagpipe	**BAG** pīp
baguette	bə **GET**
Baguio	**BAHG** ee **OH**
Bahai	bah **HĪ**
Bahaism	bah **HĪ** iz əm
Bahaist	bah **HĪ** ist
Bahama	bə **HAH** mə
Bahia	bə **HEE** ə
Bahrain	bah **RAYN**
Baikal	bī **KAHL**
bailey, B-	**BAY** lee
bailiff	**BAY** ləf
bailiwick	**BAY** lə wik
Bairam	bī **RAHM**

---

o on, oh oat, oi boy, oo soon, oor poor, or for, ow cow, sh shush,
th thin, *th* this, u up, ur spur, uu book, *zh* pleasure

Bairiki	bī REE kee
bairn	bairn
baize	bayz
Bakelite	BAY kə LĪT
Bakhtiar	BOK tee ahr
baksheesh	BAK sheesh
Baku	bah KOO
Balaam	BAY ləm
balaclava	BAL ə KLAH və
Balaguer, Joaquín	bah lah GAIR, hwah KEEN
balalaika	BAL ə LĪ kə
Balanchine	BAL ən SHEEN
Balaton	BAH lah TAWN
Balboa	bal BOH ə
balbriggan	bal BRIG ən
balcony	BAL kə nee
baldachin	BAL də kən
Balder	BAWL dər
balderdash	BAWL dər DASH
baldpate	BAWLD payt
baldric	BAWL drik
Baldwin	BAWLD wən
bale	bayl
Bâle	bahl
Balearic	BAL ee AR ik
baleen	bə LEEN
baleful	BAYL fəl
Balenciaga	ba LEN see AH gə
Baleta, Abdi	bah LAY tah, AHB dee
Balewa, Abubakar Tafawa	ba LAY wah, a BOO ba kahr ta FAH wah
Balfour	BAL fuur
Bali	BAH lee
Balikpapan	BAH leek PAH pahn
Balinese	BAH lə NEEZ
balk	bawk
Balkan	BAWL kən
ballad	BAL əd
ballade	bə LAHD
balladeer	BAL ə DEER
balladry	BAL ə dree
Ballantine	BAL ən tīn
ballast	BAL əst

ə ago, a at, ah calm, ahr dark, air care, aw saw, ay say, ch church
e bet, ee me, eer beer, hw what, i is, ī my, *n* French final n vin,

ballerina	BAL ə REE nə
ballet	ba LAY
Balliol	BAL yəl
ballistic	bə LIS tik
Ballo in Maschera	BAH loh een MAHS kay rah
balloon	bə LOON
ballyhoo	BAL ee HOO
balm	bahm
Balmoral, b-	bal MAWR əl
baloney	bə LOH nee
balsa	BAWL sə
balsam	BAWL səm
Balthazar	bal THAY zər
Baltic	BAWL tik
Baltimore	BAWL tə MOR
Baluchistan	bə LOO chə STAN
baluster	BAL ə stər
balustrade	BAL ə STRAYD
Balzac	BAL zak
Bamako	BAM ə KOH
bambino	bam BEE noh
bamboo	bam BOO
bamboozle	bam BOO zəl
banal	bə NAHL
banality	bə NAL ə tee
Banda	BAHN dah
bandage	BAN dij
bandanna	ban DAN ə
bandeau	ban DOH
Bandoeng, Bandung	BAHN duung
bandolier	BAN də LEER
bandy-legged	BAN dee LEG əd
bane	bayn
baneberry	BAYN BER ee
baneful	BAYN fəl
Banff	bamf
bangalore, B-	BANG gə LOHR
Bangkok	BANG kok
Bangladesh	ʒANG glə DESH
bangle	BANG gəl
Bangui	bahng GEE
Bani-Sadr, Abolhassan	BAH nee SAH dər, AH buul hah SAHN
banister	BAN ə stər

o on, oh oat, oi boy, oo soon, oor poor, or for, ow cow, sh shush,
th thin, *th* this, u up, ur spur, uu book, *zh* pleasure

Banjermasin	**BAHN** jər **MAH** sən
banjo	**BAN** joh
Banjul	**BAHN** juul
bankruptcy	**BANGK** rupt see
bannock	**BAN** ək
banns	banz
banquet	**BANG** kwət
Banquo	**BANG** kwoh
banshee	**BAN** shee
Bantu	**BAN** too
banyan	**BAN** yən
Banyuwangi	**BAHN** yoo **WAHNG** ee
banzai	bahn **ZĪ**
baobab	**BAY** oh **BAB**
Bao Dai	bow dī (bow as in *cow*)
baptism	**BAP** tiz əm
baptismal	bap **TIZ** məl
baptist, B-	**BAP** təst
baptistery	**BAP** tə stree
baptize	**BAP** tīz
Barabbas	bə **RAB** əs
Baraca	bə **RAH** kə
Baraka, Amiri	bah **RAH** kah, ah **MEER** ee
Baranof	**BA** rə **NAWF**
Barbados	bahr **BAY** dohs
barbarian	bahr **BAIR** ee ən
barbaric	bahr **BAR** ik
barbarism	**BAHR** bə **RIZ** əm
barbarity	bahr **BAR** ə tee
Barbarossa	**BAHR** bə **RAWS** ə
barbarous	**BAHR** bə rəs
Barbary	**BAHR** bə ree
barbecue	**BAHR** bə **KYOO**
barbed	bahrbd
barberry	**BAHR BER** ee
Barbiere di Siviglia	bahr **BYE** re dee see **VEE** lyah
barbiturate	bahr **BICH** ə rət
barbituric	**BAHR** bə **TUUR** ik
Barbuda	bahr **BOO** də
barcarole	**BAHR** kə **ROHL**
Barcelona	**BAHR** sə **LOH** nə
Barco Vargas, Virgilio	**BAHR** koh **VAHR** gahs, veer **HEE** lee oh
Bardot, Brigitte	bahr **DOH**, bri **ZH**EET

ə ago, a at, ah calm, ahr dark, air care, aw saw, ay say, ch church
e bet, ee me, eer beer, hw what, i is, ī my, *n* French final n vin,

barefaced	bair fayst
bareheaded	BAIR HED əd
barely	BAIR lee
Barents	BA rənts
bargain	BAHR gən
barge	bahrj
bargeman	BAHRJ mən
baritone	BA rə TOHN
barium	BA ree əm
barkentine	BAHR kən TEEN
barker	BAHR kər
Bar-le-Duc	BAHR lə DUUK
barley	BAHR lee
barleycorn, B-	BAHR lee KORN
barm	bahrm
Barma, Ramadane	BAHR mə, RAH mə DAHN
bar mitzvah	bahr MITS və
barmy	BAHR mee
Barnabas	BAHR nə bəs
barnacle	BAHR nə kəl
Barnard	BAHR nərd
Barnegat	BAHR ni gət
Barnouw	BAHR noh
Barnstable	BAHRN stə bəl
barnstorm	BAHRN storm
barnyard	BAHRN yahrd
barometer	bə ROM ə tər
barometric	BA rə MET rik
baroness	BA rə nəs
baronet	BA rə nət
baronetcy	BA rə nət see
baronial	bə ROH nee əl
baroque	bə ROHK
barouche	bə ROOSH
barque	bahrk
barquentine	BAHR kən TEEN
barracks	BA rəks
barracuda	BA rə KOO də
barrage	bə RAHZH
barranca, B-	bə RANG kə
Barranquilla	BA rən KEE ə
Barrault	ba ROH
Barré, Mohamed	ba RAY, mə HAH məd

o on, oh oat, oi boy, oo soon, oor poor, or for, ow cow, sh shush,
th thin, *th* this, u up, ur spur, uu book, *zh* pleasure

barred	bahrd
barren	**BA** rən
barricade	**BA** rə **KAYD**
barrier	**BA** ree ər
barrio	**BAHR** ee oh
barrister	**BA** rə stər
barroom	**BAHR ROOM**
Bartholdi	bahr **THOL** dee
Bartholomew	bahr **THOL** ə **MYOO**
Bartlett	**BAHRT** lət
Bartók, Béla	**BAHR** tok, **BAY** lə
Baruch (Bible)	**BAIR** ək
Baruch, Bernard	bə **ROOK**
Baryshnikov, Mikhail	bah **REESH** ni **KOF**, mi kah **EEL**
Barzun, Jacques	**BAHR** zən, _zh_ ahk
basal	**BAY** səl
basalt	bə **SAWLT**
base	bays
Basel	**BAH** zəl
baseless	**BAYS** ləs
basement	**BAYS** mənt
baseness	**BAYS** nəs
basenji	bə **SEN** jee
bases (pl of _base_)	**BAY** səz
bases (pl of _basis_)	**BAY** seez
bashful	**BASH** fəl
Bashkir	bahsh **KEER**
Basho	bah shoh
basic	**BAY** sik
basil, B-	**BAZ** əl
basilar	**BAS** ə lər
basilic	bə **SIL** ik
basilica	bə **SIL** i kə
basilisk	**BAZ** ə lisk
basis	**BAY** səs
bas mitzvah	bahs **MITS** və
basque, B-	bask
Basra	**BUS** rə
bas-relief	**BAH** ri **LEEF**
bass (fish)	bas
bass (sound)	bays
basset	**BAS** ət
basso	**BAS** oh

ə ago, a at, ah calm, ahr dark, air care, aw saw, ay say, ch church
e bet, ee me, eer beer, hw what, i is, ī my, _n_ French final n vin,

bassoon	bə SOON
basso profundo	BAS oh proh FUUN doh
bastard	BAS tərd
bastardize	BAS tər DĪZ
bastardy	BAS tərd ee
baste	bayst
bastille, B-	ba STEEL
bastinado	BAS tə NAY doh
bastion	BAS chən
Bastogne	ba STOHN
Bataan	bə TAN
Batang	bah tahng
Batavia	bə TAY vee ə
bateau	ba TOH
bated	BAY təd
bath	bath
bathe	bay*th*
batholith	BATH ə lith
bathos	BAY thos
Bathsheba	bath SHEE bə
bathyscaphe	BATH ə SKAYF
bathysphere	BATH ə SFEER
batik	ba TEEK
batiste	ba TEEST
bat mitzvah	baht MITS və
baton	ba TON
Baton Rouge	BAT ən ROOZ*H*
batrachian, B-	bə TRAY kee ən
battalion	bə TAL yən
batten	BAT ən
battery	BAT ə ree
battledore	BAT əl DOR
battue	ba TOO
Batum	bah TUUM
bauble	BAW bəl
baud	bawd
Baudelaire	BOHD ə LAIR
Baudouin	boh DWAN (DWAN French final *n*)
Bauhaus	BOW hows (BOW as in *cow*)
Baumann	BOW mən (BOW as in *cow*)
bauxite	BAWK sīt
Bavaria	bə VAIR ee ə
Bavarian	bə VAIR ee ən

o **on**, oh **oat**, oi **boy**, oo **soon**, oor **poor**, or **for**, ow **cow**, sh **shush**,
th **thin**, *th* **this**, u **up**, ur **spur**, uu **book**, *zh* **pleasure**

Bayard	**BAY** ərd
Bayard (French)	bah **YAHR**
bayberry	**BAY BER** ee
Bayeux	bah **YUU**
bayonet	**BAY** ə nət
Bayonne (France)	bah **YUN**
Bayonne (US)	bay **YOHN**
bayou	**BĪ** oo
Bayreuth	**BĪ** roit
bazaar, bazar	bə **ZAHR**
Bazargan	**BAH** zahr gahn
bazooka	bə **ZOO** kə
bdellium	**DEL** ee əm
beacon	**BEE** kən
Beaconsfield	**BEE** kənz **FEELD**
beadle	**BEED** əl
beagle	**BEE** gəl
beanie	**BEE** nee
bear	bair
bearing	**BAIR** ing
béarnaise	**BAY** ər **NAYZ**
beatific	**BEE** ə **TIF** ik
beatification	bee **AT** ə fə **KAY** shən
beatify	bee **AT** ə **FĪ**
beatitude	bee **AT** ə **TOOD**
beatnik	**BEET** nik
Beatrice	**BEE** ə trəs
beau	boh
Beau Brummel	boh **BRUM** əl
Beauchamp	**BEE** chəm
Beaufort (scale)	**BOH** fərt
Beaufort (North Carolina)	**BOH** fərt
Beaufort (South Carolina)	**BYOO** fərt
beau geste	boh **ZHEST**
Beauharnais	boh ahr **NAY**
beau ideal	**BOH** ī **DEE** əl
Beaujolais	**BOH** zhoh **LAY**
Beaulac	**BOH** lak
Beaulieu (England)	**BYOO** lee
beau monde	boh **MAWND**
Beaumont	**BOH** mont

ə ago, a at, ah calm, ahr dark, air care, aw saw, ay say, ch church
e bet, ee me, eer beer, hw what, i is, ī my, *n* French final n vin,

beauteous	BYOO tee əs
beautician	byoo TISH ən
beautification	BYOO tə fə KAY shən
beautiful	BYOO ti fəl
beautify	BYOO tə FĪ
beauty	BYOO tee
Beauvoir, Simone de	bohv WAHR, see MUN də
beaux	bohz
beaux (French)	boh
beaux arts	boh ZAHR
bebop	BEE BOP
becalm	bi KAHM
béchamel	BAY shə MEL
bêche-de-mer	BESH də MAIR
Bechuana	BECH oo AH nə
Bechuanaland	BECH oo AH nə LAND
Becket	BEK ət
Beckett	BEK ət
beckon	BEK ən
becloud	bi KLOWD
become	bi KUM
Becquerel	be KREL
bedaub	bi DAWB
Bedaux	bə DOH
bedazzle	bi DAZ əl
bedclothes	BED klohz
bedeck	bi DEK
bedevil	bi DEV əl
Bedford	BED fərd
Bedivere	BED ə VEER
bedizen	bi DĪ zən
bedlam	BED ləm
Bedloe	BED loh
Bedouin	BED oo ən
bedraggled	bi DRAG əld
beefeater	BEEF ee tər
Beelzebub	bee EL zə BUB
been	bin
Beerbohm, Max	BIR bohm
Beersheba	beer SHEE bə
Beethoven	BAY toh vən
befall	bi FAWL
befitting	bi FIT ing

o on, oh oat, oi boy, oo soon, oor poor, or for, ow cow, sh shush,
th thin, *th* this, u up, ur spur, uu book, *zh* pleasure

befog	bi FOG
beforehand	bi FOR HAND
befoul	bi FOWL
Begin, Menachem	BE geen, me NAHK əm (BE as in *bet*, me as in *met*)
beginning	bi GIN ing
begone	bi GAWN
begonia	bi GOHN yə
begot	bi GOT
begrudge	bi GRUJ
beguile	bi GĪL
beguine	bi GEEN
begum	BEE gəm
behalf	bi HAF
Behan, Brendan	BEE ən, BREN dən
behavior	bi HAYV yər
behaviorism	bi HAYV yə RIZ əm
behemoth	bi HEE məth
Behistun	BAY his TOON
Behn	bayn
behoove	bi HOOV
beige	bay*zh*
Beijing	bay jeeng
Beirut	bay ROOT
Bekaa	bi KAH
Békésy, Georg von	BAY ke shee, gay ORG fawn
belabor	bi LAY bər
Belafonte	BEL ə FON tee
Belasco	bə LAS koh
Belaunde Terry, Fernando	bel ow OON day TER ee, fer NAHN doh
bel canto	bel KAHN toh
beldam	BEL dəm
Belfast	BEL fast
belfry	BEL free
Belgian	BEL jən
Belgic	BEL jik
Belgium	BEL jəm
Belgrade	bel GRAYD
Belgravia	bel GRAY vee ə
Belial	BEE lee əl
belie	bi LĪ
belief	bə LEEF

ə ago, a at, ah calm, ahr dark, air care, aw saw, ay say, ch church
e bet, ee me, eer beer, hw what, i is, ī my, *n* French final n vin,

believe	bə LEEV
belittle	bi LIT əl
Beliveau	be li VOH
Belize	bə LEEZ
belladonna	BEL ə DON ə
Bellamy	BEL ə mee
belle	bel
Belleau	be LOH
Belleek	bə LEEK
Bellerophon	bə LER ə fən
belles-lettres	bel LET rə
bellhop	BEL hop
bellicose	BEL ə KOHS
belligerence	bə LIJ ə rəns
belligerent	bə LIJ ə rənt
Bellini	bə LEE nee
bellman	BEL mən
bellow	BEL oh
bellows	BEL ohz
bellwether	BEL WETH ər
Belmondo	bel MOHN doh
Belmopan	BEL moh PAN
beloved (a)	bi LUVD
beloved (a, n)	bi LUV əd
Bel Paese	BEL pah AY zə
Belshazzar	bel SHAZ ər
beluga	bə LOO gə
belvedere, B-	BEL və DEER
Belvoir (castle)	BEE vər
Belvoir (US)	BEL vwahr
bemoan	bi MOHN
bemuse	bi MYOOZ
Benacerraf, Baruj	BAY nah se RAHF, bah ROOK
Benares	bə NAHR əs
Ben Bella	ben BEL lah
Bendjedid, Chadli	BEN JED eed, CHAHD lee
beneath	bi NEETH
benedick, B-	BEN ə dik
benedict, B-	BEN ə dikt
Benedictine (monk, nun)	BEN ə DIK tən
Benedictine (liqueur)	BEN ə DIK TEEN
benediction	BEN ə DIK shən

---

o on, oh oat, oi boy, oo soon, oor poor, or for, ow cow, sh shush,
th thin, *th* this, u up, ur spur, uu book, *zh* pleasure

benedictory	BEN ə DIK tə ree
Benedictus	BEN ə DIK təs
benefaction	BEN ə FAK shən
benefactor	BEN ə FAK tər
benefic	bə NEF ik
benefice	BEN ə fəs
beneficence	bə NEF ə səns
beneficent	bə NEF ə sənt
beneficial	BEN ə FISH əl
beneficiary	BEN ə FISH ee ER ee
benefit	BEN ə fit
Benelux	BEN ə LUKS
Benét	bə NAY
benevolence	bə NEV ə ləns
benevolent	bə NEV ə lənt
Bengal	ben GAWL
Bengalese	BEN gə LEEZ
Bengali	ben GAW lee
bengaline	BENG gə LEEN
Bengasi, Benghazi	ben GAH zee
Bengelloun, Ali	ben GEE loon, AH lee
Ben-Gurion	ben GUUR ee ən
benighted	bi NĪ təd
benign	bi NĪN
benignant	bi NIG nənt
benignity	bi NIG nə tee
Benin	bə NEEN
benison	BEN ə zən
Benites, Leopoldo	be NEE tes, lay oh POHL doh
Benjamin	BEN jə mən
Ben Khedda, Benyoussef	ben KAY də, ben YOO səf
Benoni	bə NOH nee
Bentham	BEN thəm
ben trovato	BEN troh VAHT oh
benumb	bi NUM
Benvenuto, b-	BEN və NOO toh
Ben Yahia, Habib	ben YAH hee ə, hah BEEB
Benzedrine	BEN zə DREEN
benzene	BEN zeen
benzine	BEN zeen
benzoate	BEN zoh AYT
benzoin	BEN zoh in

ə ago, a at, ah calm, ahr dark, air care, aw saw, ay say, ch church
e bet, ee me, eer beer, hw what, i is, ī my, n French final n vin,

benzol	**BEN** zohl
Beowulf	**BAY** ə **WUULF**
bequeath	bi **KWEE***TH*
bequest	bi **KWEST**
berate	bi **RAYT**
Berber	**BUR** bər
berceuse	ber **SUZ**
Berchtesgaden	**BERK** təs **GAHD** ən
Berdyaev	ber **DYAH** yef
Berea	bə **REE** ə
bereave	bi **REEV**
bereft	bi **REFT**
Berenson	**BER** ən sən
beret	bə **RAY**
bergamot	**BUR** gə **MOT**
Berganza	ber **GAHN** zə
Bergen (Norway)	**BER** gən
Bergen (US)	**BUR** gən
Bergerac	ber *zh*ə **RAK**
Bergman	**BURG** mən
Bergonzi, Carlo	bair **GOHN** dzee, **KAHR** loh
Bergson, Henri	berg **SAWN**, ahn **REE** (**SAWN** French final *n*)
Beria (Russian)	**BER** ee ə
beriberi	**BER** ee **BER** ee
Bering	**BEER** ing
Berkeley (California)	**BURK** lee
Berkeley (London)	**BAHRK** lee
Berkshire	**BURK** shir
Berlin (Germany)	bər **LIN**
Berlin (US)	**BUR** lən
Berlioz	**BER** lee **OHZ**
berm	burm
Bermuda	bər **MYOO** də
Bermúdez	ber **MOO** *th*ays
Bern, Berne	burn
Bernadotte	**BUR** nə **DOT**
Bernardin, Joseph Louis	**BER** nar **DAN** (**DAN** French final *n*)
Bernardine	**BUR** nər deen
Bernhardt	**BURN** hahrt
Bernice	bur **NEES**
Bernini	ber **NEE** nee

o on, oh oat, oi boy, oo soon, oor poor, or for, ow cow, sh shush, th thin, *th* this, u up, ur spur, uu book, *zh* pleasure

Bernoulli	bər **NOO** lee
Bernstein	**BURN** stīn
berserk	bər **SURK**
berth	burth
Bertha	**BUR** thə
Bertillon, Alphonse	**BER** tee **YOHN** (**YOHN** French final *n*)
Bertillon system	**BUR** tə **LON**
beryl	**BER** əl
beryllium	bə **RIL** ee əm
beseech	bi **SEECH**
beset	bi **SET**
beshrew	bi **SHROO**
besides	bi **SĪDZ**
besiege	bi **SEEJ**
besom	**BEE** zəm
Besoyan	bə **SOI** yən
Bessarabia	**BES** ə **RAY** bee ə
Bessemer	**BES** ə mər
besotted	bi **SOT** əd
bestial	**BES** chəl
bestiality	**BES** chee **AL** ə tee
bestiary	**BES** chee **ER** ee
bestir	bi **STUR**
bestow	bi **STOH**
bestride	bi **STRĪD**
beta	**BAY** tə
Betancourt	**BET** ən **KUUR**
Betancur, Belisario	bay tahn **KOOR**, bay lee **SAHR** ee oh
betatron	**BAY** tə **TRON**
betel	**BEE** təl
Betelgeuse	**BET** əl **JOOZ**
bête noire	bet **NWAHR**
Bethany	**BETH** ə nee
Bethe	**BAY** tə
Bethel	**BETH** əl
Bethesda	bə **THEZ** də
bethink	bi **THINGK**
Bethlehem	**BETH** li **HEM**
Bethmann-Hollweg	**BAYT** mahn **HAWL** vayk
Bethsaida	beth **SAY** ə də
betimes	bi **TĪMZ**
bêtise	be **TEEZ**
Betjeman	**BECH** ə mən

ə ago, a at, ah calm, ahr dark, air care, aw saw, ay say, ch church
e bet, ee me, eer beer, hw what, i is, ī my, *n* French final n vin,

betoken	bi TOH kən
betray	bi TRAY
betroth	bi TROH*TH*
betrothal	bi TROH *th*əl
betrothed (a, n)	bi TROH*TH*D
betta	BET ə
better, bettor	BET ər
Beulah	BYOO lə
beverage	BEV ə rij
Beverwijk	BAY vər VĪK
bevy	BEV ee
bewail	bi WAYL
beware	bi WAIR
Bewick, Thomas	BYOO ik
bewildered	bi WIL dərd
bewitched	bi WICHT
bey	bay
Beyle	bayl
beyond	bee OND
bezant	BEZ ənt
bezel	BEEZ əl
bezique	bə ZEEK
Bhagavad-Gita	BUG ə vəd GEE tah
bhang	bang
Bhatt, Uddhav Deo	baht, oo DAHV DAY oh
Bhopal, Bhopol	boh PAHL
Bhumibol, Adulyadej	POO mee POHN, a DUUN lə DAYT
Bhutan	boo TAHN
Bhutto, Benazir	BOO toh, BEN ə ZEER
Biafra	bee AF rə
Biaggi	bee AH jee
bialy	bee AH lee
Bialystok	bee AH li STAWK
biannual	bī AN yoo əl
Biarritz	BEE ə RITS
bias	BĪ əs
biathlon	bī ATH lon
bibelot	BIB loh
biblical, B-	BIB li kəl
bibliographer	BIB lee OG rə fər
bibliography	BIB lee OG rə fee
bibliophile	BIB lee ə FĪL
bibulous	BIB yə ləs

o on, oh oat, oi boy, oo soon, oor poor, or for, ow cow, sh shush,
th thin, *th* this, u up, ur spur, uu book, *zh* pleasure

bicameral	bī **KAM** ər əl
bicarbonate	bī **KAHR** bə nət
bicentenary	bī **SEN** tə **NER** ee
bicentennial	**BĪ** sen **TEN** ee əl
biceps	**BĪ** seps
bichloride	bī **KLOHR** īd
bicker	**BIK** ər
bicuspid	bī **KUS** pəd
bicycle	**BĪ** si kəl
bicycling	**BĪ** si kling
bicyclist	**BĪ** si kləst
bidden	**BID** ən
biddy	**BID** ee
bidet	bee **DAY**
biennial	bī **EN** ee əl
bier	beer
bifilar	bī **FĪ** lər
bifocal	bī **FOH** kəl
bifurcate	**BĪ** fər **KAYT**
bifurcation	**BĪ** fər **KAY** shən
bigamist	**BIG** ə məst
bigamy	**BIG** ə mee
bight	bīt
Bignone, Reynaldo Benito	been **YOHN** ay, ray **NAHL** doh bay **NEE** toh
bignonia	big **NOH** nee ə
bigot	**BIG** ət
bigoted	**BIG** ə təd
bigotry	**BIG** ə tree
Bihać	**BEE** hahch
Bihar	bi **HAHR**
bijou	**BEE** *zh*oo
Bikaner	**BEE** kə **NER**
Bikel	bi **KEL**
bikini, B-	bə **KEE** nee
bilateral	bī **LAT** ə rəl
Bilbao	bil **BAH** oh
Bildad	**BIL** dad
bile	bīl
bilge	bilj
bilingual	bī **LING** gwəl
bilious	**BIL** yəs
billet	**BIL** ət

ə ago, a at, ah calm, ahr dark, air care, aw saw, ay say, ch church
e bet, ee me, eer beer, hw what, i is, ī my, *n* French final n vin,

billet-doux	BIL ay DOO
billiards	BIL yərds
billingsgate, B-	BIL ingz GAYT
Biloxi	bə LUK see
bimetallism	bī MET ə LIZ əm
bimonthly	bī MUNTH lee
binary	BĪ nə ree
binaural	bi NOR əl
binder	BĪN dər
bindery	BĪN də ree
Bindzi, Benoit	BIND zee, BEN wah
Binet	bi NAY
binge	binj
Bingen	BING ən
bingo	BING goh
binnacle	BIN ə kəl
binoculars	bə NOK yə lərz
binomial	bi NOH mee əl
biochemical	BĪ oh KEM i kəl
biodegradable	BĪ oh di GRAY də bəl
biogenesis	BĪ oh JEN ə səs
biogenic	BĪ oh JEN ik
biographer	bi OG rə fər
biography	bi OG rə fee
Bioko	bee OH koh
biological	BĪ ə LOJ i kəl
biology	bi OL ə jee
biomass	BĪ oh MAS
biome	BĪ ohm
bionics	bi ON iks
bionomics	BĪ ə NOM iks
biophysics	BĪ oh FIZ iks
biopsy	BĪ op see
biorhythm	BĪ oh RITH əm
biosynthesis	BĪ oh SIN thə səs
biotin	BĪ ə tən
bipartisan	bi PAHR tə zən
bipartite	bi PAHR tīt
biped	BĪ ped
Birabhongse Kasemsri	PEE rah pohng kah SEM sree
birch	burch
bird's-eye	BURDZ ī
bireme	BĪ reem

o on, oh oat, oi boy, oo soon, oor poor, or for, ow cow, sh shush,
th thin, *th* this, u up, ur spur, uu book, *zh* pleasure

biretta	bə **RET** ə
Birmingham (Alabama)	**BUR** ming **HAM**
Birmingham (England)	**BUR** ming əm
Bisayas	bee **SAH** yahs
Biscay	**BIS** kay
biscuit	**BIS** kət
bisect	bī **SEKT**
bisexual	bī **SEK** shoo əl
Bisho	**BEE** shoh
bishop	**BISH** əp
bishopric	**BISH** əp rik
Bismarck	**BIZ** mahrk
bismuth	**BIZ** məth
bison	**BĪ** sən
bisque	bisk
Bissau	bi **SOW** (**SOW** as in *cow*)
bissextile	bi **SEKS** təl
bistable	bī **STAY** bəl
bister	**BIS** tər
bistro	**BEES** troh
bisulfate	bī **SUL** fayt
Bitsios, Dimitri	**BEET** see ohs, dee **MEE** tree
bittern	**BIT** ərn
bitumen	bə **TOO** mən
bituminous	bə **TOO** mə nəs
bivalence	bī **VAY** ləns
bivalent	bī **VAY** lənt
bivalve	**BĪ** valv
bivouac	**BIV** oo ak
biweekly	bī **WEEK** lee
bizarre	bə **ZAHR**
Bizerte	bə **ZUR** tee
Bizet	bee **ZAY**
blab	blab
blackguard	**BLAG** ərd
blamable	**BLAY** mə bəl
blanch	blanch
blancmange	blə **MAHNJ**
Blanco, Salvador Jorge	**BLAHN** koh, sahl vah **DAWR HOR** hay
bland	bland
blandishment	**BLAN** dish mənt

ə ago, a at, ah calm, ahr dark, air care, aw saw, ay say, ch church
e bet, ee me, eer beer, hw what, i is, ī my, *n* French final n vin,

blanket	**BLANG** kət
blare	blair
Blasco-Ibáñez	**BLAH** skoh ee **BAH** nyeth
blasé	blah **ZAY**
blaspheme	blas **FEEM**
blasphemous	**BLAS** fə məs
blasphemy	**BLAS** fə mee
blastula	**BLAS** chuu lə
blatancy	**BLAY** tən see
blatant	**BLAYT** ənt
blatherskite	**BLA***TH* ər **SKĪT**
Blavatsky	blə **VAHT** skee
blazon	**BLAY** zən
Blenheim	**BLEN** əm
Blériot	**BLAY** ree oh
blessed (a)	**BLES** əd
blessed (v)	blest
blight	blīt
blissful	**BLIS** fəl
blithe	blī*th*
blithering	**BLI***TH* ə ring
blitz	blits
blitzkrieg	**BLITS** kreeg
blizzard	**BLIZ** ərd
bloc	blok
blockade	blo **KAYD**
Bloembergen, Nicolaas	**BLOOM** **BUR** gən, **NIK** ə ləs
Bloemfontein	**BLOOM** fon **TAYN**
Blois	blwah
blond, blonde	blond
blotter	**BLOT** ər
blouse	blows
blowzy	**BLOW** zee (**BLOW** as in *cow*)
blubber	**BLUB** ər
blucher	**BLOO** chər
bludgeon	**BLUJ** ən
Bluebeard	**BLOO** beerd
bluestocking	**BLOO** **STOK** ing
bluish	**BLOO** ish
Blum, Yehuda	**BLOOM**, yə **HOO** də
blunderbuss	**BLUN** dər **BUS**
bluster	**BLUS** tər

o **on**, oh **oat**, oi **boy**, oo **soon**, oor **poor**, or **for**, ow **cow**, sh **shush**,
th **thin**, *th* **this**, u **up**, ur **spur**, uu **book**, *zh* **pleasure**

B'nai B'rith	bə NAY BRITH
boa	BOH ə
Boabdil	BOH ahb *TH*EEL
Boadicea	BOH ad ə SEE ə
boar	bor
board	bord
boarish	BOR ish
Boas	BOH az
boatswain	BOH sən
Boaz	BOH az
bobbin	BOB ən
bobolink	BOB ə LINGK
bobsled	BOB sled
Boca Raton	BOH kə rə TOHN
Boccaccio, Giovanni	boh KAH chee OH, JEE ə VAH nee
boche, B-	bosh
bock	bok
bodega	boh DAY gə
Bodensee	BOH dən ZAY
bodice	BOD əs
bodily	BOD ə lee
bodkin	BOD kən
Bodleian	bod LEE ən
Boeing	BOH ing
Boeotia	bee OH shee ə
Boeotian	bee OH shən
Boer	bohr
Boethius	boh EE thee əs
Bogan	BOH gən
bogey	BOH gee
boggle	BOG əl
bogie	BOH gee
Bogota (NJ)	bə GOH tə
Bogotá (Colombia)	BOH gə TAH
bogy	BOH gee
Bohan, Marc	boh AHN, MAHRK
bohème	boh EM
Bohemia	boh HEE mee ə
Bohol	boh HAWL
Bohr, Nils	bohr, neels
Boise	BOI zee
boisterous	BOI stə rəs
Bokhara	boh KAHR ə

ə ago, a at, ah calm, ahr dark, air care, aw saw, ay say, ch church
e bet, ee me, eer beer, hw what, i is, ī my, *n* French final n vin,

bola	**BOH** lə
bolas	**BOH** ləz
Bole, Filipe Nagera	**BOH** lay, fi **LEE** pee nahn **GER** ay
bolero	bə **LAIR** oh
Boleyn	buu **LIN**
bolivar (coin)	**BOL** ə vər
Bolívar, Simón	baw **LEE** vahr, see **MAWN**
Bolivia, b-	bə **LIV** ee ə
Bolivian	bə **LIV** ee ən
boll	bohl
Böll, Heinrich	**BUL, HĪN** rik
bollard	**BOL** ərd
bolo	**BOH** loh
Bologna (Italy)	bə **LOHN** yə
bologna (sausage)	bə **LOH** nee
Bolognese	**BOH** lən **YEEZ**
bolometer	boh **LOM** ə tər
boloney	bə **LOH** nee
bolshevik, B-	**BOHL** shə vik
Bolshoi	**BOHL** shoi
bolster	**BOHL** stər
bolus	**BOH** ləs
Bolzano, Bernhard	bohl **TSAH** noh, **BERN** hahrt
Bomani, Paul	baw **MAHN** ee
bomb	bom
bombard	bom **BAHRD**
bombardier	**BOM** bər **DEER**
bombast	**BOM** bast
bombastic	bom **BAS** tik
Bombay	bom **BAY**
Bombay duck	**BOM** bay **DUK**
bombazine	**BOM** bə **ZEEN**
bombe	bawmb
bomber	**BOM** ər
Bombois	bohm **BWAH**
Bomboko	bəm **BOH** koh
bombproof	**BOM** proof
bombshell	**BOM** shel
bona fide	**BOH** nə **FĪD**
bona fides	**BOH** nə **FĪ** deez
bonanza	bə **NAN** zə
Bonaparte	**BOH** nə **PAHRT**
Bonaventura	**BON** ə ven **CHUUR** ə

o **on**, oh **oat**, oi **boy**, oo **soon**, oor **poor**, or **for**, ow **cow**, sh **shush**,
th **thin**, *th* **this**, u **up**, ur **spur**, uu **book**, *zh* **pleasure**

Bonaventure, Saint	**BON** ə **VEN** chər
bonbon	**BON** bon
bondage	**BON** dij
bonfire	**BON** fīr
bongo	**BONG** goh
Bongo, El Hadj Omar	**BAWNG** goh, el **HAH** jee oh **MAHR**
Bonheur	bah **NUR**
bonhomie	**BON** ə **MEE**
Bonin	**BOH** nən
bonito	bə **NEE** toh
bonjour	bawn **ZHOOR** (bawn French final *n*)
bon mot	bawn **MOH** (bawn French final *n*)
Bonn	bon
Bonnard	baw **NAHR**
bonnet	**BON** ət
bonsai	**BON** sī
bonsoir	bawn **SWAHR** (bawn French final *n*)
bonus	**BOH** nəs
bon vivant	bawn vee **VAHN** (bawn and **VAHN** French final *n*)
bon voyage	bawn vwah **YAHZH** (bawn French final *n*)
Bonynge	**BON** ing
bonze	bonz
booby	**BOO** bee
boodle	**BOO** dəl
boogie-woogie	**BUUG** ee **WUUG** ee
Boolean	**BOO** lee ən
boomerang	**BOO** mə **RANG**
boondocks	**BOON** doks
boondoggle	**BOON** dah gəl
Boorstin	**BOORS** tən
Boötes	boh **OH** teez
booth, B-	booth
booths	boo*th*z
bootless	**BOOT** ləs
Bophuthatswana	**BOH** poo taht **SWAH** nə
boracic	bə **RAS** ik
borate	**BOR** ayt
borax	**BOR** aks
Borch, Otto	bork
Bordeaux	bor **DOH**
bordelaise	**BAWR** də **LAYZ**

ə ago, a at, ah calm, ahr dark, air care, aw saw, ay say, ch church
e bet, ee me, eer beer, hw what, i is, ī my, *n* French final n vin,

bordello	bor **DEL** oh
boreal	**BOR** ee əl
borealis	**BOR** ee **AL** əs
Boreas	**BOR** ee əs
Borg, Bjorn	borg, jorn
Borges, Jorge Luis	**BOR** hays, **HOR** hay loo **EES**
Borghese	bor **GAY** zay
Borgia	**BOR** jə
Borglum	**BOR** gləm
boric	**BOR** ik
Boris	**BOR** is
Borisoglebsk	**BAW** ree saw **GLEPSK**
Borja, Jacinto Castel	**BOR** hah, hah **SEEN** toh kah **STEL**
Borlaug, Norman	**BOR** lawg
borne	born
Borneo	**BOR** nee **OH**
Bornholm	**BORN** hohm
Borodin	**BOR** ə **DEEN**
boron	**BOR** on
borough	**BUR** oh
borrow	**BAH** roh
borsch	borsh
borscht	borsht
borzoi	**BOR** zoi
boscage	**BOS** kij
Bosch, Hieronymus	**BOSH, HEE** ə **ROH** nə məs
Bose	bohs
bosh	bosh
Bosley	**BOZ** lee
Bosnia	**BOZ** nee ə
bosom	**BUUZ** əm
boson	**BOH** sahn
Bosphorus	**BOS** fər əs
Bosporus	**BOS** pər əs
Bossuet	baw **SWAY**
Boston, b-	**BAW** stən
bosun	**BOH** sən
botanical	bə **TAN** i kəl
botany	**BOT** ə nee
botch	boch
Botha, Pieter	bwə **TAH, PEE** tər
Botha, Roelof	bwə **TAH**, roo **LAWF**
Bothe, Walter	**BOH** tə

---

o on, oh oat, oi boy, oo soon, oor poor, or for, ow cow, sh shush,
th thin, *th* this, u up, ur spur, uu book, *zh* pleasure

bother	**BAH** *th*ər
Botswana	bot **SWAH** nə
Bottegari	boh tə **GAH** ree
Botticelli	**BOT** ə **CHEL** ee
Botticini	**BOT** ə **CHEE** nee
botulism	**BOCH** ə LIZ əm
Botvinnik, Mikhail	**BAWT** vee nik, mi kah **EEL**
Boucher, François	boo **SHAY**, frahn **SWAH** (frahn French final *n*)
bouclé	boo **KLAY**
boudoir	**BOO** dwahr
bougainvillaea	**BOO** gən **VIL** ee ə
Bougainville (island)	**BOO** gən **VIL**
bough	bow (as in *cow*)
bought	bawt
bougie	**BOO** jee
Bouguereau	boog ə **ROH**
bouillabaisse	**BOO** yə **BAYS**
bouillon	**BOOL** yon
Boulanger	boo lahn **ZHAY** (lahn French final *n*)
boulder, B-	**BOHL** dər
boulevard	**BUUL** ə **VAHRD**
Boulogne	boo **LAWN** yə
Boumédienne	**BOO** may **DYEN**
bounteous	**BOWN** tee əs
bountiful	**BOWN** tə fəl
bouquet (aroma)	boo **KAY**
bouquet (flowers)	boh **KAY**
Bourbon (European)	**BOOR** bən
Bourbon, b- (US; whiskey)	**BUR** bən
bourgeois	boor **ZHWAH**
bourgeoise	boor **ZHWAHZ**
bourgeoisie	**BOOR** *zh*wah **ZEE**
Bourget	boor **ZHAY**
Bourguiba, Habib	buur **GEE** bah, hah **BEEB**
Bourke	burk
Bournemouth	**BOORN** məth
bourse	boors
Bouterse, Desire	**BOW** ter sə, **DAY** see ray
boutonniere	**BOOT** tə **NEER**
Bouvet	**BOO** vay
bouzouki	bə **ZOO** kee

ə ago, a at, ah calm, ahr dark, air care, aw saw, ay say, ch church
e bet, ee me, eer beer, hw what, i is, ī my, *n* French final n vin,

Bovary	**BOH** vah ree
Bovet, Daniel	boh **VAY**, dah **NYEL**
bovine	**BOH** vīn
bow (prow; nod)	bow (as in *cow*)
bow (weapon; curve; knot)	boh
Bowdich, Bowditch	**BOW** DICH (**BOW** as in *cow*)
Bowdler	**BOHD** lər
bowdlerize	**BOHD** lə RĪZ
Bowdoin	**BOHD** ən
bowel	**BOW** əl (**BOW** as in *cow*)
bower (arbor; cards; anchor)	**BOW** ər (**BOW** as in *cow*)
bower (violinist)	**BOH** ər
bowery, B-	**BOW** ə ree (**BOW** as in *cow*)
bowie, B-	**BOO** ee
bowl	bohl
bowlegged	**BOH** LEG əd
bowler	**BOH** lər
bowline	**BOH** lən
bowman (archer)	**BOH** mən
bowman (oarsman)	**BOW** mən (**BOW** as in *cow*)
bowsprit	**BOW** sprit (**BOW** as in *cow*)
bowstring	**BOH** string
boxer	**BOK** sər
Boya, Thomas Setondji	**BOH** yə, TOM əs sə **TOON** jee
boyar	boh **YAHR**
boycott	**BOI** kot
Boyd, Aquilino	**BOID**, ah kee **LEE** noh
Bo Yibo	baw yee baw
boysenberry	**BOI** zən BER ee
bra	brah
Brabant	brə **BANT**
brace	brays
bracelet	**BRAYS** lət
bracero	brah **SAIR** oh
brachial	**BRAY** kee əl
brachiopod	**BRAY** kee ə POD
brachium	**BRAY** kee əm
brachycephalic	**BRAK** ee sə FAL ik
bracken	**BRAK** ən
brackish	**BRAK** ish
brae	bray

---

o on, oh oat, oi boy, oo soon, oor poor, or for, ow cow, sh shush,
th thin, *th* this, u up, ur spur, uu book, *zh* pleasure

Braganca	brah **GAHN** sə
braggadocio	**BRAG** ə **DOH** shee **OH**
braggart	**BRAG** ərt
Brahe, Tycho	**BRAH, TEE** koh
Brahma, b-	**BRAH** mə
Brahman	**BRAH** mən
Brahmaputra	**BRAH** mə **POO** trə
Brahmin	**BRAH** mən
Brahms	brahmz
braid	brayd
braille, B-	brayl
braise	brayz
Bramante	brah **MAHN** tay
Braña	**BRAH** nyah
Brancusi	brahn **KOO** see
Brandeis	**BRAN** dīs
Brandenburg	**BRAN** dən **BURG**
brandied	**BRAN** deed
brandish	**BRAN** dish
Brandt, Willy	**BRAHNT, VIL** ee
Braque, Georges	**BRAHK,** zhawrzh
Brasília	brə **ZIL** yə
brass	bras
brassard	**BRAS** ərd
brasserie	**BRAS** ə **REE**
brassiere	brə **ZEER**
Bratislava	**BRAH** tə **SLAH** və
Brattain, Walter	**BRAT** ən
Braun	brown
Braunschweiger	**BROWN** shwī gər
bravado	brə **VAH** doh
bravo	**BRAH** voh
bravura	brə **VYOOR** ə
brawny	**BRAW** nee
braze	brayz
brazier	**BRAY** zhər
Brazil	brə **ZIL**
Brazzaville	**BRAZ** ə **VIL**
breach	breech
breadth	bredth
breadthways	**BREDTH** wayz
breadthwise	**BREDTH** wīz
breakage	**BRAY** kij

ə ago, a at, ah calm, ahr dark, air care, aw saw, ay say, ch church
e bet, ee me, eer beer, hw what, i is, ī my, *n* French final n vin,

breakfast	**BREK** fəst
bream	breem
breast	brest
breath	breth
breathalyzer	**BRETH** ə lī zər
breathe	bree*th*
breathed	bree*th*d
breathing	**BREE*TH*** ing
breathy	**BRETH** ee
breccia	**BRECH** ee ə
Brecht, Bertolt	**BREKT, BER** tohlt
breech	breech
breeches (trousers)	**BRICH** əz
breeches buoy	**BREE** chəz **BOO** ee
breechloader	**BREECH LOH** dər
Bremen (Germany)	**BRAY** mən
Bremen (US)	**BREE** mən
Brenner	**BREN** ər
Brentano	bren **TAH** noh
Brescia	**BRE** shah
Breslau	**BRES** low (low as in *cow*)
Bressoud	bre **SUUD**
Brest	brest
Brest-Litovsk	**BREST** lə **TAWFSK**
brethren	**BRE*TH*** rən
Breton	**BRET** ən
Bretton	**BRET** ən
Breughel	**BROI** gəl
breve	breev
brevet	brə **VET**
breviary	**BREE** vee **ER** ee
brevier	brə **VEER**
brevity	**BREV** ə tee
brewery	**BROO** ə ree
Brezhnev, Leonid	**BREZ*H*** nef, **LAY** oh nid
Briand, Aristide	bree **AHN**, ah ree **STEED** (**AHN** French final *n*)
Briareus	brī **AIR** ee əs
bribery	**BRĪ** bə ree
bric-a-brac	**BRIK** ə **BRAK**
bridal	**BRĪD** əl
bridegroom	**BRĪD** groom
bridesmaid	**BRĪDZ** mayd

o on, oh oat, oi boy, oo soon, oor poor, or for, ow cow, sh shush,
th thin, *th* this, u up, ur spur, uu book, *zh* pleasure

bridle	**BRĪD** əl
Brie	bree
brier	**BRĪ** ər
brigade	bri **GAYD**
brigadier	BRIG ə **DEER**
brigand	**BRIG** ənd
brigantine	**BRIG** ən TEEN
brilliance	**BRIL** yəns
brilliant	**BRIL** yənt
brilliantine	**BRIL** yən TEEN
Brindisi	**BREEN** də zee
brindled	**BRIN** dəld
brioche	bree **OHSH**
briquette	bri **KET**
Brisbane (Australia)	**BRIZ** bən
Briseis	brī **SEE** əs
brisket	**BRIS** kət
brisling	**BRIZ** ling
bristle	**BRIS** əl
Bristol	**BRIS** təl
Britannia	bri **TAN** ee ə
Britannic	bri **TAN** ik
Briticism	**BRIT** ə SIZ əm
Britisher	**BRIT** i shər
Briton	**BRIT** ən
Brno	**BUR** noh
broach	brohch
broad gauge	brawd gayj
Brobdingnag	**BROB** ding NAG
Brobdingnagian	BROB ding **NAG** ee ən
brocade	broh **KAYD**
broccoli	**BROK** ə lee
broché	broh **SHAY**
brochette	broh **SHET**
brochure	broh **SHUUR**
brogan	**BROH** gən
Broglio	**BROH** lee oh
brogue	brohg
brokerage	**BROH** kə rij
brome	brohm
bromide	**BROH** mīd
bromine	**BROH** meen
bronchial	**BRONG** kee əl

ə ago, a at, ah calm, ahr dark, air care, aw saw, ay say, ch church
e bet, ee me, eer beer, hw what, i is, ī my, *n* French final n vin,

bronchitis	brong **KĪ** təs
bronchoscope	**BRONG** kə **SKOHP**
bronco	**BRONG** koh
Brontë	**BRON** tee
brontosaurus	**BRON** tə **SOR** əs
Bronx	brongks
bronze	bronz
brooch	brohch
brothel	**BRAHTH** əl
brotherhood	**BRU***TH* ər **HUUD**
brougham	broom
brouhaha	**BROO** hah hah
Broun	broon
browbeat	**BROW BEET** (**BROW** as in *cow*)
browse	browz
Broz	brawz
brucellosis	**BROO** sə **LOH** səs
Bruckner, Anton	**BRUUK** nər, **AN** tohn
Brueghel	**BROI** gəl
Bruges	broo*zh*
bruin	**BROO** ən
bruise	brooz
bruiser	**BROO** zər
bruit	broot
Brumaire	bruu **MAIR**
brumal	**BROO** məl
brume	broom
Brumel, Valery	**BRUU** mil, vah **LAI** ree
Brunei	bruu **NĪ**
Brunelleschi	**BROON** ə **LES** kee
brunet	broo **NET**
Brunetière	**BRUU** nə **TYAIR**
Brunhild	**BRUUN** hilt
Brunnhilde	bruun **HIL** də
brusque	brusk
Brussels	**BRUS** əlz
brut	broot
brute	broot
Bruxelles	broo **SEL**
Bruyère	bruu **YAIR**
Bryansk	bree **AHNSK**
Brynhild	**BRIN** hild
Bryn Mawr	brin **MAHR**

o on, oh oat, oi boy, oo soon, oor poor, or for, ow cow, sh shush,
th thin, *th* this, u up, ur spur, uu book, *zh* pleasure

bryophyte	**BRĪ** ə **FĪT**
Brython	**BRITH** ən
Brythonic	bri **THON** ik
Brzezinski, Zbigniew	brə **ZH**IN skee, zə **BIG** nəf
Buali, Abdulaziz	**BOO** lee, ahb **DOOL** ah **SEEZ**
Buber, Martin	**BOO** bər
Bubiriza, Pascal	boo bee **REE** zah, **PAH** skahl
bubo	**BYOO** boh
buboes	**BYOO** bohz
bubonic	byoo **BON** ik
buccal	**BUK** əl
buccaneer	**BUK** ə **NEER**
buccinator	**BUK** sə **NAY** tər
Bucephalus	byoo **SEF** ə ləs
Buchanan	byoo **KAN** ən
Buchan, John	**BUK** ən
Bucharest	**BOO** kə **REST**
Buchenwald	**BOOK** ən **VAHLT**
Buchholz, Horst	**BUK** hohlts, **HAWRST**
Buchman	**BUUK** mən
Buchmanism	**BUUK** mə **NIZ** əm
Buchmanite	**BUUK** mə **NĪT**
Buchwald	**BOOK** wawld
buckaroo	**BUK** ə **ROO**
Buckeye, b-	**BUK** ī
Buckingham	**BUK** ing əm
bucko	**BUK** oh
buckram	**BUK** rəm
buckwheat	**BUK** hweet
bucolic	byoo **KOL** ik
Bucovina	**BOO** kə **VEE** nə
Bucyk	**BYUU** sik
Budapest	**BOO** də **PEST**
Buddha	**BOO** də
Buddhism	**BOOD** iz əm
buddleia	**BUD** lee ə
Budenny	boo **DEN** ee
budgerigar	**BUJ** ə ree **GAHR**
Budo, Halim	**BUU** doh, **HAL** leem
Budweiser	**BUD** wī zər
Buell	**BYOO** əl
Buenaventura	**BWAY** nə ven **TUUR** ə
Buenos Aires	**BWAY** nəs **ĪR** eez

ə ago, a at, ah calm, ahr dark, air care, aw saw, ay say, ch church
e bet, ee me, eer beer, hw what, i is, ī my, *n* French final n vin,

buffalo, B-	**BUF** ə loh
buffet (blow)	**BUF** ət
buffet (sideboard; meal)	bə **FAY**
buffo	**BOO** foh
buffoon	bə **FOON**
buffoonery	bə **FOO** nə ree
Bug (river)	boog
bugaboo	**BUG** ə **BOO**
Buganda	boo **GAN** də
bugle	**BYOO** gəl
bugloss	**BYOO** glaws
Buitenzorg	**BĪT** ən **ZORG**
Bujumbura	**BOO** jəm **BUUR** ə
Bukharin	boo **KAH** rən
bulbous	**BUL** bəs
bulbul	**BUUL** buul
Bulganin	buul **GAHN** ən
Bulgar	**BUL** gər
Bulgaria	buul **GAIR** ee ə
bulgur	**BUUL** gər
bulimia	byoo **LIM** ee ə
bulkhead	**BULK** hed
bulldoze	**BUUL** dohz
bullion	**BUUL** yən
Bull Moose	buul moos
Bull, Ole	**BOOL, OH** lə
bullock	**BUUL** ək
bulrush	**BUUL** rush
bulwark	**BUUL** wərk
bumblebee	**BUM** bəl **BEE**
bumpkin	**BUM** kən
bumptious	**BUMP** shəs
Buna	**BOO** nə
Bunche	bunch
bunco	**BUNG** koh
buncombe	**BUNG** kəm
Bund	buund
Bundesrat	**BUUN** dəs **RAHT**
Bundestag	**BUUN** dəs **TAHG**
Bundeswehr	**BUUN** dəs **VAIR**
bungalow	**BUNG** gə **LOH**
bunghole	**BUNG** **HOHL**

Bunin	**BOON** ən
bunion	**BUN** yən
bunkum	**BUNG** kəm
Bunsen	**BUN** sən
bunting	**BUN** ting
Buñuel, Luis	**BUUN** yoo **EL**, loo **EES**
Bunyan	**BUN** yən
buoy	**BOO** ee
buoyancy	**BOI** ən see
buoyant	**BOI** ənt
Burbage	**BUR** bij
Burbank	**BUR** bank
Burberry	**BUR** bə ree
burdock	**BUR** dok
bureau	**BYOOR** oh
bureaucracy	byuu **ROK** rə see
burette	byuu **RET**
burgeon	**BUR** jən
burgess	**BUR** jəs
burgher	**BUR** gər
Burghley	**BUR** lee
burglar	**BUR** glər
burglarize	**BUR** glə **RĪZ**
burglary	**BUR** glə ree
burgomaster	**BUR** gə **MAS** tər
burgoo	bur **GOO**
Burgoyne	bər **GOIN**
burgrave	**BUR** grayv
Burgundian	bər **GUN** dee ən
Burgundy	**BUR** gən dee
burial	**BER** ee əl
burin	**BYUUR** ən
burka	**BUUR** kə
burl	burl
burlap	**BUR** lap
Burleigh	**BUR** lee
burlesque	bər **LESK**
burley, B-	**BUR** lee
burly	**BUR** lee
Burma	**BUR** mə
Burmese	bər **MEEZ**
burnoose, burnous	bər **NOOS**
burnsides	**BURN** **SĪDZ**

ə ago, a at, ah calm, ahr dark, air care, aw saw, ay say, ch church
e bet, ee me, eer beer, hw what, i is, ī my, n French final n vin,

burro	**BUR** oh
burrow	**BUR** oh
bursa	**BUR** sə
bursae	**BUR** see
bursar	**BUR** sər
bursitis	bər **SĪ** təs
Burundi	buu **RUUN** dee
bury	**BER** ee
busby	**BUZ** bee
bushel	**BUUSH** əl
bushido, B-	boo shee doh
bushwhacker	**BUUSH** hwak ər
business	**BIZ** nəs
businessman	**BIZ** nəs **MAN**
buskin	**BUS** kən
Bustamante	**BOO** stah **MAHN** tay
Bustamente	**BOO** stah **MEN** tay
bustard	**BUS** tərd
bustle	**BUS** əl
Busuanga	boo **SWAHNG** gə
busy	**BIZ** ee
busyness	**BIZ** ee nəs
butadiene	**BYOO** tə **DĪ** een
butane	**BYOO** tayn
butchery	**BUUCH** ə ree
Butor, Michel	buu **TAWR**, mee **SHEL**
butt	but
butte, B-	byoot
butterwort	**BUT** ər **WURT**
buttock	**BUT** ək
buttress	**BUT** rəs
butyl	**BYOO** təl
butyrate	**BYOO** tə **RAYT**
butyric	byoo **TIR** ik
buxom	**BUK** səm
buzzard	**BUZ** ərd
Bwakira, Melchior	bgah **TEER** rah, **MEL** kee or (bgah *b* barely pronounced)
bwana	**BWAH** nə
Bydgoszcz	**BID** gawsh
bye	bī
Byelorussia	**BYEL** oh **RUSH** ə
Byelorussian	**BYEL** oh **RUSH** ən

---

o on, oh oat, oi boy, oo soon, oor poor, or for, ow cow, sh shush,
th thin, *th* this, u up, ur spur, uu book, *zh* pleasure

bylaw, byelaw	**BĪ** law
by-line	**BĪ** līn
Byong Hion Lew	byong hyon loo
Byron	**BĪ** rən
Byronic	bī **RON** ik
Bysshe	bish
bystander	**BĪ** stan dər
byte	bīt
Byzantine	**BIZ** ən **TEEN**
Byzantium	bə **ZAN** shee əm

C

cabal	kə **BAL**
cabala	**KAB** ə lə
cabalistic	**KAB** ə **LIS** tik
caballero	**KAB** əl **YAIR** oh
Caballero Tamayo, Jaime	kah bah **YAIR** oh tah **MAH** yoh, **HĪ** may
cabana	kə **BAN** ə
cabaret	**KAB** ə **RAY**
cabbala	**KAB** ə lə
Cabell	**KAB** əl
cabinet	**KAB** ə nət
cabochon	**KAB** ə **SHON**
caboodle	kə **BOO** dəl
caboose	kə **BOOS**
Cabot	**KAB** ət
Cabrera	ka **BRAY** rə
cabriole	**KAB** ree **OHL**
cabriolet	**KAB** ree ə **LAY**
cacao	kə **KAY** oh
Caccia	**KAH** chə
cache	kash
cachet	ka **SHAY**
cachou	kə **SHOO**
cachucha	kə **CHOO** chə
cacique	kə **SEEK**
cacophonous	kə **KOF** ə nəs
cacophony	kə **KOF** ə nee
cacti	**KAK** tī

ə ago, a at, ah calm, ahr dark, air care, aw saw, ay say, ch church
e bet, ee me, eer beer, hw what, i is, ī my, *n* French final n vin,

cactus	**KAK** təs
cadaver	kə **DAV** ər
cadaverous	kə **DAV** ər əs
caddie, caddy	**KAD** ee
cadence	**KAY** dəns
cadenza	kə **DEN** zə
cadet	kə **DET**
cadge	kaj
cadi	**KAH** dee
Cádiz	kə **DIZ**
Cadmean	kad **MEE** ən
cadmium	**KAD** mee əm
Cadmus	**KAD** məs
cadre	**KAD** ree
caduceus	kə **DOO** see əs
Caedmon	**KAD** mən
Caedmonian	kad **MOH** nee ən
Caen	kahn (French final *n*)
Caerleon	kahr **LEE** ən
Caesar	**SEE** zər
Caesarea	SEE zə **REE** ə
Caesarean	si **ZAIR** ee ən
caesura	si **ZHOOR** ə
café	ka **FAY**
café au lait	ka **FAY** oh **LAY**
café noir	ka **FAY NWAHR**
cafeteria	KAF ə **TEER** ee ə
caffeine	ka **FEEN**
caftan	**KAF** tən
cagey, cagy	**KAY** jee
Cagliostro	kah **LYAWS** troh
cahoots	kə **HOOTS**
Caiaphas	**KAY** ə fəs
Caicos	**KAY** kəs
caiman	**KAY** mən
caïque	kah **EEK**
cairn	kairn
Cairo (Egypt)	**KĪ** roh
Cairo (Illinois)	**KAIR** oh
caisson	**KAY** sən
caitiff	**KAY** tif
Caitlin	**KAYT** lin
Caius	**KAY** əs

o on, oh oat, oi boy, oo soon, oor poor, or for, ow cow, sh shush,
th thin, *th* this, u up, ur spur, uu book, *zh* pleasure

Caius (college)	keez
cajole	kə JOHL
cajolery	kə JOH lə ree
Cajun	KAY jən
calabash	KAL ə BASH
calaboose	KAL ə BOOS
Calabria	kə LAH bree ə
caladium	kə LAY dee əm
Calais (France)	ka LAY
Calais (US)	KA lis
calamari	KAHL ə MAHR ee
calamary	KAL ə MER ee
calamine	KAL ə MĪN
calamitous	kə LAM ə təs
calamity	kə LAM ə tee
calamus	KAL ə məs
calash	kə LASH
calcareous	kal KAR ee əs
calceolaria	KAL see ə LAIR ee ə
calces	KAL seez
calcify	KAL sə FĪ
calcimine	KAL sə MĪN
calcine	KAL sīn
calcite	KAL sīt
calcium	KAL see əm
calculable	KAL kyə lə bəl
calculate	KAL kyə LAYT
calculation	KAL kyə LAY shən
calculator	KAL kyə LAY tər
calculous	KAL kyə ləs
calculus	KAL kyə ləs
Calcutta	kal KUT ə
Calderon (English)	KAWL dər ən
Calderón (Spanish)	KAHL de RAWN
caldron	KAWL drən
Caleb	KAY ləb
calèche	ka LESH
Caledonia	KAL i DOH nee ə
Caledonian	KAL ə DOH nee ən
calendar	KAL ən dər
calender	KAL ən dər
calends	KAL əndz
calendula	kə LEN jə lə
calf	kaf

ə ago, a at, ah calm, ahr dark, air care, aw saw, ay say, ch church
e bet, ee me, eer beer, hw what, i is, ī my, *n* French final n vin,

Cali	**KAH** lee
Caliban	**KAL** ə **BAN**
caliber	**KAL** ə bər
calibrate	**KAL** ə **BRAYT**
calices	**KAL** i **SEEZ**
calico	**KAL** ə **KOH**
calif	**KAY** lif
California	**KAL** ə **FOR** nyə
californium	**KAL** ə **FOR** nee əm
caliper	**KAL** ə pər
caliph	**KAY** lif
caliphate	**KAL** ə **FAYT**
calisthenic	**KAL** əs **THEN** ik
calix	**KAY** liks
calk	kawk
calla	**KAL** ə
Callaghan	**KAL** ə han
Callao	kah **YAH** oh
Callas	**KAL** əs
Callejas, Rafael Leonardo	cah **YAY** hahs, rah fi **EL** lay or **NAHR** doh
calligraphy	kə **LIG** rə fee
calliope, C-	kə **LĪ** ə **PEE**
Callisto	kə **LIS** toh
callous	**KAL** əs
callow	**KAL** oh
callus	**KAL** əs
calm	kahm
calmative	**KAHM** ə tiv
calomel	**KAL** ə **MEL**
caloric	kə **LAW** rik
calorie	**KAL** ə ree
calumet	**KAL** yə **MET**
calumniate	kə **LUM** nee **AYT**
calumniator	kə **LUM** nee **AY** tər
calumny	**KAL** əm nee
Calvary	**KAL** və ree
Calvin	**KAL** vin
Calvinism	**KAL** və **NIZ** əm
Calvinist	**KAL** və nist
Calvo Sotelo, Leopoldo	**KAHL** boh soh **TEL** oh, lay oh **POHL** doh
calx	kalks

o on, oh oat, oi boy, oo soon, oor poor, or for, ow cow, sh shush,
th thin, *th* this, u up, ur spur, uu book, *zh* pleasure

calyces	KAY lə SEEZ
calycle	KAL i kəl
Calydon	KAL i DON
Calypso, c-	kə LIP soh
calyx	KAY liks
calyxes	KAY liks əz
Camacho	kah MAH choh
Camaguey	KAM ə GWAY
camaraderie	KAH mə RAH də ree
Camargue	kə MAHRG
camarilla	KAM ə RIL ə
camber	KAM bər
cambium	KAM bee əm
Cambodia	kam BOH dee ə
Cambrai	kahm BRAY
Cambrian	KAM bree ən
cambric	KAYM brik
Cambridge	KAYM brij
camellia	kə MEEL yə
Camelot	KAM ə LOT
Camembert	KAM əm BAIR
cameo	KAM ee oh
camera	KAM ə rə
camerlengo	KAM ər LING goh
Cameroon	KAM ə ROON
camisole	KAM i SOHL
camomile	KAM ə MEEL
Camorra	kə MAW rə
camouflage	KAM ə FLAHZH
campagna, C-	kam PAHN yə
campaign	kam PAYN
Campania	kam PAY nee ə
campanile	KAM pə NEE lee
campanula	kam PAN yə lə
Campeche	kam PEE chee
camphor	KAM fər
campion, C-	KAM pee ən
campo	KAM poh
Campora	kahm PAW rah
campus	KAM pəs
Camus	ka MUU
Cana	KAY nə
Canaan	KAY nən

ə ago, a at, ah calm, ahr dark, air care, aw saw, ay say, ch church
e bet, ee me, eer beer, hw what, i is, ī my, n French final n vin,

Canada	KAN ə də
Canadian	kə NAY dee ən
canaille	kə NĪ
canalization	kə NAL i ZAY shən
canapé	KAN ə pee
canard	kə NAHRD
Canary, c-	kə NAIR ee
Cañas	KAH nyahs
canasta	kə NAS tə
Canaveral	kə NAV ər əl
Canberra	KAN bər ə
Canby	KAN bee
cancan	KAN kan
cancelable	KAN sə lə bəl
cancellation	KAN sə LAY shən
candela	kan DEE lə
candelabra	KAN də LAH brə
candelabrum	KAN də LAH brəm
candescent	kan DES ənt
candid	KAN did
Candida	KAN di də
candidacy	KAN di də SEE
candidate	KAN di DAYT
Candide	kahn DEED
Candlemas	KAN dəl məs
candor	KAN dər
candytuft	KAN dee TUFT
Canetti	ka NET ee
canine	KAY nīn
Canis	KAY nis
canister	KAN ə stər
canker	KANG kər
canna	KAN ə
cannabis	KAN ə bəs
cannel	KAN əl
cannelloni	KAN ə LOH nee
Cannes	kan
canoe	kə NOO
canon	KAN ən
cañon	KAN yən
canonical	kə NON i kəl
canonize	KAN ə NĪZ
Canopic	kə NOH pik

o on, oh oat, oi boy, oo soon, oor poor, or for, ow cow, sh shush,
th thin, *th* this, u up, ur spur, uu book, *zh* pleasure

Canopus	kə **NOH** pəs
Canossa	kə **NOS** ə
cant	kant
can't	kant
cantabile	kahn **TAH** bi **LAY**
Cantabrigian	**KAN** tə **BRIJ** ee ən
cantaloupe	**KAN** tə **LOHP**
cantankerous	kan **TANG** kər əs
cantata	kən **TAH** tə
canteen	kan **TEEN**
canter	**KAN** tər
Canterbury	**KAN** tər **BER** ee
canticle	**KAN** ti kəl
cantilever	**KAN** tə **LEE** vər
cantina	kan **TEE** nə
canto	**KAN** toh
Canton (China)	kan **TON**
Canton (US)	**KAN** tən
canton	**KAN** tən
Cantonese	**KAN** tə **NEEZ**
cantonment	kan **TON** mənt
cantor	**KAN** tər
Canuck	kə **NUK**
canvas	**KAN** vəs
canvass	**KAN** vəs
canyon	**KAN** yən
canzone	kahn **TSOH** nay
Caodaism	kow **DĪ** iz əm
capacious	kə **PAY** shəs
capacitance	kə **PAS** ə təns
capacitor	kə **PAS** ə tər
caparison	kə **PAR** ə sən
Capek, Karel	**CHAH** pek, **KAH** rəl
Capella	kə **PEL** ə
caper	**KAY** pər
Capetian	kə **PEE** shən
Cape Verde	**KAYP VURD**
Capezio	kə **PEE** zee oh
capillary	**KAP** ə **LER** ee
capitulate	kə **PICH** ə **LAYT**
capitulation	kə **PICH** ə **LAY** shən
capo	**KAH** poh
capon	**KAY** pon

ə ago, a at, ah calm, ahr dark, air care, aw saw, ay say, ch church
e bet, ee me, eer beer, hw what, i is, ī my, *n* French final n vin,

Caporetto	KAP ə RET oh
Capote	kə POH tee
cappuccino	KAP ə CHEE noh
capriccio	kə PREE chee OH
caprice	kə PREES
capricious	kə PRISH əs
Capricorn	KAP rə KORN
capriole	KAP ree OHL
capsize	KAP sīz
capstan	KAP stən
capsule	KAP səl
captain	KAP tən
caption	KAP shən
captious	KAP shəs
captivate	KAP tə VAYT
captor	KAP tər
capture	KAP chər
Capucci	kah PUU chee
capuchin, C-	KAP yə chin
Capucine	ka pyoo SEEN
Capulet	KAP yə lət
Caputo	kə POOT oh
carabao	KAHR ə BAH oh
carabiniere	KA rə bən YAIR ay
caracal	KA rə KAL
Caracalla	KA rə KAL ə
Caracas	kə RAH kəs
caracul	KA rə kəl
carafe	kə RAF
Caramanlis	KA rə MAN lis
caramel	KA rə məl
caramelize	KA rə mə LĪZ
carapace	KA rə PAYS
carat	KA rət
Caravaggio	KAH rah VAHD joh
caravan	KA rə VAN
caravansary	KA rə VAN sə ree
caravanserai	KA rə VAN sə RĪ
caravel	KA rə VEL
caraway	KA rə WAY
Carazo, Rodrigo	kah RAH soh, rawd REE goh
carbide	KAHR bīd
carbine	KAHR been

o on, oh oat, oi boy, oo soon, oor poor, or for, ow cow, sh shush,
th thin, *th* this, u up, ur spur, uu book, *zh* pleasure

carbohydrate	**KAHR** boh **HĪ** drayt
carbolic	kahr **BOL** ik
carbon	**KAHR** bən
carbonaceous	**KAHR** bə **NAY** shəs
Carbonari	**KAHR** bə **NAHR** ee
carboniferous, C-	**KAHR** bə **NIF** ər əs
carbonize	**KAHR** bə **NĪZ**
carborundum, C-	**KAHR** bə **RUN** dəm
carbuncle	**KAHR** bung kəl
carburetor	**KAHR** bə **RAY** tər
carcass	**KAHR** kəs
Carcassonne	kahr ka **SAWN**
carcinogen	kahr **SIN** ə jən
carcinoma	**KAHR** sə **NOH** mə
cardamom	**KAHR** də məm
Cárdenas	**KAHR** day nahs
cardiac	**KAHR** dee **AK**
Cardiff	**KAHR** dif
cardigan, C-	**KAHR** də gən
Cardin	kahr **DAN** (**DAN** French final *n*)
cardinal	**KAHR** də nəl
Cardinale, Claudia	kahr dee **NAH** le, **KLOW** dee ah
Cardoso, Mario	kahr **DOH** soh, **MAH** ree oh
Cardozo	kahr **DOH** zoh
Carducci	kahr **DOO** chee
careen	kə **REEN**
career	kə **REER**
caress	kə **RES**
caret	**KA** rət
Carew	kə **ROO**
Caria	**KAIR** ee ə
Carías	kah **REE AHS**
Caribbean	**KA** rə **BEE** ən
caribou	**KA** rə **BOO**
caricature	**KA** rə kə **CHUUR**
caricaturist	**KA** rə kə **CHUUR** əst
caries	**KAIR** eez
carillon	**KA** rə **LON**
carioca	**KA** ree **OH** kə
Carlisle	kahr **LĪL**
Carlos (US)	**KAHR** ləs
Carlos (Spain)	**KAHR** lohs
Carlovingian	**KAHR** lə **VINJ** ee ən

ə ago, a at, ah calm, ahr dark, air care, aw saw, ay say, ch church
e bet, ee me, eer beer, hw what, i is, ī my, *n* French final n vin,

Carlsbad	**KAHRLZ** bad
Carlstadt	**KAHRL** stat
Carlyle	kahr **LĪL**
Carmel (California)	kahr **MEL**
Carmel (mountain in Israel)	**KAHR** məl
Carmelite	**KAHR** mə **LĪT**
Carmen	**KAHR** mən
Carmichael	**KAHR** mī kəl
carmine	**KAHR** mən
Carmona	kahr **MOH** nə
carnage	**KAHR** nij
carnal	**KAHR** nəl
Carnarvon	kahr **NAHR** vən
carnation	kahr **NAY** shən
carnauba	kahr **NAW** bə
Carnegie, Andrew	kahr **NAY** gee
Carnegie Hall	**KAHR** nə gee
carnelian	kahr **NEEL** yən
carnival	**KAHR** nə vəl
Carnivora	kahr **NIV** ər ə
carnivore	**KAHR** nə **VOR**
carnivorous	kahr **NIV** ər əs
Carolina	**KA** rə **LĪN** ə
Caroline	**KA** rə lin
Carolingian	**KA** rə **LIN** jee ən
Carolinian	**KA** rə **LIN** ee ən
carom	**KA** rəm
carotene	**KA** rə **TEEN**
carotid	kə **ROT** əd
carousal	kə **ROW** zəl (**ROW** as in *cow*)
carouse	kə **ROWZ** (**ROWZ** as in *cows*)
carousel	**KA** rə **SEL**
Carpaccio	kahr **PAHT** choh
Carpathia	kahr **PAY** thee ə
Carpathian	kahr **PAY** thee ən
Carpatho-Ukraine	kahr **PAY** thoh yoo **KRAIN**
carpe diem	**KAHR** pe **DEE** em
Carracci, Annibale	kah **RAHT** chee, ahn **NEE** bah le
Carradine	**KA** rə deen
Carrara	kə **RAHR** ə
carrel	**KA** rəl
Carreon, Camilio	kah rah **OHN**, kah **MEE** lyoh

---

o on, oh **o**at, oi b**o**y, oo s**oo**n, oor p**oo**r, or f**o**r, ow c**o**w, sh **sh**u**sh**,
th **th**in, *th* **th**is, u **u**p, ur sp**ur**, uu b**oo**k, *zh* plea**s**ure

carriage	**KA** rij
carrier	**KA** ree ər
Carrillo Flores, Antonio	kah **REE** yoh **FLAW** res, ahn **TOH** nyoh
carrion	**KA** ree ən
carrot	**KA** rət
carrousel	**KA** rə **SEL**
Carstens	**KAHR** stəns
Cartagena	**KAHR** tə **HAY** nə
carte	kahrt
carte blanche	kahrt blahnsh
carte du jour	**KAHRT** də **ZH**UUR
cartel	kahr **TEL**
Cartesian	kahr **TEE** zhən
Carthage	**KAHR** thij
Carthaginian	**KAHR** thə **JIN** ee ən
Carthusian	kahr **THOO** zhən
Cartier (French)	kahr **TYAY**
Cartier (US)	**KAHR** tee ay
Cartier-Bresson	kahr tyay bre **SAWN** (**SAWN** French final *n*)
cartilage	**KAHR** tə lij
cartilaginous	**KAHR** tə **LAJ** ə nəs
cartographer	kahr **TOG** rə fər
cartography	kahr **TOG** rə fee
carton	**KAHR** tən
cartoon	kahr **TOON**
cartouche	kahr **TOOSH**
cartridge	**KAHR** trij
Caruso	kə **ROO** soh
Carvalho Silos, Geraldo de	ker **VAH** lyuu **SEE** luush, *zh*ə **RAHL** duu də
carvel	**KAHR** vəl
caryatid	**KA** ree **AT** əd
casaba	kə **SAH** bə
Casablanca	**KAH** sah **BLAHNG** kah
Casals	kah **SAHLZ**
Casanova	**KAZ** ə **NOH** və
Casbah	**KAHZ** bah
cascara	kas **KA** rə
casein	**KAY** seen
casement	**KAYS** mənt
cashew	**KASH** oo
cashmere	**KAZH** meer

ə ago, a at, ah calm, ahr dark, air care, aw saw, ay say, ch church
e bet, ee me, eer beer, hw what, i is, ī my, *n* French final n vin,

Cashmere (India)	kash **MEER**
Casimir	**KAZ** ə mir
Casoria	ka **SOR** ee ə
Caspian	**KAS** pee ən
casque	kask
cassaba	kə **SAH** bə
Cassandra	kə **SAN** drə
Cassatt, Mary	kə **SAT**
cassava	kə **SAH** və
Cassel, Jean-Pierre	kah **SEL**, *zh*ahn pyair (*zh*ahn French final *n*)
casserole	**KAS** ə ʀᴏʜʟ
cassette	kə **SET**
cassia	**KASH** ə
Cassin, René	ka **SAN**, rə **NAY** (SAN French final *n*)
Cassini	kə **SEE** nee
Cassiopeia	ᴋᴀs ee ə **PEE** ə
cassiterite	kə **SIT** ə ʀ**Ī**ᴛ
cassock	**KAS** ək
cassowary	**KAS** ə **WER** ee
Castaneda, Jorge	kahs tahn **YAY** dah, **HOR** hee
castanet	ᴋᴀs tə **NET**
castaway	**KAS** tə **WAY**
caste	kast
Castelo Branco, Humberto	kahs **TE** luu **BRAHN** kuu, oom **BER** tuu
caster	**KAS** tər
castigate	**KAS** tə ɢᴀʏᴛ
Castiglione	ᴋᴀʜ stee **LYAW** ne
Castiglioni	ᴋᴀʜ stee **LYAW** nee
Castile (Spain)	ka **STEEL**
Castile (NY)	ka **ST**Ĭ**L**
Castilian	ka **STIL** yən
Castillo	kahs **TEE** yaw
castle	**KAS** əl
castor, C-	**KAS** tər
castrate	**KAS** trayt
castrato	ka **STRAH** toh
Castries	ka **STREEZ**
Castro	**KAS** troh
casual	**KAZ***H* oo əl
casualty	**KAZ***H* oo əl tee
casuist	**KAZ***H* ə wəst

o on, oh oat, oi boy, oo soon, oor poor, or for, ow cow, sh shush,
th thin, *th* this, u up, ur spur, uu book, *zh* pleasure

casuistry	**KAZH** ə wəs tree
casus belli	**KAY** səs **BEL** ī
catabolism	kə **TAB** ə LIZ əm
catachresis	**KAT** ə **KREE** səs
cataclysm	**KAT** ə KLIZ əm
catacomb	**KAT** ə KOHM
catafalque	**KAT** ə FAWK
Catalan	**KAT** ə LAN
catalectic	**KAT** ə **LEK** tik
catalepsy	**KAT** ə LEP see
cataleptic	**KAT** ə **LEP** tik
catalog	**KAT** ə LAWG
catalpa	kə **TAL** pə
catalyses	kə **TAL** ə SEEZ
catalysis	kə **TAL** ə səs
catalyst	**KAT** ə ləst
catamaran	**KAT** ə mə **RAN**
catamite	**KAT** ə MĪT
catapult	**KAT** ə pəlt
cataract	**KAT** ə RAKT
catarrh	kə **TAHR**
catastrophe	kə **TAS** trə fee
catastrophic	**KAT** ə **STROF** ik
catatonic	**KAT** ə **TON** ik
Catawba, c-	kə **TAW** bə
catchup	**KACH** əp
catechism	**KAT** ə KIZ əm
categorical	**KAT** ə **GOR** i kəl
categorize	**KAT** ə gə **RĪZ**
category	**KAT** ə GOH ree
catenary	**KAT** ə NER ee
catercorner	**KAT** ər KOR nər
caterer	**KAY** tər ər
caterpillar	**KAT** ə PIL ər
caterwaul	**KAT** ər WAWL
catharsis	kə **THAHR** səs
cathartic	kə **THAHR** tik
Cathay	ka **THAY**
cathedral	kə **THEE** drəl
Cather, Willa	**KATH** ər, WIL ə
catheter	**KATH** ə tər
cathode	**KATH** ohd
catholicism, C-	kə **THOL** ə SIZ əm

ə ago, a at, ah calm, ahr dark, air care, aw saw, ay say, ch church
e bet, ee me, eer beer, hw what, i is, ī my, n French final n vin,

catholicity	**KATH** ə **LIS** ə tee
cation	**KAT** $\bar{\text{i}}$ ən
Cato	**KAY** toh
Catroux	ka **TROO**
catsup	**KAT** səp
catty-cornered	**KAT** ee **KOR** nərd
Catullus	kə **TUL** əs
Caucasia	kaw **KAY** zhə
Caucasian	kaw **KAY** zhən
Caucasus	**KAW** kə səs
caucus	**KAW** kəs
caudal	**KAWD** əl
caudillo, C-	kaw **DEEL** yoh
caudle	**KAWD** əl
caul	kawl
cauldron	**KAWL** drən
cauliflower	**KAW** lə **FLOW** ər (**FLOW** as in *cow*)
caulk	kawk
causal	**KAW** zəl
causality	kaw **ZAL** ə tee
causative	**KAW** zə tiv
cause célèbre	kohz say **LEB** rə
causerie	**KOHZ** ə **REE**
causeway	**KAWZ** **WAY**
caustic	**KAWS** tik
cauterize	**KAW** tə **RĪZ**
cautionary	**KAW** shə **NER** ee
cavalcade	**KAV** əl **KAYD**
cavalier, C-	**KAV** ə **LEER**
Cavalleria Rusticana	**KAV** ə lə **REE** ə **RUUS** tə **KAHN** ə
cavalry	**KAV** əl ree
cavatina	**KAV** ə **TEE** nə
caveat	**KAV** ee **AT**
caveat emptor	**KAV** ee **AT** **EMP** tər
caveat venditor	**KAV** ee **AT** **VEN** di tər
Cavell	**KAV** əl
Cavendish	**KAV** ən dish
cavern	**KAV** ərn
cavernous	**KAV** ər nəs
cavetto	kə **VET** oh
caviar	**KAV** ee **AHR**
cavil	**KAV** əl
cavitation	**KAV** ə **TAY** shən

o on, oh oat, oi boy, oo soon, oor poor, or for, ow cow, sh shush,
th thin, *th* this, u up, ur spur, uu book, *zh* pleasure

Cavite	kah VEE te
cavort	kə VORT
Cavour	kah VUUR
Cawdor	KAW dər
Caxton	KAK stən
cayenne, C-	kī EN
cayman, C-	KAY mən
Cayuga	kay YOO gə
cayuse, C-	kī YOOS
Ceausescu, Nicolae	CHOW oo SHES koo, NEE koh LĪ ə
Cebu	say BOO
Cecil (US)	SEE səl
Cecil (British)	SE səl
cecum	SEE kəm
cedilla	si DIL ə
celandine	SEL ən DĪN
Celebes	SEL ə BEEZ
celebrant	SEL ə brənt
Celebrezze	se lə BREE zee
celebrity	sə LEB rə tee
celerity	sə LER ə tee
celesta	sə LES tə
celeste, C-	sə LEST
celestial	sə LES chəl
celiac	SEE lee AK
celibacy	SEL ə bə see
celibate	SEL ə bət
cellar	SEL ər
Cellini	chə LEE nee
cellist	CHEL əst
cello	CHEL oh
cellophane	SEL ə FAYN
cellular	SEL yə lər
celluloid, C-	SEL yə LOID
cellulose	SEL yə LOHS
Celsius	SEL see əs
Celt	kelt
Celtic	KEL tik
Celtics (team)	SEL tiks
Cenci	CHEN chee
Cenis	sə NEE
cenobite	SEN ə BĪT
cenotaph	SEN ə TAF

ə ago, a at, ah calm, ahr dark, air care, aw saw, ay say, ch church
e bet, ee me, eer beer, hw what, i is, ī my, n French final n vin,

Cenozoic	SEE nə ZOH ik
censer	SEN sər
censor	SEN sər
censorable	SEN sər ə bəl
censorious	sen SOR ee əs
censorship	SEN sər SHIP
censure	SEN shər
census	SEN səs
centaur, C-	SEN tor
Centaurus	sen TOR əs
centavo	sen TAH voh
centenary	SEN tə NER ee
centennial	sen TEN ee əl
centigrade	SEN tə GRAYD
centime	sahn TEEM
centimeter	SEN tə MEE tər
centipede	SEN tə PEED
centrifugal	sen TRIF yə gəl
centrifuge	SEN trə FYOOJ
centripetal	sen TRIP ə təl
centrist	SEN trəst
centurion	sen TUUR ee ən
century	SEN chə ree
cephalic	sə FAL ik
cephalopod	SEF ə lə POD
Cephalus	SEF ə ləs
cepheid	SEE fee əd
Cepheus	SEE fee əs
Ceram	say RAHM
ceramic	sə RAM ik
ceramist	SE rə məst
Cerberus	SUR bər əs
cere	seer
cereal	SEER ee əl
cerebellum	SER ə BEL əm
cerebral	SER ə brəl
cerebrate	SER ə BRAYT
cerebrum	SER ə brəm
cerement	SEER mənt
ceremonial	SER ə MOH nee əl
Ceres	SEER eez
cerise	sə REES
cerium	SEER ee əm

o on, oh oat, oi boy, oo soon, oor poor, or for, ow cow, sh shush,
th thin, *th* this, u up, ur spur, uu book, *zh* pleasure

cermet	SUR met
certification	SUR tə fə KAY shən
certiorari	SUR shee ə RAIR ee
certitude	SUR tə TOOD
cerulean	sə ROO lee ən
cerumen	sə ROO mən
Cervantes	ser VAN teez
cervelat	SUR və LAHT
cervical	SUR vi kəl
cervix	SUR viks
cesium	SEE zee əm
cessation	se SAY shən
cetane	SEE tayn
ceteris paribus	KAY te REES PAH ri BUUS
Cetus	SEE təs
Ceuta	SAY OOT ə
Ceylon	si LON
Ceyx	SEE iks
Cézanne	say ZAHN
chablis, C-	sha BLEE
cha-cha	CHAH chah
Chaco	CHAH koh
chaconne	shah KAWN
Chad	chad
chafe	chayf
chaff	chaf
chaffinch	CHAF inch
Chagall	shah GAHL
Chagres	CHAH gres
chagrin	shə GRIN
Chahar	chah hahr
chaise	shayz
chaise longue	shayz LAWNG
Chai Zemin	chī zu meen
Chakiris	chah KEE ris
Chakravarty	chah krah vahr TEE
Chalcedon	KAL si DON
chalcedony	kal SED ə nee
chalcopyrite	KAL kə PĪ rīt
Chaldea	kal DEE ə
Chaldean	kal DEE ən
Chaldee	kal DEE
chalet	sha LAY

ə ago, a at, ah calm, ahr dark, air care, aw saw, ay say, ch church
e bet, ee me, eer beer, hw what, i is, ī my, n French final n vin,

Chaliapin	shah **LYAH** pin
chalice	**CHAL** is
chalk	chawk
challis	**SHAL** ee
chamberlain, C-	**CHAYM** bər lən
chambray	**SHAM** bray
chameleon	kə **MEEL** yən
chamfer	**CHAM** fər
chamois	**SHAM** ee
Chamonix	SHAM ə **NEE**
Chamorro	chə **MAW** roh
champagne, C-	sham **PAYN**
champaign, C-	sham **PAYN**
champion	**CHAM** pee ən
Champlain	sham **PLAYN**
Champs Elysées	shahnz ay lee **ZAY**
chancel	**CHAN** səl
chancellery	**CHAN** sə lə ree
chancellor	**CHAN** sə lər
chancery	**CHAN** sə ree
chancre	**SHANG** kər
chandelier	SHAN də **LEER**
Chanderli, Abdelkader	chahn dər **LEE**, ahb dəl **KAH** dər
Chandigarh	CHUN di **GUR**
Chand, Lokendra Bahadur	**CHAHND**, loh **KEN** drə bah hah **DOOR**
Chanel	shə **NEL**
changeable	**CHAYN** jə bəl
changeling	**CHAYNJ** ling
chanson	shahn **SAWN** (both syllables French final *n*)
chanteuse	shahn **TUUZ** (shahn French final *n*)
chantey	**SHAN** tee
chanticleer	**CHAN** tə KLEER
Chantilly, c-	shahn tee **YEE** (shahn French final *n*)
chanty	**SHAN** tee
Chanukah	**HAH** nə kə
chaos	**KAY** os
chaotic	kay **OT** ik
chaparajos	SHAP ə **RAY** ohs
chaparral	SHAP ə **RAL**
chapbook	**CHAP** buuk
chapeau	sha **POH**

---

o on, oh oat, oi boy, oo soon, oor poor, or for, ow cow, sh shush,
th thin, *th* this, u up, ur spur, uu book, *zh* pleasure

chaperon	SHAP ə ROHN
chaplain	CHAP lən
Chaplin	CHAP lən
Chapultepec	chə PUUL tə PEK
charabanc	SHAR ə BANG
characteristic	KAR ik tə RIS tik
charade	shə RAYD
charcoal	CHAHR KOHL
chard	chahrd
Chardin, Jean	shar DAN, zhahn (DAN, zhahn French final n)
chargeable	CHAHR jə bəl
chargé d'affaires	shahr ZHAY da FAIR
charioteer	CHA ree ə TEER
charisma	kə RIZ mə
charismatic	KA rəz MAT ik
charivari	shə RIV ə REE
charlatan	SHAHR lə tən
Charlemagne	SHAHR lə MAYN
Charles (French)	shahrl
Charleston	CHAHRL stən
Charlotte, c-	SHAHR lət
Charolais	SHA rə LAY
Charon	KAIR ən
Chartism	CHAHR tiz əm
Chartres	SHAHR trə
chartreuse, C-	shahr TRUUZ
chary	CHAIR ee
Charybdis	kə RIB dəs
chasm	KAZ əm
chassé	sha SAY
chassis	SHAS ee
chaste	chayst
chasten	CHAY sən
chastise	chas TĪZ
chastisement	chas TĪZ mənt
chastity	CHAS tə tee
chasuble	CHAZ yə bəl
château	sha TOH
chateaubriand	shah TOH bree AHN (AHN French final n)
chatelaine	SHAT ə LAYN
Chatham	CHAT əm
Chattahoochee	CHAT ə HOO chee

ə ago, a at, ah calm, ahr dark, air care, aw saw, ay say, ch church
e bet, ee me, eer beer, hw what, i is, ī my, n French final n vin,

Chattanooga	**CHAT** ə **NOO** gə
chattel	**CHAT** əl
Chaucer	**CHAW** sər
Chaucerian	chaw **SEER** ee ən
Chaudet	shoh **DAY**
chauffeur	shoh **FUR**
chaulmoogra	chawl **MOO** grə
Chautauqua	shə **TAW** kwə
chauvinism	**SHOH** və nız əm
chauvinistic	shoh və **NIS** tik
Chaves	**CHAH** ves
Chavez	**CHAH** vez
Chebrikov, Viktor	**CHEB** ree kawf, **VEEK** tor
Cheddar, c-	**CHED** ər
cheetah	**CHEE** tə
chef	shef
chef-d'oeuvre	she **DURV** rə
Chehab, Fuad	shə **HAB**, **FOO** ahd
Cheka	**CHE** kah
Chekhov	**CHE** kawf
Chekiang	jəj ee ahng
Chelsea	**CHEL** see
chemise	shə **MEEZ**
Chemnitz	**KEM** nits
chemurgy	**KEM** ər jee
Chen-chiang	jun jee ahng
Cheney	**CHAY** nee
Chengdu	chung doo
Chenier	shay **NYAY**
chenille	shə **NEEL**
Chenoweth	**CHEN** oh weth
Chen Pixian	chun pee shee ahn
Chen Yun	chun yuun
cheongsam	**CHAWNG** sahm
Cheops	**KEE** ops
Cherbourg	**SHAIR** buurg
cherchez la femme	sher **SHAY** la **FAM**
Cherenkov, Pavel	chə **RENG** kof, **PAH** vəl
Chernenko, Konstantin	chər **NYEN** kə, **KON** stan **TEEN**
Cherokee	**CHER** ə **KEE**
cheroot	shə **ROOT**
chert	churt
cherub	**CHER** əb

o on, oh oat, oi boy, oo soon, oor poor, or for, ow cow, sh shush,
th thin, *th* this, u up, ur spur, uu book, *zh* pleasure

cherubic	chə **ROO** bik
chervil	**CHUR** vəl
Chesapeake	**CHES** ə PEEK
Cheshire	**CHESH** ər
chestnut	**CHES** nut
Chetnik	chet **NEEK**
chevalier	SHEV ə **LEER**
Chevalier	shə **VAL** yay
cheviot (cloth)	**SHEV** ee ət
cheviot, C- (sheep; Hills)	**CHEV** ee ət
Chevrolet	SHEV rə **LAY**
chevron	**SHEV** rən
Cheyenne	shī **EN**
Cheysson, Claude	shay **SAWN, KLOHD** (**SAWN** French final *n*)
chez	shay
chi	kī
Chiang Ching-kuo	jee ahng jeeng kwoh
Chiang Kai-shek	jee ahng kī shek
Chianti	kee **AHN** tee
Chiari	kee **AH** ree
chiaroscuro	kee AHR ə **SKYUUR** oh
chic	sheek
Chicago	shi **KAH** goh
chicane	shi **KAYN**
chicanery	shi **KAY** nə ree
Chicano	chi **KAH** noh
Chiceri, Caruncho	chee **CHAIR** ee, kah **RUUN** choh
Chichén-Itzá	chə CHEN ət **SAH**
chichi	**SHEE** shee
Chichibu	chee chee boo
chickadee	**CHIK** ə DEE
chicle	**CHIK** əl
Chico, c-	**CHEE** koh
chicory	**CHIK** ə ree
chide	chīd
chieftain	**CHEEF** tən
chiffon	shi **FON**
chiffonier	SHIF ə **NEER**
chigger	**CHIG** ər
chignon	**SHEEN** yon
chigoe	**CHIG** oh

ə ago, a at, ah calm, ahr dark, air care, aw saw, ay say, ch church
e bet, ee me, eer beer, hw what, i is, ī my, *n* French final n vin,

Chihuahua, c-	chi **WAH** wah
chilblain	**CHIL** BLAYN
Chile	**CHIL** ee
chile con carne	**CHIL** ee kon **KAHR** nee
chili	**CHIL** ee
Chillon	shə **LON**
chimera	kə **MIR** ə
chimerical	kə **MER** i kəl
chimpanzee	CHIM pan **ZEE**
China	**CHĪ** nə
chinch	chinch
chinchilla	chin **CHIL** ə
Chincoteague	SHING kə **TEEG**
Chindit	**CHIN** dit
Chindwin	chin dwin
chine	chīn
Chinese	chī **NEEZ**
Chinghai	jing hī
chino	**CHEE** noh
Chinook	shi **NUUK**
chintz	chints
Chios	**KĪ** os
Chipamaunga, Edmund	CHEE pah mah **OONG** gah
Chippendale	**CHIP** ən DAYL
Chippewa	**CHIP** ə WAH
Chiquita	chə **KEE** tə
Chiriboga	chee ree **BAW** gah
Chirico, Giorgio de	**KEE** ree koh, **JOR** joh də
chiromancy	**KĪ** rə MAN see
Chiron	**KĪ** ron
chiropodist	kə **ROP** ə dəst
chiropody	kə **ROP** ə dee
chiropractor	**KĪ** rə PRAK tər
chirrup	**CHIR** əp
chisel	**CHIZ** əl
Chisholm	**CHÍZ** əm
chiton	**KĪT** ən
Chitradurga	CHIT rə **DUR** gə
chitterlings	**CHIT** lənz
chivalric	shə **VAL** rik
chivalrous	**SHIV** əl rəs
chivalry	**SHIV** əl ree

o on, oh oat, oi boy, oo soon, oor poor, or for, ow cow, sh shush, th thin, *th* this, u up, ur spur, uu book, *zh* pleasure

chive	chīv
chivy	**CHIV** ee
Chloe, Chloë	**KLOH** ee
chlorate	**KLOR** ayt
chloride	**KLOR** īd
chlorinate	**KLOR** ə **NAYT**
chlorine	**KLOR** een
chloroform	**KLOR** ə **FORM**
chlorophyll	**KLOR** ə fil
Choate	choht
chock-full	chok fuul
chocolate	**CHOK** lət
Choctaw	**CHOK** taw
choir	kwīr
Choiseul	shwah **ZUL**
choler	**KOL** ər
cholera	**KOL** ə rə
choleric	**KOL** ə rik
cholesterol	kə **LES** tə **ROHL**
Cholmondeley	**CHUM** lee
Chongjin	chawng jin
Chongqing	chuung ching
Chookasian, Lili	chuu **KAH** syahn, **LEE** lee
Chopin	**SHOH** pan (pan French final *n*)
chop suey	**CHOP SOO** ee
choral (a)	**KOR** əl
chorale (n)	kə **RAL**
Chorazin	koh **RAY** zin
chordate	**KOR** dayt
chore	chor
chorea	kə **REE** ə
choreographer	**KOR** ee **OG** rə fər
choreography	**KOR** ee **OG** rə fee
choric	**KOR** ik
chorine	**KOR** **EEN**
chorister	**KOR** ə stər
chortle	**CHOR** təl
Choudhury, Humayun Rasheed	**CHOW** də ree, **HOO** mah **YOON** rah **SHEED**
Chou En-lai	joh en lī
chow	chow (as in *cow*)
chowchow	**CHOW** chow
chowder	**CHOW** dər

ə ago, a at, ah calm, ahr dark, air care, aw saw, ay say, ch church
e bet, ee me, eer beer, hw what, i is, ī my, *n* French final n vin,

chow mein	chow **MAYN**
chrestomathy	kre **STOM** ə thee
chrism	**KRIZ** əm
christen	**KRIS** ən
Christendom	**KRIS** ən dəm
Christian	**KRIS** chən
Christiania	**KRIS** chee **AN** ee ə
Christianity	**KRIS** chee **AN** ə tee
Christmas	**KRIS** məs
Christophe	kree **STAWF**
Christopher	**KRIS** tə fər
chromatic	kroh **MAT** ik
chromatin	**KROH** mə tin
chrome	krohm
chromium	**KROH** mee əm
chromosome	**KROH** mə **SOHM**
chromosphere	**KROH** mə **SFEER**
chronic	**KRON** ik
chronicle	**KRON** ə kəl
chronograph	**KRON** ə **GRAF**
chronological	**KRON** ə **LOJ** i kəl
chronology	krə **NOL** ə jee
chronometer	krə **NOM** ə tər
chrysalis	**KRIS** ə lis
chrysanthemum	kri **SAN** thə məm
Chryseis	krī **SEE** is
Chrysler	**KRĪS** lər
Chrysostom	**KRIS** ə stəm
chukker	**CHUK** ər
Chun Doo-Hwan	juun doh hwahn
Churchill	**CHUR** chil
churchman	**CHURCH** mən
Chust	koost
chute	shoot
chutney	**CHUT** nee
chutzpah	**HUUT** spə
ciao	chow
Ciardi	**CHAHR** dee
Cibber, Colley	**SIB** ər, **KOL** ee
Cibola	**SEE** bə lə
ciborium	sə **BOR** ee əm
cicada	sə **KAY** də
cicala	sə **KAH** lə

o on, oh oat, oi boy, oo soon, oor poor, or for, ow cow, sh shush,
th thin, *th* this, u up, ur spur, uu book, *zh* pleasure

cicatrix	SIK ə TRIKS
Cicero	SIS ə ROH
cicerone	SIS ə ROH nee
Ciceronian	SIS ə ROH nee ən
Cid	sid
ci-devant	seed ə VAHN (VAHN French final *n*)
Cienfuegos	syen FWE gohs
cigarette	SIG ə RET
Cilicia	sə LISH ə
Cimabue	CHEE mah BOO ay
Cimarron	SIM ə RON
Cimbri	SIM bri
Cimmerian	si MER ee ən
cinchona	sin KOH nə
Cincinnati	SIN sə NAT ee
Cincinnatus	SIN sə NAT əs
cincture	SINGK chər
cinema	SIN ə mə
Cinerama	SIN ə RAM ə
cinnabar	SIN ə BAHR
cinnamon	SIN ə mən
cinquefoil	SINGK FOIL
Cinque Ports	singk ports
Cinzano	chin ZAH noh
cipher	SĪ fər
circa	SUR kə
circadian	sər KAY dee ən
Circassian	sər KASH ən
Circe	SUR see
circuit	SUR kət
circuitous	sər KYOO ə təs
circuitry	SUR kə tree
circular	SUR kyə lər
circulation	SUR kyə LAY shən
circulatory	SUR kyə lə TOR ee
circumcise	SUR kəm SĪZ
circumference	sər KUM fə rəns
circumflex	SUR kəm FLEKS
circumlocution	SUR kəm loh KYOO shən
circumnavigate	SUR kəm NAV ə GAYT
circumscribe	SUR kəm SKRĪB
circumspect	SUR kəm SPEKT
circumstance	SUR kəm STANS

ə ago, a at, ah calm, ahr dark, air care, aw saw, ay say, ch church
e bet, ee me, eer beer, hw what, i is, ī my, *n* French final n vin,

circumstantial	sᴜʀ kəm **STAN** shəl
circumvent	sᴜʀ kəm **VENT**
cirque	surk
cirrhosis	sə **ROH** səs
cirrus	**SIR** əs
cisalpine	sis **AL** pīn
Ciskei	**SIS** kī
Cistercian	sis **TUR** shən
cistern	**SIS** tərn
citadel	**SIT** ə dəl
citation	sī **TAY** shən
citizen	**SIT** ə zən
citizenry	**SIT** ə zən ree
citrate	**SI** trayt
citric	**SI** trik
Citroen	sɪ troh **EN**
citron	**SI** trən
citronella	sɪ trə **NEL** ə
citrus	**SI** trəs
Città Vecchia	cheet **TAH VEK** yah
Ciudad, c-	syoo **DAHD**
civet	**SIV** ət
civvies	**SIV** eez
claimant	**KLAY** mənt
clairvoyance	klair **VOI** əns
clairvoyant	klair **VOI** ənt
clamant	**KLAY** mənt
clamber	**KLAM** bər
clamor	**KLAM** ər
clandestine	klan **DES** tən
clangor	**KLANG** ər
clapboard	**KLAB** ərd
claque	klak
claret	**KLAR** ət
Claretian	klə **REE** shən
clarification	**KLAR** ə fə **KAY** shən
clarinet	**KLAR** ə **NET**
clarion	**KLAR** ee ən
clarity	**KLAR** ə tee
clastic	**KLAS** tik
Claudel	kloh **DEL**
Clausewitz, von	**KLOW** zə vits, fawn
claustrophobia	ᴋʟᴀᴡs trə **FOH** bee ə

o on, oh oat, oi boy, oo soon, oor poor, or for, ow cow, sh shush,
th thin, *th* this, u up, ur spur, uu book, *zh* pleasure

clavichord	**KLAV** ə **KORD**
clavicle	**KLAV** ə kəl
clavier	klə **VEER**
cleanliness	**KLEN** lee nəs
cleanly (a)	**KLEN** lee
cleanly (adv)	**KLEEN** lee
cleanse	klenz
cleavage	**KLEE** vij
clef	klef
clematis	**KLEM** ə təs
Clemenceau	**KLEM** ən **SOH**
clemency	**KLEM** ən see
Clemens	**KLEM** ənz
clement, C-	**KLEM** ənt
Cleon	**KLEE** on
Cleone	klee **OH** nee
Cleopatra	**KLEE** ə **PA** trə
clerihew	**KLER** i **HYOO**
Cleveland	**KLEEV** lənd
clew	kloo
Cliburn	**KLĪ** burn
cliché	klee **SHAY**
Clichy	klee **SHEE**
Clicquot	**KLEE** koh
client	**KLĪ** ənt
clientele	**KLĪ** ən **TEL**
climacteric	klī **MAK** tə rik
climactic	klī **MAK** tik
climatology	**KLĪ** mə **TOL** ə jee
climax	**KLĪ** maks
clinician	kli **NISH** ən
Clio	**KLĪ** oh
clique	kleek
clitoris	**KLIT** ə ris
clobber	**KLOB** ər
cloche	klohsh
clod	klod
Cloete	**KLOO** tee
cloisonné	**KLOI** zə **NAY**
cloister	**KLOI** stər
clone	klohn
close (a, adv)	klohs
close (v, n)	klohz

ə ago, a at, ah calm, ahr dark, air care, aw saw, ay say, ch church
e bet, ee me, eer beer, hw what, i is, ī my, *n* French final n vin,

closure	**KLOH** *zh*ər
cloth	klawth
clothe	kloh*th*
clothes	klohz
clothier	**KLOH***TH* yər
cloture	**KLOH** chər
clout	klowt
Clouzot	kloo **ZOH**
cloven	**KLOH** vən
Clovis	**KLOH** vis
Cluj	kluu*zh*
Cluny	**KLOO** nee
Cluytens	klee **TAHNS**
Clydesdale	**KLĪDZ** dayl
Clytemnestra	KLĪ təm **NES** trə
Cnidia	**NĪ** dee ə
coadjutor	koh **AJ** ə tər
coagulate	koh **AG** yə **LAYT**
Coahuila	KOH ə **WEE** lə
coalesce	KOH ə **LES**
coalition	KOH ə **LISH** ən
coarse	kors
coauthor	koh **AW** thər
coax (v)	kohks
coax (electrical)	**KOH** aks
coaxial	koh **AK** see əl
cobalt	**KOH** bawlt
cobbler	**KOB** lər
Cóbh	kohv
Coblenz	**KOH** blents
COBOL	**KOH** bawl
cobra	**KOH** brə
coca	**KOH** kə
cocaine	koh **KAYN**
coccidiosis	kok **SID** ee **OH** səs
coccus	**KOK** əs
coccyx	**KOK** siks
Cochin, c-	**KOH** chən
cochineal	**KOCH** ə neel
cochlea	**KOK** lee ə
Cockaigne	ko **KAYN**
cockatoo	**KOK** ə TOO
cockatrice	**KOK** ə trəs

o on, oh oat, oi boy, oo soon, oor poor, or for, ow cow, sh shush,
th thin, *th* this, u up, ur spur, uu book, *zh* pleasure

Cockburn	**KOH** burn
cocker	**KOK** ər
cockerel	**KOK** ər əl
cockeyed	**KOK** īd
cockney, C-	**KOK** nee
coco	**KOH** koh
cocoa	**KOH** koh
coconut	**KOH** kə **NUT**
cocoon	kə **KOON**
cocotte	koh **KAWT**
Cocteau	kawk **TOH**
Cocytus	koh **SĪ** təs
coda	**KOH** də
code	kohd
codeine	**KOH** deen
codex	**KOH** deks
Codex Juris Canonici	**KOH** deks **JOO** ris kə **NON** i **SĪ**
codger	**KOJ** ər
codicil	**KOD** ə səl
codify	**KOD** ə **FĪ**
coefficient	**KOH** ə **FISH** ənt
coelacanth	**SEE** lə **KANTH**
coelenterate	si **LENT** ə **RAYT**
Coelho	koo **AY** lyoo
coeliac	**SEE** lee **AK**
coerce	koh **URS**
coercion	koh **UR** shən
Coeur d'Alene	**KORD** ə **LAYN**
Coeur de Lion	**KUR** də **LĪ** ən
coeval	koh **EE** vəl
coexist	**KOH** ig **ZIST**
coffee	**KAW** fee
cogency	**KOH** jən see
cogent	**KOH** jənt
cogitate	**KOJ** ə **TAYT**
cogitation	**KOJ** ə **TAY** shən
cogito ergo sum	**KOH** gi **TOH** **ER** goh **SUUM**
cognac	**KOHN** yak
cognate	**KOG** nayt
cognition	kog **NISH** ən
cognitive	**KOG** nə tiv
cognizable	**KOG** nə zə bəl
cognizance	**KOG** nə zəns

ə ago, a at, ah calm, ahr dark, air care, aw saw, ay say, ch church
e bet, ee me, eer beer, hw what, i is, ī my, n French final n vin,

cognizant	**KOG** nə zənt
cognomen	kog **NOH** mən
cognoscenti	**KON** yə **SHEN** tee
cohabit	koh **HAB** ət
Cohan, George	**KOH** han
Cohen	**KOH** ən
coherence	koh **HEER** əns
coherent	koh **HEER** ənt
cohesion	koh **HEE** *zh*ən
cohesive	koh **HEE** siv
Cohoes	kə **HOHZ**
cohort	**KOH** hort
coif (head covering)	koif
coif (coiffure)	kwahf
coiffeur	kwah **FUR**
coiffure	kwah **FYUUR**
coincide	**KOH** ən **SĪD**
coincidentally	koh **IN** sə **DEN** tə lee
coitus	**KOH** ə təs
cola	**KOH** lə
colander	**KUL** ən dər
Colbert	kohl **BAIR**
Colchester	**KOHL** **CHES** tər
colchicum	**KOL** chə kəm
Colchis	**KOL** kis
Coleridge	**KOHL** rij
coleus	**KOH** lee əs
colic	**KOL** ik
Coligny	kaw lee **NYEE**
Colima	kə **LEE** mə
coliseum	**KOL** ə **SEE** əm
colitis	kə **LĪ** təs
collaborator	kə **LAB** ə **RAY** tər
collage	kə **LAHZ***H*
collagen	**KOL** ə jən
collard	**KOL** ərd
collate	koh **LAYT**
collateral	kə **LAT** ə rəl
collation	kə **LAY** shən
colleague	**KOL** eeg
collectivism	kə **LEK** tə **VIZ** əm
colleen	kol **EEN**
collegian	kə **LEE** jən

---

o on, oh oat, oi boy, oo soon, oor poor, or for, ow cow, sh shush,
th thin, *th* this, u up, ur spur, uu book, *zh* pleasure

collegiate	kə **LEE** jət
collier	**KOL** yər
Collier, Gershon	**KOL** yər, **GUR** shən
colliery	**KOL** yə ree
collimate	**KOL** ə **MAYT**
collimator	**KOL** ə **MAY** tər
collinear	kə **LIN** ee ər
collins, C-	**KOL** ənz
collision	kə **LIZH** ən
collodion	kə **LOH** dee ən
colloid	**KOL** oid
colloquial	kə **LOH** kwee əl
colloquium	kə **LOH** kwee əm
colloquy	**KOL** ə kwee
Collossians	kə **LOSH** ənz
collude	kə **LOOD**
collusion	kə **LOO** zhən
collusive	kə **LOO** siv
cologne, C-	kə **LOHN**
Colombia	kə **LOHM** bee ə
Colombo	kə **LUM** boh
colon	**KOH** lən
Colón	koh **LOHN**
colonel	**KURN** əl
colonelcy	**KURN** əl see
colonnade	**KOL** ə **NAYD**
colony	**KOL** ə nee
colophon	**KOL** ə fən
Colorado	**KOL** ə **RAD** oh
coloratura	**KUL** ə rə **TUUR** ə
colossal	kə **LOS** əl
Colosseum	**KOL** ə **SEE** əm
colossus	kə **LOS** əs
colostomy	kə **LOS** tə mee
colostrum	kə **LOS** trəm
Colton	**KOHL** tən
Columba	kə **LUM** bə
Columbia	kə **LUM** bee ə
columbine, C-	**KOL** əm **BĪN**
Columbus	kə **LUM** bəs
column	**KOL** əm
columnar	kə **LUM** nər
columnist	**KOL** əm nəst

ə ago, a at, ah calm, ahr dark, air care, aw saw, ay say, ch church
e bet, ee me, eer beer, hw what, i is, ī my, *n* French final n vin,

colure	kə LUUR
colza	KOL zə
Colzani, Anselmo	kohlt SAH nee, ahn SEL moh
Coma Berenices	KOH mə BER ə NĪ seez
Comanche	kə MAN chee
comatose	KOH mə TOHS
Comay	koh MĪ
comb	kohm
combat (n, a)	KOM bat
combat (v)	kəm BAT
combatant	kəm BAT ənt
combative	kəm BAT iv
combine (n)	KOM bīn
combine (v)	kəm BĪN
combings	KOH mingz
combustible	kəm BUS tə bəl
combustion	kəm BUS chən
comedian	kə MEE dee ən
comedienne	kə MEE dee EN
comedo	KOM ə DOH
comely	KUM lee
Comenius	kə MEE nee əs
comestible	kə MES tə bəl
comfortable	KUMF tə bəl
comforter	KUM fə tər
Comines	kaw MEEN
Cominform	KOM ən FORM
Comintern	KOM ən TURN
comity	KOM ə tee
comma	KOM ə
commandant	KOM ən DANT
commandment	kə MAND mənt
commando	kə MAN doh
comme il faut	KUM eel FOH
commemorate	kə MEM ə RAYT
commemorative	kə MEM ə rə tiv
commencement	kə MENS mənt
commendable	kə MEN də bəl
commendation	KOM ən DAY shən
commendatory	kə MEN də TOR ee
commensurable	kə MEN sə rə bəl
commensurate	kə MEN sə rət
commentary	KOM ən TER ee

---

o on, oh oat, oi boy, oo soon, oor poor, or for, ow cow, sh shush,
th thin, *th* this, u up, ur spur, uu book, *zh* pleasure

commentator	**KOM** ən **TAY** tər
commerce	**KOM** ərs
commercial	kə **MUR** shəl
Commines	kaw **MEEN**
commingle	kə **MING** gəl
commiserate	kə **MIZ** ə **RAYT**
commiseration	kə **MIZ** ə **RAY** shən
commissar	**KOM** ə **SAHR**
commissariat	**KOM** ə **SAIR** ee ət
commissary	**KOM** ə **SER** ee
commissionaire	kə **MISH** ə **NAIR**
commissioned	kə **MISH** ənd
commissioner	kə **MISH** ə nər
commit	kə **MIT**
committee	kə **MIT** ee
commode	kə **MOHD**
commodious	kə **MOH** dee əs
commodity	kə **MOD** ə tee
commodore	**KOM** ə **DOR**
common	**KOM** ən
commons	**KOM** ənz
commonweal	**KOM** ən **WEEL**
commonwealth	**KOM** ən **WELTH**
communal	kə **MYOO** nəl
commune (n)	**KOM** yoon
commune (v)	kə **MYOON**
communicable	kə **MYOO** ni kə bəl
communicant	kə **MYOO** ni kənt
communicate	kə **MYOO** nə **KAYT**
communication	kə **MYOO** nə **KAY** shən
communicative	kə **MYOO** nə kə tiv
communion	kə **MYOON** yən
communiqué	kə **MYOO** nə **KAY**
commutable	kə **MYOO** tə bəl
commutation	**KOM** yə **TAY** shən
commute	kə **MYOOT**
Como	**KOH** moh
Comoro	**KOM** ə **ROH**
compact (a, v)	kəm **PAKT**
compact (n)	**KOM** pakt
comparable	**KOM** pə rə bəl
comparative	kəm **PAR** ə tiv
compare	kəm **PAIR**

ə ago, a at, ah calm, ahr dark, air care, aw saw, ay say, ch church
e bet, ee me, eer beer, hw what, i is, ī my, *n* French final n vin,

comparison	kəm **PAR** ə sən
compass	**KUM** pəs
compatibility	kəm **PAT** ə **BIL** ə tee
compatible	kəm **PAT** ə bəl
compatriot	kəm **PAY** tree ət
compeer	kəm **PEER**
compendium	kəm **PEN** dee əm
compensate	**KOM** pən **SAYT**
compensatory	kəm **PEN** sə **TOR** ee
competence	**KOM** pə təns
competency	**KOM** pə tən see
competitor	kəm **PET** ə tər
Compiègne	kohm **PYAIN**
compilation	**KOM** pə **LAY** shən
complacence	kəm **PLAY** səns
complacency	kəm **PLAY** sən see
complacent	kəm **PLAY** sənt
complaisance	kəm **PLAY** səns
complaisant	kəm **PLAY** sənt
complement (n)	**KOM** plə mənt
complement (v)	**KOM** plə **MENT**
complementary	**KOM** plə **MEN** tə ree
complex (a)	kom **PLEKS**
complex (n)	**KOM** pleks
complexion	kəm **PLEK** shən
compliance	kəm **PLĪ** əns
compliant	kəm **PLĪ** ənt
complicate	**KOM** plə **KAYT**
complicity	kəm **PLIS** ə tee
compliment (n)	**KOM** plə mənt
compliment (v)	**KOM** plə **MENT**
complimentary	**KOM** plə **MEN** tə ree
component	kəm **POH** nənt
comport	kəm **PORT**
compose	kəm **POHZ**
composite	kəm **POZ** ət
composition	**KOM** pə **ZISH** ən
compositor	kəm **POZ** ə tər
compos mentis	**KOM** pəs **MEN** təs
compost	**KOM** pohst
composure	kəm **POH** *zh*ər
compote	**KOM** poht
compound (a, n)	**KOM** pownd

---

o **on**, oh **oat**, oi **boy**, oo **soon**, oor **poor**, or **for**, ow **cow**, sh **shush**, th **thin**, *th* **this**, u **up**, ur **spur**, uu **book**, *zh* **pleasure**

compound (v)	kəm **POWND**
comprehend	**KOM** pri **HEND**
comprehensible	**KOM** pri **HEN** sə bəl
comprehension	**KOM** pri **HEN** shən
comprehensive	**KOM** pri **HEN** siv
compress (n)	**KOM** pres
compress (v)	kəm **PRES**
compressor	kəm **PRES** ər
comprise	kəm **PRĪZ**
compromise	**KOM** prə **MĪZ**
Compton	**KOMP** tən
comptroller	kən **TROH** lər
compulsion	kəm **PUL** shən
compulsory	kəm **PUL** sə ree
compunction	kəm **PUNGK** shən
computable	kəm **PYOOT** ə bəl
comrade	**KOM** rad
Comus	**KOH** məs
Conakry	**KON** ə kree
con amore	kawn ah **MAW** ray
conative	**KON** ə tiv
concatenation	kon **KAT** ə **NAY** shən
concave	kon **KAYV**
concavity	kon **KAV** ə tee
conceal	kən **SEEL**
concede	kən **SEED**
conceit	kən **SEET**
conceivable	kən **SEE** və bəl
conceive	kən **SEEV**
concentrate	**KON** sən **TRAYT**
concentration	**KON** sən **TRAY** shən
concentric	kən **SEN** trik
Concepción	kən **SEP** see **OHN**
concert (n)	**KON** sərt
concert (v)	kən **SURT**
Concertgebouw	kon **SERT** gə **BOW** (**BOW** as in *cow*)
concertina	**KON** sər **TEE** nə
concertino	**KON** chər **TEE** noh
concertmaster	**KON** sərt **MAS** tər
concerto	kən **CHER** toh
concessionaire	kən **SESH** ə **NAIR**
conch	kongk
concha	**KONG** kə

ə ago, a at, ah calm, ahr dark, air care, aw saw, ay say, ch church
e bet, ee me, eer beer, hw what, i is, ī my, n French final n vin,

conchoidal	kong **KOID** əl
concierge	kohn **SYERZ***H*
conciliate	kən **SIL** ee **AYT**
conciliatory	kən **SIL** ee ə **TOR** ee
concise	kən **SĪS**
conclave	**KON** klayv
conclude	kən **KLOOD**
conclusion	kən **KLOO** *zh*ən
conclusive	kən **KLOO** siv
concoct	kən **KOKT**
concomitant	kən **KOM** ə tənt
concord, C- (US other than Massachusetts)	**KON** kord
Concord Massachusetts)	**KONG** kərd
concordance	kən **KOR** dəns
concordat	kən **KOR** **DAT**
Concorde	kon **KORD**
Concordia	kən **KOR** dee ə
concourse	**KON** kors
concrete	kon **KREET**
concubinage	kon **KYOO** bə nij
concubine	**KONG** kyə **BĪN**
concupiscence	kon **KYOO** pə səns
concur	kən **KUR**
concurrence	kən **KUR** əns
concurrent	kən **KUR** ənt
concussion	kən **KUSH** ən
Conde, Mamadi Lamine	**KOHN** dee, **MAH** mah dee lah **MEEN**
condensation	**KON** den **SAY** shən
condescend	**KON** di **SEND**
condign	kən **DĪN**
condiment	**KON** də mənt
condole	kən **DOHL**
condolence	kən **DOH** ləns
condom	**KUN** dəm
condominium	**KON** də **MIN** ee əm
condone	kən **DOHN**
condor	**KON** dər
condottiere	**KON** də **TYAIR** ee
conduct (n)	**KON** dukt
conduct (v)	kən **DUKT**

---

o on, oh oat, oi boy, oo soon, oor poor, or for, ow cow, sh shush,
th thin, *th* this, u up, ur spur, uu book, *zh* pleasure

conductive	kən **DUK** tiv
conductor	kən **DUK** tər
conduit	**KON** doo ət
Conestoga	**KON** ə **STOH** gə
coney, C-	**KOH** nee
confabulate	kən **FAB** yə **LAYT**
confectionery	kən **FEK** shə **NER** ee
confederate, C- (a, n)	kən **FED** ə rət
confederate (v)	kən **FED** ə **RAYT**
confederation	kən **FED** ə **RAY** shən
conference	**KON** fə rəns
confetti	kən **FET** ee
confidant	**KON** fə **DANT**
confidence	**KON** fə dəns
confident	**KON** fə dənt
confidential	**KON** fə **DEN** shəl
configuration	kən **FIG** yə **RAY** shən
confine (n)	**KON** fin
confine (v)	kən **FĪN**
confirmation	**KON** fər **MAY** shən
confirmatory	kən **FUR** mə **TOR** ee
confiscate	**KON** fə **SKAYT**
confiscatory	kən **FIS** kə **TOR** ee
confiture	**KON** fə **TYUUR**
conflagration	**KON** flə **GRAY** shən
conflict (n)	**KON** flikt
conflict (v)	kən **FLIKT**
confluence	**KON** floo əns
conformation	**KON** for **MAY** shən
confound	kən **FOWND**
confounded	kən **FOWN** dəd
confraternity	**KON** frə **TUR** nə tee
confrere	**KON** frair
confront	kən **FRUNT**
Confucius	kən **FYOO** shəs
confused	kən **FYOOZD**
confusion	kən **FYOO** *zh*ən
confute	kən **FYOOT**
conga	**KONG** gə
congé	kohn *ZHAY*
congeal	kən **JEEL**
congenial	kən **JEEN** yəl
congenital	kən **JEN** ə təl

ə ago, a at, ah calm, ahr dark, air care, aw saw, ay say, ch church
e bet, ee me, eer beer, hw what, i is, ī my, n French final n vin,

conger	KONG gər
congeries	KON jə reez
conglomerate (a, n)	kən GLOM ə rət
conglomerate (v)	kən GLOM ə RAYT
Congo	KONG goh
Congolese	KONG gə LEEZ
congratulate	kən GRACH ə LAYT
congratulatory	kən GRACH ə lə TOR ee
congregant	KON grə gənt
congregate (a)	KONG grə gət
congregate (v)	KONG grə GAYT
congregation	KONG grə GAY shən
congress, C-	KONG grəs
congressional	kən GRESH ə nəl
Congreve	KON greev
congruent	KONG groo ənt
congruity	kən GROO ə tee
congruous	KONG groo əs
conic	KON ik
conical	KON i kəl
conifer	KON ə fər
coniferous	kə NIF ər əs
conjecture	kən JEK chər
conjoin	kən JOIN
conjugal	KON jə gəl
conjugate (a, n)	KON jə gət
conjugate (v)	KON jə GAYT
conjugation	KON jə GAY shən
conjunction	kən JUNGK shən
conjure (entreat)	kən JUUR
conjure (summon)	KON jər
Connacht	KON ət
connate	KON ayt
Connaught	KON awt
Connecticut	kə NET ə kət
Connemara	KON ə MAHR ə
connivance	kə NĪV əns
connoisseur	KON ə SUR
connotation	KON ə TAY shən
connotative	KON ə TAYT iv
connubial	kə NOO bee əl
conqueror	KONG kər ər
conquest	KON kwest

o **on**, oh **oat**, oi **boy**, oo **soon**, oor **poor**, or **for**, ow **cow**, sh **shush**, th **thin**, *th* **this**, u **up**, ur **spur**, uu **book**, *zh* **pleasure**

conquistador	kon KWIS tə DOR
consanguineous	KON sang GWIN ee əs
consanguinity	KON sang GWIN ə tee
conscience	KON shəns
conscientious	KON shee EN shəs
conscionable	KON shə nə bəl
consciousness	KON shəs nəs
conscript (a, n)	KON skript
conscript (v)	kən SKRIPT
consecrate	KON sə KRAYT
consensus	kən SEN səs
consent	kən SENT
consequence	KON sə KWENS
consequently	KON sə KWENT lee
conservatoire	kən SUR və TWAHR
conservatory	kən SUR və TOR ee
conserve (n)	KON surv
conserve (v)	kən SURV
considerable	kən SID ə rə bəl
consign	kən SĪN
consignee	KON sī NEE
consignor	kən SĪ nər
consistency	kən SIS tən see
consistory	kən SIS tə ree
consolation	KON sə LAY shən
console (n)	KON sohl
console (v)	kən SOHL
consommé	KON sə MAY
consonant	KON sə nənt
consort (n)	KON sort
consort (v)	kən SORT
consortium	kən SOR shee əm
conspectus	kən SPEK təs
conspicuous	kən SPIK yoo əs
conspiracy	kən SPIR ə see
conspirator	kən SPIR ə tər
conspire	kən SPĪR
constable	KON stə bəl
Constable, John	KUN stə bəl
constabulary	kən STAB yə LER ee
constancy	KON stən see
constantan	KON stən TAN
Constantinople	KON stan tə NOH pəl

ə ago, a at, ah calm, ahr dark, air care, aw saw, ay say, ch church
e bet, ee me, eer beer, hw what, i is, ī my, n French final n vin,

constellation	KON stə LAY shən
consternation	KON stər NAY shən
constituency	kən STICH oo ən see
constituent	kən STICH oo ənt
constitution	KON sti TOO shən
constraint	kən STRAYNT
constrictor	kən STRIK tər
construe	kən STROO
consul	KON səl
consular	KON səl ər
consulate	KON səl ət
consultant	kən SUL tənt
consume	kən SOOM
consummate (a)	kən SUM ət
consummate (v)	KON sə MAYT
consumption	kən SUMP shən
consumptive	kən SUMP tiv
contagion	kən TAY jən
contagious	kən TAY jəs
contaminant	kən TAM ə nənt
contaminate	kən TAM ə NAYT
contamination	kən TAM ə NAY shən
conté (crayon)	KON tee
Conte, Silvio	KON tee, SIL vee oh
contemplate	KON təm PLAYT
contemplation	KON təm PLAY shən
contemplative	kən TEM plə tiv
contemporaneous	kən TEM pə RAY nee əs
contempt	kən TEMPT
contemptible	kən TEMP tə bəl
contemptuous	kən TEMP choo əs
contend	kən TEND
content (what is contained)	KON tent
content (except what is contained)	kən TENT
contention	kən TEN shən
conterminous	kən TUR mə nəs
contest (n)	KON test
contest (v)	kən TEST
contestant	kən TES tənt
context	KON tekst
contextual	kən TEKS choo əl

o on, oh oat, oi boy, oo soon, oor poor, or for, ow cow, sh shush,
th thin, _th_ this, u up, ur spur, uu book, _zh_ pleasure

contiguity	KON tə GYOO ə tee
contiguous	kən TIG yoo əs
continent	KON tə nənt
contingency	kən TIN jən see
contingent	kən TIN jənt
continuance	kən TIN yoo əns
continuation	kən TIN yoo AY shən
continue	kən TIN yoo
continuity	KON tə NOO ə tee
continuum	kən TIN yoo əm
contort	kən TORT
contour	KON tuur
contra	KON trə
contraband	KON trə BAND
contrabass	KON trə BAYS
contrabassoon	KON trə bə SOON
contract (n)	KON trakt
contract (v)	kən TRAKT
contradictory	KON trə DIK tə ree
contradistinction	KON trə di STINGK shən
contrail	KON trayl
contraindicate	KON trə IN də KAYT
contralto	kən TRAL toh
contrapuntal	KON trə PUN təl
contrariwise	KON trer ee wīz
contrary	KON trer ee
contrast (n)	KON trast
contrast (v)	kən TRAST
contravene	KON trə VEEN
contretemps	KON trə TAHN (TAHN French final *n*)
contributory	kən TRIB yə TOR ee
contrite	kən TRĪT
controller	kən TROH lər
controversial	KON trə VUR shəl
controversy	KON trə VUR see
controvert	KON trə VURT
contumacious	KON tə MAY shəs
contumacy	KON tə mə see
contumely	kon TOO mə lee
contusion	kən TOO *zh*ən
conundrum	kə NUN drəm
convalescence	KON və LES əns
convalescent	KON və LES ənt

ə ago, a at, ah calm, ahr dark, air care, aw saw, ay say, ch church
e bet, ee me, eer beer, hw what, i is, ī my, *n* French final n vin,

convection	kən VEK shən
convene	kən VEEN
converge	kən VURJ
conversant	kən VUR sənt
converse (a, v)	kən VURS
converse (n)	KON vurs
conversely	kən VURS lee
conversion	kən VUR zhən
convert (n)	KON vurt
convert (v)	kən VURT
converter	kən VUR tər
convertible	kən VUR tə bəl
conveyance	kən VAY əns
convict (n)	KON vikt
convict (v)	kən VIKT
conviction	kən VIK shən
convince	kən VINS
convivial	kən VIV ee əl
convocation	KON və KAY shən
convoke	kən VOHK
convolution	KON və LOO shən
convoy	KON voi
convulsion	kən VUL shən
cookie	KUUK ee
coolant	KOO lənt
coolie, cooly	KOO lee
cooper, C-	KOO pər
cooperate	koh OP ə RAYT
cooperative	koh OP ə rə tiv
coopt	koh OPT
coordination	koh OR də NAY shən
cootie	KOO tee
Copacabana	KOH pə kə BA nə
copacetic	KOH pə SET ik
copal	KOH pəl
copeck	KOH pek
Copenhagen	KOH pən HAY gən
Copernican	koh PUR ni kən
Copernicus	koh PUR ni kəs
copier	KOP ee ər
coping	KOH ping
copious	KOH pee əs
Copland	KOHP lənd

o on, oh oat, oi boy, oo soon, oor poor, or for, ow cow, sh shush, th thin, *th* this, u up, ur spur, uu book, *zh* pleasure

Copley	**KOP** lee
copolymer	koh **POL** ə mər
copper	**KOP** ər
coppice	**KOP** əs
copra	**KOH** prə
copse	kops
Copt	kopt
Coptic	**KOP** tik
copula	**KOP** yə lə
copulate	**KOP** yə **LAYT**
copulative	**KOP** yə lə tiv
copyist	**KOP** ee əst
copyright	**KOP** ee **RĪT**
coquet	koh **KET**
coquetry	**KOH** kə tree
coquette	koh **KET**
coquille	koh **KEEL**
coquina	koh **KEE** nə
coquito	koh **KEE** toh
coracle	**KOR** ə kəl
coral	**KOR** əl
coram populo	**KOH** rəm **POP** yə **LOH**
corbel	**KOR** bəl
Corbett	**KOR** bət
Corcoran	**KOR** kər ən
cordage	**KOR** dij
cordate	**KOR** dayt
Corday	kor **DAY**
Cordelia	kor **DEEL** yə
cordial	**KOR** jəl
cordiality	kor **JAL** ə tee
cordillera	**KOR** dəl **YAIR** ə
cordite	**KOR** dīt
cordoba	**KOR** də bə
Córdoba	**KOR** daw vah
cordon	**KOR** dən
cordon bleu	kor dawn **BLUU** (dawn French final *n*)
Cordova	**KOR** də və
cordovan	**KOR** də vən
corduroy	**KOR** də **ROI**
Corelli	koh **REL** ee
coreopsis	**KOR** ee **OP** səs
corespondent	**KOH** ri **SPON** dənt

ə ago, a at, ah calm, ahr dark, air care, aw saw, ay say, ch church
e bet, ee me, eer beer, hw what, i is, ī my, *n* French final n vin,

Corfu	**KOR** foo
corgi	**KOR** gee
coriander	**KOR** ee **AN** dər
Corinth (Greece)	**KOR** ənth
Corinth (US)	kə **RINTH**
Corinthian	kə **RIN** thee ən
Coriolanus	**KOR** ee ə **LAY** nəs
Coriolis, c-	**KOR** ee **OH** ləs
cork, C-	kork
cormorant	**KOR** mə rənt
cornea	**KOR** nee ə
Corneille	kor **NAY**
cornel	**KOR** nəl
cornelian	kor **NEEL** yən
Cornelius	kor **NEEL** yəs
cornet	kor **NET**
cornice	**KOR** nəs
Cornish	**KOR** nəsh
cornucopia	**KOR** nyə **KOH** pee ə
corolla, C-	kə **ROHL** ə
corollary	**KOR** ə **LER** ee
corona	kə **ROH** nə
coronal (a)	kə **ROH** nəl
coronal (n)	**KOR** ə nəl
coronary	**KOR** ə **NER** ee
coroner	**KOR** ə nər
coronet	**KOR** ə **NET**
Corot	kaw **ROH**
corporal	**KOR** pə rəl
corporate	**KOR** pə rət
corporeal	kor **POR** ee əl
corps (sing)	kor
corps (pl)	korz
corpse	korps
corpulence	**KOR** pyə ləns
corpulent	**KOR** pyə lənt
Corpus Christi	**KOR** pəs **KRIS** tee
corpuscle	**KOR** pə səl
corpus delicti	**KOR** pəs di **LIK** tī
corral	kə **RAL**
Correggio	kor **REJ** oh
Corregidor	kə **REG** ə **DOR**
correlate	**KOR** ə **LAYT**

o on, oh oat, oi boy, oo soon, oor poor, or for, ow cow, sh shush,
th thin, *th* this, u up, ur spur, uu book, *zh* pleasure

correlation	**KOR** ə **LAY** shən
correlative	kə **REL** ə tiv
correspond	**KOR** ə **SPOND**
correspondent	**KOR** ə **SPON** dənt
corridor	**KOR** ə dər
corrigenda	**KOR** ə **JEN** də
corrigendum	**KOR** ə **JEN** dəm
corrigible	**KOR** ə jə bəl
corroborate	kə **ROB** ə **RAYT**
corroborative	kə **ROB** ə **RAY** tiv
corrode	kə **ROHD**
corrosion	kə **ROH** *zh*ən
corrosive	kə **ROH** siv
corrugate	**KOR** ə **GAYT**
corrugated	**KOR** ə **GAY** təd
corrugation	**KOR** ə **GAY** shən
corruptible	kə **RUP** tə bəl
corsage	kor **SAH***Z***H**
corsair, C-	**KOR** sair
Corsica	**KOR** sə kə
Corsican	**KOR** sə kən
cortege	kor **TEZ***H*
Cortes (parliament)	**KOR** tes
Cortés (name)	kor **TEZ**
cortex	**KOR** teks
cortical	**KOR** ti kəl
cortices	**KOR** tə seez
Cortines	kor **TEE** nes
cortisone	**KOR** tə **ZOHN**
corundum	kə **RUN** dəm
coruscate	**KOR** ə **SKAYT**
coruscation	**KOR** ə **SKAY** shən
corvée	kor **VAY**
corvette, C-	kor **VET**
Corvus	**KOR** vəs
Corydon	**KOR** ə dən
coryza	kə **RĪ** zə
Cos, c-	kos
cosecant	**KOH** **SEE** kant
cosignatory	koh **SIG** nə **TOR** ee
cosine	**KOH** sīn
cosmic	**KOZ** mik
cosmogony	koz **MOG** ə nee

ə ago, a at, ah calm, ahr dark, air care, aw saw, ay say, ch church
e bet, ee me, eer beer, hw what, i is, ī my, *n* French final n vin,

cosmology	koz **MOL** ə jee
cosmonaut	**KOZ** mə nawt
cosmopolitan	**KOZ** mə **POL** ə tən
cosmopolite	koz **MOP** ə **LĪT**
cosmos	**KOZ** məs
cosmotron	**KOS** mə **TRON**
Cossack	**KOS** ak
costal	**KOS** təl
co-star	**KOH STAHR**
Costa Rica	**KOS** tə **REE** kə
Costello (Ireland)	**KOS** tə **LOH**
Costello (US)	ko **STEL** oh
costermonger	**KOS** tər **MUNG** gər
costume (n)	**KOS** tyoom
costume (v)	kos **TYOOM**
costumer	kos **TYOO** mər
cotangent	**KOH TAN** jənt
coterie	**KOH** tə ree
coterminous	**KOH TUR** mə nəs
cotillion	kə **TIL** yən
Cotswold	**KOTS** wohld
couchant	**KOW** chənt
Coué	koo **AY**
cougar	**KOO** gər
cough	kawf
coulee	**KOO** lee
Coulibaly, Sori	kuu lee **BU** lee, **SAW** ree
coulisse	koo **LEES**
coulomb	**KOO** lom
Coumbassa, Djebel	koom **BAH** sah, **JE** bel
council	**KOWN** səl
councillor	**KOWN** sə lər
counsel	**KOWN** səl
counselor	**KOWN** sə lər
countenance	**KOWN** tə nəns
counterfeit	**KOWN** tər fit
countertenor	**KOWN** tər **TEN** ər
countrified	**KUN** tri **FĪD**
coup	koo
coup de grâce	koo də **GRAHS**
coup d'état	**KOO** day **TAH**
coupe	koop
coupé	koo **PAY**

---

o on, oh oat, oi boy, oo soon, oor poor, or for, ow cow, sh shush,
th thin, *th* this, u up, ur spur, uu book, *zh* pleasure

couplet	**KUP** lət
coupon	**KOO** pon
coups d'état	ᴋᴏᴏ day **TAH**
courage	**KUR** ij
courant	**KUUR** ənt
Courant (Institute)	kə **RAHNT**
courante	kuu **RAHNT**
Courbet	koor **BAY**
courier	**KUUR** ee ər
Cournand, André	kuur **NAHN**, ahn **DRAY** (ahn and **NAHN** French final *n*)
courteous	**KUR** tee əs
courtesan	**KOR** tə zən
courtesy	**KUR** tə see
courtier	**KOR** tee ər
courtly	**KORT** lee
Cousteau	koo **STOH**
Coutts	koots
couturier	koo **TUU** ree ᴀʏ
couvade	koo **VAHD**
covalent	koh **VAY** lənt
Covarrubias	ᴋᴏʜ və **ROO** bee əs
covenant	**KUV** ə nənt
Coventry	**KUV** ən tree
covert (n)	**KUV** ərt
covert (a)	**KOH** vərt
covet	**KUV** ət
covetous	**KUV** ə təs
covey	**KUV** ee
coward	**KOW** ərd
cowardice	**KOW** ər dəs
cowl	kowl
Cowley	**KOW** lee
Cowper	**KOO** pər
cowrie	**KOW** ree
coxcomb	**KOKS** kohm
Coxey	**KOK** see
Coxsackie	kok **SAK** ee
coxswain	**KOK** sən
coyote	kī **OH** tee
cozen	**KUZ** ən
Cozumel	ᴋᴏʜ zə **MEL**
Cozzens	**KUZ** ənz

ə ago, a at, ah calm, ahr dark, air care, aw saw, ay say, ch church
e bet, ee me, eer beer, hw what, i is, ī my, *n* French final n vin,

Cracow	**KRAK** ow
cranium	**KRAY** nee əm
crape	krayp
crapulent	**KRAP** yə lənt
crapulous	**KRAP** yə ləs
Crashaw	**KRA** shaw
crater, C-	**KRAY** tər
cravat	krə **VAT**
craven	**KRAY** vən
crawfish	**KRAW** fish
crayfish	**KRAY** fish
crayon	**KRAY** on
creamery	**KREE** mə ree
crease	krees
creative	kree **AY** tiv
creator, C-	kree **AY** tər
creature	**KREE** chər
crèche	kresh
Crécy	kray **SEE**
credence	**KREED** əns
credential	kri **DEN** shəl
credenza	kri **DEN** zə
credible	**KRED** ə bəl
creditable	**KRED** ət ə bəl
credo	**KREE** doh
credulity	kri **DOO** lə tee
credulous	**KREJ** ə ləs
creek, C-	kreek
creel	kreel
creese	krees
cremate	**KREE MAYT**
crematorium	**KREE** mə **TOR** ee əm
crematory	**KREE** mə **TOR** ee
crème de menthe	**KREM** də **MAHNT**
Cremona	kri **MOH** nə
crenelated	**KREN** ə **LAY** təd
creole, C-	**KREE** ohl
Creon	**KREE** on
creosote	**KREE** ə **SOHT**
crepe de Chine	**KRAYP** də **SHEEN**
crêpe suzette	**KRAYP** soo **ZET**
crepuscular	kri **PUS** kyə lər
crescendo	krə **SHEN** doh

---

o on, oh oat, oi boy, oo soon, oor poor, or for, ow cow, sh shush,
th thin, *th* this, u up, ur spur, uu book, *zh* pleasure

crescent	**KRES** ənt
Crespin, Régine	kres **PAN**, ray **ZHEEN** (PAN French final *n*)
Crespo-Zaldumbide, Ricardo	**KRES** poh **SAL** duum **BEE** day, ree **KAHR** doh
Cressida	**KRES** ə də
Cressy	**KRES** ee
cretaceous	kri **TAY** shəs
Cretan	**KREE** tən
Crete	kreet
cretin	**KREE** tən
cretinism	**KREE** tə **NIZ** əm
cretonne	kri **TON**
Creüsa	kree **OO** sə
crevasse	krə **VAS**
crevice	**KREV** əs
crewel	**KROO** əl
cribbage	**KRIB** ij
Crichton	**KRĪT** ən
Crimea	krī **MEE** ə
crimson	**KRIM** zən
crinoline	**KRIN** ə lən
crises	**KRĪ** seez
Criseyde	kri **SAY** də
crisis	**KRĪ** səs
Cristóbal	kris **TOH** bəl
criteria	krī **TEER** ee ə
criterion	krī **TEER** ee ən
criticism	**KRIT** ə **SIZ** əm
critique	krə **TEEK**
Croat	**KROH** at
Croatia	kroh **AY** shə
Croatian	kroh **AY** shən
Croce, Benedetto	**KROH** chay, **BE** ne **DET** toh
crochet	kroh **SHAY**
Crockett	**KROK** ət
crocodile	**KROK** ə **DĪL**
Croesus	**KREE** səs
croissant	krwah **SAHN** (SAHN French final *n*)
croix de guerre	krwah də **GAIR**
Cro-Magnon	kroh **MAG** nən
Cromwell	**KROM** wəl
Cronin	**KROH** nən

ə ago, a at, ah calm, ahr dark, air care, aw saw, ay say, ch church
e bet, ee me, eer beer, hw what, i is, ī my, *n* French final n vin,

Cronyn	**KROH** nən
croquet	kroh **KAY**
croquette	kroh **KET**
crosier	**KROH** zhər
crotchet	**KROCH** ət
croup	kroop
croupier	**KROO** pee **AY**
crouton	**KROO** ton
Crowell	**KROH** əl
crozier	**KROH** zhər
cruces	**KROO** seez
crucial	**KROO** shəl
crucifixion	**KROO** sə **FIK** shən
crucify	**KROO** sə **FĪ**
cruel	**KROO** əl
cruelty	**KROO** əl tee
cruet	**KROO** ət
cruise	krooz
cruiser	**KROO** zər
cruller	**KRUL** ər
crumpet	**KRUM** pət
crusade	kroo **SAYD**
crustacean	krus **TAY** shən
crux	kruks
Cruz	krooz
cruzeiro	kroo **ZAIR** oh
cryogenics	**KRĪ** ə **JEN** iks
cryptic	**KRIP** tik
cryptogram	**KRIP** tə **GRAM**
crystalline	**KRIS** tə lən
crystallization	**KRIS** tə lə **ZAY** shən
Csatorday, Karoly	**CHAH** tohr dī, **KAH** raw lyi
Csongrád	**CHAWNG** grahd
Cuba	**KYOO** bə
Cuban	**KYOO** bən
cubical	**KYOO** bi kəl
cubicle	**KYOO** bi kəl
Cuchulainn, Cuchullin	kuu **KUL** in
cuckold	**KUK** əld
cuckoo	**KOO** koo
cucumber	**KYOO** kum bər
cue	kyoo
Cuernavaca	**KWER** nə **VAHK** ə

o on, oh oat, oi boy, oo soon, oor poor, or for, ow cow, sh shush,
th thin, *th* this, u up, ur spur, uu book, *zh* pleasure

cui bono	KWEE BOH noh
cuirass	kwi RAS
cuirassier	KWEER ə SEER
cuisine	kwi ZEEN
cul-de-sac	KUL də SAK
Culiacán	KOOL yə KAHN
culinary	KYOO lə NER ee
culminate	KUL mə NAYT
culottes	koo LOTS
culpability	KUL pə BIL ə tee
culprit	KUL prət
cultivator	KUL tə VAY tər
cultural	KUL chə rəl
culture	KUL chər
culvert	KUL vərt
Cumae	KYOO mee
Cumaean	kyuu MEE ən
cumbersome	KUM bər səm
cumin	KUM ən
cum laude	kuum LOWD ə (LOWD as in *crowd*)
cumulative	KYOO myə lə tiv
cumulus	KYOO myə ləs
Cunard	kyuu NAHRD
cuneiform	kyuu NEE ə FORM
cunnilingus	KUN ə LING gəs
Cuomo, Mario	KWOH moh, MAHR ee oh
cupboard	KUB ərd
Cupid	KYOO pəd
cupidity	kyuu PID ə tee
cupola	KYOO pə lə
Curaçao	KUUR ə SOW (SOW as in *cow*)
curaçao	KYUUR ə SOH
curare	kyuu RAHR ee
curate	KYUUR ət
curative	KYUUR ə tiv
curator	KYUUR ay tər
curé	kyuu RAY
curettage	KYUUR ə TAHZH
curette	kyuu RET
curfew	KUR fyoo
curia, C-	KYUUR ee ə
curie, C-	KYUUR ee
curium	KYUUR ee əm

ə ago, a at, ah calm, ahr dark, air care, aw saw, ay say, ch church
e bet, ee me, eer beer, hw what, i is, ī my, n French final n vin,

curlew	**KUR** loo
curlicue	**KUR** li **KYOO**
curmudgeon	kər **MUJ** ən
currant	**KUR** ənt
current	**KUR** ənt
curricle	**KUR** i kəl
curriculum	kə **RIK** yə ləm
cursive	**KUR** siv
cursor	**KUR** sər
cursorily	**KUR** sə rə lee
cursory	**KUR** sə ree
curtail	kər **TAYL**
curtsy	**KURT** see
curvaceous	kər **VAY** shəs
curvature	**KUR** və chər
curvet	**KUR** vət
cushion	**KUUSH** ən
cuspidor	**KUS** pə dor
cussed (a)	**KUS** əd
cussed (v)	kusd
custodian	kus **TOH** dee ən
custody	**KUS** tə dee
cutaneous	kyuu **TAY** nee əs
cuticle	**KYOO** tə kəl
Cuticura	kyoo tə **KYUU** rə
cutlass	**KUT** ləs
Cuvier	**KYOO** vee **AY**
Cuyp	koip
Cuzco	**KOOS** koh
Cvejic, Biserka	**TSVAY** ich, **BI** sər kah
cyanamide	sī **AN** ə məd
cyanide	**SĪ** ə **NĪD**
cyanosis	sī ə **NOH** sis
Cybele	**SIB** ə **LEE**
cybernetics	sī bər **NET** iks
Cyclades	**SIK** lə **DEEZ**
cyclamate	**SĪ** klə **MAYT**
cyclamen	**SĪ** klə mən
cyclic	**SĪ** klik
cyclical	**SĪ** kli kəl
cyclone	**SĪ** klohn
cyclonic	sī **KLON** ik
Cyclopean	sī klə **PEE** ən

Cyclops	**SĪ** klops
cyclotron	**SĪ** klə **TRON**
cygnet	**SIG** nət
Cygnus	**SIG** nəs
cylinder	**SIL** ən dər
cymbal	**SIM** bəl
Cymbeline	**SIM** bə **LEEN**
Cymric	**KUM** rik
Cynewulf	**KIN** ə **WUULF**
cynic	**SIN** ik
cynical	**SIN** i kəl
cynicism	**SIN** ə **SIZ** əm
cynosure, C-	**SĪ** nə **SHUUR**
Cynthia	**SIN** thee ə
cypress	**SĪ** prəs
Cyprian	**SIP** ree ən
Cyprus	**SĪ** prəs
Cyrankiewicz, Jozef	tsee rahn **KAY** vich, **YOO** zef
Cyrano	**SI** rə **NOH**
Cyrenaica	**SI** rə **NAY** i kə
Cyrillic	sə **RIL** ik
Cyrus	**SĪ** rəs
cyst	sist
cystitis	sis **TĪ** təs
Cytherea	**SITH** ə **REE** ə
cytology	sī **TOL** ə jee
czar	zahr
czardas	**CHAHR** dahsh
czarevitch	**ZAHR** ə vich
czarina	zah **REE** nə
czarism	**ZAHR** iz əm
Czech ·	chek
Czechoslovak	**CHEK** oh **SLOH** vak
Czechoslovakia	**CHEK** ə sloh **VAH** kee ə
Czeladź	**CHE** lahj
Czerny	**CHER** nee
Czestochowa	**CHEN** stə **KOH** və
Czortkow	**CHAWRT** kuuf

ə ago, a at, ah calm, ahr dark, air care, aw saw, ay say, ch church
e bet, ee me, eer beer, hw what, i is, ī my, *n* French final n vin,

D

da capo	dah **KAH** poh
dacha	**DAH** chə
Dachau	**DAHK** ow
Daché, Lilly	da **SHAY**
dachshund	**DOKS** huund
Dacko, David	**DAK** oh
da Costa, Sérgio Corrêa	da **CAWSH** tə, **SER** *zh*oh kor **HAY** yə
Dacron	**DAY** kron
dactyl	**DAK** təl
Daddah, Abdellah Ould	**DAH** dah, **AHB** də lah **OOL**
Daddah, Moktar	**DAH** dah, **MOHK** tahr
Dadet, Emmanuel	da **DAY**, ə mahn yoo **EL**
Daedalus	**DED** ə ləs
daffodil	**DAF** ə dil
daguerreotype	də **GER** ə **TĪP**
dahlia	**DAL** yə
Dahomey	də **HOH** mee
Dail Eireann	doil **AIR** ən
Daimler	**DĪM** lər
daimyo	**DĪ** myoh
Dai Nippon	**DĪ** ni **PON**
Daiquiri, d-	**DĪ** kə ree
Dairen	dī ren
dais	**DAY** əs
Dakar	da **KAHR**
Daladier	da la **DYAY**
Dalai Lama	**DAH** lī **LAH** mə
Dalhousie	dal **HOO** zee
Dali, Salvador	**DAH** lee, **SAL** və ɾ ʀ
Dallas	**DAL** əs
Dalles, The	dalz
dalliance	**DAL** ee əns
Damascus	də **MAS** kəs
damask	**DAM** əsk
D'Amato, Alphonse	də **MAH** toh, **AL** fons
D'Amboise, Jacques	dahm **BWAHZ**, *ZH***AHK**

---

o on, oh oat, oi boy, oo soon, oor poor, or for, ow cow, sh shush,
th thin, *th* this, u up, ur spur, uu book, *zh* pleasure

Dambovita	**DUM** baw veet sah
Damien	**DAYM** yən
Damietta	**DAM** ee **ET** ə
Damocles	**DAM** ə **KLEEZ**
Damon	**DAY** mən
damsel	**DAM** zəl
damson	**DAM** zən
Danilova	dah **NEE** loh vah
Danish	**DAY** nish
d'Annunzio, Gabriele	dah **NOON** tsyoh, **GAH** bree **E** le
danseur	dahn **SUUR** (dahn French final *n*)
danseuse	dahn **SUUZ** (dahn French final *n*)
Dante	**DAHN** tay
Danube	**DAN** yoob
Danzig	**DANT** sig
Daphne	**DAF** nee
Daphnis	**DAF** nəs
d'Arc	dahrk
Dardanelles	**DAHR** də **NELZ**
Dar es Salaam	**DAHR ES** sə **LAHM**
Darian	**DAR** ee ən
Darien	**DAR** ee **EN**
Darius (Persian king)	də **RĪ** əs
Darius (modern name)	**DAR** ee əs
Darmstadt	**DAHRM** stat
Darrieux	dar **YUU**
Darwin	**DAHR** win
Darwinian	dahr **WIN** ee ən
dashiki	də **SHEE** kee
da Silveira, Antonio Azeredo	da sil **VAIR** ə, ahn **TOH** nyoh ah zay **RAY** doh
Dassin, Jules	da **SAN**, **ZHOOL** (SAN French final *n*)
data	**DAYT** ə
dative	**DAYT** iv
datum	**DAYT** əm
daub	dawb
d'Aubuisson, Roberto	**DOW** bee sawn, roh **BER** toh
Daudet	doh **DAY**
Daumier	doh **MYAY**
daunt	dawnt
dauphin	doh **FAN** (FAN French final *n*)
Dauphin, Claude	doh **FAN**, **KLOHD** (FAN French final *n*)

ə ago, a at, ah calm, ahr dark, air care, aw saw, ay say, ch church
e bet, ee me, eer beer, hw what, i is, ī my, *n* French final n vin,

dauphine	doh **FEEN**
David (European)	da **VEED**
Davin, Jean	**DAV** ən, **ZH**AHN (**ZH**AHN French final *n*)
da Vinci	də **VIN** chee
davit	**DAV** it
Davos	dah **VOHS**
Dawalibi, Maarouf	dah wah **LEE** bee, mah **ROOF**
Dayak	DĪ ak
Dayan, Moshe	dah **YAHN**, moh **SHE**
dearth	durth
Deauville	**DOH** vil
debacle	di **BAH** kəl
debar	di **BAHR**
de Barentzen	də bah rend **ZEN**
debark	di **BAHRK**
debase	di **BAYS**
debauch	di **BAWCH**
debenture	di **BEN** chər
debilitate	di **BIL** ə **TAYT**
debility	di **BIL** ə tee
debit	**DEB** ət
debonair	**DEB** ə **NAIR**
Deborah	**DEB** ər ə
debouch	di **BOWCH**
Debré	də **BRAY**
debrief	dee **BREEF**
debris	də **BREE**
Debussy	**DAYB** yuu **SEE**
debut	**DAY** byoo
debutante	**DEB** yuu **TAHNT**
Debye	də BĪ
decadence	**DEK** ə dəns
decadent	**DEK** ə dənt
decaffeinated	dee **KAF** ə **NAY** təd
decal	**DEE** kal
decant	di **KANT**
decapitate	di **KAP** ə **TAYT**
decathlon	di **KATH** lən
Decatur	di **KAY** tər
Deccan	**DEK** ən
decedent	di **SEE** dənt
December	di **SEM** bər

o on, oh oat, oi boy, oo soon, oor poor, or for, ow cow, sh shush,
th thin, *th* this, u up, ur spur, uu book, *zh* pleasure

decentralization	dee SEN trə lə ZAY shən
decibel	DES ə bəl
deciduous	di SIJ oo əs
decisive	di SĪ siv
declamatory	di KLAM ə TOR ee
declaration	DEK lə RAY shən
déclassé	DAY kla SAY
décolletage	DAY kahl TAHZH
décolleté	DAY kahl TAY
decompose	DEE kəm POHZ
DeConcini	DEE kon SEEN ee
décor	day KOR
decorative	DEK ə rə tiv
decorous	DEK ə rəs
decorum	di KOR əm
découpage	DAY koo PAHZH
decoy (n)	DEE koi
decoy (v)	di KOI
decrease (n)	DEE krees
decrease (v)	di KREES
decrepitude	di KREP ə TOOD
decrescendo	DAY krə SHEN doh
dedicatory	DED i kə TOR ee
deduce	di DOOS
de facto	di FAK toh
defalcate	di FAL kayt
defalcation	DEE fal KAY shən
defamatory	di FAM ə TOR ee
defense	di FENS
deference	DEF ə rəns
Defferre, Gaston	də FAIR, ga STAWN (STAWN French final *n*)
deficit	DEF ə sət
defile	di FĪL
definite	DEF ə nət
Defoe	di FOH
defoliation	dee FOH lee AY shən
defunct	di FUNGKT
dégagé	day ga ZHAY
degas	di GAS
Degas	də GAH
De Gaulle	də GOHL
degauss	dee GOWS (GOWS as in *mouse*)

ə ago, a at, ah calm, ahr dark, air care, aw saw, ay say, ch church
e bet, ee me, eer beer, hw what, i is, ī my, *n* French final n vin,

degenerate (a, n)	di JEN ə rət
degenerate (v)	di JEN ə RAYT
dehydrate	dee HĪ drayt
deify	DEE ə FĪ
deign	dayn
Deimos	DĪ mos
Deiphobus	dee IF ə bəs
Deirdre	DEER drə
déjà vu	day zhah VOO
De Jong	də YAWNG
de jure	dee JUUR ee
De Klerk, F. W.	də KLURK
de Kooning, Willem	də KOON ing, VIL əm
Delacroix	də la KRWAH
de la Madrid Hurtado, Miguel	day lah mah DRID oor TAH doh, mee GEL
de la Mare	də lə MAIR
de Larosière, Jacques	də lah roh ZYAIR, ZHAHK
Delaware	DEL ə WAIR
delectation	DEE lek TAY shən
delegate (n)	DEL ə gət
delegate (v)	DEL ə GAYT
deleterious	DEL ə TEER ee əs
Delhi	DEL ee
deliberate (a)	di LIB ə rət
deliberate (v)	di LIB ə RAYT
deliberative	di LIB ə RAY tiv
Delibes	də LEEB
Delilah	di LĪ lə
deliquesce	DEL ə KWES
Delius	DEE lee əs
Dellums	DEL əmz
Delock	də LOK
Delorean	də LOR ee ən
Delos	DEE los
De Los Angeles, Victoria	day lohs AHN je lez, vik TAW ree ə
delphinium	del FIN ee əm
Delphinus	del FĪ nəs
Delpree-Crespo, Juan Carlos	del PRAY KRES poh, hwahn KAHR lohs
delude	di LOOD
deluge	DEL yooj
delusion	di LOO zhən

o on, oh oat, oi boy, oo soon, oor poor, or for, ow cow, sh shush, th thin, *th* this, u up, ur spur, uu book, *zh* pleasure

delusive	di **LOO** siv
de luxe	di **LUUKS**
Delvecchio	del **VEK** ee oh
demagogue	**DEM** ə GOG
demarcation	DEE mahr **KAY** shən
démarche	day **MAHRSH**
de Medina, Rui Barbosa	duu mə **DEE** nə, **ROO** ee bahr **BOH** zə
dementia praecox	di **MEN** shə **PREE** koks
Demerol	**DEM** ə ROHL
demesne	di **MAYN**
Demeter	di **MEE** tər
Demetrius	də **MEE** tree əs
Demichev, Pyotr N.	DE mi chəf, **PYOH** tər
demimonde	**DEM** ee MOND
demise	di **MĪZ**
demitasse	**DEM** ee TAS
demoiselle	DEM wah **ZEL**
demoniac	di **MOH** nee AK
demoniacal	DEE mə **NĪ** ə kəl
demonology	DEE mə **NOL** ə jee
demonstrable	di **MON** strə bəl
demonstrate	**DEM** ən STRAYT
demonstrative	di **MON** strə tiv
Demosthenes	di **MOS** thə NEEZ
demur	di **MUR**
demure	di **MYOOR**
demurrer	di **MUR** ər
Demuth	də **MOOTH**
dendritic	den **DRIT** ik
Deneb	**DEN** eb
Deng Liqun	dəng lee choon
dengue	**DENG** gee
Deng Xiaoping	dəng show ping (show as in *how*)
Deng Yingchao	dəng yeeng chow
denier (coin)	də **NEER**
denier (one who denies	də **NĪ** ər
denier (unit of fineness)	**DEN** yər
denigrate	**DEN** ə GRAYT
denim	**DEN** əm
denizen	**DEN** ə zən

ə ago, a at, ah calm, ahr dark, air care, aw saw, ay say, ch church
e bet, ee me, eer beer, hw what, i is, ī my, *n* French final n vin,

Denmark	**DEN** mahrk
denotation	DEE noh **TAY** shən
denote	di **NOHT**
dénouement	DAY noo **MAHN** (**MAHN** French final *n*)
de nouveau	də noo **VOH**
de novo	day **NOH** voh
dentifrice	**DEN** tə frəs
denunciation	di NUN see **AY** shən
De Oliveira Campos, Roberto	də oh lee **VAIR** ə **KAHMP** ush, rə **BAIR** toh
deoxyribonucleic	dee OK si **RĪ** boh noo **KLEE** ik
de Piniés, Jaime	day pee **NYAYS**, **HĪ** may
depletion	di **PLEE** shən
deponent	di **POH** nənt
deposition	DEP ə **ZISH** ən
depot (military)	**DEP** oh
depot (railroad)	**DEE** poh
deprecate	**DEP** rə KAYT
depreciate	di **PREE** shee AYT
depreciation	di PREE shee **AY** shən
depredate	**DEP** rə DAYT
depredation	DEP rə **DAY** shən
deprivation	DEP rə **VAY** shən
de profundis	day proh **FUUN** dees
depute	də **PYOOT**
deputy	**DEP** yə tee
de Quay, Jan	də **KWĪ**, **YAHN**
derby, D-	**DUR** bee
derby, D- (British)	**DAHR** bee
derelict	**DER** ə likt
dereliction	DER ə **LIK** shən
de rigueur	də ree **GUR**
derisive	di **RĪ** siv
derivation	DER ə **VAY** shən
dermatologist	DUR mə **TOL** ə jəst
dermatology	DUR mə **TOL** ə jee
dernier cri	der nyay **KREE**
derogatory	di **ROG** ə TOR ee
Derounian	de **ROO** nee ən
descant	**DES** kant
Descartes	day **KAHRT**
Desdemona	DEZ də **MOH** nə

o on, oh oat, oi boy, oo soon, oor poor, or for, ow cow, sh shush,
th thin, *th* this, u up, ur spur, uu book, *zh* pleasure

desert (n)	**DEZ** ərt
desert (v)	di **ZURT**
deshabille	**DES** ə **BEEL**
De Sica, Vittorio	də **SEE** kə, vi **TOR** ee **OH**
desiccate	**DES** i **KAYT**
desideratum	di **SID** ə **RAY** təm
designate (a)	**DEZ** ig nət
designate (v)	**DEZ** ig **NAYT**
Des Moines	də **MOIN**
desolate (a)	**DES** ə lət
desolate (v)	**DES** ə **LAYT**
Désormière	day zawr **MYAIR**
desperado	**DES** pə **RAH** doh
despicable	**DES** pi kə bəl
Des Plaines	des **PLAYNZ**
Dessau	**DES** ow (ow as in *cow*)
dessert	di **ZURT**
Dessès	də **SE**
de Stijl, D-	də **STĪL**
desuetude	**DES** wi **TOOD**
desultory	**DES** əl **TOR** ee
detail	di **TAYL**
detent	**DEE** tent
détente	day **TAHNT**
deter	di **TUR**
detergent	di **TUR** jənt
deteriorate	di **TIR** ee ə **RAYT**
determinism	di **TUR** mə **NIZ** əm
deterrent	di **TUR** ənt
de Tocqueville	də **TOHK** vil
detonate	**DET** ə **NAYT**
detonator	**DET** ə **NAY** tər
detour	di **TOOR**
detoxify	dee **TOK** si **FĪ**
Detroit	di **TROIT**
de trop	də **TROH**
deuce	doos
Deukmejian, George	duuk **MAY** jən
deus ex machina	**DE** uus eks **MAH** ki **NAH**
deuterium	doo **TIR** ee əm
Deuteronomy	**DOO** tə **RON** ə mee
Deutsch	doich
Deutschland	**DOICH** lahnt

ə ago, a at, ah calm, ahr dark, air care, aw saw, ay say, ch church
e bet, ee me, eer beer, hw what, i is, ī my, *n* French final n vin,

De Valera, Eamon	DEV ə LAIR ə, AY mən
Devanagari	DAY və NAH gə REE
devastate	DEV ə STAYT
Dev, Birendra Bir Bikram Shah	DEV, bee REN drə beer bee KRAHM shah
Dever, Edmond	də VAIR, ed MAWN (MAWN French final *n*)
deviant	DEE vee ənt
deviate (a, n)	DEE vee ət
deviate (v)	DEE vee AYT
deviationism	DEE vee AY shə NIZ əm
devise	di VĪZ
Devonshire	DEV ən shər
devotee	DEV ə TEE
De Vries, Hugo	də VREES
De Vries, Peter	də VREEZ
dexterous, dextrous	DEK strəs
dextrose	DEK strohs
Dhaka, Dacca	DAK ə
dharma	DAHR mə
dhow	dow (as in *cow*)
Dia, Abdourahmane	JAH, AHB doo rah MAHN
diabetes	DĪ ə BEET eez
diabolic	DĪ ə BOL ik
diacritical	DĪ ə KRIT ə kəl
diadem	DĪ ə DEM
diaeresis	di ER ə səs
diagnose	DĪ əg NOHS
diagnosis	DĪ əg NOH səs
dialectics	DĪ ə LEK tiks
Diallo Telli	dee AH loh TE lee
dialogue, dialog	DĪ ə LAWG
dialysis	di AL ə səs
diameter	di AM ə tər
Diana	di AN ə
dianthus	di AN thəs
diapason	DĪ ə PAY zən
diaphragm	DĪ ə FRAM
diarrhea	DĪ ə REE ə
Diaspora	di AS pər ə
diastole	di AS tə LEE
diastolic	DĪ ə STOL ik
diatom	DĪ ə TOM

---

o **on**, oh **oat**, oi **boy**, oo **soon**, oor **poor**, or **for**, ow **cow**, sh **shush**,
th **thin**, *th* **this**, u **up**, ur **spur**, uu **book**, *zh* **pleasure**

diatomaceous	DĪ ə tə MAY shəs
diatonic	DĪ ə TON ik
diatribe	DĪ ə TRĪB
Diaz	DEE ahs
dichotomy	dī KOT ə mee
didactic	dī DAK tik
Diderot	DEE də ROH
Dido, d-	DĪ doh
Diefenbaker	DEE fən BAY kər
Diego	dee AY goh
Diels	deelz
Dien Bien Phu	dyen byen foo
Dieppe	dee EP
dieresis	dī ER ə səs
diesel, D-	DEE zəl
Dies Irae	DEE ays EER ay
diethylstilbestrol	dī ETH əl stil BES trohl
Dietrich, Marlene	DEE trik, mahr LAY nə
differentiate	DIF ə REN shee AYT
differentiation	DIF ə REN shee AY shən
diffident	DIF ə dənt
diffuse (a)	di FYOOS
diffuse (v)	di FYOOZ
digest (n)	DĪ jest
digest (v)	di JEST
digestion	di JES chən
digitalis	DIJ ə TAL is
digress	di GRES
Dilantin	di LAN tin
dilapidated	di LAP ə DAYT əd
dilate	dī LAYT
dilatory	DIL ə TOR ee
dilemma	di LEM ə
dilettante	DIL ə TAHNT
dilettanti	DIL ə TAHN tee
dilute	də LOOT
dimension	də MEN shən
diminish	də MIN ish
diminuendo	də MIN yoo EN doh
diminution	DIM ə NOO shən
Dimitrov	di MEE trof
dimity	DIM ə tee
Dinesen, Isak	DEE nə sən, EE sahk

ə ago, a at, ah calm, ahr dark, air care, aw saw, ay say, ch church
e bet, ee me, eer beer, hw what, i is, ī my, n French final n vin,

dinghy	**DING** gee
diocesan	dī **OS** ə sən
diocese	**DĪ** ə sis
diode	**DĪ** ohd
dioecious	dī **EE** shəs
Diogenes	dī **OJ** ə **NEEZ**
Diomede	**DĪ** ə **MEED**
Diomedes	**DĪ** ə **MEE** deez
Dione	dī **OH** nee
Dionysius	**DĪ** ə **NISH** ee əs
Dionysus	**DĪ** ə **NĪ** səs
Diop, Ousmane Soce	**DYAHP**, oos **MAHN** soh **SAY**
diopter	dī **OP** tər
Dior	dee **OR**
diorama	**DĪ** ə **RAM** ə
Diori, Hamani	dee **AW** ree, **HAH** mah nee
diorite	**DĪ** ə **RĪT**
Dioscuri	**DĪ** ə **SKYUUR** ī
Diouf, Abdou	**JOOF**, **AHB** doo
dioxin	**DĪ OK** sən
diphtheria	dif **THEER** ee ə
diphthong	**DIF** thawng
diplomacy	də **PLOH** mə see
diplomat	**DIP** lə **MAT**
diplomate	**DIP** lə **MAYT**
diplomatist	də **PLOH** mə təst
dipsomania	**DIP** sə **MAY** nee ə
diptych	**DIP** tik
direct	də **REKT**
direction	də **REK** shən
directly	də **REKT** lee
directorate	də **REK** tə rət
dirge	durj
dirigible	**DIR** ə jə bəl
dirndl	**DURN** dəl
Diroc	di **ROK**
disable	dis **AY** bəl
disaccharide	dī **SAK** ə **RĪD**
disarm	dis **AHRM**
disaster	di **ZAS** tər
disburse	dis **BURS**
discern	di **SURN**
discernible	di **SUR** nə bəl

o on, oh oat, oi boy, oo soon, oor poor, or for, ow cow, sh shush,
th thin, *th* this, u up, ur spur, uu book, *zh* pleasure

discernment	di SURN mənt
discharge (n)	DIS chahrj
discharge (v)	dis CHAHRJ
Dischinger	DI shing gər
disciplinary	DIS ə plə NER ee
disclosure	dis KLOH zhər
disconsolate	dis KON sə lət
discordant	dis KOR dənt
discothèque	DIS koh TEK
discount (n)	DIS kownt
discount (v)	dis KOWNT
discourse (n)	DIS kors
discourse (v)	dis KORS
discourteous	dis KUR tee əs
discreet	di SKREET
discrepancy	di SKREP ən see
discrepant	di SKREP ənt
discrete	di SKREET
discretion	di SKRESH ən
discursive	dis KUR siv
disdain	dis DAYN
disease	di ZEEZ
diseased	di ZEEZD
disenfranchise	DIS ən FRAN chīz
disfranchise	dis FRAN chīz
disfranchisement	dis FRAN chīz mənt
disgorge	dis GORJ
dishabille	DIS ə BEEL
disheveled	di SHEV əld
disillusion	DIS ə LOO zhən
disintegrate	dis IN tə GRAYT
disinterested	dis IN trəs təd
dismal	DIZ məl
dismantle	dis MAN təl
dismay	dis MAY
dismember	dis MEM bər
disown	dis OHN
disparage	dis PA rij
disparate	DIS pə rət
dispersion	dis PUR zhən
dispossess	dis pə ZES
disputable	dis PYOOT ə bəl
disputant	DIS pyət ənt

ə ago, a at, ah calm, ahr dark, air care, aw saw, ay say, ch church
e bet, ee me, eer beer, hw what, i is, ī my, *n* French final n vin,

disputatious	DIS pyə TAY shəs
Disraeli	diz RAY lee
disreputable	dis REP yə tə bəl
dissect	di SEKT
dissemble	di SEM bəl
disseminate	di SEM ə NAYT
dissident	DIS ə dənt
dissociate	di SOH shee AYT
dissociation	di SOH shee AY shən
dissoluble	di SOL yə bəl
dissolute	DIS ə LOOT
dissolution	DIS ə LOO shən
dissolve	di ZOLV
dissolvent	di ZOL vənt
dissuade	di SWAYD
dissyllabic	DIS ə LAB ik
distich	DIS tik
distillate	DIS tə lət
distingué	dees tang GAY
distrait	di STRAY
distraught	di STRAWT
dither	DI*TH* ər
dithyramb	DITH i RAM
dithyrambic	DITH i RAM bik
diuresis	DĪ yə REE səs
diuretic	DĪ yə RET ik
diurnal	di UR nəl
diva	DEE və
divagation	DĪ və GAY shən
divan	di VAN
diverge	də VURJ
divergence	də VUR jəns
divers	DĪ vərz
diverse	də VURS
diversion	də VUR *zh*ən
divert	də VURT
divest	də VEST
divination	DIV ə NAY shən
divot	DIV ət
divulge	də VULJ
Djakarta	jə KAHR tə
Djibouti	jə BOO tee
Djilas, Milovan	JEE lahs, MEE loh vahn

o on, oh oat, oi boy, oo soon, oor poor, or for, ow cow, sh shush,
th thin, *th* this, u up, ur spur, uu book, *zh* pleasure

Dlamini, Bhekimpi	lah **MEE** nee, bay **GEEM** pee
Dlamini, Mabandla	lah **MEE** nee, mah **BAHND** lah
Dnepr	**NEE** pər
Dnepropetrovsk	nye praw pye **TRAWFSK**
Dnestr	**NEE** stər
Dniester	**NEE** stər
Dobi, Istvan	**DOH** bee, **ISHT** vahn
Dobrynin, Anatoly	doh **BREE** nyin, ah nah **TOH** lee
docent	**DOH** sənt
docile	**DOS** əl
doctrinaire	dok trə **NAIR**
Dodecanese	doh **DEK** ə neez
Dodgson	**DOJ** sən
doff	dof
doge	dohj
dogged (a)	**DAW** gəd
dogged (v)	dawgd
doggerel	**DAWG** ə rəl
dogma	**DAWG** mə
Doha	**DOH** hah
Dolby	**DAWL** bee
dolce far niente	**DOHL** chay fahr **NYEN** tay
dolce vita	**DOHL** chay **VEE** tah
doldrums	**DOHL** drəmz
Dolgikh, Vladimir	dohl **GEEK**, vlah **DEE** meer
dollop	**DOL** əp
dolman	**DOHL** mən
dolmen	**DOHL** mən
dolomite	**DOH** lə mīt
doloroso	doh lə **ROH** soh
dolorous	**DOH** lə rəs
Dolukhanova, Zara	doh loo **KAH** noh vah, **ZAH** rah
Domenici, Pete	də **MEN** ə chee
Domesday Book	**DOOMZ** day
domicile	**DOM** ə sīl
Dominica	dom ə **NEE** kə
Dominican	də **MIN** i kən
Domrémy	dohn ray **MEE** (dohn French final *n*)
Do Muoi	doh moy
Donatello	don ə **TEL** oh
Donau	**DOH** now
Donegal	**DON** i gawl
Donets	dah **NETS**

ə ago, a at, ah calm, ahr dark, air care, aw saw, ay say, ch church
e bet, ee me, eer beer, hw what, i is, ī my, *n* French final n vin,

Don Giovanni	DON joh VAH nee
Donizetti	DON ə ZET ee
Don Juan (Byron)	don JOO ən
Don Juan (Spanish)	dawn HWAHN
donkey	DONG kee
Donna, d-	DON ə
Donne	dun
Donnybrook	DON ee BRUUK
Don Pasquale	don pah SKWAH lay
Don Quixote (English)	don KWIK sət
Don Quixote (Spanish)	DAWN kee HOH tay
dopa	DOH pə
Doppelgänger, d-	DOP əl GANG ər
doppler, D-	DOP lər
Dorcas	DOR kəs
Doré	daw RAY
Doremus	də REE məs
Dorothea	DOR ə THEE ə
Dórticos	DOR ti kaws
dory	DOR ee
dosimeter	doh SIM ə tər
Dos Passos	dohs PAS ohs
dos Santos, José Eduardo	dohs SAN tohs, ZHUU zay ED wahr doh
dossier	DOS ee AY
Dostoevski	DAWS tə YEF skee
dotage	DOHT ij
dotard	DOHT ərd
doth	duth
Douai, Douay	doo AY
douane	dwahn
double entendre	doo blahn TAHN drə
doublet	DUB lət
doubloon	du BLOON
douceur	doo SUR
douche	doosh
doughty	DOW tee
Doukhobors	DOO kə BORZ
Dountas, Mihalis	THOON təs, mee HAH lis
dour	door (as in *poor*)
Dover	DOH vər
dowager	DOW i jər
dowry	DOW ree

o on, oh oat, oi boy, oo soon, oor poor, or for, ow cow, sh shush, th thin, *th* this, u up, ur spur, uu book, *zh* pleasure

Dowson	**DOW** sən
doxology	dok **SOL** ə jee
doxy	**DOK** see
doyen	**DOI** ən
D'Oyly Carte	**DOI** lee **KAHRT**
drachm	dram
drachma	**DRAK** mə
Draco	**DRAY** koh
Draconian, d-	dray **KOH** nee ən
draconic, D-	dray **KON** ik
dragoon	drə **GOON**
Dragosavac, Dušan	DRAH goh **SAH** vahts, **DOO** shahn
drama	**DRAH** mə
Dramamine	**DRAM** ə MEEN
dramatic	drə **MAT** ik
dramatis personae	**DRAM** ə təs pər **SOH** nee
dramatist	**DRAM** ə təst
dramaturgy	**DRAM** ə TURJ ee
Drambuie	dram **BOO** ee
Drammen	**DRAH** mən
draught	draft
Drava	**DRA** və
Dravidian	drə **VID** ee ən
Dravidic	drə **VID** ik
Drees	drays
Dreier	**DRĪ** ər
Dreiser	**DRĪ** sər
Dresden	**DREZ** dən
dressage	drə **SAHZ***H*
Dreyfus	**DRAY** fəs
drivel	**DRIV** əl
drogue	drohg
droll	drohl
drollery	**DROH** lə ree
dromedary	**DROM** ə DER ee
Drori, Amir	**DRAW** ree, ah **MEER**
droshky	**DROSH** kee
drought	drowt
drouth	drowth
Drozniak	**DRUZ***H* nyak
druid, D-	**DROO** əd
Druse	drooz
Drusilla	droo **SIL** ə

ə ago, a at, ah calm, ahr dark, air care, aw saw, ay say, ch church
e bet, ee me, eer beer, hw what, i is, ī my, *n* French final n vin,

Druze	drooz
dryad, D-	DR$\overline{\text{I}}$ əd
dual	DOO əl
dualism	DOO ə LIZ əm
Duarte	DWAHR tay
Dubcek	DUUB chɛk
dubiety	duu B$\overline{\text{I}}$ ə tee
dubious	DOO bee əs
Dublin	DUB lən
Dubois, W.E.B.	doo BOIZ
dubonnet, D-	DOO bə NAY
Dubuque	də BYOOK
ducat	DUK ət
duce, D-	DOO chay
Duchamp, Marcel	doo SHAHN, mahr SEL (SHAHN French final *n*)
duchy	DUCH ee
Duclos	doo KLOH
ductile	DUK təl
dude	dood
dudgeon	DUJ ən
Dudintsev, Vladimir	doo DEENT sef, VLAH də meer
duenna	doo EN ə
duet	doo ET
Dufy, Raoul	doo FEE, rah OOL
Dukakis	də KOK əs
Dukhobors	DOO kə BORZ
dulcet	DUL sət
dulcimer	DUL sə mər
Dulcinea	DUL sə NEE ə
Dulles	DUL əs
Duluth	də LOOTH
duma	DOO mə
Dumas	doo MAH
Du Maurier	də MAW ree ay
Dungeness	dunj nɛs
Dunkirk	DUN kurk
Dunsany	dun SAY nee
Duns Scotus	DUNZ SKOH təs
duodenal	DOO ə DEEN əl
duodenum	DOO ə DEEN əm
duomo	DWAW moh
Dupas	doo PAH

o on, oh oat, oi boy, oo soon, oor poor, or for, ow cow, sh shush,
th thin, *th* this, u up, ur spur, uu book, *zh* pleasure

Duplessis	duu ple **SEE**
duplicate (a, n)	**DOO** pli kət
duplicate (v)	**DOO** pli **KAYT**
Duquesne	doo **KAYN**
durance	**DUUR** əns
durbar	**DUR** bahr
Durenberger	**DUUR** ən **BURG** ər
Dürer, Albrecht	**DUUR** ər, **AHL** brekt
duress	duu **RES**
Durham	**DUR** əm
during	**DUUR** ing
Durocher	də **ROH** shər
Durrell	**DUUR** əl
Dürrenmatt, Friedrich	**DUUR** ən **MAHT**, **FREE** drish
durum	**DUUR** əm
Dussault, Nancy	**DOO** sawlt, **NAN** see
Düsseldorf	**DUUS** əl **DAWRF**
duteous	**DOO** tee əs
Dutra	**DOO** trə
Duvalier, Jean-Claude	duu **VAHL YAY**, ᴢʜᴀᴡɴ **KLOHD**
	(ᴢʜᴀᴡɴ French final *n*)
duvet	duu **VAY**
Dvina	vi **NAH**
Dvinsk	veensk
Dvořák	**DVAWR** *zh*ahk
Dyak	**DĪ** ak
dybbuk	**DIB** ək
Dylan	**DIL** ən
dynamic	dī **NAM** ik
dynamite	**DĪ** nə **MĪT**
dynamo	**DĪ** nə **MOH**
dynamometer	**DĪ** nə **MOM** ə tər
dynast	**DĪ** nast
dynastic	dī **NAS** tik
dynasty	**DĪ** nəs tee
dynatron	**DĪ** nə **TRON**
dyne	dīn
dysentery	**DIS** ən **TER** ee
dyslexia	dis **LEK** see ə
dyslexic	dis **LEK** sik
dysmenorrhea	**DIS MEN** ə **REE** ə
dyspepsia	dis **PEP** see ə
dysprosium	dis **PROH** zee əm

ə ago, a at, ah calm, ahr dark, air care, aw saw, ay say, ch church
e bet, ee me, eer beer, hw what, i is, ī my, *n* French final n vin,

dystrophy	DIS trə fee
Dzhugashvili	JOO gəsh VEE lee

E

Eakins	AY kənz
Eanes, Antonio Ramalho	ee AHN es, ahn TOH nyoh rah MAHL luu
Earhart	AIR hahrt
eau	oh
Eban, Abba	EE bən, AH bə
ebon	EB ən
ebony	EB ə nee
Ebro	EE broh
ebullient	i BUUL yənt
ebullition	EB ə LISH ən
ecce homo	EK e HOH moh
eccentric	ik SEN trik
eccentricity	EK sen TRIS ə tee
Ecclesiastes	i KLEE zee AS teez
ecclesiastical	i KLEE zee AS ti kəl
Ecclesiasticus	i KLEE zee AS ti kəs
ecdysiast	ek DIZ ee AST
Ecevit, Bulent	ay jay VEET, byoo LENT
echelon	ESH ə LON
Echeverria Alvarez, Luis	AY chə və REE ə AHL vah REZ, LWEES
echidna	i KID nə
echinoderm	i KĪ nə DURM
echoic	e KOH ik
éclair	ay KLAIR
éclat	ay KLAH
eclectic	i KLEK tik
eclecticism	i KLEK tə SIZ əm
eclipse	i KLIPS
ecliptic	i KLIP tik
eclogue	EK lawg
École des Beaux Arts	ay KUL day boh ZAHR
ecological	EK ə LOJ ə kəl
ecology	i KOL ə jee
economic	EE kə NOM ik

---

o on, oh oat, oi boy, oo soon, oor poor, or for, ow cow, sh shush,
th thin, *th* this, u up, ur spur, uu book, *zh* pleasure

economical	EE kə NOM i kəl
economics	EE kə NOM iks
economist	i KON ə mist
economy	i KON ə mee
ecotype	EK ə TĪP
ecru	EK roo
ecstasy	EK stə see
ecstatic	ek STAT ik
ectoplasm	EK tə PLAZ əm
Ecuador	EK wə DOR
ecumenical	EK yə MEN i kəl
eczema	EG zə mə
Edam	EED əm
Edda	ED ə
eddy, E-	ED ee
edelweiss	AYD əl vīs
edema	i DEE mə
Eden	EED ən
edict	EE dikt
edifice	ED ə fəs
Edinburg (US)	ED ən BURG
Edinburgh (Scotland)	ED ən BUR oh
Edo	E doh
Edom	EE dəm
educate	EJ ə KAYT
education	EJ ə KAY shən
eerie	EER ee
effect	i FEKT
effectual	i FEK choo əl
effeminacy	i FEM ə nə see
effeminate	i FEM ə nət
effendi	e FEN dee
efferent	EF ə rənt
effervescent	EF ər VES ənt
effete	i FEET
efficacious	EF ə KAY shəs
efficacy	EF ə kə see
effigy	EF ə jee
efflorescence	EF lə RES əns
effluent	EF loo ənt
effrontery	i FRUN tə ree
effulgence	i FUL jəns
effulgent	i FUL jənt

ə ago, a at, ah calm, ahr dark, air care, aw saw, ay say, ch church
e bet, ee me, eer beer, hw what, i is, ī my, n French final n vin,

effusion	i **FYOO** *zh*ən
effusive	i **FYOO** siv
Efremov	E frə mawf
egad	i **GAD**
Eger	**AY** gər
Egeria	i **JEE** ree ə
eglantine	**EG** lən **TĪN**
ego	**EE** goh
egoism	**EE** goh **IZ** əm
egoist	**EE** goh əst
egotism	**EE** goh **TIZ** əm
egotist	**EE** goh təst
egregious	i **GREE** jəs
egregiously	i **GREE** jəs lee
egress	**EE** gres
egret	**EE** grət
Egypt	**EE** jipt
Egyptian	i **JIP** shən
Egyptology	**EE** jip **TOL** ə jee
Ehrenburg	**AIR** ən **BUURG**
Ehrlich (Germany)	**AIR** lik
Ehrlich (US)	**UR** lik
Eichmann	**ĪK** mahn
eider	**Ī** dər
eidetic	i **DET** ik
eidolon	i **DOH** lən
Eiffel	**Ī** fəl
eighth	ayth
Eilat	ay **LAHT**
Einstein	**ĪN** stīn
Eire	**AIR** ə
Eisenstein	**Ī** zen **STĪN**
Eissa, Omer Salih	**EE** sah, oo **MAHR SAH** lee
eisteddfod	i **STE***TH* vod
either	**EE** thər
ejaculate (v)	i **JAK** yə **LAYT**
ejaculate (n)	i **JAK** yə lət
ejaculation	i **JAK** yə **LAY** shən
eject	i **JEKT**
eke	eek
Eke, Abudu Yesufu	**EE** kay, ah **BOO** doo ye **SOO** foo
ekistics	i **KIS** tiks
elaborate (a)	i **LAB** ə rət

---

o on, oh oat, oi boy, oo soon, oor poor, or for, ow cow, sh shush,
th thin, *th* this, u up, ur spur, uu book, *zh* pleasure

elaborate (v)	i **LAB** ə **RAYT**
Elaine	i **LAYN**
El Al	el al
El Alamein	el **AL** ə **MAYN**
Elamite	**EE** lə **MĪT**
élan	ay **LAHN** (**LAHN** French final *n*)
eland	**EE** lənd
Elath	**EE** lath
Elberfeld	**EL** bər **FELT**
El Dorado, Eldorado	**EL** də **RAH** doh
Eleatic	**EL** ee **AT** ik
Eleazar, Eleazer	**EL** ee **AY** zər
elector	i **LEK** tər
electoral	i **LEK** tə rəl
electorate	i **LEK** tə rət
Electra	i **LEK** trə
electrocardiogram	i **LEK** troh **KAHR** dee ə **GRAM**
electrocute	i **LEK** trə **KYOOT**
electrode	i **LEK** trohd
electrolysis	i lek **TROL** ə səs
electrolyte	i **LEK** trə **LĪT**
electromagnet	i **LEK** troh **MAG** nət
electromagnetic	i **LEK** troh mag **NET** ik
electromotive	i **LEK** trə **MOH** təv
electrostatics	i **LEK** trə **STAT** iks
electrovalent	i **LEK** troh **VAY** lənt
eleemosynary	**EL** ə **MOS** ə **NER** ee
elegance	**EL** ə gəns
elegant	**EL** ə gənt
elegiac	**EL** ə **JĪ** ək
elegize	**EL** ə **JĪZ**
elegy	**EL** ə jee
Elekdag, Sukru	el **EK** dah, **SHUUK** ruu
elephantiasis	**EL** ə fən **TĪ** ə səs
elephantine	**EL** ə **FAN** teen
Eleusinian	**EL** yuu **SIN** ee ən
Eleusis	i **LOO** sis
Eleuthera	ə **LOO** thə rə
El-Fattal, Dia-Allah	el fah **TEL**, dyu **OOL** lah
Elgin	**EL** jən
Elgin (British)	**EL** gən
El Greco	el **GREK** oh
Eli	**EE** lī

ə ago, a at, ah calm, ahr dark, air care, aw saw, ay say, ch church
e bet, ee me, eer beer, hw what, i is, ī my, *n* French final n vin,

Elia	EE lee ə
Elias	i LĪ əs
elicit	i LIS ət
elide	i LĪD
eligibility	EL ə jə BIL ə tee
eligible	EL ə jə bəl
Elihu	EL ə HYOO
Elihu (Bible)	i LĪ hyoo
Elijah	i LĪ jə
Elisha	i LĪ shə
elision	i LI zhən
Elisir d'Amore	AY lee ZEER da MOH ray
elite	i LEET
elixir	i LIK sər
Eliza	i LĪ zə
Elizabethan	i LIZ ə BEE thən
Elizalde	e lee SAHL de
Elkanah	el KAH nə
el-Kodsi, Nazem	ahl KOH tsee, NAH zem
Ellice	EL is
ellipse	i LIPS
ellipses	i LIP seez
ellipsis	i LIP səs
elliptical	i LIP ti kəl
Elmi, Hassan Nur	EL mee, HAH sən NOOR
Elmira	el MĪ rə
elocution	EL ə KYOO shən
Elohim	E loh HEEM
Elohistic	E loh HIS tik
elongate	i LAWNG gayt
eloquence	EL ə kwəns
El Paso	el PAS oh
Elsa	EL sə
El Salvador	el SAL və DOR
elsewhere	ELS hwair
Elsie	EL see
Éluard, Paul	AY loo AHR, POHL
elucidate	i LOO sə DAYT
elude	i LOOD
elusion	i LOO zhən
elusive	i LOO siv
elusory	i LOO sə ree
elves	elvz

---

o on, oh oat, oi boy, oo soon, oor poor, or for, ow cow, sh shush,
th thin, *th* this, u up, ur spur, uu book, *zh* pleasure

Elvira	el VĪR ə
Ely (given name)	EE lī
Ely (place name)	EE lee
Elysian	i LIZH ən
Elysium	i LIZH ee əm
Elytis, Odysseus	ay LEE tees, oh *th*ee SAY əs
emaciate	i MAY shee AYT
emaciation	i MAY shee AY shən
emanate	EM ə NAYT
emanation	EM ə NAY shən
emasculate (a)	i MAS kyə lət
emasculate (v)	i MAS kyə LAYT
embalm	im BAHM
embarrass	im BA rəs
embezzle	im BEZ əl
emblazon	im BLAY zən
emblematic	EM blə MAT ik
embodiment	im BOD i mənt
embolism	EM bə LIZ əm
embolus	EM bə ləs
emboss	im BAWS
embouchure	AHM buu SHUUR
embrasure	im BRAY *zh*ər
embrocate	EM broh KAYT
embroidery	im BROI də ree
embryo	EM bree OH
embryology	EM bree OL ə jee
embryonic	EM bree ON ik
emendation	EE men DAY shən
emerald	EM ə rəld
emerita	i MER ə tə
emeritus	i MER ə təs
emesis	EM ə səs
emetic	i MET ik
émeute	ay MYOOT
emigrant	EM ə grənt
emigrate	EM ə GRAYT
émigré	EM ə GRAY
Emilio	ay MEE lyoh
emir	ə MEER
emirate	EM ə rət
emissary	EM ə SER ee
emission	ə MISH ən

ə ago, a at, ah calm, ahr dark, air care, aw saw, ay say, ch church
e bet, ee me, eer beer, hw what, i is, ī my, *n* French final n vin,

emissivity	EM ə SIV ə tee
Emmaus	e MAY əs
emollient	i MOL yənt
emolument	i MOL yə mənt
empathy	EM pə thee
emphasis	EM fə səs
emphatic	em FAT ik
emphysema	EM fə SEE mə
empiric	em PIR ik
empirical	em PIR i kəl
empiricism	em PIR ə SIZ əm
employee	em PLOI ee
Emporia	em POR ee ə
emporium	em POR ee əm
empyrean	EM pə REE ən
emu	EE myoo
emulate	EM yə LAYT
emulation	EM yə LAY shən
emulsify	i MUL sə FĪ
emulsion	i MUL shən
enamor	i NAM ər
enceinte	ahn SANT (ahn French final *n*)
Enceladus	en SEL ə dəs
encephalitis	en SEF ə LĪ tis
encephalograph	en SEF ə lə GRAF
encephalography	en SEF ə LOG rə fee
encephalon	en SEF ə LON
encina	en SEE nə
Enckell	ENG kel
enclave	EN klayv
enclitic	en KLIT ik
enclosure	en KLOH *zh*ər
encomium	en KOH mee əm
encompass	in KUM pəs
encore	AHN kor
encroach	in KROHCH
encumbrance	in KUM brəns
encyclical	in SIK li kəl
encyclopedia	in sĪ klə PEE dee ə
encyclopedist	in sĪ klə PEE dəst
endeavor	in DEV ər
endemic	in DEM ik
endive	EN dīv

o on, oh oat, oi boy, oo soon, oor poor, or for, ow cow, sh shush,
th thin, *th* this, u up, ur spur, uu book, *zh* pleasure

endocrine	EN də krən
endocrinology	EN də krə **NOL** ə jee
endodontia	EN də **DON** shə
endogenous	en **DOJ** ə nəs
Endor	EN dor
endorse	in **DORS**
endowment	in **DOW** mənt
endure	in **DOOR** (**DOOR** as in *poor*)
Endymion	en **DIM** ee ən
enervate	EN ər **VAYT**
Enesco	e **NES** koh
enfant terrible	ahn **FAHN** te **REE** blə (ahn and **FAHN** French final *n*)
enfilade	EN fə **LAYD**
enfranchise	en **FRAN** chīz
enfranchisement	en **FRAN** chīz mənt
engagé	ahn gah **ZHAY** (ahn French final *n*)
Engels	EN gəlz
England	**ING** glənd
English	**ING** glish
engram	EN gram
engross	in **GROHS**
enhance	in **HANS**
Enid	EE nid
enigma	i **NIG** mə
enigmatic	EN ig **MAT** ik
Eniwetok	EN ə **WEE** tok
enjambment	in **JAM** mənt
enlightenment	in **LĪT** ən mənt
enliven	in **LĪ** vən
en masse	ahn **MAS**
enmity	EN mə tee
ennui	ahn wee
Enoch	EE nək
enormity	i **NOR** mə tee
Enos	EE nəs
enow	i **NOW**
en route	ahn **ROOT**
ensconce	in **SKONS**
ensemble	ahn **SAHM** bəl
ensign	EN sən
ensilage	EN sə lij
ensue	in **SOO**

ə ago, a at, ah calm, ahr dark, air care, aw saw, ay say, ch church
e bet, ee me, eer beer, hw what, i is, ī my, *n* French final n vin,

entablature	in **TAB** lə chər
Entebbe	en **TEB** ee
entente	ahn **TAHNT**
entente cordiale	ahn **TAHNT** kawr **DYAHL** (ahn and **TAHNT** French final *n*)
enteric	en **TER** ik
Entezam, Nasrollah	en tə **ZAHM**, nahs **ROH** lah
enthalpy	**EN** thal pee
enthrall	in **THRAWL**
enthusiasm	in **THOO** zee AZ əm
enthusiast	in **THOO** zee AST
enthusiastic	in THOO zee **AS** tik
enthymeme	**EN** thə MEEM
entirety	in **TĪR** tee
entomb	in **TOOM**
entomology	EN tə **MOL** ə jee
entourage	AHN tuu **RAHZ***H*
entr'acte	**AHN** trakt
entrails	**EN** traylz
entrance (n)	**EN** trəns
entrance (v)	in **TRANS**
entrechat	AHN trə **SHAH**
entree	**AHN** tray
entremets	AHN trə **MAY**
entre nous	AHN trə **NOO**
entrepreneur	AHN trə prə **NUR**
entresol	**EN** trə SOL
entropy	**EN** trə pee
enunciate	i **NUN** see AYT
enuresis	**EN** yə REE səs
envelop (v)	in **VEL** əp
envelope (n)	**EN** və lohp
enviable	**EN** vee ə bəl
environ	in **VĪ** rən
environment	in **VĪ** rən mənt
environs	in **VĪ** rənz
envisage	in **VIZ** ij
envoy	**EN** voi
enzyme	**EN** zīm
Eocene	**EE** ə SEEN
Eolian	ee **OH** lee ən
eon	**EE** ən
eparch	**EP** ahrk

o on, oh oat, oi boy, oo soon, oor poor, or for, ow cow, sh shush,
th thin, *th* this, u up, ur spur, uu book, *zh* pleasure

epaulet	EP ə LET
épée	ay PAY
ephedrine	i FED rən
ephemeral	i FEM ə rəl
Ephesian	i FEE zhən
Ephesus	EF ə səs
ephor	EF ər
Ephraim	EE free əm
epicene	EP ə SEEN
Epictetus	EP ik TEE təs
epicure	EP ə kyuur
epicurean, E-	EP i kyuu REE ən
Epicurus	EP ə KYUUR əs
epidemiology	EP ə DEE mee OL ə jee
epidermis	EP ə DUR məs
epiglottis	EP ə GLOT əs
epigram	EP ə GRAM
epilepsy	EP ə LEP see
epilogue	EP ə LAWG
epinephrine	EP ə NEF rən
Epiphany, e-	i PIF ə nee
Epirus	i PĪ rəs
episcopacy	i PIS kə pə see
episcopal, E-	i PIS kə pəl
episcopate	i PIS kə pət
episodic	EP ə SOD ik
epistemology	i PIS tə MOL ə jee
epistle, E-	i PIS əl
epistolary	i PIS tə LER ee
epitaph	EP ə TAF
epithelium	EP ə THEE lee əm
epithet	EP ə THET
epitome	i PIT ə mee
epizootic	EP ə zoh OT ik
e pluribus unum	e PLOO rə bəs OO nəm
epoch	EP ək
epochal	EP ə kəl
epode	EP ohd
eponym	EP ə nim
eponymous	ə PON ə məs
epopee	EP ə PEE
epos	EP os
epoxy	e POK see

ə ago, a at, ah calm, ahr dark, air care, aw saw, ay say, ch church
e bet, ee me, eer beer, hw what, i is, ī my, n French final n vin,

epsilon	EP sə LON
Epsom	EP səm
equability	EK wo BIL ə tee
equable	EK wə bəl
equality	i KWOL ə tee
equalization	EE kwə lə ZAY shən
equanimity	EE kwə NIM ə tee
equate	i KWAYT
equator	i KWAY tər
equatorial	EE kwə TOR ee əl
equerry	EK wə ree
equestrian	i KWES tree ən
equestrienne	i KWES tree EN
equidistant	EE kwə DIS tənt
equilateral	EE kwə LAT ər əl
equilibrium	EE kwə LIB ree əm
equine	EE kwīn
equinoctial	EE kwə NOK shəl
equinox	EE kwə NOKS
equipage	EK wə pij
equipoise	EK wə POIZ
equipotential	EE kwə pə TEN shəl
equitable	EK wə tə bəl
equity	EK wə tee
equivalent	i KWIV ə lənt
equivocal	i KWIV ə kəl
equivocate	i KWIV ə KAYT
equivocation	i KWIV ə KAY shən
Equuleus	i KWOO lee əs
era	EER ə
Erasmus	i RAZ məs
erasure	i RAY shər
Erato	ER ə TOH
Eratosthenes	ER ə TOS thə NEEZ
erbium	UR bee əm
Erdreich	AIRD rīsh
ere	air
Erebus	E rə bəs
Erechtheum	i REK thee əm
Erechtheus	i REK thee əs
erectile	i REK təl
Erede, Alberto	e RAY day, ahl BER toh
eremite	ER ə MĪT

---

o on, oh oat, oi boy, oo soon, oor poor, or for, ow cow, sh shush,
th thin, *th* this, u up, ur spur, uu book, *zh* pleasure

Erewhon	**ER** ə hwən
Erfurt	**AIR** fuurt
erg	urg
ergo	**ER** goh
ergosterol	ur **GOS** tə ROHL
ergot	**UR** gət
Erhard, Ludwig	**AIR** hahrt, **LUUT** vig
Eric	**ER** ik
Eridanus	i **RID** ən əs
Erie	**IR** ee
Erin	**ER** in
eristic	i **RIS** tik
Eritrea	**ER** i **TREE** ə
Erlander, Tage	er **LAHN** dair, **TAH** gi
erlking	**URL** king
ermine	**UR** mən
Ernani	air **NAH** nee
erogenous	i **ROJ** ə nəs
Eros, e-	**ER** ahs
erosion	i **ROH** _zh_ən
erosive	i **ROH** siv
erotic	i **ROT** ik
err	er
errand	**ER** ənd
errant	**ER** ənt
errata	e **RAH** tə
erratic	i **RAT** ik
erratum	e **RAH** təm
erroneous	i **ROH** nee əs
ersatz	**AIR** zahts
Erse	urs
Érsekújvár	**AYR** she **KOO** i VAHR
Erskine	**UR** skin
erudite	**ER** yə DĪT
Ervin	**UR** vin
Ervine	**UR** vīn
erysipelas	**ER** ə **SIP** ə ləs
erythematosus	**ER** ə **THEE** mə **TOH** səs
erythrocyte	i **RITH** rə SĪT
Esau	**EE** saw
escadrille	**ES** kə **DRIL**
escalator	**ES** kə `LAY tər
escallop	i **SKOL** əp

ə ago, a at, ah calm, ahr dark, air care, aw saw, ay say, ch church
e bet, ee me, eer beer, hw what, i is, ī my, _n_ French final n vin,

escapade	ES kə PAYD
escargot	es kahr GOH
escargots	es kahr GOH
escarole	ES kə ROHL
escarpment	e SKAHRP mənt
eschatology	ES kə TOL ə jee
escheat	es CHEET
eschew	es CHOO
Escorial	e SKOR ee əl
escort (n)	ES kort
escort (v)	es KORT
escritoire	ES krə TWAHR
escrow	ES kroh
escudo	e SKOO doh
Escurial	e SKYUUR ee əl
escutcheon	e SKUCH ən
Esdraelon	ES drə EE lən
Esdras	EZ drəs
Eshkol, Levi	ESH kawl, LAY vee
Eshowe	ESH ə WAY
Esmeralda	EZ mə RAL də
esophagus	i SOF ə gəs
esoteric	ES ə TER ik
espalier	i SPAL yay
especial	i SPESH əl
Esperanto	ES pə RAHN toh
espionage	ES pee ə NAHZH
Espíritu Santo (Brazil)	ə SPIR ə TOO SAN too
Espíritu Santo (New Hebrides)	ə SPIR ə TOO SAN toh
esplanade	ES plə NAHD
espousal	i SPOW zəl
espouse	i SPOWZ
espresso	e SPRES oh
Espriella, Ricardo de la	ES pree AY yə, ree KAHR doh day lah
esprit	es PREE
esprit de corps	es PREE də KOR
esquire, E-	ES kwīr
essay (n)	ES ay
essay (v)	e SAY
essayist	ES ay əst
Essegian	ə SEE jən

o on, oh oat, oi boy, oo soon, oor poor, or for, ow cow, sh shush,
th thin, *th* this, u up, ur spur, uu book, *zh* pleasure

Essen	ES ən
Essene	i SEEN
Essequibo	ES ə KWEE boh
Essex	ES iks
Essy, Amara	AY see, ah MAHR ə
Este	ES te
Esther	ES tər
esthete	ES theet
estimate (n)	ES tə mət
estimate (v)	ES tə MAYT
Estonia	e STOH nee ə
estovers	e STOH vərz
estrange	e STRAYNJ
Estremadura	ES tre mah *TH*OO rah
estrogen	ES trə jən
estrogenic	ES trə JEN ik
estrone	ES trohn
estrus	ES trəs
estuary	ES choo ER ee
eta	AY tə
étagère	ay tah *ZH*AIR
Étaples	ay TAH plə
et cetera	et SET ə rə
Eteocles	i TEE ə KLEEZ
Ethan	EE thən
ethanol	ETH ə NAWL
ether	EE thər
ethereal	i THEER ee əl
Ethiopia	EE thee OH pee ə
Ethiopian	EE thee OH pee ən
ethnic	ETH nik
ethnicity	eth NIS ə tee
ethnocentric	ETH noh˙ SEN trik
ethnology	eth NOL ə jee
ethos	EE thos
ethylene	ETH ə LEEN
etiolate	EE tee ə LAYT
etiology	EE tee OL ə jee
etiquette	ET i kət
Etna	ET nə
Eton	EET ən
Etruria	i TRUUR ee ə
Etrurian	i TRUUR ee ən

ə ago, a at, ah calm, ahr dark, air care, aw saw, ay say, ch church
e bet, ee me, eer beer, hw what, i is, ī my, *n* French final n vin,

Etruscan	i **TRUS** kən
et tu, Brute	et **TOO BROO** te
étude	**AY** tood
etui	ay **TWEE**
etymology	**ET** ə **MOL** ə jee
Euboea	yoo **BEE** ə
eucalyptus	**YOO** kə **LIP** təs
Eucharist	**YOO** kə rəst
euchre	**YOO** kər
Euclid	**YOO** kləd
Euclidean	yuu **KLID** ee ən
Eugene Onegin	yoo **JEEN** oh **NAY** gin
eugenic	yuu **JEN** ik
Euler, Ulf von	**OY** lər, **UULF** fawn
eulogia	yuu **LOH** jee ə
eulogium	yuu **LOH** jee əm
eulogy	**YOO** lə jee
Eumenides	yoo **MEN** ə **DEEZ**
Eunice	**YOO** nis
Eunomia	yoo **NOH** mee ə
eunuch	**YOO** nək
euphemism	**YOO** fə **MIZ** əm
euphonious	yuu **FOH** nee əs
euphony	**YOO** fə nee
euphorbia	yuu **FOR** bee ə
euphoria	yuu **FOR** ee ə
Euphrates	yoo **FRAY** teez
Euphrosyne	yoo **FROS** ə **NEE**
euphuism	**YOO** fyoo **IZ** əm
Eurasia	yuu **RAY** *zh*ə
Euratom	yuu **RAT** əm
eureka	yuu **REE** kə
eurhythmic	yuu **RI***TH* mik
Euripides	yuu **RIP** ə **DEEZ**
Euroclydon	yuu **ROK** li **DON**
Eurodollar	**YUUR** oh **DOL** ər
Europa	yuu **ROH** pə
Europe	**YUUR** əp
European	**YUUR** ə **PEE** ən
Eurydice	yuu **RID** ə **SEE**
Eurystheus	yuu **RIS** thee əs
eurythmic	yuu **RI***TH* mik
Eustace	**YOOS** təs

o on, oh oat, oi boy, oo soon, oor poor, or for, ow cow, sh shush,
th thin, *th* this, u up, ur spur, uu book, *zh* pleasure

Eustachian	yuu **STAY** shən
eutectic	yuu **TEK** tik
Euterpe	yoo **TUR** pee
euthanasia	**YOO** thə **NAY** *zh*ə
eutrophic	yuu **TROH** fik
eutrophy	**YOO** trə fee
evanescent	**EV** ə **NES** ənt
evangelical	**EE** van **JEL** i kəl
Evangeline (name)	i **VAN** jə **LEEN**
Evangeline (poem)	i **VAN** jə lin
evangelism	i **VAN** jə **LIZ** əm
evasion	i **VAY** *zh*ən
evasive	i **VAY** siv
Eve	eev
evening (n)	**EEV** ning
evening (v)	**EE** vən ing
eventual	i **VEN** choo əl
evidential	**EV** ə **DEN** shəl
evidently	**EV** ə dənt lee
evince	i **VINS**
eviscerate	i **VIS** ə **RAYT**
evocative	i **VOK** ə tiv
evolution	**EV** ə **LOO** shən
evolve	i **VOLV**
Evren, Kenan	**EV** ren, ke **NAHN**
ewe	yoo
Ewell	**YOO** əl
ewer	**YOO** ər
Ewing	**YOO** ing
exacerbate	ig **ZAS** ər **BAYT**
exactitude	ig **ZAK** tə **TOOD**
exaggerate	ig **ZAJ** ə **RAYT**
exalt	ig **ZAWLT**
exarch	**EK** sahrk
exasperate	ig **ZAS** pə **RAYT**
Excalibur	ek **SKAL** ə bər
ex cathedra	**EKS** kə **THEE** drə
excellency, E-	**EK** sə lən see
excelsior	ik **SEL** see ər
excerpt (n)	**EK** surpt
excerpt (v)	ek **SURPT**
excess (a)	**EK** ses
excess (n)	ik **SES**

ə ago, a at, ah calm, ahr dark, air care, aw saw, ay say, ch church
e bet, ee me, eer beer, hw what, i is, ī my, *n* French final n vin,

exchequer, E-	EKS CHEK ər
excise (n)	EK sīz
excise (v)	ik SĪZ
excitant	ik SĪT ənt
excitatory	ik SĪ tə TOR ee
exclamation	EKS klə MAY shən
exclamatory	iks KLAM ə TOR ee
exclusive	iks KLOO siv
excommunicate	EKS kə MYOO nə KAYT
excoriate	ek SKOR ee AYT
excrement	EK skrə mənt
excrescence	ik SKRES əns
excretive	ik SKREE tiv
excretory	EK skrə TOR ee
excruciate	ik SKROO shee AYT
exculpate	EK skul PAYT
excursion	ik SKUR zhən
excusatory	ik SKYOO zə TOR ee
execrable	EK si crə bəl
executant	ig ZEK yə tənt
executive	ig ZEK yə tiv
executor (performer)	EK sə KYOO tər
executor (of a will)	ig ZEK yə tər
executrix	ig ZEK yə triks
exegesis	EK sə JEE səs
exegete	EK sə JEET
exemplar	ig ZEM plər
exemplary	ig ZEM plə ree
exemplify	ig ZEM plə FĪ
exempli gratia	ig ZEM plee GRAH tee AH
exempt	ig ZEMPT
exequies	EK sə kweez
exertion	ig ZUR shən
exeunt	EK see ənt
exeunt omnes	EK see ənt OM neez
exfoliate	eks FOH lee AYT
exhalation	EKS hə LAY shən
exhilarate	ig ZIL ə RAYT
exhort	ig ZORT
exhortation	EG zor TAY shən
exhortative	ig ZOR tə tiv
exhume	ig ZOOM
exigence	EK sə jəns

o on, oh oat, oi boy, oo soon, oor poor, or for, ow cow, sh shush,
th thin, *th* this, u up, ur spur, uu book, *zh* pleasure

exigency	**EK** sə jən see
exigent	**EK** sə jənt
exiguous	ig **ZI** gyoo əs
exile	**EG** zīl
existential	**EG** zis **TEN** shəl
existentialism, E-	**EG** zis **TEN** shə **LIZ** əm
existentialist, E-	**EG** zis **TEN** shə ləst
ex libris	eks **LEE** brəs
exodus, E-	**EK** sə dəs
ex officio	eks ə **FISH** ee **OH**
exonerate	ig **ZON** ə **RAYT**
exophthalmic	**EK** sof **THAL** mik
exorable	**EK** sər ə bəl
exorbitance	ig **ZOR** bə təns
exorbitant	ig **ZOR** bə tənt
exorcise	**EK** sor **SĪZ**
exorcism	**EK** sor **SIZ** əm
exorcist	**EK** sor **SIST**
exorcize	**EK** sor **SĪZ**
exordium	ig **ZOR** dee əm
exosphere	**EK** sə **SFEER**
exoteric	**EK** sə **TER** ik
exotic	ig **ZOT** ik
ex parte	eks **PAHR** tee
expatiate	ek **SPAY** shee **AYT**
expatriate (a, n)	ek **SPAY** tree ət
expatriate (v)	eks **PAY** tree **AYT**
expectorant	ik **SPEK** tə rənt
expectorate	ik **SPEK** tə **RAYT**
expedient	ik **SPEE** dee ənt
expedite	**EK** spə **DĪT**
expenditure	ik **SPEN** di chər
experiential	ik **SPEER** ee **EN** chəl
experiment	ik **SPER** ə mənt
expert	**EK** spurt
expiable	**EK** spee ə bəl
expiate	**EK** spee **AYT**
expiation	**EK** spee **AY** shən
expiatory	**EK** spee ə **TOR** ee
expiration	**EK** spə **RAY** shən
expiratory	ik **SPĪR** ə **TOR** ee
expire	ik **SPĪR**
explanatory	ik **SPLAN** ə **TOR** ee

ə ago, a at, ah calm, ahr dark, air care, aw saw, ay say, ch church
e bet, ee me, eer beer, hw what, i is, ī my, *n* French final n vin,

expletive	EK splə tiv
explicable	EK splə kə bəl
explicative	EK splə KAY tiv
explicit	ik SPLIS ət
exploit (n)	EK sploit
exploit (v)	ik SPLOIT
exploratory	ik SPLOR ə TOR ee
exponent	ik SPOH nənt
exponential	EK spə NEN shəl
export (n)	EK sport
export (v)	ik SPORT
expose	ik SPOHZ
exposé	EK spoh ZAY
exposition	EK spə ZISH ən
expository	ik SPOZ ə TOR ee
ex post facto	EKS POHST FAK toh
expostulate	ik SPOS chə LAYT
expropriate	eks PROH pree AYT
expulsion	ik SPUL shən
expunge	ik SPUNJ
expurgate	EK spər GAYT
exquisite	EKS kwiz it
extant	EK stənt
extemporaneous	ek STEM pə RAY nee əs
extempore	ik STEM pə REE
extensor	ik STEN sər
extenuate	ik STEN yoo AYT
extinct	ik STINGKT
extirpate	EK stər PAYT
extol	ik STOHL
extortion	ik STOR shən
extract (n)	EK strakt
extract (v)	ik STRAKT
extradite	EK strə DĪT
extradition	EK strə DISH ən
extrados	EK strə DOS
extramural	EK strə MYUUR əl
extraneous	ek STRAY nee əs
extraordinary	ik STROR də NER ee
extrapolate	ik STRAP ə LAYT
extrasensory	EK strə SEN sə ree
extravagance	ik STRAV ə gəns
extravagancy	ik STRAV ə gən see

---

o on, oh oat, oi boy, oo soon, oor poor, or for, ow cow, sh shush,
th thin, *th* this, u up, ur spur, uu book, *zh* pleasure

extravaganza	ik **STRAV** ə **GAN** zə
extraversion	**EK** strə **VUR** *zh*ən
extravert	**EK** strə **VURT**
extremity	ik **STREM** ə tee
extricate	**EK** strə **KAYT**
extrinsic	ek **STRIN** zik
extroversion	**EK** strə **VUR** *zh*ən
extrovert	**EK** strə **VURT**
extrude	ik **STROOD**
exuberance	ig **ZOO** bər əns
exuberant	ig **ZOO** bə rənt
exude	ig **ZOOD**
exult	ig **ZULT**
exultation	**EG** zəl **TAY** shən
exurb	**EK** surb
Eyadéma, Gnassingbé	ay **YAH** day mah, gah **SING** bee
Eyck, van	**ĪK**, van
eyre, E-	air
eyrie	**AIR** ee
Eyskens, Gaston	**AY** skinz, gah **STOHN**
Eytan, Rafael	ay **TAHN**, **RE** fah el
Ezekiel	ə **ZEE** kyəl
Ezra	**EZ** rə

F

Faber	**FAY** bər
Fabian	**FAY** bee ən
Fabiani	fah bee **AH** nee
Fabianism	**FAY** bee ə **NI** zəm
Fabiola	fah bee **OH** lah
Fabius	**FAY** bee əs
fabliau	**FAB** lee **OH**
Fabre	**FA** brə
fabricate	**FAB** ri **KAYT**
fabulist	**FAB** yə ləst
fabulous	**FAB** yə ləs
facade	fə **SAHD**
facet	**FAS** ət
facetious	fə **SEE** shəs
facia	**FAYSH** ə

ə ago, a at, ah calm, ahr dark, air care, aw saw, ay say, ch church
e bet, ee me, eer beer, hw what, i is, ī my, *n* French final n vin,

facial	**FAY** shəl
facile	**FAS** əl
facilitate	fə **SIL** ə **TAYT**
facility	fə **SIL** ə tee
Facio, Gonzalo	fah **SEE** oh, gohn **ZAH** loh
facsimile	fak **SIM** ə lee
factious	**FAK** shəs
factitious	fak **TISH** əs
factor	**FAK** tər
factotum	fak **TOHT** əm
factual	**FAK** choo əl
faculty	**FAK** əl tee
Fadh ibn Abdul Aziz al Saud	**FED** ə **IB** ən **AHB** duul ah **ZEEZ** el **SOWD**
Faeroe	**FAIR** oh
Fafnir	**FAHV** nir
Fagin	**FAY** gən
fagot	**FAG** ət
Fahrenheit	**FA** rən **HĪT**
faience	fay **AHNS**
Faisal	**FĪ** səl
fait accompli	**FAYT** ə **KOM PLEE**
Faiyum	fi **YOOM**
faker	**FAY** kər
fakir	fə **KIR**
Falangist	fə **LAN** jəst
Falasha	fə **LAHSH** ə
falcate	**FAL** kayt
falcon	**FAL** kən
falconer	**FAL** kə nər
falconry	**FAL** kən ree
falderal	**FAL** də **RAL**
falderol	**FAL** də **ROL**
Falkland	**FAWK** lənd
fallacious	fə **LAY** shəs
fallacy	**FAL** ə see
Fälldin	**FEL** din
fallible	**FAL** ə bəl
Fallopian	fə **LOH** pee ən
fallow	**FAL** oh
falsetto	fawl **SET** oh
falsify	**FAWL** sə **FĪ**
Falstaff	**FAWL** staf

o on, oh oat, oi boy, oo soon, oor poor, or for, ow cow, sh shush,
th thin, *th* this, u up, ur spur, uu book, *zh* pleasure

familiarity	fə MIL YA rə tee
familiarize	fə MIL yə RĪZ
famine	FAM ən
fanaticism	fə NAT ə SIZ əm
fancier	FAN see ər
fancy	FAN see
fandango	fan DANG goh
Faneuil	FAN yəl
Fanfani, Amintore	fahn FAH nee, ah MIN taw re
fanfare	FAN fair
fanfaronade	FAN fə rə NAYD
Fang Lizhi	fahng lee jər
Fang Yi	fahng yee
fantasy	FAN tə see
farad	FA rəd
faraday, F-	FA rə day
Farah	fə RAH
farandole	FA rən DOHL
farce	fahrs
farina	fə REE nə
faro	FAIR oh
Faroe	FAIR oh
farrago	fə RAH goh
Farragut	FA rə gət
Farrah	FA rə
Farrar	fə RAHR
farrier	FA ree ər
farrow	FA roh
Farsi	FAHR see
farthing	FAHR thing
farthingale	FAHR thən GAYL
Fascell	fay SEL
fasces	FAS eez
fascicle	FAS i kəl
fascinate	FAS ə NAYT
fascism, F-	FASH iz əm
fascist	FASH əst
Fascisti	fah SHEE stee
Fassi, Allal El	FAH see, ah LAHL el
fasten	FAS ən
fastidious	fa STID ee əs
fatal	FAY təl
fata morgana	FAH tə mor GAH nə

ə ago, a at, ah calm, ahr dark, air care, aw saw, ay say, ch church
e bet, ee me, eer beer, hw what, i is, ī my, *n* French final n vin,

fathom	**FA***TH* əm
fatigue	fə **TEEG**
Fatima	**FA** tə mə
fatuity	fə **TOO** ə tee
fatuous	**FACH** oo əs
faucet	**FAW** sit
Faulkner	**FAWK** nər
fault	fawlt
faun	fawn
fauna	**FAW** nə
Faure	fohr
Fauré	foh **RAY**
Faust	fowst
Faustus	**FOW** stəs
faute de mieux	foht də **MYUU**
fauve, F-	fohv
Fauvist	**FOH** vəst
faux pas	foh **PAH**
favor	**FAY** vər
favorite	**FAY** və rət
Fawkes	fawks
Faya-Largeau	**FĪ** yah lahr **ZHOO**
fealty	**FEE** əl tee
feasible	**FEE** zə bəl
feature	**FEE** chər
febrile	**FEB** rīl
February	**FEB** roo **ER** ee
fecal	**FEE** kəl
feces	**FEE** seez
fecund	**FEE** kənd
fecundity	fi **KUN** də tee
fedayeen	fe dah **YEEN**
federal, F-	**FED** ə rəl
federalist, F-	**FED** ə rə ləst
federation	**FED** ə **RAY** shən
fedora	fi **DOR** ə
Fedorchuk, Vitaly	fee dohr **CHOOK**, vee **TAH** lee
Fedorenko, Nikolai	fe daw **RENG** koh, nee koh **LĪ**
feign	fayn
Feikema, Feike	**FĪ** kə mə, **FĪ** ki
Fekini, Mohieddine	fe **KEE** nee, moh hye **DEEN**
Felice	fə **LEES**
felicitous	fi **LIS** ə təs

o on, oh oat, oi boy, oo soon, oor poor, or for, ow cow, sh shush, th thin, *th* this, u up, ur spur, uu book, *zh* pleasure

felicity	fi LIS ə tee
feline	FEE līn
Felix	FEE liks
fellah	FEL ə
fellatio	fə LAY shee OH
felon	FEL ən
felonious	fə LOH nee əs
felony	FEL ə nee
felucca	fə LOO kə
feminine	FEM ə nən
femininity	FEM ə NIN ə tee
feminism	FEM ə NIZ əm
femme fatale	FEM fə TAL
femoral	FEM ə rəl
femur	FEE mər
Fénelon	fay nə LAWN (LAWN French final *n*)
fenestration	FEN ə STRAY shən
Fenian	FEE nee ən
fennel	FEN əl
Fenoaltea, Sergio	fe noh AHL tay ah, SAIR jee oh
feoff	fef
feral	FEER əl
fer de lance	FER də LANS
ferment (n)	FUR ment
ferment (v)	fər MENT
Fermi	FER mee
fermium	FER mee əm
Fernandes	fair NAHN des
Fernandez	fer NAN diz
Fernós-Isern	fayr NOHS EE sern
ferocious	fə ROH shəs
ferocity	fə ROS ə tee
Ferrara	fə RAHR ə
Ferrer	fə RAIR
ferret	FER ət
ferrous	FER əs
ferrule	FER əl
ferry	FER ee
fertile	FUR təl
ferule	FER əl
fervent	FUR vənt
fervid	FUR vəd
fervor	FUR vər

ə ago, a at, ah calm, ahr dark, air care, aw saw, ay say, ch church
e bet, ee me, eer beer, hw what, i is, ī my, *n* French final n vin,

Fescennine	**FES** ə **NĪN**
fescue	**FES** kyoo
festoon	fe **STOON**
festschrift	**FEST** shrift
Festung	**FES** tuung
Festus	**FES** təs
fetal	**FEE** təl
fete	fayt
fête champêtre	fet shahn **PE** trə (shahn French final *n*)
fetid	**FET** əd
fetish	**FET** ish
fetor	**FEE** tər
fettuccine Alfredo	**FET** ə **CHEE** nee al **FRAYD** oh
fetus	**FEE** təs
feud	fyood
feudal	**FYOO** dəl
fever	**FEE** vər
fey	fay
fez, F-	fez
Ffrangcon-Davies	**FRANG** kən **DAY** veez
fiacre	fee **AH** krə
fiancé, fiancée	**FEE** ahn **SAY**
Fianna Fail	**FEE** ə nə **FOIL**
fiasco	fee **AS** koh
fiat	**FEE** at
fibrillate	**FIB** rəl **AYT**
fibrin	**FĪ** brən
fibrosis	fi **BROH** səs
fibula	**FIB** yə lə
fiche	feesh
Fichte	**FIK** tə
fichu	**FISH** oo
fictitious	fik **TISH** əs
Fidel	fə **DEL**
Fidelio	fi **DAYL** yoh
fidelity	fi **DEL** ə tee
fiducial	fi **DOO** shəl
fiduciary	fi **DOO** shee **ER** ee
fief	feef
fiery	**FĪ** ə ree
Fiesole	**FYE** zaw le
fiesta	fee **ES** tə
fife	fif

o on, oh oat, oi boy, oo soon, oor poor, or for, ow cow, sh shush,
th thin, *th* this, u up, ur spur, uu book, *zh* pleasure

figment	**FIG** mənt
Figueiredo, João Baptista	**FEE** ger **AY** doo **ZH**WOWN ba **TEESH** tə
figurative	**FIG** yə rə tiv
figurine	**FIG** yə **REEN**
Fiji	**FEE** jee
Fijian	**FEE** jee ən
filament	**FIL** ə mənt
filariasis	**FIL** ə **RĪ** ə səs
filbert	**FIL** bərt
filch	filch
filet	fi **LAY**
filial	**FIL** ee əl
filibuster	**FIL** ə **BUS** tər
filigree	**FIL** ə **GREE**
Filipino	**FIL** ə **PEE** noh
fille de joie	**FEE** də **ZH**WAH
fillet (band)	**FIL** it
fillet (slice)	fi **LAY**
fillip	**FIL** əp
fils	fees
finagle	fə **NAY** gəl
finale	fə **NAL** ee
finalist	**FĪ** nə ləst
finality	fi **NAL** ə tee
finance	fə **NANS**
financier	**FIN** ən **SEER**
fin de siècle	fan də **SYE** klə (fan French final *n*)
fines herbes	**FEEN ERB**
finis	**FIN** əs
Finisterre	**FIN** i **STAIR**
finite	**FĪ** nīt
Finland	**FIN** lənd
Finlandia	fin **LAN** dee ə
finnan haddie	**FIN** ən **HAD** ee
Finnbogadottir	**FIN BOH** gə **DAWT** ər
Finno-	**FIN** oh
Finsteraarhorn	**FIN** stər **AHR** horn
Fiona	fee **OH** nə
fiord	fyord
Fiorello	**FEE** ə **REL** oh
Firenze	fee **REND** ze
firing	**FĪR** ing

ə ago, a at, ah calm, ahr dark, air care, aw saw, ay say, ch church
e bet, ee me, eer beer, hw what, i is, ī my, *n* French final n vin,

firkin	FUR kən
firth	furth
fiscal	FIS kəl
Fischer-Dieskau	FISH ər DEE skow
fission	FISH ən
fissionable	FISH ə nə bəl
fissure	FISH ər
fistula	FIS chə lə
Fiume	FYOO me
fjord	fyord
flabellum	flə BEL əm
flaccid	FLAK sid
flagellant	FLAJ ə lənt
flagellate (v)	FLAJ ə LAYT
flagellate (n, a)	FLAJ ə lət
flagellum	flə JEL əm
flageolet	FLAJ ə LET
flagitious	flə JISH əs
flagon	FLAG ən
flagrant	FLAY grənt
Flagstad	FLAG stad
flambé	flahm BAY
flambeau	FLAM boh
flamboyant	flam BOI ənt
flamenco	flə MENG koh
flamingo	flə MING goh
Flanagan	FLAN ə gən
flaneur	flah NUR
flange	flanj
flatulence	FLACH ə ləns
flatus	FLAY təs
Flaubert	floh BAIR
flaunt	flawnt
flautist	FLOWT əst
flavor	FLAY vər
fleur-de-lis (sing)	FLUR də LEE
fleurs-de-lis (pl)	FLUR də LEE
flexion	FLEK shən
Flexner	FLEKS nər
flexure	FLEK shər
flibbertigibbet	FLIB ər tee JIB ət
Fliegende Holländer, der	FLEE gen də HOH layn dair, dair

---

o on, oh oat, oi boy, oo soon, oor poor, or for, ow cow, sh shush,
th thin, *th* this, u up, ur spur, uu book, *zh* pleasure

flier	**FLĪ** ər
flimsy	**FLIM** zee
flippancy	**FLIP** ən see
flippant	**FLIP** ənt
flirtatious	flər **TAY** shəs
flitch	flich
floe	floh
floozy	**FLOO** zee
Flora, f-	**FLOR** ə
floral	**FLOR** əl
Florence	**FLOR** əns
Florentine	**FLOR** ən **TEEN**
Flores	**FLAW** res
Flores Avendaño, Guillermo	**FLAW** res ah ben **TH**AH nyoh, gee **LYAIR** moh
florescence	flor **RES** əns
florid	**FLOR** id
Florida	**FLOR** ə də
Floridian	flə **RID** ee ən
florin	**FLOR** ən
Florio	**FLOR** ee oh
florist	**FLOR** əst
flotation	floh **TAY** shən
flotilla	floh **TIL** ə
Flotow	**FLOH** toh
flotsam	**FLOT** səm
flounce	flowns
flourish	**FLUR** ish
flout	flowt
fluctuate	**FLUK** choo **AYT**
fluctuation	**FLUK** choo **AY** shən
flue	floo
fluent	**FLOO** ənt
fluke	flook
flume	floom
flummery	**FLUM** ə ree
fluorescent	**FLOO** ə **RES** ənt
fluoridate	**FLUUR** ə **DAYT**
fluoride	**FLUUR** īd
fluoridize	**FLUUR** ə **DĪZ**
fluorine	**FLUUR** **EEN**
fluoroscope	**FLUUR** ə **SKOHP**
fluoroscopy	fluu **ROS** kə pee

ə ago, a at, ah calm, ahr dark, air care, aw saw, ay say, ch church
e bet, ee me, eer beer, hw what, i is, ī my, n French final n vin,

flurry	**FLUR** ee
flute	floot
flutist	**FLOO** təst
fluvial	**FLOO** vee əl
flux	fluks
fluxion	**FLUK** shən
focal	**FOH** kəl
Foch	fawsh
focus	**FOH** kəs
Fogg	fog
fogy	**FOH** gee
foible	**FOI** bəl
foie gras	fwah **GRAH**
foist	foist
Fokine	foh **KEEN**
Fokker	**FOK** ər
folderol	**FOL** də **ROL**
foliage	**FOH** lee ij
foliation	**FOH** lee **AY** shən
Folies Bergères	foh **LEE** bair **ZH**AIR
folk	fohk
folklore	**FOHK** lor
follicle	**FOL** i kəl
foment	foh **MENT**
fomentation	**FOH** men **TAY** shən
fondant	**FON** dənt
fondue	fon **DOO**
Fonseka, Ignatius	fon **SAY** kə
Fontainebleau	**FONT** ən **BLOH**
fontanel	**FON** tə **NEL**
Fonteyn	fon **TAYN**
foolscap	**FOOLZ** kap
forage	**FOR** ij
forbad, forbade	fər **BAD**
forbear (n)	**FOR** bair
forbear (v)	for **BAIR**
force majeure	fawrs ma **ZH**UR
forcemeat	**FORS** meet
forceps	**FOR** səps
forebear	**FOR** bair
forecastle	**FOHK** səl
forehead	**FOR** əd
foreign	**FOR** ən

o on, oh oat, oi boy, oo soon, oor poor, or for, ow cow, sh shush,
th thin, *th* this, u up, ur spur, uu book, *zh* pleasure

forensic	fə REN sik
foreshorten	for SHOR tən
forestation	FOR ə STAY shən
forfeit	FOR fət
forfeiture	FOR fə chər
forgery	FOR jə ree
formaldehyde	for MAL də HĪD
formalin	FOR mə lən
format	FOR mat
formative	FOR mə tiv
formidable	FOR mə də bəl
Formosa	for MOH sə
formula	FOR myə lə
formulae	FOR myə lee
Forquet	fawr KAY
forsooth	for SOOTH
forsythia	for SITH ee ə
Fortaleza	FAWR tə LAY zə
forte (a, adv)	FOR tay
forte (n)	fort
forthwith	forth WI*TH*
fortissimo	for TIS ə MOH
fortitude	FOR tə TOOD
fortuitous	for TOO ə təs
Fortuna	for TOO nə
fortune	FOR chən
forum	FOR əm
forward	FOR wərd
Forza del Destino	FORT sah del de STEE noh
fossa	FOS ə
Foucault	foo KOH
Fouché	foo SHAY
foulard	fuu LAHRD
foulmouthed	fowl mow*th*d (mow as in *cow*)
Fourie, Bernardus	FOO ree, ber NAHR daws
Fourier	FUUR ee AY
Fournier	fuur NYAY
foyer	FOI ər
Fra Angelico	frah ahn JAI li koh
fracas	FRAY kəs
fractious	FRAK shəs
fracture	FRAK chər
Fra Diavolo	frah DYAH voh loh

ə ago, a at, ah calm, ahr dark, air care, aw saw, ay say, ch church
e bet, ee me, eer beer, hw what, i is, ī my, *n* French final n vin,

fragile	**FRAJ** əl
fragmentary	**FRAG** mən **TER** ee
Fragonard	fra gaw **NAHR**
fragrant	**FRAY** grənt
frailty	**FRAYL** tee
Fra Lippo Lippi	frah **LIP** oh **LIP** ee
franc	frangk
Françaix	frahn **SAY** (frahn French final *n*)
France	frans
Francesca	frahn **CHES** kə
Francescatti	**FRAHN** che **SKAH** tee
Franceschi	frahn **CHE** skee
franchise	**FRAN** chīz
Franciscan	fran **SIS** kən
francium	**FRAN** see əm
Franck, César	**FRAHNK**, say **ZAHR**
Franco-	**FRANG** koh
Franconia	frang **KOH** nee ə
Francophile	**FRANG** kə **FĪL**
Francophobe	**FRANG** kə **FOHB**
frangible	**FRAN** jə bəl
frangipane	**FRAN** jə **PAYN**
frangipani	**FRAN** jə **PAN** ee
Franglais	frahn **GLAY**
Franjieh, Suleiman	fran **JEE** ə, **SOO** lay man
Frankenstein	**FRANG** kən **STĪN**
Frankfort	**FRANGK** fərt
Frankfurt am Main	**FRAHNGK** fuurt ahm **MĪN**
frankfurter, F-	**FRANGK** fər tər
frankincense	**FRANGK** ən **SENS**
franklin, F-	**FRANGK** lən
Franz (American)	franz
Franz (European)	frahnts
frappé	fra **PAY**
Fraser	**FRAY** zər
fraternize	**FRAT** ər **NĪZ**
fratricide	**FRAT** rə **SĪD**
Frau	frow
fraud	frawd
fraudulent	**FRAW** jə lənt
Frauen	**FROW** ən
fraught	frawt
Fräulein	**FROI** līn

---

o on, oh oat, oi boy, oo soon, oor poor, or for, ow cow, sh shush,
th thin, *th* this, u up, ur spur, uu book, *zh* pleasure

Frazer	**FRAY** zər
freak	freek
Fredericton	**FRED** ər ik tən
Fredonia	frə **DOHN** yə
freesia	**FREE** *zh*ə
Freiburg (Germany)	**FRĪ** buurk
Frelinghuysen	**FREE** ling **HĪ** zən
Freneau	fri **NOH**
frenetic	frə **NET** ik
frenum	**FREE** nəm
Freon	**FREE** on
frequency	**FREE** kwən see
frequent (a)	**FREE** kwənt
frequent (v)	fri **KWENT**
frequentative	fri **KWEN** tə tiv
frère	frair
fresco	**FRES** koh
freshet	**FRESH** ət
Fresnel	fray **NEL**
Fresno	**FREZ** noh
Freud	froid
Freudian	**FROI** dee ən
Freundlich	**FROIND** lik
Frey	fray
Freya	**FRAY** ə
friable	**FRĪ** ə bəl
friar	**FRĪ** ər
fricassee	**FRIK** ə **SEE**
Frick	frik
Friedan	free **DAN**
Fries	freez
Friesian	**FREE** *zh*ən
frieze	freez
frigate	**FRIG** ət
Frigg	frig
Frigga	**FRIG** ə
frigid	**FRIJ** əd
frijole	free **HOH** lee
Friml	**FRIM** əl
Frisch, Max	frish, mahks
Frisian	**FRIZ***H* ən
frivolity	fri **VOL** ə tee
frivolous	**FRIV** ə ləs

ə ago, a at, ah calm, ahr dark, air care, aw saw, ay say, ch church
e bet, ee me, eer beer, hw what, i is, ī my, *n* French final n vin,

Frobisher	**FROH** bi shər
Froebel	**FROI** bəl
Froissart	frwah **SAHR**
Fromm	frohm
Fronde	frawnd
Frondizi	fron **DEE** zee
frontage	**FRUN** tij
Frontenac	**FRON** tə **NAK**
frontier	frun **TEER**
frontispiece	**FRUN** təs **PEES**
fronton	**FRON** ton
frottage	fraw **TAHZ***H*
Froude	frood
froufrou	**FROO** froo
frow	froh
Fruchtman	**FRUUKT** mən
fructify	**FRUK** tə **FĪ**
frugal	**FROO** gəl
fruition	froo **ISH** ən
Frunze	**FROON** ze
frustrate	**FRUS** trayt
frustum	**FRUS** təm
Fuad	foo **AHD**
Fuchs	fyooks
fuchsia	**FYOO** shə
fuchsine	**FUUK** sən
Fuegian	fyoo **EE** ji ən
fuehrer	**FYUUR** ər
fuel	**FYOO** əl
Fuentes	**FWEN** tays
fugacious	fyoo **GAY** shəs
fugitive	**FYOO** jə tiv
fugue	fyoog
führer, F-	**FYUUR** ər
Fuji	**FOO** jee
Fujiyama	**FOO** jee **YAH** mah
Fukien	foo kyen
Fukuda, Takeo	foo koo dah, tah kay oh
Fukui	foo koo ee
Fukuoka	foo koo oh kah
Fula	**FOO** lə
Fulani	**FOO** lah nee
fulcrum	**FUUL** krəm

o on, oh oat, oi boy, oo soon, oor poor, or for, ow cow, sh shush,
th thin, *th* this, u up, ur spur, uu book, *zh* pleasure

fulgent	**FUL** jənt
fulminant	**FUUL** mə nənt
fulminate	**FUUL** mə **NAYT**
fulsome	**FUUL** səm
fumarole	**FYOO** mə **ROHL**
fumigate	**FYOO** mə **GAYT**
Funafuti	**FOO** nə **FOO** tee
funambulist	fyuu **NAM** byə ləst
Funchal	fuun **SHAHL**
function	**FUNGK** shən
functionary	**FUNGK** shə **NER** ee
Fundy	**FUN** dee
funeral	**FYOO** nə rəl
funereal	fyuu **NIR** ee əl
fungi	**FUN** jī
fungicide	**FUN** ji **SĪD**
fungus	**FUNG** gəs
funicular	fyuu **NIK** yə lər
furbelow	**FUR** bə **LOH**
furcation	**FUR** **KAY** shən
furlough	**FUR** loh
furor	**FYUUR** ər
furrier	**FUR** ee ər
furrow	**FUR** oh
Furtwängler	**FUURT** veng lər
furze	furz
fusel	**FYOO** zəl
fuselage	**FYOO** sə **LAHZH**
Fushun	foo shuun
fusil	**FYOO** zəl
fusilier, fusileer	**FYOO** zə **LEER**
fusillade	**FYOO** sə **LAYD**
fusion	**FYOO** *zh*ən
fustian	**FUS** chən
futile	**FYOO** təl
Futuna	fə **TOO** nə
future	**FYOO** chər
futurist	**FYOO** chər əst
futurity	fyuu **TUUR** ə tee
Fuzhou	foo joh

ə ago, a at, ah calm, ahr dark, air care, aw saw, ay say, ch church
e bet, ee me, eer beer, hw what, i is, ī my, *n* French final n vin,

G

gabardine	**GAB** ər **DEEN**
gabbro	**GAB** roh
Gabès	**GAHB** əs
gabion	**GAY** bee ən
gable	**GAY** bəl
Gabon	ga **BOHN**
Gabor	gə **BOR**
Gaboriau	ga baw **RYOH**
Gabriel	**GAY** bree əl
Gabrilowitsch	**GAH** bri **LUV** ich
Gaea	**JEE** ə
Gaekwar	**GĪK** wahr
Gaelic	**GAY** lik
Gaetano	**GAH** e **TAH** noh
Gagarin	gah **GAH** rən
gage	gayj
Gagliano	gah **LYAH** noh
Gaillard (France)	gī **YAHR**
gaillardia	gə **LAHR** dee ə
gainsay	gayn **SAY**
Gainsborough	**GAYNZ** bur ə
Gaius	**GAY** əs
Gajdusek, Daniel	**GĪ** də **SHEK**
gala	**GAY** lə
galactic	gə **LAK** tik
Galahad	**GAL** ə **HAD**
Galápagos	gə **LAH** pə gəs
Galatea	**GAL** ə **TEE** ə
Galatia	gə **LAY** shə
Galatians	gə **LAY** shənz
galaxy, G-	**GAL** ək see
Galbraith	**GAL** brayth
Galen	**GAY** lən
galena	gə **LEE** nə
Galicia	gə **LISH** ə
Galilee	**GAL** ə **LEE**
Galileo	**GAL** ə **LEE** oh
Galitzine	gah leed **ZIN**

o on, oh oat, oi boy, oo soon, oor poor, or for, ow cow, sh shush,
th thin, *th* this, u up, ur spur, uu book, *zh* pleasure

Gallanos	gə LAH nohs
gallant (a)	GAL ənt
gallant (n, v)	gə LANT
gallantly	GAL ənt lee
gallantry	GAL ən tree
Gallaudet	GAL ə DET
Gallegos	gah YAY gohs
galleon	GAL ee ən
galleria	GAL ə REE ə
gallery	GAL ə ree
Gallic	GAL ik
Gallicism	GAL ə sIZ əm
gallimaufry	GAL ə MAW free
Gallin-Douathe, Michel	gah LAN doh WAHT, mee SHEL
galliot	GAL ee ət
Gallipoli	gə LIP ə lee
Gallipolis (Ohio)	GAL ə pə LEES
gallium	GAL ee əm
gallivant	GAL ə vANT
Gallo	GAL oh
gallop	GAL əp
Galloway	GAL ə wAY
gallows	GAL ohz
galop	GAL əp
galore	gə LOR
galosh	gə LOSH
Galsworthy	GAWLZ wUR thee
Galtieri	gahl TYAIR ee
Galton	GAWL tən
Galuppi	gah LOOP ee
Galvani	gahl VAH nee
galvanic	gal VAN ik
Galveston	GAL və stən
Galvez	gahl VES
Galway	GAWL way
Gama	GAM ə
Gamaliel	gə MAY lee əl
Gamarra	gah MAH rah
gamba	GAHM bə
gambado	gam BAY doh
Gambetta	gam BET ə
Gambia	GAM bee ə

ə ago, a at, ah calm, ahr dark, air care, aw saw, ay say, ch church
e bet, ee me, eer beer, hw what, i is, ī my, n French final n vin,

gambier, G-	**GAM** bir
gambit	**GAM** bət
gamble	**GAM** bəl
gamboge	gam **BOHJ**
gambol	**GAM** bəl
gambrel	**GAM** brəl
Gambrell	gam **BREL**
Gambrinus	gam **BRĪ** nəs
gamete	**GAM** eet
gamin	**GAM** ən
gamma	**GAM** ə
gamut	**GAM** ət
gamy	**GAY** mee
Gandhi, Indira	**GAHN** dee, **IN** də rə
Ganev, Dimiter	**GAH** nef, **DI** mi tər
Ganges	**GAN** jeez
ganglion	**GANG** glee ən
gangrene	**GANG** green
gangrenous	**GANG** grə nəs
Gannett, g-	**GAN** ət
Gansu	gahn soo
gantlet	**GAWNT** lət
gantry, G-	**GAN** tree
Ganymede	**GAN** i **MEED**
gaol	jayl
gaoler	**JAYL** ər
garage	gə **RAHZ***H*
Garamond	**GAR** ə **MOND**
Garand	**GAR** ənd
Garango, Tiemoko	gah **RAHN** goh, **TEE** ay **MOH** koh
Garcia	gahr **SEE** ə
Garcia del Solar, Lucio	gahr **SEE** ə **DEL** soh **LAHR**, **LOO** syoh
Garcia Márquez, Gabriel	gahr **SEE** ə **MAHR** kez, gah bree **EL**
Garcia Robles, Alfonso	gahr **SEE** ə **ROH** bles, al **FON** soh
garçon	gahr **SAWN** (**SAWN** French final *n*)
gardener	**GAHRD** nər
gardenia	gahr **DEEN** yə
Gardiner	**GAHRD** nər
Gareth	**GAR** əth
Garfield	**GAHR** feeld
Gargantua	gahr **GAN** choo ə

o on, oh oat, oi boy, oo soon, oor poor, or for, ow cow, sh shush,
th thin, *th* this, u up, ur spur, uu book, *zh* pleasure

gargoyle	**GAHR** goil
Garibaldi, g-	GA rə **BAWL** dee
Garin, Vasco Vieira	gah **RAN, VAHSH** koh vee **AY** rə
garish	**GA** rish
garner	**GAHR** nər
garnet	**GAHR** nət
garnishee	GAHR nə **SHEE**
garniture	**GAHR** nə chər
Garonne	ga **RUN**
garotte	gə **ROT**
garret	**GA** rət
Garrick	**GA** rik
Garrigues	gah **REE** ges
garrison, G-	**GA** rə sən
garrote	gə **ROT**
garrulity	gə **ROO** lə tee
garrulous	**GA** rə ləs
Garźon	gahr **SOHN**
Gascon	**GAS** kən
gasconade	GAS kə **NAYD**
Gascony	**GAS** kə nee
gaseous	**GAS** ee əs
gasohol	**GAS** ə HAWL
gasoline	**GAS** ə LEEN
gasometer	gas **OM** ə tər
Gaspé	ga **SPAY**
Gasperi, Alcide De	**GAHS** pe ree, ahl **CHEE** de de
Gastonia	ga **STOH** nee ə
gastric	**GAS** trik
gastritis	gas **TRĪ** təs
gastronomy	ga **STRON** ə mee
gastropod	**GAS** trə POD
Gath	gath
gather	**GA***TH* ər
Gatling	**GAT** ling
Gatun	gah **TOON**
gauche	gohsh
gaucho, G-	**GOW** choh
gaudeamus igitur	GOW day **AH** muus **IG** ə TUUR
gauge	gayj
Gauguin	goh **GAN** (GAN French final *n*)
Gaul	gawl
gauleiter, G-	**GOW** LĪ tər

ə ago, a at, ah calm, ahr dark, air care, aw saw, ay say, ch church
e bet, ee me, eer beer, hw what, i is, ī my, *n* French final n vin,

gaunt	gawnt
gauntlet	**GAWNT** lət
gauss	gows
Gaussian	**GOW** see ən
Gautama	**GOW** tə mə
Gautier	goh **TYAY**
gauze	gawz
Gaviria, Fernando	gah **VEE** ree ə, fer **NAN** doh
gavotte	gə **VOT**
Gawain	**GAH** win
Gaza	**GAH** zə
gazebo	gə **ZEE** boh
gazelle	gə **ZEL**
gazette	gə **ZET**
gazetteer	ɢᴀᴢ ə **TEER**
gazpacho	gəz **PAH** choh
Gazzara	gə **ZA** rə
Gbeho, James Victor	**GBE** hoh (**GBE** *G* barely pronounced)
Gbenye, Christophe	gə **BENG** yay, **KREE** stawf
Gdansk	gə **DAHNSK**
Gdynia	gə **DIN** yə
Gebre-Egzy, Tesfaye	**GAB** rə **EG** zee, tahs **FĪ** ay
Gedda	**GED** ə
Geddes	**GED** eez
gefilte	gə **FIL** tə
Gehenna	gi **HEN** ə
Geiger	**GĪ** gər
geisha	**GAY** shə
Geissler	**GĪS** lər
gel	jel
gelatin	**JEL** ət ən
gelatinous	jə **LAT** ən əs
gelding	**GEL** ding
gelid	**JEL** əd
gelignite	**JEL** ig **NĪT**
Gemara	gə **MAHR** ə
Gemayel, Amin	jə **MĪ** əl, a **MEEN**
Gemini	**JEM** ə **NĪ**
gemutlich	gə **MUUT** lik
gendarme	*ZH*AHN dahrm
genealogy	ᴊᴇᴇ nee **AL** ə jee
genera	**JEN** ə rə
generic	jə **NER** ik

---

o on, oh oat, oi boy, oo soon, oor poor, or for, ow cow, sh shush,
th thin, *th* this, u up, ur spur, uu book, *zh* pleasure

Genesee	JEN ə SEE
Geneseo	JEN ə SEE oh
genesis, G-	JEN ə səs
genet	JEN ət
Genêt	*zh*ə NAY
geneticist	jə NET ə səst
Geneva	jə NEE və
Genghis Khan	JENG gəs KAHN
genial	JEEN yəl
genie	JEE nee
genii	JEE nee ī
genius	JEEN yəs
genius loci	JEE nee əs LOH sī
Genoa	JEN oh ə
genocide	JEN ə SĪD
genre	*ZH*AHN rə
gens	jenz
Genscher, Hans Dietrich	GEN shər, HAHNS DEE trish
gentian	JEN shən
gentile, G-	JEN tīl
Gentoo	JEN too
gentrification	JEN trə fə KAY shən
gentrify	JEN trə FĪ
gentry	JEN tree
genuflection	JEN yə FLEK shən
genuine	JEN yoo ən
genus	JEE nəs
geocentric	JEE oh SEN trik
geodesy	jee OD ə see
geodetic	JEE ə DET ik
Geoffrey	JEF ree
Geoffrion	JEF ree ən
geography	jee OG rə fee
geology	jee OL ə jee
geometer	jee OM ə tər
geometric	JEE ə MET rik
geometry	jee OM ə tree
geophysical	JEE ə FIZ i kəl
geophysics	JEE ə FIZ iks
geopolitics	JEE oh POL ə tiks
geoponic	JEE ə PON ik
Georgetown	JORJ town

ə ago, a at, ah calm, ahr dark, air care, aw saw, ay say, ch church
e bet, ee me, eer beer, hw what, i is, ī my, *n* French final n vin,

georgette	jor **JET**
Georgia	**JOR** jə
Georgian	**JOR** jən
geotropism	jee **OT** rə **PIZ** əm
Geraint	jə **RAYNT**
Geraldine	**JER** əl **DEEN**
geranium	jə **RAY** nee əm
Gerard	jə **RAHRD**
Gerasimov, Gennadi	gyə **RAH** see mohv, gyə **NAH** jee
gerbil	**JUR** bəl
Gerhardsen, Einar	ge **RAHRD** sen, Ī nahr
geriatrics	**JER** ee **A** triks
Géricault	*zh*ay ree **KOH**
germane	jər **MAYN**
germanium	jər **MAY** nee əm
Germany	**JUR** mə nee
germicide	**JUR** mə **SĪD**
germinate	**JUR** mə **NAYT**
Geronimo	jə **RON** ə **MOH**
gerontocracy	**JER** ən **TOK** rə see
gerontology	**JER** ən **TOL** ə jee
Gerry	**GER** ee
gerrymander	**JER** i **MAN** dər
Gershwin	**GURSH** wən
gerund	**JER** ənd
Geryon	**JER** ee ən
gesso	**JES** oh
gest	jest
Gestalt	gə **SHTAHLT**
Gestapo	gə **STAH** poh
Gesta Romanorum	**JES** tə **ROH** mə **NOR** əm
gestation	je **STAY** shən
gesture	**JES** chər
gesundheit	gə **ZUUNT** hīt
Gethsemane, g-	geth **SEM** ə nee
Gettysburg	**GET** iz **BURG**
gewgaw	**GYOO** gaw
gewürztraminer	gə **VUURTS** **TRAHM** ə nər
geyser	**GĪ** zər
geyser (heater, British)	**GEE** zər
Gezira	jə **ZEER** ə
Ghana	**GAH** nə
ghastly	**GAST** lee

---

o on, oh oat, oi boy, oo soon, oor poor, or for, ow cow, sh shush,
th thin, *th* this, u up, ur spur, uu book, *zh* pleasure

ghat, G-	gawt
Ghazala, Abdel Halim Abu	gah **ZAH** lə, ahb **DEL** hah **LEEM** ah **BOO**
Gheber, Ghebre	**GAY** bər
ghee	gee
Ghent	gent
Gheorghiu-Dej, Georghe	dyawr **DYOO** de*zh*, **DYAWR** dyay
gherkin	**GUR** kən
ghetto	**GET** oh
Ghibelline	**GIB** ə lən
Ghiberti	gee **BAIR** tee
Ghirlandajo	**GEER** lahn **DAH** yoh
Ghorbal, Ashraf	**GOR** bahl, **AHSH** rahf
Ghotbzadeh, Sadegh	**KOHT** bə **ZA** də, **SAH** dək ə
ghoul	gool
Giaever, Ivar	**YAY** vər, **EE** vahr
Giaimo	**JĪ** moh
Giaiotti, Bonaldo	jī **OH** tee, boh **NAHL** doh
Giannini	jah **NEE** nee
giantism	**JĪ** ən **TIZ** əm
giaour	jowr
Giauque, William	jee **OHK**
gibber	**JIB** ər
gibberish	**JIB** ə rish
gibbet	**JIB** ət
gibbon, G-	**GIB** ən
gibbous	**GIB** əs
gibe	jīb
Gibeon	**GIB** ee ən
giblet	**JIB** lət
Gibraltar	jə **BRAWL** tər
Gibran, Kahlil	jə **BRAHN**, kah **LEEL**
Gide	*zh* eed
Gideon	**GID** ee ən
Gideonse	**GID** ee ənz
Gielgud	**GEEL** guud
gigantic	jī **GAN** tik
gigolo	**ZHIG** ə **LOH**
gigot	*zh* ee **GOH**
gigue	*zh* eeg
Gila	**HEE** lə
Gilboa	gil **BOH** ə

ə ago, a at, ah calm, ahr dark, air care, aw saw, ay say, ch church
e bet, ee me, eer beer, hw what, i is, ī my, *n* French final n vin,

Gilchrist	**GIL** krist
Gilead	**GIL** ee əd
Giles	jīlz
gilgai	**GIL** gī
Gilgamesh	**GIL** gə MESH
gill (anatomy; ravine)	gil
gill (measure)	jil
Gillespie	gə **LES** pee
Gillette	jə **LET**
gillie	**GIL** ee
gillyflower	**JIL** ee **FLOW** ər (**FLOW** as in *cow*)
gimbals	**GIM** bəls
gimcrack	**JIM** krak
gimlet	**GIM** lət
gimmick	**GIM** ik
gimp	gimp
gin	jin
ginger	**JIN** jər
gingham	**GING** əm
gingivitis	**JIN** jə **VĪ** təs
Gingold, Hermione	**GING** gohld, hər **MĪ** ə nee
ginkgo	**GING** koh
Ginn	gin
ginseng	**JIN** seng
Ginza	**GEEN** zah
Gioconda, la	joh **KON** də, lah
Giorgione	jor **JOH** ne
Giotto	**JAWT** toh
Giovanni	joh **VAH** ni
giraffe, G-	ji **RAF**
girandole	**JIR** ən **DOHL**
Girard	jə **RAHRD**
Giraudoux	*ZH*EE roh **DOO**
Gironde	*zh*ee **RAWND**
Girondist	jə **RON** dəst
Girosi	ji **RAW** see
Giscard d'Estaing, Valéry	*zh*ees **KAHR** des **TAN**, va lay **REE** (**TAN** French final *n*)
gittern	**GIT** ərn
Giuseppe	joo **ZEP** pay
Givenchy	*ZH*EE vahn shee
Gizenga, Antoine	gi **ZENG** gə, ahn **TWAHN**
Gjellerup	**GEL** ə ruup

---

o on, oh oat, oi boy, oo soon, oor poor, or for, ow cow, sh shush,
th thin, *th* this, u up, ur spur, uu book, *zh* pleasure

glabrous	**GLAY** brəs
glacé	gla **SAY**
glacial	**GLAY** shəl
glacier	**GLAY** shər
gladiator	**GLAD** ee **AY** tər
gladiolus	**GLAD** ee **OH** ləs
Gladstone	**GLAD** stohn
Glamis (Scotland)	glahmz
Glamis (Shakespeare)	**GLAH** mis
glamour	**GLAM** ər
glance	glans
Glarus (Switzerland)	**GLAHR** əs
Glarus (Wisconsin)	**GLA** rəs
Glasgow	**GLAS** goh
Glasnost	**GLAZ** nost
Glaspell	**GLAS** pel
glassine	gla **SEEN**
glaucoma	glow **KOH** mə (glow as in *cow*)
glaze	glayz
glazier	**GLAY** *zh*ər
Glazunov	**GLAZ** ə **NAWF**
glebe	gleeb
Glemp, Jozef	**GLEMP, YOO** zef
Glengarry, g-	glen **GAR** ee
Glinka	**GLING** kə
glissade	gli **SAHD**
glissando	gli **SAHN** doh
gloaming	**GLOH** ming
global	**GLOH** bəl
globin	**GLOH** bən
globular	**GLOB** yə lər
globule	**GLOB** yool
glockenspiel	**GLOK** ən **SHPEEL**
Gloucester (England, Massachusetts)	**GLOS** tər
glow	gloh
glower	**GLOW** ər (**GLOW** as in *cow*)
gloxinia	glok **SIN** ee ə
Gluck	gluuk
glucose	**GLOO** kohs
gluten	**GLOOT** ən
gluteus	**GLOOT** ee əs
glutinous	**GLOOT** ə nəs

ə ago, a at, ah calm, ahr dark, air care, aw saw, ay say, ch church
e bet, ee me, eer beer, hw what, i is, ī my, *n* French final n vin,

glycerin	GLIS ə rən
glycine	GLĪ seen
glycol	GLĪ kohl
glyph	glif
gnarled	nahrld
gnash	nash
gnat	nat
gnathic	NATH ik
gnaw	naw
Gneisenau	gə NĪ zə now
gneiss	nīs
gnome	nohm
gnomic	NOH mik
gnosis	NOH səs
gnostic, G-	NOS tik
gnu	noo
Goa	GOH ə
gobbledygook	GOB əl dee GUUK
Gobelin	GOH bə lən
Gobi	GOH bee
Godiva	gə DĪ və
Godunov	GUUD ə NAWF
Goebbels	GAIR bəlz
Goering	GAIR ing
Goethals	GOH thəlz
Goethe	GAIR tə
Goetz	gets
Gog	gog
Gogh, van	van GOH
Gogol	GOH gəl
Goidelic	goi DEL ik
goiter	GOIT ər
Golan	GOH lahn
Golconda	gol KON də
Goldhaber, Maurice	GOHLD hay bər, maw REES
Goldmark	GOHLD mahrk
Goldoni	gawl DOH nee
golem, G-	GOH ləm
Golembiewski	gah ləm BYOO skee
Golgi	GAWL jee
Golgotha	GOL gə thə
goliard	GOHL yərd
goliardic	gohl YAHR dik

---

o on, oh oat, oi boy, oo soon, oor poor, or for, ow cow, sh shush,
th thin, *th* this, u up, ur spur, uu book, *zh* pleasure

Goliath	gə LĪ əth
Gollancz	gə LANS
Golovanov	gə lah VAH nəf
Goma	GOH mə
Gómez	GOH mez
Gomorrah	gə MOR ə
Gompers	GOM pərz
Gomulka	gə MUUL kə
gonad	GOH nad
Goncourt	gawn KOOR
Gond	gond
Gondi	GON dee
gondola	GON də lə
gondolier	GON də LEER
Goneril	GON ər il
gonfalon	GON fə lən
gonorrhea	GON ə REE ə
Gonzalez	gawn SAH les
googol	GOO gawl
googolplex	GOO gawl PLEKS
gook	guuk
goon	goon
goop	goop
gooseberry	GOOS BER ee
Gopallawa	goh pah LAH wah
gopher	GOH fər
Gorbach, Alfons	GOR bahk, AHL fəns
Gorbachev, Mikhail	gor bah CHAWF, mee hī EEL
Gorgas	GOR gəs
gorget	GOR jət
gorgon	GOR gən
Gorgonzola	GOR gən ZOH lə
Gorky	GOR kee
Gorno-Badakhshan	GOR noh bah dahk SHAHN
goshawk	GOS hawk
Goshen	GOH shən
gosling	GOZ ling
Gosplan	GAWS plahn
gospodin	GOS pə DEEN
gossamer	GOS ə mər
Gosse	gaws
Gotay	goh TĪ
Göteborg	YU tə BOR yə

ə ago, a at, ah calm, ahr dark, air care, aw saw, ay say, ch church
e bet, ee me, eer beer, hw what, i is, ī my, *n* French final n vin,

Goth	goth
Gotham	**GOTH** əm
Gothenburg	**GOTH** ən **BURG**
Gothic	**GOTH** ik
Gotland	**GAHT** land
Götterdämmerung	**GAIRT** ər **DEM** ə **RUUNG**
Göttingen	**GAIR** ting ən
Gottwald	**GAWT** vahld
gouache	gwahsh
Goucher	**GOW** chər
Gouda	**GOO** də
Goudge	guuj
Goudy	**GOW** dee
gouge	gowj
Goukouni Oueddei	goo **KOO** nee **WAH** dee
Goulart, João	**GOO** lahr, **ZH**WOWN
goulash	**GOO** lahsh
Gould	goold
Gounod	**GOO** noh
gourami	**GUUR** ə mee
gourd	goord
gourmand	**GUUR** mahnd
gourmet	**GUUR** may
Gouverneur	**GOO** vər **NUUR**
government	**GUV** ərn mənt
governor	**GUV** ər nər
Gower	**GOW** ər
Gowon, Yakubu	goh **WAHN**, yah **KOO** boo
Goya	**GOI** ə
graben	**GRAHB** ən
Gracchus	**GRAK** əs
gracious	**GRAY** shəs
gradient	**GRAY** dee ənt
gradual	**GRAJ** oo əl
graduate (a, n)	**GRAJ** oo ət
graduate (v)	**GRAJ** oo **AYT**
gradus	**GRAY** dəs
Graf	grahf
graffiti	grə **FEET** ee
graffito	grə **FEET** oh
graft	graft
graham, G-	**GRAY** əm
Grail	grayl

---

o on, oh oat, oi boy, oo soon, oor poor, or for, ow cow, sh shush,
th thin, *th* this, u up, ur spur, uu book, *zh* pleasure

Grainger	**GRAYN** jər
gramercy	grə **MUR** see
Gramercy Park	**GRAM** ər see
Granada	grə **NAH** də
Granados, Enrique	grah **NAH** dohs, en **REE** ke
granary	**GRAN** ə ree
Gran Chaco	grahn **CHAH** koh
Grand Coulee	grand **KOO** lee
grandee	gran **DEE**
grandeur	**GRAN** jər
grandiloquent	gran **DIL** ə kwənt
grandiose	**GRAN** dee **OHS**
Grand Pré	gran pray
Grand Prix	grahn **PREE** (grahn French final *n*)
Grand Teton	grand **TEE** tahn
granule	**GRAN** yool
grapnel	**GRAP** nəl
grappa	**GRAHP** pah
Gratian	**GRAY** shən
Gratiano	grahsh **YAH** noh
gratis	**GRAT** əs
gratitude	**GRAT** ə **TOOD**
Grattan	**GRAT** ən
gratuitous	grə **TOO** ə təs
gratuity	grə **TOO** ə tee
Grau San Martin	**GROW** san mahr **TEEN** (**GROW** as in *cow*)
Graustark	**GROW** stahrk (**GROW** as in *cow*)
gravamen	grə **VAY** mən
graven	**GRAY** vən
gravity	**GRAV** ə tee
gravure	grə **VYUUR**
Graziano	**GRAHT** see **AH** noh
grazier	**GRAY** *zh*ər
grease	grees
greasy	**GREE** see
grebe	greeb
Grecian	**GREE** shən
Greco-	**GREK** oh
Greece	grees
Greeley	**GREE** lee
Greenland	**GREEN** lənd
Greenock	**GREE** nək
Greenough	**GREE** noh

ə ago, a at, ah calm, ahr dark, air care, aw saw, ay say, ch church
e bet, ee me, eer beer, hw what, i is, ī my, *n* French final n vin,

Greensboro	**GREENZ** bur oh
Greenwich (England)	**GRIN** ij
Greenwich Village	**GREN** ich
gregarious	gri **GA** ree əs
Gregorian	gri **GOR** ee ən
Gregory	**GREG** ə ree
Grenada	grə **NAY** də
grenade	grə **NAYD**
grenadier	gren ə **DIR**
grenadine, G-	gren ə **DEEN**
Grendel	**GREN** dəl
Grenoble	grə **NOH** bəl
Grenville	**GREN** vil
Gresham	**GRESH** əm
Gretna	**GRET** nə
gridiron	**GRID** ī ərn
Grieg	greeg
grievance	**GREE** vəns
grievous	**GREE** vəs
griffin, G-	**GRIF** ən
griffon	**GRIF** ən
grimace	**GRIM** əs
Grimes	grīmz
grimly	**GRIM** lee
Grimm	grim
Grimsby	**GRIMZ** bee
grimy	**GRĪ** mee
gringo	**GRING** goh
Grinnell	gri **NEL**
griot	**GREE** ət
gripe	grīp
grippe	grip
Gris, Juan	grees, hwahn
grisaille	gri **ZĪ**
Griselda	gri **ZEL** də
grisette	gri **ZET**
gris-gris	**GREE** gree
Grishin, Viktor	**GREESH** in, **VEEK** tər
grisly	**GRIZ** lee
gristle	**GRIS** əl
Griva	**GREE** və
Griz Nez	gree **NAY**
grizzly	**GRIZ** lee

o on, oh oat, oi boy, oo soon, oor poor, or for, ow cow, sh shush,
th thin, *th* this, u up, ur spur, uu book, *zh* pleasure

groat	groht
Grofé, Ferde	**GROH** fay, **FURD** ee
grogram	**GROG** rəm
groin	groin
Grolier	**GROH** lee ər
Gromyko	grə **MEE** koh
Gronchi	**GRONG** kee
Groningen	**GROH** ning ən
Gropius	**GROH** pee əs
grosbeak	**GROHS** beek
groschen	**GROH** shən
grosgrain	**GROH** grayn
gross	grohs
Grosvenor	**GROHV** nər
Grosz	grohs
grotesque	groh **TESK**
Grotius	**GROH** shee əs
Groton	**GROT** ən
grotto	**GROT** oh
groundsel	**GROWN** səl (**GROWN** as in *town*)
grovel	**GRUV** əl
Grozny	**GRAWZ** ni
Grudziadz	**GRUU** jawnts
Gruen	**GROO** ən
Grundy	**GRUN** dee
Grünert, Horst	**GRUUN** ərt, **HORST**
Grunitzky, Yao	groo **NEES** kee, **YOW**
Grus	grus
Gruyère	groo **YAIR**
guacharo	**GWAHCH** ə ʀoʜ
Guadalajara	ɢᴡᴀʜᴅ ə lə **HAHR** ə
Guadalcanal	ɢᴡᴀʜ dəl kə **NAL**
Guadalquivir	ɢᴡᴀʜ dəl kee **VEER**
Guadalupe	ɢᴡᴀʜ də **LOOP**
Guadeloupe	ɢᴡᴀʜ də **LOOP**
Guadiana	ɢᴡᴀʜ dee **AH** nah
Guadix	gwah **DEESH**
Guam	gwahm
Guanajuato	ɢᴡᴀʜ nah **HWAH** taw
Guangdong	gwahng dawng
Guangxi	gwahng shee
Guangzhou	gwahng joh
guano	**GWAH** noh

ə ago, a at, ah calm, ahr dark, air care, aw saw, ay say, ch church
e bet, ee me, eer beer, hw what, i is, ī my, *n* French final n vin,

Guantánamo	gwahn TAHN ə MOH
Guaporé	GWAH paw RAY
Guarani, g-	GWAHR ə NEE
guarantee	GA rən TEE
guarantor	GA rən TOR
guaranty	GA rən TEE
Guardi, Francesco	GWAHR dee, frahn CHES koh
guardian	GAHR dee ən
Guarneri	gwahr NAIR ee
Guarnerius	gwahr NAIR ee əs
Guatemala	GWAH tə MAH lə
guava	GWAH və
Guayaquil	GWĪ ah KEEL
guayule	gwah YOO lee
gubernatorial	GOO bə nə TOR ee əl
Gubner	GOOB nər
Gubser	GOOB sər
Gudrun	GUUD roon
Gueden, Hilde	GOO dən, HIL də
Guelich	GYOO lik
Guelph, Guelf	gwelf
Guerard	gay RAHRD
guerdon	GUR dən
Guerin	GAIR in
Guernsey, g-	GURN zee
guerre	gair
guerrilla	gə RIL ə
Guevara	ge VAH rah
Guggenheim	GUUG ən HĪM
Guglielmo	goo YEL moh
Guiana	gee AN ə
Guido	GWEE doh
Guido, José Maria	GEE doh, hoh SAY mah REE ah
guidon	GĪ dən
guild	gild
guilder	GIL dər
guile	gīl
Guilford	GIL fərd
Guillaume	gee YOHM
Guillemin	gee yə MAN (MAN French final *n*)
guillemot	GIL ə MOT
Guillermo Garcia, José	gə LYAIR moh gahr SEE ah, hoh SAY
guillotine	GIL ə TEEN

---

o on, oh oat, oi boy, oo soon, oor poor, or for, ow cow, sh shush,
th thin, *th* this, u up, ur spur, uu book, *zh* pleasure

Guinea, g-	**GIN** ee
Guinea-Bissau	**GIN** ee bi **SOW** (**SOW** as in *cow*)
Guinevere	**GWIN** ə **VEER**
Guipuzcoa	gee **POOTH** kə wə
guise	gīz
Guise	geez
guitar	gə **TAHR**
Guiyang	gwee yahng
Guizhou	gwee joh
Guizot	gee **ZOH**
Gujarat	**GUUJ** ə **RAHT**
Gujarati	**GUUJ** ə **RAH** tee
gulden	**GUUL** dən
gules	gyoolz
Gullah	**GUL** ə
gullet	**GUL** ət
gullible	**GUL** ə bəl
Gulliver	**GUL** ə vər
gumbo	**GUM** boh
gumption	**GUMP** shən
Gu Mu	goo moo
Gunnar	**GUUN** nahr
Gunther	**GUN** thər
gunwale	**GUN** əl
guppy	**GUP** ee
Gurev, Guriev	**GUUR** yef
Gurkha	**GUR** kə
Gurko	**GUR** koh
Gursel, Cemal	gər **SEL**, ke **MAHL**
guru	**GOO** roo
Gusev, Gussev	**GOO** sef
gusset	**GUS** ət
Gustaf	**GOO** stahf
gustatory	**GUS** tə **TOR** ee
Gustave	**GUS** tahv
Gustavus	gə **STAY** vəs
Gutenberg	**GOOT** ən **BURG**
Gutierrez	guu **TYER** res
gutta-percha	**GUT** ə **PUR** chə
Guyana	gī **AN** ə
Guzmán Blanco	goos **MAHN** **BLAHN** koh
Gwinnett	gwi **NET**
Gwyn	gwin

ə ago, a at, ah calm, ahr dark, air care, aw saw, ay say, ch church
e bet, ee me, eer beer, hw what, i is, ī my, *n* French final n vin,

gymkhana	jim **KAH** nə
gymnasium (European school)	gim **NAH** zee **UUM**
gymnasium (sports)	jim **NAY** zee əm
gymnast	**JIM** nast
gymnastics	jim **NAS** tiks
gymnosophist	jim **NOS** ə fəst
gymnosperm	**JIM** nə **SPURM**
gynandrous	ji **NAN** drəs
gynecology	**GĪ** nə **KOL** ə jee
Gyöngyös	**DYUN** dyush
Győr	dyur
gypsophila	jip **SOF** ə lə
gypsum	**JIP** səm
gypsy	**JIP** see
gyrate	**JĪ** rayt
gyre	**JĪ** ər
gyrfalcon	**JUR FAL** kən
gyroscope	**JĪ** rə **SKOHP**
gyve	jīv

H

Haakon	**HAW** kuun
Haarlem	**HAHR** ləm
Habakkuk	hə **BAK** ək
habanera	**HAH** bə **NYAIR** ə
habeas corpus	**HAY** bee əs **KOR** pəs
Haber, Fritz	**HAH** bər
habergeon	**HAB** ər jən
Habib	ha **BEEB**
habiliment	hə **BIL** ə mənt
habitat	**HAB** ə **TAT**
habituation	hə **BICH** oo **AY** shən
habitué	hə **BICH** oo **AY**
Habre, Hissen	**HAH** bray, **HEE** sahn
Habsburg	**HAPS** burg
Habyarimana, Juvénal	**HAHB** yah ree **MAHN** ah, *zh*oo ve **NAHL**
hacienda	**HAH** see **EN** də
hackney	**HAK** nee

o on, oh oat, oi boy, oo soon, oor poor, or for, ow cow, sh shush,
th thin, *th* this, u up, ur spur, uu book, *zh* pleasure

Hadassah	hah **DAH** sə
Haddad, Saad	hah **DED, SAHD**
hadj	haj
hadji	**HAJ** ee
Hadrian	**HAY** dree ən
Haeckel	**HEK** əl
Ha-erh-pin	hah er bin
hafiz, H-	hah **FIZ**
hafnium	**HAF** nee əm
Haganah	**HAH** gah **NAH**
Hagar	**HAY** gər
Haggadah	hah **GAH** dah
Haggai	**HAG** ee ī
haggard, H-	**HAG** ərd
haggis	**HAG** əs
hagiocracy	**HAG** ee **OK** rə see
Hagiographa	**HAG** ee **OG** rə fə
hagiography	**HAG** ee **OG** rə fee
Hague	hayg
Hahnemann	**HAH** nə mən
hahnium	**HAHN** ee əm
Haidalla, Mohamed Khouna Ould	**HĪ** də lah, moh **HAHM** ed **HOO** nə **OOL**
Haifa	**HĪ** fə
Haig	hayg
haik	hīk
haiku	**HĪ** koo
Haile-Mariam, Mengistu	**HAY** lee **MAIR** ee əm, men **GIT** soo
Haile Selassie	**HĪ** lee sə **LAS** ee
Hailey, Haley	**HAY** lee
Hainan	hī nahn
Hainaut	ay **NOH**
Haiphong	hī fawng
Haiti	**HAY** tee
Haitian	**HAY** shən
Hajek, Jiri	**HAH** yek, **YEE** ree
Hakim, Georges	hah **KEEM, ZH**AWR**ZH**
Hakluyt	**HAK** loot
Halakah, Halacha	hah **LAHK** ə
halakist	**HAH** lə kəst
Halasz	**HAH** lahsh
halberd	**HAL** bərd

ə ago, a at, ah calm, ahr dark, air care, aw saw, ay say, ch church
e bet, ee me, eer beer, hw what, i is, ī my, *n* French final n vin,

halcyon	HAL see ən
Haldane	HAWL dayn
Haleakala	HAH lay ah kah LAH
halfpenny	HAYP ə nee
halibut	HAL ə bət
halide	HAL īd
Halifax	HAL ə FAKS
halite	HAL īt
halitosis	HAL ə TOH səs
Hallam	HAL əm
Halle	HAHL ə
Halleck	HAL ək
hallelujah	HAL ə LOO yə
Halley	HAL ee
hallo	hə LOH
halloo	hə LOO
hallucination	hə LOO sə NAY shən
hallucinogen	hə LOO sə nə jən
Halmahera	HAHL mə HAIR ə
halogen	HAL ə jən
Hals, Frans	hahlz, frahns
halvah	hahl VAH
halve	hav
halyard	HAL yərd
Hamadan	HAM ə DAN
Hamadou, Barkat Gourad	HAH mah doo, BAHR kaht GOO rahd
hamadryad	HAM ə DRĪ əd
hamal	hə MAHL
Haman	HAY mən
Hambletonian	HAM bəl TOH nee ən
Hambro, Edvard Isak	HAHM broh, ED vahrt EE sak
Hamburg	HAM burg
Hämeenlinna	HA mayn li nə
Hamelin	HAM ə lin
Hamilcar	hə MIL kahr
Hamitic	ha MIT ik
hamlet, H-	HAM lət
Hammarskjöld, Dag	HAH mər SHOHLD, DAHG
Hammerfest	HAHM ər FEST
Hammerschmidt	HAM ər SHMIT
Hammerstein	HAM ər STĪN
Hammurabi	HAH muu RAH bee

o on, oh oat, oi boy, oo soon, oor poor, or for, ow cow, sh shush,
th thin, *th* this, u up, ur spur, uu book, *zh* pleasure

Hamody, Mohamed Said Ould	hah **MOH** dee, moh **HAHM** ed sah **EED OOL**
Hampden	**HAM** dən
Hampshire	**HAMP** shər
hamster	**HAM** stər
Hamsun, Knut	**HAHM** sən, **KNUUT**
Hamtramck	ham **TRAM** ik
Han	hahn
Handel	**HAN** dəl
handful	**HAND** fuul
handkerchief	**HANG** kər chəf
handsome	**HAN** səm
hangar	**HANG** ər
Hangchow	hang chow
hanger	**HANG** ər
Hangzhou	hahng joh
Hankow	hang kow
Hannibal	**HAN** ə bəl
Hanoi	hah **NOI**
Hanover	**HAN** oh vər
Hansard	**HAN** sərd
Hanseatic	**HAN** see **AT** ik
Hänsel and Gretel	**HAN** səl and **GRET** əl
Hansen	**HAHN** sən
hansom	**HAN** səm
Hanukkah	**HAH** nə kə
Hapsburg	**HAPS** burg
Harad	**HAHR** əd
Harada, Masahiko	hah rah dah, mah sah hee koh
hara-kiri	**HAHR** ə **KEER** ee
harangue	hə **RANG**
harass	hə **RAS**
harassed	hə **RAST**
harassment	hə **RAS** mənt
Harbin	**HAHR** bən
harbinger	**HAHR** bən jər
harebell	**HAIR** bel
harem	**HA** rəm
haricot	**HA** ri **KOH**
Harleian	**HAHR** lee ən
Harlem	**HAHR** ləm
harlequin, H-	**HAHR** li kwən
harlequinade	**HAHR** li kwə **NAYD**

ə ago, a at, ah calm, ahr dark, air care, aw saw, ay say, ch church
e bet, ee me, eer beer, hw what, i is, ī my, *n* French final n vin,

Harley Street	**HAHR** lee
harlot	**HAHR** lət
harmonic	hahr **MON** ik
harmonica	hahr **MON** i kə
harmonious	hahr **MOH** nee əs
harpsichord	**HAHRP** si **KORD**
harquebus	**HAHR** kwi bəs
harridan	**HA** rə dən
Harrovian	ha **ROH** vee ən
Harrow, h-	**HA** roh
Harte	hahrt
hartebeest	**HAHRT** ə **BEEST**
Harz	hahrtz
Hasdrubal	**HAZ DROO** bəl
Haseganu, Mihail	hah say **GAH** noo, mi hah **EEL**
hasenpfeffer	**HAH** sən **FEF** ər
Hašhek, Jaroslav	**HAH** shek, **YAH** raw **SLAHF**
Hashemite	**HASH** ə **MĪT**
hashish	**HASH** eesh
Hassam	**HAS** əm
Hassan	**HAH** sahn
hasta la vista	**AH** stah lah **VEE** stah
hasta mañana	**AH** stah mah **NYAH** nah
hasten	**HAY** sən
Hastings	**HAY** stingz
Hathor	**HATH** awr
Hatoyama	hah toh yah mah
Hatteras	**HAT** ər əs
Hatvan	**HAHT** vahn
hauberk	**HAW** burk
Haugesund	**HOW** gə suun
Haughey, Charles	**HAWK** ee
haughty	**HAW** tee
haul	hawl
haunch	hawnch
haunt	hawnt
Hauptmann	**HOWPT** mahn
Hausa	**HOW** sə
hausfrau	**HOWS** frow
hautboy	**HOH** boi
haute couture	oht koo **TUUR**
haute cuisine	oht kwee **ZEEN**
hauteur	hoh **TUR**

o on, oh oat, oi boy, oo soon, oor poor, or for, ow cow, sh shush,
th thin, *th* this, u up, ur spur, uu book, *zh* pleasure

haut monde	oh **MAWND**
Havana	hə **VAN** ə
Havel, Vaclav	**HAH** vel, **VAHTS** lahv
havelock, H-	**HAV** lok
Haverford	**HAV** ər fərd
Haverhill	**HAY** vrəl
haversack	**HAV** ər sak
havoc	**HAV** ək
Havre (France)	**AH** vrə
Havre (US)	**HAV** ər
Havre de Grace	**HAV** ər də **GRAS**
Hawaii	hə **WAH** ee
Hawaiian	hə **WAH** yən
hawser	**HAW** zər
Hawthorne	**HAW** thorn
Haya de la Torre	**Ī** yah day lah **TAW** ray
Hayakawa	hah yah **KAH** wah
Hayashi, Teru	hah yah **SHEE**, **TE** roo
Hayden	**HAYD** ən
Haydn	**HĪD** ən
Hayek	**HĪ** yək
Hayes	hayz
hazardous	**HAZ** ər dəs
Házi, Vencel	**HAH** zee, **VEN** sel
Hazlitt	**HAZ** lət
headcheese	**HED** cheez
hearken	**HAHR** kən
Hearn, Lafcadio	**HURN**, laf **KAD** ee oh
hearse	hurs
Hearst	hurst
hearth	hahrth
heath, H-	heeth
heathen	**HEE** *th*ən
heather	**HE***TH* ər
Hebbel	**HEB** əl
hebdomadal	heb **DOM** ə dəl
Hebe	**HEE** bee
Hebei	hə bay
Hébert	ay **BAIR**
Hebraic	hi **BRAY** ik
Hebrew	**HEE** broo
Hebrides	**HEB** rə **DEEZ**
Hebron	**HEE** brən

ə ago, a at, ah calm, ahr dark, air care, aw saw, ay say, ch church
e bet, ee me, eer beer, hw what, i is, ī my, *n* French final n vin,

Hecate	HEK ə tee
Hecate (Shakespeare)	HEK ət
hecatomb	HEK ə TOHM
Hechler	HEK lər
Hecht	hekt
hectare	HEK tair
hector, H-	HEK tər
Hecuba	HEK yuu bə
Hedemann, Knut	HED ə MAHN, KNOOT
Hedmark	HED mahrk
hedonism	HEE də NIZ əm
Hedwig	HED vig
Hegel	HAY gəl
Hegelian	hay GAY lee ən
hegemony	hi JEM ə nee
hegira, H-	hi JĪ rə
Heidegger	HĪD i gər
Heidelberg	HĪD əl BURG
heifer	HEF ər
Heifetz, Jascha	HĪ fits, YAH shə
height	hīt
Heijo	hay joh
heil	hīl
Heilbroner	HĪL BROHN ər
Heilbronn	HĪL brawn
Heilongjiang	hay luung jee ahng
Heilungkiang	hay luung jee ahng
Heimdall	HAYM dahl
Heine	HĪ nə
Heinlein	HĪN līn
heinous	HAY nəs
Heinsohn	HĪN sohn
Heinz	hīnz
heir	air
heirloom	AIR loom
Hejaz	hej AZ
heldentenor	HEL dən TEN ər
Helena	HEL ə nə
Helgason, Hördur	HEL gə SOON, HAHR *th*ər
Helgoland	HEL goh LAND
helianthus	HEE lee AN thəs
Helicon, h-	HEL ə KON
helicopter	HEL ə KOP tər

o on, oh oat, oi boy, oo soon, oor poor, or for, ow cow, sh shush,
th thin, *th* this, u up, ur spur, uu book, *zh* pleasure

Heligoland	HEL ə goh LAND
heliocentric	HEE lee oh SEN trik
Heliogabalus	HEE lee ə GAB ə ləs
heliometer	HEE lee OM ə tər
heliotherapy	HEE lee oh THER ə pee
heliotrope	HEE lee ə TROHP
heliport	HEL ə PORT
helium	HEE lee əm
helix	HEE liks
hellebore	HEL ə BOR
Hellenic	he LEN ik
Hellespont	HEL ə SPONT
hellion	HEL yən
Helmholtz	HELM hohlts
helot, H-	HEL ət
helotry	HEL ə tree
helpmate	HELP mayt
Helsingfors	HEL sing FORZ
Helsinki	HEL sing kee
Helvetia	hel VEE shə
Helvetii	hel VEE shee ī
Hemans	HEM ənz
hematin	HEM ə tən
hematite	HEE mə TĪT
hematology	HEE mə TOL ə jee
hematoma	HEE mə TOH mə
Hemingway	HEM ing WAY
hemiplegia	HEM i PLEE jee ə
hemistich	HEM i STIK
hemoglobin	HEE mə GLOH bən
hemophilia	HEE mə FIL ee ə
Henan	hu nahn
Henar, Lucien	hay NAHR, loo SYEN
hendiadys	hen DĪ ə dəs
Hengist	HENG gist
Henley	HEN lee
henna	HEN ə
Henslowe	HENZ loh
heparin	HEP ə rən
hepatic	hi PAT ik
hepatica	hi PAT i kə
hepatitis	HEP ə TĪ təs
Hephaestus	hi FES təs

ə ago, a at, ah calm, ahr dark, air care, aw saw, ay say, ch church
e bet, ee me, eer beer, hw what, i is, ī my, n French final n vin,

Hephzibah	HEF zə bə
Hepplewhite	HEP əl HWĪT
Heptateuch	HEP tə TYOOK
Hepzibah	HEP zə bə
Hera	HIR ə
Heracles	HE rə KLEEZ
Heraclitus	HE rə KLĪ təs
heraldic	hə RAL dik
heraldry	HE rəl dree
herb	urb
herbaceous	hur BAY shəs
herbage	UR bij
herbarium	hur BAIR ee əm
herbivore	HUR bə VOR
herbivorous	hur BIV ə rəs
Herculaneum	HUR kyə LAY nee əm
Herculean, h-	HUR kyə LEE ən
Hercules, h-	HUR kyə LEEZ
hereditary	hə RED ə TER ee
herein	hir IN
heresy	HE rə see
heretic	HE rə tik
heretical	hə RET i kəl
heritage	HE rə tij
hermaphrodite	hur MAF rə DĪT
hermeneutics	HUR mə NOO tiks
Hermes	HUR meez
Hermes, Peter	HER məs, PAY tər
Hermione	hur MĪ ə NEE
hermitage	HUR mə tij
Hermon	HUR mən
Hermosa	hər MOH sə
Hernandez	er NAHN des
hernia	HUR nee ə
hero, H-	HEE roh
Herod	HE rəd
Herodiade	ay roh dee AD
Herodias	hi ROH dee əs
Herodotus	hi ROD ə təs
heroic	hi ROH ik
heroin	HE roh ən
heroine	HE roh ən
heroism	HE roh IZ əm

o on, oh oat, oi boy, oo soon, oor poor, or for, ow cow, sh shush,
th thin, _th_ this, u up, ur spur, uu book, _zh_ pleasure

heron	HE rən
herpes	HUR peez
herpetology	HUR pə TOL ə jee
Herr	hair
Herrenvolk	HAIR ən FAWLK
Herrera Campins, Luis	ay RER ə kam PEENZ, loo EES
Herrick	HE rik
herring	HE ring
Herriot, Édouard	e RYOH, ay DWAHR
Herriot, James	HE ree ət
Herschel	HUR shəl
Hersey	HUR see
Herter	HUR tər
Hertford (England)	HAHR fərd
Hertford (US)	HURT fərd
Hertz, h-	hurts
Hertzog	HAIRT zawg
Herzegovina	HAIR tsə goh VEE nə
Herzl	HAIRT səl
Herzog	HAIRT zawg
Heshvan	HESH vən
Hesiod	HEE see əd
hesitant	HEZ ə tənt
hesitate	HEZ ə TAYT
Hesperia	he SPI ree ə
Hesperides	he SPE rə DEEZ
Hesperus	HES pər əs
Hess	hes
Hesse	HES ə
Hessellund-Jensen, Aage	HE se lun YEN sen, AW gə
Hessian	HESH ən
hetaera	hi TIR ə
heterodox	HET ər ə DOKS
heterodoxy	HET ər ə DOK see
heterodyne	HET ər ə DĪN
heterogamy	HET ə ROG ə mee
heterogeneity	HET ə roh jə NEE ə tee
heterogeneous	HET ər ə JEE nee əs
Heteroousian	HET ər oh OO see ən
heterosexual	HET ə rə SEK shoo əl
heuristic	hyuu RIS tik

ə ago, a at, ah calm, ahr dark, air care, aw saw, ay say, ch church
e bet, ee me, eer beer, hw what, i is, ī my, n French final n vin,

Hevesy, Georg	HE ve shee, GAY org
hexagonal	hek SAG ə nəl
hexameter	hek SAM ə tər
hey	hay
heyday	HAY day
Heyerdahl, Thor	HĪ ər DAHL, THOR
Heyrovsky, Jaroslav	HAY RAWF skee, YAH raw SLAHF
Heyse	HĪ zə
Heywood	HAY wuud
Hezekiah	HEZ ə KĪ ə
Hialeah	HĪ ə LEE ə
hiatus	hī AY təs
Hiawatha	HĪ ə WAH thə
hibernate	HĪ bər NAYT
Hibernian	hī BUR nee ən
hibiscus	hī BIS kəs
hiccup	HIK əp
hidalgo, H-	hi DAL goh
hideous	HID ee əs
hierarchical	HĪ ə RAHR ki kəl
hierarchy	HĪ ə RAHR kee
hieratic	HĪ ə RAT ik
hieroglyph	HĪ ə rə GLIF
hieroglyphic	HĪ ə rə GLIF ik
Hieronymus	HĪ ə RON ə məs
highboy	HĪ boi
highfalutin	HĪ fə LOOT ən
highland, H-	HĪ lənd
highwayman	HĪ way mən
Hiiumaa	HEE uu MAH
hilarious	hi LA ree əs
hilarity	hi LA rə tee
Hilary	HIL ə ree
Hildebrand	HIL də BRAND
Hillyer	HIL yər
Hilo	HEE loh
Himachal Pradesh	hi MAH chəl prə DAYSH
Himalaya	HIM ə LAY ə
Himalayan	HIM ə LAY ən
Hinckley	HINGK lee
Hindemith	HIN də məth
Hindenburg	HIN dən BURG
Hindi	HIN dee

o on, oh oat, oi boy, oo soon, oor poor, or for, ow cow, sh shush,
th thin, *th* this, u up, ur spur, uu book, *zh* pleasure

hindrance	HIN drəns
Hindu	HIN doo
Hindustan	HIN doo STAN
Hindustani	HIN duu STAN ee
hinterland	HIN tər LAND
Hipparchus	hi PAHR kəs
Hippocrates	hi POK rə TEEZ
Hippocratic	HIP ə KRAT ik
Hippocrene	HIP ə KREEN
hippodrome	HIP ə DROHM
hippogriff	HIP ə GRIF
Hippolytus	hi POL ə təs
Hippomenes	hi POM ə NEEZ
hippopotamus	HIP ə POT ə məs
Hiram	HĪ rəm
Hirohito	HI roh HEE toh
Hiroshige	HI roh SHEE gə
Hiroshima	HI roh SHEE mə
Hirshhorn	HURSH horn
hirsute	HUR soot
Hispaniola	HIS pən YOH lə
histamine	HIS tə MEEN
histology	hi STOL ə jee
historian	hi STOR ee ən
historical	hi STOR i kəl
historiographer	hi STOR ee OG rə fər
history	HIS tə ree
histrionic	HIS tree ON ik
hither	HITH ər
Hitler	HIT lər
Hitlerism	HIT lə RIZ əm
Hittite	HI tīt
hives	hīvz
Hjalmar	YAHL mahr
hoagie	HOH gee
hoary	HOR ee
Hobart (Tasmania)	HOH bərt
Hobart (US)	HOH bahrt
Hobbes	hobz
Hoboken	HOH boh kən
Ho Chi Minh	hoh chee min
Hochoy, Solomon	hoh CHOI, SOL ə mən
Hoeven	HOH vən

ə ago, a at, ah calm, ahr dark, air care, aw saw, ay say, ch church
e bet, ee me, eer beer, hw what, i is, ī my, *n* French final n vin,

Hoffmann	HOF mən
Hofstadter	HOF STAT ər
Hofstra	HOF strə
hogan	HOH gahn
Hogan	HOH gən
Hogarth	HOH gahrth
Hohenzollern	HOH ən ZOL ərn
hoi polloi	HOI pə LOI
hoity-toity	HOI tee TOI tee
Hokkaido	hoh KĪ doh
hokku	HOK oo
Holbein	HOHL bīn
Holinshed	HOL inz HED
holism	HOH LIZ əm
holistic	hoh LIS tik
Holland	HOL ənd
hollandaise	HOL ən DAYZ
hollyhock	HOL ee HOK
holm	hohm
Holmes	hohmz
holocaust	HOL ə KAWST
Holocene	HOH lə SEEN
Holofernes	HOL ə FUR neez
hologram	HOH lə GRAM
holograph	HOH lə GRAF
Holstein, h-	HOHL stīn
Holyhead	HAH lee HED
Holyoake	HOH lee OHK
Holyoke	HOHL yohk
Massachusetts)	
homage	HOM ij
hombre	OM bray
Homburg, h-	HOM burg
Home (earls of)	hyoom
homely	HOHM lee
homeopath	HOH mee ə PATH
homeopathic	HOH mee ə PATH ik
homeopathy	HOH mee OP ə thee
homer, H-	HOH mər
Homeric	hoh MER ik
homicide	HOM ə SĪD
homiletic	HOM ə LET ik
homily	HOM ə lee

o on, oh oat, oi boy, oo soon, oor poor, or for, ow cow, sh shush,
th thin, *th* this, u up, ur spur, uu book, *zh* pleasure

hominid	**HOM** ə nid
hominy	**HOM** ə nee
homo, H-	**HOH** moh
homogeneity	**HOH** mə jə **NEE** ə tee
homogeneous	**HOH** mə **JEE** nee əs
homologous	hoh **MOL** ə gəs
homonym	**HOM** ə nim
Homoousian	**HOH** moh **OO** see ən
homophone	**HOM** ə **FOHN**
Homo sapiens	**HOH** moh **SAY** pee ənz
Honan	hoh nan
Honda	**HON** də
Honduras	hon **DUUR** əs
Honecker, Erich	**HOH** nə kər, **AY** rik
Honegger	**HOH** ne gər
Hong Kong	**HONG** kong
Honiara	**HOH** nee **AHR** ə
Honolulu	**HON** ə **LOO** loo
honorable	**ON** ə rə bəl
honorarium	**ON** ə **RAIR** ee əm
honorific	**ON** ə **RIF** ik
Honshu	hon shoo
hooch	hooch
Hooch, Pieter de	**HOHK**, **PEE** tər də
hoodlum	**HUUD** ləm
hoodoo	**HOO** doo
hoodwink	**HUUD** wingk
hoof	huuf
hook	huuk
hookah	**HUUK** ə
hooker	**HUUK** ər
hooligan	**HOO** li gən
hoop	huup
hoopla	**HOO** plah
hoosegow, hoosgow	**HOOS** gow
Hoosier	**HOO** zhər
hootch	hooch
hootenanny	**HOOT** ə **NAN** ee
hooves	hoovz
Hopeh	hoh pay
Hopi	**HOH** pee
Horace	**HAW** rəs
Horatio	hə **RAY** shoh

ə ago, a at, ah calm, ahr dark, air care, aw saw, ay say, ch church
e bet, ee me, eer beer, hw what, i is, ī my, *n* French final n vin,

Horatius	hə **RAY** shəs
Horeb	**HOH** reb
horizon	hə **RĪ** zən
horizontal	**HOR** ə **ZON** təl
hormone	**HOR** mohn
Hormuz	**HOR** məz
hornblende	**HORN** blend
Horney	**HOR** nī
horologist	hə **ROL** ə jəst
horoscope	**HOR** ə **SKOHP**
Horowitz	**HOR** ə wits
horrendous	haw **REN** dəs
horrible	**HOR** ə bəl
horrid	**HOR** əd
horror	**HOR** ər
Horsa	**HOR** sə
hors de combat	or də kohn **BAH** (kohn French final *n*)
hors d'oeuvre	or **DURV**
hors d'oeuvres	or **DURV**
Horst Wessel	**HORST VES** əl
Horszowski, Mieczyslaw	hawr **SHUF** skee, mye **CHI** swahf
hosanna	hoh **ZAN** ə
Hosea	hoh **ZEE** ə
hosiery	**HOH** *zh*ə ree
Hosmer	**HAWZ** mər
hospice	**HOS** pəs
hospitable	**HOS** pi tə bəl
hostage	**HOS** tij
hostel	**HOS** təl
hostelry	**HOS** təl ree
hostile	**HOS** təl
hostler	**HOS** lər
hotel	hoh **TEL**
hôtel de ville	oh **TEL** də **VEEL**
Houdini	hoo **DEE** nee
Houdon	oo **DAWN** (DAWN French final *n*)
Hough	huf
Houghton	**HOHT** ən
Hounsfield, Godfrey	**HOWNZ** feeld, **GAHD** free
houri	**HUUR** ee
Housatonic	**HOO** sə **TAHN** ik
Housman	**HOWS** mən

o on, oh oat, oi boy, oo soon, oor poor, or for, ow cow, sh shush,
th thin, *th* this, u up, ur spur, uu book, *zh* pleasure

Houston (English botanist and Scotland)	**HOO** stən
Houston (New York street and Georgia county)	**HOW** stən
Houston (Texas soldier and city)	**HYOO** stən
Houyhnhnm	**HWIN** əm
hovel	**HUV** əl
hover	**HUV** ər
Hovey	**HUV** ee
howdah	**HOW** də
howdy	**HOW** dee
Howe	how
Howells	**HOW** əlz
howitzer	**HOW** ət sər
hoyden	**HOI** dən
Hoyle	hoil
Hrdlička	**HURD** lich **KAH**
Hua Guofeng	hwah gwoh feng
Huang Ho	hwahng hoh
huarache	wə **RAH** chee
Huascarán	**WAH** skah **RAHN**
Hubbard	**HUB** ərd
hubbub	**HUB** ub
Hubei	hoo bay
hubris	**HYOO** brəs
huckster	**HUK** stər
Hudibras	**HYOO** də **BRAS**
Huelva	**WEL** vah
Huerta, Victoriano	**WER** tah, **BEEK** taw **RYAH** naw
Huesca	**WES** kah
Hughes	hyooz
Huguenot	**HYOO** gə **NOT**
Huila	**WEE** lah
Hui-tsung	hwee dzuung
hula-hula	**HOO** lə **HOO** lə
hullabaloo	**HUL** ə bə **LOO**
hullo	hə **LOH**
Hulme (British)	hyoom
Hulme (US)	hulm
humane	hyoo **MAYN**

ə ago, a at, ah calm, ahr dark, air care, aw saw, ay say, ch church
e bet, ee me, eer beer, hw what, i is, ī my, *n* French final n vin,

humanism, H-	HYOO mə NIZ əm
humanitarian	hyoo MAN ə TAIR ee ən
humanization	HYOO mə nə ZAY shən
Humber	HUM bər
humble	HUM bəl
Humboldt	HUM bohlt
humdrum	HUM drum
Hume	hyoom
humerus	HYOOM ə rəs
humid	HYOO məd
humidity	hyoo MID ə tee
humidor	HYOO mə DOR
humiliate	hyoo MIL ee AYT
humiliation	hyoo MIL ee AY shən
humility	hyoo MIL ə tee
hummock	HUM ək
hummus	HUM əs
humor	HYOO mər
humorist	HYOO mər əst
humorous	HYOO mə rəs
Humperdinck	HUUM pər DINGK
humus	HYOO məs
Hunan	hoo nahn
hundred	HUN drəd
hundredth	HUN drədth
Huneker	HUN ə kər
Hungarian	hung GAIR ee ən
Hungary	HUNG gə ree
hunger	HUNG gər
Hungnam	huung nahm
hungry	HUNG gree
Hupeh	hoo be
Hu Qili	hoo chee lee
Huron	HYUUR ən
hurrah	hə RAH
hurray	hə RAY
hurricane	HUR ə KAYN
Hurtado Larrea, Osvaldo	oor TAH doh lah RAY ah, aws VAHL doh
Husák, Gustav	HOO sahk, GUUS tahf
husky	HUS kee
Huss	hus
hussar	hə ZAHR

o on, oh oat, oi boy, oo soon, oor poor, or for, ow cow, sh shush, th thin, *th* this, u up, ur spur, uu book, *zh* pleasure

Hussein	hoo **SAYN**
hussy	**HUS** ee
hustings	**HUS** tingz
hustle	**HUS** əl
Huston	**HYOO** stən
Huszt	hoost
Huxley	**HUKS** lee
Hu Yaobang	hoo yah oh bahng
Huygens	**HĪ** gənz
Huysmans (Dutch)	**HOIS** mahns
Huysmans (French)	wees **MAHNS**
huzzah	hə **ZAH**
Hwang Hai	hwahng hī
Hwang Ho	hwahng hoh
hyacinth	**HĪ** ə sinth
Hyacinthus	**HĪ** ə **SIN** thəs
Hyades	**HĪ** ə **DEEZ**
Hyannis	hī **AN** is
hybrid	**HĪ** brəd
hybridization	**HĪ** brə də **ZAY** shən
Hyderabad	**HĪ** dər ə **BAD**
Hydra, h-	**HĪ** drə
hydrangea	hī **DRAYN** jə
hydraulic	hī **DRAW** lik
hydrocephalic	**HĪ** droh sə **FAL** ik
hydrocephalus	**HĪ** droh **SEF** ə ləs
hydrogen	**HĪ** drə jən
hydrogenate	hī **DROJ** ə **NAYT**
hydrographic	**HĪ** drə **GRAF** ik
hydrography	hī **DROG** rə fee
hydrology	hī **DROL** ə jee
hydrometer	hī **DROM** ə tər
hydropathy	hī **DROP** ə thee
hydrophobia	**HĪ** drə **FOH** bee ə
hydroplane	**HĪ** drə **PLAYN**
hydroponic	**HĪ** drə **PON** ik
hydroxyl	hī **DROK** səl
Hydrozoa	**HĪ** drə **ZOH** ə
Hydrus	**HĪ** drəs
hyena	hī **EE** nə
Hygeia	hī **JEE** ə
hygiene	**HĪ** jeen
hygienic	**HĪ** jee **EN** ik

ə ago, a at, ah calm, ahr dark, air care, aw saw, ay say, ch church
e bet, ee me, eer beer, hw what, i is, ī my, *n* French final n vin,

hygienist	hī JEE nəst
Hyksos	HIK sohs
Hymen, h-	HĪ mən
hymeneal	HĪ mə NEE əl
Hymettus	HĪ MET əs
hymn	him
hymnal	HIM nəl
hyperbaric	HĪ pər BA rik
hyperbola	hī PUR bə lə
hyperbole	hī PUR bə lee
hyperbolic	HĪ pər BOL ik
hyperborean, H-	HĪ pər BOR ee ən
hypercritical	HĪ pər KRIT i kəl
hyperesthesia	HĪ pər es THEE zhə
hypergolic	HĪ pər GOL ik
Hyperion	hī PIR ee ən
hyperopia	HĪ pər OH pee ə
hypertension	HĪ pər TEN shən
hyperthyroid	HĪ pər THĪ roid
hypertrophy	hī PUR trə fee
Hypnos	HIP nos
hypnosis	hip NOH səs
hypnotic	hip NOT ik
hypnotism	HIP nə TIZ əm
hypnotist	HIP nə təst
hypochondria	HĪ pə KON dree ə
hypochondriac	HĪ pə KON dree AK
hypochondriacal	HĪ pə kən DRĪ ə kəl
hypocrisy	hi POK rə see
hypocrite	HIP ə krit
hypodermic	HĪ pə DUR mik
hypoglycemia	HĪ poh glī SEE mee ə
hypostasis	hī POS tə səs
hypotenuse	hī POT ə NOOS
hypothecate	hī POTH ə KAYT
hypothecation	hī POTH ə KAY shən
hypothermia	HĪ poh THUR mee ə
hypotheses	hī POTH ə SEEZ
hypothesis	hī POTH ə səs
hypothetical	HĪ pə THET i kəl
hypothyroid	HĪ poh THĪ roid
hypoxia	hī POK see ə
Hypseus	HIP see əs

---

o on, oh oat, oi boy, oo soon, oor poor, or for, ow cow, sh shush,
th thin, *th* this, u up, ur spur, uu book, *zh* pleasure

Hypsipyle	hip **SIP** ə **LEE**
hyrax	**HĪ** raks
Hyrcania	hər **KAY** nee ə
hyson	**HĪ** sən
hyssop	**HIS** əp
hysterectomy	**HIS** tə **REK** tə mee
hysteresis	**HIS** tə **REE** səs
hysteria	hi **STI** ree ə
hysterics	hi **STER** iks
hysterotomy	**HIS** tə **ROT** ə mee

I

Iago	ee **AH** goh
iamb	**Ī** amb
Iambe	**Ī** əm **BEE**
iambic	ī **AM** bik
Iapetus	ī **AP** ə təs
iatrogenic	ī **A** trə **JEN** ik
Ibadan	ee **BAH** dahn
Ibañez	ee **BAH** nyeth
Iberia	ī **BIR** ee ə
Iberian	ī **BIR** ee ən
ibidem	**IB** ə **DEM**
ibis	**Ī** bis
Ibiza	ee **VEE** zə
Ibn Saud, i-	**IB** ən sah **OOD**
Ibo	**EE** boh
Ibrahim, Mohamed Hamid	**IB** rə **HIM**, moh **HAHM** ed hahm **ID**
Ibsen	**IB** sən
Icarian	i **KAIR** ee ən
Icarus	**IK** ər əs
Iceland	**ĪS** lənd
Iceni	ī **SEE** nī
Ichabod	**IK** ə **BOD**
ich dien	ik **DEEN**
I Ching	ee jeeng
ichneumon	ik **NOO** mən
ichor	**Ī** kor
ichthyology	**IK** thee **OL** ə jee

ə ago, a at, ah calm, ahr dark, air care, aw saw, ay say, ch church
e bet, ee me, eer beer, hw what, i is, ī my, *n* French final n vin,

ichthyosaurus	IK thee ə SAW rəs
ichthyosis	IK thee OH sis
icicle	Ī si kəl
icon	Ī kon
iconoclasm	ī KON ə KLAZ əm
iconoclast	ī KON ə KLAST
iconolatry	Ī kə NOL ə tree
icosahedron	ī KOH sə HEE drən
icterus	IK tər əs
ictus	IK təs
Ida	Ī də
Idaho	Ī də HOH
idea	ī DEE ə
ideal	ī DEE əl
idealism	ī DEE ə LIZ əm
ideality	Ī dee AL ə tee
idée fixe	ee day FEEKS
idem	Ī dem
identically	ī DEN ti kə lee
ideogram	ID ee ə GRAM
ideograph	ID ee ə GRAF
ideologue	Ī dee ə LOG
ideology	Ī dee OL ə jee
ides	īdz
id est	id est
idiocy	ID ee ə see
idiom	ID ee əm
idiomatic	ID ee ə MAT ik
idiosyncrasy	ID ee ə SING krə see
idiosyncratic	ID ee oh sin KRAT ik
idiot	ID ee ət
idiot savant	EE DYOH sa VAHN (VAHN French final n)
Ido	EE doh
idolater	ī DOL ə tər
idolum	ī DOH ləm
Idomeneo	EE doh mə NAY oh
Idomeneus	ī DOM ə NOOS
Idris Senussi	i DREES se NOO see
idyll	Ī dəl
idyllic	ī DIL ik
Idzumbuir, Theodore	id zuum BWEER, tay oh DAWR
Ifni	IF nee

---

o on, oh oat, oi boy, oo soon, oor poor, or for, ow cow, sh shush,
th thin, *th* this, u up, ur spur, uu book, zh pleasure

Igdrasil	**IG** drə sil
igitur	**IG** ə **TUUR**
Ignacio-Pinto, Louis	ig **NAH** see oh **PEEN** toh, **LWEES**
Ignatia	ig **NAY** shə
Ignatius	ig **NAY** shəs
igneous	**IG** nee əs
ignis fatuus	**IG** nəs **FACH** oo əs
ignition	ig **NISH** ən
ignoble	ig **NOH** bəl
ignominious	**IG** nə **MIN** ee əs
ignominy	**IG** nə **MIN** ee
ignoramus	**IG** nə **RAY** məs
Igorot	**IG** ə **ROHT**
Igraine	i **GRAYN**
iguana	i **GWAH** nə
Iguassú	**EE** gwah **SOO**
ihram	ee **RAHM**
Ijssel	**Ī** səl
Ijsselmeer	**Ī** səl **MAIR**
ikebana	**EE** ke **BAH** nah
Ikeda	ee ke dah
Ileana	eel **YAH** nə
île de France	eel də **FRAHNS**
ileitis	**IL** ee **Ī** təs
Ileo	i **LAY** oh
ileum	**IL** ee əm
ilex	**Ī** leks
Iliad	**IL** ee əd
Iliescu, Ion	il ee **ES** koo, **YAHN**
Ilium, i-	**IL** ee əm
Illampu	ee **YAHM** poo
illative	**IL** ə tiv
illegible	i **LEJ** ə bəl
illegitimate	**IL** ə **JIT** ə mit
illicit	i **LIS** ət
Illimani	**EE** yee **MAH** nee
Illinois	**IL** ə **NOI**
illiterate	i **LIT** ə rət
Illueca, Jorge	eel **WEK** ah, **HOR** hay
illuminate	i **LOO** mə **NAYT**
illumination	i **LOO** mə **NAY** shən
illusion	i **LOO** *zh*ən
illusive	i **LOO** siv

ə ago, a at, ah calm, ahr dark, air care, aw saw, ay say, ch church
e bet, ee me, eer beer, hw what, i is, ī my, *n* French final n vin,

illusory	i **LOO** sə ree
illustrate	**IL** ə **STRAYT**
illustrative	i **LUS** tro tiv
illustrator	**IL** ə **STRAY** tər
illustrious	i **LUS** tree əs
Illyria	i **LEER** ee ə
Iloniemi, Jaakko	**EE** loh **NEE** mee, **YAH** koh
image	**IM** ij
imagery	**IM** ij ree
imago	i **MAY** goh
imam	i **MAHM**
imamate	i **MAH** mayt
imbecile	**IM** bə səl
imbecility	**IM** bə **SIL** ə tee
imbroglio	im **BROHL** yoh
imbue	im **BYOO**
immaculate	i **MAK** yə lət
immanent	**IM** ə nənt
Immanuel	i **MAN** yoo əl
immature	**IM** ə **CHUUR**
immeasurable	i **MEZ***H* ə rə bəl
immerse	i **MURS**
immersion	i **MUR** *zh*ən
immigrant	**IM** ə grənt
immigrate	**IM** ə **GRAYT**
imminent	**IM** ə nənt
immiscible	i **MIS** ə bəl
immobile	i **MOH** bəl
immolate	**IM** ə **LAYT**
immoral	i **MOR** əl
immortality	**IM** or **TAL** ə tee
immune	i **MYOON**
immunization	**IM** yə nə **ZAY** shən
immunize	**IM** yə **NĪZ**
immunology	**IM** yə **NOL** ə jee
immure	i **MYUUR**
immutable	i **MYOO** tə bəl
Imogen	**IM** ə **JEN**
Imogene	**IM** ə **JEEN**
impala	im **PAL** ə
impartial	im **PAHR** shəl
impartiality	im **PAHR** shee **AL** ə tee
impasse	**IM** pas

o on, oh oat, oi boy, oo soon, oor poor, or for, ow cow, sh shush,
th thin, *th* this, u up, ur spur, uu book, *zh* pleasure

impasto	im PAS toh
impatience	im PAY shəns
impatiens	im PAY shənz
impeccable	im PEK ə bəl
impecunious	IM pə KYOO nee əs
impedance	im PEE dəns
impediment	im PED ə mənt
impedimenta	im PED ə MEN tə
impenetrable	im PEN ə trə bəl
impenitent	im PEN ə tənt
imperial	im PIR ee əl
imperialism	im PIR ee ə LIZ əm
imperialistic	im PIR ee ə LIS tik
impertinent	im PUR tə nənt
imperturbable	IM pər TUR bə bəl
impervious	im PUR vee əs
impetigo	IM pə TĪ goh
impetuosity	im PECH oo OS ə tee
impetuous	im PECH oo əs
impetus	IM pə təs
Imphal	IMP həl
impiety	im PĪ ə tee
impious	IM pee əs
impiousness	IM pee əs nəs
implacable	im PLAK ə bəl
implement (n)	IM plə mənt
implement (v)	IM plə MENT
implicate	IM plə KAYT
implicit	im PLIS ət
import (n)	IM port
import (v)	im PORT
important	im POR tənt
importunate	im POR chə nət
importune	IM pər TOON
impostor	im POS tər
impotence	IM pə təns
impotency	IM pə tən see
impotent	IM pə tənt
imprecatory	IM prə kə TOR ee
impregnate	im PREG nayt
impresario	IM prə SAHR ee OH
impress (n)	IM pres
impress (v)	im PRES

ə ago, a at, ah calm, ahr dark, air care, aw saw, ay say, ch church
e bet, ee me, eer beer, hw what, i is, ī my, *n* French final n vin,

imprimatur	IM prə MAH tuur
impromptu	im PROMP too
improvisation	im PROV ə ZAY shən
improvvisatore	EEM prawv VEE zah TAW re
imprudent	im PROO dənt
impudence	IM pyə dəns
impudent	IM pyə dənt
impugn	im PYOON
impuissance	im PYOO ə səns
impunity	im PYOO nə tee
impute	im PYOOT
in absentia	IN ab SEN shə
inadvertent	IN əd VUR tənt
inalienable	in AYL yə nə bəl
inane	i NAYN
inanition	IN ə NISH ən
inanity	i NAN ə tee
Inanna	ee NAH nah
inapplicable	in AP li kə bəl
inarticulate	IN ahr TIK yə lət
inaugural	in AW gyə rəl
inaugurate	in AW gyə RAYT
inauspicious	IN aw SPISH əs
Inca	ING kə
incandescence	IN kən DES əns
incandescent	IN kən DES ənt
incarnate (a)	in KAHR nət
incarnate (v)	in KAHR nayt
incendiary	in SEN dee ER ee
incense (n)	IN sens
incense (anger)	in SENS
incestuous	in SES choo əs
inchoate	in KOH ət
incinerate	in SIN ə RAYT
incipient	in SIP ee ənt
incision	in SIZH ən
incisive	in SĪ siv
incisor	in SĪ zər
inclement	in KLEM ənt
incline (n)	IN klīn
incline (v)	in KLĪN
inclusion	in KLOO zhən
inclusive	in KLOO siv

o on, oh oat, oi boy, oo soon, oor poor, or for, ow cow, sh shush,
th thin, *th* this, u up, ur spur, uu book, *zh* pleasure

incognito	IN KOG NEE toh
incoherent	IN koh HIR ənt
incommensurate	IN kə MEN shər ət
incommodious	IN kə MOH dee əs
incommunicado	IN kə MYOO nə KAH doh
incomparable	in KOM pə rə bəl
incompatibility	IN kəm PAT ə BIL ə tee
incompatible	IN kəm PAT ə bəl
incompetence	in KOM pə təns
incompetent	in KOM pə tənt
incongruity	IN kong GROO ə tee
incongruous	in KONG groo əs
inconsequential	in KON sə KWEN shəl
inconsolable	IN kən SOH lə bəl
incontinent	in KON tə nənt
incontrovertible	in KON trə VUR tə bəl
incorporate (a)	in KOR pə rət
incorporate (v)	in KOR pə RAYT
incorporeal	IN kor POR ee əl
incorrigible	in KOR ə jə bəl
increase (n)	IN krees
increase (v)	in KREES
incredible	in KRED ə bəl
incredulity	IN krə DOO lə tee
incredulous	in KREJ ə ləs
increment	IN krə mənt
incremental	IN krə MENT əl
incubate	IN kyə BAYT
incubator	IN kyə BAY tər
incubus	IN kyə bəs
inculcate	in KUL kayt
inculpable	in KUL pə bəl
inculpate	in KUL payt
incumbent	in KUM bənt
incunabula	IN kyə NAB yə lə
incursion	in KUR zhən
incus	ING kəs
indecorous	in DEK ə rəs
indefatigable	IN di FAT ə gə bəl
indelible	in DEL ə bəl
indenture	in DEN chər
independence	IN də PEN dəns
indescribable	IN di SKRĪ bə bəl

ə ago, a at, ah calm, ahr dark, air care, aw saw, ay say, ch church
e bet, ee me, eer beer, hw what, i is, ī my, *n* French final n vin,

India	IN dee ə
Indian	IN dee ən
Indiana	IN dee AN ə
Indianapolis	IN dee ə NAP ə ləs
Indic	IN dik
indicative	in DIK ə tiv
indices	IN də SEEZ
indicia	in DISH ee ə
indict	in DĪT
indictable	in DĪ tə bəl
indictment	in DĪT mənt
indigenous	in DIJ ə nəs
indigent	IN di jənt
indignant	in DIG nənt
indigo	IN də GOH
indiscreet	IN di SKREET
indiscrete	IN di SKREET
indiscretion	IN di SKRESH ən
indiscriminate	IN di SKRIM ə nət
indisputable	IN di SPYOO tə bəl
indissoluble	IN di SOL yə bəl
indite	in DĪT
indium	IN dee əm
indivisible	IN də VIZ ə bəl
Indo-	IN doh
Indochina	IN doh CHĪ nə
indolence	IN də ləns
indomitable	in DOM ə tə bəl
Indonesia	IN də NEE zhə
Indore	in DOR
Indra	IN drə
indubitable	in DOO bə tə bəl
induce	in DOOS
Indus	IN dəs
Indy, d'	dan DEE (dan French final n)
inebriate (a, n)	in EE bree ət
inebriate (v)	in EE bree AYT
inebriation	in EE bree AY shən
inedible	in ED ə bəl
ineffable	in EF ə bəl
ineffectual	IN ə FEK choo əl
inefficacy	in EF i kə see
inefficient	IN ə FISH ənt

o on, oh oat, oi boy, oo soon, oor poor, or for, ow cow, sh shush,
th thin, *th* this, u up, ur spur, uu book, *zh* pleasure

ineluctable	IN ə LUK tə bəl
inequity	in EK wə tee
ineradicable	IN ə RAD i kə bəl
inert	i NURT
inertia	i NUR shə
inestimable	in ES tə mə bəl
inevitable	in EV ə tə bəl
inexorable	in EK sə rə bəl
inexplicable	in EK splik ə bəl
in extremis	IN ik STREE məs
inextricable	in EK strik ə bəl
Inez	Ī nez
infallible	in FAL ə bəl
infamous	IN fə məs
infamy	IN fə mee
infancy	IN fən see
infanta	in FANT ə
infante	in FANT ee
infanticide	in FAN tə SĪD
infantile	IN fən TĪL
infarction	in FAHRK shən
inference	IN fə rəns
inferiority	in FIR ee OR ə tee
infernal	in FUR nəl
inferno	in FUR noh
infest	in FEST
infidel	IN fə dəl
infiltrate	in FIL trayt
infiltration	IN fil TRAY shən
infinite	IN fə nət
infinitesimal	IN fin ə TES ə məl
infinity	in FIN ə tee
in flagrante delicto	in flah GRAHN te di LIK toh
inflammable	in FLAM ə bəl
inflammation	IN flə MAY shən
inflexible	in FLEK sə bəl
inflorescence	IN flə RES əns
influential	IN floo EN shəl
influenza	IN floo EN zə
informative	in FOR mə tiv
infra dignitatem	IN frah DIG ni TAH tem
infrangible	in FRAN jə bəl
infrared	IN frə RED

ə ago, a at, ah calm, ahr dark, air care, aw saw, ay say, ch church
e bet, ee me, eer beer, hw what, i is, ī my, *n* French final n vin,

Infusoria	IN fyuu SOR ee ə
Inge	inj
Ingelow	IN jə LOH
Ingeman, -n	ING gə mən
Ingemar	ING gə MAHR
ingenious	in JEEN yəs
ingenue	AN jə NOO
ingenuity	IN jə NOO ə tee
ingenuous	in JEN yoo əs
inglenook	ING gəl NUUK
Ingold	IN gohld
Ingoldsby	ING gəlz bee
ingot	ING gət
Ingram	ING grəm
ingrate	IN grayt
ingratiate	in GRAY shee AYT
ingredient	in GREE dee ənt
Ingres	AN grə (AN French final *n*)
ingress	IN gres
inguinal	ING gwə nəl
inhere	in HIR
inherent	in HIR ənt
inheritance	in HE rə təns
inhibition	IN ə BISH ən
inhospitable	in HOS pi tə bəl
inimical	i NIM i kəl
inimitable	i NIM ə tə bəl
iniquitous	i NIK wə təs
iniquity	i NIK wə tee
initiate (a, n)	i NISH ee ət
initiate (v)	i NISH ee AYT
initiation	i NISH ee AY shən
initiative	i NISH ə tiv
injudicious	IN juu DISH əs
injunction	in JUNGK shən
inlay	IN lay
in loco parentis	in LOH koh pə REN təs
in medias res	in MAY dee AHS RAYS
in memoriam	IN mə MOR ee əm
Inness	IN əs
innocent, I-	IN ə sənt
innocuous	i NOK yoo əs
innovate	IN ə VAYT

o on, oh oat, oi boy, oo soon, oor poor, or for, ow cow, sh shush,
th thin, *th* this, u up, ur spur, uu book, *zh* pleasure

Innsbruck	**INZ** bruuk
innuendo	**IN** yoo **EN** doh
Innuit	**IN** yoo ət
innumerable	i **NOO** mə rə bəl
Inönü	**EE** noh noo
inordinate	in **OR** də nət
Inouye	i **NOO** ay
in perpetuum	**IN** pər **PET** yoo əm
inquest	**IN** kwest
inquire	in **KWĪR**
inquiry	in **KWĪR** ee
inquisition, I-	**IN** kwə **ZISH** ən
inquisitive	in **KWIZ** ə tiv
inquisitor	in **KWIZ** ə tər
in re	in **RAY**
insalubrious	**IN** sə **LOO** bree əs
insatiable	in **SAY** shə bəl
insatiate	in **SAY** shee ət
inscrutable	in **SKROO** tə bəl
insecticide	in **SEK** tə **SĪD**
Insectivora	**IN** sek **TIV** ər ə
insectivore	in **SEK** tə **VOR**
insentient	in **SEN** shənt
insert (n)	**IN** surt
insert (v)	in **SURT**
insidious	in **SID** ee əs
insigne	in **SIG** nee
insignia	in **SIG** nee ə
insinuation	in **SIN** yoo **AY** shən
insipid	in **SIP** əd
in situ	in **SĪ** too
insolent	**IN** sə lənt
insomnia	in **SOM** nee ə
insomniac	in **SOM** nee **AK**
insouciance	in **SOO** see əns
insouciant	in **SOO** see ənt
in statu quo	in **STAH** too **KWOH**
instinct (a)	in **STINGKT**
instinct (n)	**IN** stingkt
institut	an stee **TOO** (an French final *n*)
institute	**IN** stə **TOOT**
insubordinate	**IN** sə **BOR** də nət
insufferable	in **SUF** ə rə bəl

ə ago, a at, ah calm, ahr dark, air care, aw saw, ay say, ch church
e bet, ee me, eer beer, hw what, i is, ī my, *n* French final n vin,

insular	**IN** sə lər
insularity	**IN** sə **LAR** ə tee
insulate	**IN** sə **LAYT**
insulation	**IN** sə **LAY** shən
insulator	**IN** sə **LAY** tər
insulin	**IN** sə lən
insult (n)	**IN** sult
insult (v)	in **SULT**
insuperable	in **SOO** pə rə bəl
insurable	in **SHUUR** ə bəl
insurgent	in **SUR** jənt
insurrectionary	**IN** sə **REK** shə **NER** ee
intact	in **TAKT**
intaglio	in **TAL** yoh
integer	**IN** tə jər
integral	**IN** tə grəl
integrate	**IN** tə **GRAYT**
integration	**IN** tə **GRAY** shən
integrity	in **TEG** rə tee
integument	in **TEG** yə mənt
intellectual	**IN** tə **LEK** choo əl
intelligentsia	in **TEL** ə **JENT** see ə
intelligible	in **TEL** ə jə bəl
intemperate	in **TEM** pə rət
inter	in **TUR**
inter alia	**IN** tər **AH** lee ə
inter alios	**IN** tər **AH** lee **OHS**
intercede	**IN** tər **SEED**
intercept (n)	**IN** tər **SEPT**
intercept (v)	**IN** tər **SEPT**
interdict (n)	**IN** tər **DIKT**
interdict (v)	**IN** tər **DIKT**
interest	**IN** trəst
interested	**IN** tə ri stid
interesting	**IN** tə ri sting
interface	**IN** tər **FAYS**
interfere	**IN** tər **FIR**
interference	**IN** tər **FIR** əns
interferon	**IN** tər **FIR** **ON**
interim	**IN** tə rəm
Interlaken	**IN** tər **LAH** kən
interlocutor	**IN** tər **LOK** yə tər
interlocutory	**IN** tər **LOK** yə **TOR** ee

o on, oh oat, oi boy, oo soon, oor poor, or for, ow cow, sh shush,
th thin, *th* this, u up, ur spur, uu book, *zh* pleasure

interloper	IN tər LOH pər
interlude	IN tər LOOD
intermediary	IN tər MEE dee ER ee
intermediate	IN tər MEE dee ət
interment	in TUR mənt
intermezzo	IN tər MET soh
interminable	in TUR mə nə bəl
intern (medical n, v)	IN turn
intern (confine, v)	in TURN
internecine	IN tər NEE sən
internist	in TUR nəst
internment	in TURN mənt
inter nos	IN tər NOHS
internship	in TURN SHIP
interpolate	in TUR pə LAYT
interpolation	in TUR pə LAY shən
interpretative	in TUR prə TAY tiv
interregnum	IN tər REG nəm
interrogatory	IN tə ROG ə TOR ee
inter se	IN tər SAY
interstice	in TUR stəs
interstices	in TUR stə SEEZ
interstitial	IN tər STISH əl
intestate	in TES TAYT
intifada	in tə FAH də
intimacy	IN tə mə see
intimate (a)	IN tə mət
intimate (v)	IN tə MAYT
intimation	IN tə MAY shən
intimidate	in TIM ə DAYT
intolerable	in TOL ə rə bəl
intonation	IN tə NAY shən
in toto	in TOH toh
intoxicant	in TOK si kənt
intrados	IN trə DOS
intransigence	in TRAN sə jəns
intrauterine	IN trə YOO tə rən
intravenous	IN trə VEE nəs
intrepid	in TREP əd
intrepidity	IN tre PID ə tee
intricacy	IN tri kə see
intricate	IN tri kət
intrigue	in TREEG

ə ago, a at, ah calm, ahr dark, air care, aw saw, ay say, ch church
e bet, ee me, eer beer, hw what, i is, ī my, n French final n vin,

intrinsic	in **TRIN** zik
introit	in **TROH** ət
introversion	IN trə **VUR** *zh*ən
introvert	IN trə **VURT**
intuition	IN too **ISH** ən
intuitive	in **TOO** ə tiv
intumescence	IN tuu **MES** əns
Inuit	IN yoo ət
inundate	IN ən **DAYT**
inure	in **YUUR**
in utero	in **YOO** tər OH
in vacuo	in **VAK** yoo OH
invalid (ill; a, n, v)	IN və ləd
invalid (void)	in **VAL** əd
Invalides	an vah **LEED** (an French final *n*)
inveigh	in **VAY**
inveigle	in **VAY** gəl
inventory	IN vən **TOR** ee
Inverness, i-	IN vər **NES**
inversion	in **VUR** *zh*ən
invert (a, n)	IN vurt
invert (v)	in **VURT**
invertebrate	in **VUR** tə brət
investiture	in **VES** tə chər
inveterate	in **VET** ə rət
invidious	in **VID** ee əs
invigorate	in **VIG** ə **RAYT**
inviolable	in **VĪ** ə lə bəl
inviolate	in **VĪ** ə lət
in vitro	in **VEE** troh
in vivo	in **VEE** voh
invoice	IN vois
involute	IN və **LOOT**
Io	**Ī** oh
iodine	**Ī** ə **DĪN**
Iola	ī **OH** lə
Iolanthe	ī ə **LAN** thee
ion	**Ī** ən
Ionesco	ee ə **NES** koh
Ionia	ī **OH** nee ə
Ionic, i-	ī **ON** ik
ionium	ī **OH** nee əm
ionize	**Ī** ə **NĪZ**

o on, oh oat, oi boy, oo soon, oor poor, or for, ow cow, sh shush,
th thin, *th* this, u up, ur spur, uu book, *zh* pleasure

ionosphere	ī ON ə SFEER
iota	ī OH tə
Iowa	Ī ə wə
Iowan	Ī ə wən
ipecac	IP i KAK
Iphigenia	IF ə jə NĪ ə
Ippolitov-Ivanov	i paw LEE tawf i VAH nawf
ipse dixit	IP see DIK sət
ipso facto	IP soh FAK toh
Ipswich	IP swich
Iran	i RAHN
Irani	i RAHN ee
Iranian	i RAY nee ən
Iraq	i RAHK
Iraqi	i RAHK ee
irascible	i RAS ə bəl
irate	ī RAYT
Irazú	EE rah ZOO
ire	īr
Ireland	ĪR lənd
Irene (not myth)	ī REEN
Irene (myth)	ī REE nee
Irgun	ir GUUN
iridescence	IR ə DES əns
iridium	ir ID ee əm
iris, I-	Ī rəs
Irish	Ī rish
iritis	ī RĪ təs
Irkutsk	ir KUUTSK
Irminger	UR ming gər
iron	Ī ərn
ironic	ī RON ik
irony	Ī rə nee
Iroquois	IR ə KWOI
irradiate	i RAY dee AYT
Irrawaddi	IR ə WOD ee
irreconcilable	i REK ən sī lə bəl
Irredentist	IR i DEN təst
irrefragable	i REF rə gə bəl
irrefutable	i REF yə tə bəl
irrelevant	i REL ə vənt
irremediable	IR i MEE dee ə bəl
irreparable	i REP ə rə bəl

ə ago, a at, ah calm, ahr dark, air care, aw saw, ay say, ch church
e bet, ee me, eer beer, hw what, i is, ī my, *n* French final n vin,

irresolute	i **REZ** ə **LOOT**
irreverent	i **REV** ə rənt
irrevocable	i **REV** ə kə bəl
irritant	**IR** ə tənt
irruption	ir **RUP** shən
Irtish	ir **TISH**
Irvine	**UR** vin
Irving	**UR** ving
Iryani, Abdel Karim	**EER** ee ah **NEE**, **AHB** del kah **REEM**
Isador, -e	**IZ** ə **DOR**
Isaiah	ī **ZAY** ə
Isaias	ī **ZAY** əs
Isar	**EE** zahr
Iscariot	i **SKAR** ee ət
ischemia	is **KEE** mee ə
Isère	ee **ZAIR**
Iseult	i **SOOLT**
Isfahan	**IS** fə **HAHN**
Ishbosheth	ish **BOH** shith
Isherwood	**ISH** ər **WUUD**
Ishihara	**ISH** ee **HAHR** ə
Ishikawa	**EE** shee **KAH** wah
Ishmael	**ISH** mee əl
Ishtar	**ISH** tahr
Isidor, -e	**IZ** ə **DOR**
isinglass	**Ī** zən **GLAS**
Isis	**Ī** səs
Islam	is **LAHM**
Islamabad	is **LAHM** ə **BAHD**
Islamic	is **LAH** mik
isle	īl
islet	**Ī** lət
Islington	**IZ** ling tən
Islip	**Ī** slip
Ismaili	**IZ** may **IL** ee
isobar	**Ī** sə **BAHR**
Isocrates	ī **SOK** rə **TEEZ**
isolate (v)	**Ī** sə **LAYT**
isolate (n)	**Ī** sə lət
isolation	**Ī** sə **LAY** shən
Isolde	i **SOHLD**
isomer	**Ī** sə mər
isometric	**Ī** sə **MET** rik

---

o on, oh oat, oi boy, oo soon, oor poor, or for, ow cow, sh shush,
th thin, *th* this, u up, ur spur, uu book, *zh* pleasure

isosceles	ī SOS ə LEEZ
isotherm	Ī sə THURM
isotonic	ī sə TON ik
isotope	Ī sə TOHP
Israel	IZ ree əl
Israeli	iz RAY lee
Israelite	IZ ree ə LĪT
issei	ees say
Issembe, Aristide	EE sem bay, A ris teed
issue	ISH oo
Istanbul	IS tan BOOL
isthmus	IS məs
Istria	IS tree ə
Italian	i TAL yən
italic, I-	ə TAL ik
italicize	ə TAL ə sīz
Italy	IT ə lee
Itasca	ī TAS kə
item	Ī təm
iterate	IT ə RAYT
iteration	IT ə RAY shən
iterative	IT ə rə tiv
Ithaca	ITH ə kə
Ithome	i THOH mee
Ithuriel	i THYUU ree əl
itinerant	ī TIN ə rənt
itinerary	ī TIN ə RER ee
Ivan	Ī vən
Ivan (Russian)	i VAHN
Ivanhoe	Ī vən HOH
Ivanovo	i VAH naw vaw
Ives	īvz
Iwo Jima	EE woh JEE mə
ixia, I-	IK see ə
Ixion	ik SĪ ən
Izmir	iz MIR
Izvestia	iz VES tee ah

ə ago, a at, ah calm, ahr dark, air care, aw saw, ay say, ch church
e bet, ee me, eer beer, hw what, i is, ī my, *n* French final n vin,

J

Jabesh	**JAY** besh
jabot	*zh*a **BOH**
jacaranda	**JAK** ə **RAN** də
jacinth	**JAY** sənth
jackal	**JAK** əl
jackanapes	**JAK** ə **NAYPS**
Jacobean	**JAK** ə **BEE** ən
Jacobin	**JAK** ə bən
Jacoby (British)	**JAK** ə bee
Jacoby (US)	jə **KOH** bee
Jacovides, Andrea	**JA** koh **VEE** deez, an **DRAY** ə
Jacquard	**JAK** ahrd
Jacqueline (French)	*zh*ahk **LEEN**
Jacqueline (US)	**JAK** ə lin
Jacqueminot	**JAK** mi noh
Jacquerie, j-	*zh*ah **KREE**
Jacques	*zh*ahk
Jacquinot	*zh*ah kee **NOH**
Jacuzzi	jə **KOO** zee
jaeger	**YAY** gər
Jael	**JAY** əl
Jaffa	**JAF** ə
Jagan, Cheddi	**HAH** gahn, **CHE** dee
jagged	**JAG** əd
jaguar	**JAG** wahr
Jahve	**YAH** ve
jai alai	**HĪ** lī
Jain	jīn
Jainism	**JĪ** niz əm
Jaipur	**JĪ** puur
Jakarta	jə **KAHR** tə
Jalapa	hah **LAH** pah
Jalisco	hah **LEES** koh
jalopy	jə **LOP** ee
jalousie	**JAL** ə **SEE**
Jamaica	jə **MAY** kə
Jamal, Jasim Yousif	jah **MAHL**, **JAH** seem **YOO** sef
Jamali	jah **MAH** lee

---

o on, oh oat, oi boy, oo soon, oor poor, or for, ow cow, sh shush,
th thin, *th* this, u up, ur spur, uu book, *zh* pleasure

jamb	jam
jambalaya	JAM bə LĪ ə
jamboree	JAM bə REE
Jamesian	JAYM zee ən
Jamestown	JAYMZ town
Jamie	JAY mee
Jammu	JUM oo
Jan (European)	yahn
Jan (US)	jan
Janáček	YA nah CHEK
jangle	JANG gəl
Janis	JA nis
janissary, J-	JAN ə SER ee
janitor	JAN ə tər
janizary, J-	JAN ə ZER ee
Jansen	JAN sən
January	JA nyoo ER ee
Janus	JAY nəs
Japan	jə PAN
Japanese	JAP ə NEEZ
jape	jayp
Japheth	JAY fəth
japonica	jə PON i kə
Japurá	ZHAHP ə RAH
Jaques (Shakespeare)	JAY kweez
jardiniere	JAHR də NEER
Jared	JA rəd
Jargalsaikhan, Bayaryn	jahr GAHL sī hahn, BĪ ah rin
jargon	JAHR gən
Jaroslav	YAH rə SLAHF
Jaroslaw	YAH rə SLAHF
Jarrell, Randall	jə REL, RAN dəl
Jarrow	JA roh
Jaruzelski, Wojciech	YAHR oo ZEL skee, VOI chek
jasmine	JAZ mən
Jason	JAY sən
jasper, J-	JAS pər
Jataka	JAH tə kə
jato	JAY toh
jaundice	JAWN dəs
jaunt	jawnt
Java	JAH və
Javanese	JAV ə NEEZ

ə ago, a at, ah calm, ahr dark, air care, aw saw, ay say, ch church
e bet, ee me, eer beer, hw what, i is, ī my, *n* French final n vin,

Javel, -le	*zh*ə VEL
javelin	JAV ə lən
Javier	hah VYER
Javits	JA vəts
Jawara, Alhaji Sir Dawda Kairaba	jah WAHR ə, ahl HAH jee shahr dah OO dah kī EER ah bah
ja wohl	yah VOHL
Jayewardene	jī yə wor di nə
Jean (French)	*zh*ahn (*zh*ahn French final *n*)
Jeanmaire	*zh*ahn MAIR (*zh*ahn French final *n*)
Jeanne (French)	*zh*ahn
jehad	ji HAHD
Jehoiakim	ji HOI ə kim
Jehol	jə HOHL
Jehoram	ji HOH rəm
Jehoshaphat	ji HOSH ə FAT
Jehovah	ji HOH və
Jehu	JEE hyoo
jejune	ji JOON
jejunum	ji JOON əm
Jekyll	JEE kəl
Jellicoe	JEL i KOH
Jemima	jə MĪ mə
Jena	YAY nah
Jenner	JEN ər
jennet	JEN ət
Jennifer	JEN ə fər
jenny, J-	JEN ee
Jensen (Danish)	YEN sən
Jensen (German)	YEN zən
Jensen (US)	JEN sən
Jens, Salome	JENZ, SAL oh may
jeopardize	JEP ər DĪZ
jeopardy	JEP ər dee
Jephthah	JEF thə
jerboa	jər BOH ə
jeremiad	JER ə MĪ əd
Jeremiah	JER ə MĪ ə
Jerez	he RETH
Jericho	JER ə KOH
Jericó (Colombia)	he ri KOH
jerkin	JUR kin
Jeroboam, j-	JER ə BOH əm

o on, oh oat, oi boy, oo soon, oor poor, or for, ow cow, sh shush,
th thin, *th* this, u up, ur spur, uu book, *zh* pleasure

Jerome	jə **ROHM**
Jersey, j-	**JUR** zee
Jerusalem	jə **ROO** sə ləm
Jervis (British)	**JAHR** vəs
Jervis (US)	**JUR** vəs
jessamine, J-	**JES** ə mən
Jesse, Jessie	**JES** ee
Jessica	**JES** i kə
Jesu	**JEE** zoo
Jesuit	**JEZ***H* oo it
jeté	*zh*ə **TAY**
Jethro	**JETH** roh
jetsam	**JET** səm
jettison	**JET** ə sən
jeu de mots	*zh*uu də **MOH**
jeu d'esprit	*zh*uu des **PREE**
jewel	**JOO** əl
jewelry	**JOO** əl ree
Jewett	**JOO** ət
Jewry	**JOO** ree
Jezebel	**JEZ** ə **BEL**
Jezreel	**JEZ** ree əl
Jhelum	**JAY** ləm
Jiangsu	jee ahng soo
Jiangxi	jee ahng shee
jibe	jīb
Jibuti	ji **BOO** tee
Jicamarca	hee kah **MAHR** kə
Jidda	**JID** ə
Jigme Dorji Wanchuk	**DYIG** me **DOR** jee **VANG** chook
jihad	ji **HAHD**
Jilin	jee leen
Jiménez	hee **MAY** nəs
jimson, J-	**JIM** sən
jingle	**JING** gəl
jingly	**JING** glee
jingo	**JING** goh
jingoism	**JING** goh **IZ** əm
jinn	jin
Jinnah	**JIN** ə
jinni	**JEE** nee
jinrikisha	jin **RIK** shaw
jipijapa	**HEE** pee **HOP** ə

ə ago, a at, ah calm, ahr dark, air care, aw saw, ay say, ch church
e bet, ee me, eer beer, hw what, i is, ī my, *n* French final n vin,

jitney	**JIT** nee
Joab	**JOH** ab
Joachim (Bible)	**JOH** ə kim
Joachim	**YOH** ə kim
Joanna	joh **AN** ə
Joanne	joh **AN**
Joaquin	wah **KEEN**
job	job
Job	johb
Jocasta	joh **KAS** tə
jocose	joh **KOHS**
jocosity	joh **KOS** ə tee
jocular	**JOK** yə lər
jocund	**JOK** ənd
Jodhpur, j-	**JOD** pər
jodhpurs	**JOD** pərz
Joel	**JOH** əl
Joffre	**ZH**AW frə
Joffrey	**JOF** ree
Jogjakarta	**JOHG** jə **KAHRT** ə
Johann (German)	**YOH** hahn
Johannes (German)	yoh **HAH** nes
Johannesburg	joh **HAN** əs **BURG**
Johore	jə **HOR**
joie de vivre	*zh*wah də **VEE** vrə
joinder	**JOIN** dər
Joinvile (Brazil)	*zh*oin **VEE** lee
Joinville (France)	*zh*wan **VEEL** (*zh*wan French final *n*)
Jókai	**YOH** koi
Joliet	**JOH** lee **ET**
Joliot-Curie	*zh*aw **LYOH** kuu **REE**
Jolo	haw law
Jonah	**JOH** nə
Jonathan	**JON** ə thən
Jones, Abeodu Bowen	**JOHNZ**, ah **BEE** doo **BOH** een
jongleur	**ZH**AWN glər
jonquil	**JONG** kwəl
Joplin	**JOP** lən
Jordaens	**YOR** dahns
Jordan	**JOR** dən
Jordanian	jor **DAY** nee ən
jorum	**JOR** əm
Josephus	joh **SEE** fəs

o on, oh oat, oi boy, oo soon, oor poor, or for, ow cow, sh shush,
th thin, *th* this, u up, ur spur, uu book, *zh* pleasure

Joshua	**JOSH** oo ə
Josiah	joh **SĪ** ə
joss	jos
jostle	**JOS** əl
Jouhaux, Léon	*zh*oo **OH**, lay **AWN** (AWN French final *n*)
Joule, j-	jool
Jourdain, Louis	*zh*uur **DAN**, loo **EE** (DAN French final *n*)
joust	just
Jove	johv
Jowett	**JOW** ət
Joyce	jois
Juan (French)	*zh*oo **AHN** (AHN French final *n*)
Juan (Spanish)	hwahn
Juanita	wah **NEE** tə
Juárez	**HWAH** res
Juba	**JOO** bah
Jubal	**JOO** bəl
Jubilate	**JOO** bə **LAY** tee
jubilate	**JOO** bə **LAYT**
jubilee	**JOO** bə **LEE**
Judaea	joo **DEE** ə
Judah	**JOO** də
Judaic	joo **DAY** ik
Judaica	joo **DAY** ə kə
Judaism	**JOO** dee **IZ** əm
Judas	**JOO** dəs
Judea	joo **DEE** ə
judgment	**JUJ** mənt
judicable	**JOO** di kə bəl
judicial	joo **DISH** əl
judiciary	joo **DISH** ee **ER** ee
judicious	joo **DISH** əs
judo	**JOO** doh
Juggernaut, j-	**JUG** ər **NAWT**
Jugnauth, Aneerood	joo **NOHT**, ah **NEE** rood
jugular	**JUG** yə lər
Juilliard	**JOO** lee ahrd
jujitsu	joo **JIT** soo
juju	**JOO** joo
jujube	**JOO** joob
jukebox	**JOOK** boks

ə ago, a at, ah calm, ahr dark, air care, aw saw, ay say, ch church
e bet, ee me, eer beer, hw what, i is, ī my, *n* French final n vin,

Jukes	jooks
julep	**JOO** ləp
julienne	**JOO** lee **EN**
junco	**JUNG** koh
juncture	**JUNGK** chər
Juneau	**JOO** noh
Jung	yuung
Jungfrau	**YUUNG** frow
Juniata	**JOO** nee **AT** ə
juniper	**JOO** nə pər
Junius	**JOON** yəs
Junker, j-	**YUUNG** kər
junket	**JUNG** kət
Juno	**JOO** noh
Junoesque	**JOO** noh **ESK**
junta	**HUUN** tə
junto	**JUN** toh
Jupiter	**JOO** pə tər
Jura	**JUUR** ə
Jurassic	juu **RAS** ik
jurat	**JUUR** at
Jurgens	**JUR** gənz
juridical	juu **RID** i kəl
jurisdiction	**JOOR** əs **DIK** shən
jurisprudence	**JOOR** əs **PROO** dəns
Juruá	*ZH*OO roo **AH**
Jusserand	*zh*oos **RAHN** (**RAHN** French final *n*)
jussive	**JUS** iv
justificatory	jə **STIF** ə kə **TOR** ee
Justin	**JUS** tin
Justinian	jə **STIN** ee ən
Jute, j-	joot
Jutish	**JOO** tish
Jutland	**JUT** lənd
Juvenal	**JOO** və nəl
juvenescence	**JOO** və **NES** əns
juvenile	**JOO** və nəl
juvenilia	**JOO** və **NIL** ee ə
juxtapose	**JUK** stə **POHZ**
juxtaposition	**JUK** stə pə **ZISH** ən

o on, oh oat, oi boy, oo soon, oor poor, or for, ow cow, sh shush,
th thin, *th* this, u up, ur spur, uu book, *zh* pleasure

K

Kaaba	**KAH** bə
Kabaiwanska	kah **BĪ** ee **VAHN** skə
Kabalevsky	**KAH** bah **LYEF** skee
kabob	kə **BOB**
Kabore, John Boureima	kah bə **REE**, **JON** boo **RAY** mə
kabuki	kə **BOO** kee
Kabul	**KAH** buul
Kabyle	kə **BĪL**
kachina	kə **CHEE** nə
Kádár, Janos	**KAH** dahr, **YAH** nohsh
Kaddish	**KOD** ish
Kadesh	**KAY** desh
Kaduna	kə **DOO** nə
Kaesong	**KAY** sawng
Kaffir, k-	**KAF** ər
Kaffraria	kə **FRAIR** ee ə
Kafir, k-	**KAF** ər
Kafka	**KAHF** kah
kaftan	**KAF** tən
Kagawa	kah gah wah
Kagoshima	kah goh shee mah
Kaifeng	kī fung
kaiser, K-	**KĪ** zər
Kakatiya	kah **KAH** tee yah
Kalahari	**KAH** lah **HAH** ree
Kalamazoo	**KAL** ə mə **ZOO**
kalanchoe	kə **LANG** koo ee
Kalat	kə **LAHT**
kaleidoscope	kə **LĪ** də **SKOHP**
kaleidoscopic	kə **LĪ** də **SKOP** ik
Kalevala	**KAH** li **VAH** lah
Kalgan	kahl gahn
Kalinin	kah **LEE** nin
Kalisz	**KAH** lish
Kalmuck	**KAL** muk
Kalonji	kah **LOHN** jee
Kamakura	kah mah koo rah

ə ago, a at, ah calm, ahr dark, air care, aw saw, ay say, ch church
e bet, ee me, eer beer, hw what, i is, ī my, n French final n vin,

Kamara, Dauda	kah MAHR ə, DOW də
Kamchatka	kam CHAT kə
Kamehameha	kə MAY ə MAY hah
Kamerad	KAH mə RAHT
kamikaze	KAH mi KAH zee
Kampala	KAHM PAHL ə
kampong	KAHM pawng
Kanaka	kə NAK ə
Kanara	kə NAHR ə
Kanarese	KAN ə REEZ
Kanazawa	kah nah zah wah
Kanchenjunga	KAHN chən JUUNG gə
Kandahar	KAN də HAHR
Kandinsky	kan DIN skee
kangaroo	KANG gə ROO
Kanin	KAY nin
Kansas	KAN zəs
Kansu	kahn soo
Kant	kahnt
Kantian	KAHN tee ən
Kantorovich, Leonid	KAHN tə RAWV ich, lye aw NYEET
kaolin	KAY ə lən
kaon	KAY on
Kapellmeister	kah PEL MĪ stər
Kapitonov, Ivan	kap ee TAWN awf, ee VAHN
Kapitsa, Pyotr	KOP yit sə, PYAW tər
Kaplan	KAP lən
kapok	KAY pok
kappa	KAP ə
kaput	kə PUUT
Kara	KAHR ə
Karachi	kə RAH chee
Karajan	KAH rah YAHN
Kara-Kalpak	kah RAH kahl PAHK
Karakoram	KAHR ə KOH rəm
karakul	KA rə kəl
Kara Kum	KA rə KUUM
Karamanlis, Constantin	KAH rə MAHN lees, KON stən teen
Karame, Rashid	KAH rə may, rah SHEED
Karandreas, Nicolas	KAHR ahn THRAY əs, nee KOH lah OHSH
karate	kə RAH tee

o on, oh oat, oi boy, oo soon, oor poor, or for, ow cow, sh shush,
th thin, *th* this, u up, ur spur, uu book, *zh* pleasure

Karelian	kə REE lee ən
Karenina, Anna	kah RE nyi nə, AH nah
Karjalainen, Ahti	KAHR yə LĪ nən, AH tee
Karlovac	KAHR lə VAHTS
Karlsbad	KAHRLZ bad
Karlsruhe	KAHRLZ ROO ə
karma	KAHR mə
Karmal, Babrak	KAHR mel, bah BRAHK
Karnak	KAHR nak
Károlyi	KAH roh lyi
Kartawidjaja, Djuanda	KAHR tah wee JĪ ə, JOO ahn də
Kasai	kə SĪ
Kasavubu	kah sah VOO boo
kasha	KAH shə
Kashmir	kash MIR
kashruth	KOSH ruut
Kassebaum, Nancy	KAS ə bowm
Kassem, Abdel-Raouf al-	KAH sim, AHB duul rah OOF el
Kassim	kah SEEM
Kastenmeier	KAH sten mī ər
Katahdin	kə TAH din
Katanga	kə TAHNG gə
Katangese	kə tahng GEEZ
Katmai	KAT mī
Katmandu	KAHT mahn DOO
Katowice	KAH toh VEET se
Katrine	KA trin
Kattegat	KAT ə GAT
katydid	KAY tee did
Kauai	KOW ī
Kauffmann	KOWF mahn
Kaufman, George S.	KAWF mən
Kaunas	KOW nahs
Kaunda, Kenneth	kah OON dah
Kavir	kə VEER
Kawabata, Yasunari	kah wah bah tah, yah soo nah ree
Kawasaki	KAH wah SAH kee
kayak	KĪ ak
Kaye	kay
Kaysone Phomvihane	kī ee SAWN puum vee HAHN
Kazak, Kazakh	kə ZAHK
Kazan	kə ZAN

ə ago, a at, ah calm, ahr dark, air care, aw saw, ay say, ch church
e bet, ee me, eer beer, hw what, i is, ī my, n French final n vin,

Kazan (USSR)	kə ZAHN
Kazbek	kaz BEK
Kazin	KAY zin
kazoo	kə ZOO
kea	KAY ə
Kean, Edmund	keen
Kean, Thomas	kayn
Kearny	KAHR nee
Keats	keets
kebab	kə BOB
kebob	kə BOB
Kedah	KAY dah
Kedar	KEE dər
kedge	kej
kedgeree	KEJ ə REE
Kedron	KEE drən
keeshond	KAYS hawnt
Keewatin	kee WAH tin
kefir	kə FIR
Keijo	kay joh
Keita, Modibo	KAY tah, maw DEE baw
Keith	keeth
Kekkonen, Urho	KEK oh NEN, OOR hoh
kelpie	KEL pee
Kelvin, k-	KEL vən
Kemal Ataturk	ke MAHL AH tah TURK
Kemi	KEM ee
Kenilworth	KEN əl WURTH
Kennebec	KEN ə BEK
Kennebunk	KEN ə BUNGK
Kennelly	KEN ə lee
kenning	KEN ing
keno	KEE noh
Kenosha	kə NOH shə
kenosis	ki NOH səs
Kensington	KEN zing tən
Kentucky	kən TUK ee
Kenya	KEN yə
Kenyatta, Jomo	ken YAH tə, JOH moh
Kenyon	KEN yən
Keokuk	KEE ə kək
Keos	KEE os
Keough	KEE oh

o on, oh oat, oi boy, oo soon, oor poor, or for, ow cow, sh shush,
th thin, *th* this, u up, ur spur, uu book, *zh* pleasure

kepi	**KAY** pee
Kepler	**KEP** lər
Kerch	kairch
kerchief	**KUR** chəf
Kérékou, Ahmed Mathieu	**KER** ə **KOO, AH** med mah tee **YOO**
Kerensky, Kerenski	kə **REN** skee
kerf	kurf
Kerguelen	**KUR** gə lən
Kermanshah	**KUR** mahn **SHAH**
kermis	**KUR** mis
Kermit	**KUR** mit
Kern	kurn
Kerouac	**KER** oo **AK**
Kerr (British)	kahr
Kerr (US)	kur
kestrel	**KES** trəl
Keszthely	**KEST** hay
ketchup	**KECH** əp
ketone	**KEE** tohn
ketosis	kee **TOH** səs
Keturah	kə **TUUR** ə
Keuka	**KYOO** kə
Kevin	**KEV** in
Kew	kyoo
kewpie, K-	**KYOO** pee
Keynes	kaynz
Keynesian	**KAYN** zee ən
Khabarovsk	kah **BAH** rofsk
Khachaturian	**KAH** chə **TUUR** ee ən
Khaibar	**KĪ** bər
khaki	**KAK** ee
Khalkha	**KAL** kə
Khamenei, Hojatolislam Ali	hah **MEE** nee, **HOH** jə **TOOL** is lam **AH** lee
khan, K-	kahn
Khanaqin	**KAN** ə kin
Kharg	karg
Kharkov	**KAHR** kawf
Khartoum, Khartum	kahr **TOOM**
Khayyám	kī **YAHM**
khedive	kə **DEEV**
Khmer	kə **MER**

ə ago, a at, ah calm, ahr dark, air care, aw saw, ay say, ch church
e bet, ee me, eer beer, hw what, i is, ī my, *n* French final n vin,

Khomeini, Ruhollah	hoh **MAY** nee, roo chol **LAH**
Khrushchev	kruush **CHAWF**
Khufu	**KOO** foo
Khurramshahr	**KOR** əm **SHAHR**
Khust	koost
Khuzistan	**KOO** zis **TAHN**
Khyber	**KĪ** bər
Kiangsi	jee ahng see
Kiangsu	jee ahng soo
Kibanda, Simon Pierre	kee **BAHN** də, see **MOHN** pyair
	(**MOHN** French final *n*)
kibbutz	ki **BUUTS**
kibei	kee bay
kibitz	**KIB** əts
kibitzer	**KIB** əts ər
kibosh	**KĪ** bosh
Kickapoo	**KIK** ə **POO**
kickshaw	**KIK** shaw
Kiddush	**KID** əsh
Kiel	keel
kielbasa	keel **BAH** sə
Kierkegaard	**KEER** kə **GAHRD**
Kiesinger, Kurt	**KEE** zing ər, **KUURT**
Kieta	kee **E** tah
Kiev	kee **EV**
Kigali	ki **GAHL** ee
Kigeri	kee **GAIR** ee
Kilauea	**KEE** low **AY** ə (low as in *cow*)
Kilimanjaro	**KIL** ə mən **JAHR** oh
Kilkenny	kil **KEN** ee
Killarney	ki **LAHR** nee
Killiecrankie	**KIL** ee **KRANG** kee
Kilmarnock	kil **MAHR** nək
kiln	kil
kilo	**KEE** loh
kilogram	**KIL** ə **GRAM**
kilometer	kə **LOM** ə tər
kilowatt	**KIL** ə **WOT**
Kimberley	**KIM** bər lee
Kim Du-bong	kim doo bohng
Kim Il-sung	kim eel sung
Kimny, Nong	**KIM** nee, **NONG**
kimono	kə **MOH** nə

o on, oh oat, oi boy, oo soon, oor poor, or for, ow cow, sh shush,
th thin, *th* this, u up, ur spur, uu book, *zh* pleasure

Kinabalu	KIN ə bə LOO
kindergarten	KIN dər GAHR tən
kinescope, K-	KIN ə SKOHP
kinesics	kə NEE siks
kinesiology	kə NEE see OL ə jee
kinesthesia	KIN əs THEE zhə
kinesthetic	KIN əs THET ik
kinetic	kə NET ik
Kingsley	KINGZ lee
Kingston	KINGZ tən
kinkajou	KING kə JOO
Kinsey	KIN zee
Kinshasa	kin SHAHS ə
Kioga	kee OH gə
kiosk	KEE osk
Kiowa	KĪ ə waw
Kiplinger	KIP ling ər
Kirca, A. Coşkun	kur JAH, jawsh KUUN
Kirchschlaeger, Rudolf	KIRK shleg ər, ROO dohlf
Kirghiz	kir GEEZ
Kiribati	KIR ə BAS
Kirilenko	ki ri LENG koh
Kirin	kee reen
kirk	kurk
Kirkcudbright	kər KOO bree
Kirkpatrick	kurk PAT rik
Kirkuk	kir KOOK
Kirman	kər MAHN
Kironde, Apollo	kee RAHN day, ah POH loh
Kirov	KEE rof
kirschwasser	KEERSH VAH sər
Kirsten	KEER stən
Kirsten (US)	KUR stən
kirtle	KUR təl
Kirwan	KUR wən
Kiselev, Tikhon	kee seel YAWF, TEE hən
Kishi, Nobusuke	KEE shee, noh BUU ske
Kishinev	KISH i nef
kishke	KISH kə
Kiska	KIS kə
kismet	KIZ mət
Kissinger	KIS ən jər
kitsch	kich

ə ago, a at, ah calm, ahr dark, air care, aw saw, ay say, ch church
e bet, ee me, eer beer, hw what, i is, ī my, n French final n vin,

Kittikachorn, Thanom	**KEE** tee kah **CHORN**, thah **NOM**
Kiwanis	kə **WAH** nəs
kiwi	**KEE** wee
Kizya, Luka	**KEE** *zh*ah, loo **KAH**
Klagenfurt	**KLAH** gən **FUURT**
Klamath	**KLAM** əth
klaxon, K-	**KLAK** sən
Kléber	klay **BAIR**
Kleberg	**KLAY** bərg
Klee	klay
kleig	kleeg
Klemperer	**KLEM** pər ər
kleptomania	**KLEP** tə **MAY** nee ə
kleptomaniac	**KLEP** tə **MAY** nee **AK**
Klestil, Thomas	**KLES** teel, **TOH** mahs
klieg	kleeg
Klingsor	**KLING** zor
Klondike	**KLON** dīk
klystron	**KLĪS** tron
knapsack	**NAP** sak
knavish	**NAY** vish
knell	nel
Kneller	**NEL** ər
Knesset	kə **NES** et
Knickerbocker	**NIK** ər **BOK** ər
knickknack	**NIK** nak
knish	kə **NISH**
knob	nob
knoll	nohl
Knopf	knahpf
Knossos	**NOS** əs
knout	nowt
knowledge	**NOL** ij
Knowles	nohlz
Knox	noks
knurl	nurl
Knut	kə **NOOT**
koala	koh **AH** lə
koan	**KOH** on
Kobe	**KOH** bee
Koblenz	**KOH** blents
Koch, Edward	koch
Kodak	**KOH** dak

o on, oh oat, oi boy, oo soon, oor poor, or for, ow cow, sh shush,
th thin, *th* this, u up, ur spur, uu book, *zh* pleasure

Kodály, Zoltán	koh **DĪ**, **ZOHL** tahn
Kodiak, k-	**KOH** dee AK
Koestler	**KEST** lər
Kohinoor	**KOH** ə NUUR
Kohl, Helmut	**KOHL**, **HEL** moot
kohlrabi	kohl **RAH** bee
Koht	koot
koine, K-	koi **NAY**
Koirala, Matrika Prasad	kaw **RAH** lah, **MAH** tri kah prah **SAHD**
Koivisto, Mauno	**KOY** vees toh, **MOW** noh
Kokoschka	kə **KAWSH** kə
Kolingba, André-Dieudonne	koh **LING** bah, ahn **DRAY** DYUU daw **NAY**
kolinsky	kə **LIN** skee
kolkhoz	kawl **KAWZ**
Kollwitz, Käthe	**KOHL** vits, **KAY** tə
Kol Nidre	kohl **NID** rə
Kolyma	kə **LEE** mə
Komarno	kaw **MAHR** naw
Komatina, Miljan	koh **MAH** tee nah, **MEEL** yahn
kona	**KOH** nə
Kondrashin	kahn **DRAH** shin
Konev	**KAW** nef
Königsberg	**KAYN** igz BURG
Konitsa	**KAW** neet SAH
Kónya, Sándor	**KAWN** yah, **SHAHN** dor
kookaburra	**KUUK** ə BUR ə
Koopmans	**KOOP** mənz
Kootenay	**KOOT** ə NAY
kopeck	**KOH** pek
Kopit	**KOH** pit
kopje	**KOP** ee
Koran	kə **RAHN**
Korea	kə **REE** ə ·
Kornegay, Horace	**KORN** gay
Koroma, Abdul	koh **ROH** mə, ahb **DOOL**
Korzybski	kor **ZIP** skee
Kościuszko, Tadeusz	kawsh **CHUUSH** koh, tah **DE** uush
kosher	**KOH** shər
Košice	**KAW** shit se
Kossuth	**KAH** sooth
Kostandov, Leonid	kah **STAHN** dawf, lee ahn **YEED**

ə ago, a at, ah calm, ahr dark, air care, aw saw, ay say, ch church
e bet, ee me, eer beer, hw what, i is, ī my, n French final n vin,

Koster	**KOS** tər
Kosygin	kə **SEE** gən
Kotka	**KAWT** kə
koto	**KOH** toh
koumis	**KOO** məs
Kountché, Seyni	**KOON** chee, **SAY** nee
Koussevitzky	**KOO** sə **VIT** skee
Kovalev, Anatoly	kah vahl **YAWF**, ah nah **TOH** lee
Kovno	**KAWV** naw
Kowalczyk, Edward	koh **VAL** chik, **ED** vahrd
kowtow	**KOW** tow (tow as in *cow*)
kraal	krahl
Krafft-Ebing	**KRAHFT AY** bing
Krag, Jens Otto	**KROW**, **YENS AH** toh
Kragerö	**KRAH** yai **RER**
Krakatoa	**KRAH** kə **TOH** ə
kraken	**KRAH** kən
Kraków (Polish)	**KRAH** kuuf
Krasnodar	**KRAHS** naw **DAHR**
Kravets, Vladimir	**KRAH** vits, vlah **DEE** mir
Krefeld	**KRAY** felt
Kreisky, Bruno	**KRĪS** kee
kremlin, K-	**KREM** lən
Kreutzer, k-	**KROIT** sər
Kreymborg, Alfred	**KRAYM** borg
krieg, K-	kreeg
Kriemhild	**KREEM** hild
kris	krees
Krishna	**KRISH** nə
Krishnan, Natarajan	**KRISH** nən, nat **RAH** jən
Kristiansand	**KRIS** tyahn **SAHN**
Kristiansund	**KRIS** tyahn **SOON**
Krk	kurk
Krnov	**KUR** nawf
Krokodil	kroh koh **DEEL**
krona	**KROH** nə
krone	**KROH** nə
Kronstadt	**KRAWN** staht
Kropotkin	krə **POT** kən
Kruger	**KROO** gər
krugerrand	**KROO** gər rand
Krupp	kruup
Kruševac	**KROO** she **VAHTS**

o on, oh oat, oi boy, oo soon, oor poor, or for, ow cow, sh shush,
th thin, *th* this, u up, ur spur, uu book, zh pleasure

Krylov	kri **LAWF**
krypton	**KRIP** tahn
Kryuchkov, Vladimir	krə yuuch **KAWF**, vlah **DEE** meer
Kuala Lumpur	**KWAH** lə luum **PUUR**
Kubango	kuu **BAHNG** goh
Kubelik	**KUUB** ə lik
Kublai Khan	**KOO** blī **KAHN**
Kubla Khan	**KOO** blə **KAHN**
Kuchel	**KEE** kəl
Kuchta	**KOOSH** tah
kudos	**KYOO** dahs
kudu	**KOO** doo
kudzu	**KUUD** zoo
Kufic	**KOO** fik
kugel	**KUUG** əl
Kuibyshev	**KWEE** bə **SHEF**
Ku Klux Klan	koo kluks klan
kulak	koo **LAHK**
Kuldiga	**KUUL** di gah
Kultur	kuul **TOOR**
kümmel	**KIM** əl
kumquat	**KUM** kwot
Kunayev, Dinmukhamed	koo **NĪ** yef, **DEEN** moo hah **MED**
Kundera, Milan	**KUUN** də rə, **MI** lan
Kundry	**KUUN** dri
Kuner	**KYOO** nər
Kung Fu-tse	kuung foo dzu
Kunming	kuun ming
Kuomintang	kwoh min tahng
Kura	kuu **RAH**
Kural, Adnan	koo **RAHL**, ahd **NAHN**
Kurdish	**KUR** dish
Kurdistan	**KUR** də **STAN**
Kure	**KOO** re
Kuril, -e	**KYUUR** il
Kurosawa	**KUUR** ə **SAH** wah
Kursk	kuursk
Kusch, Polycarp	**KUUSH**, **POL** i **KAHRP**
Kush (India)	kuush
Kuwait	kə **WAYT**
Kuwatly, Shukri Al	koo **WAHT** lee, **SHOO** kree ahl
Kuznetsk	kuuz **NETSK**

ə ago, a at, ah calm, ahr dark, air care, aw saw, ay say, ch church
e bet, ee me, eer beer, hw what, i is, ī my, *n* French final n vin,

Kuznetsov, Vasily	kooz nyits **AWF**, vah **SEEL** ee
Kuznets, Simon	**KUZ** nets
Kwajalein	**KWAHJ** ə **LAYN**
Kwakiutl	**KWAH** kee **OOT** əl
Kwangchowan	gwahng joh wahn
Kwangsi Chuang	gwahng see jwahng
Kwangtung	gwahng duung
Kwantung	gwahn duung
kwashiorkor	**KWASH** ee **OR** kər
Kweichow	gway joh
Kweilin	kway lin
Kweiyang	gway yahng
Kyd	kid
Kymry	**KIM** ree
Ky, Nguyen Cao	**KEE, NOO** yen kow
Kyoto	kee **OH** toh
kyphosis	kī **FOH** səs
Kyprianou, Spyros	**KEE** pree **AH** noo, **SPEE** rohs
Kyrie eleison	**KIR** ee **AY** ə **LAY** ə **SAHN**
Kyushu	**KYOO** shoo

L

laager	**LAH** gər
Laban	**LAY** bən
labia	**LAY** bee ə
labial	**LAY** bee əl
labium	**LAY** bee əm
laboratory	**LAB** rə **TOR** ee
Labrador	**LAB** rə dor
Labuan	**LAH** boo **AHN**
laburnum	lə **BUR** nəm
labyrinth, L-	**LAB** ə rinth
labyrinthine	**LAB** ə **RIN** thən
Laccadive	**LAK** ə **DĪV**
laccolith	**LAK** ə lith
Lacedaemon	**LAS** ə **DEE** mən
Lacedaemonian	**LAS** ə di **MOH** nee ən
Lachaise, La Chaise	la **SHEZ**
Lacharrière, Guy Ladreit de	lah shahr **YAIR, GEE** lah **DRAY** də

---

o on, oh oat, oi boy, oo soon, oor poor, or for, ow cow, sh shush,
th thin, *th* this, u up, ur spur, uu book, *zh* pleasure

laches	LACH əz
Lachesis	LAK ə sis
lachrymal	LAK rə məl
lachrymose	LAK rə MOHS
lackadaisical	LAK ə DAY zi kəl
Lackawanna	LAK ə WAH nə
lackey	LAK ee
Laconia	lə KOH nee ə
laconic	lə KON ik
lacquer	LAK ər
lacrosse	lə KRAWS
lactation	lak TAY shən
lactose	LAK tohs
lacuna	lə KYOO nə
lacunae	lə KYOO nee
Ladakh	lah DAHK
Ladin	lə DEEN
Ladino, l-	lə DEE noh
Ladoga	LAD ə gə
Ladrone, l-	lə DROHN
Lae	LAH ay
Laertes	lay ER teez
Laetare	lay TAH ree
laetrile	LAY ə tril
La Farge	lə FAHRZH
Lafayette (French general)	lah fah YET
Lafayette (US)	LAF ee ET
Lafcadio	laf KAD ee oh
Lafitte, Laffite	lə FEET
La Fontaine	la fon TEN
lager	LAH gər
lagniappe	lan YAP
lagoon	lə GOON
Lagos (Nigeria)	LAH gohs
Lagting, Lagthing	LAHG ting
La Guardia, Fiorello	lə GWAHR dee ə, FEE ə REL oh
Lahore	lə HOR
laic	LAY ək
laird	laird
laissez-faire	LES ay FAIR
laity	LAY ə tee
Laius	LAY əs

ə ago, a at, ah calm, ahr dark, air care, aw saw, ay say, ch church
e bet, ee me, eer beer, hw what, i is, ī my, n French final n vin,

La Jolla	lə HOI ə
Lakmé	lak MAY
Lalo	la LOH
lama, L-	LAH mə
Lamarck	lə MAHRK
Lamartine	la mahr TEEN
lamasery	LAH mə SER ee
Lamaze	lə MAHZ
lambaste	lam BAYST
lambda	LAM də
lambent	LAM bənt
Lambeth	LAM bəth
lamé	la MAY
Lamech	LAY mək
lament	lə MENT
lamentable	LAM ən tə bəl
laminate (a, n)	LAM ə nət
laminate (v)	LAM ə NAYT
Lamont	lə MONT
lampoon	lam POON
lamprey	LAM pree
Lamy	la MEE
lanai, L-	lə NĪ
Lanark	LAN ərk
Lancashire	LANG kə SHIR
Lancaster	LANG kə stər
Lancastrian	lang KAS tree ən
Lancelot	LAN sə lət
lancet	LAN sət
Lanchow	lahn joh
landau	LAN dow
Ländler	LENT lər
Landsbergis, Vytautas	LAHNZ ber gis, vee TOW təs
Lange (North European)	LAHNG ə
Langer	LANG ər
Langland	LANG lənd
Langley	LANG lee
Langmuir	LANG myuur
langue d'oc	lahng DAWK
langue d'oïl	lahng daw EEL
languid	LANG gwəd
languish	LANG gwish
languor	LANG gər

Lanier	lə NEER
lanthanide	LAN thə NĪD
lanthanum	LAN thə nəm
Lantos	LAN tohs
lanugo	lə NOO goh
lanyard	LAN yərd
Lanzhou	lahn joh
Lao	low (as in *cow*)
Laoag	lah WAHG
Laocoön	lay AHK ə wahn
Laodamia	lay OD ə MĪ ə
Laodicea	lay OD ə SEE ə
Laodicean	lay OD ə SEE ən
Laomedon	lay OM ə DON
Laos	LAH ohs
Lao-tzu	lowd zu (ow as in *cow*)
La Paz	lə PAHZ
lapel	lə PEL
lapidary	LAP ə DER ee
lapis lazuli	LAP əs LAZ ə lee
Lapland	LAP land
La Plata	lah PLAH tah
Lapp	lap
lapsus linguae	LAP səs LING gwee
Laputa	lə PYOO tə
Laramie	LA rə mee
larboard	LAHR bərd
larcenous	LAHR sə nəs
larceny	LAHR sə nee
lardoon	lahr DOON
Laredo	lə RAY doh
lares	LAIR eez
largess	lahr ZHES
larghetto	lahr GET oh
largo	LAHR goh
lariat	LA ree ət
La Rocca, Umberto	lah RAWK ah, oom BAIR toh
Laroche	lah ROHSH
La Rochefoucauld	lah RUSH foo KOH
Larousse	lah ROOS
Larvik	LAHR veek
laryngeal	lə RIN jee əl
laryngectomy	LA rən JEK tə mee

ə ago, a at, ah calm, ahr dark, air care, aw saw, ay say, ch church
e bet, ee me, eer beer, hw what, i is, ī my, *n* French final n vin,

laryngitis	**LA** rən **JĪ** təs
laryngology	**LA** rən **GOL** ə jee
larynx	**LA** ringks
lasagna	lə **ZAHN** yə
La Salle	lə **SAL**
La Scala	lah **SKAH** lah
lascivious	lə **SIV** ee əs
Las Cruces	lahs **KROO** səs
laser	**LAY** zər
Lashio	**LAHSH** yoh
La Spezia	lah **SPET** syah
Lassen	**LAS** ən
lassie	**LAS** ee
lasso	**LAS** oh
Las Vegas	lahs **VAY** gəs
Latakia	**LAH** tah **KEE** ah
lateen	la **TEEN**
latent	**LAY** tənt
Lateran	**LAT** ər ən
latex	**LAY** teks
lath	lath
lathe	lay*th*
lather (soap)	**LA*TH*** ər
lather (worker)	**LATH** ər
Latimer	**LAT** ə mər
Latium	**LAY** shee əm
Latona	lə **TOH** nə
Latourette	la too **RET**
Latvia	**LAT** vee ə
laud, L-	lawd
laudanum	**LAW** də nəm
Lauder	**LAW** dər
launch	lawnch
laureate	**LOR** ee ət
laurel	**LOR** əl
Laurencin	law rahn **SAN** (rahn and **SAN** French final *n*)
Laurentian	law **REN** shən
Laurents	**LAW** rents
Laurie	**LAWR** ee
Lausanne	loh **ZAN**
Lautenberg	**LOWT** ən **BURG**

o on, oh oat, oi boy, oo soon, oor poor, or for, ow cow, sh shush, th thin, *th* this, u up, ur spur, uu book, *zh* pleasure

Lautrec	loh **TREK**
lava	**LAH** və
lavaliere	**LAV** ə **LIR**
lavatory	**LAV** ə **TOR** ee
lave	layv
Laver	**LAY** vər
Lavoisier	la vwah **ZYAY**
Laxalt	**LAKS** awlt
Laxness, Halldór	**LAHKS** nes, **HAHL** dohr
Layamon	**LAY** ə mən
lazar	**LAY** zər
lazaret	**LAZ** ə **RET**
lazaretto	**LAZ** ə **RET** oh
Lazarus	**LAZ** ər əs
Lazear	lə **ZEER**
lazulite	**LAZ** ə **LĪT**
lazzarone	**LAZ** ə **ROH** nay
leaden	**LED** ən
league	leeg
Leah	**LEE** ə
Leahy	**LAY** hee
Leander	lee **AN** dər
Lear	leer
learned (a)	**LUR** nəd
leash	leesh
leaven	**LEV** ən
Leavenworth	**LEV** ən **WURTH**
Leavis	**LEEV** əs
Lebanese	**LEB** ə **NEEZ**
Lebanon	**LEB** ə nən
Lebensraum	**LAY** bəns **ROWM** (**ROWM** as in *cow*)
Lebrija	le **BREE** hah
Lech (river)	lek
lecher	**LECH** ər
Lechuga, Carlos	lay **CHOO** gah, **KAHR** lohs
lecithin	**LES** ə thən
Leconte	lə **KAWNT**
Le Corbusier	lə kor buu **ZYAY**
lectern	**LEK** tərn
lecture	**LEK** chər
Leczyca	lan **CHIT** sah
Leda	**LEE** də
Lederberg, Joshua	**LAY** dər **BURG**, **JOSH** ə wə

ə ago, a at, ah calm, ahr dark, air care, aw saw, ay say, ch church
e bet, ee me, eer beer, hw what, i is, ī my, *n* French final n vin,

lederhosen	LAY dər HOH zən
Lederle	LED ər lee
Lee Huan	lee wan
Lee Kuan Yew	lee kwahn yoo
Lee Teng-hui	lee dung way
Leeuwenhoek	LAY vən HOOK
leeward, L-	LEE wərd
leeward (nautical)	LOO ərd
Lefevre (French)	lə FEV
legacy	LEG ə see
Le Gallienne	lə GAL yən
legate (n)	LEG ət
legate (v)	li GAYT
legatee	LEG ə TEE
legato	li GAH toh
legend	LEJ ənd
legendary	LEJ ən DER ee
Léger	lay ZHAY
legerdemain	LEJ ər də MAYN
Leghorn (Italy)	LEG horn
leghorn, L- (poultry)	LEG ərn
legible	LEJ ə bəl
legionnaire	LEE jə NAIR
legislature	LEJ əs LAY chər
Legree	li GREE
legume	LEG yoom
Legwaila, Legwaila Joseph	lee kwī EEL ah, lee kwī EEL ah JOH səf
Lehár	LAY hahr
Le Havre	lə HAH vrə
Lehigh	LEE hī
lei	lay
Leibnitz	LĪB nits
Leica	LĪ kə
Leicester	LES tər
Leiden	LĪ dən
Leif	leef
Leigh	lee
Leinsdorf	LĪNZ dorf
Leinster	LEN stər
Leipzig	LĪP sig
leisure	LEE zhər
Leith	leeth

o on, oh oat, oi boy, oo soon, oor poor, or for, ow cow, sh shush,
th thin, *th* this, u up, ur spur, uu book, *zh* pleasure

leitmotiv	**LĪT** moh **TEEF**
Leland	**LEE** lənd
Lely	**LEE** lee
leman	**LEM** ən
Leman	**LEE** mən
Le Mans	lə **MAHN** (**MAHN** French final *n*)
Lemass, Sean	lə **MAHS**, **SHAWN**
lemming	**LEM** ing
Lemnitzer	**LEM** nit sər
Lemnos	**LEM** nos
Lemoyne	lə **MOIN**
Lemuel	**LEM** yoo əl
lemur	**LEE** mər
Lemuria	li **MYOO** ree ə
Lena (river)	**LYE** nah
Lendl, Ivan	**LEN** dəl, **EE** vahn
L'Enfant	lahn **FAHN** (lahn and **FAHN** French final *n*)
length	lengkth
leniency	**LEE** nee ən see
lenient	**LEE** nee ənt
Lenin	**LEN** in
Leningrad	**LEN** in **GRAD**
lenity	**LEN** ə tee
Lenox, Lennox	**LEN** əks
lens	lenz
lentil	**LEN** təl
lento	**LEN** toh
Lenya, Lotte	**LAY** nyə, **LAH** tə
Leo	**LEE** oh
Leonard	**LEN** ərd
Leonardo	**LEE** ə **NAHR** doh
Leoncavallo	lay **AWN** kah **VAH** loh
Leonid	**LEE** ə nid
Leonidas	lee **ON** ə dəs
Leontief	lee **AWN** tyef
Leopardi, Giacomo	**LAY** aw **PAHR** dee, **JAH** kaw maw
Léopoldville	**LEE** ə pohld **VIL**
leotard	**LEE** ə **TAHRD**
Lepanto	li **PAN** toh
Lepidus	**LEP** i dəs
Lepontine	li **PON** tin
leprechaun	**LEP** rə **KAWN**

ə ago, a at, ah calm, ahr dark, air care, aw saw, ay say, ch church
e bet, ee me, eer beer, hw what, i is, ī my, *n* French final n vin,

leprosy	**LEP** rə see
Lepus	**LEE** pəs
Lermontov	**LER** mən **TAWF**
lesbian, L-	**LEZ** bee ən
Lesbos	**LEZ** bos
Leschetizky	**LE** she **TIT** skee
lese majesty	**LEEZ MAJ** ə stee
lesion	**LEE** *zh*ən
Leslie (American)	**LES** lee
Leslie (British)	**LEZ** lee
Lesotho	lay **SOO** too
Lesseps	**LES** əps
Le Sueur	lə **SUUR**
lethal	**LEE** thəl
lethargic	lə **THAHR** jik
lethargy	**LETH** ər jee
Lethe, l-	**LEE** thee
Letitia	li **TISH** ə
leucocyte	**LOO** kə **SĪT**
leukemia	loo **KEE** mee ə
Levant	lə **VANT**
Levantine	lə **VAN** tin
levee	**LEV** ee
lever	**LEV** ər
leverage	**LEV** ə rij
Levi	**LEE** vī
leviathan, L-	lə **VĪ** ə thən
Levice	**LE** vit **SE**
Levine	lə **VEEN**
Levit, -t	**LE** vit
Leviticus	lə **VIT** ə kəs
levity	**LEV** ə tee
levy	**LEV** ee
Levy	**LEE** vee
lexicography	**LEK** sə **KOG** rə fee
lexicon	**LEK** sə **KON**
lex talionis	**LEKS TAL** ee **OH** nəs
Leyden	**LĪ** dən
Leydig	**LĪ** dig
Leyte	**LAY** tee
Lhasa	**LAH** sə
Lhasa apso	**LAH** sə **AP** soh
liability	**LĪ** ə **BIL** ə tee

---

o on, oh oat, oi boy, oo soon, oor poor, or for, ow cow, sh shush,
th thin, *th* this, u up, ur spur, uu book, *zh* pleasure

liable	LĪ ə bəl
liaison	LEE ə ZON
liana	lee AH nə
Liao	lyow
Liaoning	lyow ning
libation	lī BAY shən
Libby	LIB ee
libelous	LĪ bə ləs
Liberia	lī BEER ee ə
libertine	LIB ər TEEN
libidinous	lə BID ə nəs
libido	lə BEE doh
libra, L-	LEE brə
librarian	lī BRAIR ee ən
librettist	lə BRET əst
libretto	lə BRET oh
Libya	LIB ee ə
Libyan	LIB ee ən
licentiate	lī SEN shee ət
licentious	lī SEN shəs
lichee	lee chee
lichen	LĪ kən
licorice	LIK ə rəs
Li Desheng	lee du shung
Lidice	LEE də CHAY
Lido	LEE doh
liebfraumilch	LEEB frow MILK
Liechtenstein	LIK tən STĪN
lied (song)	leed
lieder (pl of *lied*, song)	LEE dər
Liederkranz	LEE dər KRAHNTS
lief, L-	leef
liege	leej
Liège	lee EZH
lien	leen
lieu	loo
lieutenant	loo TEN ənt
lieutenant (British army)	lef TEN ənt
Ligachev, Egor	lee gah CHAWF, yer GOR
ligament	LIG ə mənt
ligature	LIG ə chər

ə ago, a at, ah calm, ahr dark, air care, aw saw, ay say, ch church
e bet, ee me, eer beer, hw what, i is, ī my, *n* French final n vin,

lightning	LĪT ning
ligneous	LIG nee əs
lignite	LIG nīt
Ligonier	LIG ə NEER
Ligurian	li GYUUR ee ən
lilac	LĪ lək
Lilith	LIL əth
Liliuokalani	lee LEE oo oh kah LAH nee
Lille	leel
Lilliput	LIL ə pət
Lilliputian	LIL ə PYOO shən
Lilongwe	li LAWNG way
lima (bean)	LĪ mə
Lima (Ohio)	LĪ mə
Lima (Peru)	LEE mə
limbo	LIM boh
Limburger (cheese)	LIM BURG ər
limerick, L-	LIM ə rik
Limoges	li MOHZ*H*
limousine	LIM ə ZEEN
limpet	LIM pət
limpid	LIM pəd
Limpopo	lim POH poh
linage	LĪ nij
lineage (family)	LIN ee ij
lineament	LIN ee ə mənt
linear	LIN ee ər
Lingayen	LING gah YEN
lingerie	LAN *zh*ə REE
Ling Qing	leeng chung
lingua franca	LING gwə FRANG kə
Linguaphone	LING gwə FOHN
linguistic	ling GWIS tik
Linley	LIN lee
Linlithgow	lin LITH goh
Linnaean	lə NEE ən
Linnaeus	lə NEE əs
linnet, L-	LIN ət
Linotype	LĪ nə TĪP
Lin Piao	leen pyow
lintel	LIN təl
Linton	LIN tən
Linus	LĪ nəs

o on, oh oat, oi boy, oo soon, oor poor, or for, ow cow, sh shush,
th thin, *th* this, u up, ur spur, uu book, *zh* pleasure

Lin Yutang	lin yoo tahng
Linz	lints
Linzer torte	**LIN** zər **TORT**
Lipari	**LIP** ə ree
Lipchitz	**LIP** shits
Li Peng	lee pung
Lippe	**LIP** ə
Lippi	**LIP** ee
Lippizaner	**LIP** it **SAH** nər
liqueur	li **KUR**
liquidity	li **KWID** ə tee
liquor	**LIK** ər
lira	**LIR** ə
lire	**LIR** ay
Lisbon	**LIZ** bən
lisle	līl
Lisle (France)	leel
Lisle (US)	līl
Lissajous	**LEE** sə **ZHOO**
lissome	**LIS** əm
Liszt	list
litany, L-	**LIT** ə nee
litchi	**LEE** chee
liter	**LEE** tər
literary	**LIT** ə **RER** ee
literate	**LIT** ə rət
literati	**LIT** ə **RAH** tee
literature	**LIT** ər ə chər
lithe	lī*th*
lithium	**LITH** ee əm
lithograph	**LITH** ə **GRAF**
lithography	li **THOG** rə fee
lithotomy	li **THOT** ə mee
Lithuania	**LITH** oo **AY** nee ə
litigant	**LIT** ə gənt
litigious	lə **TIJ** əs
litmus	**LIT** məs
litotes	**LĪ** tə **TEEZ**
litterateur	**LIT** ə rə **TUR**
littoral	**LIT** ə rəl
liturgical	lə **TUR** ji kəl
liturgy	**LIT** ər jee
Liu Shao-chi	lee oo show chee (show as in *cow*)

ə ago, a at, ah calm, ahr dark, air care, aw saw, ay say, ch church
e bet, ee me, eer beer, hw what, i is, ī my, *n* French final n vin,

livable	**LIV** ə bəl
livelihood	**LĪV** lee **HUUD**
livelong	liv lawng
liven	**LĪ** vən
liver	**LIV** ər
Liverpudlian	**LIV** ər **PUD** lee ən
liverwort	**LIV** ər **WURT**
liverwurst	**LIV** ər **WUURST**
livery	**LIV** ə ree
Livia	**LIV** ee ə
livid	**LIV** əd
Livonia	li **VOH** nee ə
Livorno	lee **VOR** noh
Livy	**LIV** ee
Li Weihan	lee way hahn
Li Xiannian	lee shee ahn nyahn
Ljubljana	lyoo **BLYAH** nah
llama	**LAH** mə
Llanelly	la **NEL** ee
Llanera	lyah **NAY** rah
Lleshi, Haxhi	**LAY** shee, hah **JEE**
Llewellyn	loo **EL** in
Llullaillaco	**YOO YĪ YAHK** oh
loach	lohch
Loanda	loh **AHN** də
loath	lohth
loathe	loh*th*
lobar	**LOH** bər
lobe	lohb
lobectomy	loh **BEK** tə mee
lobelia	loh **BEEL** yə
Lobito	loo **BEE** too
loblolly	**LOB LOL** ee
Lobo, l-	**LOH** boh
lobotomy	loh **BOT** ə mee
locale	loh **KAL**
Locarno	loh **KAHR** noh
locative	**LOK** ə tiv
loch, L-	lok
lochia	**LOH** kee ə
Lochinvar	**LOK** in **VAHR**
Locke	lok
loco	**LOH** koh

o on, oh oat, oi boy, oo soon, oor poor, or for, ow cow, sh shush,
th thin, *th* this, u up, ur spur, uu book, *zh* pleasure

locum tenens	LOH kəm TEN ənz
locus	LOH kəs
locution	loh KYOO shən
locutory	LOK yə TOR ee
Lodge, l-	loj
Lodi (Italy)	LAW dee
Lodi (US)	LOH dī
Lodz	luuj
Loeb	lohb
Loeffler	LEF lər
loess	LOH es
Loesser	LES ər
Loew	loh
Loewe	loh
Loewy	LOH ee
Lofoten	LOH FUUT ən
Logan	LOH gən
logarithm	LAW gə RITH əm
loge	loh*zh*
loggia	LOHJ ə
logic	LOJ ik
logistic	loh JIS tik
logo	LOH goh
logomachy	loh GOM ə kee
logos, L-	LOH gos
logy	LOH gee
Lohengrin	LOH ən grin
Loire	lwahr
Loki	LOH kee
Lokoloko, Tore	LOH koh LOH koh, TOR ay
Lola	LOH lə
Lolita	loh LEET ə
loll	lol
Lollard	LOL ərd
Lollobrigida, Gina	law law BREE *zh*ee dah, ZHEE nah
Lombard	LOM bərd
Lombardy	LOM bər dee
Lombrosian	lom BROH zee ən
Lomé	loh MAY
Lomond	LOH mənd
Loncar, Budimir	LAWN chər, BUU dee meer
London	LUN dən
longevity	lon JEV ə tee

ə ago, a at, ah calm, ahr dark, air care, aw saw, ay say, ch church
e bet, ee me, eer beer, hw what, i is, ī my, *n* French final n vin,

Longinus	lon JĪ nəs
longitude	LON jə TOOD
long-lived	lawng līvd
Longobardi	LON goh BAHR dee
López	LOH pez
López Mateos, Adolfo	LOH pez mah TAY ohs, ah DAWL foh
López Portillo, José	LOH pez por TEE yoh, hoh SAY
loquacious	loh KWAY shəs
loquacity	loh KWAS ə tee
Lorain	lə RAYN
loran, L-	loh RAN
Lorca	LOR kə
lordosis	lor DOH səs
Lorelei	LOR ə LĪ
Loren, Sophia	LAW ren, soh FEE ah
lorgnette	lorn YET
Lorica	law REE kə
Loridan	law ree DAHN
lorry	LOR ee
Los Alamos	law SAL ə MOHS
Los Angeles	law SAN jə ləs
Los Gatos	law SGAT əs
L'Osservatore Romano	loh SER vah TAW re roh MAH noh
Lothario	loh THA ree oh
Lothian	LOH thee ən
Loti	loh TEE
Loudon	LOW dən (LOW as in cow)
lough	lok
Louis (English)	LOO is
Louis (French)	lwee
Louisiana	loo EE zee AN ə
Louisville	LOO ee VIL
lour	lowr (as in sour)
Lourdes	luurd
Louvain	loo VAN (VAN French final n)
louver	LOO vər
Louvre	LOO vrə
Loveland	LUV lənd
Lowell	LOH əl
lower (scowl)	LOW ər (LOW as in cow)
lox	loks
Loyola	loi OH lə

o on, oh oat, oi boy, oo soon, oor poor, or for, ow cow, sh shush,
th thin, th this, u up, ur spur, uu book, zh pleasure

lozenge	**LOZ** ənj
Luanda	loo **AHN** də
Luang Prabang	loo **AHNG** prah **BAHNG**
luau	**LOO** ow
Lubang	loo **BAHNG**
Lubavitcher	luu **BAHV** əch ər
Lubbers, Jan Hendrik	**LUUB** ərs, yahn **HEN** drik
Lubbock	**LUB** ək
Lübeck	**LOO** bek
Lübke, Heinrich	**LOOP** kə, **HĪN** rish
Lublin	**LOO** blin
lubricity	loo **BRIS** ə tee
Lucan	**LOO** kən
Lucania	loo **KAY** nee ə
Lucas	**LOO** kəs
luce, L-	loos
Lucenec	**LOO** che **NETS**
Lucerne, l-	loo **SURN**
Lucia (Italian)	loo **CHEE** ah
Lucian	**LOO** shən
lucid	**LOO** səd
Lucifer, l-	**LOO** sə fər
Lucite	**LOO** sīt
Lucius	**LOO** shəs
Lucknow	**LUK** now
lucrative	**LOO** krə tiv
lucre	**LOO** kər
Lucrece	loo **KREES**
Lucretius	loo **KREE** shəs
Lucrezia	loo **KRAYT** see ə
lucubrate	**LOO** kyə **BRAYT**
lucubration	**LOO** kyə **BRAY** shən
Lucullan	loo **KUL** ən
Lucullus	loo **KUL** əs
Lüda	loo dah
Luddite	**LUD** īt
ludicrous	**LOO** də krəs
Ludwiczak, Zdzislaw	**LOOD** vee chak, **ZDEE** slahv
Ludwig	**LUD** wig
lues	**LOO** eez
Luftwaffe	**LUUFT** vah fə
Luger	**LOO** gər
lugubrious	luu **GOO** bree əs

ə ago, a at, ah calm, ahr dark, air care, aw saw, ay say, ch church
e bet, ee me, eer beer, hw what, i is, ī my, n French final n vin,

Lukow	**LUU** kuuf
Lully	luu **LEE**
lumbago	lum **BAY** goh
lumbar	**LUM** bər
Luminal	**LOO** mə nəl
luminescence	**LOO** mə **NES** əns
luminous	**LOO** mə nəs
lummox	**LUM** əks
Lumumba, Patrice	luu **MUUM** bə, pa **TREES**
lunar	**LOO** nər
lunette	loo **NET**
Lupercalia	**LOO** pər **KAY** lee ə
lupine (plant)	**LOO** pən
lupine (wolfish)	**LOO** pīn
lupus	**LOO** pəs
lure	luur
lurid	**LUUR** əd
Lusaka	loo **SAHK** ə
Lusitania	**LOO** sə **TAY** nee ə
lustrous	**LUS** trəs
Lü-ta	loo dah
lutanist, lutenist	**LOOT** ə nəst
lute	loot
Lutece	lyoo **TES**
lutetium	loo **TEE** shee əm
Luthuli	loo **THOO** lee
Lutsk	lootsk
lux, L-	luks
luxe	luuks
Luxembourg	**LUK** səm **BURG**
Luxor	**LUK** sor
luxuriance	lug **ZH**UUR ee əns
luxurious	lug **ZH**UUR ee əs
luxury	**LUG** zhə ree
Luzon	loo **ZON**
Lvov, Lwów	lə **VAWF**
Lwoff, André	**LWAWF**, **AHN** dray
lycanthropy	lī **KAN** thrə pee
Lycaon	lī **KAY** ən
Lycaonia	**LĪ** kay **OH** nee ə
lycée	lee **SAY**
lyceum	lī **SEE** əm
Lycian	**LISH** ee ən

o on, oh oat, oi boy, oo soon, oor poor, or for, ow cow, sh shush,
th thin, *th* this, u up, ur spur, uu book, *zh* pleasure

Lycidas	**LIS** ə dəs
Lycurgus	lī **KUR** gəs
Lydgate	**LID GAYT**
Lyle	līl
Lyly	**LIL** ee
lymph	limf
lymphocyte	**LIM** fə **SĪT**
lymphogranulomatosis	**LIM** foh **GRAN** yə **LOH** mə **TOH** səs
Lyndon	**LIN** dən
lynx	lingks
Lyon (France)	lee **AWN** (**AWN** French final *n*)
lyonnaise	**LĪ** ə **NAYZ**
Lyonnesse	**LĪ** ə **NES**
Lyons (France)	lee **AWN** (**AWN** French final *n*)
Lyons (US)	**LĪ** ənz
Lyra	**LĪ** rə
lyre	līr
lyric	**LIR** ik
Lysander	lī **SAN** dər
Lysenko	lə **SENG** koh
lysergic	lə **SUR** jik
Lysistrata	**LIS** i **STRAH** tə
lyssophobia	**LIS** ə **FOH** bee ə
Lystra	**LIS** trə
Lytton	**LIT** ən

M

ma'am	mam
Maas	mahs
Maastricht	**MAHS** trikt
Mabinogion	**MAB** ə **NOH** gee ən
macabre	mə **KAH** brə
macadam	mə **KAD** əm
macadamia	**MAK** ə **DAY** mee ə
Macao	mə **KOW**
Macapagal, Diosdado	**MAH** kah pah **GAHL, DEE** ohs **DAH** doh
macaque	mə **KAHK**
macaroni	**MAK** ə **ROH** nee
macaronic	**MAK** ə **RON** ik

ə ago, a at, ah calm, ahr dark, air care, aw saw, ay say, ch church
e bet, ee me, eer beer, hw what, i is, ī my, *n* French final n vin,

macaroon	MAK ə ROON
Macassar	mə KAS ər
Macaulay	mə KAW lee
macaw	mə KAW
Maccabaeus	MAK ə BEE əs
Maccabean	MAK ə BEE ən
Maccabees	MAK ə BEEZ
Macchiarola, Frank	MAK ee ə ROH lə
McCulloch	mə KUL ək
MacDiarmid	mək DUR məd
McDougal, -l	mək DOO gəl
MacDowell	mək DOW əl
macédoine	ma say DWAHN
Macedonia	MAS ə DOH nee ə
maceration	MAS ə RAY shən
McGuffey	mə GUF ee
Mach	mahk
Machel, Samora Moisés	mah SHEL, sah MOR ah MOH zəz
machete	mə SHET ee
Machiavelli	MAK ee ə VEL ee
machination	MAK ə NAY shən
machismo	mah CHEEZ moh
macho	MAH choh
machree	mə KREE
Machu Picchu	MAH choo PEEK choo
Maciejowice	MAH che yaw VEET se
Mackehenie, Carlos	mah KE nee, KAHR lohs
Mackinac	MAK ə NAW
Mackinaw	MAK ə NAW
MacLean, McLean	mə KLAYN
MacLeish	mək LEESH
Macleod, McLeod	mə KLOWD
MacMahon, McMahon	mik MAN
MacMillan, Macmillan	mək MIL ən
MacMonnies	mək MON eez
McNamara	MAK nə MA rə
McNaughton	mək NAWT ən
Macon	MAY kən
MacPherson	mək FUR sən
macramé	MAK rə MAY
Macris	MA kris
macrobiotic	MAK roh bī OT ik

o on, oh oat, oi boy, oo soon, oor poor, or for, ow cow, sh shush, th thin, *th* this, u up, ur spur, uu book, *zh* pleasure

Macrobius	mə **KROH** bee əs
macrocosm	**MAK** rə ᴋoz əm
macron	**MAY** kron
macula	**MAK** yə lə
macushla	mə **KUUSH** lə
Madagascar	ᴍᴀᴅ ə **GAS** kər
madam	**MAD** əm
madame (French)	ma **DAHM**
Madang	mah **DAHNG**
Madariaga	ᴍᴀʜ *th*ah **RYAH** gah
Madeira	mə **DEER** ə
Madeleine, m-	**MAD** ə lən
mademoiselle	ᴍᴀᴅ ə mə **ZEL**
Madhya Bharat	**MUD** yə **BU** rət
Madhya Pradesh	**MUD** yə prə **DAYSH**
madonna, M-	mə **DON** ə
madras	**MAD** rəs
Madras	mə **DRAS**
Madrid (Spain)	mə **DRID**
madrigal	**MAD** ri gəl
madrilène	ᴍᴀ drə **LEN**
Madura (India)	**MAJ** uu rə
Madura (Indonesia)	mah **DUUR** ah
Maecenas	mi **SEE** nəs
maelstrom, M-	**MAYL** strəm
maenad	**MEE** nad
maestoso	ᴍᴀʜ es **TOH** soh
maestro	**MĪ** stroh
Maeterlinck	**MAY** tər ʟɪɴɢᴋ
Mafeking	**MAH** fə ᴋɪɴɢ
mafia, M-	**MAH** fee ə
Maga, Hubert	**MAH** gah, yoo **BAIRT**
Magallanes	ᴍᴀʜ gah **YAH** nes
Magaña, Alvaro	mah **GAH** nyah, **AHL** vah roh
Magdalen (Oxford)	**MAWD** lin
Magdalena	ᴍᴀʜɢ *th*ah **LE** nah
Magdalene, m-	**MAG** də ʟᴇᴇɴ
Magdalene Cambridge)	**MAWD** lin
Magdeburg	**MAG** də ʙᴜʀɢ
Magellan	mə **JEL** ən
Magellanic	ᴍᴀᴊ ə **LAN** ik
Magen David	ᴍᴀᴡ gən **DAW** vəd

ə ago, a at, ah calm, ahr dark, air care, aw saw, ay say, ch church
e bet, ee me, eer beer, hw what, i is, ī my, *n* French final n vin,

magenta	mə **JEN** tə
Maggiore	mə **JOH** ree
Magi	**MAY** jī
Magindanao	mah GEEN dah **NAH** oh
Maginot	**MA** zhə NOH
magisterial	MAJ ə **STIR** ee əl
Magister Ludi	**MAH** gis tər **LOO** dee
magistracy	**MAJ** i strə see
Magloire	mah **GLWAHR**
magma	**MAG** mə
Magna Charta	**MAG** nə **KAHR** tə
magna cum laude	**MAHG** nə kuum **LOWD** ə (**LOWD** as in *crowd*)
Magnani	mahn **YAH** nee
magnanimity	MAG nə **NIM** ə tee
magnanimous	mag **NAN** ə məs
magnate	**MAG** nət
Magnavox	**MAG** nə voks
magnesium	mag **NEE** zee əm
magnet	**MAG** nət
magneto	mag **NEE** toh
magnetometer	MAG nə **TOM** ə tər
magnetron	**MAG** nə TRON
Magnificat, m-	mag **NIF** i KAT
magnifico	mag **NIF** ə KOH
magniloquent	mag **NIL** ə kwənt
Magnin	**MAG** nən
magnitude	**MAG** nə TOOD
magnolia	mag **NOHL** yə
magnum	**MAG** nəm
magnum opus	MAG nəm **OH** pəs
Magnus	**MAG** nəs
Magog	**MAY** gog
Magsaysay, Ramón	mahg **SĪ** sī, rah **MOHN**
Magus, m-	**MAY** gəs
Magyar	**MAG** yahr
Magyarorszag	**MAWD** yahr AWR sahg
Mahabharata	mə HAH BAHR ə tə
Mahan	mə **HAN**
maharaja	MAH hə RAHJ ə
maharani	MAH hə RAH nee
mahatma, M-	mə **HAHT** mə
Mahayana	MAH hə YAH nə

o on, oh oat, oi boy, oo soon, oor poor, or for, ow cow, sh shush,
th thin, *th* this, u up, ur spur, uu book, *zh* pleasure

Mahdi	MAH dee
Mahendra Bir Bikram Shah Deva	mə HEN drah BEER bee KRUM SHAH dee VAH
mahjong	MAH zhahng
Mahler	MAH lər
mahout	mə HOWT
Mahovlich	mah HAHV lich
Mahratti, Mahrati	mə RAT ee
Maia	MAY yə
Maidanek	MĪ də NEK
maigre	MAY gər
Mailliard	MĪ yahrd
Maillol	mah YAWL
maillot	mī YOH
maim	maym
Maimonides	mī MON ə DEEZ
Mainbocher	man boh SHAY
mainsail (nautical)	MAYN səl
maintain	mayn TAYN
maintenance	MAYN tə nəns
Mainz	mīntz
Maitama-Sule, Alhaji	mī TAH mə SOO lay, ahl HAH jee
maître d'hôtel	ME trə doh TEL
Majali, Abdul Hadi	mah JEL lee, AHB duul HEH dee
Majlis	MUHJ lis
majolica	mə JOL i kə
Majorca	mə YOR kah
major-domo	MAY jər DOH moh
majuscule	MAJ ə SKYOOL
Makarios	mah KAH ree aws
Makarova, Natalia	mah KAH rə və, nə TAL yə
Makeka, Thabo	mah KAY kah, TAH boh
Makhachkala	mə KAHCH kə LAH
Malabar	MAL ə BAHR
Malabo	mə LAH boh
Malacca	mə LAK ə
Malachi	MAL ə KĪ
malachite	MAL ə KĪT
maladroit	MAL ə DROIT
Málaga	MAH lah GAH
Malagasy	MAL ə GAS ee
malagueña	MAH lah GAY nyah
malaise	mə LAYZ

ə ago, a at, ah calm, ahr dark, air care, aw saw, ay say, ch church
e bet, ee me, eer beer, hw what, i is, ī my, n French final n vin,

Malalasekera, Gunapala Piyasena	MAH lah lah SAY kə rə, GOO nə PAH lə PEE yə SAY nə
Malamud	MAL ə MUUD
malamute	MAL ə MYOOT
Malaprop	MAL ə PROP
malapropism	MAL ə PROP IZ əm
malaria	mə LAIR ee ə
malarkey	mə LAHR kee
malathion	MAL ə THĪ ən
Malawi	mah LAH wee
Malay	MAY lay
Malaya	mə LAY ə
Malayalam	MAL ə YAH ləm
Malaysia	mə LAY zhə
mal de mer	MAL də MAIR
Malden	MAWL dən
Maldive	MAWL deev
Male	MAHL ee
malediction	MAL ə DIK shən
malefactor	MAL ə FAK tər
Malenkov	MAL ən KAWF
malevolent	mə LEV ə lənt
malfeasance	mal FEE zəns
Malherbe	mal ERB
Mali	MAH lee
malign	mə LĪN
malignant	mə LIG nənt
Malinga, Norman	mah LING gə
malinger	mə LING gər
Malinovsky	MAL ə NAWF skee
Malinowski	MAL ə NAWF skee
Malita, Mircea	mah LEET sah, MEERT chah
mall	mawl
mallard	MAL ərd
Mallarmé	ma lahr MAY
malleable	MAL ee ə bəl
Mallorca	mah YOR kah
Mallory	MAL ə ree
Malmédy	mal may DEE
Malmesbury	MAHMZ bə ree
Malmö	MAL moh
malmsey	MAHM zee

o on, oh oat, oi boy, oo soon, oor poor, or for, ow cow, sh shush,
th thin, *th* this, u up, ur spur, uu book, *zh* pleasure

Malory	MAL ə ree
Malraux	mal ROH
Malta	MAWL tə
Malthus	MAL thəs
Malthusian	mal THOO zhən
maltreat	mal TREET
Mamaroneck	mə MA rə NEK
mamba	MOM bə
mambo	MOM boh
Mameluke, m-	MAM ə LOOK
mammary	MAM ə ree
Mammon, m-	MAM ən
Managua	mah NAH gwah
Manama	mə NAM ə
mañana	mah NYAH nah
Manassas	mə NAS əs
Manasseh	mə NAS ə
manatee	MAN ə TEE
Manchu	man choo
Manchukuo	man choo kwoh
Manchuria	man CHUUR ee ə
Mancunian	man KYOO nee ən
mandala	MUN də lə
Mandalay	MAN də LAY
mandamus	man DAY məs
mandarin, M-	MAN də rən
mandate	MAN dayt
mandatory	MAN də TOR ee
Mandeville	MAN də vil
Mandingo	man DING goh
mandolin	MAN də lin
manège	ma NEZH
manes, M-	MAY neez
Manet	ma NAY
maneuver	mə NOO vər
manganese	MANG gə NEEZ
Mangano, Silvana	mahn GAH noh, seel VAH nah
manger	MAYN jər
mango	MANG goh
Mangope, Chief Lucas	mahn GOHP ee, cheef LOO kahs
mangrove	MANG grohv
mania	MAY nee ə
maniacal	mə NĪ ə kəl

ə ago, a at, ah calm, ahr dark, air care, aw saw, ay say, ch church
e bet, ee me, eer beer, hw what, i is, ī my, n French final n vin,

Manichean	MAN ə KEE ən
manifesto	MAN ə FES toh
manifold	MAN ə FOHLD
Manila	mə NIL ə
manioc	MAN ee OK
Manipur	MUN i PUUR
Manitoba	MAN ə TOH bə
manitou	MAN ə TOO
Manitoulin	MAN ə TOO lən
Mankiewicz	MANG kə wits
mankind	man kīnd
Mann (Thomas)	mahn
Mann (Horace)	man
manna	MAN ə
mannequin	MAN i kən
Mannheim	MAN hīm
Manoah	mə NOH ə
Manolete	MAHN oh LAY tay
manometer	mə NOM ə tər
Manon Lescaut	ma NAWN le SKOH (NAWN French final *n*)
manqué	mahn KAY (mahn French final *n*)
mansard	MAN sahrd
Manson	MAN sən
mansuetude	MAN swi TOOD
manta	MAN tə
manteau	man TOH
Mantegna	mahn TE nyah
mantel	MAN təl
mantilla	man TEE ə
mantle	MAN təl
Mantoux (test)	MAN too
mantra	MAN trə
Mantua, m-	MAN choo ə
manumission	MAN yə MISH ən
Manutius	mə NYOO shee əs
Manx, m-	mangks
Manzanillo	MAHN sah NEE yaw
manzanita	MAN zə NEE tə
Manzoni	mahn DZOH nee
Manzù	mahn ZOO
Maori	MOW ree (MOW as in *cow*)
Mao Zedong	mow dzə duung (mow as in *cow*)
Mapai	mah PĪ

o on, oh oat, oi boy, oo soon, oor poor, or for, ow cow, sh shush,
th thin, *th* this, u up, ur spur, uu book, *zh* pleasure

Maputo	mə POOT oh
maquillage	ma kee YAHZ*H*
Maquis, m-	mah KEE
Mara	MAHR ə
marabou	MA rə BOO
maraca	mə RAH kə
Maracaibo	MA rə KĪ boh
Marajó	MAHR ə ZH*AW*
maraschino	MA rə SKEE noh
Marasesti	mə rə SHESHT
Marat	mah RAH
Maratha	mə RAH tə
Marathi	mə RAH tee
Marathon, m-	MAR ə THON
maraud	mə RAWD
Marawi	mə RAH wee
Marceau, Marcel	mahr SOH, mahr SEL
Marceline	MAHR sə LEEN
marchesa	mahr KAY zə
marchese	mahr KAY zay
marchioness	MAHR shə nəs
Marcia	MAHR shə
Marckwardt, Marckwart	MAHR kwahrt
Marconi	mahr KOH nee
Marcos, Ferdinand	MAHR kohs
Mardi Gras	MAHR dee GRAH
mare (sea; moon area)	MAHR ay
Marengo	mə RENG goh
margarine	MAHR jə rən
Margesson	MAHR jə sən
marginalia	MAHR jə NAY lee ə
Margolin	MAHR gə lin
maria (seas)	MAHR ee ə
Maria	mə REE ə
Maria (Black Maria)	mə RĪ ə
Mariana Islands	MA ree AN ə
Marietta	MA ree ET ə
marigold	MA rə GOHLD
marijuana	MA rə WAH nə
marimba	mə RIM bə
marina	mə REE nə
marinade	MA rə NAYD

ə ago, a at, ah calm, ahr dark, air care, aw saw, ay say, ch church
e bet, ee me, eer beer, hw what, i is, ī my, *n* French final n vin,

marinara	MAHR ə NAHR ə
marinate	MA rə NAYT
marine, M-	mə REEN
mariner	MA rə nər
Marinescu, Teodor	MAH ree NES koo, TAY oh DOR
Marisol	MA rə SOHL
Maritain	ma ree TAN (TAN French final *n*)
marital	MA rə təl
maritime, M-	MA rə TĪM
Mariveles	mah ree VE les
Marjai, Jozsef	MAHR yah ee, YOH *zh*ef
marjoram	MAHR jə rəm
Markevitch	mahr KAY vich
Markham	MAHR kəm
Marlborough (British)	MAWL brə
Marlborough (US)	MAHRL bə rə
Marmara, Marmora	MAHR mə rə
marmoset	MAHR mə SET
marmot	MAHR mət
maroon	mə ROON
Marquand	mahr KWAHND
Marquardt, Marquart	MAHR kwahrt
marquee	mahr KEE
Marquesas Islands	mahr KAY zəs
marquess	MAHR kwəs
marquetry	MAHR kə tree
Marquette	mahr KET
marquis, M-	MAHR kwəs
marquis (French)	mahr KEE
marquise	mahr KEEZ
marquisette	MAHR kə ZET
Marrakech, Marrakesh	MA rə KESH
Marriott (hotels)	MA ree ət
marron	MA rən
Marryat	MA ree ət
Marsala	mahr SAH lə
Marschner	MAHRSH nər
Marseillaise	MAHR say EZ
Marseille (French)	mahr SAY
Marseilles	mahr SAY
marshal, M-	MAHR shəl
marshmallow	MAHRSH MEL oh
marsupial	mahr SOO pee əl

o on, oh oat, oi boy, oo soon, oor poor, or for, ow cow, sh shush,
th thin, *th* this, u up, ur spur, uu book, *zh* pleasure

Martaban	MAHR tə BAHN
Martel	mahr TEL
Martello, m-	mahr TEL oh
marten	MAHR tən
martial, M-	MAHR shəl
Martian	MAHR shən
Martineau	MAHR ti NOH
Martinelli	MAHR ti NEL ee
martinet	MAHR tə NET
Martínez	mahr TEE nes
martingale	MAHR tən GAYL
martini, M-	mahr TEE nee
Martinique	MAHR tə NEEK
Martini Urdaneta,	mahr TEE nee oor dah NAY tah,
Alberto	al BER toh
martyr	MAHR tər
Marvell	MAHR vəl
marzipan	MAHR zə PAN
Masaccio	mah SAHT chaw
Masahiro	mah sah hee roh
Masai	mah SĪ
Masaryk	MAS ə rik
Masbate	mahz BAH tee
Mascagni	mahs KAH nyee
mascara	ma SKA rə
maser	MAY zər
Maseru	MAZ ə ROO
Masharbrum,	MUSH ər BRUUM
Masherbrum	
Mashingaidze, Elleck	mah SHEE ən gah YEE dzee, AY lek
Masire, Quett	ma SEE ray, KWET
masochism	MAS ə KIZ əm
masochist	MAS ə kəst
Masonic, m-	mə SON ik
Masonite	MAY sə NĪT
Masora	mə SOR ə
Masorete	MAS ə REET
masque	mask
Massachusetts	MAS ə CHOO səts
massacre	MAS ə kər
massage	mə SAHZH
Massenet	MAS ə NAY
masseur	ma SUUR

ə ago, a at, ah calm, ahr dark, air care, aw saw, ay say, ch church
e bet, ee me, eer beer, hw what, i is, ī my, n French final n vin,

masseuse	ma SUUZ
massif	ma SEEF
Massine	ma SEEN
mastaba	MAS tə bə
mastectomy	ma STEK tə mee
mastodon	MAS tə DON
mastoid	MAS toid
Mastroianni, Marcello	MAH stroh YAH nee, mahr CHE loh
Matabele	MAT ə BEE lee
matador	MAT ə DOR
Matagalpa	MAT ə GAL pə
Mata Hari	MAH tə HAHR ee
Matamoros	MAT ə MOR əs
Matanuska	MAT ə NOOS kə
Matanzima, Kaiser Daliwonga	mah TAHN zee mah, KĪ zər DAH lee WAHNG gah
Matawan	MAT ə WAHN
matelote	MAT ə LOHT
Mateos	mah TE aws
mater	MAY tər
material	mə TIR ee əl
materia medica	mə TIR ee ə MED i kə
materiel	mə TIR ee EL
Mather	MA*TH* ər
Mathias	mə THĪ əs
matin, M-	MAT ən
matinee	MAT ə NAY
Matisse	ma TEES
Mato Grosso	MAT ə GROH soh
matriarch	MAY tree AHRK
matricide	MAT rə sĪD
matrix	MAY triks
matronly	MAY trən lee
Matsas	MAHT sahs
Matsch, Franz	mahtch, frahns
Matsu	maht soo
Matsui, Robert	mat SOO ee
Matsunaga	mah tsoo nah gah
Matsuoka	mah tsoo oh kah
Matsushita	mah tsoo shee tah
Matterhorn	MAT ər HORN
mature	mə CHUUR
matzo	MAHT sə

o on, oh oat, oi boy, oo soon, oor poor, or for, ow cow, sh shush,
th thin, *th* this, u up, ur spur, uu book, *zh* pleasure

matzos	**MAHT** zəs
matzoth	**MAHT** soht
maudlin	**MAWD** lən
Maugham, Somerset	**MAWM, SUM** ər **SET**
Maui	**MOW** ee (**MOW** as in *cow*)
Mau Mau	mow mow (as in *cow*)
Maumee	maw **MEE**
Mauna Kea	**MOW** nah **KAY** ah (**MOW** as in *cow*)
Mauna Loa	**MOW** nah **LOH** ah (**MOW** as in *cow*)
maunder	**MAWN** dər
Maundy	**MAWN** dee
Maupassant	**MOH** pə **SAHN** (**SAHN** French final *n*)
Mauriac	mawr **YAHK**
Maurice	**MOR** əs
Maurice (French)	moh **REES**
Mauritania, Mauretania	**MOR** ə **TAY** nee ə
Mauritius	maw **RISH** əs
Maurois	mohr **WAH**
Mauroy, Pierre	mohr **WAH, PYAIR**
Mauser, m-	**MOW** zər (**MOW** as in *cow*)
mausoleum, M-	**MAW** sə **LEE** əm
mauve	mohv
maven	**MAY** vən
maverick	**MAV** ə rik
mavis, M-	**MAY** vəs
mavourneen	mə **VUUR** neen
maxim, M-	**MAK** səm
Maxim (French)	mak **SEEM**
Maxime	mak **SEEM**
Maximilian	**MAK** sə **MIL** yən
Maya	**MAH** yə
Mayaguez	**MAH** yah **GWES**
Mayakovsky, Vladimir	**MĪ** ah **KUV** skee, **VLAH** də meer
Mayan	**MAH** yən
Mayer, Maria Goeppert	**MĪ** ər, mah **REE** ə **GEP** ərt
Mayo	**MAY** oh
Mayon	mah **YAWN**
mayonnaise	**MAY** ə **NAYZ**
mayoralty	**MAY** ər əl tee
Mayotte	mah **YAHT**
Mazarin	**MAZ** ə rin

ə ago, a at, ah calm, ahr dark, air care, aw saw, ay say, ch church
e bet, ee me, eer beer, hw what, i is, ī my, *n* French final n vin,

Mazatlán	MAH saht LAHN
Mazda, m-	MAZ də
mazel tov	MAH zəl TAWF
mazer	MAY zər
Mazowiecki, Tadeusz	mah zoh VYET skee, tah DAY uush
mazurka	mə ZUUR kə
Mazzini	maht TSEE nee
M'Ba, Leon	əm BAH, lee AHN
Mbabane	EM bə BAHN
Mbaye, Kéba	əm BAH ee, KEE bah
Mbogua, John	əm BOH gwah (gwah g barely pronounced)
Mboya	əm BOI ə
mea culpa	MAY ə KUUL pə
mead, M-	meed
meager	MEE gər
meander, M-	mee AN dər
meatus	mee AY təs
Mébiame, Léon	mə bee AHM, lay AWN (AWN French final n)
Mecca, m-	MEK ə
mechanize	MEK ə NĪZ
Mechlin	MEK lin
Mecklenburg, Mecklenberg	MEK lən BURG
Medaglia d'Oro	mə DAL yə DOR oh
medallion	mə DAL yən
Mede	meed
Medea	mə DEE ə
Medellín	me de YEEN
media, M-	MEE dee ə
median, M-	MEE dee ən
mediant	MEE dee ənt
mediate (a)	MEE dee ət
mediate (v)	MEE dee AYT
medicament	mi DIK ə mənt
Medici	MED ə chee
medicinal	mə DIS ə nəl
medicine	MED ə sən
medico	MED i KOH
medieval	MEE dee EE vəl
Medina (Saudi Arabia)	mə DEE nə
Medina (US)	mə DĪ nə

o on, oh oat, oi boy, oo soon, oor poor, or for, ow cow, sh shush,
th thin, th this, u up, ur spur, uu book, zh pleasure

mediocre	MEE dee OH kər
mediocrity	MEE dee OK rə tee
Mediterranean	MED ə tə RAY nee ən
medley	MED lee
Médoc	may DAHK
medulla	mə DUL ə
medullary	MED ə LER ee
Medusa, m-	mə DOO sə
Meehan	MEE ən
meerschaum	MEER shəm
Mefitus	mə FĪ tis
megabyte	MEG ə BĪT
megacycle	MEG ə sī kəl
Megaera	mə JEER ə
megahertz	MEG ə HURTS
megalomania	MEG ə loh MAY nee ə
megalopolis	MEG ə LOP ə ləs
Meganthropus	mə GAN thrə pəs
megaton	MEG ə TUN
Megiddo	mə GID oh
megillah	mə GIL ə
megohm	MEG ohm
megrim	MEE grəm
Meguid, Ahmed Esmat Abdel	MAY good, AH med ES maht AHB del (good as in *food*)
Mehta, Ved	MEH tə, VED
Meiji	may jee
Mein Kampf	mīn KAHMPF
meiosis	mī OH səs
Meir, Golda	ME eer, GOHL də
Meissen	MĪ sən
Meistersinger	MĪ stər ZING ər
Meitner, Lise	MĪT nər, LEE zə
Mejias, Roman	mə HEE əs, roh MAHN
Mejia Victores, Oscar	may HEE ə VIK tor es, AWS kər
Méjico	ME hee koh
Meklong	may klawng (klawng *g* barely pronounced)
Meknès	mek NES
Mekong	may kawng (kawng *g* barely pronounced)
melancholia	MEL ən KOH lee ə
melancholy	MEL ən KOL ee

ə ago, a at, ah calm, ahr dark, air care, aw saw, ay say, ch church
e bet, ee me, eer beer, hw what, i is, ī my, *n* French final n vin,

Melanchthon, Melancthon	mə LANGK thən
Melanesia	MEL ə NEE zhə
mélange	may LAHNZH
Melba	MEL bə
Melbourne	MEL bərn
Melchers	MEL chərz
Melchizedek, Melchisedec	mel KIZ ə DEK
Meleager	MEL ee AY jər
melee	MAY lay
Melilla	mə LEE yə
meliorate	MEEL yə RAYT
mellifluous	mə LIF loo əs
Mellon	MEL ən
Melnik (Czechoslovakia)	MYEL neek
melodeon	mə LOH dee ən
melodrama	MEL ə DRAH mə
Melos	MEE los
Melpomene	mel POM ə nee
Melville	MEL vil
membrane	MEM brayn
membranous	MEM brə nəs
Memel	MAY məl
memento	mə MEN toh
memento mori	mə MEN toh MOR ī
Memnon	MEM non
memoir	MEM wahr
memorabilia	MEM ə rə BIL ee ə
memorable	MEM ər ə bəl
Memphis	MEM fəs
memsahib	MEM sah ib
ménage	may NAHZH
ménage à trois	may NAHZH a TRWAH
menagerie	mə NAJ ə ree
Menam	me NAHM
Menander	mə NAN dər
menarche	mə NAHR kee
Mencius	MEN shee əs
Mencken	MENG kən
mendacious	men DAY shəs
mendacity	men DAS ə tee

o on, oh oat, oi boy, oo soon, oor poor, or for, ow cow, sh shush,
th thin, *th* this, u up, ur spur, uu book, *zh* pleasure

Mendeleev	MEN də LAY əf
mendelevium	MEN də LEE vee əm
Mendelian	men DEE lee ən
Mendelssohn	MEN dəl sən
Menderes	MEN de RES
mendicant	MEN də kənt
Mendocino	MEN də SEE noh
Menelaus	MEN ə LAY əs
Menelik	MEN ə lik
menhaden	men HAY dən
menhir	MEN hir
menial	MEE nee əl
meninges	mə NIN jeez
meningitis	MEN in JĪ təs
meninx	MEN ingks
meniscus	mə NIS kəs
Menninger	MEN ing ər
Mennonite	MEN ə NĪT
Menomoñee	mə NOM ə nee
Menomonie	mə NOM ə nee
Menotti, Gian-Carlo	mə NOT ee, jahn KAHR loh
menses	MEN seez
menshevik, M-	MEN shə vik
Menshikov, Mikhail	MEN shi kuf, mi KĪL
menstrual	MEN stroo əl
menstruation	MEN stroo AY shən
mensuration	MEN sə RAY shən
menthol	MEN thawl
mentor	MEN tər
menu	MEN yoo
Menuhin, Yehudi	MEN yoo ən, yə HOO dee
Menzies	MEN zeez
Mephisto	mə FIS toh
Mephistopheles	MEF ə STOF ə LEEZ
mephitic	mə FIT ik
mephitis	mə FĪ təs
mercantile	MUR kən TEEL
mercaptan	mər KAP tan
Mercator	mər KAY tər
mercenary	MUR sə NER ee
mercer, M-	MUR sər
merci	mair SEE
Mercian	MUR shee ən

ə ago, a at, ah calm, ahr dark, air care, aw saw, ay say, ch church
e bet, ee me, eer beer, hw what, i is, ī my, n French final n vin,

Mercier (French)	mair **SYAY**
Mercouri, Melina	mer **KOO** ree, mə **LEE** nə
mercurial	mər **KYUUR** ee əl
mercury, M-	**MUR** kyə ree
Mercutio	mər **KYOO** shee oh
merengue	mə **RENG** gay
meretricious	**MER** ə **TRISH** əs
Mérida	**ME** ree dah
meridian	mə **RID** ee ən
Mérimée	may ree **MAY**
meringue	mə **RANG**
merino	mə **REE** noh
mermaid	**MUR** mayd
Merovingian	**MER** ə **VIN** jee ən
Merrimac, -k	**MER** ə **MAK**
merry	**MER** ee
Mersey	**MUR** zee
mesa, M-	**MAY** sə
Mesabi	mə **SAHB** ee
mescal	mes **KAL**
mescaline	**MES** kə **LEEN**
mesdames	may **DAHM**
mesenteric	**MEZ** ən **TER** ik
Meshach	**MEE** shak
Meshed	mə **SHED**
meshuga	mə **SHUUG** ə
mesial	**MEE** zee əl
Mesmer	**MEZ** mər
mesmerize	**MEZ** mə **RĪZ**
mesne	meen
mesomorph	**MEZ** ə **MORF**
meson (elementary particle)	**MEE** zon
Mesopotamia	**MES** ə pə **TAY** mee ə
mesothelium	**MEZ** ə **THEE** lee əm
mesotron	**MEZ** ə **TRON**
Mesozoic	**MES** ə **ZOH** ik
mesquite	me **SKEET**
Messalina	**MES** ə **LĬ** nə
messaline	**MES** ə **LEEN**
Messiah, m-	mə **SĪ** ə
messieurs	may **SYUU**
Messina	mə **SEE** nə

---

o **on**, oh **oat**, oi **boy**, oo **soon**, oor **poor**, or **for**, ow **cow**, sh **shush**,
th **thin**, *th* **this**, u **up**, ur **spur**, uu **book**, *zh* **pleasure**

Messrs.	**MES** ərz
mestiza	me **STEE** zə
mestizo	me **STEE** zoh
Meštrović	**MESH** traw **VICH**
metabolism	mə **TAB** ə **LIZ** əm
metallic	mə **TAL** ik
metallurgy	**MET** ə **LUR** jee
metamorphoses	**MET** ə **MOR** fə **SEEZ**
metamorphosis	**MET** ə **MOR** fə səs
metaphor	**MET** ə **FOR**
metaphorical	**MET** ə **FOR** i kəl
metaphysical	**MET** ə **FIZ** i kəl
metaphysics	**MET** ə **FIZ** iks
metastases	mə **TAS** tə seez
metastasis	mə **TAS** tə səs
metatarsal	**MET** ə **TAHR** səl
metathesis	mə **TATH** ə səs
Metaxas	mə **TAK** səs
metempsychosis	**MET** əm sī **KOH** səs
meteor	**MEE** tee ər
meteorite	**MEE** tee ə **RĪT**
meteorology	**MEE** tee ə **ROL** ə jee
methane	**METH** ayn
Methodist	**METH** ə dəst
Methuen	mə **THYOO** ən
Methuselah	mə **THOO** zə lə
methyl	**METH** əl
meticulous	mə **TIK** yə ləs
métier	may **TYAY**
métis	may **TEE**
métisse	may **TEES**
metonymy	mə **TON** ə mee
metronome	**MET** rə **NOHM**
metropolis	mə **TROP** ə ləs
metropolitan	**MET** rə **POL** ə tən
Metternich	**MET** ər nik
Metuchen	mə **TUCH** ən
Metz	mets
Metzenbaum, Howard	**METS** ən **BOWM** (**BOWM** as in *cow*)
meunière	mun **YAIR**
Meursault	mur **SOH**
Meuse	muuz
Mexico	**MEK** sə **KOH**

ə ago, a at, ah calm, ahr dark, air care, aw saw, ay say, ch church
e bet, ee me, eer beer, hw what, i is, ī my, *n* French final n vin,

Meyerbeer	**MĪ** ər **BEER**
mezuza	mə **ZUUZ** ə
mezzanine	**MEZ** ə **NEEN**
mezzo	**MET** soh
mezzotint	**MET** soh **TINT**
mho	moh
Miami	mī **AM** ee
miasma	mī **AZ** mə
mica	**MĪ** kə
Micah	**MĪ** kə
Micajah	mī **KAY** yə
Micawber	mi **KAW** bər
Michaux	mee **SHOH**
Michel, Robert	**MĪK** əl
Michelangelo	**MĪ** kəl **AN** jə **LOH**
Michener, James	**MICH** nər
Michigan	**MISH** ə gən
Michiko	**MI** chi koh
microbe	**MĪ** krohb
microcephalic	**MĪ** kroh sə **FAL** ik
microcosm	**MĪ** krə **KOZ** əm
microfiche	**MĪ** krə **FEESH**
micrography	mī **KROG** rə fee
micrometer	mī **KROM** ə tər
Micronesia	**MĪ** krə **NEE** zhə
microscope	**MĪ** krə **SKOHP**
microscopy	mī **KROS** kə pee
microwave	**MĪ** kroh **WAYV**
micturate	**MIK** chə **RAYT**
Midas	**MĪ** dəs
Middlebury	**MID** əl **BER** ee
Midi	mee **DEE**
Midianite	**MID** ee ə **NĪT**
Midlothian	mid **LOH** *th*ee ən
midwifery	**MID** **WĪF** ree
mien	meen
Mies van der Rohe	**MEES VAHN** də **ROH**
Mifune, Toshiro	mee fuu ne, toh shee roh
mignon	meen **YAWN** (**YAWN** French final *n*)
mignonette	**MIN** yə **NET**
migraine	**MĪ** grayn
migrant	**MĪ** grənt
migratory	**MĪ** grə **TOR** ee

o on, oh oat, oi boy, oo soon, oor poor, or for, ow cow, sh shush,
th thin, *th* this, u up, ur spur, uu book, *zh* pleasure

Miguel	mee GEL
mikado, M-	mi KAH doh
Miki, Takeo	mee kee, tah kay oh
mikvah	MIK və
Milan	mi LAN
milanaise	mee lah NEZ
Milanese	MI lə NEEZ
Milano	mee LAH naw
Milanov, Zinka	MEE lah NAWF, ZING kah
milch	milch
Miletus	mī LEET əs
Milhaud, Darius	mee YOH, da RYUUS
milieu	meel YUU
militant	MIL i tənt
militia	mə LISH ə
Milla Bermudez	MEE lyah bair MOO dez
Millais	mi LAY
Millard	MIL ərd
Millay	mi LAY
millennium	mə LEN ee əm
millet	MIL ət
Millet, Jean François	mee YAY, ZHAHN frahn SWAH
	(ZHAHN and frahn French final n)
milliampere	MIL ee AM pir
Millikan	MIL ə kən
millimeter	MIL ə MEE tər
millimicron	MIL ə MĪ kron
millinery	MIL ə NER ee
Milne	miln
milo, M-	MĪ loh
Milo	MEE loh
Milosz	MEE lawsh
milquetoast, M-	MILK tohst
Miltiades	mil TĪ ə DEEZ
Miltonic	mil TON ik
Milwaukee	mil WAW kee
Mimas	MĪ məs
mime	mīm
mimeograph, M-	MIM ee ə GRAF
mimesis	mə MEE səs
mimetic	mə MET ik
mimic	MIM ik
mimicry	MIM ik ree

ə ago, a at, ah calm, ahr dark, air care, aw saw, ay say, ch church
e bet, ee me, eer beer, hw what, i is, ī my, n French final n vin,

Mimieux, Yvette	mee MYUU, ee VET
Mimir	MEE mir
mimosa	mə MOH sə
minaret	MIN ə RET
minatory	MIN ə TOR ee
Mindanao	MIN də NAH oh
Mindoro	min DOR oh
Mineola	MIN ee OH lə
mineralogy	MIN ə RAL ə jee
Minerva	mə NUR və
minestrone	MIN ə STROH nee
Mineta	mi NET ə
Ming	ming
miniature	MIN ee ə chər
minion	MIN yən
Minneapolis	MIN ee AP ə lis
minnesinger	MIN i SING ər
Minnesota	MIN ə SOH tə
Minoan	mə NOH ən
Minorca, m-	mə NOR kə
Minos	MĪ nəs
Minotaur	MIN ə TOR
Minow	MIN oh
Minsk	minsk
minuend	MIN yoo END
minuet	MIN yoo ET
Minuit	MIN yoo ət
minuscule	MIN ə SKYOOL
minute (a)	mī NOOT
minute (n, v)	MIN ət
minutia	mə NOO shee ə
minutiae	mə NOO shee EE
Miocene	MĪ ə SEEN
miotic	mī OT ik
Miquelon	meek ə LAWN (LAWN French final n)
Mirabeau	MIR ə BOH
mirabile dictu	mee RAH bi LE DIK too
Miraflores	MEE rah FLAW res
mirage	mə RAHZH
Miranda	mə RAN də
Miriam	MIR ee əm
Miró Cardona	mee ROH kahr DOH nə
Miró, Joan	mee ROH, zhuu AHN

---

o on, oh oat, oi boy, oo soon, oor poor, or for, ow cow, sh shush,
th thin, th this, u up, ur spur, uu book, zh pleasure

Mirvish	**MUR** vish
misalliance	MIS ə **LĪ** əns
misanthrope	MIS ən **THROHP**
miscegenation	mi **SEJ** ə **NAY** shən
miscellaneous	MIS ə **LAY** nee əs
miscellany	MIS ə **LAY** nee
mischief	**MIS** chəf
mischievous	**MIS** chə vəs
miscible	**MIS** ə bəl
miscreant	**MIS** kree ənt
misdemeanor	MIS də **MEE** nər
mise en scène	mee zahn **SEN** (zahn French final *n*)
Misérables, Les	mee zay **RAH** blə, lay
Miserere, m-	MIZ ə **RAIR** ee
misericord	mə **ZER** ə **KORD**
mishap	**MIS** hap
misnomer	mis **NOH** mər
misogamy	mə **SOG** ə mee
misogynist	mə **SOJ** ə nəst
misprision	mis **PRIZ***H* ən
missal	**MIS** əl
missile	**MIS** əl
missilery	**MIS** əl ree
Missouri	mə **ZUUR** i
mistletoe	**MIS** əl **TOH**
mistral	mi **STRAHL**
miter	**MĪ** tər
Mitford	**MIT** fərd
Mithridates	MITH rə **DAY** teez
mitigate	**MIT** ə **GAYT**
mitosis	mī **TOH** səs
Mitsubishi	mit soo **BISH** ee
Mitterrand, François	**MEET** rahn, frahn **SWAH** (rahn and frahn French final *n*)
mittimus	**MIT** ə məs
mitzvah	**MITS** və
Mizere, N. T.	mee **ZER** ee
Mizpah	**MIZ** pə
Mlada Boleslav	mə **LAH** dah **BAW** le slahf
Mladenov, Petar	**MLAH** den awf, **PE** tahr
Mmabatho	mah **BAH** toh
mnemonic	ni **MON** ik
Mnemosyne	ni **MOS** ə **NEE**

ə ago, a at, ah calm, ahr dark, air care, aw saw, ay say, ch church
e bet, ee me, eer beer, hw what, i is, ī my, *n* French final n vin,

moa	MOH ə
Moab	MOH ab
mobile (a)	MOH bəl
mobile (sculpture)	moh BEEL
Mobile	moh BEEL
mobilize	MOH bə LĪZ
Möbius	MOH bee əs
Mobutu Sese Seko	mə BOO too SAY say SAY koh
Mocha, m-	MOH kə
modal	MOHD əl
modem	MOH dem
Modena	MAWD ə nə
moderato	MOD ə RAH toh
modern	MOD ərn
modicum	MOD ə kəm
Modigliani	MAW dee LYAH nee
modiste	moh DEEST
Modred	MOH drid
Modrow, Hans	MO drawf, hahnz (MO as in *hot*)
modulate	MOJ ə LAYT
modulation	MOJ ə LAY shən
module	MOJ ool
modulus	MOJ ə ləs
modus operandi	MOH dəs OP ə RAN dee
modus vivendi	MOH dəs vi VEN dee
Mogadishu	MOG ə DISH oo
Mogen David	MAW gən DAW vəd
Mogul, m-	MOH gəl
Mohács	MOH hach
Mohamad, Mahathir	moh HAH məd, mah HAH teer
Mohammed	moh HAM əd
Mohammed Da'ud	moh HAM əd dah OOD
Mohammed Na'im	moh HAM əd nah EEM
Mohammed Zahir	moh HAM əd zah EER
Mohave	mə HAH vee
mohel	MOH əl
Mohican	moh HEE kən
Mohieddin, Ahmad Fuad	moh HEE din, AH mahd fwahd
Moho	MOH hoh
Moholy-Nagy	MOH hoi NOD yə
Mohorovičić	MOH hə ROH və chich
Mohs (scale)	mohz

---

o on, oh oat, oi boy, oo soon, oor poor, or for, ow cow, sh shush, th thin, *th* this, u up, ur spur, uu book, *zh* pleasure

Mohyeddin, Zia	moi YED in, TSEE ah
Moi, Daniel arap	MAW ee, DAN yəl AR əp
moiety	MOI ə tee
Moira	MOI rə
moire	mwahr
moiré	mwah RAY
Mojave	mə HAH vee
Moji	moh jee
molar	MOH lər
molasses	mə LAS əz
Moldau	MAWL dow
Moldavia	mol DAY vee ə
Molech	MOH lek
molecular	mə LEK yə lər
molecule	MOL ə KYOOL
molest	mə LEST
molestation	MOH le STAY shən
Molière	mohl YAIR
Molina	mə LEE nə
Moline	moh LEEN
mollify	MOL ə FĪ
mollusk	MOL əsk
Molnár, Ferenc	MOHL nahr, FE rənts
Moloch	MOH lok
Molokai	MOH loh KĪ
Molotov	MOL ə TAWF
Molucca	mə LUK ə
moly	MOH lee
molybdenum	mə LIB də nəm
Mombasa	mahm BAH sə
momentous	moh MEN təs
momentum	moh MEN təm
Momus	MOH məs
Monaco	MON ə KOH
monad	MOH nad
monadnock, M-	mə NAD NOK
Monaghan (Ireland)	MON ə gən
Monaghan (family name)	MON ə han
Mona Lisa	MOH nə LEE zə
monarchical	mə NAHR ki kəl
monaural	mon OR əl
Mondjo, Nicolas	MAWN joh, NIK oh LAH

ə ago, a at, ah calm, ahr dark, air care, aw saw, ay say, ch church
e bet, ee me, eer beer, hw what, i is, ī my, n French final n vin,

Mondrian, Piet	MAWN dree AHN, PEET
Monel	moh NEL
Monet, Claude	moh NAY, KLOHD
monetarism	MON ə tə RIZ əm
Monge, Luis Alberto	MAWNG hay, loo EES ahl BER toh
monger	MUNG gər
Mongol	MONG gəl
Mongolia	mong GOH lee ə
mongoloid, M-	MONG gə LOID
mongoose	MONG goos
mongrel	MUNG grəl
Monique	moh NEEK
monitor	MON ə tər
Monmouth	MON məth
Monnet	maw NAY
monocle	MON ə kəl
monocoque	MON ə KOK
Monod, Jacques	maw NOH, ZHAHK
monody	MON ə dee
monogamy	mə NOG ə mee
monogram	MON ə GRAM
monograph	MON ə GRAF
monogyny	mə NOJ ə nee
monolatry	mə NOL ə tree
monolith	MON ə lith
monologue	MON ə LAWG
monologuist	MON ə LAWG əst
monomania	MON ə MAY nee ə
monomial	mə NOH mee əl
Monongahela	mə NONG gə HEE lə
mononucleosis	MON oh NOO klee OH səs
monophonic	MON ə FON ik
Monophysite	mə NOF ə sIT
monoplane	MON ə PLAYN
monopoly	mə NOP ə lee
monosyllabic	MON ə sə LAB ik
monotheism	MON ə thee IZ əm
monotony	mə NOT ə nee
monotype	MON ə TIP
monovalent	MON ə VAY lənt
Monrovia	mən ROH vee ə
Monsarrat	MAHN sə RAHT

---

o on, oh oat, oi boy, oo soon, oor poor, or for, ow cow, sh shush,
th thin, *th* this, u up, ur spur, uu book, *zh* pleasure

Monseigneur, m-	**MOHN** sayn **YUR** (**MOHN** French final *n*)
Monsieur, m-	mə **SYUU**
Monsignor, m-	mon **SEEN** yər
Monson	**MUN** sən
monsoon	mon **SOON**
mons veneris	**MONZ VEN** ə rəs
montage	mohn **TAHZ***H*
Montagu, -e	**MON** tə **GYOO**
Montaigne	mohn **TEN** yə (mohn French final *n*)
Montale, Eugenio	mohn **TAH** lay, ay oo **JAYN** yoh
Montana	mon **TAN** ə
Montand, Yves	mohn **TAHN, EEV** (mohn and **TAHN** French final *n*)
Montauk	**MON** tawk
Mont Blanc	mohn **BLAHN** (mohn and **BLAHN** French final *n*)
Montcalm	mont **KAHM**
monte	**MON** tee
Monte Cassino	**MAWN** te kah **SEE** noh
Montego Bay	mon **TEE** goh
Montenegro	**MON** tə **NEE** groh
Monterey, Monterrey	**MON** tə **RAY**
Montespan	**MON** tə **SPAN**
Montesquieu	**MOHN** tə **SKYUU** (**MOHN** French final *n*)
Montessori	**MON** tə **SOH** ree
Monteverdi	**MAWN** tə **VAIR** dee
Montevideo	**MON** tə və **DAY** oh
Montezuma	**MON** tə **ZOO** mə
Montfort (English)	**MONT** fərt
Montfort (French)	mohn **FOR** (mohn French final *n*)
Montgomery	munt **GUM** ə ree
Monticello	**MON** tə **SEL** oh
Montmartre	mohn **MAHR** trə (mohn French final *n*)
Montpelier (Vermont)	mont **PEEL** yər
Montpellier (France)	mohn pe **LYAY** (mohn French final *n*)
Montreal	**MON** tree **AWL**
Montserrat	**MONT** sə **RAT**
Mont Tremblant	**MOHN** trahn **BLAHN** (all syllables French final *n*)
moped	**MOH** ped

ə ago, a at, ah calm, ahr dark, air care, aw saw, ay say, ch church
e bet, ee me, eer beer, hw what, i is, ī my, *n* French final n vin,

moraine	mə **RAYN**
moral	**MOR** əl
morale	mə **RAL**
Morales	maw **RAH** les
Morandi	maw **RAHN** dee
morass	mə **RAS**
Morava	**MAW** rah vah
Moravia	mə **RAY** vee ə
moray	**MOR** ay
morbidity	mor **BID** ə tee
mordant	**MOR** dənt
Mordecai	**MOR** də ᴋɪ̄
mordent	**MOR** dənt
Mordovian	mor **DOH** vee ən
Mordred	**MOR** drid
Morea	moh **REE** ə
Moreau	maw **ROH**
morel	mə **REL**
Morelos	mə **RAY** ləs
mores	**MOR** ayz
Moresby	**MORZ** bee
Morgan	**MOR** gən
morganatic	**MOR** gə **NAT** ik
Morgenthau	**MOR** gən **THAW**
Moriah	mə **RĪ** ə
Moriarty	maw ree **AHR** tee
moribund	**MOR** ə bənd
Moriches	mə **RICH** əz
Morinigo	maw **REE** nee gaw
Morisot, Berthe	maw ree **ZOH**, **BAIRT**
Mormon	**MOR** mən
Mornay	mor **NAY**
Morocco, m-	mə **ROK** oh
moron	**MOR** on
Moron	mə **RAWN**
morose	mə **ROHS**
morpheme	**MOR** feem
morphemic	mor **FEE** mik
Morpheus	**MOR** fee əs
morphine	**MOR** feen
morphology	mor **FOL** ə jee
morphosis	mor **FOH** səs
mortadella	**MOR** tə **DEL** ə

o on, oh oat, oi boy, oo soon, oor poor, or for, ow cow, sh shush,
th thin, *th* this, u up, ur spur, uu book, *zh* pleasure

mortgage	**MOR** gij
mortician	mor **TISH** ən
Mortimer	**MOR** tə mər
mortise	**MOR** təs
mortuary	**MOR** choo **ER** ee
mosaic, M-	moh **ZAY** ik
Moscoso	mohs **KOH** zoh
Moscow	**MOS** kow
Moselle	moh **ZEL**
Moshoeshoe	moh **SHOO** shoo
Moslem	**MOZ** ləm
Moson	**MAW** shawn
mosque	mosk
mosquito	mə **SKEET** oh
Moss	maws
Mossadegh	**MOH** sah **DEK**
Mössbauer	**MAWS** bow ər (bow as in *cow*)
Mosul	moh **SOOL**
motet	moh **TET**
Motherwell	**MU***TH* ər **WEL**
motif	moh **TEEF**
motile	**MOH** təl
motive	**MOH** tiv
motley	**MOT** lee
motorcycle	**MOH** tər **sī** kəl
moue	moo
moulin, M-	moo **LAN** (**LAN** French final *n*)
moulins, M-	moo **LAN** (**LAN** French final *n*)
Moulmein	muul **MAYN**
moult	mohlt
mountainous	**MOWN** tə nəs
mountebank	**MOWN** tə **BANGK** (**MOWN** as in *town*)
mouser	**MOW** zər (**MOW** as in *cow*)
Moushoutas, Constantine	moo **SHOO** tahs, **KON** stən teen
Moussa	**MOO** sah
mousse	moos
mousseline	moos **LEEN**
Moussorgsky	muu **SORG** skee
mouton	**MOO** ton
mow (cut)	moh
mow (grimace; stack)	mow (as in *cow*)

ə ago, a at, ah calm, ahr dark, air care, aw saw, ay say, ch church
e bet, ee me, eer beer, hw what, i is, ī my, *n* French final n vin,

Mowgli	MOW glee (MOW as in *cow*)
moxie	MOK see
Mozambique	MOH zəm BEEK
Mozart	MOHT sahrt
mozzarella	MAWT sə REL ə
Mphephu, Patrick	əm PAY poo
Mrs.	MIS əz
Msuya, Cleopa	əm SOO ye, klee OH pə
Mubarak, Hosni	muu BAHR ək, HOZ ni
mucilage	MYOO sə lij
mucilaginous	MYOO sə LAJ ə nəs
mucous, mucus	MYOO kəs
Mueller	MYOO lər
Muenster	MUN stər
muezzin	myoo EZ ən
mufti, M-	MUF tee
Mugabe, Robert	muu GAH bee
mugwump	MUG wump
Muir	myuur
Mukacevo	MOOK ə CHEV aw
Mukden	MUUK dən
mukluk	MUK luk
mulatto	mə LAT oh
mulct	mulkt
Muldoon, Robert	mul DOON
muliebrity	MYOO lee EB rə tee
mullah	MUL ə
mullein	MUL ən
Muller	MUL ər
Müller	MUUL ər
mullet	MUL ət
mulligan, M-	MUL i gən
mulligatawny	MUL i gə TAW nee
mullion	MUL yən
multifarious	MUL tə FA ree əs
multiparous	MUL TIP ə rəs
multiplicity	MUL tə PLIS ə tee
multitudinous	MUL tə TOO də nəs
multum in parvo	MUL təm in PAHR voh
Munch, Edvard	MUUNGK, ED vahrd
Münch	muunsh
Munchausen	MUN CHOW zən
Muncie	MUN see

---

o on, oh oat, oi boy, oo soon, oor poor, or for, ow cow, sh shush,
th thin, *th* this, u up, ur spur, uu book, *zh* pleasure

mundane	mun **DAYN**
Mundia, Nalumino	muun **DEE** yə, NAL oo **MEE** noh
Munich	**MYOO** nik
municipal	myuu **NIS** ə pəl
municipality	myuu NIS ə **PAL** ə tee
munificent	myuu **NIF** ə sənt
munition	myuu **NISH** ən
Muñiz, Carlos Manuel	moo **NEEZ**, **KAHR** lohs **MAHN** wel
Muñoz Ledo, Porfirio	moo **NYOHZ LAY** doh, por **FEE** ree oh
Muñoz Marín	moon **YAW** smah **REEN**
Munro	mən **ROH**
Münster (Germany)	**MIN** stər
Munster (Ireland)	**MUN** stər
muon	**MYOO** on
mural	**MYUUR** əl
Murasaki	MOO rah **SAH** kee
Murat (river)	moo **RAHT**
Murdoch, Rupert	**MUR** dok
Murfreesboro	**MUR** freez BUR ə
muriatic	MYUUR ee **AT** ik
Murillo	myuu **RIL** oh
Murman	muur **MAHN**
Murmansk	muur **MAHNSK**
murmur	**MUR** mər
murrain	**MUR** ən
Musa	**MOO** sah
Musca	**MUS** kə
muscadine	**MUS** kə **DĪN**
muscat, M-	**MUS** kat
muscatel	MUS kə **TEL**
muscle	**MUS** əl
Muscovite, m-	**MUS** kə **VĪT**
Muscovy	**MUS** kə vee
muscular dystrophy	**MUS** kyə lər **DIS** trə fee
muse, M-	myooz
musette	myuu **ZET**
museum	myuu **ZEE** əm
musicale	MYOO zi **KAL**
Musici, I	**MOO** zee chee, ee
muskeg	**MUS** keg
Muskegon	mə **SKEE** gən
muskellunge	**MUS** kə LUNJ

ə ago, a at, ah calm, ahr dark, air care, aw saw, ay say, ch church
e bet, ee me, eer beer, hw what, i is, ī my, *n* French final n vin,

Muskogee	mus **KOH** gee
muskrat	**MUSK** rat
Muslim	**MUUZ** ləm
muslin	**MUZ** lən
mussel	**MUS** əl
Musset	myoo **SAY**
Mussolini	**MOO** sə **LEE** nee
mustache	**MUS** tash
mustang	**MUS** tang
mutant	**MYOO** tənt
mutation	myoo **TAY** shən
mutineer	**MYOO** tə **NEER**
Mutsuhito	muu tsuu hee toh
mutual	**MYOO** choo əl
muu-muu	**MOO** moo
muzhik	moo **ZH**EEK
Muzorewa	**MUUZ** ə **RAY** wə
Mwambutsa, Mwami	mwahm **BOO** tsah, **MWAH** mee
Mweru	**MWAY** roo
myasthenia	**MĪ** əs **THEE** nee ə
Mycenae	mī **SEE** nee
mycosis	mī **KOH** səs
myelitis	**MĪ** ə **LĪ** təs
myelogram	**MĪ** ə lə **GRAM**
Myint, U Kyee	myint, oo kee
Mykonos	**MEE** kə **NAWS**
mynah	**MĪ** nə
Mynheer, m-	mīn **IIAIR**
myopia	mī **OH** pee ə
Myra	**MĪ** rə
Myrdal	**MIR** dahl
myriad	**MIR** ee əd
Myrmidon, m-	**MUR** mə **DON**
Myron	**MĪ** rən
myrrh	mur
Mysore	mī **SOR**
mysticism	**MIS** tə **SIZ** əm
mythical	**MITH** i kəl
Mytilene	**MIT** ə **LEE** nee

o on, oh oat, oi boy, oo soon, oor poor, or for, ow cow, sh shush,
th thin, *th* this, u up, ur spur, uu book, *zh* pleasure

N

Naaman	NAY ə mən
nabob	NAY bob
Nabokov	nə BAW kəf
Naboth	NAY bahth
nacelle	nə SEL
Na Champassak, Sisouk	nah shahm PAH sahk, see SOOK
Nacogdoches	NAK ə DOH chəz
nacre	NAY kər
nacreous	NAY kree əs
Nader	NAY dər
nadir	NAY dir
Naga	NAH gah
Nagasaki	NAH gə SAH kee
Nagoya	nah GAW yah
Nagy (Hungarian)	NOD yə
Nahant	nə HANT
Nahua	NAH wah
Nahuatl	NAH wah təl
Nahuatlan	nah WAHT lən
Nahum	NAY əm
naiad	NAY əd
naïf	nah EEF
Naipaul	NĪ pawl
Nairobi	nī ROH bee
naive	nah EEV
naiveté	nah EEV TAY
Najibullah	nah jee BUUL lah
Nakagawa, Ichiro	nah kah gah wah, ee chee roh
Nakasone, Yasuhiro	nah kah soh ne, yah suu hee roh
Nakhichevan	nah KEE chə VAHN
Nama	NAH mah
Namaqua	nah MAH kwə
Namibia	nə MIB ee ə
Nampula	nam POO lə
Nanda Devi	NUN dah DAY vee
Nanga Parbat	NUNG gah PUR bət
Nanjing	nahn jeeng
nankeen	nan KEEN

ə ago, a at, ah calm, ahr dark, air care, aw saw, ay say, ch church
e bet, ee me, eer beer, hw what, i is, ī my, n French final n vin,

Nanking	nan king
Nansen, Fridtjof	**NAHN** sən, **FREET** yawf
Nansen Sound	**NAN** sən
Nantes	nahnt
Nantucket	nan **TUK** ət
Naomi	nay **OH** mee
napalm	**NAY** pahm
nape	nayp
napery	**NAY** pə ree
Naphtali	**NAF** tə **LĪ**
naphtha	**NAF** thə
Napier	**NAY** pee ər
Naples	**NAY** pəlz
napoleon, N-	nə **POH** lee ən
Nara	nah rah
Narasimhan	nah rah sim **HAHN**
Narayan	na **RĪ** an
Narayanan, K. R.	nə **RĪ** ə nən
Narbonne	nahr **BUN**
narcissism	**NAHR** sə **SIZ** əm
narcissus, N-	nahr **SIS** əs
narcolepsy	**NAHR** kə **LEP** see
narcosis	nahr **KOH** səs
narcotic	nahr **KOT** ik
narcotize	**NAHR** kə **TĪZ**
Narragansett	**NAR** ə **GAN** sət
narrate	na **RAYT**
Narva	**NAHR** vah
Narvik	**NAHR** vik
narwhal	**NAHR** wəl
narwhale	**NAHR** hwayl
nascent	**NAY** sənt
Nashua	**NASH** oo ə
Nassau	**NA** saw
Nastase, Ilie	nah **STAHZ** ee, **EE** lee
nasturtium	nə **STUR** shəm
natal	**NAY** təl
Natal	nə **TAL**
natatorium	**NAY** tə **TOR** ee əm
Natchez	**NACH** əz
Natchitoches	**NAK** ə **TOSH**
nates	**NAY** teez
Nathan	**NAY** thən

o on, oh oat, oi boy, oo soon, oor poor, or for, ow cow, sh shush,
th thin, *th* this, u up, ur spur, uu book, *zh* pleasure

Natick	NAY tik
national	NASH ə nəl
nativity, N-	nə TIV ə tee
naturalization	NACH ə rə lə ZAY shən
naturally	NACH ə rə lee
Naugatuck	NAW gə TUK
naught	nawt
Nauru	nah OO roo
nausea	NAW zee ə
nauseate	NAW zee AYT
nauseous	NAW shəs
Nausicaä	naw SIK ee ə
nautch	nawch
nautical	NAW ti kəl
nautilus	NAW tə ləs
Navaho	NAV ə HOH
Navajo	NAV ə HOH
naval	NAY vəl
Navarra	nə VAH rə
Navarre	nə VAHR
navel	NAY vəl
Navon, Yitzhak	nah VAWN, YITS hahk
Navratilova, Martina	NAH vrə tə LOH və, mahr TEEN ə
nawab, N-	nə WAWB
Nawaz, S. Shah	nah WAHZ, shah hə
Naxos	NAH ksaws
Nazarene	NAZ ə REEN
Nazi	NAHT see
N'Djamena	ən JAH may nah
Neanderthal	nee AN dər THAWL
Neapolitan	NEE ə POL ə tən
Nebiim	NEB ee EEM
Nebo	NEE boh
Nebraska	nə BRAS kə
Nebuchadnezzar	NEB ə kəd NEZ ər
nebular	NEB yə lər
nebulous	NEB yə ləs
necessarily	NES ə SER ə lee
necessary	NES ə SER ee
necklace	NEK ləs
necrology	nə KROL ə jee
necromancer	NEK rə MAN sər
necrophilia	NEK rə FIL ee ə

ə ago, a at, ah calm, ahr dark, air care, aw saw, ay say, ch church
e bet, ee me, eer beer, hw what, i is, ī my, n French final n vin,

necropolis	nə KROP ə ləs
necrosis	nə KROH səs
necrotic	nə KROT ik
nectar	NEK tər
nectarine	NEK tə REEN
née	nay
Needham	NEED əm
Néel, Louis	nay EL, LWEE
ne'er-do-well	NAIR doo WEL
nefarious	ni FA ree əs
Nefertiti	NEF ər TEE tee
negate	ni GAYT
Negev	NEG ev
negligee	NEG lə ZHAY
negligence	NEG li jəns
negotiable	ni GOH shə bəl
negotiate	ni GOH shee AYT
negotiation	ni GOH shee AY shən
Negrillo	ni GRIL oh
Negri Sembilan	NAY gree SEM bee LAHN
Negrito	nə GREE toh
Negro	NEE groh
Negroponte, John	ne groh PON tee
Negro, Río	NAY groh, REE oh
Negros (island)	NAY grohs
negus, N-	NEE gəs
Nehemiah	NEE ə MĪ ə
Nehru	NAY roo
Neilson	NEEL sən
Neiman-Marcus	NEE mən MAHR kəs
Nei Monggol	NAY MON gohl
neither	NEE thər
Nejd	nejd
nematode	NEM ə TOHD
Nembutal	NEM byə TAWL
Nemea	NEE mee ə
nemesis, N-	NEM ə səs
Neocene	NEE ə SEEN
neolithic	NEE ə LITH ik
neologism	nee OL ə JIZ əm
neomycin	NEE oh MĪ sin
neophyte	NEE ə FĪT
neoprene	NEE ə PREEN

---

o on, oh oat, oi boy, oo soon, oor poor, or for, ow cow, sh shush,
th thin, th this, u up, ur spur, uu book, zh pleasure

Nepal	nə PAWL
Nepalese	NEP ə LEEZ
nepenthe	nə PEN thee
nephew	NEF yoo
nephritis	nə FRĪ təs
nephrosis	nə FROH səs
ne plus ultra	nay pluus UUL trah
nepotism	NEP ə TIZ əm
Neptune	NEP tyoon
Nereid	NIR ee əd
Nereus	NIR ee əs
Nero	NEER oh
Neruda	nay ROO *th*ah
Nesselrode, n-	NES əl ROHD
Nessus	NES əs
n'est-ce pas	nes PAH
nestle	NES əl
Nestor	NES tər
Nestorian	ne STOR ee ən
nether	NE*TH* ər
Netherlands	NE*TH* ər lənds
Neuchâtel	nuu shah TEL
Neufchâtel	nuu shah TEL
Neuilly	nuu YEE
neuralgia	nuu RAL jə
neurasthenia	NUUR əs THEE nee ə
neuritis	nuu RĪ təs
neuroses (pl)	nuu ROH seez
neurosis	nuu ROH səs
neurotic	nuu ROT ik
neutrino	noo TREE noh
neutron	NOO tron
Neva	NEE və
Nevada (state)	nə VAD ə
nevus	NEE vəs
Newark (Delaware)	NOO ahrk
Newark (New Jersey)	NOO ərk
Newcastle	NOO KAS əl
New Delhi	NOO DEL ee
Newfoundland	noo FOWND lənd
Ne Win	nay win
New Orleans	NOO OR lee ənz
New Rochelle	NOO roh SHEL

ə ago, a at, ah calm, ahr dark, air care, aw saw, ay say, ch church
e bet, ee me, eer beer, hw what, i is, ī my, *n* French final n vin,

Nez Percé	nez purs
Ngaio	NĪ oh
Ngarukiyintwali, François	GAHR oo KEE in WAHL ee, frahn SWAH (frahn French final *n*)
Ngonda, Putteho	ən GOHN dah, puu TAY hoh
Nguyen Van Lihn	nwin vahn ling
niacin	NĪ ə sən
Niagara	nī AG rə
Niamey	nee AHM ay
Nibelung	NEE bə LUUNG
Nibelungenlied	NEE bə LUUNG ən LEED
Nicaea	nī SEE ə
Nicaragua	NIK ə RAH gwə
Nice (France)	nees
Nicene	nī SEEN
nicety	NĪ sə tee
niche	nich
Nicobar	NIK ə BAHR
Nicodemus	NIK ə DEEM əs
Nicole	ni KOHL
Nicosia	NIK ə SEE ə
nicotine	NIK ə TEEN
nictitation	NIK tə TAY shən
nidus	NĪ dəs
Niebuhr	NEE buur
Nielsen, Sivert	NEEL sen, SEE vərt
Nietzsche	NEE chə
Nigel	NĪ jəl
Niger	NĪ jər
Nigeria	nī JIR ee ə
nightingale, N-	NĪT ən GAYL
nightshade	NĪT shayd
nihilism	NĪ ə LIZ əm
nihilist	NĪ ə ləst
Nihon	nee hawn
Niihau	NEE ee HAH oo
Nijinsky	nə JIN skee
Nijmegen	NĪ MAY gən
Nike	NĪ kee
Niksic	NEE shich
Nikula, Pentti	NI koo lah, PEN tee
Nile	nīl
Nilotic	nī LOT ik

o on, oh oat, oi boy, oo soon, oor poor, or for, ow cow, sh shush, th thin, *th* this, u up, ur spur, uu book, *zh* pleasure

Nilsson, Birgit	**NEEL** sohn, **BEER** git
nimbus	**NIM** bəs
Nimeiry, Gaafar Mohammed al-	nee **MER** ee, **GAF** ahr moh **HAHM** ed ahl
Nîmes	neem
Nineveh	**NIN** ə və
Ningxia Huizu	neeng shee ah hwee zuu
Niobe	**NĪ** ə **BEE**
niobium	nī **OH** bee əm
Nippon	**NIP** ahn
Nipponese	**NIP** ə **NEEZ**
nirvana	nir **VAH** nə
nisei, N-	nee say
Nishapur	**NEE** shah **PUUR**
nisi	**NĪ** sī
Nissen	**NIS** ən
niter	**NĪ** tər
nitric	**NĪ** trik
nitrogen	**NĪ** trə jən
nitrogenous	nī **TROJ** ə nəs
nitroglycerin	**NĪ** trə **GLIS** ə rən
nitrous	**NĪ** trəs
Niue	nee **OO** ay
Ni Zhifu	nee jee fuu
Nkrumah, Kwame	ən **KROO** mah, **KWAH** mee
Noah	**NOH** ə
Nobel	noh **BEL**
nobelium	noh **BEL** ee əm
noblesse oblige	noh **BLES** oh **BLEEZ***H*
nocturnal	nok **TUR** nəl
nocturne	**NOK** turn
nocuous	**NOK** yoo əs
nodal	**NOHD** əl
nodule	**NOJ** ool
Noel (personal name)	**NOH** əl
Noel, n- (Christmas)	noh **EL**
noesis	noh **EE** sis
noetic	noh **ET** ik
Nogales	noh **GAL** əs
Noguchi	noh **GOO** chee
noisome	**NOI** səm
nolens volens	**NOH** lenz **VOH** lenz
noli me tangere	**NOH** lee me **TAHNG** ge re

ə ago, a at, ah calm, ahr dark, air care, aw saw, ay say, ch church
e bet, ee me, eer beer, hw what, i is, ī my, *n* French final n vin,

nolle prosequi	NOL ee PROS ə KWĪ
nolo contendere	NOH loh kən TEN də ree
nol-pros	nol PROS
nomad	NOH mad
nomadic	noh MAD ik
nom de guerre	NOM də GAIR
nom de plume	NOM də PLOOM
Nome	nohm
nomenclature	NOH mən KLAY chər
nominal	NOM ə nəl
nomogram	NOH mə GRAM
nonchalance	NON shə LAHNS
nonchalant	NON shə LAHNT
noncombatant	non KOM bə tənt
non compos mentis	non KOM pəs MEN təs
nonconformist	NON kən FOR məst
nondescript	NON di SKRIPT
nonentity	non EN tə tee
nones	nohnz
nonpareil	NON pə REL
nonplus	non PLUS
non sequitur	non SEK wə tər
nook	nuuk
Norbert	NOR bərt
Nordaustlandet	noord OWST lahn det
Norfolk	NOR fək
Noriega, Manuel	NAW ree AY gah, mah noo EL
normalcy	NOR məl see
Norman	NOR mən
Norodom Sihanouk	noh roh DUM SEE ə NUUK
Norse	nors
Northumberland	nor THUM bər lənd
Norton	NOR tən
Norwalk	NOR wawk
Norwegian	nor WEE jən
Norwich (Connecticut)	NOR wich
Norwich (England)	NAHR ij
Nosavan, Phoumi	noh sah VAHN, POO mee
nosology	noh SOL ə jee
nostalgia	nah STAL jə
Nostradamus	NOS trə DAY məs
Nostrand	NOH strənd
nostril	NAHS trəl

o on, oh oat, oi boy, oo soon, oor poor, or for, ow cow, sh shush,
th thin, *th* this, u up, ur spur, uu book, *zh* pleasure

nostrum	NAHS trəm
nota bene	NOH tah BAY nay
noteworthy	NOHT wur *th*ee
notion	NOH shən
notoriety	NOH tə RĪ ə tee
Notre Dame (Paris)	NAW trə DAHM
Notre Dame (US)	NOH tər DAYM
Nottingham	NOT ing əm
Nouakchott	nuu AHK SHAHT
nougat	NOO gət
nought	nawt
Nouméa	noo MAY ə
noumenon	NOO mə NON
nourish	NUR ish
nouveau riche	NOO voh REESH
nouveaux riches	NOO voh REESH
nova, N-	NOH və
Nova Scotia	NOH və SKOH shə
Novaya Zemlya	NAW vah yah ZEM lyah
novel	NOV əl
novella	noh VEL ə
November	noh VEM bər
novena	noh VEE nə
Novgorod	NOV gə ROD
Novi	NOH vī
novice	NOV is
Novi Sad	NAW vee SAHD
novitiate	noh VISH ət
Novocain	NOH və KAYN
novocaine	NOH və KAYN
Novorossiisk	NAW vaw raw SEESK
Novosibirsk	NAW vaw si BIRSK
Novotna	nə VOT nə
Novotny, Antonin	nah VUT nee, ahn TOH neen
Nowak, Jerzy	NOH vahk, YER *zh*e
Nox	noks
noxious	NOK shəs
Noyes	noiz
nuance	NOO ahns
Nuba	NOO bə
Nubian	NOO bee ən
nubile	NOO bəl
nuclear	NOO klee ər

ə ago, a at, ah calm, ahr dark, air care, aw saw, ay say, ch church
e bet, ee me, eer beer, hw what, i is, ī my, n French final n vin,

nuclei (pl)	NOO klee ī
nucleic	noo KLEE ik
nucleon	NOO klee ON
nucleonics	NOO klee ON iks
nucleotide	NOO klee ə TĪD
nucleus	NOO klee əs
nude	nood
nudnik	NUUD nik
Nuevo León	NWAY voh lay OHN
nugatory	NOO gə TOR ee
nugget	NUG ət
nuisance	NOO səns
Nukualofa	NOO koo ə LAW fə
Nuku Hivā	NOO koo HEE və
null	nul
nullity	NUL ə tee
numeral	NOO mə rəl
Numidia	noo MID ee ə
numismatic	NOO məz MAT ik
numismatist	noo MIZ mə təst
nunc dimittis	NUNGK di MIT is
nuncio	NUUN see oh
Nuñez	NOO nyes
nuptial	NUP shəl
Nuremberg	NUUR əm BURG
Nureyev, Rudolph	nuu RAY yəf
Nurmi	NUUR mee
Nur, Mohamud Haji	NOOR, moo HAH mood HAH jee
nurture	NUR chər
Nuseibeh, Hazem	noo SAY i bə, HAZ im
nutation	noo TAY shən
nutrient	NOO tree ənt
nutriment	NOO trə mənt
nutrition	nuu TRISH ən
nux vomica	nuks VOM i kə
Nuyen, France	noo YEN, FRANS
Nyack	NĪ ak
Nyasa, Nyassa	nī AS ə
Nyerere	nyə RAIR ay
Nygaard, Hjalmar	NĪ gord, YAHL mahr
Nygaarsdvold	NĪ gawrs vawl
Nyiregyhaza	NYI rej HAH zaw
nymph	nimf

o on, oh oat, oi boy, oo soon, oor poor, or for, ow cow, sh shush,
th thin, *th* this, u up, ur spur, uu book, *zh* pleasure

nymphet	nim **FET**
nymphomania	**NIM** fə **MAY** nee ə
nystagmus	ni **STAG** məs
Nyx	niks

O

Oahu	ə **WAH** hoo
oases	oh **AY** seez
oasis	oh **AY** səs
Oates	ohts
oath	ohth
Oaxaca	wah **HAH** kah
Ob	ohb
Obadiah	**OH** bə **DĪ** ə
obbligato	**OB** lə **GAH** toh
obdurate	**OB** duu rət
obeah	**OH** bee ə
obeisance	oh **BEE** səns
obelisk	**OB** ə lisk
Oberammergau	**OH** bər **AH** mər **GOW**
Oberon	**OH** bə **RON**
obese	oh **BEES**
obesity	oh **BEE** sə tee
obfuscate	**OB** fə **SKAYT**
obi	**OH** bee
Obie	**OH** bee
obiit	**OH** bee **IT**
obit	**OH** bit
obiter dictum	**OHB** ə tər **DIK** təm
obituary	ə **BICH** oo **ER** ee
object (n)	**OB** jikt
object (v)	əb **JEKT**
objet d'art	aw *zh*ay **DAHR**
objet trouvé	aw *zh*ay troo **VAY**
objurgate	**OB** jər **GAYT**
oblation	ə **BLAY** shən
obligato	**OB** lə **GAH** toh
obligatory	ə **BLIG** ə **TOR** ee
oblige	ə **BLĪj**
oblique	ə **BLEEK**

ə ago, a at, ah calm, ahr dark, air care, aw saw, ay say, ch church
e bet, ee me, eer beer, hw what, i is, ī my, *n* French final n vin,

oblique (military)	ə BLĪK
obliquity	ə BLIK wə tee
obliterate	ə BLIT ə RAYT
oblivion	ə BLIV ee ən
oblivious	ə BLIV ee əs
oblong	OB lawng
obloquy	OB lə kwee
oboe	OH boh
Obote, Milton	aw BAW te
Obregón	OH bray GAWN
obscenity	əb SEN ə tee
obscurantism	əb SKYOOR ən TIZ əm
obsequies	OB sə kweez
obsequious	əb SEE kwee əs
obsequy	OB sə kwee
obsidian	əb SID ee ən
obsolescent	OB sə LES ənt
obsolete	OB sə LEET
obstacle	OB stə kəl
obstetric	əb STET rik
obstetrician	OB stə TRISH ən
obstinate	OB stə nət
obstreperous	əb STREP ə rəs
obtrusive	əb TROO siv
obtuse	əb TOOS
obverse	OB vurs
obviate	OB vee AYT
ocarina	OK ə REE nə
O'Casey, Sean	oh KAY see, SHAWN
Occam	OK əm
occasion	ə KAY zhən
occident, O-	OK sə dənt
occipital	ok SIP ə təl
occult	ə KULT
occultation	OK əl TAY shən
Oceania	OH shee AN ee ə
oceanographer	OH shə NOG rə fər
Oceanus	oh SEE ə nəs
ocher	OH kər
Ochoa, Severo	oh CHOH ə, sə VAIR oh
Ockham	OK əm
octagon	OK tə GON
octagonal	ok TAG ə nəl

o on, oh oat, oi boy, oo soon, oor poor, or for, ow cow, sh shush,
th thin, *th* this, u up, ur spur, uu book, *zh* pleasure

octahedron	OK tə HEE drən
octameter	ok TAM ə tər
octane	OK tayn
Octans	OK tanz
octant	OK tənt
octave	OK tiv
Octavia	ok TAY vee ə
Octavius	ok TAY vee əs
octavo	ok TAY voh
octet	ok TET
octogenarian	OK tə jə NAIR ee ən
octopus	OK tə pəs
ocular	OK yə lər
oculist	OK yə ləst
odalisque	OHD ə lisk
Oda, Shigeru	oh dah, shee ge roo
Odegard	OH də gahrd
Oder	OH dər
Odessa	oh DES ə
odeum	oh DEE əm
Odin	OH din
odious	OH dee əs
odium	OH dee əm
Odoacer	OH doh AY sər
odoriferous	OH də RIF ər əs
odorous	OH dər əs
Odysseus	oh DIS ee əs
Odyssey	OD ə see
Oedipal, o-	ED ə pəl
Oedipus	ED ə pəs
oenology	ee NOL ə jee
Oenone	ee NOH nee
oenophile	EE nə fil
oersted	UR stəd
oeuvre	UUV rə
O'Faoláin, Seán	oh FAL ən, SHAWN
Offenbach	AW fən BAHK
official	ə FISH əl
officious	ə FISH əs
O'Flaherty, Liam	oh FLA ər tee, LEE əm
often	AW fən
Ogbomosho	OG bə MOH shoh
ogee	OH jee

ə ago, a at, ah calm, ahr dark, air care, aw saw, ay say, ch church
e bet, ee me, eer beer, hw what, i is, ī my, n French final n vin,

ogham	OG əm
Ogilvie	OH gəl vee
ogive	OH jīv
Oglala	oh GLAH lə
ogle	OH gəl
Oglethorpe	OH gəl THORP
ogre	OH gər
Ohira, Masayoshi	oh hee rah, mah sah yoh shee
ohm, O-	ohm
Oireachtas	AIR ək thəs
Oise	wahz
Oistrakh	OI strahk
Ojibwa	oh JIB way
okapi	oh KAH pee
Okawara, Yoshio	oh kah wah rah, yoh shee oh
Okazaki, Katsuo	oh kah zah kee, kaht soo oh
Okeechobee	OH kə CHOH bee
Okhotsk	oh KOTSK
Okinawa	OH kə NAH wə
Oklahoma	OH klə HOH mə
okra	OH krə
Olav	OH lahf
Oldham	OHL dəm
Olduvai	AWL duu VĪ
oleaginous	OH lee AJ ə nəs
oleander	OH lee AN dər
olefin	OH lə fən
oleo	OH lee oh
oleomargarine	OH lee oh MAHR jə rən
olfactory	ahl FAK tə ree
oligarchy	AHL ə GAHR kee
Oligocene	AHL ə goh SEEN
oligopoly	ahl ə GOP ə lee
olio	OH lee oh
Olivier	oh LIV ee AY
Ollenauer, Erich	AW lən ow ər, AIR ish
Olmedo	ohl MAY doh
Olympia	oh LIM pee ə
Omaha	OH mə HAH
O'Mahoney	oh MA ə nee
Oman	oh MAHN
Omar Khayyám	OH mahr kī YAHM
ombudsman	OM BUUDZ mən

---

o on, oh oat, oi boy, oo soon, oor poor, or for, ow cow, sh shush,
th thin, *th* this, u up, ur spur, uu book, *zh* pleasure

Omdurman	AHM dər MAN
omen	OH mən
omicron	OM ə KRON
ominous	OM ə nəs
omnibus	OM nə bəs
omnifarious	OM nə FA ree əs
omnipotent	om NIP ə tənt
omnipresent	OM nə PREZ ənt
omniscience	om NISH əns
omniscient	om NISH ənt
omnivorous	om NIV ə rəs
Omphale	OM fə LEE
Omsk	awmsk
Onan	OH nən
onanism	OH nə NIZ əm
Onassis	oh NAS əs
Ondias-Souna, Hubert	awn DEE ahs SOO nə, oo BAIR
Ondine	awn DEEN
Onega	oh NEE gə
Onegin	oh NAY gin
Oneida	oh NĪ də
Oneonta	OH nee ON tə
onerous	ON ə rəs
Ong Yoke Lin, Dató	ohng yoh KAY leen, dah TOH
onomatopoeia	ON ə MAT ə PEE ə
Onondaga	ON ən DAH gə
Onsager, Lars	OON sah gər, lahrs
Ontario	on TAIR ee OH
ontogenesis	ON tə JEN ə sis
ontogeny	on TOJ ə nee
ontological	ON tə LOJ ə kəl
ontology	on TOL ə jee
onus	OH nəs
onyx	ON iks
oolite	OH ə LĪT
oolitic	OH ə LIT ik
oolong	OO lawng
opacity	oh PAS ə tee
opal	OH pəl
opaque	oh PAYK
opera	OP ər ə
Opéra	oh pay RAH
opéra bouffe	OP ər ə BOOF

ə ago, a at, ah calm, ahr dark, air care, aw saw, ay say, ch church
e bet, ee me, eer beer, hw what, i is, ī my, *n* French final n vin,

opera buffa	OP ər ə BOO fə
operative (a)	OP ə rə tiv
operative (n)	OP ə RAY tiv
operculum	oh PUR kyə ləm
operetta	OP ə RET ə
Ophelia	oh FEEL yə
Ophir	OH fər
Ophiuchus	AH fi YOO kəs
ophthalmologist	AHF thal MOL ə jəst
opiate (a, n)	OH pee ət
opine	oh PĪN
opium	OH pee əm
Oporto	oh POR toh
opossum	ə POS əm
opportune	OP ər TOON
opportunism	OP ər TOO NIZ əm
opportunity	OP ər TOO nə tee
oppressor	ə PRES ər
opprobrious	ə PROH bree əs
opprobrium	ə PROH bree əm
optician	op TISH ən
optimism	OP tə MIZ əm
optimum	OP tə məm
option	OP shən
optometrist	op TOM ə trəst
optometry	op TOM ə tree
opulent	OP yə lənt
opuntia	oh PUN shə
opus	OH pəs
oracular	aw RAK yə lər
Oradea	aw RAH dyah
oral, O-	OH rəl
orangutan	ə RANG ə TAN
orator	OR ə tər
oratorio	OR ə TOR ee OH
oratory	OR ə TOR ee
orbital	OR bə təl
orchestra	OR kə strə
orchestral	or KES trəl
orchid	OR kəd
orchidaceous	OR kə DAY shəs
ordeal	or DEEL
ordinal	OR də nəl

o on, oh oat, oi boy, oo soon, oor poor, or for, ow cow, sh shush,
th thin, *th* this, u up, ur spur, uu book, *zh* pleasure

ordinance	OR də nəns
ordinarily	OR də NER ə lee
ordinary	OR də NER ee
ordinate	OR də nət
ordnance	ORD nəns
Ordoñez, Antonio	awr DOHN yez, ahn TOH nee oh
Ordovician	OR də VISH ən
ordure	OR jər
Ordzhonikidze	or jaw ni KEED ze
oread	OR ee AD
orectic	oh REK tik
oregano	ə REG ə NOH
Oregon	OR ə gən
Oregonian	OR ə GOH nee ən
Orel	oh REL
Oreopithicus	OR ee oh PITH ə kəs
Orestes	ə RES teez
organdy, organdie	OR gən dee
orgiastic	OR jee AS tik
orgy	OR jee
oriel	OR ee əl
orient, O- (a, n)	OR ee ənt
orient (v)	OR ee ENT
oriental, O-	OR ee EN təl
orientation	OR ee ən TAY shən
Oriente	OR ee EN te
orifice	OR ə fəs
oriflamme	OR ə FLAM
origami	OR ə GAH mee
origan	OR ə gən
Origen	OR ə jən
origin	OR ə jən
Orinoco	OR ə NOH koh
oriole	OR ee OHL
Orion	ə RĪ ən
Oriskany	oh RIS kə nee
orison	OR ə zən
Orissa	oh RIS ə
Orizaba	OR ee ZAH bah
Orkney	ORK nee
Orlando	or LAN doh
Orleans	OR lee ənz
Orléans	or lay AHN (AHN French final *n*)

ə ago, a at, ah calm, ahr dark, air care, aw saw, ay say, ch church
e bet, ee me, eer beer, hw what, i is, ī my, *n* French final n vin,

Orlich	or LEECH
Orlon	OR lon
Orly	or LEE
Ormazd	OR məzd
ormolu	OR mə LOO
Ormuz	OR məz
Ormsby-Gore	ORMZ bee gawr
ornithology	OR nə THOL ə jee
ornithorhynchus	OR nə thə RING kəs
orography	aw ROG rə fee
orology	aw ROL ə jee
Orosius	aw ROH zhee əs
orotund	OR ə TUND
Orozco	aw RAW skaw
Orpen	OR pən
orphan	OR fən
Orpheus	OR fee əs
orris, orrice	OR əs
Ortega Saavedra, Daniel	or TAY gah sah VAYD rah
Ortega y Gasset, José	or TAY gə EE gah SET, haw SE
orthicon	OR thi KON
orthoclase	OR thə KLAYS
orthodontia	OR thə DON shə
orthodox	OR thə DOKS
orthodoxy	OR thə DOK see
orthoepist	or THOH ə pəst
orthoepy	or THOH ə pee
orthographic	OR thə GRAF ik
orthography	or THOG rə fee
orthopedic	OR thə PEE dik
Ortiz, Carlos	awr TEES, KAHR lohs
Orvieto	or VYAY toh
Osage	oh SAYJ
Osaka	oh SAH kə
Osborn, -e	OZ bərn
Oscan	OS kən
Osceola	os ee OH lə
oscillate	OS ə LAYT
oscilloscope	ə SIL ə SKOHP
Osco-Umbrian	OS koh UM bree ən
osculate	OS kyə LAYT
Oshkosh	OSH kosh

o on, oh oat, oi boy, oo soon, oor poor, or for, ow cow, sh shush,
th thin, *th* this, u up, ur spur, uu book, *zh* pleasure

osier	OH *zh*ər
Osijek	AW see YEK
Osiris	oh SĪ rəs
Oslo	OZ loh
Osman, Aden Abdulla	OHS mən, AH dən ahb DOO lə
osmosis	oz MOH səs
Osnaburg	OZ nə BURG
Ospina	aw SPEE nah
osprey	OS pree
Ossa	OS ə
Ossetia	ah SEE shə
Ossian	OSH ən
Ossietzky	os ee ET skee
ossify	OS ə FĪ
Ossining	OS ə ning
Ostend	ah STEND
ostensible	ə STEN sə bəl
ostentatious	os ten TAY shəs
osteopath	OS tee ə PATH
osteopathy	os tee OP ə thee
Ostia	OS tee ə
ostler	OS lər
Ostmark	AWST mahrk
ostracize	OS trə SĪZ
Ostrava	AW strah vah
Ostrogoth	OS trə GOTH
Ostrowiec	aw STRAW vyets
Ostwald	OHST vahlt
Ostyak, Ostiak	OS tee AK
Oswego	ah SWEE goh
Oswiecim	awsh VYANT sim
otalgia	oh TAL jee ə
Othello	ə THEL oh
otiose	OH shee OHS
otitis	oh TĪ təs
otology	oh TOL ə jee
Otranto	oh TRAHN toh
Otsego	aht SEE goh
ottava rima	oh TAH və REE mə
Ottawa	OT ə wə
Ottoman	OT ə mən
Otunnu, Olara	aw TOO noo, aw LAR rah
Ouachita	WOSH i TAW
Ouagadougou	WAH gə DOO goo

ə ago, a at, ah calm, ahr dark, air care, aw saw, ay say, ch church
e bet, ee me, eer beer, hw what, i is, ī my, *n* French final n vin,

oubliette	oo blee **ET**
Oueddei, Goukouni	**WAH** dee, goo **KOO** nee
Ouedraogo, Jean-Baptiste	**WED** drah oh **GOH**, *zh*ahn bah **TEEST** (*zh*ahn French final *n*)
ought	awt
Ouida	**WEE** də
Ouija	**WEE** jə
Oulu	**OH** loo
Oumarou, Idé	oo mah **ROO**, **EE** day
outré	oo **TRAY**
ouzel, ousel	**OO** zəl
ouzo	**OO** zoh
ovarian	oh **VA** ree ən
ovary	**OH** və ree
overt	oh **VURT**
overthrow (v)	**OH** vər **THROH**
overthrow (n)	**OH** vər **THROH**
overture	**OH** vər chər
overwrought	**OH** vər **RAWT**
Ovid	**OV** əd
Oviedo	aw **VYE** *th*aw
oviparous	oh **VIP** ə rəs
ovoid	**OH** void
ovulate	**OV** yə **LAYT**
ovule	**OH** vyool
ovum	**OH** vəm
oxalic	ok **SAL** ik
Oxford	**OKS** fərd
oxidant	**OK** sə dənt
oxidation	**OK** sə **DAY** shən
oxidize	**OK** sə **DĪZ**
Oxnard	**OKS** nahrd
Oxonian	ok **SOH** nee ən
oxyacetylene	**OK** see ə **SET** ə **LEEN**
oxymoron	**OK** si **MOH** ron
Oyono, Ferdinand Léopold	oh **YOH** noh, **FUR** di **NAND** **LEE** oh pohld
Ozark	**OH** zahrk
Ozawa, Seiji	oh **ZAH** wə, **SAY** jee
ozone	**OH** zohn
Ozores Typaldos, Carlos	**OH** soh res tee **PAHL** dohs, **KAHR** lohs

---

o on, oh oat, oi boy, oo soon, oor poor, or for, ow cow, sh shush,
th thin, *th* this, u up, ur spur, uu book, *zh* pleasure

P

pabulum	**PAB** yə ləm
Pacelli	pah **CHE** lee
Pachachi, Adnan	pə **SHAH** shee, ahd **NAHN**
pachisi	pə **CHEE** zee
pachyderm	**PAK** i ᴅᴜʀᴍ
pacification	ᴘᴀs ə fə **KAY** shən
pacifism	**PAS** ə ꜰɪᴢ əm
pacify	**PAS** ə ꜰɪ̄
Packard	**PAK** ərd
Padang	pah **DAHNG**
paddock	**PAD** ək
paddy, P-	**PAD** ee
Paderewski, Ignace Jan	ᴘᴀᴅ ə **REF** skee, ee **NYAS YAHN**
Padilla	pah **DEE** yah
padishah	**PAH** di ꜱʜᴀʜ
padre	**PAH** dray
padrone	pah **DROH** nay
Padua	**PAJ** oo ə
Paducah	pə **DOO** kə
paean	**PEE** ən
Paestum	**PES** təm
pagan	**PAY** gən
Paganini	ᴘᴀɢ ə **NEE** nee
pageant	**PAJ** ənt
Paget	**PAJ** ət
paginate	**PAJ** ə ɴᴀʏᴛ
Pagliacci	pah **LYAHT** chee
Pagliaroni	pa glee ə **ROH** nee
pagoda	pə **GOH** də
Pago Pago	**PAHNG** oh **PAHNG** oh
Pahang	pah **HAHNG**
Pahlavi, p-	**PAH** lə ᴠᴇᴇ
paillette	pī **YET**
paisley, P-	**PAYZ** lee
Paiute	**PĪ** yoot
Pakistan	**PAK** i ꜱᴛᴀɴ
Pakistani	ᴘᴀᴋ i **STAN** ee

ə ago, a at, ah calm, ahr dark, air care, aw saw, ay say, ch church
e bet, ee me, eer beer, hw what, i is, ī my, *n* French final n vin,

palabra	pah **LAH** brah
paladin	**PAL** ə dən
palaestra	pə **LES** trə
Palafox, Antonio	**PA** lə fahks, an **TOH** nee oh
Palais-Royal	**PA** lay roi **YAL**
Palamon	**PA** lə mən
palanquin	**PAL** ən **KEEN**
Palar, Lambertus	pah **LAHR**, lahm **BER** təs
palatable	**PAL** ə tə bəl
palatal	**PAL** ə təl
palate	**PAL** ət
palatial	pə **LAY** shəl
palatinate, P-	pə **LAT** ə nət
palatine, P-	**PAL** ə **TĪN**
Palau	pah **LOW** (**LOW** as in *cow*)
palaver	pə **LAV** ər
Palawan	pah **LAH** wahn
palazzo	pah **LAHT** soh
Palembang	**PAH** lem **BAHNG**
Palenque	pah **LENG** kay
Paleocene	**PAY** lee ə **SEEN**
paleography	**PAY** lee **OG** rə fee
paleolithic	**PAY** lee ə **LITH** ik
paleontology	**PAY** lee ən **TOL** ə jee
Paleozoic	**PAY** lee ə **ZOH** ik
Palermo	pah **LER** moh
Palestine	**PAL** ə **STĪN**
palestra	pə **LES** trə
Palestrina	**PAL** ə **STREE** nə
palette	**PAL** ət
palfrey	**PAWL** free
Palgrave	**PAWL** grayv
Pali	**PAH** lee
palimony	**PAL** ə **MOH** nee
palimpsest	**PAL** əm **SEST**
palindrome	**PAL** ən **DROHM**
palisade, P-	**PAL** ə **SAYD**
Palladian	pə **LAY** dee ən
Palladino, Nunzio	**PAH** lah **DEEN** oh, **NUUN** tsee oh
Palladio	pah **LAHD** yoh
palladium, P-	pə **LAY** dee əm
Pallas	**PAL** əs

---

o on, oh oat, oi boy, oo soon, oor poor, or for, ow cow, sh shush,
th thin, *th* this, u up, ur spur, uu book, *zh* pleasure

pallet	PAL ət
palliasse	pal YAS
palliative	PAL yə tiv
pallid	PAL əd
pall-mall, Pall Mall	pel mel
palm	pahm
Palma	PAHL mah
Palmas	PAHL mahs
Palme, Olof	PAHL mə, OH lawf
palmer, P-	PAH mər
palmetto	pal MET oh
palmistry	PAH mə stree
Palmyra, p-	pal MĪ rə
Palo Alto	PAL oh AL toh
Palomar	PAL ə MAHR
palomino	PAL ə MEE noh
palooka	pə LOO kə
Palos	PAH laws
palpable	PAL pə bəl
palpitation	PAL pə TAY shən
palsy	PAWL zee
palter	PAWL tər
paltry	PAWL tree
Pamela	PAM ə lə
Pamir	pah MIR
Pamlico	PAM lə KOH
pampa, P-	PAHM pə
pampas	PAHM pəz
pampero	pahm PE roh
pamphlet	PAM flət
panacea	PAN ə SEE ə
panache	pə NASH
Panama, p-	PAN ə MAH
Panamanian	PAN ə MAY nee ən
panatella	PAN ə TEL ə
Panay	pah NĪ
panchromatic	PAN kroh MAT ik
pancreas	PAN kree əs
pancreatic	PAN kree AT ik
panda	PAN də
Pandarus	PAN dər əs
pandect, P-	PAN dekt
pandemic	pan DEM ik

ə ago, a at, ah calm, ahr dark, air care, aw saw, ay say, ch church
e bet, ee me, eer beer, hw what, i is, ī my, n French final n vin,

pandemonium, P-	PAN də MOH nee əm
pandit, P-	PUN dət
Pandora	pan DOR ə
pandowdy	pan DOW dee
panegyric	PAN ə JIR ik
panegyrist	PAN ə JIR əst
panegyrize	PAN ə jə RĪZ
panelist	PAN ə ləst
Pango Pango	PAHNG oh PAHNG oh
Panhellenic	PAN hə LEN ik
Panjabi	pun JAH bee
panjandrum	pan JAN drəm
Panmunjom	pahn muun JUM
pannier	PAN yər
pannikin	PAN i kən
panocha	pə NOH chə
panoply	PAN ə plee
panorama	PAN ə RAM ə
Pantagruel	pan TA groo EL
Pantelleria	pahn TE le REE ə
pantheism	PAN thee IZ əm
pantheon, P-	PAN thee ON
Panthéon	pahn tay OHN (pahn and OHN French final *n*)
pantomime	PAN tə MĪM
pantomimic	PAN tə MIM ik
pantothenic	PAN tə THEN ik
Panurge	pan URJ
panzer, P-	PAN zər
papacy	PAY pə see
Papadopoulos, George	PAH pə DOP ə ləs
Papajorgji, Justin	PAH pah YOHR gee, JUUS tin
papal	PAY pəl
Papandreou, Andreas	PAH pahn *TH*RAY oo, ahn DRAY əs
Papanicalaou	PAH pə NEE kə LOW (LOW as in *cow*)
paparazzi	PAH pə RAHT tsee
Papas	PA pəs
papaw	PAW paw
papaya	pə PAH yə
Papeete	PAH pee AY tay
papeterie	PAP ə tree
papier-mâché	PAY pər mə SHAY
papilla	pə PIL ə

---

o on, oh oat, oi boy, oo soon, oor poor, or for, ow cow, sh shush,
th thin, *th* this, u up, ur spur, uu book, *zh* pleasure

papillary	PAP ə LER ee
papilloma	PAP ə LOH mə
papillon	PAP ə LON
papist	PAY pəst
papoose	pa POOS
Papoulias, George	pah POOL yahs
paprika	pə PREE kə
Papua	PAP yoo ə
papule	PAP yool
papyrus	pə PĪ rəs
Pará	pah RAH
parable	PA rə bəl
parabola	pə RAB ə lə
parabolic	PA rə BOL ik
Paracelsus	PA rə SEL səs
paraclete	PA rə KLEET
paradichlorobenzene	PA rə dī KLOR ə BEN zeen
paradigm	PA rə DĪM
paradigmatic	PA rə dig MAT ik
paradise, P-	PA rə DĪS
paradisiac	PA rə DIZ ee AK
paradisiacal	PA rə də SĪ ə kəl
paradox	PA rə DOKS
paradoxical	PA ṛə DOK si kəl
paraffin	PA rə fən
paragon	PA rə GON
Paraguay	PA rə GWAY
parakeet	PA rə KEET
parallax	PA rə LAKS
parallel	PA rə LEL
parallelogram	PA rə LEL ə GRAM
paralysis	pə RAL ə səs
paralytic	PA rə LIT ik
Paramaribo	PA rə MA rə BOH
paramecium	PA rə MEE see əm
parameter	pə RAM ə tər
paramount	PA rə MOWNT
paramour	PA rə MUUR
Paramus	pə RAM əs
Paraná	PA rə NAH
paranoia	PA rə NOI ə
paranoiac	PA rə NOI AK
Paranthropus	PA rən THROH pəs

ə ago, a at, ah calm, ahr dark, air care, aw saw, ay say, ch church
e bet, ee me, eer beer, hw what, i is, ī my, *n* French final n vin,

parapet	**PA** rə pət
paraphernalia	**PA** rə fə **NAYL** yə
paraphrase	**PA** rə **FRAYZ**
paraphrastic	**PA** rə **FRAS** tik
paraplegia	**PA** rə **PLEE** jə
paraplegic	**PA** rə **PLEE** jik
parapsychology	**PA** rə sī **KOL** ə jee
parasite	**PA** rə **SĪT**
parasitic	**PA** rə **SIT** ik
parasitism	**PA** rə sə **TIZ** əm
parasol	**PA** rə **SAWL**
parataxis	**PA** rə **TAK** səs
parathyroid	**PA** rə **THĪ** roid
Paray	pah **RAY**
parboil	**PAHR** boil
Parcae	**PAHR** see
Parcheesi, p-	pahr **CHEE** zee
paregoric	**PA** rə **GOR** ik
paresis	pə **REE** səs
par excellence	**PAHR EK** sə **LAHNS**
parfait	pahr **FAY**
parhelion	pahr **HEE** lee ən
pariah	pə **RĪ** ə
Paricutín	pah ree koo **TEEN**
parietal	pə **RĪ** ə təl
pari-mutuel	**PA** ri **MYOO** choo əl
pari passu	**PAH** ree **PAHS** soo
Paris	**PA** rəs
parish	**PA** rish
parishioner	pə **RISH** ə nər
Parisian	pə **REE** *zh* ən
parka	**PAHR** kə
Park Chung Hee	pahrk chung hee
parlance	**PAHR** ləns
parlay	**PAHR** lay
parley	**PAHR** lee
parliament	**PAHR** lə mənt
parliamentarian	**PAHR** lə mən **TAIR** ee ən
parliamentary	**PAHR** lə **MEN** tə ree
Parma	**PAHR** mə
Parmesan	**PAHR** mə **ZAHN**
parmigiana	**PAHR** mi **JAH** nə
Parnassian	pahr **NAS** ee ən

o on, oh oat, oi boy, oo soon, oor poor, or for, ow cow, sh shush,
th thin, *th* this, u up, ur spur, uu book, *zh* pleasure

Parnassus	pahr NAS əs
Parnu	PAR noo
parochial	pə ROH kee əl
parody	PA rə dee
parole	pə ROHL
paroxysm	PA rək SIZ əm
parquet	pahr KAY
parquetry	PAHR kə tree
Parran	PA rən
parricide	PA rə SĪD
parrot	PA rət
parry, P-	PA ree
parse	pahrs
parsec	PAHR sek
Parsi	PAHR see
Parsifal	PAHR si FAHL
parsimonious	PAHR sə MOH nee əs
parsimony	PAHR sə MOH nee
parsley	PAHRS lee
parsnip	PAHR snəp
parterre	pahr TAIR
parthenogenesis	PAHR thə noh JEN ə səs
Parthenon	PAHR thə NON
Parthenope	pahr THEN ə PEE
Parthenos	PAHR thə NOS
Parthian	PAHR thee ən
participial	PAHR tə SIP ee əl
participle	PAHR tə SIP əl
particular	pər TIK yə lər
partisan	PAHR tə zən
partite	PAHR tīt
partitive	PAHR tə tiv
partridge	PAHR trij
parturient	pahr TYUUR ee ənt
parturition	PAHR chə RISH ən
parvenu	PAHR və NOO
pas (French)	pah
Pasadena	PAS ə DEE nə
Pascal, Blaise	pas KAL, BLEZ
paschal	PAS kəl
pasha	PAH shə
Pashayan	pə SHAY ən
Pashto	PUSH toh (PUSH as in *slush*)

ə ago, a at, ah calm, ahr dark, air care, aw saw, ay say, ch church
e bet, ee me, eer beer, hw what, i is, ī my, *n* French final n vin,

Pasiphaë	pə SIF ə EE
paso doble	PAH soh DOH blay
Pasquale	pah SKWAH lay
passacaglia	PAH sə KAHL yə
passade	pə SAYD
passado	pə SAH doh
Passaic	pə SAY ik
Passamaquoddy	PAS ə mə KWOD ee
passé	pa SAY
passel	PA səl
passementerie	pas MEN tree
passe-partout	PAS pahr TOO
passerine	PAS ə RĪN
passim	PAS əm
passivity	pa SIV ə tee
Passover	PAS OH vər
passus	PAS əs
Passy	pa SEE
pasta	PAH stə
pastel	pa STEL
Pasternak	PAS tər NAK
Pasteur	pa STUR
pasteurize	PAS chə RĪZ
pasticcio	pa STEE choh
pastiche	pa STEESH
pastille	pa STEEL
pastime	PAS tīm
Pastinen, Ilkka Olavi	PAHS tee nən, EEL kə OH lah vee
Pasto	PAHS taw
pastoral	PAS tə rəl
pastorale	PAS tə RAL
pastorate	PAS tə rət
pastrami	pə STRAH mee
Patachou	pah tah SHOO
Patagonia	PAT ə GOH nee ə
Patchogue	PA chog
patchouli	PA chuu lee
pate	payt
pâté	pah TAY
pâté de foie gras	pah TAY də FWAH GRAH
patella	pə TEL ə
paten	PAT ən
patent (obvious)	PAY tənt

o on, oh oat, oi boy, oo soon, oor poor, or for, ow cow, sh shush,
th thin, *th* this, u up, ur spur, uu book, *zh* pleasure

patent (except obvious)	**PAT** ənt
patently	**PAY** tənt lee
Pater, p-	**PAY** tər
paterfamilias	**PAT** ər fə **MIL** ee əs
paternoster, Pater Noster	**PAH** tər **NOS** tər
Paterson	**PAT** ər sən
pathetic	pə **THET** ik
Pathet Lao	**PAH** tət **LAH** oh
pathogen	**PATH** ə jən
pathogenesis	**PATH** ə **JEN** ə səs
pathological	**PATH** ə **LOJ** ə kəl
pathology	pə **THOL** ə jee
pathos	**PAY** thos
Patiala	**PUT** ee **AH** lə
patina	pə **TEE** nə
Patiño	pah **TEE** nyaw
patio	**PAT** ee **OH**
patisserie	pah tees **REE**
Patmos	**PAT** məs
Patna	**PUT** nə (**PUT** as in *but*)
patois	**PA** twah
Paton, Alan	**PAYT** ən
Patras	pə **TRAS**
patriarch	**PAY** tree **AHRK**
patriarchal	**PAY** tree **AHR** kəl
patrician	pə **TRISH** ən
patricidal	**PA** trə **SĪ** dəl
patricide	**PA** tri **sĪD**
patrimony	**PA** trə **MOH** nee
patriot	**PAY** tree ət
patriotic	**PAY** tree **OT** ik
patriotism	**PAY** tree ə **TIZ** əm
patristic	pə **TRIS** tik
Patroclus	pə **TROH** kləs
patronage	**PAY** trə nij
patroness	**PAY** trə nəs
patronize	**PAY** trə **NĪZ**
patronymic	**PA** trə **NIM** ik
patroon	pə **TROON**
paucity	**PAW** sə tee
Pauli, Wolfgang	**POW** lee, **VUULF** gahng

ə ago, a at, ah calm, ahr dark, air care, aw saw, ay say, ch church
e bet, ee me, eer beer, hw what, i is, ī my, *n* French final n vin,

Pauling, Linus	**PAW** ling, **LĪ** nəs
Paumotu	pah uu **MOH** too
paunch	pawnch
pauper	**PAW** pər
Pausanias	paw **SAY** nee əs
pavane	pa **VAHN**
Pavarotti, Luciano	**PAH** vah **RAW** tee, loo **CHAH** noh
pavé	pa **VAY**
Pavia	pah **VEE** ah
Pavicevic, Miso	pah **VI** chay vich, **MEE** shoh
pavilion	pə **VIL** yən
Pavlov	**PAHV** lawf
Pavlova	pahv **LOH** və
Pawnee	paw **NEE**
Pawtucket	pə **TUK** ət
Pax Romana	**PAHKS** roh **MAH** nah
pax vobiscum	**PAHKS** woh **BIS** kuum
payola	pay **OH** lə
Paz Estenssoro	**PAHS** es ten **SAW** roh
Pazhwak, Abdul Rahman	pa*z*h **WAWK**, ahb **DUUL** rah **MAHN**
Paz Zamora, Jaime	**PAHS** zah **MOR**ə, **HĪ** may
Pearson	**PIR** sən
Peary	**PIR** ee
pease	peez
pecan	pi **KAHN**
peccadillo	**PEK** ə **DIL** oh
peccary	**PEK** ə ree
peccavi	pe **KAY** vee
Pecksniffian	pek **SNIF** ee ən
Pecos	**PAY** kəs
Pecs	paych
pectin	**PEK** tən
pectoral	**PEK** tə rəl
peculation	**PEK** yə **LAY** shən
peculiar	pi **KYOOL** yər
peculiarity	pi **KYOOL YA** rə tee
pecuniary	pi **KYOO** nee **ER** ee
pedagogue	**PED** ə **GOG**
pedagogy	**PED** ə **GOH** jee
pedant	**PED** ənt
pedantic	pi **DAN** tik
pedantry	**PED** ən tree

o on, oh oat, oi boy, oo soon, oor poor, or for, ow cow, sh shush, th thin, *th* this, u up, ur spur, uu book, *z*h pleasure

pederast	**PED** ə **RAST**
pediatric	**PEE** dee **AT** rik
pediatrician	**PEE** dee ə **TRISH** ən
pediatrist	**PEE** dee **AT** rəst
pedicure	**PED** ə **KYUUR**
pedology	pi **DOL** ə jee
pedometer	pi **DOM** ə tər
peduncle	pi **DUNG** kəl
peerage	**PEER** ij
Pegasus	**PEG** ə səs
pegmatite	**PEG** mə **TĪT**
peignoir	payn **WAHR**
Pei, I. M.	pay
Peiping	pay ping
pejorative	pi **JOR** ə tiv
Pekin, p-	**PEE** kin
Peking	pee king
Pekingese	**PEE** kə **NEEZ**
pekoe	**PEE** koh
pelage	**PEL** ij
pelagic	pə **LAJ** ik
pelargonium	**PEL** ahr **GOH** nee əm
Pele	**PE** lay
Pelée	pə **LAY**
Peleliu	**PEL** ə lyoo
Peleus	**PEE** lee əs
Pelew	pee **LOO**
Pelham	**PEL** əm
Pelias	**PEE** lee əs
pelican	**PEL** i kən
Pelion	**PEE** lee ən
pelisse	pə **LEES**
pellagra	pə **LAY** grə
Pelletier, Gérard	pel **TYAY**, *zh*ay **RAHR**
pellmell	pel mel
pellucid	pə **LOO** səd
Peloponnesian	**PEL** ə pə **NEE** *zh*ən
Peloponnesus	**PEL** ə pə **NEE** səs
Pelops	**PEE** lops
pelota	pə **LOH** tə
Pelshe, Arvid	**PEL** shə, **AHR** vid
Pemba	**PEM** bə
pemmican	**PEM** i kən

ə ago, a at, ah calm, ahr dark, air care, aw saw, ay say, ch church
e bet, ee me, eer beer, hw what, i is, ī my, *n* French final n vin,

Peña	**PE** nyah
penal	**PEE** nəl
penalize	**PEE** nə **LĪZ**
penalty	**PEN** əl tee
penance	**PEN** əns
Penang	pi **NANG**
penates	pə **NAY** teez
penchant	**PEN** chənt
pendant	**PEN** dənt
pendragon, P-	pen **DRAG** ən
pendulous	**PEN** jə ləs
pendulum	**PEN** jə ləm
Penelope	pə **NEL** ə pee
Peneus	pə **NEE** əs
penguin	**PEN** gwən
Peng Zhen	pung jun
penicillin	**PEN** ə **SIL** ən
peninsula	pə **NIN** sə lə
penitence	**PEN** ə təns
penitentiary	**PEN** ə **TEN** shə ree
Pennario	pe **NAH** ree oh
Pennine	**PEN** in
pennon	**PEN** ən
Pennsylvania	**PEN** səl **VAY** nyə
Penobscot	pə **NOB** skot
penology	pi **NOL** ə jee
Pensacola	**PEN** sə **KOH** lə
pensée	pahn **SAY**
Penseroso	**PEN** sə **ROH** soh
pension (boarding house)	pahn **SYAWN** (pahn and **SYAWN** French final *n*)
penstemon	pen **STEE** mən
pentagon, P-	**PEN** tə **GON**
pentameter	pen **TAM** ə tər
Pentateuch	**PEN** tə **TYOOK**
Pentecost	**PEN** ti **KAWST**
pentimento	**PEN** tə **MEN** toh
Pentothal	**PEN** tə **THAWL**
pentstemon	pent **STEE** mən
penuche	pə **NOO** chee
penult	**PEE** nult
penultimate	pi **NUL** tə mət
penumbra	pə **NUM** brə

o on, oh oat, oi boy, oo soon, oor poor, or for, ow cow, sh shush,
th thin, *th* this, u up, ur spur, uu book, *zh* pleasure

penurious	pə NUUR ee əs
penury	PEN yə ree
Penzance	pen ZANS
Penzias, Arno	PENT see əs, AHR noh
peon	PEE ən
peonage	PEE ə nij
peony	PEE ə nee
Pepin	PEP ən
peplum	PEP ləm
pepperidge	PEP ər ij
peptic	PEP tik
peptide	PEP tīd
Pepys	peeps
Pequot	PEE kwot
Perak	PE rak
per annum	pər AN əm
percale	pər KAYL
per capita	pər KAP ə tə
percentile	pər SEN tīl
Perceval	PUR sə vəl
Percheron	PUR chə RON
percipient	pər SIP ee ənt
Percival, -e	PUR sə vəl
percolate	PUR kə LAYT
percolator	PUR kə LAY tər
percussion	pər KUSH ən
per diem	pər DEE əm
perdition	pər DISH ən
père, P-	pair
peregrinate	PER ə grə NAYT
peregrination	PER ə grə NAY shən
peregrine	PER ə grən
pereira	pə RAIR ə
Pereira	pe RAY rah
Perelman	PURL mən
peremptory	pə REMP tə ree
perennial	pə REN ee əl
Peres, Shimon	PE res, SHI mawn
Perestroika	PERə STROY kə
Perez	pə REZ
Pérez de Cuellar, Javier	PAY rez day KWAY yahr, hah VYAIR
Pérez Esquivel, Aldolpho	PAY rez ES kee VEL, a DAWL foh

ə ago, a at, ah calm, ahr dark, air care, aw saw, ay say, ch church
e bet, ee me, eer beer, hw what, i is, ī my, *n* French final n vin,

Pérez Jiménez, Marcos	**PAY** rez hee **MAY** nez, **MAHR** kohs
perfect (a)	**PUR** fikt
perfect (v)	pər **FEKT**
perfecto	pər **FEK** toh
perfervid	pər **FUR** vəd
perfidious	pər **FID** ee əs
perfidy	**PUR** fə dee
perforate (a)	**PUR** fə rət
perforate (v)	**PUR** fə **RAYT**
perforce	pər **FORS**
perfume (n)	**PUR** fyoom
perfume (v)	pər **FYOOM**
perfunctory	pər **FUNGK** tə ree
pergola	**PUR** gə lə
Pergolesi	**PAIR** gə **LAY** see
perhaps	pər **HAPS**
pericardium	**PE** rə **KAHR** dee əm
Periclean	**PE** rə **KLEE** ən
Pericles	**PE** rə **KLEEZ**
pericranium	**PE** rə **KRAY** nee əm
perigee	**PE** rə jee
perihelion	**PE** rə **HEE** lee ən
peril	**PE** ril
perimeter	pə **RIM** ə tər
perineum	**PE** rə **NEE** əm
periodic	**PEER** ee **OD** ik
periodical	**PEER** ee **OD** i kəl
periosteum	**PE** ree **OS** tee əm
peripatetic	**PE** rə pə **TET** ik
periphery	pə **RIF** ə ree
periphrasis	pə **RIF** rə səs
periphrastic	**PE** rə **FRAS** tik
periscope	**PE** rə **SKOHP**
perish	**PE** rish
peristalsis	**PE** rə **STAWL** səs
peristyle	**PE** rə **STĪL**
peritoneum	**PE** rə tə **NEE** əm
peritonitis	**PE** rə tə **NĪ** təs
perjure	**PUR** jər
perjury	**PUR** jə ree
Perlis	pər **LIS**
perlite	**PUR** līt
perm	purm

---

o on, oh oat, oi boy, oo soon, oor poor, or for, ow cow, sh shush,
th thin, *th* this, u up, ur spur, uu book, *zh* pleasure

Perm (USSR)	perm
permalloy	**PUR** mə LOI
permanganate	pər **MANG** gə NAYT
permeability	**PUR** mee ə **BIL** ə tee
permeable	**PUR** mee ə bəl
permeate	**PUR** mee AYT
Permian	**PUR** mee ən
permit (n)	**PUR** mit
permit (v)	pər **MIT**
permutation	**PUR** myə **TAY** shən
Pernambuco	**PUR** nəm **BYOO** koh
pernicious	pər **NISH** əs
Pernod	pair **NOH**
Perón	pe **ROHN**
peroration	**PE** rə **RAY** shən
perpetual	pər **PECH** oo əl
perpetuity	**PUR** pə **TOO** ə tee
perquisite	**PUR** kwə zət
Perrault	pe **ROH**
Perrier	**PE** ree ay
per se	pər **SAY**
Perseid	**PUR** see əd
Persephone	pər **SEF** ə nee
Persepolis	pər **SEP** ə ləs
Perse, St.-John	**PURS, SIN** jən
Perseus	**PUR** see əs
perseverance	**PUR** sə **VIR** əns
persevere	**PUR** sə **VIR**
Pershing	**PUR** shing
Persia	**PUR** zhə
Persian	**PUR** zhən
persiflage	**PUR** sə **FLAHZH**
persimmon	pər **SIM** ən
persist	pər **SIST**
persona	pər **SOH** nə
personae	pər **SOH** nee
personal	**PUR** sə nəl
persona non grata	pər **SOH** nə nohn **GRAH** tə
personification	pər **SON** ə fə **KAY** shən
personify	pər **SON** ə **FĪ**
personnel	**PUR** sə **NEL**
perspective	pər **SPEK** tiv
perspicacious	**PUR** spə **KAY** shəs

ə ago, a at, ah calm, ahr dark, air care, aw saw, ay say, ch church
e bet, ee me, eer beer, hw what, i is, ī my, *n* French final n vin,

perspicacity	PUR spə KAS ə tee
perspicuity	PUR spə KYOO ə tee
perspicuous	pər SPIK yoo əs
perspiration	PUR spə RAY shən
perspire	pər SPĪR
persuade	pər SWAYD
persuasion	pər SWAY zhən
persuasive	pər SWAY siv
Perth	purth
pertinacious	PUR tə NAY shəs
pertinacity	PUR tə NAS ə tee
pertinent	PUR tə nənt
Pertini, Alessandro	pair TEE nee, AH lay SAHN droh
perturbation	PUR tər BAY shən
pertussis	pər TUS əs
Peru	pə ROO
Perugia	pe ROO jah
Perugino	PE roo JEE noh
peruke	pə ROOK
perusal	pə ROO zəl
peruse	pə ROOZ
Perutz	PE rəts
Peruvian	pə ROO vee ən
pervasive	pər VAY siv
perverse	pər VURS
perversion	pər VUR zhən
pervert (n)	PUR vurt
pervert (v)	pər VURT
pervious	PUR vee əs
Pesach	PAY sahk
Pescadores	PES kah DOR es
peseta	pə SAY tə
Peshawar	pe SHAH wər
peso	PAY soh
Pestalozzi	PES tə LOT see
pestiferous	pe STIF ə rəs
pestilence	PES tə ləns
pestilential	PES tə LEN shəl
pestle	PES əl
pesto	PES toh
petard	pə TAHRD
petiole	PET ee OHL
petit	PET ee

o on, oh oat, oi boy, oo soon, oor poor, or for, ow cow, sh shush,
th thin, *th* this, u up, ur spur, uu book, *zh* pleasure

petite	pə TEET
petit four	PET ee FOR
petition	pə TISH ən
petit point	PET ee POINT
petits pois	pə tee PWAH
Petöfi, Sándor	PE tuu fee, SHAHN dor
Petran, Janos	PET ran, YAH nohsh
Petrarch	PEE trahrk
Petrarchan	pi TRAHR kən
petrel	PE trəl
petri	PEE tree
Petrides, Avra	pe TREE *this*, AH vrah
Petrie	PEE tree
petrify	PET rə FĪ
Petrignani, Rinaldo	pe treen YAH nee, ree NAHL doh
petroglyph	PET rə GLIF
Petrograd	PE trə GRAD
petrography	pə TROG rə fee
petrol	PET rəl
petrolatum	PET rə LAY təm
petroleum	pə TROH lee əm
petrology	pə TROL ə jee
Petronius	pi TROH nee əs
Petropavlovsk	PE traw PAHV lawfsk
Petrosani	PE traw SHAHN
Petrouchka	pə TROOSH kə
Petrozavodsk	PE trə zə VAHTSK
Petruchio	pə TROO kee oh
Petsamo	PET sah maw
pettifoggery	PET ee FOG ə ree
petulance	PECH ə ləns
petulant	PECH ə lənt
petunia	pə TOO nyə
pewter	PYOO tər
peyote	pay OH tee
Pfeiffer	FĪ fər
pfennig	FEN ig
Pfizer	FĪ zər
Phaedra	FEE drə
Phaëthon	FAY ə thən
phaeton	FAY ə tən
phagocyte	FAG ə SĪT
phalanx	FAY langks

phalarope	FAL ə ROHP
phallic	FAL ik
phallus	FAL əs
Pham Van Dong	fahm vahn dahng
phantasm	FAN TAZ əm
phantasmagoria	fan TAZ mə GOR ee ə
phantasmal	fan TAZ məl
phantom	FAN təm
Pharaoh	FAIR oh
Pharaonic	FAIR ay ON ik
pharisaic, P-	FA rə SAY ik
Pharisee, p-	FA rə SEE
pharmaceutical	FAHR mə SOO ti kəl
pharmacopoeia	FAHR mə kə PEE ə
Pharos, p-	FAI rahs
Pharpar	FAHR pahr
Pharsalus	fahr SAY ləs
pharyngeal	fə RIN jee əl
pharyngitis	FA rən JĪ təs
pharynx	FA ringks
Phebe	FEE bee
Phèdre	FE drə
phenacetin	fə NAS ə tən
phenobarbital	FEE noh BAHR bə tawl
phenol	FEE nohl
phenology	fi NOL ə jee
phenomena	fi NOM ə nə
phenomenal	fi NOM ə nəl
phenomenon	fi NOM ə NON
phial	FĪ əl
Phidias	FID ee əs
philanderer	fə LAN də rər
philanthropic	FIL ən THROP ik
philanthropist	fə LAN thrə pəst
philanthropy	fə LAN thrə pee
philatelic	FIL ə TEL ik
philatelist	fə LAT ə ləst
philately	fə LAT ə lee
Philemon	fə LEE mən
philharmonic	FIL hahr MON ik
Philippi	fə LIP ī
Philippian	fə LIP ee ən
Philippic, p-	fə LIP ik

o on, oh oat, oi boy, oo soon, oor poor, or for, ow cow, sh shush,
th thin, *th* this, u up, ur spur, uu book, *zh* pleasure

Philippine	FIL ə PEEN
Philistine	FIL ə STEEN
philodendron	FIL ə DEN drən
philogyny	fə LOJ ə nee
philologian	FIL ə LOH jən
philologist	fə LOL ə jəst
philology	fə LOL ə jee
philomel	FIL ə MEL
Philomela	FIL ə MEE lə
philosophical	FIL ə SOF i kəl
philosophy	fə LOS ə fee
philter	FIL tər
Phineas	FIN ee əs
phlebitis	flə BĪ təs
phlebotomy	flə BOT ə mee
Phlegethon	FLEG ə THON
phlegm	flem
phlegmatic	fleg MAT ik
phlogiston	floh JIS tən
phlox	floks
Phnom Penh	nom pen
phobia	FOH bee ə
Phobos	FOH bos
phocomelia	FOH koh MEE lee ə
Phoebe, p-	FEE bee
Phoebus	FEE bəs
Phoenicia	fə NEE shə
Phoenix, p-	FEE niks
phonation	foh NAY shən
phoneme	FOH neem
phonemic	fə NEE mik
phonetic	fə NET ik
phonetician	FOH nə TISH ən
phonic	FON ik
phosgene	FOZ jeen
phosphate	FOS fayt
phosphorescence	FOS fə RES əns
phosphoric	fos FOR ik
phosphorous (a)	FOS fə rəs
phosphorus (n)	FOS fə rəs
photogenic	FOH tə JEN ik
photography	fə TOG rə fee
photogravure	FOH tə grə VYUUR

ə ago, a at, ah calm, ahr dark, air care, aw saw, ay say, ch church
e bet, ee me, eer beer, hw what, i is, ī my, n French final n vin,

photolytic	FOH tə LIT ik
photometer	foh TOM ə tər
photometry	foh TOM ə tree
photon	FOH tahn
photostat, P-	FOH tə STAT
phraseology	FRAY zee OL ə jee
phrenetic	fri NET ik
phrenic	FREN ik
phrenology	fri NOL ə jee
Phrygia	FRIJ ee ə
phthalic	THAL ik
phthisic	TIZ ik
phthisis	TIS əs
Phyfe	fif
phylactery	fə LAK tə ree
phylogeny	fī LOJ ə nee
phylum	FĪ ləm
physiatrist	FIZ ee A trəst
physiognomy	FIZ ee OG nə mee
physiography	FIZ ee OG rə fee
physiological	FIZ ee ə LOJ i kəl
physiology	FIZ ee OL ə jee
physiotherapy	FIZ ee oh THER ə pee
physique	fə ZEEK
pi	pī
Piacenza	pyah CHEN tsah
Piaget	pyah ZHAY
pianissimo	PEE ə NIS ə MOH
pianist	pee AN əst
piano (a, adv)	pee AH noh
piano (n)	pee AN oh
pianoforte	pee AN oh FOR tay
piaster	pee AS tər
piazza	pee AZ ə
Piazza Navone	PYAHT sah nah VOH ne
pibroch	PEE brok
pica	PĪ kə
picador	PIK ə DOR
Picardy	PIK ər dee
picaresque	PIK ə RESK
Picasso	pi KAH soh
picayune	PIK ə YOON
Piccadilly	PIK ə DIL ee

o on, oh oat, oi boy, oo soon, oor poor, or for, ow cow, sh shush,
th thin, *th* this, u up, ur spur, uu book, *zh* pleasure

Piccadilly Circus	PIK ə DIL ee SUR kəs
piccalilli	PIK ə LIL ee
Piccard, Auguste	pee KAR, oh GUUST
piccolo	PIK ə loh
Pickwickian	pik WIK ee ən
picot	PEE koh
Pict	pikt
Pictor	PIK tər
pictorial	pik TOR ee əl
picture	PIK chər
picturesque	PIK chə RESK
picul	PIK əl
Pidgin, p-	PIJ ən
piebald	PĪ bawld
pièce de résistance	PYES də ray zees TAHNS (TAHNS French final *n*)
Pieck	peek
pied	pīd
pied-à-terre	pye da TAIR
Piedmont, p-	PEED mont
Piemonte	pye MAWN te
Pierian	pī IR ee ən
Pierre	pyair
Pierre (South Dakota)	pir
Pierrot	PEE ə ROH
Piers Plowman	PEERZ PLOW mən
Piestany	PYESH tyah nee
Pietà, p-	PEE ay TAH
Pietermaritzburg	PEE tər MA rits BURG
pietism	PĪ ə TIZ əm
pietistic	PĪ ə TIS tik
piety	PĪ ə tee
piezoelectric	pee AY zoh ə LEK trik
Pigalle	pee GAL
pigeon	PIJ ən
Pigmy, p-	PIG mee
pignoli	peen YOH lee
pignolia	peen YOH lee ə
pilaf	PEE lahf
pilaster	pə LAS tər
Pilate, Pontius	PĪ lət, PON chəs
pilau	PEE lahf
pilchard	PIL chərd

ə ago, a at, ah calm, ahr dark, air care, aw saw, ay say, ch church
e bet, ee me, eer beer, hw what, i is, ī my, *n* French final n vin,

Pilcomayo	**PEEL** kaw **MAH** yaw
pileus	**PĪ** lee əs
pilgrimage	**PIL** grə mij
pili	pee **LEE**
pillion	**PIL** yən
pillory	**PIL** ə ree
pilose	**PĪ** lohs
pilot	**PĪ** lət
Pilote, Pierre	pee **LAHT, PYAIR**
Pilsen	**PIL** zən
Pilsudski	pil **SOOT** skee (**SOOT** as in *boot*)
Piltdown	**PILT** down
Pima	**PEE** mə
pimento	pə **MEN** toh
pimiento	pə **MEN** toh
pimpernel, P-	**PIM** pər **NEL**
piña	**PEE** nyah
pinaceous	pī **NAY** shəs
pinafore	**PIN** ə **FOR**
piñata	peen **YAH** tah
pince-nez	**PANS** nay
pincers	**PIN** sərz
Pindar	**PIN** dahr
Pindaric	pin **DA** rik
pineal	**PIN** ee əl
Pinero	pə **NE** roh
Piñero	pee **NYE** roh
pinion	**PIN** yən
pinnace	**PIN** əs
pinnacle	**PIN** ə kəl
pinnate	**PIN** ayt
Pinochet Ugarte, Augusto	**PEE** noh **CHET** oo **GAHR** tay, ow **GOOS** toh
pinochle	**PEE NUK** əl
pinole	pi **NOH** lee
Pinot	**PEE** noh
pinta	**PIN** tə
Pinta	**PEEN** tah
pintle	**PIN** təl
pion	**PĪ** on
pioneer	**PĪ** ə **NIR**
pious	**PĪ** əs
pipette	pī **PET**

---

o **on**, oh **oat**, oi **boy**, oo **soon**, oor **poor**, or **for**, ow **cow**, sh **shush**, th **thin**, *th* **this**, u **up**, ur **spur**, uu **book**, *zh* **pleasure**

pipit	**PIP** ət
Pippa	**PIP** ə
Piqua	**PIK** way
piquancy	**PEE** kən see
piquant	**PEE** kənt
pique	peek
piqué	pi **KAY**
piquet	pi **KAY**
piracy	**PĪ** rə see
Piraeus	pī **REE** əs
piragua	pə **RAH** gwə
Pirandello	**PIR** ən **DEL** oh
Piranesi	**PEE** rah **NAY** zee
piranha	pə **RAHN** yə
piratical	pə **RAT** i kəl
Pirithous	pī **RITH** oh əs
pirogen	pə **RUG** ən
pirogue	**PEE** rohg
piroshki	pə **RUSH** kee
pirouette	**PIR** oo **ET**
Pisa	**PEE** zə
pis aller	pee za **LAY**
Pisano	pee **ZAH** noh
piscatorial	**PIS** kə **TOR** ee əl
Pisces	**PĪ** seez
piscine	**PĪ** seen
Pisgah	**PIZ** gə
Pisistratus	pi **SIS** trə təs
pismire	**PIS** mīr
Pissarro	pi **SAHR** oh
pissoir	pee **SWAHR**
pistachio	pə **STASH** ee oh
piston	**PIS** tən
Pitcairn	**PIT** kairn
pitchblende	**PICH** blend
piteous	**PIT** ee əs
Pithecanthropus	**PITH** i **KAN** thrə pəs
pithy	**PITH** ee
pitiable	**PIT** ee ə bəl
piton	**PEE** ton
Pitot	**PEE** toh
Pitri	**PI** tree
pittance	**PIT** əns

ə ago, a at, ah calm, ahr dark, air care, aw saw, ay say, ch church
e bet, ee me, eer beer, hw what, i is, ī my, *n* French final n vin,

pituitary	pə TOO ə TER ee
Pius	PĪ əs
pivot	PIV ət
pivotal	PIV ə təl
pixie	PIK see
Pizarro	pə ZAHR oh
pizza	PEET sə
pizzeria	PEET sə REE ə
pizzicato	PIT si KAH toh
placable	PLAK ə bəl
placard	PLAK ahrd
placate	PLAY kayt
placebo	plə SEE boh
placenta	plə SEN tə
placet	PLAY sit
placid	PLAS əd
placket	PLAK ət
plagiarism	PLAY jə RIZ əm
plagiarize	PLAY jə RĪZ
plague	playg
plaice	plays
plaid	plad
plaint	playnt
plaintiff	PLAYN təf
plait	playt
planarian	plə NA ree ən
planchette	plan SHET
Planck, Max	plahngk, maks
planetarium	PLAN ə TAIR ee əm
planetary	PLAN ə TER ee
planetesimal	PLAN ə TES ə məl
plangent	PLAN jənt
planimeter	plə NIM ə tər
Planinc, Milka	plah NEENS, MEEL kə
planish	PLAN ish
plankton	PLANGK tən
planometer	plə NOM ə tər
Plantagenet	plan TAJ ə nət
plantain	PLAN tən
plaque	plak
plasma	PLAZ mə
plasmodium	plaz MOH dee əm
Plassey	PLAH see

o on, oh oat, oi boy, oo soon, oor poor, or for, ow cow, sh shush,
th thin, *th* this, u up, ur spur, uu book, *zh* pleasure

plastic	**PLAS** tik
plasticity	plas **TIS** ə tee
Plata	**PLAH** tah
plat du jour	**PLAH** də **ZHOOR**
plateau	pla **TOH**
Plate, Juan	**PLAH** tay, **HWAHN**
platen	**PLAT** ən
platinum	**PLAT** ə nəm
platitude	**PLAT** ə **TOOD**
platitudinous	**PLAT** ə **TOO** də nəs
Plato	**PLAY** toh
Platonic, p-	plə **TON** ik
Platonism	**PLAYT** ən **IZ** əm
platoon	plə **TOON**
Plattdeutsch	**PLAHT** doich
Platte	plat
platy	**PLAT** ee
platypus	**PLAT** i pəs
Platzer, Wilfried	**PLAHT** sər, **VIL** freet
plaudit	**PLAW** dət
plausible	**PLAW** zə bəl
Plautus	**PLAW** təs
playa	**PLĪ** ə
plaza	**PLAZ** ə
Plaza (Latin America)	**PLAH** sah
pleasant	**PLEZ** ənt
pleasure	**PLEZ**H ər
pleat	pleet
pleb	pleb
plebe	pleeb
plebeian	plə **BEE** ən
plebiscite	**PLEB** ə **SĪT**
plebs	plebz
plectrum	**PLEK** trəm
Pleiades	**PLEE** ə **DEEZ**
Pleistocene	**PLĪ** stə **SEEN**
plenary	**PLEE** nə ree
plenipotentiary	**PLEN** ə pə **TEN** shee **ER** ee
plenitude	**PLEN** ə **TOOD**
plenteous	**PLEN** tee əs
plenum	**PLE** nəm
pleonasm	**PLEE** ə **NAZ** əm
pleonastic	**PLEE** ə **NAS** tik

ə ago, a at, ah calm, ahr dark, air care, aw saw, ay say, ch church
e bet, ee me, eer beer, hw what, i is, ī my, n French final n vin,

plesiosaur	PLEE see ə SAWR
plesiosaurus	PLEE see ə SOR əs
plethora	PLETH ə rə
plethoric	plə THOR ik
pleurisy	PLUUR ə see
Plexiglas	PLEK si GLAS
plexus	PLEK səs
pliable	PLĪ ə bəl
pliant	PLĪ ənt
plié	plee AY
Plimsoll	PLIM səl
plinth	plinth
Pliny	PLIN ee
Pliocene	PLĪ ə SEEN
Plisetskaya, Maya	plee SETS KĪ ə, MĪ ə
Ploesti	plaw YESHT
Plotinus	ploh TĪ nəs
Plovdiv	PLAWV dif
plover	PLUV ər
plow	plow
plumb	plum
plumbago	plum BAY goh
plumber	PLUM ər
plummet	PLUM ət
plumose	PLOO mohs
plumule	PLOOM yool
pluperfect	ploo PUR fikt
plural	PLUUR əl
plurality	pluu RAL ə tee
Plutarch	PLOO tahrk
Pluto	PLOO toh
plutocracy	ploo TOK rə SEE
plutocrat	PLOO tə KRAT
Plutonic, p-	ploo TON ik
plutonium	ploo TOH nee əm
Plutus	PLOO təs
pluvial	PLOO vee əl
Pluvius	PLOO vee əs
ply	plī
Plymouth	PLIM əth
pneumatic	nuu MAT ik
pneumoconiosis	NOO moh KOH nee OH səs
pneumonectomy	NOO mə NEK tə mee

o on, oh oat, oi boy, oo soon, oor poor, or for, ow cow, sh shush,
th thin, *th* this, u up, ur spur, uu book, *zh* pleasure

pneumonia	nuu **MOHN** yə
Pnom-Penh	nom pen
Pnyx	niks
Po	poh
Pocahontas	**POH** kə **HON** təs
pococurante	**POH** koh kuu **RAN** tee
podagra	pə **DAG** rə
podesta	poh **DES** tə
Podgorny, Nikolai	pod **GAWR** nee, nee koh **LĪ**
podiatrist	pə **DĪ** ə trəst
podium	**POH** dee əm
podsol	**POD** sol
Podunk	**POH** dungk
podzol	**POD** zol
poem	**POH** əm
Poena	**PEE** nə
poesy	**POH** ə zee
poet	**POH** ət
poetaster	**POH** ət **AS** tər
poetess	**POH** ət əs
poetic	poh **ET** ik
poet laureate	**POH** ət **LOR** ee ət
poetry	**POH** ə tree
pogrom	**POH** grəm
Pohai	poh **HĪ**
poi	poi
poignancy	**POIN** yən see
poignant	**POIN** yənt
poilu	pwah **LOO**
poinciana	**POIN** see **AN** ə
poinsettia	poin **SET** ee ə
pointillism	**POIN** tə **LIZ** əm
Poisson	pwah **SAWN** (**SAWN** French final *n*)
Poitier	**PWAH** tyay
Poitiers	pwah **TYAY**
Poitou	pwah **TOO**
polacca	poh **LAK** ə
Poland	**POH** lənd
polar	**POH** lər
Polaris	pə **LAR** əs
polarity	pə **LAR** ə tee
Polaroid	**POH** lə **ROID**
polder	**POHL** dər

ə ago, a at, ah calm, ahr dark, air care, aw saw, ay say, ch church
e bet, ee me, eer beer, hw what, i is, ī my, *n* French final n vin,

polemic	pə LEM ik
polenta	poh LEN tə
polio	POH lee OH
poliomyelitis	POH lee oh MĪ ə LĪ təs
Politburo	POL it BYUUR oh
politesse	POL i TES
Politian	poh LISH ən
politic	POL ə tik
politico	pə LIT i KOH
polity	POL ə tee
Polk	pohk
polka (dance)	POHL kə
polka (dot)	POH kə
poll	pohl
pollack	POL ək
pollen	POL ən
polliwog	POL ee WOG
Pollock	POL ək
pollute	pə LOOT
Pollux	POL əks
polonaise	POL ə NAYZ
polonium	pə LOH nee əm
Polonius	pə LOH nee əs
Pol Pot	pol pot
Poltava	pol TAH vah
poltergeist	POHL tər GĪST
poltroon	pol TROON
polyandry	POL ee AN dree
Polybius	pə LIB ee əs
Polycarp	POL i KAHRP
polychrome	POL i KROHM
polyclinic	POL i KLIN ik
Polyclitus, Polycleitus	POL i KLĪ təs
Polycrates	pə LIK rə TEEZ
polydactyl	POL i DAK təl
Polydorus	POL i DOR əs
polyester	POL ee ES tər
polyethylene	POL ee ETH ə LEEN
polygamy	pə LIG ə mee
polyglot	POL i GLOT
Polygnotus	POL ig NOH təs
polygon	POL i GON
polygraph	POL i GRAF

polygyny	pə LIJ ə nee
Polyhymnia	POL i HIM nee ə
polymer	POL ə mər
polymerization	pə LIM ər ə ZAY shən
Polymnia	pə LIM nee ə
Polynesia	POL ə NEE zhə
Polynices	POL i NĪ seez
polynomial	POL ee NOH mee əl
polyp	POL əp
Polyphemus	POL ə FEE məs
polyphonic	POL i FON ik
polyphony	pə LIF ə nee
polypropylene	POL i PROH pə LEEN
polyptych	POL əp TIK
polystyrene	POL i STĪ reen
polysyllabic	POL i sə LAB ik
polysyllable	POL i SIL ə bəl
polytechnic	POL i TEK nik
polytheism	POL i thee IZ əm
Polyxena	pə LIK sə nə
pomade	pə MAYD
pomander	POH MAN dər
pomegranate	POM ə GRAN ət
pomelo	POM ə LOH
Pomerania	POM ə RAY nee ə
pommel	PUM əl
pomology	poh MOL ə jee
Pomona	pə MOH nə
pompadour, P-	POM pə DOR
Pompeii	pom PAY
Pompeius	pom PEE əs
Pompey	POM pee
Pompidou, Georges	pohm pee DOO, *ZHAWRZH*
pom-pom	POM pom
pompon	POM pon
pomposity	pom POS ə tee
pompous	POM pəs
Ponca	PONG kə
ponce	pons
Ponce	PAWN se
Ponce de León	PAWN sə day le AWN
Ponchielli	pawng KYEL ee
poncho	PON choh

ə ago, a at, ah calm, ahr dark, air care, aw saw, ay say, ch church
e bet, ee me, eer beer, hw what, i is, ī my, *n* French final n vin,

ponderous	PON dər əs
Pondicherry	PON di CHER ee
pongee	pon JEE
poniard	PON yərd
Ponomaryov, Boris	PON ə mahr YAWF, bah REES
pons, P-	ponz
Ponta Delgada	PAWN tə del GAH də
Pontchartrain	PON chər TRAYN
Pontiac	PON tee AK
pontifex	PON tə FEKS
pontifical	pon TIF i kəl
pontificate (n)	pon TIF i kət
pontificate (v)	pon TIF ə KAYT
Pontius	PON chəs
pontoon	pon TOON
Pontoppidan	pon TOP i DAHN
Pontus	PON təs
Poona	POO nə
poplar	POP lər
poplin	POP lən
Popocatepetl	POH pə KAT ə PET əl
Popovic	PAW paw vich
populace	POP yə ləs
popular	POP yə lər
popularity	POP yə LAR ə tee
populous	POP yə ləs
porcelain	POR sə lən
porcine	POR sin
porcupine	POR kyə PIN
porgy, P-	POR gee
Pori	POR ee
pornographic	POR nə GRAF ik
pornography	por NOG rə fee
porosity	pə ROS ə tee
porous	POR əs
porphyry	POR fə ree
porpoise	POR pəs
porridge	POR ij
porringer	POR ən jər
Porsena, Lars	POR si nə, LAHRZ
Port-au-Prince	PORT oh PRINS
portcullis	port KUL əs
Port du Salut	POR də sal OO

o on, oh oat, oi boy, oo soon, oor poor, or for, ow cow, sh shush,
th thin, *th* this, u up, ur spur, uu book, *zh* pleasure

porte-cochère	**PORT** koh **SHAIR**
portend	por **TEND**
Porteño	por **TAY** nyoh
portent	**POR** tent
portentous	por **TEN** təs
portfolio	port **FOH** lee **OH**
Portia	**POR** shə
portico	**POR** ti **KOH**
portiere	por **TYAIR**
Portland	**PORT** lənd
portmanteau	port **MAN** toh
Porto (Portugal)	**POR** tuu
Porto Alegre	**POR** tuu ah **LE** gri
portrait	**POR** trət
portraiture	**POR** trə **CHUUR**
Port Said	**PORT** sah **EED**
Portsmouth	**PORTS** məth
Portugal	**POR** chə gəl
Portuguese	**POR** chə **GEEZ**
portulaca	**POR** chə **LAK** ə
Porumbeanu	**PAW** rəm bee **AH** noo
Poseidon	pə **SĪ** dən
Posen	**POH** zən
poseur	poh **ZUR**
posit	**POZ** ət
positive	**POZ** ə tiv
positively	**POZ** ə tiv lee
positively (emphatic)	**POZ** ə **TIV** lee
positron	**POZ** ə **TRON**
posse	**POS** ee
possess	pə **ZES**
possession	pə **ZESH** ən
posset	**POS** ət
possible	**POS** ə bəl
possum	**POS** əm
post bellum	**POHST BEL** əm
postdiluvian	**POHST** də **LOO** vee ən
posterity	pos **TER** ə tee
postern	**POH** stərn
post hoc ergo propter hoc	pohst **HOHK AIR** goh **PROHP** tər **HOHK**
posthumous	**POS** chuu məs
postiche	paw **STEESH**

ə ago, a at, ah calm, ahr dark, air care, aw saw, ay say, ch church
e bet, ee me, eer beer, hw what, i is, ī my, n French final n vin,

postilion, postillion	poh **STIL** yən
postmeridian	**POHST** mə **RID** ee ən
post meridiem	**POHST** mə **RID** ee əm
postmortem	pohst **MOR** təm
postprandial	pohst **PRAN** dee əl
postulant	**POS** chə lənt
postulate (n)	**POS** chə lət
postulate (v)	**POS** chə **LAYT**
posture	**POS** chər
posy	**POH** zee
potable	**POH** tə bəl
potage	poh **TAHZ***H*
potash	**POT** ash
potassium	pə **TAS** ee əm
potato	pə **TAY** toh
pot-au-feu	poht oh **FUU**
poteen	poh **TEEN**
Potemkin	pə **TEM** kən
potency	**POH** tən see
potent	**POH** tənt
potentate	**POH** tən **TAYT**
potential	pə **TEN** shəl
potentiality	pə **TEN** shee **AL** ə tee
potentially	pə **TEN** shə lee
potentiometer	pə **TEN** shee **OM** ə tər
potheen	poh **THEEN**
pother	**PO***TH* ər
potherb	**POT** urb
potiche	poh **TEESH**
potion	**POH** shən
Potiphar	**POT** ə fər
Potomac	pə **TOH** mək
Potosi	pə **TOH** see
Potosí	**PAW** taw **SEE**
potpie	**POT** pī
potpourri	**POH** puu **REE**
Potsdam	**POTS** dam
potsherd	**POT** shurd
pottage	**POT** ij
pouf	poof
Poughkeepsie	pə **KIP** see
Poulenc	poo **LANGK**
poult	pohlt

---

o on, oh oat, oi boy, oo soon, oor poor, or for, ow cow, sh shush,
th thin, *th* this, u up, ur spur, uu book, *zh* pleasure

poultice	**POHL** təs
pourboire	puur **BWAHR**
pourparler	puur pahr **LAY**
pousse-café	**POOS** ka **FAY**
Poussin	poo **SAN** (**SAN** French final *n*)
Powhatan	**POW** ə **TAN**
Powys	**POH** əs
Pozarevac	**PAW** *zh*ah re vahts
Pozega	**PAW** *zh*e gah
Poznań	**PAWZ** nahn yə
practitioner	prak **TISH** ə nər
Pradhan, Om	prah **DAHN**, awm
praetor	**PREE** tər
praetorian, P-	pree **TOR** ee ən
pragmatic	prag **MAT** ik
pragmatism	**PRAG** mə **TIZ** əm
Prague	prahg
Praha	**PRAH** hah
Praia	**PRĪ** ə
prairie	**PRAIR** ee
Prajadhipok	prə **CHAH** ti **POK**
Prakrit	**PRAH** krit
praline	**PRAY** leen
prance	prans
prandial	**PRAN** dee əl
praseodymium	**PRAY** zee oh **DIM** ee əm
pratfall	**PRAT** fawl
pratique	pra **TEEK**
Pravda	**PRAHV** dah
praxis	**PRAK** səs
Praxiteles	prak **SIT** ə **LEEZ**
prayer (act of praying)	prair
prayer (one who prays)	**PRAY** ər
prebendary	**PREB** ən **DER** ee
Precambrian	pree **KAM** bree ən
precarious	pri **KA** ree əs
precatory	**PREK** ə **TOR** ee
precedence	pri **SEED** əns
precedent (a)	pri **SEED** ənt
precedent (n)	**PRES** ə dənt
precept	**PREE** sept
preceptor	pri **SEP** tər

ə ago, a at, ah calm, ahr dark, air care, aw saw, ay say, ch church
e bet, ee me, eer beer, hw what, i is, ī my, *n* French final n vin,

precession	pree SESH ən
precinct	PREE singkt
preciosity	PRES ee OS ə tee
precipice	PRES ə pəs
precipitant	pri SIP ə tənt
precipitate (v)	pri SIP ə TAYT
precipitate (a, n)	pri SIP ə tit
precipitous	pri SIP ə təs
précis	pray SEE
precise	pri SĪS
precisely	pri SĪS lee
precision	pri SIZH ən
preclude	pri KLOOD
precocious	pri KOH shəs
precocity	pri KOS ə tee
precognition	PREE kog NISH ən
precursor	pri KUR sər
predator	PRED ə tər
predatory	PRED ə TOR ee
predecessor	PRED ə SES ər
predestination	pree DES tə NAY shən
predicament	pri DIK ə mənt
predicate (a, n)	PRED ə kət
predicate (v)	PRED ə KAYT
predilection	PRED ə LEK shən
preeminence	pree EM ə nəns
preempt	pree EMPT
preface	PREF əs
prefatory	PREF ə TOR ee
prefect	PREE fekt
prefecture	PREE FEK chər
preferable	PREF ər ə bəl
preferably	PREF ər ə blee
preference	PREF ər əns
preferential	PREF ə REN shəl
prefix (n)	PREE fiks
prefix (v)	pree FIKS
pregnancy	PREG nən see
prehensile	pree HEN səl
prehistory	pree HIS tə ree
prejudge	pree JUJ
prejudice	PREJ ə dəs
prejudicial	PREJ ə DISH əl

o on, oh oat, oi boy, oo soon, oor poor, or for, ow cow, sh shush,
th thin, *th* this, u up, ur spur, uu book, *zh* pleasure

prelacy	**PREL** ə see
prelate	**PREL** ət
preliminary	pri **LIM** ə **NER** ee
Prelog, Vladimir	**PRE** lohg, **VLA** də mir
prelude	**PREL** yood
Premadasa, Ranasinghe	pree mə dah sə, rah nah sing ə
premature	**PREE** mə **CHUUR**
premier	pri **MIR**
premiere	pri **MYER**
premise	**PREM** əs
premium	**PREE** mee əm
premonition	**PREE** mə **NISH** ən
Prem Tinsulanonda	praym **TIN** suul ah **NON**
prenatal	pree **NAYT** əl
Prentice	**PREN** təs
Prentiss	**PREN** təs
preparative	pri **PA** rə tiv
preparatory	pri **PA** rə **TOR** ee
preponderance	pri **PON** dər əns
preposition	**PREP** ə **ZISH** ən
prepossession	**PREE** pə **ZESH** ən
preposterous	pri **POS** tər əs
prepuce	**PREE** pyoos
Pre-Raphaelite	pree **RAF** ee ə **LĪT**
prerequisite	pri **REK** wə zət
prerogative	pri **ROG** ə tiv
presage (n)	**PRES** ij
presage (v)	pri **SAYJ**
presbyter	**PREZ** bə tər
Presbyterian	**PREZ** bə **TEER** ee ən
presbytery	**PRES** bə **TER** ee
prescience	**PRESH** əns
prescient	**PRESH** ənt
Prescott	**PRES** kət
present (a, n)	**PREZ** ənt
present (v)	pri **ZENT**
presentation	**PREZ** ən **TAY** shən
presentiment	pri **ZEN** tə mənt
preside	pri **ZĪD**
presidency	**PREZ** ə dən see
presidential	**PREZ** ə **DEN** shəl
presidio	pri **SID** ee **OH**

ə ago, a at, ah calm, ahr dark, air care, aw saw, ay say, ch church
e bet, ee me, eer beer, hw what, i is, ī my, *n* French final n vin,

presidium	pri SID ee əm
pressure	PRESH ər
prestidigitation	PRES tə DIJ ə TAY shən
prestidigitator	PRES tə DIJ ə TAY tər
prestige	pre STEEZ*H*
prestissimo	pre STIS ə MOH
presto	PRES toh
Preston	PRES tən
presume	pri ZOOM
presumptive	pri ZUM tiv
presumptuous	pri ZUM choo əs
presupposition	PREE SUP ə ZISH ən
pretense	PREE tens
pretentious	pri TEN shəs
preterit	PRET ər ət
preternatural	PREE tər NACH ə rəl
pretext	PREE tekst
Pretoria	pri TOR ee ə
pretzel	PRET səl
prevalence	PREV ə ləns
prevalent	PREV ə lənt
prevaricator	pri VAR ə KAY tər
preventive	pri VEN tiv
Prévost	pray VOH
Priam	PRĪ əm
priapic	prī AY pik
priapism	PRĪ ə PIZ əm
Priapus, p-	prī AY pəs
Pribilof	PRIB ə LOF
prie-dieu	pree dyuu
Prigogine, Ilya	prə GOH zh ən, EEL yə
prima	PREE mə
primacy	PRĪ mə see
prima donna	PRĪ mə DON ə
prima facie	PRĪ mə FAY shee
primarily	prī MER ə lee
primary	PRĪ MER ee
primate	PRĪ mayt
primer (book)	PRIM ər
primer (except book)	PRĪ mər
primeval	prī MEE vəl
primipara	prī MIP ə rə
primogenitor	PRĪ mə JEN ə tər

---

o on, oh oat, oi boy, oo soon, oor poor, or for, ow cow, sh shush,
th thin, *th* this, u up, ur spur, uu book, *zh* pleasure

primogeniture	PRĪ mə JEN ə chər
primordial	prī MOR dee əl
primula	PRIM yə lə
primus, P-	PRĪ məs
primus inter pares	PREE məs IN tər PA reez
prince	prins
princes	PRINS əz
princess	PRINS əs
princesses	PRINS əs əz
Princeton	PRINS tən
principal	PRIN sə pəl
principality	PRIN sə PAL ə tee
Principe	PRIN sə pee
principle	PRIN sə pəl
prior, P-	PRĪ ər
priorate	PRĪ ər ət
prioress	PRĪ ər əs
priority	prī OR ə tee
priory	PRĪ ə ree
Pripet	PREE pet
Priscian	PRISH ən
prism	PRIZ əm
prismatic	priz MAT ik
pristine	PRIS teen
prithee	PRI*TH* ee
privacy	PRĪ və see
privateer	PRĪ və TEER
privation	prī VAY shən
privet	PRIV ət
privilege	PRIV ə lij
privy	PRIV ee
prix fixe	pree feeks
probably	PROB ə blee
probate	PROH bayt
probationary	proh BAY shə NER ee
probity	PROH bə tee
problematical	PROB lə MAT ə kəl
pro bono publico	proh BOH noh POOB lə KOH
proboscis	proh BOS əs
procaine	PROH kayn
procedural	prə SEE jər əl
procedure	prə SEE jər
proceeds (goes forward)	proh SEEDS

ə ago, a at, ah calm, ahr dark, air care, aw saw, ay say, ch church
e bet, ee me, eer beer, hw what, i is, ī my, *n* French final n vin,

proceeds (money)	**PROH** seeds
process	**PROS** es
Prochnik	**PRAHCH** nik
proclitic	proh **KLIT** ik
proclivity	proh **KLIV** ə tee
Procne	**PROK** nee
Procopius	proh **KOH** pee əs
procrastinate	proh **KRAS** tə **NAYT**
procreant	**PROH** kree ənt
Procrustean	proh **KRUS** tee ən
Procrustes	proh **KRUS** teez
proctology	prok **TOL** ə jee
proctor	**PROK** tər
procurance	prə **KYUUR** əns
procuration	**PROK** yə **RAY** shən
procurator	**PROK** yə **RAY** tər
procure	prə **KYUUR**
procurer	prə **KYUUR** ər
procuress	prə **KYUUR** əs
Procyon	**PROH** see **ON**
prodigal	**PROD** ə gəl
prodigality	**PROD** ə **GAL** ə tee
prodigious	prə **DIJ** əs
prodigy	**PROD** ə jee
produce (n)	**PROD** oos
produce (v)	prə **DOOS**
proem	**PROH** em
profanation	**PROF** ə **NAY** shən
profane	proh **FAYN**
profanity	proh **FAN** ə tee
profess	prə **FES**
profession	prə **FESH** ən
professorial	**PROH** fə **SOR** ee əl
proffer	**PROF** ər
proficiency	prə **FISH** ən see
proficient	prə **FISH** ənt
profile	**PROH** fil
profiteer	**PROF** ə **TIR**
profligacy	**PROF** lə gə see
profligate	**PROF** lə gət
pro forma	proh **FOR** mə
profound	prə **FOWND**
profundity	prə **FUN** də tee
profuse	prə **FYOOS**

o on, oh oat, oi boy, oo soon, oor poor, or for, ow cow, sh shush,
th thin, *th* this, u up, ur spur, uu book, *zh* pleasure

profusion	prə FYOO *zh*ən
progenitor	proh JEN ə tər
progeny	PROJ ə nee
progesterone	proh JES tə ROHN
prognathous	PROG nə thəs
prognosis	prog NOH səs
prognostic	prog NOS tik
prognosticate	prog NOS tə KAYT
program	PROH gram
programmatic	PROH grə MAT ik
progress (n)	PROG rəs
progress (v)	prə GRES
progression	prə GRESH ən
progressive	prə GRES iv
prohibition	PROH ə BISH ən
prohibitive	proh HIB ə tiv
project (n)	PROJ ekt
project (v)	prə JEKT
projectile	prə JEK təl
Prok Amaranand	prohk AHM ah rah NAHN
Prokofieff, Prokofiev	praw KAW fyef
Prokopievsk	praw kaw PYEFSK
prolapse	proh LAPS
prolegomenon	PROH li GOM ə NON
prolepsis	proh LEP səs
proletarian	PROH lə TAIR ee ən
proletariat	PROH lə TAIR ee ət
proliferate	prə LIF ə RAYT
prolific	prə LIF ik
prolix	proh LIKS
prolixity	proh LIK sə tee
prolocutor	proh LOK yə tər
prologue	PROH lawg
prolong	prə LAWNG
prolongation	PROH lawng GAY shən
promenade	PROM ə NAYD
Promethean	prə MEE thee ən
Prometheus	prə MEE thee əs
prominence	PROM ə nəns
prominent	PROM ə nənt
promiscuity	PROM ə SKYOO ə tee
promiscuous	prə MIS kyoo əs
promissory	PROM ə SOR ee

ə ago, a at, ah calm, ahr dark, air care, aw saw, ay say, ch church
e bet, ee me, eer beer, hw what, i is, ī my, *n* French final n vin,

promontory	PROM ən TOR ee
promulgate	PROM əl GAYT
promulgation	PROM əl GAY shən
promulgator	PROM əl GAY tər
pronto	PRON toh
pronunciamento	proh NUN see ə MEN toh
pronunciation	prə NUN see AY shən
propaganda	PROP ə GAN də
propagate	PROP ə GAYT
propane	PROH payn
propel	prə PEL
propellant	prə PEL ənt
propensity	prə PEN sə tee
Propertius	proh PUR shəs
prophecy (n)	PROF ə see
prophesy (v)	PROF ə sī
prophet	PROF ət
prophetic	prə FET ik
prophylactic	PROH fə LAK tik
prophylaxis	PROH fə LAK səs
propinquity	prə PING kwə tee
propitiate	prə PISH ee AYT
propitious	prə PISH əs
proponent	prə POH nənt
proportionate (a)	prə POR shə nət
proportionate (v)	prə POR shə NAYT
proprietary	prə PRĪ ə TER ee
proprietor	prə PRĪ ə tər
propriety	prə PRĪ ə tee
propulsion	prə PUL shən
pro rata	proh RAY tə
prorogue	prə ROHG
prosaic	proh ZAY ik
proscenium	proh SEE nee əm
prosciutto	proh SHOO toh
proselyte	PROS ə LĪT
proselytize	PROS ə lə TĪz
Proserpina	prə SUR pə nə
Proserpine	PROS ər PĪN
prosit	PROH zət
prosodic	prə SOD ik
prosodist	PROS ə dəst
prosody	PROS ə dee

---

o on, oh oat, oi boy, oo soon, oor poor, or for, ow cow, sh shush,
th thin, *th* this, u up, ur spur, uu book, *zh* pleasure

prospectus	prə **SPEK** təs
Prospero	**PROS** pə **ROH**
prostate	**PROS** tayt
prostatitis	**PROS** tə **TĪT** əs
prosthesis	pros **THEE** səs
prosthetic	pros **THET** ik
Prostigmin, p-	proh **STIG** min
prostitute	**PROS** tə **TOOT**
prostrate	**PROS** trayt
prostyle	**PROH** stīl
prosy	**PROH** zee
protactinium	**PROH** tak **TIN** ee əm
protagonist	proh **TAG** ə nəst
Protagoras	proh **TAG** ər əs
protamine	**PROH** tə **MEEN**
protean, P-	**PROH** tee ən
protectorate	prə **TEK** tə rət
protégé	**PROH** tə **ZHAY**
protein	**PROH** teen
pro tempore	proh **TEM** pə **RE**
Proterozoic	**PROT** ər ə **ZOH** ik
protest (n)	**PROH** test
protest (v)	prə **TEST**
Protestant, p-	**PROT** ə stənt
protestation	**PROT** ə **STAY** shən
Proteus	**PROH** tee əs
prothalamion	**PROH** thə **LAY** mee **ON**
prothesis	**PROTH** ə səs
protium	**PROH** tee əm
protocol	**PROH** tə **KAWL**
proton	**PROH** ton
protoplasm	**PROH** tə **PLAZ** əm
prototype	**PROH** tə **TĪP**
Protozoa	**PROH** tə **ZOH** ə
protozoan	**PROH** tə **ZOH** ən
protract	proh **TRAKT**
protrude	proh **TROOD**
protrusion	proh **TROO** *zh*ən
protrusive	proh **TROO** siv
protuberance	proh **TOO** bə rəns
Proudhon	proo **DAWN** (**DAWN** French final *n*)
Proust	proost
provenance	**PROV** ə nəns

ə ago, a at, ah calm, ahr dark, air care, aw saw, ay say, ch church
e bet, ee me, eer beer, hw what, i is, ī my, *n* French final n vin,

Provençal	proh vahn **SAHL**
Provence	proh **VAHNS**
provender	**PROV** ən dər
proverb	**PROV** urb
proverbial	prə **VUR** bee əl
providence, P-	**PROV** ə dəns
provident	**PROV** ə dənt
province	**PROV** əns
provincial	prə **VIN** shəl
provision	prə **VIZH** ən
proviso	prə **VĪ** zoh
Provo	**PROH** voh
provocation	**PROV** ə **KAY** shən
provocative	prə **VOK** ə tiv
provolone	**PROH** və **LOH** nee
provost	**PROH** vohst
provost (military)	**PROH** voh
prowess	**PROW** əs
proximal	**PROK** sə məl
proximate	**PROK** sə mət
proximity	prok **SIM** ə tee
proximo	**PROK** sə **MOH**
proxy	**PROK** see
prudery	**PROO** də ree
Prud'hon	proo **DAWN** (**DAWN** French final *n*)
prudish	**PROOD** ish
prunella	proo **NEL** ə
prurient	**PRUUR** ee ənt
Prussia	**PRUSH** ə
Prussian	**PRUSH** ən
prussic	**PRUS** ik
Pruszkow	**PRUUSH** kuuf
Prut, -h	proot
Prynne	prin
psalm	sahm
psalmodist	**SAH** mə dəst
psalmody	**SAH** mə dee
psalter, P-	**SAWL** tər
psaltery, P-	**SAWL** tə ree
pseudo	**SOO** doh
pseudonym	**SOO** də nim
pseudonymous	soo **DON** ə məs
pseudopod	**SOO** də **POD**

---

o on, oh oat, oi boy, oo soon, oor poor, or for, ow cow, sh shush,
th thin, *th* this, u up, ur spur, uu book, *zh* pleasure

pseudopodium	soo də POH dee əm
pshaw	shaw
psi	sī
psilocybin	SĪL ə SĪ bən
psittacosis	SIT ə KOH səs
psoriasis	sə RĪ ə səs
psyche, P-	SĪ kee
psychedelic	sī kə DEL ik
psychiatric	sī kee AT rik
psychiatrist	si KĪ ə trəst
psychiatry	si KĪ ə tree
psychic	SĪ kik
psychoanalysis	sī koh ə NAL ə səs
psychoanalyst	sī koh AN ə ləst
psychogenic	sī koh JEN ik
psychological	sī kə LOJ i kəl
psychologist	si KOL ə jəst
psychology	si KOL ə jee
psychometry	si KOM ə tree
psychoneuroses	sī koh nuu ROH seez
psychoneurosis	sī koh nuu ROH səs
psychopath	SĪ kə PATH
psychopathic	sī kə PATH ik
psychopathology	sī koh pə THOL ə jee
psychoses	si KOH seez
psychosis	si KOH səs
psychosomatic	sī kə sə MAT ik
psychotherapy	sī koh THER ə pee
psychotic	si KOT ik
Ptah	pə TAH
ptarmigan	TAHR mi gən
pterodactyl	TER ə DAK təl
pteropod	TER ə POD
Ptolemaic	TOL ə MAY ik
Ptolemy	TOL ə mee
ptomaine	TOH mayn
ptosis	TOH səs
puberty	PYOO bər tee
pubescent	pyoo BES ənt
pubic	PYOO bik
publican	PUB li kən
Pucci, Emilio	POO chee, ay MEE lyoh
Puccini	poo CHEE nee

ə ago, a at, ah calm, ahr dark, air care, aw saw, ay say, ch church
e bet, ee me, eer beer, hw what, i is, ī my, n French final n vin,

puce	pyoos
pudendum	pyuu **DEN** dəm
Puebla	**PWE** blah
pueblo, P-	**PWEB** loh
puerile	**PYUUR** əl
puerperal	pyoo **UR** pə rəl
Puerto Rican	**PWER** toh **REE** kən
Puerto Rico	**PWER** toh **REE** koh
Puerto Vallarta	**PWER** toh vah **YAHR** tah
puffin	**PUF** ən
Puget	**PYOO** jit
puggaree	**PUG** ə ree
pugilist	**PYOO** jə ləst
pugnacious	pug **NAY** shəs
pugree	**PUG** ree
puisne	**PYOO** nee
puissance	**PYOO** ə səns
puissant	**PYOO** ə sənt
pukka	**PUK** ə
Pulaski	pə **LAS** kee
pulchritude	**PUL** krə **TOOD**
pulchritudinous	**PUL** krə **TOO** də nəs
pule	pyool
puli	**POO** lee
Pulitzer	**PUUL** ət sər
pullet	**PUUL** ət
Pullman	**PUUL** mən
pullulate	**PUL** yɔ **LAYT**
pulmonary	**PUUL** mə **NER** ee
pulpit	**PUUL** pit
pulque	**PUUL** kay
pulsate	**PUL** sayt
Pultusk	**PUUL** tuusk
pulverize	**PUL** və **RĪZ**
puma	**PYOO** mə
pumice	**PUM** əs
pummel	**PUM** əl
pumpernickel	**PUM** pər **NIK** əl
pumpkin	**PUMP** kən
puna	**POO** nah
puncheon	**PUN** chən
punchinello, P-	**PUN** chə **NEL** oh
punctilio	pungk **TIL** ee **OH**

o on, oh oat, oi boy, oo soon, oor poor, or for, ow cow, sh shush,
th thin, *th* this, u up, ur spur, uu book, *zh* pleasure

punctilious	pungk TIL ee əs
punctual	PUNGK choo əl
punctuality	PUNGK choo AL ə tee
punctuate	PUNGK choo AYT
punctuation	PUNGK choo AY chən
puncture	PUNGK chər
pundit	PUN dət
pungent	PUN jənt
Punic	PYOO nik
punitive	PYOO nə tiv
Punjab	pun JAHB
Punjabi	pun JAH bee
punkah	PUNG kə
Punta Arenas	POON tah ah RE nahs
Punxsutawney	PUNGK sə TAW nee
puny	PYOO nee
pupa	PYOO pə
Pupin	pyuu PEEN
puppet	PUP ət
Puppis	PUP is
purblind	PUR blind
Purcell (composer)	PUR səl
purdah	PUR də
purée	pyuu RAY
purgative	PUR gə tiv
purgatory	PUR gə TOR ee
Purim	PUUR im
puritanical, P-	PYUUR ə TAN i kəl
Puritanism, p-	PYUUR ə tə NIZ əm
purl	purl
purlieu	PURL yoo
purloin	pər LOIN
purport (n)	PUR port
purport (v)	pər PORT
purposive	PUR pə siv
purpura	PUR pyə rə
purslane	PURS lən
pursuance	pər SOO əns
pursuant	pər SOO ənt
pursue	pər SOO
pursuit	pər SOOT
pursuivant	PUR swi vənt
purulence	PYUUR ə ləns

ə ago, a at, ah calm, ahr dark, air care, aw saw, ay say, ch church
e bet, ee me, eer beer, hw what, i is, ī my, n French final n vin,

purulent	**PYUUR** ə lənt
purveyor	pər **VAY** ər
purview	**PUR** vyoo
Pusan	poo sahn
Pusey	**PYOO** zee
Pushkin	**PUUSH** kən
Pushto	**PUSH** toh (**PUSH** as in *hush*)
Pushtu	**PUSH** too (**PUSH** as in *hush*)
pusillanimity	**PYOO** sə lə **NIM** ə tee
pusillanimous	**PYOO** sə **LAN** ə məs
pustule	**PUS** chool
putative	**PYOO** tə tiv
Putnam	**PUT** nəm
putrefaction	**PYOO** trə **FAK** shən
putrescent	pyoo **TRES** ənt
putrid	**PYOO** trəd
Putsch, p-	puuch
putt	put (as in *nut*)
puttee	pu **TEE**
putty	**PUT** ee (**PUT** as in *nut*)
Putumayo	**POO** too **MAH** yaw
Pu-yi	poo yee
Pydna	**PID** nə
pyelitis	**PĪ** ə **LĪ** təs
pyemia	pī **EE** mee ə
Pygmalion	pig **MAYL** yən
Pygmy, p-	**PIG** mee
pyknic	**PIK** nik
pylon	**PĪ** lon
pylorus	pī **LOR** əs
Pylos	**PĪ** lahs
Pynchon	**PINCH** ən
Pyongyang	pyung yahng
pyorrhea	**PĪ** ə **REE** ə
pyramid	**PIR** ə mid
pyramidal	pə **RAM** ə dəl
Pyramus	**PIR** ə məs
pyre	pīr
Pyrenean	**PIR** ə **NEE** ən
Pyrenees	**PIR** ə **NEEZ**
pyretic	pī **RET** ik
Pyrex	**PĪ** reks
pyrexia	pī **REK** see ə

o on, oh oat, oi boy, oo soon, oor poor, or for, ow cow, sh shush,
th thin, *th* this, u up, ur spur, uu book, *zh* pleasure

pyridine	**PIR** ə DEEN
pyridoxine	**PIR** ə **DOK** seen
pyriform	**PIR** ə **FORM**
pyrite	**PĪ** rīt
pyrites	pə **RĪ** teez
pyrogenic	**PĪ** rə **JEN** ik
pyrography	pī **ROG** rə fee
pyrolysis	pī **ROL** ə sis
pyrolyze	**PĪ** rə **LĪZ**
pyromania	**PĪ** rə **MAY** nee ə
pyrophobia	**PĪ** rə **FOH** bee ə
pyrosis	pī **ROH** səs
pyrotechnic	**PĪ** rə **TEK** nik
Pyrrha	**PIR** ə
pyrrhic, P-	**PIR** ik
Pyrrhonism	**PIR** ə NIZ əm
Pyrrhus	**PIR** əs
Pythagoras	pə **THAG** ər əs
Pythagorean	pə THAG ə **REE** ən
Pythia	**PITH** ee ə
Pythian	**PITH** ee ən
Pythias	**PITH** ee əs
python, P-	**PĪ** thon
pythoness	**PĪ** thə nəs
pyuria	pī **YUUR** ee ə
pyx	piks
Pyxis, p-	**PIK** səs

Q

Qaddafi, Muammar al-	kə **DAHF** ee, **MOO** ə MAHR ahl
Qantas	**KWON** təs
Qara Qum	kah **RAH** KUUM
Qatar	**KAH** tahr
Qattara	kah **TAH** rah
Qeshm	**KESH** əm
Qingdao	ching dow
Qinghai	ching hī
Qin Shi Huang	chin shuu hwahng
Qirghiz	kir **GEEZ**
Qishm	**KISH** əm

ə ago, a at, ah calm, ahr dark, air care, aw saw, ay say, ch church
e bet, ee me, eer beer, hw what, i is, ī my, *n* French final n vin,

Qizil Qum	ki ZIL KUUM
qua	kwah
Quaalude	KWAY lood
quad	kwod
quadragenarian	KWOD rə jə NA ree ən
Quadragesima	KWOD rə JES ə mə
quadrangle	KWOD rang əl
quadrangular	kwod RANG gyə lər
quadrant	KWOD rənt
quadraphonic	KWOD rə FON ik
quadrate	KWOD rayt
quadrate (v)	KWOD rayt
quadratic	kwo DRAT ik
quadrature	KWOD rə chər
quadrennial	kwo DREN ee əl
quadricentennial	KWOD rə sen TEN ee əl
quadrille	kwo DRIL
quadriplegia	KWOD rə PLEE jee ə
quadriplegic	KWOD rə PLEE jik
quadrivium	kwo DRIV ee əm
quadroon	kwo DROON
Quadros, Jânio	KWAH drohsh, ZHA nee oh
quadruped	KWOD rə PED
quadruple	kwo DROO pəl
quadruplet	KWOD rə plət
quadruplicate (a, n)	kwo DROO plə kət
quadruplicate (v)	kwo DROO plə KAYT
quaestor	KWES tər
quaff	kwahf
quagmire	KWAG mīr
quahog	KWAW hawg
Quai d'Orsay	KAY dor SAY
quaint	kwaynt
Quaison-Sackey, Alex	KWE sən SA kay, A leks
qualitative	KWOL ə TAY tiv
qualm	kwahm
quandary	KWON də ree
quandong	KWON dong
quant	kwant
quanta	KWON tə
quantic	KWON tik
quantitative	KWON tə TAY tiv
quantity	KWON tə tee

o on, oh oat, oi boy, oo soon, oor poor, or for, ow cow, sh shush,
th thin, *th* this, u up, ur spur, uu book, *zh* pleasure

quantum	KWON təm
quarantine	KWOR ən TEEN
quark	kwork (as in *stork*)
Quarnero	kwahr NE raw
quarrel	KWOR əl
quarry	KWOR ee
quart (measure)	kwort (as in *sort*)
quartan	KWOR tən
quartile	KWOR tīl
quarto	KWOR toh
quartz	kworts (as in *sorts*)
quasar	KWAY zahr
quash	kwosh
quasi	KWAY zī
Quasimodo, Salvatore	KWAH zee MAW daw, SAHL vah TAW re
quassia	KWOSH ə
quaternary	KWAH tər NER ee
Quathlamba	kwaht LAHM bah
quatrain	KWAH trayn
quatrefoil	KAT ər FOIL
quattrocento	KWAH troh CHEN toh
quay	kee
queasy	KWEE zee
Quebec	kwi BEK
Quebecois	KAY be KWAH
quebracho	kay BRAH choh
Quechua	KECH wə
Quechuan	KECH wən
Queensland	KWEENZ lənd
Quelpart	KWEL pahrt
Quemoy	kee MOI
quenelle	kə NEL
Querétaro	ke RE tah ROH
querulous	KWER ə ləs
query	KWIR ee
questionnaire	KWES chə NAIR
questor	KWES tər
Quetta	KWET ah
quetzal	ket SAHL
Quetzalcoatl	ket SAHL KWAHT əl
queue	kyoo
Quezon	KAY zon
quiche	keesh

ə ago, a at, ah calm, ahr dark, air care, aw saw, ay say, ch church
e bet, ee me, eer beer, hw what, i is, ī my, *n* French final n vin,

Quiché	kee **CHAY**
quiddity	**KWID** ə tee
quidnunc	**KWID** nungk
quid pro quo	**KWID** proh **KWOH**
quién sabe	kyen **SAH** be
quiescence	kwī **ES** əns
quiescent	kwī **ES** ənt
quietude	**KWĪ** ə **TOOD**
quietus	kwī **EE** təs
quinacrine	**KWIN** ə **KREEN**
quincunx	**KWIN** kungks
Quincy (Illinois)	**KWIN** see
Quincy (Massachusetts)	**KWIN** zee
quindecagon	kwin **DEK** ə **GON**
quindecennial	**KWIN** di **SEN** ee əl
quinidine	**KWIN** ə **DEEN**
quinine	**KWĪ** nīn
quinquagenarian	**KWING** kwə jə **NA** ree ən
Quinquagesima	**KWING** kwə **JES** ə mə
quinquennial	kwin **KWEN** ee əl
quinquennium	kwin **KWEN** ee əm
quinquereme	**KWING** kwə **REEM**
quinsy	**KWIN** zee
quintal	**KWIN** təl
Quintana Roo	keen **TAHN** ə **ROO**
quintessence	kwin **TES** əns
quintessential	**KWIN** tə **SEN** shəl
Quintilian	kwin **TIL** yən
quintillion	kwin **TIL** yən
quintuple	kwin **TOO** pəl
quintuplet	**KWIN** tə plət
quire	kwīr
Quirinal	**KWIR** ə nəl
Quirinus	kwə **RĪ** nəs
Quirites	kwə **RĪ** teez
quirk	kwurk
quirt	kwurt
quisling	**KWIZ** ling
Quito	**KEE** toh
qui vive	kee **VEEV**
Quixote (see Don Quixote)	
quixotic	kwik **SOT** ik

o on, oh oat, oi boy, oo soon, oor poor, or for, ow cow, sh shush,
th thin, *th* this, u up, ur spur, uu book, *zh* pleasure

Qum	kuum
Qumran	kuum **RAHN**
quo animo	**KWOH AH** ni **MOH**
quodlibet	**KWOD** lə **BET**
quoin	koin
quoit	kwoit
quondam	**KWON** dəm
Quonset	**KWON** sət
quorum	**KWOR** əm
quota	**KWOH** tə
quotation	kwoh **TAY** shən
quoth	kwohth
quotidian	kwoh **TID** ee ən
Quo Vadis	kwoh **WAH** dəs

R

Ra	rah
Rabat	rah **BAHT**
Rabaul	rah **BOWL** (**BOWL** as in *howl*)
Rabbath	**RAB** əth
rabbi	**RAB** ī
Rabbinic, r-	rə **BIN** ik
rabbinical	rə **BIN** i kəl
rabbinist	**RAB** ə nəst
Rabelais	**RAB** ə **LAY**
Rabelaisian	**RAB** ə **LAY** *zh*ən
rabid	**RAB** əd
rabies	**RAY** beez
Rabi, I. I.	**RAH** bee
Rabin, Yitzhak	rah **BEEN**, **YEETS** hahk
raccoon	ra **KOON**
raceme	ray **SEEM**
Rachel	**RAY** chəl
Rachel (French)	ra **SHEL**
rachis	**RAY** kəs
rachitic	rə **KIT** ik
rachitis	rə **KĪ** təs
Rachmaninoff, Rachmaninov	rahk **MAH** nə **NAWF**
Racine (Wisconsin)	rə **SEEN**

ə ago, a at, ah calm, ahr dark, air care, aw saw, ay say, ch church
e bet, ee me, eer beer, hw what, i is, ī my, *n* French final n vin,

Racine, Jean Baptiste	ra SEEN, *zh*ahn ba TEEST (*zh*ahn French final *n*)
racket	RAK ət
Rackham	RAK əm
racon	RAY kon
raconteur	RAK on TUR
racquet	RAK ət
Rácz, Pál	rahs, pal
radar	RAY dahr
Radauti	RAHD ə OOTS
Radek	RAH dek
Radhakrishnan	rah dah KRISH nən
radial	RAY dee əl
radian	RAY dee ən
radiant	RAY dee ənt
radiate	RAY dee AYT
radiation	RAY dee AY shən
radiator	RAY dee AY tər
radical	RAD i kəl
radii (pl)	RAY dee Ī
radioactive	RAY dee oh AK tiv
radiogram	RAY dee oh GRAM
radiography	RAY dee OG rə fee
radioisotope	RAY dee oh Ī sə TOHP
radiology	RAY dee OL ə jee
radiosonde	RAY dee oh SOND
radium	RAY dee əm
radius	RAY dee əs
radix	RAY diks
Radnor	RAD nər
Radom	RAH dawm
radome	RAY dohm
radon	RAY don
Radrodro, J. F.	rahn draw DOH
Radványi, János	ROHD vah nyee, YAH nohsh
raffia	RAF ee ə
raffinate	RAF ə NAYT
raffish	RAF ish
Rafsanjani, Hashemi	ruf sen JAN ee, HASH ə mee
raga	RAH gə
ragamuffin	RAG ə MUF ən
ragged	RAG əd
raglan	RAG lən

o on, oh oat, oi boy, oo soon, oor poor, or for, ow cow, sh shush,
th thin, *th* this, u up, ur spur, uu book, *zh* pleasure

Ragnarok	**RAHG** nə **ROK**
ragout	ra **GOO**
Ragusa	rah **GOO** zah
raillery	**RAY** lə ree
raiment	**RAY** mənt
Raimondi	rī **MOHN** dee
Rainier (Mount)	rə **NEER**
Rainier (Prince)	re **NYAY**
raison d'être	**RAY** zohn **DET** rə (zohn French final *n*)
raj	rahj
raja	**RAH** jə
Rajaie-Khorassani, Said	rah **JE** ee **HOH** rah **SEN** ee, sah **EED**
Rajasthan	**RAH** jə **STAHN**
Rajput	**RAHJ** poot
Rajputana	**RAHJ** puu **TAH** nə
raki	rah **KEE**
rakish	**RAY** kish
Rakotomalala, Louis	**RAH** koh toh **MAH** lahl, loo **EE**
Rakowski, Mieczyslaw	rah **KOF** skee, **MYE** chi swahf
Raleigh	**RAW** lee
rallentando	**RAH** lən **TAHN** doh
Ralston	**RAWL** stən
Rama	**RAH** mə
Ramachandra	**RAH** mə **CHUN** drə
Ramadan	**RAM** ə **DAHN**
Ramapo	**RAM** ə poh
Rama Rau, Santha	**RAH** mah **ROW**, **SAHN** tə (**ROW** as in *cow*)
Ramayana	rah **MAH** yə nə
Rambouillet	rahn boo **YAY** (rahn French final *n*)
rambunctious	ram **BUNGK** shəs
Ramdat-Misier, Lachmipersad	**RAHM** daht mis **EER**, **LAHCH** mee pər **SAHD**
Rameau	ra **MOH**
ramekin	**RAM** ə kən
Rameses	**RAM** ə **SEEZ**
ramification	**RAM** ə fə **KAY** shən
Ramirez Pane, Ruben	rah **MEER** ez **PAH** nay, **ROO** ben
Ramón	rah **MAWN**
ramose	**RAY** mohs
rampage (n)	**RAM** payj

ə ago, a at, ah calm, ahr dark, air care, aw saw, ay say, ch church
e bet, ee me, eer beer, hw what, i is, ī my, *n* French final n vin,

rampage (v)	ram **PAYJ**
rampant	**RAM** pənt
Ramsay	**RAM** zee
Ramses	**RAM** seez
Ramsey	**RAM** zee
ramshackle	**RAM SHAK** əl
ranchero	rahn **CHAIR** oh
rancho	**RAHN** choh
rancid	**RAN** səd
rancor	**RANG** kər
random	**RAN** dəm
ranee	**RAH** nee
Rangel	**RANG** gəl
Rangoon	rang **GOON**
rani	**RAH** nee
Rank, Otto	rahnk
Rankine	**RANG** kən
ransack	**RAN** sak
ranunculus	rə **NUNG** kyə ləs
Raoul, Raúl	ra **OOL**
rapacious	rə **PAY** shəs
rapacity	rə **PAS** ə tee
Rapacki, Adam	rah **PAHT** see, ah **DAHM**
Rapallo	rah **PAH** law
Raphael	**RAY** fee əl
Raphael (painter)	**RAH** fah el
Rapidan	**RAP** ə **DAN**
rapidity	rə **PID** ə tee
rapier	**RAY** pee ər
rapine	**RAP** ən
Rappahannock	**RAP** ə **HAN** ək
rappel	rə **PEL**
rapport	ra **POR**
rapprochement	ra prohsh **MAHN** (**MAHN** French final *n*)
rapscallion	rap **SKAL** yən
rapture	**RAP** chər
rapturous	**RAP** chər əs
rara avis	**RAR** ə **AY** vəs
rarebit	**RAR** bət
rarefaction	**RAR** ə **FAK** shən
rarefy	**RAR** ə **FĪ**
Raritan	**RAR** ət ən
rarity	**RAR** ə tee

o on, oh oat, oi boy, oo soon, oor poor, or for, ow cow, sh shush,
th thin, *th* this, u up, ur spur, uu book, *zh* pleasure

Rarotonga	RAR ə TONG gə
rascality	ra SKAL ə tee
rasher	RASH ər
Rashi	RAH shee
Rashidov, Sharaf	rah SHEE dof, shah RAHF
Rasmussen, Knud	RAHS muu sən, KNOO*TH*
raspberry	RAZ BER ee
Rasputin	ra SPYOO tən
Rastafarian	RAS tə FA ree ən
raster	RAS tər
ratafia	RAT ə FEE ə
ratatouille	rah tah TOO yə
ratchet	RACH ət
rather	RA*TH* ər
rathskeller	RAHT SKEL ər
ratiné	RAT ə NAY
ratio	RAY shee oh
ratiocinate	RASH ee OS ə NAYT
ratiocination	RASH ee OS ə NAY shən
ration	RASH ən
rational	RASH ə nəl
rationale	RASH ə NAL
rationalism	RASH ən əl IZ əm
rationality	RASH ə NAL ə tee
rationalization	RASH ən əl ə ZAY shən
ratline	RAT lən
ratsbane	RATS bayn
Ratsiraka, Didier	RAHT see RAH kah, dee dee AY
rattan	ra TAN
raucous	RAW kəs
Rauschenburg	ROW shən BURG (ROW as in *cow*)
rauwolfia	raw WUUL fee ə
ravage	RAV ij
ravel	RAV əl
Ravel	ra VEL
raven (n, a)	RAY vən
raven (v)	RAV ən
Ravenna	rə VEN ə
ravenous	RAV ə nəs
ravigote	ra vee GAWT
ravine	rə VEEN
ravioli	RAV ee OH lee
ravish	RAV ish

ə ago, a at, ah calm, ahr dark, air care, aw saw, ay say, ch church
e bet, ee me, eer beer, hw what, i is, ī my, *n* French final n vin,

Rawalpindi	RAH wəl PIN dee
rayah	RAH yə
Rayburn	RAY bərn
Rayleigh	RAY lee
rayon	RAY on
Re, r-	ray
reactance	ree AK təns
reaction	ree AK shən
reactionary	ree AK shə NER ee
reactor	re AK tər
Reading (Pennsylvania, England)	RED ing
Reading Gaol	RED ing JAYL
Reagan	RAY gən
reagent	ree AY jənt
real	REE əl
realign	REE ə LĪN
realism	REE ə LIZ əm
reality	ree AL ə tee
realization	REE ə lə ZAY shən
really	REE ə lee
realm	relm
realpolitik	ray AHL POH li TEEK
realtor, R-	REE əl tər
realty	REE əl tee
Réaumur	RAY oh MYUUR
rebec	REE bek
Rebecca, Rebekah	ri BEK ə
rebel (n)	REB əl
rebel (v)	ri BEL
rebellion	ri BEL yən
rebellious	ri BEL yəs
rebozo, R-	ri BOH zoh
rebuke	ri BYOOK
rebus	REE bəs
rebut	ri BUT
rebuttal	ri BUT əl
recalcitrance	ri KAL sə trəns
recalcitrant	ri KAL sə trənt
recall	ri KAWL
recamier	RAY kə MYAY
Récamier	ray ka MYAY

---

o on, oh oat, oi boy, oo soon, oor poor, or for, ow cow, sh shush,
th thin, *th* this, u up, ur spur, uu book, *zh* pleasure

recant	ri KANT
recapitulate	REE kə PICH ə LAYT
receipt	ri SEET
recency	REE sən see
recension	ri SEN shən
receptacle	ri SEP ti kəl
recess (n)	REE ses
recess (v)	ri SES
recessional	ri SESH ə nəl
réchauffé	ray shoh FAY
recherché	rə SHAIR SHAY
recidivism	ri SID ə viz əm
recidivist	ri SID ə vəst
Recife	re SEE fə
recipe	RES ə PEE
recipient	ri SIP ee ənt
reciprocal	ri SIP rə kəl
reciprocate	ri SIP rə KAYT
reciprocity	RES ə PROS ə tee
recital	ri SĪ təl
recitation	RES ə TAY shən
recitative (music)	RES ə tə TEEV
reclamation	REK lə MAY shən
recluse	REK loos
reclusive	ri KLOO siv
recognition	REK əg NISH ən
recognizable	REK əg NĪ zə bəl
recognizance	ri KOG nə zəns
recoil (v)	ri KOIL
recoil (n)	REE koil
recollect (recall)	REK ə LEKT
re-collect (collect again)	REE kə LEKT
recollection	REK ə LEK shən
recombinant	ree KOM bə nənt
recompense	REK əm PENS
reconcilable	REK ən SĪ lə bəl
reconciliation	REK ən SIL ee AY shən
recondite	REK ən DĪT
reconnaissance	ri KON ə səns
reconnoiter	REE kə NOI tər
record (a, n)	REK ərd
record (v)	ri KORD

ə ago, a at, ah calm, ahr dark, air care, aw saw, ay say, ch church
e bet, ee me, eer beer, hw what, i is, ī my, *n* French final n vin,

recorder	ri **KOR** dər
recoup	ri **KOOP**
recourse	**REE** kors
recreant	**REK** ree ənt
recreate (relax)	**REK** ree **AYT**
re-create (create again)	**REE** kree **AYT**
recreation (relaxation)	**REK** ree **AY** shən
re-creation (creation anew)	**REE** kree **AY** shən
recrimination	ri **KRIM** ə **NAY** shən
recriminatory	ri **KRIM** ə nə **TOR** ee
recrudesce	**REE** kroo **DES**
recrudescence	**REE** kroo **DES** əns
recruit	ri **KROOT**
rectangle	**REK TANG** gəl
rectangular	rek **TANG** gyə lər
rectify	**REK** tə **FĪ**
rectilinear	**REK** tə **LIN** ee ər
rectitude	**REK** tə **TOOD**
recto	**REK** toh
rector	**REK** tər
rectory	**REK** tə ree
rectum	**REK** təm
recumbent	ri **KUM** bənt
recuperate	ri **KOO** pə **RAYT**
recuperative	ri **KOO** pər ə tiv
recur	ri **KUR**
recurrence	ri **KUR** əns
recusant	**REK** yə zənt
redact	ri **DAKT**
redaction	ri **DAK** shən
Reddy, Sanjiva	**RED** ee, sən **JEE** və
redeploy	**REE** di **PLOI**
redingote	**RED** ing **GOHT**
redolent	**RED** ə lənt
Redon, Odilon	rə **DOHN**, oh dee **LOHN** (**DOHN** and **LOHN** French final *n*)
redoubt	ri **DOWT**
redoubtable	ri **DOW** tə bəl
redound	ri **DOWND**
redress	ri **DRES**
reductio ad absurdum	ri **DUUK** tee oh ad ab **SUURD** əm

---

o on, oh oat, oi boy, oo soon, oor poor, or for, ow cow, sh shush,
th thin, *th* this, u up, ur spur, uu book, *zh* pleasure

redundancy	ri **DUN** dən see
redundant	ri **DUN** dənt
reefer	**REE** fər
refectory	ri **FEK** tə ree
referee	REF ə **REE**
reference	**REF** ə rəns
referendum	REF ə **REN** dəm
referent	**REF** ə rənt
referential	REF ə **REN** shəl
referral	ri **FUR** əl
reflection	ri **FLEK** shən
reflector	ri **FLEK** tər
reflex	**REE** fleks
reflexive	ri **FLEK** siv
reflux (n)	**REE** fluks
reflux (v)	ri **FLUKS**
reforestation	ree FOR ə **STAY** shən
reformation	REF ər **MAY** shən
reformatory	ri **FOR** mə TOR ee
refraction	ri **FRAK** shən
refractory	ri **FRAK** tə ree
refrain	ri **FRAYN**
refrangible	ri **FRAN** jə bəl
refuge	**REF** yooj
refugee	REF yuu **JEE**
refulgent	ri **FUL** jənt
refund (n)	**REE** fund
refund (v)	ri **FUND**
refurbish	ri **FUR** bish
refusal	ri **FYOO** zəl
refuse (a, n)	**REF** yoos
refuse (v)	ri **FYOOZ**
refutable	ri **FYOO** tə bəl
refutation	REF yuu **TAY** shən
refute	ri **FYOOT**
regal	**REE** gəl
regale	ri **GAYL**
regalia	ri **GAYL** yə
Regan	**REE** gən
regatta	ri **GAT** ə
Régence	ray **ZH**AHNS
regency, R-	**REE** jən see
regenerate (n)	ri **JEN** ər ət

ə ago, a at, ah calm, ahr dark, air care, aw saw, ay say, ch church
e bet, ee me, eer beer, hw what, i is, ī my, *n* French final n vin,

regenerate (v)	ri JEN ə RAYT
Regensburg	RAY gənz burg
regent	REE jənt
Reggio di Calabria	RE jaw DEE kah LAH bree ah
regicide	REJ ə SĪD
regime	rə ZHEEM
regimen	REJ ə mən
regiment (n)	REJ ə mənt
regiment (v)	REJ ə MENT
Regina	ri JĪ nə
region	REE jən
régisseur	ray zhee SUR
registrant	REJ ə strənt
registrar	REJ ə STRAHR
registry	REJ ə stree
regius, R-	REE jəs
regnant	REG nənt
regress (n)	REE gres
regress (v)	ri GRES
regression	ri GRESH ən
regular	REG yə lər
regularity	REG yə LAR ə tee
regularly	REG yə lər lee
regulatory	REG yə lə TOR ee
Regulus, r-	REG yə ləs
regurgitate	ri GUR jə TAYT
rehabilitate	REE hə BIL ə TAYT
rehabilitation	REE hə BIL ə TAY shən
Rehan	REE ən
rehash (n)	REE hash
rehash (v)	ree HASH
rehearsal	ri HUR səl
Rehnquist, William	REN kwist
Rehoboam	REE ə BOH əm
Rehoboth	rə HOH bəth
Rehovot	rə HOH voht
Reich	rīk
Reichstag	RĪKS tahg
Reichstein, Tadeus	RĪK stīn, tah DE uush
Reichswehr	RĪKS vair
Reifel	RĪ fəl
reify	REE ə fī
Reik	rīk

---

o on, oh oat, oi boy, oo soon, oor poor, or for, ow cow, sh shush,
th thin, *th* this, u up, ur spur, uu book, *zh* pleasure

Reikjavik	**RAY** kyə **VEEK**
Reims	rans (rhymes with *dance*)
reindeer	**RAYN** deer
reiterate	ree **IT** ə **RAYT**
reiteration	ree **IT** ə **RAY** shən
rejoinder	ri **JOIN** dər
rejuvenate	ri **JOO** və **NAYT**
rejuvenescence	ri **JOO** və **NES** əns
relativism	**REL** ə ti **VIZ** əm
relativity	**REL** ə **TIV** ə tee
relaxation	**REE** lak **SAY** shən
relay (a, n)	**REE** lay
relay (pass along)	**REE** lay
relay (lay again)	ree **LAY**
relegate	**REL** ə **GAYT**
relegation	**REL** ə **GAY** shən
relent	ri **LENT**
relevance	**REL** ə vəns
relevant	**REL** ə vənt
reliable	ri **LĪ** ə bəl
relic	**REL** ik
relict	**REL** ikt
relief	ri **LEEF**
relieve	ri **LEEV**
relievo	rel **YAY** voh
religieuse	ray lee **ZH**UUZ
religieux	ray lee **ZH**UU
religiosity	ri **LIJ** ee **OS** ə tee
relinquish	ri **LING** kwish
reliquary	**REL** ə **KWER** ee
reliquiae	ri **LIK** wi **EE**
remanent	**REM** ə nənt
Remarque	ri **MAHRK**
Rembrandt van Rijn	**REM** brahnt vahn **RĪN**
remedial	ri **MEE** dee əl
remedy	**REM** ə dee
remembrance	ri **MEM** brəns
reminisce	**REM** ə **NIS**
reminiscence	**REM** ə **NIS** əns
remiss	ri **MIS**
remission	ri **MISH** ən
remittance	ri **MIT** əns
remnant	**REM** nənt

ə ago, a at, ah calm, ahr dark, air care, aw saw, ay say, ch church
e bet, ee me, eer beer, hw what, i is, ī my, *n* French final n vin,

remonstrance	ri **MON** strəns
remonstrate	ri **MON STRAYT**
remonstrative	ri **MON** strə tiv
remora	**REM** ər ə
remorse	ri **MORS**
rémoulade	**RAY** moo **LAHD**
remuneration	ri **MYOO** nə **RAY** shən
remunerative	ri **MYOO** nər ə tiv
Remus	**REE** məs
Renais, Alain	rə **NAY**, ah **LAN** (**LAN** French final *n*)
Renaissance	**REN** ə **SAHNS**
renaissance	ri **NAY** səns
renal	**REE** nəl
Renan, Joseph	rə **NAHN**, *zh*oh **SEF** (**NAHN** French final *n*)
Renard	**REN** ərd
renascence, R-	ri **NAY** səns
Renata	rə **NAH** tə
Renault	rə **NOH**
rendezvous (n, v)	**RAHN** day **voo**
rendezvous (n pl)	**RAHN** day **voo**
René, Renée	rə **NAY**
renegade	**REN** ə **GAYD**
renege	ri **NEG**
Reni, Guido	**RE** nee, **GWEED** oh
Rennes	ren
rennet	**REN** ət
rennin	**REN** ən
Renoir	rə **NWAHR**
renovate	**REN** ə **VAYT**
renown	ri **NOWN**
renowned	ri **NOWND**
Rensselaer	**REN** sə **LEER**
rentier	rahn **TYAY**
renunciation	ri **NUN** see **AY** shən
repairable	ri **PAIR** ə bəl
reparable	**REP** ər ə bəl
reparation	**REP** ə **RAY** shən
repartee	**REP** ahr **TAY**
repast	ri **PAST**
repatriate (v)	ree **PAY** tree **AYT**
repatriate (n)	ree **PAY** tree ət
repay	ree **PAY**

o on, oh oat, oi boy, oo soon, oor poor, or for, ow cow, sh shush,
th thin, *th* this, u up, ur spur, uu book, *zh* pleasure

repellent	ri PEL ənt
repercussion	REE pər KUSH ən
repertoire	REP ər TWAHR
repertory	REP ər TOR ee
repetitive	ri PET ə tiv
repine	ri PĪN
replete	ri PLEET
repletion	ri PLEE shən
replevin	ri PLEV ən
replica	REP li kə
replicate (a, n)	REP li kət
replicate (v)	REP lə KAYT
replicative	REP li KAY tiv
reportage	REP or TAHZH
reportorial	REP ər TOR ee əl
repository	ri POZ ə TOR ee
repoussé	rə poo SAY
Repplier	REP lir
reprehend	REP ri HEND
reprehensible	REP ri HEN sə bəl
reprehension	REP ri HEN shən
representation	REP ri zen TAY shən
representative	REP ri ZEN tə tiv
reprieve	ri PREEV
reprimand	REP rə MAND
reprint (n)	REE print
reprint (v)	ree PRINT
reprisal	ri PRĪ zəl
reprise (law)	ri PRĪZ
reprise (music)	ri PREEZ
reprobate	REP rə BAYT
reprobation	REP rə BAY shən
reproof	ri PROOF
reprove	ri PROOV
reptile	REP təl
reptilian	rep TIL ee ən
republic	ri PUB lik
république, R-	ray puu BLEEK
repudiate	ri PYOO dee AYT
repugnance	ri PUG nəns
repugnant	ri PUG nənt
repulse	ri PULS
repulsion	ri PUL shən

ə ago, a at, ah calm, ahr dark, air care, aw saw, ay say, ch church
e bet, ee me, eer beer, hw what, i is, ī my, n French final n vin,

repulsive	ri **PUL** siv
reputable	**REP** yə tə bəl
reputation	**REP** yə **TAY** shən
repute	ri **PYOOT**
requiem, R-	**REK** wee əm
requiescat in pace	**RE** kwee **ES** kaht in **PAH** kay
requisite	**REK** wə zət
requisition	**REK** wə **ZISH** ən
requital	ri **KWĪT** əl
requite	ri **KWĪT**
reredos	**RIR** dos
rescind	ri **SIND**
rescission	ri **SIZH** ən
research	ri **SURCH**
resemblance	ri **ZEM** bləns
resent	ri **ZENT**
reserpine	ri **SUR** peen
reservist	ri **ZUR** vəst
reservoir	**REZ** ər **VWAHR**
residence	**REZ** ə dəns
residential	**REZ** ə **DEN** shəl
residual	ri **ZIJ** oo əl
residue	**REZ** ə **DOO**
residuum	ri **ZIJ** oo əm
resignation	**REZ** ig **NAY** shən
resilient	ri **ZIL** yənt
resin	**REZ** ən
resistor	ri **ZIS** tər
resolute	**REZ** ə **LOOT**
resolution	**REZ** ə **LOO** shən
resolve	ri **ZOLV**
resolvent	ri **ZOL** vənt
resonance	**REZ** ə nəns
resonant	**REZ** ə nənt
resonator	**REZ** ə **NAY** tər
resort	ri **ZORT**
resound	ri **ZOWND**
resource	**REE** sors
resourceful	ri **SORS** fəl
Respighi	re **SPEE** gee
respirable	**RES** pər ə bəl
respiration	**RES** pə **RAY** shən
respirator	**RES** pə **RAY** tər

o on, oh oat, oi boy, oo soon, oor poor, or for, ow cow, sh shush,
th thin, *th* this, u up, ur spur, uu book, zh pleasure

respiratory	**RES** pə rə **TOR** ee
respite	**RES** pət
resplendent	ri **SPLEN** dənt
respondent	ri **SPON** dənt
responsory	ri **SPON** sə ree
res publica	rays **POO** bli **KAH** (rays ryhmes with *space*)
restaurant	**RES** tə rənt
restaurateur	**RES** tə rə **TUR**
restitution	**RES** tə **TOO** shən
Reston	**RES** tən
restoration	**RES** tə **RAY** shən
restorative	ri **STOR** ə tiv
resume	ri **ZOOM**
résumé	**REZ** ə **MAY**
resumption	ri **ZUMP** shən
resurgam	re **SOOR** gahm
resurgence	ri **SUR** jəns
resurrect	**REZ** ə **REKT**
resuscitate	ri **SUS** ə **TAYT**
resuscitation	ri **SUS** ə **TAY** shən
retail	**REE** tayl
retailer	**REE** tayl ər
retake (n)	**REE** tayk
retake (v)	ree **TAYK**
retaliate	ri **TAL** ee **AYT**
retaliatory	ri **TAL** ee ə **TOR** ee
retard	ri **TAHRD**
retardant	ri **TAHR** dənt
retardation	**REE** tahr **DAY** shən
reticence	**RET** ə səns
reticent	**RET** ə sənt
reticle	**RET** i kəl
reticular	ri **TIK** yə lər
reticule	**RET** i **KYOOL**
reticulum, R-	ri **TIK** yə ləm
retina	**RET** ə nə
retinitis pigmentosa	**RET** ən **ĪT** əs **PIG** mən **TOH** sə
retinue	**RET** ən **YOO**
retort	ri **TORT**
retrench	ri **TRENCH**
retribution	**RE** trə **BYOO** shən
retrieve	ri **TREEV**

ə ago, a at, ah calm, ahr dark, air care, aw saw, ay say, ch church
e bet, ee me, eer beer, hw what, i is, ī my, *n* French final n vin,

retroactive	RET roh AK tiv
retroflex	RET rə FLEKS
retrograde	RET rə GRAYD
retrogress	RET rə GRES
retrospect	RET rə SPEKT
retroussé	rə TROO SAY
Reuben	ROO bin
Réunion	ree YOON yən
Reuss	rois
Reuters	ROI tərz
reveille	REV ə lee
revel	REV əl
revenue	REV ən YOO
reverberatory	ri VUR bər ə TOR ee
revere, R-	ri VEER
reverence	REV ər əns
reverend	REV ər ənd
reverent	REV ər ənt
reverential	REV ə REN shəl
reverie	REV ə ree
reversion	ri VUR zhən
revetment	ri VET mənt
revision	ri VIZH ən
revival	ri VĪ vəl
revivify	ri VIV ə FĪ
revocable	REV ə kə bəl
revocation	REV ə KAY shən
revolt	ri VOHLT
revue	ri VYOO
revulsion	ri VUL shən
rex, R-	reks
Rexist	REKS əst
Reye's syndrome	RĪZ SIN drohm
Reykjavik	RAY kyə VEEK
Reymont	RAY mont
Reynard	RAY nahrd
Reynolds	REN əldz
Reza Shah Pahlavi	ri ZAH SHAH pah lah VEE
rhabdomancy	RAB də MAN see
Rhadamanthine, r-	RAD ə MAN thən
Rhadamanthus, Rhadamanthys	RAD ə MAN thəs
Rhaetian	REE shən

---

o on, oh oat, oi boy, oo soon, oor poor, or for, ow cow, sh shush,
th thin, *th* this, u up, ur spur, uu book, *zh* pleasure

Rhaetic	**REE** tik
Rhaeto-Romanic	REE toh roh **MAN** ik
rhapsodic	rap **SOD** ik
rhapsody	**RAP** sə dee
rhatany	**RAT** ə nee
Rhea	**REE** ə
Rheims	rans (rhymes with *dance*)
Rhein	rīn
Rheingold	**RĪN** gohld
rhematic	ri **MAT** ik
Rhenish	**REN** ish
rhenium	**REE** nee əm
rheostat	**REE** ə STAT
rhesus, R-	**REE** səs
rhetoric	**RET** ər ik
rhetorical	ri **TOR** i kəl
rhetorician	RET ə **RISH** ən
rheumatic	ruu **MAT** ik
rheumatism	**ROO** mə TIZ əm
rhinal	**RĪN** əl
Rhine	rīn
rhinestone	**RĪN** stohn
rhinitis	rī **NĪ** təs
rhinoceros	rī **NOS** ə rəs
rhinology	rī **NOL** ə jee
rhizome	**RĪ** zohm
rhizotomy	rī **ZOT** ə mee
rho	roh
Rhoda	**ROH** də
Rhodes	rohdz
Rhodesia	roh **DEE** *zh*ə
rhodium	**ROH** dee əm
rhododendron	ROH də **DEN** drən
rhodolite	**ROH** də LĪT
rhodonite	**ROH** də NĪT
Rhodope, Rhodopi	**ROD** ə pee
rhombic	**ROM** bik
rhombus	**ROM** bəs
rhonchus	**RONG** kəs
Rhone	rohn
rhubarb	**ROO** bahrb
rhumb	rum
rhumba	**RUUM** bə

ə ago, a at, ah calm, ahr dark, air care, aw saw, ay say, ch church
e bet, ee me, eer beer, hw what, i is, ī my, *n* French final n vin,

rhyme	rīm
rhyolite	**RĪ** ə **LĪT**
Rhys	rees
rhythm	**RI***TH* əm
Riad, Mahmoud	ree **AHD, MAH** mood
Rialto	ree **AL** toh
riant	**RĪ** ənt
riata	ree **AH** tə
ribald	**RIB** əld
ribaldry	**RIB** əl dree
Ribas Reig, Oscar	ree **BAHS RAY, OS** kahr
riboflavin	**RĪ** bə **FLAY** vən
ribonucleic	**RĪ** boh nuu **KLEE** ik
ribose	**RĪ** bohs
ribosome	**RĪ** bə **SOHM**
Ricardo	ri **KAHR** doh
Ricci	**REE** chee
Riccio	**REE** choh
Richard, Henri	ree **SHAHR, AHN** ree (**AHN** French final *n*)
Richelieu	reesh ə **LYUU**
Richter	**RIK** tər
rickets	**RIK** əts
rickettsia	ri **KET** see ə
rickettsial	ri **KET** see əl
rickety	**RIK** ə tee
rickey	**RIK** ee
Rickover, Hyman	**RIK** oh vər, **HĪ** mən
ricksha	**RIK** shaw
ricochet	**RIK** ə **SHAY**
ricotta	ree **KAWT** tah
Riegger	**REEG** ər
Riegle	**REEG** əl
Rienzi	ree **EN** zee
Riesling	**REEZ** ling
Rifa'i, Abdul Monem	ree **FĪ, AHB** dəl moh **NEM**
Riga	**REE** gə
rigamarole	**RIG** ə mə **ROHL**
righteous	**RĪ** chəs
rigmarole	**RIG** mə **ROHL**
Rigoletto	**RIG** ə **LET** oh
rigor	**RIG** ər
rigorous	**RIG** ər əs

o on, oh oat, oi boy, oo soon, oor poor, or for, ow cow, sh shush, th thin, *th* this, u up, ur spur, uu book, zh pleasure

Rigsdag	**RIGZ** dahg
Rig-Veda	rig **VAY** də
Riis	rees
Rikhoff	**RIK** hawf
Riksdag	**RIKS** dahg
rilievo	ril **YE** voh
Rilke, Rainer	**RIL** kə, **RĪ** nər
rill	ril
Rimbaud	ran **BOH** (ran French final *n*)
Rimini	**RIM** ə nee
Rimmon	**RIM** ən
Rimsky-Korsakov	**RIM** skee **KOR** sə ᴋᴀᴡꜰ
Rinaldo	ri **NAL** doh
rind	rīnd
Rio Bravo	**REE** oh **BRAH** voh
Rio de Janeiro	**REE** oh day *zh*ə **NAIR** oh
Rio de Oro	**REE** oh de **AW** raw
Rio Gallegos	**REE** oh gah **YAY** gəs
Rio Grande (Brazil)	**REE** uu **GRAHN** di
Rio Grande (US)	**REE** oh **GRAND**
Rio Muni	**REE** aw **MOO** nee
Ríos Montt, Efraín	**REE** ohs **MONT**, ᴇꜰ rah **EEN**
riotous	**RĪ** ə təs
riparian	ri **PAIR** ee ən
Ripon	**RIP** ən
riposte	ri **POHST**
risibility	ʀɪᴢ ə **BIL** ə tee
risible	ʀɪᴢ ə bəl
Risorgimento	ʀᴇᴇ sor jee **MEN** toh
risotto	ree **SAW** toh
risqué	ri **SKAY**
rissole	**RI** sohl
rissolé	ree saw **LAY**
ritardando	ʀᴇᴇ tahr **DAHN** doh
ritual	**RICH** oo əl
Rivas	**REE** vahs
Rivas-Gallont, Ernesto	**REE** vahs ga **LAWNT**, air **NES** toh
Rivera	ree **VE** rah
rivet	**RIV** ət
Riviera, r-	ʀɪᴠ ee **AIR** ə
rivière	ree **VYAIR**
rivulet	**RIV** yə lət
Riyadh	ree **YAHD**

ə ago, a at, ah calm, ahr dark, air care, aw saw, ay say, ch church
e bet, ee me, eer beer, hw what, i is, ī my, *n* French final n vin,

riyal	ree **YAHL**
Rizal	ree **SAHL**
Rizzio	**REET** see **OH**
Rizzo	**RIZ** oh
Roanoke	**ROH** ə **NOHK**
Robbia	**ROH** bee ə
Robeson	**ROHB** sən
Robespierre	**ROHBZ** pyair
robot	**ROH** bot
roburite	**ROH** bə **RĪT**
robust	roh **BUST**
rocambole	**ROK** əm **BOHL**
Rocha	**RAW** chah
Rochambeau (French)	raw shahn **BOH** (shahn French final *n*)
Rochambeau (US)	**ROH** sham **BOH**
Rochdale	**ROCH** dayl
Rochefoucauld, La	rawsh foo **KOH**, la
Rochelle	roh **SHEL**
Rockefeller	**ROK** ə **FEL** ər
rococo	rə **KOH** koh
rodent	**ROHD** ənt
rodeo	**ROH** dee **OH**
rodeo (southwestern US)	roh **DAY** oh
Rodin	roh **DAN** (**DAN** French final *n*)
rodomontade	**ROD** ə mon **TAYD**
Roebling	**ROH** bling
roentgen, R-	**RENT** gən
Roethke, Theodore	**RET** kee
rogation	roh **GAY** shən
Roget	roh *ZH***AY**
rogue	rohg
roguery	**ROH** gə ree
roguish	**ROH** gish
Roh Tae Woo	roh tay woo
roil	roil
roister	**ROI** stər
Rojas	**ROH** hahs
role	rohl
roll	rohl
Rolland, Romain	raw **LAHN**, raw **MAN** (**LAHN** and **MAN** French final *n*)

---

o **on**, oh **oat**, oi **boy**, oo **soon**, oor **poor**, or **for**, ow **cow**, sh **shush**, th **thin**, *th* **this**, u **up**, ur **spur**, uu **book**, *zh* **pleasure**

Rollo	**ROL** oh
Rölvaag, Ole	**ROHL** vahg, **OH** lə
roly-poly	**ROH** lee **POH** lee
Romaic	roh **MAY** ik
romaine	roh **MAYN**
Romains, Jules	raw **MAN**, *ZH*UUL (**MAN** French final *n*)
Roman	**ROH** mən
roman	roh **MAHN** (**MAHN** French final *n*)
roman à clef	roh **MAHN** ah **KLAY** (**MAHN** French final *n*)
romance, R-	roh **MANS**
Romanesque	ROH mə **NESK**
Romania	roh **MAY** nee ə
Romanic	roh **MAN** ik
Romanism	**ROH** mə NIZ əm
Romano	roh **MAHN** oh
Romanov, Romanoff	**ROH** mə NAWF
Romansh	roh **MANSH**
romantic	roh **MAN** tik
Romany	**ROM** ə nee
Rome	rohm
Romeo	**ROH** mee OH
romero	roh **MAIR** oh
Rommany	**ROM** ə nee
Rommel	**ROM** əl
Romney	**ROM** nee
Romola	**ROM** ə lə
Romualdez, Benjamin	rom **WAHL** dez
Romulo	**ROM** yuu LOH
Romulus	**ROM** yə ləs
Roncalli, Angelo Giuseppe	rohn **KAH** lee, **AHN** jə loh jə **ZEP** ee
Roncesvalles	**RAHN** sə VALZ
rondeau	**RON** doh
rondel	**RON** dəl
rondo	**RON** doh
Ronsard	rohn **SAHR** (rohn French final *n*)
Röntgen, r-	**RENT** gən
rood, R-	rood
Roodepoort-Maraisburg	**ROO** də PUURT mah **RAY** burk
rook	ruuk

ə ago, a at, ah calm, ahr dark, air care, aw saw, ay say, ch church
e bet, ee me, eer beer, hw what, i is, ī my, *n* French final n vin,

rookery	**RUUK** ə ree
rookie	**RUUK** ee
Roosevelt	**ROH** zə **VELT**
roque	rohk
Roquefort	**ROHK** fərt
roquet	roh **KAY**
rorqual	**ROR** kwəl
Rorschach	**ROR** shok
rosaceous	roh **ZAY** shəs
Rosales-Rivera, Mauricio	roh **SAH** les ree **VER** ə, maw **REE** see oh
Rosario	roh **ZAHR** ee **OH**
rosary	**ROH** zə ree
rosé	roh **ZAY**
Roseau	roh **ZOH**
Rosecrans	**ROHZ** krans
roseola	**ROH** zee **OH** lə
Rosetta	roh **ZET** ə
rosette	roh **ZET**
Rosh Hashana	**ROHSH** hah **SHAH** nah
Rosicrucian	**ROH** zə **KROO** shən
rosin	**ROZ** ən
Rosina	roh **ZEE** nə
Rosinante	**ROZ** ə **NAN** tee
Roslyn	**ROZ** lən
rosolio	roh **ZAW** lyoh
Rossel, Agda	**RU** sel, **AHG** dah
Rossetti	roh **SET** ee
Rossides, Zenon	roh **SEE** *th*ees, **ZEE** nuun
Rossi-Drago	**ROH** see **DRAH** goh
Rossini	roh **SEE** nee
Rostand	raw **STAHN** (**STAHN** French final *n*)
Rostenkowski, Daniel	**ROS** tən **KOW** skee
roster	**ROS** tər
Rostock	**ROS** tok
Rostov	**ROS** tof
Rostropovich, Mstislav	rah strah **PAW** veech, stis **LAHV**
rostrum	**ROS** trəm
rota, R-	**ROH** tə
Rotarian	roh **TAIR** ee ən
rotary, R-	**ROH** tə ree
rotative	**ROH** **TAY** tiv
rotatory	**ROH** tə **TOR** ee

---

o on, oh oat, oi boy, oo soon, oor poor, or for, ow cow, sh shush,
th thin, *th* this, u up, ur spur, uu book, *zh* pleasure

rote	roht
Rothschild	**RAWTH** chĭld
Rothschild (French)	rawt **SHEELD**
rotifer	**ROH** tə fər
rotisserie	roh **TIS** ə ree
rotl	**ROT** əl
rotogravure	ROH tə grə **VYUUR**
rotor	**ROH** tər
Rotterdam	**ROT** ər DAM
rotund	roh **TUND**
rotunda	roh **TUN** də
Rouault	roo **OH**
Roubaix	roo **BE**
rouble	**ROO** bəl
roué	roo **AY**
Rouen	roo **AHN** (**AHN** French final *n*)
rouge	roo*zh*
Rouget de Lisle	roo *ZH*AY də **LEEL**
roulade	roo **LAHD**
rouleau	roo **LOH**
Rouleau, Raymond	roo **LOH**, ray **MOHN** (**MOHN** French final *n*)
roulette	roo **LET**
Roumania	roo **MAY** nee ə
roundel	**ROWN** dəl
roundelay	**ROWN** də **LAY**
roup	roop
rouse	rowz
Rousseau	roo **SOH**
Roussillon	ROO see **YOHN** (**YOHN** French final *n*)
route	root
routine	roo **TEEN**
roux	roo
Rovno	**RAWV** naw
rowan	**ROH** ən
rowdy	**ROW** dee (**ROW** as in *cow*)
Rowe	roh
rowel	**ROW** əl (**ROW** as in *cow*)
rowen	**ROW** ən (**ROW** as in *cow*)
Rowena	roh **WEE** nə
Rowne	**RUUV** ne
Roxana	rok **SAN** ə
Roxane	rok **SAN**

ə ago, a at, ah calm, ahr dark, air care, aw saw, ay say, ch church
e bet, ee me, eer beer, hw what, i is, ī my, *n* French final n vin,

Roxas	**ROH** hahs
Ruanda-Urundi	roo **AHN** də uu **RUUN** dee
Rubaiyat	**ROO** bī **YAHT**
rubato	roo **BAH** toh
rubble	**RUB** əl
rubefacient	**ROO** bə **FAY** shənt
rubella	roo **BEL** ə
Rubens	**ROO** bənz
rubeola	**ROO** bee **OH** lə
rubescent	ruu **BES** ənt
Rubicon	**ROO** bi **KON**
rubicund	**ROO** bi kənd
rubidium	ruu **BID** ee əm
rubiginous	ruu **BIJ** ə nəs
ruble	**ROO** bəl
rubric	**ROO** brik
ruche	roosh
rucksack	**RUK** sak
ruckus	**RUK** əs
ruction	**RUK** shən
rudbeckia	rud **BEK** ee ə
rudiment	**ROO** də mənt
rudimentary	**ROO** də **MEN** tə ree
Rudyard	**RUD** yərd
rue	roo
rueful	**ROO** fəl
ruffian	**RUF** ee ən
rufous	**ROO** fəs
Rugby	**RUG** bee
rugose	**ROO** gohs
Ruhr	ruur
ruinous	**ROO** ə nəs
Ruis	ruu **EES**
Ruisdael	**ROIS** dahl
Rukeyser	**ROO** kī zər
Rumania	roo **MAY** nee ə
rumba	**RUUM** bə
Rumelia	roo **MEEL** yə
ruminate	**ROO** mə **NAYT**
rummage	**RUM** ij
rummy	**RUM** ee
Rumpelstiltskin	**RUM** pəl **STILT** skin
runcible	**RUN** sə bəl

o on, oh oat, oi boy, oo soon, oor poor, or for, ow cow, sh shush,
th thin, *th* this, u up, ur spur, uu book, *zh* pleasure

runcinate	RUN sə NAYT
rune	roon
runic	ROO nik
runnel	RUN əl
Runnymede	RUN i MEED
Runyon	RUN yən
rupee	roo PEE
rupiah	roo PEE ə
Rupia, Paul Milyango	roo PEE ya, pawl mee lee YAHN goh
rupture	RUP chər
rural	RUUR əl
Rurik	RUUR ik
Rusakov, Konstantin	roo sah KAWF, kon ston TYEEN
ruse	rooz
Rushdie, Salman	RUSH dee, SAHL man
Ruskin	RUS kən
russet	RUS ət
Russia	RUSH ə
Russian	RUSH ən
Russophile	RUS ə FĪL
Russophobe	RUS ə FOHB
rustic	RUS tik
rusticate	RUS ti KAYT
rusticity	rus TIS ə tee
rustle	RUS əl
Ryzhkov, Nikolai	rizh KAWF, nee koh LĪ
rutabaga	ROO tə BAY gə
ruth, R-	rooth
Ruthenia	roo THEE nee ə
ruthenium	roo THEE nee əm
Rutherford, Rutherfurd	RUTH ər fərd
rutherfordium	RUTH ər FOR dee əm
ruthless	ROOTH ləs
Rutland	RUT lənd
Rutledge	RUT lij
Ruwenzori	ROO wən ZOR ee
Ruysdael	ROIS dahl
Ruyter	ROI tər
Ruzicka, Leopold	ROO zheech kah, LAY oh pawlt
Rwanda	ruu WAHN də
Ryazan	ryah ZAHN
Ryder	RĪ dər

ə ago, a at, ah calm, ahr dark, air care, aw saw, ay say, ch church
e bet, ee me, eer beer, hw what, i is, ī my, *n* French final n vin,

ryot	**RĪ** ət
Ryswick	**RIZ** wik
Ryukyu	ryoo kyoo
Ruutel, Arnold	**ROO** tel, **AHR** nəld
Rzeszow	*ZH*E shuuf

S

Saar	sahr
Saarbrucken	**SAHR** bruuk ən
Saarinen	**SAHR** ə nən
Saba	**SAY** bə
Sabac	**SHAH** bahts
Sabaean	sə **BEE** ən
Sabaoth	**SAB** ee oth
sabbath	**SAB** əth
Sabbatical, s-	sə **BAT** i kəl
Sabean	sə **BEE** ən
Sabena	sə **BEE** nə
saber	**SAY** bər
Sabin	**SAY** bin
Sabina	sə **BEE** nə
Sabine (ancient Italy)	**SAY** bīn
Sabine (Texas)	sə **BEEN**
sabot	**SA** boh
sabotage	**SAB** ə TAH*ZH*
saboteur	sab ə **TUR**
sabra, S-	**SAH** brə
sabre	**SAY** bər
sabretache	**SAY** bər TASH
Sabrina	sə **BREE** nə
sac, S-	sak
Sacagawea	sak ə jə **WEE** ə
saccharide	**SAK** ə RĪD
saccharine	**SAK** ə rən
Sacco	**SAK** oh
sacerdotal	sas ər **DOHT** əl
sachem	**SAY** chəm
sachet	sa **SHAY**
Sacheverell	sə **SHEV** ər əl
Sachs (German)	zahks
Sachs (US)	saks

---

o on, oh oat, oi boy, oo soon, oor poor, or for, ow cow, sh shush,
th thin, *th* this, u up, ur spur, uu book, *zh* pleasure

sacral (near the sacrum)	SAK rəl
sacral (holy)	SAYK rəl
sacrament	SAK rə mənt
sacramental	SAK rə MEN təl
Sacramento	SAK rə MEN toh
sacrarium	sə KRAIR ee əm
sacrifice	SAK rə FĪS
sacrificial	SAK rə FISH əl
sacrilege	SAK rə lij
sacrilegious	SAK rə LEE jəs
sacristan	SAK rə stən
sacristy	SAK rə stee
sacroiliac	SAK roh IL ee AK
sacrosanct	SAK roh SANGT
sacrum	SAK rəm
Sadat, Anwar	sah DOT, ON wahr
Sadducean	SAJ ə SEE ən
Sadducee	SAJ ə SEE
Sade	sahd
sadism	SAY diz əm
sadist	SAY dəst
sadistic	sə DIS tik
Sadowa	SAH daw VAH
safari	sə FAHR ee
saffron	SAF rən
Safid Rud	sa FEED ROOD
Safire, William	SAF ir
saga	SAH gə
sagacious	sə GAY shəs
sagacity	sə GAS ə tee
sagamore	SAG ə MOR
Sagan, Carl	SAY gən
Sagan, Françoise	sa GAHN, frahn SWAHZ (GAHN and frahn French final *n*)
Saghalien	SAH gahl YEN
Saginaw	SAG ə NAW
Sagitta	sə JIT ə
sagittal	SAJ ə təl
Sagittarius	SAJ ə TAIR ee əs
sago, S-	SAY goh
saguaro	sə WAH roh
Saguenay	SAG ə NAY

ə ago, a at, ah calm, ahr dark, air care, aw saw, ay say, ch church
e bet, ee me, eer beer, hw what, i is, ī my, *n* French final n vin,

Sahara	sə HAR ə
sahib, S-	SAH ib
said	sed
Saida	SAH ee DAH
saiga	SĪ gə
Saigon	sī GON
St. Albans	saynt AWL bənz
St. Augustine	saynt AW gə STEEN
Saint Bernard	SAYNT bər NAHRD
St.-Cloud (France)	san KLOO (san French final *n*)
St. Cloud (US)	saynt KLOWD (KLOWD rhymes with *loud*)
St. Croix	saynt KROI
St. Denis	SAN də NEE (SAN French final *n*)
Ste. Anne de Beaupré	saynt AN də boh PRAY
Sainte-Beuve	sant BUUV
St.-Étienne	SAN tay TYEN (SAN French final *n*)
Saint-Exupéry	SAN teg zuu pay REE (SAN French final *n*)
Saint-Gaudens	saynt GAWD ənz
St.-Germain	san *zh*air MAN (san and MAN French final *n*)
St. Gotthard	saynt GOT ərd
St. Helena	SAYNT hə LEE nə
St. Helier	saynt HEL yər
St. Laurent	san loh RAHN (san and RAHN French final *n*)
St.-Lô	san LOH (san French final *n*)
St. Louis (Missouri)	saynt LOO əs
Saint Lucia	saynt LOO shə
St.-Malo	san ma LOH (san French final *n*)
St.-Mihiel	san mee YEL (san French final *n*)
St.-Moritz	SAYNT mə RITS
St.-Nazaire	san na ZAIR (san French final *n*)
St.-Ouen	san TWAHN (san and TWAHN French final *n*)
St.-Pierre	san PYAIR (san French final *n*)
Saint-Saëns	san SAHN (san and SAHN French final *n*)
Saintsbury	SAYNTS bə ree
Saint-Simon	san see MAWN (san and MAWN French final *n*)
St. Tropez	san troh PAY (san French final *n*)

o on, oh oat, oi boy, oo soon, oor poor, or for, ow cow, sh shush,
th thin, *th* this, u up, ur spur, uu book, *zh* pleasure

Saipan	sī PAN
saith	seth
sake (drink)	SAH ke
Sakhalin	SAK ə LEEN
Sakharov, Andrei	SAH kə RAWF, ahn DRAY
Saki	SAH kee
Sakurauchi, Yoshio	sah koo rah oo chee, yoh shee oh
salaam	sə LAHM
salacious	sə LAY shəs
salacity	sə LAS ə tee
Saladin	SAL ə din
Salado	sah LAH doh
Salam, Abdus	sah LAHM, AHB duus
Salamanca	SAL ə MANG kə
salamander	SAL ə MAN dər
Salambria	sə LAM bree ə
salami	sə LAH mee
Salamis	SAL ə mis
Sala y Gómez	SAHL ə ee GOH MAYS
Salazar	SAL ə ZAHR
Salcedo, Luis Moreno	sal SAY doh, loo EES moh RE noh
Saleh, Ali Abdullah	SAH lay, AH lee AHB doo lah
Salem	SAY ləm
saleratus	SAL ə RAY təs
Salerno	sə LER noh
Salesian	sə LEE zhən
Salic	SAY lik
salicylate	sə LIS ə LAYT
Salida	sə LĪ də
salience	SAY lyəns
salient	SAY lyənt
Salim, Salim Ahmed	sah LEEM, sah LEEM AH med
Salina, s-	sə LĪ nə
Salinas	sə LEE nəs
Salinas de Gortari, Carlos	sah LEE nahs day gor TAHR ee, KAHR lohs
saline	SAY leen
Salinger	SAL ən jər
Salisbury	SAWLZ ber ee
Salish	SAY lish
Salishan	SAY lish ən
saliva	sə LĪ və
salivary	SAL ə VER ee

ə ago, a at, ah calm, ahr dark, air care, aw saw, ay say, ch church
e bet, ee me, eer beer, hw what, i is, ī my, *n* French final n vin,

salivate	SAL ə VAYT
Salk	sawk
Sallah, Ousman	SAH lah, OOS mahn AH mah doo Ahmadou
Sallam, Mohamed Abdulaziz	sah LAHM, moh HAHM ed AHB dool ah SEEZ
Sallust	SAL əst
salmagundi	SAL mə GUN dee
salmi	SAL mee
salmon, S-	SAM ən
salmonella	SAL mə NEL ə
Salome	sə LOH mee
Salomé (opera)	SAL ə MAY
salon	sə LON
Salonika	SAL ə NEE kə
salsa	SAWL sə
salsify	SAL sə FĪ
saltarello	SAL tə REL oh
Saltillo	sahl TEE yaw
Salton	SAWL tən
salubrious	sə LOO bree əs
salubrity	sə LOO brə tee
Saluki	sə LOO kee
Salus	SAY ləs
salutary	SAL yə TER ee
salutation	SAL yə TAY shən
salutatorian	sə LOO tə TOR ee ən
salute	sə LOOT
Salvador, El	SAL və DOR, el
salvage	SAL vij
salve (hail)	SAHL way
salve (ointment)	sav
salve (salvage)	salv
salver	SAL vər
salvia	SAL vee ə
salvo	SAL voh
Salween	SAL ween
Salzburg	SAWLZ burg
samadhi	sə MAH dee
Samantha	sə MAN thə
Samar	SAH mahr
Samaria	sə MA ree ə
Samaritan	sə MA rə tən
samarium	sə MA ree əm

o on, oh oat, oi boy, oo soon, oor poor, or for, ow cow, sh shush,
th thin, *th* this, u up, ur spur, uu book, *zh* pleasure

Samarkand	SAM ər KAND
Samarra	sə MAHR ə
samarskite	sə MAHR skīt
samba	SAHM bə
samisen	SAM ə SEN
samite	SAM īt
samizdat	SAH meez DOT
Samoa	sə MOH ə
Samos	SAY mos
Samothrace	SAM ə THRAYS
samovar	SAM ə VAHR
Samoyed	SAM ə YED
sampan	SAM pan
Sampang	SAHM pahng
samphire	SAM fīr
Samson	SAM sən
Samsun	sahm SUUN
samurai	SAM ə RĪ
Sanaa, San'a	sah NAH
San Agustín	sahn AH guu STEEN
San Andreas	san an DRAY əs
San Andrés	sahn ahn DRES
San Angelo	san AN jə loh
San Antonio	SAN an TOH nee oh
sanatorium	SAN ə TOR ee əm
San Benito	SAN bə NEE toh
San Bernardino	SAN BUR nər DEE noh
Sancho Panza	SAHN choh PAHN zə
San Clemente	SAN klə MEN tee
San Cristóbal	SAN kris TOH bəl
sanctify	SANGK tə FĪ
sanctimonious	SANGK tə MOH nee əs
sanctimony	SANGK tə MOH nee
sanctuary	SANGK choo ER ee
sanctum	SANGK təm
sanctum sanctorum	SANGK təm SANGK TOR əm
Sanctus	SANGK təs
sandarac	SAN də RAK
Sandefjord	SAH nə FYOR
sandhi	SAN dee
San Diego	SAN dee AY goh
Sandinist	SAN də nəst
Sandinista	SAN də NEES tə

ə ago, a at, ah calm, ahr dark, air care, aw saw, ay say, ch church
e bet, ee me, eer beer, hw what, i is, ī my, *n* French final n vin,

Sandino, Augusto César	sahn DEE noh, ow GOOS toh SAY sahr
Sándor, Šandor	SHAHN dor
Sandor (US)	SAN dər
Sandusky	san DUS kee
Sandys, Duncan	SANDZ, DUNG kən
San Fernando	SAN fər NAN doh
San Francisco	SAN frən SIS koh
San Gabriel	san GAY bree əl
sangaree	SANG gə REE
San Gennaro	SAN jen NAIR oh
Sanger	SANG ər
sang-froid	sahn FRWAH (sahn French final *n*)
Sangre de Cristo	SANG gre de KRIS toh
sangria	sang GREE ə
Sangsomsack, Bounkeut	sahng suum sahk, boon kuut
sanguinary	SANG gwə NER ee
sanguine	SANG gwən
sanguineous	sang GWIN ee əs
Sanhedrin	san HED rən
sanitarium	SAN ə TAIR ee əm
sanitary	SAN ə TER ee
sanitation	SAN ə TAY shən
sanity	SAN ə tee
San Jacinto	SAN jə SIN toh
San Joaquín	SAN waw KEEN
San Jorge	sahn HAWR he
San Jose (California)	SAN hoh ZAY
San José (Spanish)	SAHN haw SE
San Juan	san HWAHN
Sankhya	SAHNG kyə
San Luis Obispo	san LOO əs ə BIS poh
San Luis Potosí	sahn loo EES paw taw SEE
San Marino	SAN mə REE noh
San Martín	SAHN mahr TEEN
San Remo	san REE moh
sans	sanz
San Salvador	san SAL və DOR
sans-culotte	sahn kuu LUT (sahn French final *n*)
San Sebastian	SAN si BAS chən
sansei	sahn say
Sanskrit	SAN skrit

---

o on, oh oat, oi boy, oo soon, oor poor, or for, ow cow, sh shush,
th thin, *th* this, u up, ur spur, uu book, *zh* pleasure

sans serif	SANZ SER əf
sans souci	sahn soo SEE (sahn French final *n*)
Santa (in English names)	SAN tə
Santa (in Spanish and Italian names)	SAHN tah
Santa Barbara	SAN tə BAHR bə rə
Santa Catalina	SAN tə KAT ə LEE nə
Santa Claus	SAN tə KLAWZ
Santa Cruz	SAN tə KROOZ
Santa Fe	SAN tə FAY
Santa María	SAHN tah mah REE ah
Santa Monica	SAN tə MON ə kə
Santander	SAHN tahn DAIR
Santayana	SAN tee AN ə
Santiago	SAN tee AH goh
Santiago de Cuba	SAHN tee AH goh de KOO bah
Santo Domingo	SAN toh də MING goh
Santos	SAHN tuus
São Francisco	SOWN frahn SEES kuu (SOWN as in *town*)
São Luiz	sown LWEES (sown as in *town*)
São Miguel	SOWN mee GEL (SOWN as in *town*)
Saône	sohn
São Paulo	sown POW luu (sown as in *town*)
Saorstat Eireann	SAIR stawt AIR ən
São Salvador	sown SAHL və DAWR (sown as in *town*)
São Tomé	SOWN tə MAY (SOWN as in *town*)
sapajou	SAP ə JOO
sapid	SAP əd
sapience	SAY pee əns
sapient	SAY pee ənt
sapodilla	SAP ə DIL ə
saponaceous	SAP ə NAY shəs
saponify	sə PON ə FĪ
sapor	SAY pər
saporific	SAP ə RIF ik
sapota	sə POH tə
sapper	SAP ər
Sapphic, s-	SAF ik
Sapphira	sə FĪ rə
sapphire	SAF īr

ə ago, a at, ah calm, ahr dark, air care, aw saw, ay say, ch church
e bet, ee me, eer beer, hw what, i is, ī my, *n* French final n vin,

sapphism	SAF iz əm
Sappho	SAF oh
Sapporo	sah poh roh
saprolite	SAP rə LĪT
saprophyte	SAP rə FĪT
sapsago	sap SAY goh
Saqqara	sə KAH rə
saraband	SA rə BAND
Saracen	SA rə sən
Saracoglu	sah RAH jaw gluu
Saragossa	SAR ə GOS ə
Sarajevo	SA rə YAY voh
Saran	sə RAN
Saranac	SAR ə NAK
Sarasota	SAR ə SOH tə
Saratoga	SAR ə TOH gə
Saratov	sah RAH tawf
Sarawak	sə RAH wahk
Sarbanes, Paul	SAHR baynz
sarcasm	SAHR kaz əm
sarcastic	sahr KAS tik
sarcenet	SAHRS nət
sarcoma	sahr KOH mə
sarcomatosis	sahr KOH mə TOH sis
sarcomatous	sahr KOH mə təs
sarcophagi	sahr KOF ə GĪ
sarcophagus	sahr KOF ə gəs
sarcous	SAHR kəs
sardine	sahr DEEN
Sardinia	sahr DIN ee ə
sardonic	sahr DON ik
sardonyx	sahr DON iks
Sardou	sahr DOO
sargasso, S-	sahr GAS oh
sargassum	sahr GAS əm
Sargent	SAHR jənt
sari	SAH ree
Sarkis, Elias	SAHR kəs
sarong	sə RONG
Sarouk	sər OOK
Sarpedon	sahr PEE dən
Sarrante, Nathalie	sah RAHNT, nah tah LEE
Sarré, Massamba	SAHR, mah SAHM bah

---

o on, oh oat, oi boy, oo soon, oor poor, or for, ow cow, sh shush,
th thin, *th* this, u up, ur spur, uu book, *zh* pleasure

sarsaparilla	SAS pə RIL ə
sarsenet	SAHRS nət
Sarto	SAHR toh
sartorial	sahr TOR ee əl
sartorius	sahr TOR ee əs
Sartre	SAHR trə
Sartzetakis, Christos	sahr dze TAHK ees, HREE stohs
sashay	sa SHAY
Saskatchewan	sas KACH ə WAHN
Saskatoon, s-	SAS kə TOON
sasquatch, S-	SAS kwach
sassaby	SAS ə bee
sassafras	SAS ə FRAS
Sassenach	SAS ə nak
Sassoon	sa SOON
Sassou-Nguesso, Denis	SA soo ən GWAY soo, də NEE
satanic, S-	sə TAN ik
Satanism, s-	SAY tə NIZ əm
sateen	sa TEEN
satiate (a)	SAY shee ət
satiate (v)	SAY shee AYT
Satie	sa TEE
satiety	sə TĪ ə tee
satire	SA tīr
satirical	sə TIR i kəl
satirize	SAT ə RĪZ
Sato, Eisaku	sah toh, ay sah koo
satori	sah TOR ee
satrap	SAY trap
satrapy	SAY trə pee
Satsuma, s-	sah tsoo mah
saturant	SACH ər ənt
saturate	SACH ə RAYT
Saturday	SAT ər DAY
Saturn	SAT ərn
Saturnalia, s-	SAT ər NAY lee ə
Saturnian, s-	sə TUR nee ən
saturnine	SAT ər NĪN
Satyagraha	SUT yə GRU hə
satyr	SAY tər
satyriasis	SAY tə RĪ ə sis
satyric	sə TIR ik
Saud	sah OOD

ə ago, a at, ah calm, ahr dark, air care, aw saw, ay say, ch church
e bet, ee me, eer beer, hw what, i is, ī my, n French final n vin,

Saudi Arabia	sah **OO** dee ə **RAY** bee ə
sauerbraten	**SOW** ər **BRAH** tən (**SOW** as in *cow*)
sauerkraut	**SOW** ər **KROWT** (**SOW** as in *cow*, **KROWT** as in *out*)
Sauk	sawk
Saúl Menem, Carlos	sah **OOL MEN** em, **DAHR** lohs
Sault Sainte Marie	**SOO SAYNT** mə **REE**
sauna	**SOW** nə (**SOW** as in *cow*)
saunter	**SAWN** tər
Saurashtra	sow **RUSH** trə (sow as in *cow*)
saurian	**SOR** ee ən
sauropod	**SOR** ə **POD**
sausage	**SAW** sij
sauté	soh **TAY**
sauterne	soh **TURN**
Sauternes	soh **TAIRN**
sauve qui peut	sohv kee **PUU**
sauvignon blanc	**SOH** veen **YAWN BLAHN** (**YAWN** and **BLAHN** French final *n*)
Sava	**SAH** vah
savage	**SAV** ij
Savaii	sah **VI** ee
Savang Vatthana	sah **VAHNG** vah **TAH** nah
savanna	sə **VAN** ə
savant	sa **VAHN** (**VAHN** French final *n*)
savate	sa **VAHT**
savior, S-	**SAY** vyər
savoir faire	**SAV** wahr **FAIR**
Savonarola	**SAV** ə nə **ROH** lə
savor	**SAY** vər
savory	**SAY** və ree
Savoy, s-	sə **VOI**
Savoyard	**SA** voi **AHRD**
savvy	**SAV** ee
Sawatch	sə **WACH**
Saw Hlaing	saw hlīng
Saw Maung	saw mawng
Saxe-Coburg-Gotha	**SAKS KOH** burg **GOH** thə
saxifrage	**SAK** sə frij
Saxon	**SAK** sən
Saxony	**SAK** sə nee
saxophone	**SAK** sə **FOHN**
Sayan	sah **YAHN**

o on, oh oat, oi boy, oo soon, oor poor, or for, ow cow, sh shush,
th thin, *th* this, u up, ur spur, uu book, *zh* pleasure

Scaasi	**SKAH** see
scabies	**SKAY** beez
scabious	**SKAY** bee əs
scabrous	**SKAB** rəs
Scafell	**SKAW** fel
scaffold	**SKAF** əld
scagliola	skal **YOH** lə
scaife	skayf
scalar	**SKAY** lər
scalawag	**SKAL** ə **WAG**
scald	skawld
scalene	**SKAY** leen
scallion	**SKAL** yən
scallop	**SKAL** əp
scallywag	**SKAL** ə **WAG**
scalpel	**SKAL** pəl
Scanderbeg	**SKAN** dər **BEG**
Scandia	**SKAN** dee ə
Scandian	**SKAN** dee ən
Scandinavia	**SKAN** də **NAY** vee ə
scandium	**SKAN** dee əm
scansion	**SKAN** shən
Scapa Flow	**SKAP** ə **FLOH**
scapegoat	**SKAYP** goht
scapula	**SKAP** yə lə
scapular	**SKAP** ə lər
scarab	**SKAR** əb
scarce	skairs
scarify	**SKAR** ə **FĪ**
Scarlatti	skahr **LAHT** ee
scathe	skay*th*
scatological	**SKAT** ə **LOJ** i kəl
scatology	skə **TOL** ə jee
scavenge	**SKAV** ənj
scavenger	**SKAV** ən jər
scenario	sə **NA** ree oh
scenic	**SEE** nik
scepter	**SEP** tər
Schaghticoke	**SKAT** ə **KOHK**
Scharnhorst	**SHAHRN** howrst
Schawlow, Arthur	**SHAW** loh
schedule	**SKEJ** ool
Scheherazade	shə **HER** ə **ZAH** də (**HER** as in *herring*)

ə ago, a at, ah calm, ahr dark, air care, aw saw, ay say, ch church
e bet, ee me, eer beer, hw what, i is, ī my, *n* French final n vin,

Scheldt	skelt
Schell	shel
Scheltema, Hugo	**SKEL** tə mə, **HYOO** hoh (**SKEL** *K* almost an *H* sound)
schema	**SKEE** mə
schematic	ski **MAT** ik
schematize	**SKEE** mə TĪZ
scheme	skeem
Schenectady	skə **NEK** tə dee
Scherchen	**SHAIR** shin
scherzando	skair **TSAHN** doh
scherzo	**SKAIR** tsoh
Scheyven	**SHI** vən
Schiaffino, Rosanna	shah **FEE** noh, roh **ZAH** nah
Schick	shik
Schiller, s-	**SHIL** ər
schilling	**SHIL** ing
schipperke	**SKIP** ər kee
Schippers	**SHIP** ərz
schism	**SIZ** əm
schismatic	siz **MAT** ik
schist	shist
schistosome	**SHIS** tə sohm
schistosomiasis	shis tə soh **MĪ** ə səs
schizoid	**SKIT** soid
schizomycete	skiz oh mī **SEET**
schizomycosis	skiz oh mī **KOH** səs
schizophrenia	skit sə **FREE** nee ə
schizophrenic	skit sə **FREN** ik
schlemiel	shlə **MEEL**
Schleswig	**SHLES** wig
Schliemann	**SHLEE** mahn
Schluter, Poul	**SHLOO** tər, pohl
schmaltz	shmahlts
Schmidt, Helmut	**SHMIT, HEL** moot
schmierkase	**SHMEER** kayz ə
schnapps	shnahps
schnauzer	**SHNOW** zər
schnitzel	**SHNIT** səl
Schnitzler	**SHNITS** lər
schnorkel	**SHNOR** kəl
schnorrer	**SHNOR** ər
Schoenberg	**SHURN** burg

o on, oh oat, oi boy, oo soon, oor poor, or for, ow cow, sh shush, th thin, *th* this, u up, ur spur, uu book, *zh* pleasure

scholastic	skə **LAS** tik
scholasticism	skə **LAS** tə **SIZ** əm
scholia	**SKOH** lee ə
scholiast	**SKOH** lee **AST**
scholium	**SKOH** lee əm
Schönberg	**SHURN** burg
schoolhouse	**SKOOL** hows
schooner	**SKOO** nər
Schoonover	**SKOO** noh vər
Schopenhauer	**SHOH** pən **HOW** ər
schottische	**SHOT** ish
Schottky	**SHOT** kee
Schrödinger	**SHRAY** ding ər
Schroeder, Patricia	**SHROHD** ər
Schubert	**SHOO** bərt
Schueler	**SHOO** lər
Schumann	**SHOO** mahn
Schurmann	**SHUR** mahn
Schurz	shurts
schuss	shuus
Schuster	**SHOO** stər
Schutzstaffel	**SHUUTS** **SHTAH** fəl
Schuyler	**SKĪ** lər
Schuylkill	**SKOOL** kil
schwa	shwah
Schwab	shwahb
Schwarzkopf	**SHVAHRTS** kupf
Schweitzer	**SHVĪT** zər
Schwengel	**SHWENG** gəl
Schwinger	**SHWING** ər
Schwitters	**SHVIT** ərz
sciamachy	sī **AM** ə kee
sciatica	sī **AT** i kə
sciential	sī **EN** shəl
scientology	**SĪ** ən **TOL** ə jee
scilicet	**SIL** i **SET**
Scilla	**SIL** ə
Scilly	**SIL** ee
scimitar	**SIM** ə tər
scintilla	sin **TIL** ə
scintillate	**SIN** tə **LAYT**
sciolism	**SĪ** ə **LIZ** əm
sciolist	**SĪ** ə ləst

ə ago, a at, ah calm, ahr dark, air care, aw saw, ay say, ch church
e bet, ee me, eer beer, hw what, i is, ī my, *n* French final n vin,

scion	**SĪ** ən
Scioto	sī **OH** tə
Scipio	**SIP** ee OH
Scituate	**SICH** oo it
scleritis	sklə **RĪ** təs
scleroma	sklə **ROH** mə
sclerosis	sklə **ROH** səs
Scofield	**SKOH** feeld
scoliosis	SKOH lee **OH** səs
sconce	skons
scone	skohn
Scone	skoon
scopolamine	skə **POL** ə MEEN
scorbutic	skor **BYOO** tik
scoria	**SKOR** ee ə
Scorpio	**SKOR** pee OH
scorpion	**SKOR** pee ən
Scorpius	**SKOR** pee əs
scotia, S-	**SKOH** shə
Scotism	**SKOH** tiz əm
Scotland	**SKOT** lənd
scotoma	skə **TOH** mə
Scourby	**SKOR** bee
scourge	skurj
Scowcroft	**SKOW** krawft (**SKOW** as in *cow*)
scrabble	**SKRAB** əl
scrag	skrag
scrapple	**SKRAP** əl
Scriabin	skree **AH** bin
scrimshaw	**SKRIM** shaw
scriptorium	skrip **TOR** ee əm
scrivener	**SKRIV** nər
scrod	skrod
scrofula	**SKROF** yə lə
scrofulous	**SKROF** yə ləs
Scrooge	skrooj
scrotum	**SKROH** təm
scrounge	skrownj
scrumptious	**SKRUM** shəs
scrunch	skrunch
scruple	**SKROO** pəl
scrupulous	**SKROO** pyə ləs
scuba	**SKOO** bə

---

o on, oh oat, oi boy, oo soon, oor poor, or for, ow cow, sh shush,
th thin, *th* this, u up, ur spur, uu book, *zh* pleasure

scull	skul
scullery	**SKUL** ə ree
scullion	**SKUL** yən
sculptor	**SKULP** tər
sculpture	**SKULP** chər
sculpturesque	**SKULP** chə **RESK**
scurrility	skə **RIL** ə tee
scurrilous	**SKUR** ə ləs
scurry	**SKUR** ee
scurvy	**SKUR** vee
Scutari	**SKOO** tah **REE**
scutcheon	**SKUCH** ən
scuttlebutt	**SKUT** əl **BUT**
scutum, S-	**SKYOO** təm
Scylla	**SIL** ə
scyphus	**SĪ** fəs
scythe	sī*th*
Scythian	**SITH** ee ən
Sealyham	**SEE** lee əm
seamstress	**SEEM** strəs
Seanad Eireann	**SAN** ahd **AIR** ən
séance	**SAY** ahns
Seattle	see **AT** əl
sebaceous	si **BAY** shəs
Sebastopol	si **BAS** tə **POHL**
Sebe, Chief Lennox	**SAY** bay, cheef **LEN** əks
seborrhea	**SEB** ə **REE** ə
Sebrell	se **BREL**
sebum	**SEE** bəm
secant	**SEE** kant
secco	**SEK** oh
secession	si **SESH** ən
seclude	si **KLOOD**
Seconal	**SEK** ə **NAWL**
second	**SEK** ənd
secondary	**SEK** ən **DER** ee
secondhand	**SEK** ənd **HAND**
secondo	si **KOHN** doh
Secrest	**SEE** krəst
secretaire	**SEK** rə **TAIR**
secretarial	**SEK** rə **TA** ree əl
secretariat	**SEK** rə **TA** ree ət
secretary	**SEK** rə **TER** ee

ə ago, a at, ah calm, ahr dark, air care, aw saw, ay say, ch church
e bet, ee me, eer beer, hw what, i is, ī my, *n* French final n vin,

secrete	si **KREET**
secretion	si **KREE** shən
secretive	**SEE** krə tiv
secretiveness	**SEE** krə tiv nəs
sectarian	sek **TA** ree ən
sector	**SEK** tər
secular	**SEK** yə lər
Secunderabad	sə **KUN** dər ə **BAD**
Sedalia	si **DAY** lee ə
sedan, S-	si **DAN**
sedate	si **DAYT**
sedation	si **DAY** shən
sedative	**SED** ə tiv
sedentary	**SED** ən **TER** ee
Seder	**SAY** dər
sediment	**SED** ə mənt
sedition	si **DISH** ən
seduce	si **DOOS**
seductive	si **DUK** tiv
sedulity	si **DYOO** lə tee
sedulous	**SEJ** ə ləs
sedum	**SEE** dəm
Seferis, Giorgos	se **FE** rees, ye **OR** ee uus
Segni, Antonio	**SAY** nyee, ahn **TOH** nyoh
segno	**SAY** nyoh
sego	**SEE** goh
Segovia	sə **GOH** vee ə
Segré, Emilio	say **GRAY**, ay **MEE** lyoh
segregate (n)	**SEG** ri gət
segregate (v)	**SEG** ri **GAYT**
segregation	**SEG** ri **GAY** shən
segregationist	**SEG** ri **GAY** shə nist
segregative	**SEG** ri **GAY** tiv
segue	**SEG** way
seguidilla	**SEG** ə **DEEL** yah
seicento	say **CHEN** toh
seiche	saysh
seidel, S-	**SID** əl
Seidlitz	**SED** ləts
seigneur	say **NYUR**
seignior	**SAYN** yər
seigniorage	**SAYN** yər ij
seigniory	**SAYN** yə ree

---

o on, oh oat, oi boy, oo soon, oor poor, or for, ow cow, sh shush,
th thin, *th* this, u up, ur spur, uu book, *zh* pleasure

Seine	sen
seine	sayn
seismic	SĪZ mik
seismograph	SĪZ mə GRAF
seismology	sīz MOL ə jee
selah	SEE lə
Selangor	sə LAHNG gawr
Selene	sə LEE nee
selenite	SEL ə NĪT
selenium	sə LEE nee əm
selenology	SEL ə NOL ə jee
Seleucus	sə LOO kəs
Seljuk	sel JOOK
Selma	SEL mə
Seltzer, s-	SELT sər
selvage	SEL vij
semantic	si MAN tik
semaphore	SEM ə FOR
Semarang	sə MAHR ahng
semasiology	si MAY see OL ə jee
semblance	SEM bləns
Sembrich	ZEM brik
semé	sə MAY
Semedo, Inacio	se MEE doo, in NAH see oh
Semele	SEM ə LEE
semen	SEE mən
Semenov, Nikolai	sə MYAW nof, nee koh LĪ
semester	sə MES tər
seminal	SEM ə nəl
seminar	SEM ə NAHR
seminary	SEM ə NER ee
Seminole	SEM ə NOHL
semiology	SEE mee OL ə jee
semiotic	SEE mee OT ik
semiotics	SEE mee OT iks
Semiramis	si MIR ə mis
Semite	SEM īt
Semitic	sə MIT ik
Semitism	SEM ə TIZ əm
semolina	SEM ə LEE nə
semper fidelis	SEM pər fə DAY ləs
semper paratus	SEM pər pə RAH təs
sempiternal	SEM pi TUR nəl

ə ago, a at, ah calm, ahr dark, air care, aw saw, ay say, ch church
e bet, ee me, eer beer, hw what, i is, ī my, n French final n vin,

senate	SEN ət
senator	SEN ə tər
Sendai	sen dī
Seneca	SEN ə kə
Senecan	SEN ə kən
Senegal	SEN ə GAWL
Senegalese	SEN ə gə LEEZ
Senegambia	SEN ə GAM bee ə
senescent	si NES ənt
seneschal	SEN ə shəl
Senghor, Leopold	seng GAWR, lee oh POHLD
senhor	si NYOR
senhora	si NYOR ə
senhorita	SEE nyə REE tə
senile	SEE nīl
senility	si NIL ə tee
Senlac	SEN lak
senna	SEN ə
Sennacherib	sə NAK ər əb
senor	sayn YOR
senora	sayn YOR ə
senorita	sayn yə REET ə
senseless	SENS ləs
sensibility	SEN sə BIL ə tee
sensorium	sen SOR ee əm
sensory	SEN sə ree
sensual	SEN shoo əl
sensuality	SEN shoo AL ə tee
sensuous	SEN shoo əs
sentential	sen TEN shəl
sententious	sen TEN shəs
sentience	SEN shəns
sentient	SEN shənt
sentimental	SEN tə MEN təl
sentinel	SEN tə nəl
sentry	SEN tree
Senusi, Senussi	se NOO see
Seoul	sohl
sepal	SEE pəl
separate (a, n)	SEP ə rət
separate (v)	SEP ə RAYT
separatist	SEP ə rə təst
Sephardic	sə FAHR dik

o on, oh oat, oi boy, oo soon, oor poor, or for, ow cow, sh shush,
th thin, *th* this, u up, ur spur, uu book, *zh* pleasure

Sephardim	sə FAHR dəm
sepia	SEE pee ə
Sepik	SAY pik
sepiolite	SEE pee ə LĪT
sepoy	SEE poi
Seppälä	SE pa la
seppuku	se poo koo
sepsis	SEP səs
September	sep TEM bər
septenary	SEP tə NER ee
septennial	sep TEN ee əl
septet	sep TET
septic	SEP tik
septicemia	SEP tə SEE mee ə
septuagenarian	SEP choo ə jə NAIR ee ən
Septuagesima	SEP choo ə JES ə mə
Septuagint	SEP too ə JINT
septum	SEP təm
septuple	SEP tə pəl
sepulcher	SEP əl kər
sepulchral	sə PUL krəl
sepulture	SEP əl chər
Sepulveda, Bernardo	sep ool VAY də, ber NAHR doh
sequacious	si KWAY shəs
sequel	SEE kwəl
sequela	si KWEL ə
sequelae	si KWEL ee
sequence	SEE kwəns
sequential	si KWEN shəl
sequester	si KWES tər
sequestration	SEK wəs TRAY shən
sequin	SEE kwən
sequoia	si KWOI ə
Serafina	SER ə FEE nə
seraglio	sə RAL yoh
serai	sə RAH ee
seral	SI rəl
Serang	se RAHNG
serape	sə RAH pee
seraph	SER əf
seraphic	sə RAF ik
seraphim	SER ə fim
Serapis	sə RAY pəs

ə ago, a at, ah calm, ahr dark, air care, aw saw, ay say, ch church
e bet, ee me, eer beer, hw what, i is, ī my, n French final n vin,

Serb	surb
Serbia	SUR bee ə
Serbo-Croatian	SUR boh kroh AY shən
sere	seer
Serena	sə REE nə
serenade	SER ə NAYD
serendipity	SER ən DIP ə tee
serene	sə REEN
Serengeti	SER ən GET ee
serenity	sə REN ə tee
serf	surf
serge, S-	surj
sergeant	SAHR jənt
seriatim	SI ree AY təm
sericulture	SER ə KUL chər
serif	SER əf
serigraph	SER ə GRAF
serigraphy	sə RIG rə fee
Serkin	SUR kin
serology	sə ROL ə jee
serous	SI rəs
Serov	SE rof
Serpens	SUR pənz
serpent	SUR pənt
serpentine	SUR pən TEEN
serpiginous	sər PIJ ə nəs
serried	SER eed
serum	SI rəm
serval	SUR vəl
serviette	SUR vee ET
servile	SUR vəl
servility	sur VIL ə tee
sesame	SES ə mee
sesquicentennial	SES kwi sen TEN ee əl
sesquipedalian	SES kwi pi DAYL yən
sesterce	SES tərs
sestet	ses TET
sestina	ses TEE nə
setaceous	si TAY shəs
settecento	se te CHEN taw
settee	se TEE
Seurat	suu RAH
Sevareid	SEV ə RĪD

---

o on, oh oat, oi boy, oo soon, oor poor, or for, ow cow, sh shush,
th thin, *th* this, u up, ur spur, uu book, *zh* pleasure

Sevastopol	sə VAS tə POHL
sever	SEV ər
several	SEV ə rəl
severance	SEV ə rəns
severe	sə VIR
severity	sə VER ə tee
Severn	SEV ərn
Severnaya Zemlya	SEV ər nə YAH ZEM lee AH
seviche	sə VEE chay
Sévigné	say vee NYAY
Sevilla	say VEE lyah
Sevilla-Sacasa,	say VEEL yah sah KAH sah, gil
Guillermo	YAIR moh
Seville	sə VIL
Sèvres	SE vrə
sewage	SOO ij
Seward	SOO ərd
sewerage	SOO ər ij
Sewrajsing, Inderdew	SOO rahj SING, IN dər DOO
sexagenarian	SEK sə jə NAIR ee ən
Sexagesima	SEK sə JES ə mə
sexennial	sek SEN ée əl
sexology	sek SOL ə jee
sextain	SEKS tayn
Sextans	SEKS tənz
sextant	SEKS tənt
sextet	seks TET
sextuple	seks TOO pəl
sextuplet	seks TUP lət
sexuality	SEK shoo AL ə tee
Seychelles	say SHELZ
Seydoux, Roger	say DOO, roh ZHAY
sforzando	sfort SAHN doh
sforzato	sfort SAH toh
Shaanxi	shahn shee
Shabuoth	shə VOO oht
shadchan	SHAHD kən
shaddock	SHAD ək
Shadrach	SHAD rak
Shaerf, Adolph	SHAIRF, AH dawlf
Shaftesbury	SHAFTS bə ree
Shagari, Alhaji Shehu	shah GAH ree, ahl HAH jee she HOO
shagreen	sha GREEN

ə ago, a at, ah calm, ahr dark, air care, aw saw, ay say, ch church
e bet, ee me, eer beer, hw what, i is, ī my, n French final n vin,

shah, S-	shah
Shahada	shah HAH dah
Shahjahanpur	SHAH jə HAHN PUUR
shaitan, S-	shī TAHN
Shakespeare	SHAYK spir
Shakespearean	shayk SPIR ee ən
shako	SHAK oh
Shakti, s-	SHUK tee
shalloon	sha LOON
shallop	SHAL əp
shallot	shə LOT
shalom	shah LOHM
shaman	SHAH mən
Shamash	SHAH mahsh
Shamir, Yitzhak	shah MEER, YITS hahk
shammes	SHAH məs
shamus	SHAY məs
Shan	shahn
Shandong	shahn dawng
shandrydan	SHAN dree DAN
shandygaff	SHAN dee GAF
Shanghai	shang HĪ
Shangri-La	SHANG gri LAH
Shansi	shahn see
shan't	shant
Shantung, s-	shan TUNG
Shanxi	shahn shi
Shara	SHAHR ə
Shari	SHAH ree
sharif	shə REEF
Sharon	SHA rən
Sharon, Ariel	shah ROHN, AHR ee əl
Sharra	SHAHR ə
shashlik	shahsh LIK
Shasta	SHAS tə
Shatt-al-Arab	SHAT al AHR ahb
Shavian	SHAY vee ən
Shavuoth	shə VOO oht
Shaw, s-	shaw
Shcharansky, Anatoly	shah RAHN skee, ah nah TOH lee
Shcherbakov	CHER bə KAWF
Shcherbitsky, Vladimir	shair BEET skee, vlah DEE mir
shea (tree)	shee

---

o on, oh oat, oi boy, oo soon, oor poor, or for, ow cow, sh shush,
th thin, *th* this, u up, ur spur, uu book, *zh* pleasure

Shea (stadium)	shay
sheath	sheeth
sheathe	shee*th*
Sheba	**SHEE** bə
shebang	shə **BANG**
shebeen	shə **BEEN**
Shebeli	shay **BE** li
Sheboygan	shi **BOI** gən
Shechinah	shə **KEE** nə
Shehu, Mehmet	**SHAY** hoo, **MEM** et
sheik (handsome man)	sheek
sheikh (Arab chief)	shayk
Sheila	**SHEE** lə
sheitel	**SHAY** təl
shekel	**SHEK** əl
Shekinah	shə **KEE** nə
Sheldov, Anatoly	**SHEL** dawf, ah nah **TOH** lee
shellac	shə **LAK**
Shenandoah	sʜᴇɴ ən **DOH** ə
shenanigan	shə **NAN** ə gən
Shensi	shen see
Shenyang	shən yahng
Sheol, s-	**SHEE** ohl
Shepard	**SHEP** ərd
shepherd	**SHEP** ərd
Sheraton	**SHER** ə tən
sherbet	**SHUR** bət
sherif	shə **REEF**
sheriff	**SHER** əf
Sherpa	**SHUR** pə
Shetland	**SHET** lənd
Shevardnadze, Eduard	shev ahrd **NAHD** zeh, ed **WAHRD**
Shevtsova, Ludmila	sheft **SOH** vah, lood **MEE** lah
Shevuoth	shə **VOO** oht
Shiah	**SHEE** ə
shiatsu	shee aht soo
shibboleth	**SHIB** ə ləth
shield	sheeld
shigellosis	sʜɪɢ ə **LOH** səs
Shih Tzu	shee **TSOO**
Shiite	**SHEE** īt
Shikoku	shee **KOH** koo
shillelagh	shə **LAY** lee

ə ago, a at, ah calm, ahr dark, air care, aw saw, ay say, ch church
e bet, ee me, eer beer, hw what, i is, ī my, *n* French final n vin,

Shillong	shi **LAWNG**
Shiloh	**SHĪ** loh
Shimizu	shi mee zoo
Shimonoseki	**SHEE** mə noh **SEK** ee
Shinnecock	**SHIN** ə kok
Shinto	**SHIN** toh
Shiraz	shee **RAHZ**
shirr	shur
shish kebab	**SHISH** kə **BOB**
shittah	**SHIT** ə
shittim	**SHIT** əm
Shiva	**SHEE** və
shivaree	**SHIV** ə **REE**
Shizuoka	shee zoo oh kah
shoal	shohl
shoat	shoht
shofar	**SHOH** fahr
shogun	**SHOH** guun
shogunate	**SHOH** gən ət
Sholapur	**SHOH** lə **PUUR**
Sholokhov	**SHAW** lə kawf
Sholom Aleichem	**SHOH** ləm ah **LAY** kəm
shone	shohn
shoran	**SHOR** an
short-lived	short līvd
Shoshone	shoh **SHOH** nee
Shostakovich	**SHOS** tə **KOH** vich
shrapnel	**SHRAP** nəl
Shreveport	**SHREEV** port
Shrewsbury	**SHROOZ** bə ree
shrive	shrīv
shrivel	**SHRIV** əl
shriven	**SHRIV** ən
Shriver	**SHRĪ** vər
Shropshire	**SHROP** shər
shroud	shrowd (rhymes with *crowd*)
Shuf (mountains)	shoof
Shukairy, Ahmed	shoo **KĪ** ree, **AH** med
Shulamite	**SHOO** lə **MĪT**
Shuster	**SHUU** stər
Shvernik	**SHVAIR** nik
Sialkot	see **AHL** koht
Siam	sī **AM**

---

o on, oh oat, oi boy, oo soon, oor poor, or for, ow cow, sh shush,
th thin, *th* this, u up, ur spur, uu book, *zh* pleasure

siamang	SEE ə MANG
Sian	shee ahn
Sibelius	sə BAYL yəs
Siberia	sī BEER ee ə
sibilant	SIB ə lənt
sibling	SIB ling
Sibomana, Jean-Marie	see boh MAH nah, zhahn mah REE (zhahn French final n)
Sibyl, s-	SIB əl
sibylline, S-	SIB ə LEEN
sic	sik
siccative	SIK ə tiv
Sichuan	sich oo ahn
Sicilian	si SIL yən
Sicily	SIS ə lee
sickle	SIK əl
sic semper tyrannis	sik SEM pər tə RAN əs
sic transit gloria mundi	sik TRAN sət GLOH ree ah MUUN dee
Siddhartha	si DAHR tə
Siddons	SID ənz
siddur	SID uur
sidereal	sī DIR ee əl
siderite	SID ə RĪT
siderosis	SID ə ROH səs
sidewinder	SĪD wĪN dər
Sidi Barrani	SEE dee bah RAH nee
Sidikou, Abdou	see dee KOO, AHB doo
sidle	SĪ dəl
Sidon	SĪ dən
Sidonian	sī DOH nee ən
Sidra	SID rə
siècle	SYE klə
Siegbahn	SEEG bahn
Siegel	SEE gəl
Siegfried	SEEG freed
Sieglinde	see GLIN də
Siemens	SEE mənz
Siena	see EN ə
sienna	see EN ə
sierra, S-	see ER ə
Sierra Leone	see ER ə lee OH nee
Sierra Madre	see ER ə MAH dray

ə ago, a at, ah calm, ahr dark, air care, aw saw, ay say, ch church
e bet, ee me, eer beer, hw what, i is, ī my, n French final n vin,

Sierra Nevada	see ER ə nə VAD ə
siesta	see ES tə
sieve	siv
Sighisoara	SEE gee SHWAH rah
Sigismund	SIJ əs mənd
sigma	SIG mə
sigmoid	SIG moid
Sigmund	SIG mənd
signatory	SIG nə TOR ee
signet	SIG nət
significance	sig NIF i kəns
signor	seen YOR
signora	seen YOR ə
signore	seen YOR ay
Signoret, Simone	see nyaw RAY, see MUN
signorina	SEEN yə REE nə
signorino	SEEN yə REE noh
Sigurd	SIG ərd
Sihanouk, Norodom	SEE ə NUUK, NOR ə DOM
Sikandarabad	see KUN də rah BAHD
Sikh	seek
Sikkim	SIK im
Sikorsky	si KOR skee
silage	SĪ lij
silenus, S-	sī LEE nəs
Siles, Hernan	SEE les, air NAN
Silesia, s-	sī LEE zhə
silhouette	SIL oo ET
silica	SIL i kə
silicate	SIL ə kayt
siliceous	sə LISH əs
silicic	sə LIS ik
silicon	SIL i kən
silicone	SIL ə KOHN
silicosis	SIL ə KOH səs
sillabub	SIL ə BUB
Sillanpää	SIL ən PA
Sillitoe	SIL i TOH
silo	SĪ loh
Siloam	sī LOH əm
Silone	si LOH nee
Silurian	sī LUUR ee ən
silva	SIL və

o on, oh oat, oi boy, oo soon, oor poor, or for, ow cow, sh shush,
th thin, *th* this, u up, ur spur, uu book, *zh* pleasure

Silvana	sil VA nə
Silvanus	sil VAY nəs
Silvia	SIL vee ə
silviculture	SIL və KUL chər
s'il vous plaît	seel voo PLE
Simchas Torah	SIMK əs TOH rə
Simenon, Georges	seem ə NAWN, ZHAWRZH (NAWN French final n)
Simeon	SIM ee ən
Simferopol	sim fe RAW pawl
simian	SIM ee ən
similar	SIM ə lər
similarity	SIM ə LAR ə tee
simile	SIM ə lee
similitude	si MIL ə TOOD
Simonetta	see moh NE tah
simoniac	sə MOH nee AK
Simonides	sī MON ə DEEZ
simonize, Simoniz	SĪ mə NĪZ
Simon Legree	SĪ mən lə GREE
Simonov, Konstantin	SEE mə nuf, kahn stahn TEEN
simony	SIM ə nee
simoom	sə MOOM
simoon	sə MOON
Simplon	SIM plon
simulacrum	SIM yə LAY krəm
simulcast	SĪ məl KAST
simultaneity	sī məl tə NEE ə tee
simultaneous	sī məl TAY nee əs
Sinai	SĪ nī
Sinaloa	SEEN ə LOH ə
Sinarquist	SIN ahr kist
Sinarquista	SIN ahr KEES tə
Sinbad	SIN bad
sincerity	sin SER ə tee
sine	sīn
sinecure	SĪ nə KYUUR
sine die	SĪ nee DĪ ee
sine qua non	SEE ne kwah NOHN
sinew	SIN yoo
sinewy	SIN yoo ee
sinfonia	SIN fə NEE ə
sinfonietta	SIN fən YET ə

ə ago, a at, ah calm, ahr dark, air care, aw saw, ay say, ch church
e bet, ee me, eer beer, hw what, i is, ī my, n French final n vin,

Singapore	SING gə POR
Singaraja, Singaradja	SING gah RAH jah
singe	sinj
Singer, Isaac Bashevis	SING ər, ĪZ ək bah SHAY vəs
Singh	sing
Singhalese	SING gə LEEZ
singularity	SING gyə LAR ə tee
Sinhalese	SIN hə LEEZ
Sinicism	SIN i SIZ əm
sinister	SIN ə stər
sinistral	SIN ə strəl
sinistrality	SIN ə STRAL ə tee
Sinitic	si NIT ik
Sinkiang Uighur	SHIN jee ahng WEE gər
Sinn Fein	shin fayn
Sino-	SĪ noh
Sinology, s-	sī NOL ə jee
Sinon	SĪ non
sinuosity	SIN yoo OS ə tee
sinuous	SIN yoo əs
sinus	SĪ nəs
sinusitis	sī nə SĪ təs
sinusoidal	sī nə SOID əl
Siouan	SOO ən
Sioux	soo
siphon	SĪ fən
Siqueiros	see KAY raws
siren	SĪ rən
Sirena	sə REE nə
sirenian	sī REE nee ən
Siret	si RET
Sirhan	SEER hahn
Sirius	SI ree əs
sirloin	SUR loin
sirocco	sə ROK oh
Siroky, Viliam	shee ROH kee, VEEL yahm
sirrah	SI rə
sisal	SĪ səl
Sisley	SIZ lee
Sismondi	sis MON dee
Sistine	SIS teen
sistrum	SIS trəm
Sisyphean	SIS ə FEE ən

---

o on, oh oat, oi boy, oo soon, oor poor, or for, ow cow, sh shush,
th thin, *th* this, u up, ur spur, uu book, *zh* pleasure

Sisyphus	**SIS** ə fəs
sitar	si **TAHR**
Sitka	**SIT** kə
sitology	sī **TOL** ə jee
sitomania	**sī** tə **MAY** nee ə
sitophobia	**sī** tə **FOH** bee ə
Sittang	**SI** tong
situate (a)	**SICH** oo ət
situate (v)	**SICH** oo **AYT**
situs	**SĪ** təs
Sitwell	**SIT** wəl
sitz	sits
Siva	**SEE** və
Sivas	see **VAHZ**
Siwa	**SEE** wə
Sixtine	**SIKS** teen
Sixtus	**SIKS** təs
sizar	**SĪ** zər
sjambok	sham **BOK**
Skagen	**SKAH** gən
Skagerrak	**SKAG** ə **RAK**
skald	skawld
skaldic	**SKAWL** dik
Skaneateles	**SKAN** ee **AT** ləs
skein	skayn
skeletal	**SKEL** ə təl
skew	skyoo
skewer	**SKYOO** ər
ski	skee
skirl	skurl
skirmish	**SKUR** mish
skiver	**SKĪ** vər
skivvy	**SKIV** ee
skoal	skohl
Skokie	**SKOH** kee
Skoplje	**SKAWP** lye
skulduggery	skul **DUG** ə ree
skulk	skulk
Skye	skī
slalom	**SLAH** ləm
slather	**SLA***TH* ər
slattern	**SLAT** ərn
Slav	slahv

ə ago, a at, ah calm, ahr dark, air care, aw saw, ay say, ch church
e bet, ee me, eer beer, hw what, i is, ī my, *n* French final n vin,

slavey	**SLAY** vee
Slavic	**SLAH** vik
slavish	**SLAY** vish
Slavonia	slə **VOH** nee ə
Slavonic	slə **VON** ik
Slavophile	**SLAH** və **FĪL**
Slavophobe	**SLAH** və **FOHB**
Slavophobia	**SLAH** və **FOH** bee ə
sleazy	**SLEE** zee
sleigh	slay
sleight	slīt
sleuth	slooth
slew	sloo
Sligo	**SLĪ** goh
Slim, Mongi	sə **LEEM, MOHN** jee
Slim, Taïeb	sə **LEEM, TĪ** yəb
slither	**SLI***TH* ər
slithery	**SLI***TH* ə ree
sliver	**SLIV** ər
slivovitz	**SLIV** ə vits
Sliwa	**SLEE** wə
sloe	sloh
Sloka	**SLAW** kah
sloth	slawth
slough (cast off)	sluf
slough (marsh)	sloo
Slough of Despond	slow (as in *cow*)
Slovak	**SLOH** vak
Slovakia	sloh **VAH** kee ə
sloven	**SLUV** ən
Slovene	**SLOH** veen
Slovenia	sloh **VEE** nee ə
slovenly	**SLUV** ən lee
sluggard	**SLUG** ərd
sluice	sloos
slur	slur
Smetana	**SMET** ə nə
Smethwick	**SME***TH* ik
smidgen	**SMIJ** ən
smilax	**SMĪ** laks
smirch	smurch
smirk	smurk
smithy	**SMITH** ee

o on, oh oat, oi boy, oo soon, oor poor, or for, ow cow, sh shush,
th thin, *th* this, u up, ur spur, uu book, *zh* pleasure

smolder	SMOHL dər
Smolensk	smo LENSK
Smollett	SMOL ət
smolt	smohlt
smooch	smooch
smooth	smoo*th*
smorgasbord	SMOR gəs BORD
smorzando	smort SAHN doh
smother	SMU*TH* ər
Smuts	smuts
Smyrna	SMUR nə
snafu	sna FOO
snivel	SNIV əl
snood	snood
snooker	SNUUK ər
snorkel	SNOR kəl
soave	soh AH vay
Sobhuza	soh BOO zə
Sobolev	SAW bah lef
sobriety	sə BRĪ ə tee
sobriquet	SOH bri KAY
soccer	SOK ər
Sochi	SAW chi
social	SOH shəl
sociality	SOH shee AL ə tee
socialize	SOH shə LĪZ
societal	sə SĪ ə təl
society	sə SĪ ə tee
Socinian	soh SIN ee ən
Socinus	soh SĪ nəs
sociological	SOH see ə LOJ i kəl
sociology	SOH see OL ə jee
sociometry	SOH see OM ə tree
sockdolager	sok DOL i jər
socket	SOK ət
sockeye	SOK ī
Socorro	sə KAW roh
Socotra	soh KOH trə
Socrates	SOK rə TEEZ
Socratic	sə KRAT ik
sodality	soh DAL ə tee
sodium	SOH dee əm
Sodom	SOD əm

ə ago, a at, ah calm, ahr dark, air care, aw saw, ay say, ch church
e bet, ee me, eer beer, hw what, i is, ī my, *n* French final n vin,

Sodomite, s-	**SOD** ə **MĪT**
sodomy	**SOD** ə mee
Soemba	**SOOM** bah
Soembawa	soom **BAH** wah
Soenda	**SOON** dah
Soerabaja	**soo** rah **BAH** yah
Soerakarta	**soo** rah **KAHR** tah
soffit	**SOF** ət
Sofia	**SOH** fee ə
soft	sawft
soften	**SAW** fən
Sogdian	**SOG** dee ən
Sogdiana	**SOG** dee **AY** nə
soggy	**SOG** ee
Soho	**SOH** hoh
soi-disant	swah dee **ZAHN** (**ZAHN** French final *n*)
soigné	swahn **YAY**
soiree	swah **RAY**
Soissons	swah **SAWN** (**SAWN** French final *n*)
sojourn (n)	**SOH** jurn
sojourn (v)	soh **JURN**
solace	**SOL** əs
solar	**SOH** lər
solarium	soh **LA** ree əm
solarize	**SOH** lə **RĪZ**
Solarz	**SOH** lahrz
solder	**SOD** ər
solecism	**SOL** ə **SIZ** əm
Soledad	**SOL** ə **DAD**
solemn	**SOL** əm
solemnify	sə **LEM** nə **FĪ**
solemnity	sə **LEM** nə tee
solemnize	**SOL** əm **NĪZ**
solenoid	**SOH** lə **NOID**
Solent	**SOH** lənt
sol-fa	sohl **FAH**
solfatara	**SOHL** fə **TAHR** ə
solfeggio	sol **FEJ** oh
solicitor	sə **LIS** ə tər
solicitous	sə **LIS** ə təs
solidarity, S-	**SOL** ə **DAR** ə tee
solidify	sə **LID** ə **FĪ**
solidity	sə **LID** ə tee

o on, oh oat, oi boy, oo soon, oor poor, or for, ow cow, sh shush,
th thin, *th* this, u up, ur spur, uu book, *zh* pleasure

solidus	**SOL** ə dəs
solifidian	**SOL** ə **FID** ee ən
soliloquist	sə **LIL** ə kwəst
soliloquize	sə **LIL** ə **KWĪZ**
soliloquy	sə **LIL** ə kwee
solipsism	**SOL** əp **SIZ** əm
solipsist	**SOL** əp səst
solitaire	**SOL** ə **TAIR**
solitary	**SOL** ə **TER** ee
solo, S-	**SOH** loh
Solomentsev, Mikhail	səl am **YENT** sef, mee hī **EEL**
Solomon	**SOL** ə mən
Solon, s-	**SOH** lən
solstice	**SOHL** stəs
Solti	**SOHL** tee
soluble	**SOL** yə bəl
solus	**SOH** ləs
solute	**SOL** yoot
solution	sə **LOO** shən
Solvay	**SOL** vay
solve	solv
solvent	**SOL** vənt
Solway Firth	**SOL** way **FURTH**
Solzhenitsyn	**SOHL** *zh*ə **NEET** sən
soma	**SOH** mə
Somali	soh **MAH** lee
Somalia	soh **MAH** lee ə
Somaliland	soh **MAH** lee **LAND**
somatic	soh **MAT** ik
somatology	**SOH** mə **TOL** ə jee
somber	**SOM** bər
sombrero	som **BRAIR** oh
somersault	**SUM** ər **SAWLT**
Somerset	**SUM** ər **SET**
Somerville	**SUM** ər **VIL**
somewhat	**SUM** hwot
Somme	sum
sommelier	**SUM** əl **YAY**
somnambulate	som **NAM** byə **LAYT**
somnambulation	som **NAM** byə **LAY** shən
somniferous	som **NIF** ər əs
somnolence	**SOM** nə ləns
Somnus	**SOM** nəs

ə ago, a at, ah calm, ahr dark, air care, aw saw, ay say, ch church
e bet, ee me, eer beer, hw what, i is, ī my, *n* French final n vin,

Somoza	saw **MAW** sah
sonant	**SOH** nənt
sonar	**SOH** nahr
sonata	sə **NAH** tə
sonatina	**SAHN** ə **TEE** nə
song	sawng
Song Renqiong	sawng run chee awng
sonic	**SAHN** ik
soniferous	sə **NIF** ər əs
Sonnambula, La	soh **NAHM** byoo **LAH**, lah
sonnet	**SAHN** ət
sonobuoy	**SAHN** oh **BOO** ee
Sonora (Mexico)	saw **NAW** rah
Sonora (US)	sə **NOR** ə
sonority	sə **NOR** ə tee
sonorous	**SAHN** ər əs
Soochow	soo joh
Soong	suung
soot	suut
sooth	sooth
soothe	soo*th*
Sophia	soh **FĪ** ə
sophism	**SOF** iz əm
sophist	**SOF** əst
sophisticate (n)	sə **FIS** ti kət
sophisticate (v)	sə **FIS** tə **KAYT**
sophistry	**SOF** ə stree
Sophocles	**SOF** ə **KLEEZ**
sophomore	**SOF** ə **MOR**
sophomoric	**SOF** ə **MOR** ik
soporific	**SOP** ə **RIF** ik
soprano	sə **PRAN** oh
Sopron	**SHAW** prawn
Sorata	saw **RAH** tə
sorbefacient	**SOR** bə **FAY** shənt
Sorbian	**SOR** bee ən
Sorbonne	sor **BUN**
sorcerer	**SOR** sə rər
sordid	**SOR** dəd
sordino	sor **DEE** noh
Sorenson	**SOR** ən sən
sorghum	**SOR** gəm
sorites	soh **RĪ** teez

o on, oh oat, oi boy, oo soon, oor poor, or for, ow cow, sh shush,
th thin, *th* this, u up, ur spur, uu book, *zh* pleasure

soroban	soh roh bahn
Soroptimist	sə **ROP** tə məst
sororicide	sə **ROR** ə **SĪD**
sorority	sə **ROR** ə tee
sorosis	sə **ROH** sis
sorrel	**SOR** əl
Sorrento	sə **REN** toh
sorrow	**SAHR** oh
sorry	**SAHR** ee
Sorsa, Kalevi	**SOR** sə, **KAH** lay vee
sortie	**SOR** tee
sortilege	**SOR** tə lij
Sosa-Rodriguez	**SOH** sah roh **DREE** gez
Sosnowiec	saws **NAW** vyets
sostenuto	**sos** tə **NOO** toh
Sotheby	SU*TH* bee
Sothern	SU*TH* ərn
sotto voce	**SOT** oh **VOH** chee
sou	soo
soubrette	soo **BRET**
soubriquet	**SOH** brə кач
souchong	soo shawng
soufflé	soo **FLAY**
sough	sow (as in *cow*)
sought	sawt
souk	sook
Soulat, Robert	**SOO** lah, roh **BAIR**
Souleymane Ould Cheikh Sidya	soo lay **MAHN OOLT** chayk **SEE** dyah
soupçon	soop **SAWN** (**SAWN** French final *n*)
Souphanouvong	suu **FAH** noo vawng
sourdough	**SOWR** doh
Sousa	**SOO** zə
sousaphone	**SOO** zə ғонн
souse	sows (as in *louse*)
soutache	soo **TASH**
soutane	soo **TAHN**
Southampton	sowth **AMP** tən
southerly	SU*TH* ər lee
southern	SU*TH* ərn
Southey	**SOW** *th*ee (**SOW** as in *cow*)
Southwark	SU*TH* ərk

ə ago, a at, ah calm, ahr dark, air care, aw saw, ay say, ch church
e bet, ee me, eer beer, hw what, i is, ī my, *n* French final n vin,

Soutine	soo **TEEN**
Souvanna Phouma	suu **VAH** nə **FOO** mə
Souvannavong	suu vah nə **VAWNG**
souvenir	**SOO** və **NEER**
sou'wester	**SOW WES** tər (**SOW** as in *cow*)
sovereign	**SOV** ə rən
sovereignty	**SOV** ər ən tee
soviet, S-	**SOH** vee **ET**
sovietize	**SOH** vee ə **TĪZ**
sow (pig)	sow (as in *cow*)
sow (plant)	soh
Sow, Adam Malick	**SOH**, ə **DAHM MA** leek
Soweto	soh **WET** oh
spa, S-	spah
spado	**SPAY** doh
Spadolini, Giovanni	**SPAHD** əl **EE** nee, joh **VAHN** ni
spaetzle	**SHPET** slə
spaghetti	spə **GET** ee
Spain	spayn
Spalato	**SPAH** lah taw
spaniel	**SPAN** yəl
spanner	**SPAN** ər
Spartacus	**SPAHR** tə kəs
spasm	**SPAZ** əm
spasmodic	spaz **MOD** ik
spasmolytic	**SPAZ** mə **LIT** ik
Spasowski, Romuald	spa **SOF** skee, rom **OO** ahld
spastic	**SPAS** tik
spatial	**SPAY** shəl
spatterdash	**SPAT** ər **DASH**
spatterdock	**SPAT** ər **DOK**
spatula	**SPACH** ə lə
spatulate	**SPACH** ə lət
spavin	**SPAV** ən
spavined	**SPAV** ənd
spécialité	spe syah lee **TAY**
specialty	**SPESH** əl tee
specie	**SPEE** shee
species	**SPEE** sheez
specific	spi **SIF** ik
specify	**SPES** ə **FĪ**
specimen	**SPES** ə mən
speciosity	**SPEE** shee **OS** ə tee

o on, oh oat, oi boy, oo soon, oor poor, or for, ow cow, sh shush, th thin, *th* this, u up, ur spur, uu book, *zh* pleasure

specious	SPEE shəs
spectacle	SPEK tə kəl
spectacular	spek TAK yə lər
spectator	SPEK tay tər
specter	SPEK tər
spectral	SPEK trəl
spectre	SPEK tər
spectroscope	SPEK trə SKOHP
spectroscopic	SPEK trə SKOP ik
spectroscopy	spek TROS kə pee
spectrum	SPEK trəm
speculate	SPEK yə LAYT
speculum	SPEK yə ləm
speedometer	spi DOM ə tər
speiss	spīs
speleology	SPEE lee OL ə jee
spelunker	spi LUNG kər
Spencer, s-	SPEN sər
Spencerian	spen SI ree ən
Spengler	SPENG glər
Spenser	SPEN sər
Spenserian	spen SEER ee ən
sperm	spurm
spermaceti	SPUR mə SET ee
spermatozoon	SPUR mə tə ZOH ən
sphagnum	SFAG nəm
sphalerite	SFAL ə RĪT
sphenic	SFEE nik
sphere	sfeer
spherical	SFER i kəl
sphericity	sfe RIS ə tee
spheroid	SFER oid
spherule	SFER ool
spherulite	SFER ə LĪT
sphincter	SFINGK tər
sphinx, S-	sfingks
sphygmograph	SFIG mə GRAF
sphygmomanometer	SFIG moh mə NOM ə tər
sphygmus	SFIG məs
spica, S-	SPĪ kə
spiccato	spi KAH toh
spicule	SPIK yool
Spiegel, Der	SHPEE gəl, der

ə ago, a at, ah calm, ahr dark, air care, aw saw, ay say, ch church
e bet, ee me, eer beer, hw what, i is, ī my, *n* French final n vin,

spiegeleisen	SPEE gəl Ī zən
spiel	speel
Spielberg	SPEEL burg
spigot	SPIG ət
spikenard	SPĪK nahrd
spillage	SPIL ij
spillikin	SPIL ə kən
spinach	SPIN ich
spinal	SPĪ nəl
spindly	SPIND lee
spinel	spə NEL
spinet	SPIN ət
spinnaker	SPIN ə kər
Spinoza	spi NOH zə
Spinozism	spi NOH ziz əm
spiracle	SPĪ rə kəl
spiral	SPĪ rəl
spirant	SPĪ rənt
spirea	spī REE ə
spirit	SPIR ət
spiritoso	SPIR ə TOH soh
spiritual	SPIR i choo əl
spirituous	SPIR i choo əs
spiritus	SPIR i təs
spirochete	SPĪ rə KEET
Spitsbergen	SPITS BUR gən
spittoon	spi TOON
spitz	spits
spitzenburg	SPIT sən BURG
splanchnic	SPLANGK nik
splanchnology	splangk NOL ə jee
splendor	SPLEN dər
splenetic	spli NET ik
splenius	SPLEE nee əs
Split	spleet
splurge	splurj
Spode	spohd
Spokane	spoh KAN
Spoleto	spoh LE toh
spoliate	SPOH lee AYT
spoliation	SPOH lee AY shən
spondaic	spon DAY ik
spondee	SPON dee

---

o on, oh oat, oi boy, oo soon, oor poor, or for, ow cow, sh shush,
th thin, *th* this, u up, ur spur, uu book, *zh* pleasure

spondylitis	SPON də LĪ təs
sponsion	SPON shən
sponson	SPON sən
spontaneity	SPON tə NEE ə tee
spontaneous	spon TAY nee əs
spoonerism	SPOO nə RIZ əm
spoor	spuur
Sporades	SPOR ə DEEZ
sporadic	spə RAD ik
spore	spor
Spotsylvania	SPOT sil VAY nee ə
springbok	SPRING bok
springe	sprinj
sprue	sproo
spumante	spoo MAHN te
spume	spyoom
spumoni	spuu MOH nee
spumous	SPYOO məs
spurious	SPYUUR ee əs
sputnik	SPUUT nik
sputum	SPYOO təm
Spuyten Duyvil	SPĪT ən DĪ vəl
squab	skwob
squad	skwod
squadron	SKWOD rən
squalid	SKWOL əd
squall	skwawl
squalor	SKWOL ər
squama	SKWAY mə
squamous	SKWAY məs
squander	SKWAHN dər
squash	skwosh
squeegee	SKWEE jee
squirearchy	SKWĪR AHR kee
squirrel	SKWUR əl
sri	shree
Sri Lanka	sree LAHNG kə
Srinagar	sree NUG ər
Srithirath, Soubanh	sree tee RAHT, soo bahn
Stabat Mater	STAH baht MAH ter
stabile (sculpture)	stay BEEL
stabilize	STAY bə LĪZ
staccato	stə KAH toh

ə ago, a at, ah calm, ahr dark, air care, aw saw, ay say, ch church
e bet, ee me, eer beer, hw what, i is, ī my, n French final n vin,

Stader	STAY dər
stadia	STAY dee ə
stadium	STAY dee əm
Staebler	STAY blər
Staël, de	STAHL, də
stagnant	STAG nənt
staid	stayd
Stakhanovism	stə KAH nə VIZ əm
Stakhanovite	stə KAH nə VĪT
stalactite	stə LAK tīt
stalag	STAHL ahg
stalagmite	stə LAG mīt
Stalin	STAH lən
Stalingrad	STAH lən GRAD
stalk	stawk
stallion	STAL yən
stalwart	STAWL wərt
Stambolić, Petar	STAHM boh leech, PET ər
Stamboul, Stambul	stahm BOOL
stamen	STAY mən
stamina	STAM ə nə
stampede	stam PEED
stanch	stawnch
stanchion	STAN chən
Standish	STAN dish
Stanford-Binet	STAN fərd bi NAY
Stanhope, s-	STAN əp
Stanislaus	STAN əs LAWS
Stanislav	stah ni SLAHF
Stanislavsky	STAN i SLAHF skee
Stanley	STAN lee
Stanovoi	STAH naw VOI
stanza	STAN zə
stanzaic	stan ZAY ik
stapes	STAY peez
staphylococci	STAF ə lə KOK sī
staphylococcus	STAF ə lə KOK əs
stasis	STAY səs
Stasiuk	STAY see ək
Staten Island	STAT ən
stationary, stationery	STAY shə NER ee
statism	STAYT iz əm
statist	STAYT əst

o on, oh oat, oi boy, oo soon, oor poor, or for, ow cow, sh shush,
th thin, *th* this, u up, ur spur, uu book, *zh* pleasure

statistic	stə **TIS** tik
statistician	**STAT** ə **STISH** ən
Statius	**STAY** shee əs
stator	**STAY** tər
statoscope	**STAT** ə **SKOHP**
statuary	**STACH** oo **ER** ee
statue	**STACH** oo
statuesque	**STACH** oo **ESK**
statuette	**STACH** oo **ET**
stature	**STACH** ər
status	**STAYT** əs
status quo	**STAYT** əs **KWOH**
status quo ante	**STAH** təs **KWOH** **AHN** tay
statute	**STACH** oot
statutory	**STACH** ə **TOR** ee
staunch	stawnch
Staunton	**STAWN** tən
Stavanger	stah **VAHNG** ər
stave	stayv
stead	sted
steak tartare	**STAYK** tahr **TAHR**
stealth	stelth
stealthy	**STEL** thee
stearic	stee **AR** ik
Stearns	sturnz
steatite	**STEE** ə **TĪT**
steatopygia	stee **AT** ə **PIJ** ee ə
steatopygic	stee **AT** ə **PIJ** ik
Steen, Jan	stayn, yahn
steenbok	**STEEN** bok
Stefanie	**STEF** ə nee
Stefansson	**STEF** ən sən
Steffens	**STEF** ənz
stegosaurus	**STEG** ə **SOR** əs
Steichen	**STĪ** kən
stein, S-	stīn
Steinbeck	**STĪN** bek
steinbok	**STĪN** bok
Steinem	**STĪN** əm
Steinmetz	**STĪN** mets
Steinway	**STĪN** way
stela	**STEE** lə
stelae	**STEE** lee

ə ago, a at, ah calm, ahr dark, air care, aw saw, ay say, ch church
e bet, ee me, eer beer, hw what, i is, ī my, *n* French final n vin,

stichic

stele (burial stone)	STEE lee
stele (botany)	steel
Stendhal	sten DAHL
stenographer	stə NOG rə fər
stenographic	STEN ə GRAF ik
stenosis	stə NOH səs
stenotype	STEN ə TĪP
stenotypy	STEN ə TĪ pee
Stentor, s-	STEN tor
stentorian	sten TOR ee ən
Stephanie	STEF ə nee
Stephen	STEE vən
steppe	step
stercoraceous	STUR kə RAY shəs
stereo	STER ee OH
stereophonic	STER ee ə FON ik
stereopticon	STER ee OP ti kən
stereoscope	STER ee ə SKOHP
stereotype	STER ee ə TĪP
sterile	STER əl
sterility	stə RIL ə tee
sterilize	STER ə LĪZ
Stern	sturn
Sterne, Laurence	STURN, LAW rəns
sternum	STUR nəm
steroid	STI roid
sterol	STI rawl
stertorous	STUR tə rəs
stet	stet
stethoscope	STETH ə SKOHP
Stettin	shte TEEN
Steuben	STOO bən
Steubenville	STOO bən vil
stevedore	STEE və DOR
steward	STOO ərd
stewardess	STOO ərd əs
Stewart	STOO ərt
sthenic	STHEN ik
Stheno	STHEE noh
stibium	STIB ee əm
stibnite	STIB nīt
stich	stik
stichic	STIK ik

o on, oh oat, oi boy, oo soon, oor poor, or for, ow cow, sh shush, th thin, *th* this, u up, ur spur, uu book, *zh* pleasure

stichomythia	**STIK** ə **MITH** ee ə
Stieglitz	**STEEG** ləts
stifle	**STĪ** fəl
stigma	**STIG** mə
stigmata	stig **MAH** tə
stigmatic	stig **MAT** ik
stigmatism	**STIG** mə **TIZ** əm
stigmatize	**STIG** mə **TĪZ**
Stikker, Dirk	**STIK** ər, **DURK**
stilbestrol	stil **BES** trawl
stiletto	stə **LET** oh
Stilton	**STIL** tən
Stilwell	**STIL** wel
stimulant	**STIM** yə lənt
stimulus	**STIM** yə ləs
stipend	**STĪ** pend
stipulation	**STIP** yə **LAY** shən
stirpes	**STUR** peez
stirpiculture	**STUR** pə **KUL** chər
stirps	sturps
stirrup	**STI** rəp
stoa	**STOH** ə
stoat	stoht
stochastic	stoh **KAS** tik
stockade	stah **KAYD**
Stockholm	**STOK** hohm
stodgy	**STOJ** ee
stogy	**STOH** gee
Stoic, s-	**STOH** ik
stoichiometric	**STOI** kee ə **MET** rik
stoichiometry	**STOI** kee **OM** ə tree
Stoicism, s-	**STOH** ə **SIZ** əm
stolid	**STOL** əd
stolidity	stə **LID** ə tee
stolon	**STOH** lən
Stoltenberg, Gerhard	**SHTOHL** tən berg, **GAIR** hahrt
stoma	**STOH** mə
stomach	**STUM** ək
stomacher	**STUM** ə kər
stomachic	stə **MAK** ik
stomata	**STOH** mə tə
stomatitis	**STOH** mə **TĪ** təs
Stonehenge	**STOHN** henj

ə ago, a at, ah calm, ahr dark, air care, aw saw, ay say, ch church
e bet, ee me, eer beer, hw what, i is, ī my, *n* French final n vin,

stony	**STOH** nee
Stoph, Willi	**SHTAWF, VEE** lee
storied	**STOR** eed
Storting, Storthing	**STOR** ting
Stouffer	**STOH** fər
stoup	stoop
Stowe	stoh
strabismus	strə **BIZ** məs
Strabo	**STRAY** boh
strabotomy	strə **BOT** ə mee
Strachey	**STRAY** chee
Stradivari	**STRAH** dee **VAH** ree
Stradivarius	**STRAD** ə **VA** ree əs
strafe	strayf
straight	strayt
strait	strayt
straitjacket	**STRAYT JAK** ət
stramonium	strə **MOH** nee əm
straphanger	**STRAP HANG** ər
strappado	strə **PAY** doh
Strasbourg	strahz **BOOR**
strata	**STRAY** tə
stratagem	**STRAT** ə jəm
strategic	strə **TEE** jik
strategist	**STRAT** ə jəst
strategy	**STRAT** ə jee
Stratford-on-Avon	**STRAT** fərd on **AY** vən
strathspey	strath **SPAY**
stratification	**STRAT** ə fə **KAY** shən
stratocracy	strə **TOK** rə see
stratocumulus	**STRAY** toh **KYOO** myə ləs
stratosphere	**STRAT** ə **SFEER**
stratum	**STRAY** təm
stratus	**STRAY** təs
Straus, -s	strows (rhymes with *louse*)
Straus, -s (German)	shtrows (rhymes with *louse*)
Stravinsky	strə **VIN** skee
Streich	strīk
Streisand	**STRĪ** sənd
strength	strengkth
strenuous	**STREN** yə wəs
streptococcal	**STREP** tə **KOK** əl
streptococci	**STREP** tə **KOK** ī

o on, oh oat, oi boy, oo soon, oor poor, or for, ow cow, sh shush,
th thin, *th* this, u up, ur spur, uu book, *zh* pleasure

streptococcus	**STREP** tə **KOK** əs
streptomycin	**STREP** tə **MĪ** sən
stretta	**STRET** ə
stretto	**STRET** oh
stria	**STRĪ** ə
striated	**STRĪ** ay təd
stricture	**STRIK** chər
stringendo	strin **JEN** doh
stroboscope	**STROH** bə **SKOHP**
Stroessner, Alfredo	**STRES** nər, ahl **FRAY** *th*oh
Stromboli	**STRAWM** baw lee
stronger	**STRAWNG** gər
strongest	**STRAWNG** gəst
strontium	**STRON** chəm
strophe	**STROH** fee
strophic	**STROF** ik
Strozzi	**STRAWT** tsee
structure	**STRUK** chər
strudel	**SHTROO** dəl
strychnine	**STRIK** nīn
Stuart	**STOO** ərt
stubborn	**STUB** ərn
stucco	**STUK** oh
studding	**STUD** ing
studdingsail (nautical)	**STUN** səl
studio	**STOO** dee **OH**
studious	**STOO** dee əs
Stuka	**STOO** kə
stultification	**STUL** tə fə **KAY** shən
stultify	**STUL** tə **FĪ**
stumpage	**STUM** pij
stupa	**STOO** pə
stupe	stoop
stupefacient	**STOO** pə **FAY** shənt
stupefaction	**STOO** pə **FAK** shən
stupefy	**STOO** pə **FĪ**
stupendous	stuu **PEN** dəs
stupid	**STOO** pəd
stupor	**STOO** pər
sturgeon	**STUR** jən
Sturm und Drang	**SHTUURM** uunt **DRAHNG**
Stuttgart	**SHTUUT** gahrt
Stuyvesant	**STĪ** və sənt

ə ago, a at, ah calm, ahr dark, air care, aw saw, ay say, ch church
e bet, ee me, eer beer, hw what, i is, ī my, *n* French final n vin,

Stygian, s-	**STIJ** ee ən
stylet	**STĪ** lət
stylite	**STĪ** līt
stylograph	**STĪ** lə **GRAF**
stylus	**STĪ** ləs
stymie, stymy	**STĪ** mee
styptic	**STIP** tik
Styr	steer
styrene	**STĪ** reen
Styrofoam	**STĪ** rə **FOHM**
Styx	stiks
Suakin	**SWAH** kin
suasion	**SWAY** zhən
suave	swahv
suavity	**SWAH** və tee
subaltern	sub **AWL** tərn
subdue	səb **DOO**
Subic	**SOO** bik
subito	**SOO** bi **TOH**
subject (a, n)	**SUB** jikt
subject (v)	səb **JEKT**
subjective	səb **JEK** tiv
sub judice	sub **JOO** di **SEE**
subjugate	**SUB** jə **GAYT**
sublimate	**SUB** lə **MAYT**
subliminal	sub **LIM** ə nəl
subordinate (a, n)	sə **BOR** də nət
subordinate (v)	sə **BOR** də **NAYT**
suborn	sə **BORN**
Subotica, Subotitsa	**SOO** **BAW** tit sah
subpoena	sə **PEE** nə
sub rosa	sub **ROH** zə
subroutine	**SUB** roo **TEEN**
subsequent	**SUB** si kwənt
subsidence	səb **SĪD** əns
subsidiary	səb **SID** ee **ER** ee
subsidy	**SUB** sə dee
substance	**SUB** stəns
substantiate	səb **STAN** shee **AYT**
substantiation	səb **STAN** shee **AY** shən
substantive	**SUB** stən tiv
subterfuge	**SUB** tər **FYOOJ**
subterranean	**SUB** tə **RAY** nee ən

o on, oh oat, oi boy, oo soon, oor poor, or for, ow cow, sh shush,
th thin, *th* this, u up, ur spur, uu book, *zh* pleasure

subtle	SUT əl
subtlety	SUT əl tee
suburb	SUB urb
suburban	sə BUR bən
suburbanite	sə BUR bə NĪT
subversion	səb VUR zhən
succedaneum	SUK sə DAY nee əm
succeed	sək SEED
success	sək SES
succinct	suk SINGKT
succor	SUK ər
succotash	SUK ə TASH
Succoth	SUUK əs
succuba	SUK yə bə
succubus	SUK yə bəs
succulent	SUK yə lənt
succumb	sə KUM
Suceava	suu CHAH vah
Süchow	soo joh
sucrose	SOO krohs
Sudan	soo DAN
Sudanese	soo də NEEZ
Sudanic	soo DAN ik
sudarium	soo DAIR ee əm
sudatorium	SOOD ə TOR ee əm
sudatory	SOOD ə TOR ee
Sudbury	SUD ber ee
Sudermann	ZOO dər MAHN
Sudeten	soo DAY tən
Sudetes	soo DEE teez
sudorific	soo də RIF ik
sue, S-	soo
suede	swayd
suet	SOO ət
Suetonius	SOO ə TOH nee əs
Suez	soo EZ
suffice	sə FĪS
sufficient	sə FISH ənt
suffix	SUF iks
suffocate	SUF ə KAYT
Suffolk	SUF ək
suffragan	SUF rə gən
suffrage	SUF rij

ə ago, a at, ah calm, ahr dark, air care, aw saw, ay say, ch church
e bet, ee me, eer beer, hw what, i is, ī my, n French final n vin,

suffragette	sUF rə JET
suffuse	sə FYOOZ
Sufi	SOO fee
Sufism	SOO fiz əm
suggest	səg JEST
suggestion	səg JES chən
Suharto	suu HAHR toh
suicidal	SOO ə SĪ dəl
suicide	SOO ə sīD
sui generis	soo ee JEN ər əs
suitable	SOO tə bəl
suite	sweet
suitor	SOO tər
Sukarno	soo KAHR noh
sukiyaki	sUUK ee YAH kee
sukkah	SUUK ə
Sukkoth	SUUK əs
Sulaiman, Sadek Jawad	soo LAY MAHN, sah DAY jah WAHD
sulcus	SUL kəs
Suleiman	SOO lay MAHN
sulfa	SUL fə
sulfadiazine	SUL fə DĪ ə ZEEN
sulfanilamide	SUL fə NIL ə MĪD
sulfapyrazine	SUL fə PIR ə ZEEN
sulfapyridine	SUL fə PIR ə DEEN
sulfate	SUL fayt
sulfathiazole	SUL fə THĪ ə ZOHL
sulfide	SUL fīd
sulfonamide	sul FON ə MĪD
sulfonate	SUL fə NAYT
sulfone	SUL fohn
sulfonic	sul FON ik
sulfur	SUL fər
sulfureous	sul FYUUR ee əs
sulfuric	sul FYUUR ik
sulfurous	SUL fə rəs
Sulla	SUL ə
sullen	SUL ən
Sully, s-	SUL ee
sulphur	SUL fər
sultan, S-	SUL tən
sultana	sul TAN ə

---

o on, oh oat, oi boy, oo soon, oor poor, or for, ow cow, sh shush, th thin, *th* this, u up, ur spur, uu book, *zh* pleasure

sultanate	SUL tə NAYT
Sulu	SOO loo
sumac	SOO mak
Sumatra	suu MAH trə
Sumba	SOOM bah
Sumbawa	soom BAH wah
Sumer	SOO mər
Sumerian	soo MER ee ən
sumi	soo mee
sumi-e	soo mee e
summa cum laude	SUUM ə kuum LOWD ə (LOWD as in *crowd*)
summary	SUM ə ree
summation	sə MAY shən
summersault	SUM ər SAWLT
summum bonum	SUUM əm BOH nəm
sumo	SOO moh
sumptuary	SUMP choo ER ee
sumptuous	SUMP choo əs
Sunda	SUN də
sundae	SUN day
Sunday	SUN day
Sunde	SUUN də
sundry	SUN dree
Sung	suung
Sun Myung Moon	sun myung moon
Sunna, -h	SUUN ə
Sunni	SUUN ee
Sunnite	SUUN it
Sununu	sə NOO noo
Sun Yat-sen	suun yaht sen
Sun Yün-hsüan	suun yuun shuu ahn
Suomenlinna	suu AW men LIN ə
Suomi	suu AW mee
superb	suu PURB
supercilious	soo pər SIL ee əs
superficial	soo pər FISH əl
superfluity	soo pər FLOO ə tee
superfluous	suu PUR floo əs
superheterodyne	soo pər HET ə rə DIN
superintendent	soo pər in TEN dənt
superior, S-	suu PIR ee ər
superiority	suu PIR ee OR ə tee

ə ago, a at, ah calm, ahr dark, air care, aw saw, ay say, ch church
e bet, ee me, eer beer, hw what, i is, ī my, *n* French final n vin,

superlative	suu PUR lə tiv
supernal	suu PUR nəl
supernova	soo pər NOH və
supernumerary	soo pər NOO mə RER ee
supersede	soo pər SEED
supersonic	soo pər SON ik
superstition	soo pər STISH ən
superstitious	soo pər STISH əs
supine (a)	suu PĪN
supine (n)	SOO pīn
supplant	sə PLANT
supple	SUP əl
supplement (n)	SUP lə mənt
supplement (v)	SUP lə MENT
supplementary	SUP lə MEN tə ree
suppliant	SUP lee ənt
supplicant	SUP lə kənt
supplication	SUP lə KAY shən
supposition	SUP ə ZISH ən
suppository	sə POZ ə TOR ee
suppurate	SUP yə RAYT
suprarenal	soo prə REEN əl
supremacy	sə PREM ə see
supreme	sə PREEM
sura	SUUR ə
Surabaya	SUUR ə BAH yə
surah	SUUR ə
Surakarta	SUUR ə KAHR tə
Surat	sə RAT
surcease	sur SEES
surcingle	SUR sing gəl
surcoat	SUR koht
surd	surd
surety	SHUUR ə tee
surface	SUR fəs
surfactant	sər FAK tənt
surfeit	SUR fət
surgeon	SUR jən
surgery	SUR jə ree
Suribachi	SUUR ə BAH chee
Surinach	SOO ri nahk
Surinam	SUUR ə NAHM
Suriname	SUUR ə NAHM ə

---

o on, oh oat, oi boy, oo soon, oor poor, or for, ow cow, sh shush,
th thin, *th* this, u up, ur spur, uu book, *zh* pleasure

surly	SUR lee
surmise	sər MĪZ
surmount	sər MOWNT (MOWNT as in *count*)
surpass	sər PAS
surplice	SUR pləs
surplus	SUR pləs
surprise	sər PRĪZ
surrealism	sə REE ə LIZ əm
surrealist	sə REE ə ləst
surrealistic	sə REE ə LIS tik
surreptitious	SUR əp TISH əs
surrey, S-	SUR ee
surrogate (a, n)	SUR ə gət
surrogate (v)	SUR ə GAYT
sursum corda	SUUR səm KOR də
surtax	SUR taks
surtout	sər TOO
surveillance	sər VAY ləns
survey (n)	SUR vay
survey (v)	sər VAY
surveyor	sər VAY ər
Susa	SOO sah
susceptible	sə SEP tə bəl
sushi	soo shee
Suslov, Mikhail	SOOS lahf, mi kah EEL
suspect (a, n)	SUS pekt
suspect (v)	sə SPEKT
suspire	sə SPĪR
Susquehanna	SUS kwə HAN ə
Sussex	SUS iks
sustain	sə STAYN
sustenance	SUS tə nəns
susurration	SOO sə RAY shən
susurrus	suu SUR əs
Sutherland	SUTH ər lənd
sutler	SUT lər
sutra	SOO trə
suttee	su TEE
Sutter	SUT ər
suture	SOO chər
Suva	SOO vah
Suvorov	suu VAW rahf
Suwannee	sə WAH nee

ə ago, a at, ah calm, ahr dark, air care, aw saw, ay say, ch church
e bet, ee me, eer beer, hw what, i is, ī my, n French final n vin,

Suwon	soo wahn
suzerain	SOO zə rən
suzerainty	SOO zə rən tee
Suzhou	soo joh
Suzuki, Zenko	sə ZOOK ee, ZEN koh
Svalbard	SVAHL bahr
svelte	sfelt
Svengali	sfen GAHL ee
Svenska	SVEN skah
Sverdlovsk	sverd LAWFSK
Svoboda	svah BAW dah
Swabia	SWAY bee ə
swaddle	SWOD əl
Swadeshi, s-	swə DAY shee
Swahili	swah HEE lee
Swai, Nsilo	SWĪ, ən SEE loh
swami	SWAH mee
Swanee	SWAH nee
Swansea	SWAHN see
swaraj, S-	swə RAHJ
sward	swawrd
swarm	swawrm
swart, S-	swawrt
swarthy	SWAWR *th*ee
swastika	SWAH sti kə
Swat, s-	swaht
swatch	swahch
swath	swahth
swathe	swah*th*
Swazi	SWAH zee
Swaziland	SWAH zee LAND
Sweden	SWEE dən
Swedenborg	SWEE dən BORG
Swedenborgian	SWEE dən BOR gee ən
sweetbread	SWEET bred
swerve	swurv
Swigert, Jack	SWĪ gərt
Swinburne	SWIN bərn
Swithin, Swithun	SWI*TH* ən
Switzerland	SWIT sər lənd
sword	sawrd
Sybarite, s-	SIB ə RĪT
Sybaritic, s-	SIB ə RIT ik

o on, oh oat, oi boy, oo soon, oor poor, or for, ow cow, sh shush,
th thin, *th* this, u up, ur spur, uu book, *zh* pleasure

Sybil	**SIB** əl
sycamore	**SIK** ə **MOR**
sycophancy	**SIK** ə fən see
sycophant	**SIK** ə fənt
sycophantic	**SIK** ə **FAN** tik
sycosis	sī **KOH** səs
Sydney	**SID** nee
syllabary	**SIL** ə **BER** ee
syllabic	si **LAB** ik
syllabify	sə **LAB** ə **FĪ**
syllabub	**SIL** ə **BUB**
syllabus	**SIL** ə bəs
syllepsis	sə **LEP** səs
syllogism	**SIL** ə **JIZ** əm
sylph	silf
sylphid	**SIL** fəd
Sylphides	seel **FEED**
sylvan	**SIL** vən
sylvite	**SIL** vīt
symbiosis	**SIM** bee **OH** sis
symbiotic	**SIM** bee **OT** ik
symbol	**SIM** bəl
symbolism	**SIM** bə **LIZ** əm
symmetrical	sə **MET** ri kəl
symmetry	**SIM** ə tree
symposium	sim **POH** zee əm
symptom	**SIMP** təm
symptomatic	**SIM** tə **MAT** ik
synagogical	**SIN** ə **GOJ** i kəl
synagogue	**SIN** ə **GOG**
Synanon	**SIN** ə **NON**
synapse	**SIN** aps
synapses	sə **NAP** seez
synapsis	sə **NAP** səs
synchronic	sin **KRON** ik
synchronism	**SING** krə **NIZ** əm
synchronize	**SING** krə **NĪZ**
synchronous	**SING** krə nəs
synchrotron	**SING** krə **TRON**
synclinal	sin **KLĪN** əl
syncline	**SIN** klīn
syncopate	**SING** kə **PAYT**
syncope	**SING** kə pee

ə ago, a at, ah calm, ahr dark, air care, aw saw, ay say, ch church
e bet, ee me, eer beer, hw what, i is, ī my, *n* French final n vin,

syncretism	SIN krə TIZ əm
syndetic	sin DET ik
syndic	SIN dik
syndicalism	SIN di kə LIZ əm
syndicate (a, n)	SIN də kət
syndicate (v)	SIN də KAYT
syndrome	SIN drohm
synecdoche	sə NEK də kee
synergism	SIN ər JIZ əm
synergistic	SIN ər JIS tik
synergy	SIN ər jee
synesis	SIN ə səs
Synge	sing
synizesis	SIN ə ZEE səs
synod	SIN əd
synodical	sə NOD i kəl
synonymity	SIN ə NIM ə tee
synonymous	sə NON ə məs
synonymy	sə NON ə mee
synopses	sə NOP seez
synopsis	sə NOP səs
syntactic	sin TAK tik
syntheses	SIN thə seez
synthesis	SIN thə səs
synthesize	SIN thə sīz
synthetic	sin THET ik
syphilis	SIF ə ləs
syphilitic	SIF ə LIT ik
syphilology	SIF ə LOL ə jee
Syracuse	SI rə KYOOS
Syr Darya	sir DAHR yah
Syria	SI ree ə
Syriac	SI ree AK
Syrian	SI ree ən
syringa	sə RING gə
syringe	sə RINJ
syrinx, S-	SI ringks
syrup	SI rəp
systaltic	si STAWL tik
systematic	SIS tə MAT ik
systematist	SIS tə mə tist
systemic	si STEM ik
systole	SIS tə LEE

---

o on, oh oat, oi boy, oo soon, oor poor, or for, ow cow, sh shush,
th thin, *th* this, u up, ur spur, uu book, *zh* pleasure

systolic	si **STOL** ik
syzygy	**SIZ** ə jee
Szczecin	**SHCHET** seen
Szechwan	sech wahn
Szent-Györgyi	saynt **JOR** jee
Szepes	**SE** pesh
Szilard	**ZIL** ahrd
Szold	zohld
Szolnok	**SAWL** nawk
Szombathely	**SAWM** baht **HAY**
Szulc	shuults
Szydlowiec	shid **LAW** vyets

T

Taal (language)	tahl
Taal (volcano)	tah **AHL**
tabard	**TAB** ərd
tabaret	**TAB** ə rət
Tabasco	tə **BAS** koh
tabes	**TAY** beez
Tabitha	**TAB** ə thə
tablature	**TAB** lə chər
tableau	**TAB** loh
tableau vivant	ta **BLOH** vee **VAHN** (**VAHN** French final *n*)
tableaux	**TAB** lohz
table d'hôte	**TAB** əl **DOHT**
taboo	tə **BOO**
tabor	**TAY** bər
taboret	**TAB** ə **RET**
Tabriz	tah **BREEZ**
tabular	**TAB** yə lər
tabula rasa	**TAB** yə lə **RAH** zə
tacet	**TAH** ket
tachistoscope	tə **KIS** tə **SKOHP**
tachometer	tə **KOM** ə tər
tachycardia	**TAK** i **KAHR** dee ə
tachymeter	ta **KIM** ə tər
tacit	**TAS** ət
taciturn	**TAS** ə **TURN**
taciturnity	**TAS** ə **TUR** nə tee

ə ago, a at, ah calm, ahr dark, air care, aw saw, ay say, ch church
e bet, ee me, eer beer, hw what, i is, ī my, *n* French final n vin,

Tacitus	**TAS** ə təs
tackle	**TAK** əl
Tacna	**TAK** nə
taco	**TAH** koh
Tacoma	tə **KOH** mə
Taconic	tə **KON** ik
taconite	**TAK** ə **NĪT**
tactical	**TAK** ti kəl
tactician	tak **TISH** ən
tactile	**TAK** təl
Tacubaya	**TAH** koo **BAH** yah
Tadzhik, Tadjik	tah **JEEK**
Taegu	tī **GOO**
taenia	**TEE** nee ə
taffeta	**TAF** ə tə
tafia	**TAF** ee ə
Tafti	**TAF** tee
Tag (German)	tahk
Tagal	tah **GAHL**
Tagalog	tə **GAH** ləg
Taganrog	**TAH** gahn **RAWK**
Taggard	**TAG** ərd
Tagliavini	**TAH** lyah **VEE** nee
Tagore, Rabindranath	tə **GOR**, rə **BIN** drə **NAHT**
Tagus	**TAYG** əs
Tahiti	tə **HEE** tee
Tahitian	tə **HEE** shən
Tahoe	**TAH** hoh
t'ai chi	tī jee
Taif	**TAH** if
taiga	**TĪ** gə
taille	tayl
Taimyr, Taimir	tī **MEER**
Tainan	tī nahn
Taine	tayn
taipan	**TĪ** pan
Taipeh, Taipei	tī pay
Taiping	tī ping
Taisho	tī shoh
Taiwan	tī wahn
Taiyuan	**TĪ** yuu **AHN**
Taiz	ta **EEZ**
Tajik	tah **JIK**

o on, oh oat, oi boy, oo soon, oor poor, or for, ow cow, sh shush,
th thin, *th* this, u up, ur spur, uu book, *zh* pleasure

Taj Mahal	TAH*ZH* mə HAHL
Takamatsu	tah kah maht soo
talapoin	TAL ə POIN
talaria	tə LAIR ee ə
Talcahuano	TAHL kah WAH noh
talcum	TAL kəm
tales (jury)	TAY leez
talesman	TAYLZ mən
Taliesin	TAL ee ES ən
talion	TAL ee ən
taliped	TAL ə PED
talipes	TAL ə PEEZ
talipot	TAL ə POT
talisman	TAL əs mən
talkathon	TAW kə THON
Talkeetna	tal KEET nə
Tallahassee	TAL ə HAS ee
Talleyrand	TAL i RAND
Tallinn	TAHL lin
tallith	TAH ləs
Tall, Maki Koreissi Aguibou	TAL, MAH kee koh REE see ah GEE boo
Talmud	TAHL muud
Talmudic	tahl MUUD ik
talon	TAL ən
Talos	TAY lahs
talus	TAY ləs
tamale	tə MAH lee
Tamar	TAY mər
Tamara	tə MAHR ə
tamarack	TAM ə RAK
tamarind	TAM ə rənd
tamarisk	TAM ə risk
tamasha	tə MAH shə
Tamatave	TAH mah TAHV
Tamaulipas	TAH mow LEE pahs (mow as in *cow*)
Tamayo	tah MAH yoh
Tambora	tahm BOR ə
tambour	TAM buur
tambourin	TAM buu rən
tambourine	TAM bə REEN
Tamerlane	TAM ər LAYN
Tamil	TAM əl

ə ago, a at, ah calm, ahr dark, air care, aw saw, ay say, ch church
e bet, ee me, eer beer, hw what, i is, ī my, *n* French final n vin,

Tammuz	**TAH** muuz
Tampa	**TAM** pə
Tampere	**TAHM** pe re
Tampico	tam **PEE** koh
tampion	**TAM** pee ən
tampon	**TAM** pon
Tana	**TAH** nah
tanager	**TAN** i jər
Tanaka, Kakuei	tah nah kah, kah kway
Tanana	**TAN** ə **NAW**
Tananarive	tə **NAN** ə **REEV**
Tancred	**TANG** krəd
tandem	**TAN** dəm
Tang (dynasty)	tahng
Tanganyika	**TAN** gən **YEE** kə
tangelo	**TAN** jə **LOH**
tangent	**TAN** jənt
tangential	tan **JEN** shəl
tangerine	**TAN** jə **REEN**
tangible	**TAN** jə bəl
Tangier	tan **JIR**
Tangiers	tan **JIRZ**
tangle	**TANG** gəl
tango	**TANG** goh
Tangshan	dahng shahn
Tanguy, Yves	tahn **GEE**, **EEV** (tahn French final *n*)
Tanis	**TAY** nis
Tanner, Väinö	**TAH** nair, **VĪ** nə
Tannhäuser	**TAHN** HOI zər
Tannu Tuva	**TAN** oo **TOO** və
Tanqueray	**TANK** ə ray
tansy	**TAN** zee
tantalum	**TAN** tə ləm
Tantalus, t-	**TAN** tə ləs
tantamount	**TAN** tə **MOWNT** (**MOWNT** as in *count*)
tant mieux	tahn **MYUU** (tahn French final *n*)
tanto	**TAHN** toh
tant pis	tahn **PEE** (tahn French final *n*)
tantra, T-	**TUN** trə
tantrum	**TAN** trəm
Tanzania	**TAN** zə **NEE** ə
Tan Zhenlin	tahn jun leen
Tao	dow

o on, oh oat, oi boy, oo soon, oor poor, or for, ow cow, sh shush,
th thin, *th* this, u up, ur spur, uu book, *zh* pleasure

Taoism	**DOW** iz əm
Taos	tows (rhymes with *louse*)
Tapajoz	**TAH** pə **ZHAWS**
taper	**TAY** pər
tapestry	**TAP** ə stree
tapioca	**TAP** ee **OH** kə
tapir	**TAY** pər
tapis	**TAP** ee
Tapuyan	tah **POO** yən
taramosalata	**TAH** rah moh sah **LAH** tah
tarantas	**TAH** rahn **TAHS**
tarantella	**TA** rən **TEL** ə
Taranto	**TAH** rahn **TOH**
tarantula	tə **RAN** chə lə
Tarawa	tah **RAH** wah
Tarazi, Salah El Dine	**TAH** rah zee, sah **LAHK** əl **DEEN**
tarboosh	tahr **BOOSH**
Tardieu	tahr **DYUU**
tardo	**TAHR** doh
tare	tair
Targoviste	**TUR** goh **VESH** te
Targum	**TAHR** guum
Tarim	tah **REEM**
tarlatan	**TAHR** lə tən
taro	**TAHR** oh
tarot	**TA** roh
tarpaulin	tahr **PAW** lən
Tarpeia	tahr **PEE** ə
tarpon	**TAHR** pən
Tarquin	**TAHR** kwin
tarragon	**TA** rə gən
tarry (like tar)	**TAHR** ee
tarry (delay)	**TA** ree
Tarshish	**TAHR** shish
tarsier	**TAHR** see ər
Tarsus, t-	**TAHR** səs
tartan	**TAHR** tən
Tartar	**TAHR** tər
tartar (sauce)	**TAHR** tər
Tartarus	**TAHR** tər əs
Tartini	tahr **TEE** nee
Tartu	**TAHR** too
Tartuffe	tahr **TUUF**

ə ago, a at, ah calm, ahr dark, air care, aw saw, ay say, ch church
e bet, ee me, eer beer, hw what, i is, ī my, *n* French final n vin,

Tashkent, Tashkend	tahsh **KENT**
Tasman	**TAZ** mən
Tasmania	taz **MAY** nee ə
tass	tas
Tass	tahs
tassel	**TAS** əl
Tasso	**TAS** oh
tatami	tah **TAH** mee
Tatar	**TAH** tər
Tatiana	tah **TYAH** nah
Tatra	**TAH** trah
tatterdemalion	**TAT** ər di **MAYL** yən
tattersall	**TAT** ər **SAWL**
tattoo	ta **TOO**
Tatum	**TAYT** əm
tau	tow (as in *cow*)
taunt	tawnt
taupe	tohp
Taurus	**TOR** əs
Taussig	**TOW** sig (**TOW** as in *cow*)
taut	tawt
tautologous	taw **TOL** ə gəs
tautology	taw **TOL** ə jee
Taxco	**TAHS** koh
taxeme	**TAK** seem
taxidermy	**TAK** sə **DUR** mee
taxonomy	tak **SON** ə mee
Taygeta	tay **IJ** i tə
Tbilisi	tə **BIL** ə see
Tchaikovsky	chī **KAWF** skee
Tchebycheff	che **BISH** ef
Tchelitchew, Tchelitsheff	**CHU** lee chef
Tcherina, Ludmila	**CHE** ree nah, lood **MEE** lə
Tchobanov, Yordan	choh **BAH** nawf, **YOR** dahn
Tczew	chef (ch as in *chest*)
tear (weep)	teer
tear (rend)	tair
Tebaldi, Renata	tə **BAHL** dee, rə **NAH** tə
technetium	tek **NEE** shee əm
technic	**TEK** nik
technique	tek **NEEK**
technocracy	tek **NOK** rə see

---

o on, oh oat, oi boy, oo soon, oor poor, or for, ow cow, sh shush,
th thin, *th* this, u up, ur spur, uu book, *zh* pleasure

tectonic	tek TAHN ik
Tecumseh	tə KUM sə
Te Deum	tay DAY əm
tedious	TEE dee əs
tedium	TEE dee əm
teepee	TEE pee
Tees	teez
teeth	teeth
teethe	tee*th*
teetotaler	tee TOH tə lər
Tegal	te GAHL
Tegucigalpa	te GOO see GAHL pah
tegument	TEG yə mənt
Tehachapi	tə HACH ə pee
Teheran, Tehran	TAY ə RAN
Tehuantepec	te WAHN tə PEK
Tehuelche	te WEL che
Teilhard de Chardin	TAY YAR də shar DAN (DAN French final *n*)
tektite	TEK tīt
Telamon, t-	TEL ə MON
telangiectasis	TEL AN jee EK tə səs
Tel Aviv	TEL ə VEEV
telecast	TEL ə KAST
telega	tə LEG ə
telegenic	TEL ə JEN ik
telegraph	TEL ə GRAF
telegrapher	tə LEG rə fər
telegraphy	tə LEG rə fee
Telegu	TEL ə GOO
telekinesis	TEL ə kə NEE səs
Telemachus	tə LEM ə kəs
Telemann	TAY lə MAHN
Telemark, t-	TEL ə MAHRK
telemeter	TEL ə MEET ər
telemetry	tə LEM ə tree
teleological	TEL ee ə LOJ i kəl
teleology	TEL ee OL ə jee
telepathic	TEL ə PATH ik
telepathy	tə LEP ə thee
telephonic	TEL ə FON ik
telephony	tə LEF ə nee
telephoto	TEL ə FOH toh

ə ago, a at, ah calm, ahr dark, air care, aw saw, ay say, ch church
e bet, ee me, eer beer, hw what, i is, ī my, *n* French final n vin,

TelePrompTer	TEL ə PROM tər
telescopic	TEL ə SKOP ik
telescopy	tə LES kə pee
telesthesia	TEL əs THEE zhə
telethon	TEL ə THON
Teletron	TEL ə TRON
televise	TEL ə vīz
telic	TEL ik
Téllez	TEL yeth
tellurian	tə LUUR ee ən
tellurium	tə LUUR ee əm
Tellus	TEL əs
telpherage	TEL fər ij
Telugu	TEL uu GOO
temblor	TEM blər
temerarious	TEM ə RAIR ee əs
temerity	tə MER ə tee
Tempe	TEM pee
tempera	TEM pər ə
temperament	TEM pə rə mənt
temperamental	TEM pə rə MEN təl
temperance	TEM pə rəns
temperate	TEM pə rət
temperature	TEM pə rə chuur
tempestuous	tem PES choo əs
tempi	TEM pee
Templar, t-	TEM plər
template	TEM plət
tempo	TEM poh
temporal	TEM pə rəl
temporarily	TEM pə RER ə lee
temporize	TEM pə RĪz
temptress	TEM trəs
tempura	TEM puu RAH
tempus fugit	TEM pəs FYOO jət
Temuco	tay MOO koh
tenable	TEN ə bəl
tenacious	tə NAY shəs
tenacity	tə NAS ə tee
Tenafly	TEN ə FLĪ
tenant	TEN ənt
tendency	TEN dən see
tendentious	ten DEN shəs

o on, oh oat, oi boy, oo soon, oor poor, or for, ow cow, sh shush,
th thin, *th* this, u up, ur spur, uu book, *zh* pleasure

tendon	TEN dən
tendonitis	TEN də NĪT əs
Tenebrae	TEN ə BREE
tenebrous	TEN ə brəs
Tenedos	TEN ə DOS
tenement	TEN ə mənt
Tenerife, Teneriffe	TEN ə REE fay
tenet	TEN ət
Teng Hsiao-p'ing	dəng show ping (show as in *how*)
Teniers	TEN yərz
Tenniel	TEN yəl
Tennyson	TEN ə sən
Tennysonian	TEN ə SOHN ee ən
tenon	TEN ən
tenonitis	TEN ə NĪ təs
tenor	TEN ər
tenorrhaphy	tə NOR ə fee
tensile	TEN səl
tension	TEN shən
tensor	TEN sər
tentacle	TEN ti kəl
tentative	TEN tə tiv
tenuis	TEN yoo əs
tenuity	ten YOO ə tee
tenuous	TEN yoo əs
tenure	TEN yər
tenuto	tə NOO toh
teocalli	TEE ə KAL ee
Teotihuacán	TAY oh TEE wah KAHN
tepee	TEE pee
tepid	TEP əd
tequila	tə KEE lah
Terah	TEER ə
teraphim	TER ə fim
teratism	TER ə TIZ əm
teratogenic	TER ə tə JEN ik
teratology	TER ə TOL ə jee
terbium	TUR bee əm
Ter Borch, Terborch	tər BORK
Terceira	ter SAY rə
tercel	TUR səl
tercentenary	tur SEN tə NER ee
tercentennial	TUR sen TEN ee əl

ə ago, a at, ah calm, ahr dark, air care, aw saw, ay say, ch church
e bet, ee me, eer beer, hw what, i is, ī my, *n* French final n vin,

tercet	**TUR** sət
teredo	tə **REE** doh
Terence	**TER** əns
Tereshkova, Valentina	TE resh **KAW** vah, **VAH** len **TEE** nah
terga	**TUR** gə
tergiversate	**TUR JIV** ər **SAYT**
tergiversation	**TUR JIV** ər **SAY** shən
tergum	**TUR** gəm
Terhune	tər **HYOON**
Terkel, Studs	**TUR** kəl
termagant	**TUR** mə gənt
terminology	**TUR** mə **NOL** ə jee
terminus	**TUR** mə nəs
ternary	**TUR** nə ree
Ternate	ter **NAH** tay
terneplate	**TURN** playt
Ter-Ovanesyan, Igor	**TER** ah ven ye **SYAHN, EE** gor
Terpsichore	turp **SIK** ə ree
terpsichorean, T-	**TURP** si kə **REE** ən
terra, T-	**TER** ə
terrace	**TER** əs
terra cotta	**TER** ə **KOT** ə
terra firma	**TER** ə **FUR** mə
terrain	tə **RAYN**
terra incognita	**TER** ə in **KOG** nə tə
Terramycin	**TER** ə **MĪ** sən
terrapin	**TER** ə pən
terrarium	tə **RA** ree əm
terrazzo	tə **RAHT** soh
Terre Haute	**TER** ə **HOHT**
terrene	te **REEN**
terreplein	**TER** ə playn
terrestrial	tə **RES** tree əl
terrible	**TER** ə bəl
terrify	**TER** ə **FĪ**
terrigenous	te **RIJ** ə nəs
terrine	tə **REEN**
territorial	**TER** ə **TOR** ee əl
territory	**TER** ə **TOR** ee
terror	**TER** ər
terrorist	**TER** ə rəst
terrorize	**TER** ə **RĪZ**
terry, T-	**TER** ee

o on, oh oat, oi boy, oo soon, oor poor, or for, ow cow, sh shush,
th thin, *th* this, u up, ur spur, uu book, *zh* pleasure

tertiary, T-	TUR shee ER ee
Tertullian	tər TUL yən
terza rima	TER tsə REE mə
Terzin	TAIR zin
Tesla	TES lə
tessellate (v)	TES ə LAYT
tessera	TES ər ə
tessitura	TES ə TUUR ə
testate	TES tayt
testator	TES TAY tər
testes	TES teez
testicle	TES ti kəl
testimonial	TES tə MOH nee əl
testimony	TES tə MOH nee
testis	TES təs
testosterone	te STOS tə ROHN
testudo	te STOO doh
Tet	tet
tetanic	te TA nik
tetanus	TET nəs
tetany	TET ə nee
tête-à-tête	TAYT ə TAYT
tête-bêche	tet besh
tether	TE*TH* ər
Tethys	TEE thəs
tetra	TET rə
tetrachloride	TET rə KLOR īd
tetrachord	TET rə KORD
tetracycline	TET rə SĪ kleen
tetraethyl	TET rə ETH əl
Tetragrammaton	TET rə GRAM ə TAHN
tetrahedron	TET rə HEE drən
tetralogy	te TRAL ə jee
tetrameter	te TRAM ə tər
tetrarch	TE trahrk
tetrarchy	TE TRAHR kee
tetrastich	TE trə stik
Tetrazzini, t-	TE trə ZEE nee
tetrode	TE trohd
tetter	TET ər
Tetuán	te TWAHN
Teufelsdröckh, Teufelsdroeckh	TOI fəlz DREK

ə ago, a at, ah calm, ahr dark, air care, aw saw, ay say, ch church
e bet, ee me, eer beer, hw what, i is, ī my, n French final n vin,

Teuton	**TOO** tən
Teutonic	too **TON** ik
Tewkesbury	**TYOOKS** ʙᴇʀ ee
Texarkana	**TEK** sahr **KAN** ə
textile	**TEKS** təl
textual	**TEKS** choo əl
texture	**TEKS** chər
Teyde, Teide	**TAY** *th* e
Teyte	tayt
Thackeray	**THAK** ə ree
Thaddeus, Thadeus	**THAD** ee əs
Thai	tī
Thailand	**TĪ** land
Thais (pl of *Thai*)	tīz
Thaïs	**THAY** is
Thaïs (opera)	tah **EES**
thalamus	**THAL** ə məs
thalassic	thə **LAS** ik
Thales	**THAY** leez
Thalia (feminine name)	**THAY** lee ə
Thalia (Muse)	thə **LĪ** ə
thalidomide	thə **LID** ə ᴍᴵᴅ
thallium	**THAL** ee əm
thallus	**THAL** əs
Thamae, Tseliso	tah **MĪ** ee, tsee **LEE** soh
Thames (Connecticut)	thaymz
Thames (England, Canada)	temz
Thanarat, Sarit	tah nah **RAHT**, sah **REET**
thanatology	**THAN** ə **TOL** ə jee
thanatophobia	**THAN** ə tə **FOH** bee ə
thanatopsis	**THAN** ə **TOP** sis
Thanatos	**THAN** ə ᴛᴏs
thane	thayn
Thapa, Bekh Bahadur	**TAH** pə, **BEK** bah hah **DOOR**
Thapa, Surya Bahadur	**TAH** pə, **SOOR** yə bah hah **DOOR**
Thapsus	**THAP** səs
Thar	tur
Thasos	**THAH** saws
thaumatology	ᴛʜᴀᴡ mə **TOL** ə jee
thaumaturge	**THAW** mə ᴛᴜʀᴊ
thaumaturgy	**THAW** mə ᴛᴜʀ jee

o on, oh oat, oi boy, oo soon, oor poor, or for, ow cow, sh shush,
th thin, *th* this, u up, ur spur, uu book, *zh* pleasure

Thea	THEE ə
theanthropic	THEE an THROP ik
theanthropism	thee AN thrə PIZ əm
thearchy	THEE ahr kee
theater	THEE ə tər
theatrical	thee AT ri kəl
Thebaid	THEE bay ĪD
Theban	THEE bən
Thebes	theebz
thé dansant	tay dahn SAHN (dahn and SAHN French final *n*)
theine	THEE in
theism	THEE iz əm
theistic	thee IS tik (IS as in *hiss*)
thematic	thi MAT ik
Themis	THEE mis
Themistocles	thə MIS tə KLEEZ
thence	*th*ens
Theobald	THEE ə BAWLD
theocracy, theocrasy	thee OK rə see
Theocritus	thee OK rə təs
theodolite	thee OD ə LĪT
Theodoric	thee OD ə rik
Theodosius	THEE ə DOH shee əs
theogony	thee OG ə nee
theologian	THEE ə LOH jən
theology	thee OL ə jee
theophany	thee AH fə NEE
Theophilus	thee AH fə ləs
Theophrastus	THEE ə FRAS təs
theorem	THEE ə rəm
theoretical	THEE ə RET i kəl
theoretician	THEE ə rə TISH ən
theory	THEE ə ree
theosophical	THEE ə SOF i kəl
theosophy	thee OS ə fee
therapeutic	THER ə PYOO tik
therapist	THER ə pəst
therapy	THER ə pee
Theravada	THER ə VAH də
theremin, T-	THER ə mən
therianthropic	THIR ee an THROP ik
theriomorphic	THIR ee ə MOR fik

ə ago, a at, ah calm, ahr dark, air care, aw saw, ay say, ch church
e bet, ee me, eer beer, hw what, i is, ī my, *n* French final n vin,

thermae	THUR mee
thermal	THUR məl
thermion	THURM Ī ən
thermionic	THURM ī ON ik
thermistor	thər MIS tər
thermocline	THUR mə KLĪN
thermocouple	THUR mə KUP əl
thermodynamic	THUR moh dī NAM ik
thermography	thər MOG rə fee
thermolysis	thər MOL ə sis
thermometer	thər MOM ə tər
thermonuclear	THUR moh NOO klee ər
Thermopylae	thər MOP ə LEE
Thermos	THUR məs
thermostat	THUR mə STAT
Thersites	thər SĪ teez
thesauri	thi SOR ī
thesaurus	thi SOR əs
Theseus	THEE see əs
Thespian, t-	THES pee ən
Thespis	THES pəs
Thessalonians	THES ə LOH nee ənz
Thessalonica	THES ə LON ə kə
Thessaly	THES ə lee
theta	THAY tə
Thetis	THEE təs
theurgy	THEE ur jee
thew	thyoo
thews	thyooz
thiamine	THĪ ə mən
thiazine	THĪ ə ZEEN
thiazole	THĪ ə ZOHL
Thibet	tə BET
Thiers	tyair
Thimbu	THIM boo
Thimphu	THIM poo
thine	*th*īn
Thisbe	THIZ bee
thistle	THIS əl
thither	THI*TH* ər
Thohoyandou	TOI yoo yon DOH
Thomism	TOH MIZ əm
Thor	thor

o on, oh oat, oi boy, oo soon, oor poor, or for, ow cow, sh shush,
th thin, *th* this, u up, ur spur, uu book, *zh* pleasure

thoracic	thə RAS ik
thorax	THOR aks
Thoreau	thə ROH
thorium	THOR ee əm
Thoroddsen, Gunnar	TOR əd sən, GUUN ər
thoron	THOR on
thorough	THUR oh
Thorshavn	tors HOWN
Thoth	thohth
Thotmes	THOHT mes
thou	*th*ow
though	*th*oh
Thracian	THRAY shən
thrall	thrawl
threnody	THREN ə dee
threshold	THRESH ohld
thrombin	THROM bən
thrombosis	throm BOH səs
thrombotic	throm BOT ik
thrombus	THROM bəs
throstle	THROS əl
throttle	THROT əl
Thucydides	thoo SID ə DEEZ
Thule (Greenland)	TOO lee
Thule (ancient world)	THOO lee
thulium	THOO lee əm
Thummim	THUM im
Thun	toon
Thunborg, Anders	TYOON bor ee, AHN ders
Thurber	THUR bər
thurible	THUUR ə bəl
Thuringia	thuu RIN jee ə
Thursday	THURZ day
Thutmose	thut MOH sə
Thyestes	thī ES teez
thylacine	THĪ lə SĪN
thyme	tīm
thymus	THĪ məs
thyroid	THĪ roid
thyrsus	THUR səs
Tia Juana	TEE ə WAH nə
Tianjin	tee ahn jeen
tiara	tee AR ə
Tiber	TĪ bər

ə ago, a at, ah calm, ahr dark, air care, aw saw, ay say, ch church
e bet, ee me, eer beer, hw what, i is, ī my, *n* French final n vin,

Tiberius	tī **BIR** ee əs
Tibet	tə **BET**
Tibetan	tə **BET** ən
tibia	**TIB** ee ə
Tibullus	tə **BUL** əs
Ticino	tee **CHEE** noh
Ticonderoga	**TĪ** kon də **ROH** gə
Tien Shan	tee en shahn
Tientsin	tin tsin
Tiepolo	**TYEP** ə loh
tierce	teers
tiercel	**TIR** səl
Tierra del Fuego	tee **ER** ə del **FWAY** goh
Tiffany	**TIF** ə nee
tiffin	**TIF** ən
Tiflis	**TIF** ləs
Tiglath-pileser	**TIG** lath pī **LEE** zər
tiglon	**TĪ** glən
Tigrinya	tə **GREEN** yə
Tigris	**TĪ** grəs
Tijuana	**TEE** ə **WAHN** ə
Tikhonov, Nikolai	**TYEE** hən əv, nee koh **LĪ**
tiki	**TEE** kee
tilde	**TIL** də
Till Eulenspiegel	**TIL OI** lən **SHPEE** gəl
Tilsit	**TIL** zət
timbal	**TIM** bəl
timbalc	**TIM** bəl
timber	**TIM** bər
timbre	**TAN** brə (**TAN** French final *n*)
Timbuktu	**TIM** buk **TOO**
Timisoara	**TEE** mee **SHWAH** rah
timocracy	tī **MOK** rə see
Timon	**TĪ** mən
Timor	**TEE** mor
timorous	**TIM** ər əs
Timotheus	tə **MOH** thee əs
Timothy	**TIM** ə thee
timpani	**TIM** pə nee
timpanist	**TIM** pə nəst
tinamou	**TIN** ə **MOO**
Tinbergen, Jan	**TIN** ber ken, yahn (ken *k* almost an *h* sound)
tincture	**TINGK** chər

o on, oh oat, oi boy, oo soon, oor poor, or for, ow cow, sh shush,
th thin, *th* this, u up, ur spur, uu book, *zh* pleasure

tinea	TIN ee ə
tinnitus	tə NĪ təs
Tintagel	tin TAJ əl
Tintern	TIN tərn
tintinnabulation	TIN tə NAB yə LAY shən
Tintoretto	TIN tə RET oh
tiny	TĪ nee
Tippecanoe	TIP ə kə NOO
Tipperary	TIP ə RAIR ee
tirade	tī RAYD
tirailleur	tee rah YUUR
Tirana, Tiranë	tee RAH nə
Tiresias	tī REE see əs
Tiros	TĪ rohs
Tirzah	TUR zə
tisane	ti ZAN
Tiselius, Arne	tee SAY lee UUS, AHR nə
Tishah b'Av	TISH ə BAWV
Tishbite	TISH bīt
Tisiphone	tə SIF ə nee
tissue	TISH oo
Tisza	TEE sah
titan, T-	TĪT ən
Titania	tə TAY nee ə
Titanic, t-	tī TAN ik
titanium	tī TAY nee əm
tithe	tīth
tithing	TĪ thing
Tithonus	ti THOH nəs
Titian	TISH ən
Titicaca	TI ti KAH kə
titillate	TIT ə LAYT
Tito	TEE toh
titubation	TICH uu BAY shən
titular	TICH ə lər
Titus	TĪ təs
Tivoli	TIV ə lee
tizzy	TIZ ee
Tlaxcala	tlahs KAHL ə
tmesis	MEE səs
tobacco	tə BAK oh
Tobago	tə BAY goh
Tobiah	tə BĪ ə

ə ago, a at, ah calm, ahr dark, air care, aw saw, ay say, ch church
e bet, ee me, eer beer, hw what, i is, ī my, n French final n vin,

Tobias	tə **BĪ** əs
Tobit	**TOH** bət
toboggan	tə **BOG** ən
Toby, t-	**TOH** bee
Tocantins	**TAW** kahn **TEENS**
toccata	tə **KAH** tə
Tocharian	toh **KA** ree ən
tocology	toh **KOL** ə jee
tocopherol	toh **KOF** ə **ROHL**
Tocqueville, de	**TOHK** vil, də
tocsin	**TOK** sən
toffee	**TAW** fee
tofu	**TOH** foo
Togo	**TOH** goh
toile	twahl
Tokay, t-	toh **KAY**
toke	tohk
Tokelau	**TOH** kə **LOW** (**LOW** as in *cow*)
Tokharian	toh **KAIR** ee ən
Tokyo	**TOH** kee **OH**
tole	tohl
Tolima	tə **LEE** mə
Tolkien	**TAHL** keen
toll	tohl
Tolstoy, Tolstoi	tawl **STOI**
Toltec	**TOL** tek
Toluca	tə **LOO** kə
toluene	**TOL** yoo **EEN**
Tomalbaye, François	toh mahl **BĪ**, frahn **SWAH** (frahn French final *n*)
Toma, Maiva Lulai	**TOH** mə, mī **AH** və **YOO** lī
tomato	tə **MAY** toh
Tomaz, Americo	**TOO** mahsh, ə **MER** i koo
Tombigbee	tom **BIG** bee
tome	tohm
tomography	tə **MOG** rə fee
Tomonaga, Shinichiro	toh moh nah gah, shee nee chee roh
tomorrow	tə **MOR** oh
Tomsk	tawmsk
tonality	toh **NAL** ə tee
Tonga, t-	**TONG** gə
tongue	tung_
tonight	tə **NĪT**

o on, oh oat, oi boy, oo soon, oor poor, or for, ow cow, sh shush, th thin, *th* this, u up, ur spur, uu book, *zh* pleasure

Tonkin, t-	tahn kin
Tonle Sap	TAHN lay SAP
tonneau	tə NOH
Tonsberg	TUNZ bair
tonsil	TAHN səl
tonsillectomy	TAHN sə LEK tə mee
tonsillitis	TAHN sə LĪ təs
tonsorial	tahn SOR ee əl
tonsure	TAHN shər
tontine	tahn TEEN
tonus	TOH nəs
toothed	toothd
topaz	TOH paz
topectomy	tə PEK tə mee
topee (helmet)	toh PEE
Topeka	tə PEE kə
Tophet, -h	TOH fət
tophus	TOH fəs
topi (antelope)	TOH pee
topiary	TOH pee ER ee
topography	tə POG rə fee
toponym	TOP ə nim
toponymy	tə PON ə mee
Toppazzini	tah pə SEE nee
topsail	TOP səl
toque	tohk
Torah	TOH rə
torchier	tor CHEER
torchon	TOR shon
Tordesillas	TOR the SEE lyahs
toreador	TOR ee ə DOR
torero	taw RAIR oh
toreutic	tə ROO tik
torii	TOH ree EE
torment (n)	TOR ment
torment (v)	tor MENT
tornadic	tor NAY dik
tornado	tor NAY doh
Tornio	TOR nee OH
toroid	TOR oid
toroidal	taw ROID əl
Toronto	tə RON toh
torpedo	tor PEE doh

ə ago, a at, ah calm, ahr dark, air care, aw saw, ay say, ch church
e bet, ee me, eer beer, hw what, i is, ī my, n French final n vin,

torpid	**TOR** pəd
torpor	**TOR** pər
torque	tork
Torquemada	**TOR** kə **MAHD** ə
torr	tor
Torrelio, Celso	toh **REL** yoh, **SEL** soh
torrefy	**TOR** ə **FĪ**
Torrens	**TOR** ənz
torrent	**TOR** ənt
Torrente	taw **REN** tay
torrential	taw **REN** shəl
Torricelli	**TOR** ə **CHEL** ee
torrid	**TOR** əd
torsade	tor **SAYD**
torsion	**TOR** shən
torso	**TOR** soh
tort	tort
torte	tort
torticollis	**TOR** tə **KOL** əs
tortilla	tor **TEE** yə
tortoise	**TOR** təs
Tortola	tor **TOH** lə
tortoni	tor **TOH** nee
Tortuga	tor **TOO** gə
tortuous	**TOR** choo əs
torture	**TOR** chər
torturous	**TOR** chə rəs
torus	**TOR** əs
Tory	**TOR** ee
Toscanini	**TOS** kə **NEE** nee
Toshiki Kaifu	toh shee kee kī foo
totalitarian	toh **TAL** ə **TAIR** ee ən
totem	**TOH** təm
Tottenham	**TOT** ən əm
toucan	**TOO** kan
touché	too **SHAY**
tough	tuf
Toulon	too **LAWN** (**LAWN** French final *n*)
Toulouse	too **LOOZ**
Toulouse-Lautrec	too **LOOZ** loh **TREK**
Toungoo	towng goo
toupee	too **PAY**
touraco	**TUUR** ə **KOH**

o on, oh oat, oi boy, oo soon, oor poor, or for, ow cow, sh shush,
th thin, *th* this, u up, ur spur, uu book, *zh* pleasure

tour de force	TUUR də FORS
Touré, Sekou	too RAY, se KOO
Tourel	too REL
tourmaline	TUUR mə lən
tournament	TUUR nə mənt
tournedos (sing)	TUUR nə DOH
tournedos (pl)	TUUR nə DOHZ
tourney	TUUR nee
tourniquet	TUR nə kət
Tours	toor
Toussaint L'Ouverture	too SAN loo ver TYUUR (SAN French final *n*)
tout	towt
tout à fait	too ta FE
tout de suite	toot SWEET
tout ensemble	too tahn SAHN blə (tahn and SAHN French final *n*)
tout le monde	too lə MAWND
tovarich	toh VAH rish
tow	toh
toward	tord
towards	tordz
towel	TOW əl (TOW as in *cow*)
towhead	TOH hed
towhee	TOH hee
towline	TOH līn
Townes	townz
Townsend	TOWN zənd
Towson	TOW sən (TOW as in *cow*)
toxemia	tok SEE mee ə
toxicology	TOK si KOL ə jee
toxicosis	TOK sə KOH səs
toxin	TOK sən
toxophilite	tok SOF ə LĪT
Toynbee	TOIN bee
trabeation	TRAY bee AY shən
trachea	TRAY kee ə
tracheal	TRAY kee əl
tracheostomy	TRAY kee OS tə mee
tracheotomy	TRAY kee OT ə mee
trachoma	trə KOH mə
tractable	TRAK tə bəl
tractile	TRAK təl

ə ago, a at, ah calm, ahr dark, air care, aw saw, ay say, ch church
e bet, ee me, eer beer, hw what, i is, ī my, *n* French final n vin,

traduce	trə DOOS
Trafalgar	trə FAL gər
tragacanth	TRAJ ə KANTH
tragedian	trə JEE dee ən
tragedienne	trə JEE dee EN
tragicomedy	TRAJ i KOM ə dee
tragus	TRAY gəs
traipse	trayps
traitorous	TRAY tər əs
Trajan	TRAY jən
trajectory	trə JEK tə ree
Tralee	trə LEE
trammel	TRAM əl
tramontane	trə MON tayn
trampoline	TRAM pə LEEN
tramway	TRAM way
tranquil	TRANG kwəl
tranquility	trang KWIL ə tee
tranquilizer	TRANG kwə LĪ zər
Transcaucasia	TRANS kaw KAY zhə
transceiver	tran SEE vər
transcendent	tran SEN dənt
transcendental	TRAN sen DEN təl
transducer	trans DOO sər
transect	tran SEKT
transept	TRAN sept
transfer (n)	TRANS fər
transfer (v)	trans FUR
transferable	trans FUR ə bəl
transference	trans FUR əns
transfiguration	trans FIG yə RAY shən
transfix	trans FIKS
transform (n)	TRANS form
transform (v)	trans FORM
transformation	TRANS fər MAY shən
transformer	trans FOR mər
transgress	trans GRES
transience	TRAN shəns
transient	TRAN shənt
transistor	tran ZIS tər
transit	TRAN sət
transition	tran ZISH ən
transitive	TRAN sə tiv

o on, oh oat, oi boy, oo soon, oor poor, or for, ow cow, sh shush,
th thin, *th* this, u up, ur spur, uu book, *zh* pleasure

transitory	TRAN sə TOR ee
Transjordan	trans JOR dən
Transjordania	TRANS jor DAY nee ə
Transkei	trans KĪ
transliterate	trans LIT ə RAYT
translucent	trans LOO sənt
transmigration	TRANS mī GRAY shən
transmission	trans MISH ən
transmitter	trans MIT ər
transmogrification	trans MOG rə fə KAY shən
transmontane	trans MON tayn
transmutation	TRANS myuu TAY shən
transoceanic	TRANS OH shee AN ik
transom	TRAN səm
transonic	trans SAHN ik
transplant (n)	TRANS plant
transplant (v)	trans PLANT
transport (n)	TRANS port
transport (v)	trans PORT
transubstantiation	TRAN səb STAN shee AY shən
Transvaal	trans VAHL
transverse	trans VURS
transvestism	trans VES tiz əm
transvestite	trans VES tīt
Transylvania	TRAN səl VAY nee ə
Traoré, Moussa	TRAH wah lay, moo SAH
Traoré, Seydou	TRAH wah lay, SAY doo
Trapani	TRAH pah nee
trapeze	tra PEEZ
trapezium	trə PEE zee əm
trapezius	trə PEE zee əs
trapezoid	TRAP ə ZOID
Trappist	TRAP əst
trauma	TROW mə (TROW as in *cow*)
traumatic	trow MAT ik (trow as in *cow*)
Träumerei	TROI mə RĪ
travail	trə VAYL
travelog, -ue	TRAV ə LAWG
traverse (n, a)	TRAV ərs
traverse (v)	trə VURS
Traverse (lake)	TRAV ərs
travertine	TRAV ər TEEN
travesty	TRAV ə stee

ə ago, a at, ah calm, ahr dark, air care, aw saw, ay say, ch church
e bet, ee me, eer beer, hw what, i is, ī my, n French final n vin,

Traviata, La	trah **VYAH** tah, lah
travois	trə **VOI**
treacherous	**TRECH** ər əs
treachery	**TRECH** ə ree
treacle	**TREE** kəl
treadle	**TRED** əl
treasure	**TREZ***H* ər
Trebizond	**TREB** ə **ZOND**
treble	**TREB** əl
Treblinka	tre **BLEENG** kah
trecento	tre **CHEN** taw
trefoil	**TREE** foil
Treiki, Ali	tray **KEE**, ah **LEE**
Treitschke	**TRĪCH** kə
trek	trek
Tremblant	trahn **BLAHN** (trahn and **BLAHN** French final *n*)
tremendous	tri **MEN** dəs
tremolite	**TREM** ə **LĪT**
tremolo	**TREM** ə **LOH**
tremor	**TREM** ər
tremulous	**TREM** yə ləs
trenchant	**TREN** chənt
Trengganu	treng **GAH** noo
Trentino	tren **TEE** naw
Trenton	**TREN** tən
trepan	tri **PAN**
Trepczynski, Stanislaw	trep **SIN** skcc, stah **NEE** slahf
trephination	**TREF** ə **NAY** shən
trephine	**TREE** fin
trepidation	**TREP** ə **DAY** shən
trespass	**TRES** pəs
trestle	**TRES** əl
Trevelyan	tri **VEL** yən
Trevor	**TREV** ər
trey	tray
triad	**TRĪ** ad
triage	**TREE** ah*zh*
trial	**TRĪ** əl
triangle	**TRĪ ANG** gəl
triangulation	trī **ANG** gyə **LAY** shən
Triangulum	trī **ANG** gyə ləm
triarchy	**TRĪ AHR** kee

o on, oh oat, oi boy, oo soon, oor poor, or for, ow cow, sh shush,
th thin, *th* this, u up, ur spur, uu book, *zh* pleasure

Trias	TRĪ əs
Triassic	trī A sik
tribade	TRIB əd
tribadism	TRIB ə DIZ əm
tribal	TRĪ bəl
tribalism	TRĪ bəl IZ əm
tribrach	TRĪ brak
tribulation	TRIB yə LAY shən
tribunal	trī BYOO nəl
tribune	TRIB yoon
tributary	TRIB yə TER ee
tribute	TRIB yoot
triceps	TRĪ seps
Triceratops	trī SER ə TOPS
trichiasis	trī KĪ ə səs
trichina	trik Ī nə
trichinosis	TRIK ə NOH səs
trichotomy	trī KOT ə mee
triclinic	trī KLIN ik
triclinium	trī KLIN ee əm
tricot	TREE koh
tricycle	TRĪ si kəl
trident, T-	TRĪD ənt
triennial	trī EN ee əl
Trier, t-	treer
Trieste	tree EST
trifle	TRĪ fəl
Trigère	tree ZHAIR
trigon	TRĪ gon
trigonometric	TRIG ə nə MET rik
trigonometry	TRIG ə NOM ə tree
trihedral	trī HEE drəl
trilateral	trī LAT ə rəl
trilingual	trī LING gwəl
trillium	TRIL ee əm
trilobate	trī LOH BAYT
trilobite	TRĪ lə BĪT
trilogy	TRIL ə jee
trimester	trī MES tər
trimeter	TRIM ə tər
trimetric	trī MET rik
Trimurti	tri MUUR tee
Trinacria	trə NAK ree ə

ə ago, a at, ah calm, ahr dark, air care, aw saw, ay say, ch church
e bet, ee me, eer beer, hw what, i is, ī my, *n* French final n vin,

trinal	TRĪN əl
trinary	TRĪ nə ree
Trincomalee	TRING koh mə LEE
Trinidad	TRIN ə DAD
trinitrotoluene	TRĪ NĪ troh TOL yoo EEN
Trinity	TRIN ə tee
trinomial	trī NOH mee əl
trio	TREE oh
triode	TRĪ ohd
triolet	TRĪ ə lət
tripartite	trī PAHR tīt
tripe	trīp
triphibian	trī FIB ee ən
triphthong	TRIF thawng
triplet	TRIP lət
triplicate (a, n)	TRIP lə kət
triplicate (v)	TRIP lə KAYT
tripod	TRĪ pod
tripodal	TRIP ə dəl
Tripoli, t-	TRIP ə lee
Tripolitania	TRIP ə lə TAYN yə
tripos	TRĪ pos
tripterous	TRIP tər əs
Triptolemus, Triptolemos	trip TOL ə məs
triptych	TRIP tik
Tripura	TRIP ə rə
trireme	TRĪ reem
trisaccharide	trī SAK ə RĪD
triskaidekaphobia	TRIS KĪ DEK ə FOH bee ə
triskelion	trī SKEL ee ən
Trismegistus	TRIS mə JIS təs
trismus	TRIZ məs
Tristan	TRIS tən
triste	treest
tristesse	trees TES
tristich	TRIS tik
Tristram	TRIS trəm
tritheism	TRĪ thee IZ əm
tritium	TRIT ee əm
Triton	TRĪT ən
triturate	TRICH ə RAYT
triumvir	trī UM vər

---

o on, oh oat, oi boy, oo soon, oor poor, or for, ow cow, sh shush,
th thin, *th* this, u up, ur spur, uu book, *zh* pleasure

triumvirate	trī UM vər ət
Trivandrum	tri VAN drəm
trivia	TRIV ee ə
trivial	TRIV ee əl
trivium	TRIV ee əm
Trnava	TUR nah vah
Trnovac	TUR naw vahts
Troad	TROH ad
Troas	TROH as
Trobriand	TROH bree AHND
Trobriander	TROH bree AHND ər
trochaic	troh KAY ik
troche	TROH kee
trochee	TROH kee
troglodyte	TROG lə DĪT
troika	TROI kə
Troilus	TROI ləs
Trois Rivières	TRWAH ree VYAIR
Trojan	TROH jən
troll	trohl
trollop	TROL əp
Trollope	TROL əp
Trombe	trawmb
trombone	trom BOHN
trompe l'oeil	trawmp LU ee
Tromsö	TRUUM soh
Trondheim	TRAWN haym
tropaeolum	trə PEE ə ləm
trope	trohp
trophy	TROH fee
tropism	TROH piz əm
tropology	troh POL ə jee
troposphere	TROHP ə SFIR
troppo	TRAW poh
Trossachs	TROS əks
troth	trawth
Trotsky	TROT skee
troubadour	TROO bə DOR
trou-de-loup (sing)	TROO də LOO
trough	trawf
trounce	trowns
troupe	troop
trous-de-loup (pl)	TROO də LOO

ə ago, a at, ah calm, ahr dark, air care, aw saw, ay say, ch church
e bet, ee me, eer beer, hw what, i is, ī my, *n* French final n vin,

trousseau	troo **SOH**
trouvère	troo **VAIR**
Trouville	troo **VEEL**
Trovatore	**TROH** vah **TOH** ray
trowel	**TROW** əl (**TROW** as in *cow*)
Troyanovsky, Oleg	**TROI** ə **NOF** skee, **OH** leg
truant	**TROO** ənt
Trucial Oman	**TROO** shəl oh **MAHN**
truculence	**TRUK** yə ləns
Trudeau, Pierre	troo **DOH**, **PYAIR**
trudgen	**TRUJ** ən
Truffaut, François	troo **FOH**, frahn **SWAH** (frahn French final *n*)
truffle	**TRUF** əl
Trujillo	truu **HEE** yoh
Truk	truk
trullisatio	**TROO** li **SAH** shoh
Trumbo	**TRUM** boh
Trumbull	**TRUM** bəl
truncheon	**TRUN** chən
Truro	**TRUUR** oh
trypanosome	trip **AN** ə **SOHM**
trypanosomiasis	trip **AN** ə sə **MĪ** ə səs
trypsin	**TRIP** sən
tryst	trist
tsar	zahr
Tsarapkin, Semyon	tse **RAHP** kin, sem **YOHN**
Tsavo	**SAHV** oh
Tschaikovsky, Tschaikowsky	chī **KAWF** skee
tsetse	**TSET** see
Tshombe, Moise	**CHOM** bay, moh **EES**
Tsiang, Tingfu	jahng, ting foo
Tsinan	jee nahn
Tsinghai	ching hī
Tsingtao	ching dow
Tsinling Shan	sin ling shahn
Tsiranana, Philibert	tsee **RUN** ən, pi lee **BAIR**
Tsongas, Paul	**SAHN** gəs
Tsouderos	soo *th*e **RAWS**
Tsountas, Chrestos	**TSOON** dahs, **KREE** staws
Tsuga	**TSOO** gə
Tsugaru	soo gah roo

---

o on, oh oat, oi boy, oo soon, oor poor, or for, ow cow, sh shush,
th thin, *th* this, u up, ur spur, uu book, *zh* pleasure

tsunami	suu **NAH** mee
Tsuruga	tsoo roo gah
Tsushima	tsoo shee mah
tsutsugamushi (disease)	**SOOT** sə gə **MOO** shee
Tsvetkov, Boris	sə vet **KAWF**, baw **REES**
Tuamotu	**TOO** ə **MOH** too
tuan	twahn
Tuapse	too ahp **SE**
Tuareg	**TWAH** reg
tuba	**TOO** bə
tubal, T-	**TOO** bəl
tube	toob
tubercle	**TOO** bər kəl
tubercular	tuu **BUR** kyə lər
tuberculin	tuu **BUR** kyə lən
tuberculosis	tuu **BUR** kyə **LOH** səs
tuberose	**TOOB** rohz
tuberosity	**TOO** bə **RAH** sə tee
tubular	**TOO** byə lər
tubule	**TOO** byool
Tucana	too **KAY** nə
Tuchman	**TUK** mən
Tucson	**TOO** sahn
Tucumcari	**TOO** kəm **KA** ree
Tudor	**TOO** dər
Tuesday	**TOOZ** day
tufa	**TOO** fə
Tuguegarao	**TOO** ge gah **ROW** (**ROW** as in *cow*)
Tuileries	**TWEE** lə reez
Tukums	**TUU** kuums
Tula	**TOO** lah
Tulagi	too **LAHG** ee
tularemia	**TOO** lə **REE** mee ə
tule	**TOO** lee
tulip	**TOO** lip
tulle	tool
Tully	**TUL** ee
Tumacacori	**TOO** mə **KAH** kə ree
tumbril	**TUM** brəl
tumefacient	**TOO** mə **FAY** shənt
tumescent	too **MES** ənt
tumor	**TOO** mər

ə ago, a at, ah calm, ahr dark, air care, aw saw, ay say, ch church
e bet, ee me, eer beer, hw what, i is, ī my, *n* French final n vin,

tumult	**TOO** məlt
tumultuous	tuu **MUL** choo əs
tumulus	**TOO** myə ləs
tuna	**TOO** nə
tundra	**TUN** drə
tune	toon
Tungliao	toong lyow
tungsten	**TUNG** stən
Tungting	duung ting
Tungus	tuun **GUUZ**
Tunguska	tuun **GUUS** kah
tunic	**TOO** nik
tunicate	**TOO** ni kət
Tunis	**TOO** nis
Tunisia	too **NEE** *zh*ə
Tupamaro	**TOO** pah **MAH** roh
tupelo	**TOO** pə **LOH**
Tupi	too **PEE**
Tupi-Guarani	too **PEE GWAHR** ə **NEE**
tu quoque	too **KWOH** kwe
Turandot	**TUUR** ən **DOT**
Turanian	tuu **RAY** nee ən
turban	**TUR** bən
turbid	**TUR** bəd
turbine	**TUR** bən
turbojet	**TUR** boh **JET**
turbot	**TUR** bət
turbulence	**TUR** byə ləns
turbulent	**TUR** byə lənt
Turco	**TUR** koh
tureen	tə **REEN**
Turgenev, Turgeniev	tuur **GE** nyəf
turgid	**TUR** jəd
Turgot	tuur **GOH**
Turin	**TUUR** ən
turista	tuu **REE** stə
Turkestan	**TUR** kə **STAN**
Turkey, t-	**TUR** kee
Turki	**TUR** kee
Turkic	**TUR** kik
Turkmen (USSR)	**TURK** mən
Turkoman	**TUR** kə mən
Turku	**TUUR** koo

o on, oh oat, oi boy, oo soon, oor poor, or for, ow cow, sh shush,
th thin, *th* this, u up, ur spur, uu book, *zh* pleasure

turmeric	TUR mər ik
turnip	TUR nəp
turnkey	TURN kee
Turnverein	TUURN fer ĪN
turpentine	TUR pən TĪN
turpitude	TUR pə TOOD
turquoise	TUR kwoiz
turret	TUR ət
Tuscaloosa	TUS kə LOO sə
Tuscan	TUS kən
Tuscany	TUS kə nee
Tuscarora	TUS kə ROR ə
Tuscumbia	tus KUM bee ə
Tuskegee	tus KEE gee
Tussaud	too SOH
tussive	TUS iv
Tutankhamen	TOOT ahngk AH mən
tutelage	TOO tə lij
tutelary	TOO tə LER ee
tutor	TOO tər
tutorial	too TOR ee əl
tutti	TOO tee
tutti-frutti	TOO ti FROO tee
tutu	TOO too
Tutuila	TOO too EE lah
Tuva	TOO və
Tuvalu	too VAHL oo
tuxedo, T-	tuk SEE doh
Tweedsmuir	TWEEDZ myuur
Twickenham	TWIK ən əm
Tyburn	TĪ bərn
Tyche	TĪ kee
tycoon	tī KOON
Tylenol	TĪ lə NOHL
tympanic	tim PAN ik
tympanites	TIM pə NĪ teez
tympanum	TIM pə nəm
Tynan	TĪ nən
Tyndale, Tyndall	TIN dəl
Tyndareus	tin DA ree əs
Tyne	tīn
Tynemouth	TĪN məth
Typee	tī PEE

ə ago, a at, ah calm, ahr dark, air care, aw saw, ay say, ch church
e bet, ee me, eer beer, hw what, i is, ī my, *n* French final n vin,

typhoid	TĪ foid
Typhon	TĪ fon
typhoon	tī FOON
typhus	TĪ fəs
typical	TIP i kəl
typify	TIP ə FĪ
typographer	tī POG rə fər
typographical	TĪ pə GRAF ik əl
typography	tī POG rə fee
typology	tī POL ə jee
Tyr	tir
tyrannical	tə RAN i kəl
tyrannize	TIR ə NĪZ
tyrannosaur	tə RAN ə SOR
tyrannous	TIR ə nəs
tyranny	TIR ə nee
tyrant	TĪ rənt
Tyre	tīr
Tyrian	TIR ee ən
tyro, T-	TĪ roh
Tyrol	tə ROHL
Tyrolean	tə ROH lee ən
Tyrolese	TIR ə LEEZ
Tyrone (place)	ti ROHN
Tyrone (boy's name)	TĪ rohn
Tyrrhenian	tə REE nee ən
tzar	zahr
Tzigane, t-	tsee GAHN

U

Ubangi	yoo BANG gee
Ubangi-Shari	yoo BANG gee SHAHR ee
Ubeda	OO be THAH
ubiety	yoo BĪ ə tee
ubiquitous	yoo BIK wə təs
Ucayali	oo kah YAH lee
Udaipur	uu DĪ PUUR
Udall (US)	YOO dawl
Udall, Udale (England)	YOOD əl
Udmurt	UUD muurt

---

o on, oh oat, oi boy, oo soon, oor poor, or for, ow cow, sh shush,
th thin, *th* this, u up, ur spur, uu book, *zh* pleasure

udometer	yoo **DOM** ə tər
Ueberroth	**YOO** bə rawth
Uele	**WAY** lee
Uelses	**YUUL** səs
Ufa	oo **FAH**
Uffizi	oo **FEE** tsee
UFOlogy, ufology	yoo **FOL** ə jee
Uganda	yoo **GAN** də
Ugaritic	oo gə **RIT** ik
ugli	**UG** lee
Ugrian	**OO** gree ən
Ugric	**OO** grik
uhlan	**OO** lahn
Uigur, Uighur	**WEE** guur
Uinta	yoo **IN** tə
uitlander, U-	**OIT** LAN dər
Ujiji	oo **JEE** jee
Ujpest	**OO** ee PESHT
ukase	yoo **KAYS**
Ukraine	yoo **KRAYN**
Ukrainian	yoo **KRAY** nee ən
ukulele	YOO kə **LAY** lee
Ulan Bator	**OO** lahn **BAH** tor
Ulanhu	oo lahn hoo
Ulan-Ude	OO LAHN uu **DAY**
Ulbricht	**UUL** brikt
ulcer	**UL** sər
ulema	oo lə **MAH**
Ulfilas	**UL** fi ləs
ullage	**UL** ij
Ulm	uulm
ulna	**UL** nə
Ulotrichi	yoo **LOT** ri kī
ulotrichous	yoo **LOT** ri kəs
Ulrica	**UL** ri kə
Ulrichsen, Wilhelm	**OOL** rik sən, **WIL** helm
Ulster, u-	**UL** stər
ulterior	ul **TIR** ee ər
ultimate	**UL** tə mət
ultima Thule	**UUL** tə MAH **TOO** le
ultimatum	UL tə **MAY** təm
ultimo	**UL** tə MOH
ultramontane	UL trə **MON** tayn

ə ago, a at, ah calm, ahr dark, air care, aw saw, ay say, ch church
e bet, ee me, eer beer, hw what, i is, ī my, *n* French final n vin,

ultrasonic	UL trə SAHN ik
ultraviolet	UL trə VĪ ə lət
ultra vires	UL trə VĪ reez
ululate	YOOL yə LAYT
Ulusu, Bülend	OOL oo SOO, buu LEND
Ulysses	yuu LIS eez
Umatilla	YOO mə TIL ə
umber	UM bər
umbilical	um BIL i kəl
umbilicus	um BIL i kəs
umbra	UM brə
umbrage	UM brij
umbrageous	um BRAY jəs
umbrella	um BREL ə
Umbria	UM bree ə
Umbriel	UM bree EL
Umeki, Myoshi	oo me kee, mee oh shee
umiak	OO mee AK
umlaut	UUM lowt (lowt as in *out*)
Umtata	uum TAHT ə
Una	OO nə
Unalaska	UN ə LAS kə
Unamuno	oo nah MOO noh
unanimity	YOO nə NIM ə tee
unanimous	yuu NAN ə məs
unbiased	UN BĪ əst
uncial	UN shəl
unconscionable	un KON shə nə bəl
uncouth	un KOOTH
unction	UNGK shən
unctuous	UNGK choo əs
undine, U-	un DEEN
undoubtedly	UN DOW təd lee
undulant	UN jə lənt
undulate (a)	UN jə lət
undulate (v)	UN jə LAYT
undulatory	UN jə lə TOR ee
unequivocal	UN i KWIV ə kəl
unerring	UN ER ing
unfrequented	UN fri KWENT əd
ungual	UNG gwəl
unguent	UNG gwənt
ungulate	UNG gyə lət

o on, oh oat, oi boy, oo soon, oor poor, or for, ow cow, sh shush,
th thin, *th* this, u up, ur spur, uu book, *zh* pleasure

Uniat, Uniate	YOO nee AT
unicameral	YOO ni KAM ə rəl
unicorn, U-	YOO nə KORN
unicycle	YOO ni sī kəl
unilateral	YOO ni LAT ə rəl
unique	yoo NEEK
unisex	YOO nə SEKS
unison	YOO nə sən
Unitarian, u-	YOO nə TAIR ee ən
unity	YOO nə tee
universal	YOO nə VUR səl
universality	YOO nə vər SAL ə tee
universe	YOO nə VURS
unmitigated	UN MIT ə GAY təd
unobtrusive	UN əb TROO siv
unprecedented	UN PRES ə DEN təd
unrighteous	UN RĪ chəs
Unruh, Jess	UN rə
unruly	UN ROO lee
unsavory	UN SAY və ree
Unter den Linden	UUN tər den LIN dən
Unterseeboot	UUN ter zay boht
untoward	un TORD
unwarranted	UN WOR ən təd
unwonted	UN WAWN təd
Upanishad	oo PAHN i SHAHD
upas	YOO pəs
upholster	up HOHL stər
upland, U-	UP lənd
uplander	UP lənd ər
Upolu	oo POH loo
Uppsala, Upsala	UP sə LAH
uproarious	up ROR ee əs
upset (n)	UP set
upset (v, a)	up SET
upshot	UP shot
upsilon	YOOP sə LON
Ur	ur
uraeus	yuu REE əs
Ural	YUUR əl
Uralic	yuu RAL ik
Urania	yuu RAY nee ə
uranic	yuu RAN ik

ə ago, a at, ah calm, ahr dark, air care, aw saw, ay say, ch church
e bet, ee me, eer beer, hw what, i is, ī my, *n* French final n vin,

Uranus	YUU rə nəs
urban, U-	UR bən
Urbana	UR BAN ə
urbane	ur BAYN
Urbanek, Karel	OOR bahn ek, KAH rel
urbanity	UR BAN ə tee
urbanize	UR bən īz
urbi et orbi	OOR bee ET OR bee
urchin	UR chən
Urdu	UUR doo
urea	yuu REE ə
uremia	yuu REE mee ə
ureter	yuu REE tər
urethra	yuu REE thrə
Urey	YUUR ee
Urfa	uur FAH
Urga	UUR gah
Uriah	yuu RĪ ə
Uriel	YUUR ee əl
Urim	YUUR əm
urinal	YUUR ə nəl
urinalysis	YUUR ə NAL ə səs
Uris	YUUR əs
Urmia	UUR mee ə
urology	yuu ROL ə jee
Urquhart	UR kərt
Ursa	UR sə
ursine	UR sīn
Ursprache	UUR SHPRAH kə
Ursula	UR sə lə
Ursuline	UR sə lən
urticaria	UR tə KA ree ə
Uruguay	UUR ə GWĪ
Urundi	uu RUUN dee
urus	YUUR əs
usage	YOO sij
U San Yu	oo sahn yoo
use (n)	yoos
use (v)	yooz
Ushant	USH ənt
Ushas	UUSH əs
Usk	usk
Uspallata	oos pah YAH tah

---

o on, oh oat, oi boy, oo soon, oor poor, or for, ow cow, sh shush,
th thin, *th* this, u up, ur spur, uu book, *zh* pleasure

usquebaugh	US kwi **BAW**
Ussuri	oo **SOO** ree
Ustinov, Peter	**YOO** stə **NAWF**
usual	**YOO** *zh*oo əl
usufruct	**YOO** zə **FRUKT**
usurer	**YOO** *zh*ə rər
usurious	yuu **ZH**UUR ee əs
usurp	yuu **SURP**
usurpation	**YOO** sər **PAY** shən
usurper	yuu **SURP** ər
usury	**YOO** *zh*ə ree
Utah	**YOO** taw
Utamaro, Kitagawa	oo tah mah roh, kee tah gah wah
Ute	yoot
utensil	yuu **TEN** səl
uterine	**YOO** tər ən
uterus	**YOO** tər əs
Uther	**YOO** thər
Utica	**YOO** ti kə
utilitarian	yoo **TIL** ə **TAIR** ee ən
utility	yoo **TIL** ə tee
utilize	**YOO** tə **LĪZ**
uti possidetis	**YOO** tī **POS** i **DEE** tis
Uto-Aztecan	**YOO** toh **AZ TEK** ən
Utopia	yuu **TOH** pee ə
Utrecht	**YOO** trekt
Utrillo	yoo **TRIL** oh
Utt	ut
Uttar Pradesh	**UUT** ər prə **DAYSH**
utterance	**UT** ər əns
Uusikaupunki	oo see **KOW** puung kee
uvea	**YOO** vee ə
uvula	**YOO** vyə lə
U Win Maung	oo win mowng (mowng as in *town*)
Uxmal	oosh **MAHL**
uxoricide	**UK** SOR ə **SĪD**
uxorious	**UK** SOR ee əs
Uzbek	**UUZ** bek
Uzbekistan	uuz **BEK** i **STAN**
Uzhorod	**UUZ***H* haw **RAWT**
Uzice	**OO** *zh*it se

ə ago, a at, ah calm, ahr dark, air care, aw saw, ay say, ch church
e bet, ee me, eer beer, hw what, i is, ī my, *n* French final n vin,

V

Vaal	vahl
Vaasa	VAH sah
vacant	VAY kənt
vacate	VAY kayt
vacation	vay KAY shən
vaccinate	VAK sə NAYT
vaccine	vak SEEN
Vachel	VAY chəl
vacillate	VAS ə LAYT
vacuity	va KYOO ə tee
vacuole	VAK yoo OHL
vacuous	VAK yoo əs
vacuum	VAK yoo əm
vade mecum	VAY dee MEE kəm
Vaduz	VAH duuts
vagary	VAY gə ree
vagina	və JĪ nə
vaginal	VAJ ə nəl
vaginitis	VAJ ə NĪT əs
vagrancy	VAY grən see
vagrant	VAY grənt
vagus	VAY gəs
Vakil, Mehdi	va KEEL, med EE
valance	VAL əns
Valdai	vahl DĪ
Valdepeñas	VAHL də PE nyahs
Valdés, Valdéz	vahl DES
Valdez (Alaska)	val DEEZ
vale (farewell)	WAH lay
valediction	VAL ə DIK shən
valedictory	VAL ə DIK tə ree
valence	VAY ləns
Valencia	və LEN see ə
Valencia, Guillermo	vah LEN syah, gee LYAIR moh
Valenciennes lace	və LEN see ENZ
Valenzuela, Enrique	VAL ən ZWAY lə, en REE kay
valerian, V-	və LIR ee ən
valeric	və LER ik

---

o on, oh oat, oi boy, oo soon, oor poor, or for, ow cow, sh shush,
th thin, *th* this, u up, ur spur, uu book, *zh* pleasure

Valerie	VAL ə ree
Valéry	va lay REE
valet	VAL ət
valetudinarian	VAL ə TOO də NER ee ən
Valga	VAHL gə
valgus	VAL gəs
Valhalla	val HAL ə
valiant	VAL yənt
valise	və LEES
Valium	VAL ee əm
Valkyrie	val KIR ee
Vallauris	VAL aw REES
Vallejo	va LAY hoh
Valletta	vahl LET tah
Vallombrosa	VAL əm BROH sə
Valmiera	VAHL myer ah
Valois	val WAH̄
Valparaiso (Chile)	VAL pə RĪ zoh
Valparaiso (Indiana)	VAL pə RAY zoh
valpolicella, V-	VAHL POH li CHEL ah
valse	vahls
valuable	VAL yə bəl
valvulitis	VAL vyə LĪ təs
vanadium	və NAY dee əm
Vanbrugh	van BROO
Van Buren	van BYUUR ən
Vancouver	van KOO vər
vandal, V-	VAN dəl
Van Deerlin	van DEER lin
Vander Jagt	VAN dər JAK
Van Dyck, Vandyke	van DĪK
Van Eyck	van ĪK
van Gogh	van GOH
vanguard	VAN gahrd
Vanier	va NYAY
vanilla	və NIL ə
vanillin	və NIL ən
Vanir, v-	VAH nir
vanquish	VANG kwish
Vansittart	van SIT ərt
vantage	VANT ij
Vanua Levu	vah NOO ah LE voo
Vanuatu	VAN ə WAHT oo

ə ago, a at, ah calm, ahr dark, air care, aw saw, ay say, ch church
e bet, ee me, eer beer, hw what, i is, ī my, n French final n vin,

van Well, Guenter	fahn **VEL, GUUN** tər
Vanzetti	van **ZET** ee
vapid	**VAP** əd
vapor	**VAY** pər
vaporetti	**VAP** ə **RET** ee
vaporetto	**VAP** ə **RET** oh
vaporous	**VAY** pər əs
vaquero	vah **KAIR** oh
varactor	va **RAK** tər
Varese	vah **RE** se
Varèse, Edgard	və **REZ**, ed **GAHR**
variable	**VA** ree ə bəl
variance	**VA** ree əns
variation	**VA** ree **AY** shən
varicocele	**VA** rə koh **SEEL**
varicose	**VA** rə **KOHS**
variegate	**VA** ree ə **GAYT**
varietal	və **RĪ** ə təl
variety	və **RĪ** ə tee
Varig	**VA** rig
variorum	**VA** ree **OR** əm
varistor	va **RIS** tər
varlet	**VAHR** lət
Varna	**VAHR** nə
Varro	**VA** roh
Varuna	**VA** ruu nə
vary	**VA** ree
vasa murrhina	**VAY** sə mə **RĪ** nə
Vasari	vah **ZAH** ree
Vasco da Gama	**VA** skoh də **GAM** ə
vascular	**VAS** kyə lər
vas deferens	**VAS DEF** ə **RENZ**
vasectomy	va **SEK** tə mee
Vaseline	**VAS** ə **LEEN**
Vashti	**VASH** tī
vasomotor	**VAS** oh **MOH** tər
vassal	**VAS** əl
vassalage	**VAS** ə lij
Vassilevsky	**VAH** si **LEF** skee
Vassiliou, George	vah **SEE** lee ohn, jorj (ohn French final *n*)
Vatican	**VAT** i kən
Vaucluse	voh **KLOOZ**
vaudeville	**VAWD** vəl

---

o on, oh oat, oi boy, oo soon, oor poor, or for, ow cow, sh shush,
th thin, *th* this, u up, ur spur, uu book, *zh* pleasure

Vaughan	vawn
vault	vawlt
vaunt	vawnt
Veblen	**VEB** lən
vector	**VEK** tər
Veda	**VAY** də
Vedanta	və **DON** tə
vedette	vi **DET**
Vedic	**VAY** dik
Vega (star)	**VEE** gə
Vega, Lope de	**VAY** gah, **LOH** pay day
vegetable	**VEJ** tə bəl
vegetarian	**VEJ** ə **TER** ee ən
Vegh-Villegaz,	**VAYG** vee *ZH*AY gahs, ahl ay **HAHN**
Aleandro	droh
vehemence	**VEE** ə məns
vehement	**VEE** ə mənt
vehicle	**VEE** i kəl
vehicular	vee **HIK** yə lər
vein	vayn
Vela	**VEE** lə
velar	**VEE** lər
Velasco	ve **LAHS** koh
Velázquez, Diego	vay **LAHTH** keth, **DYAY** goh
Velázquez, Guaroa	bay **LAHS** kez, gwah **ROH** ah
veld, veldt	velt
velleity	və **LEE** ə tee
vellum	**VEL** əm
velocipede	və **LOS** ə **PEED**
velocity	və **LOS** ə tee
velour	və **LUUR**
velouté	və loo **TAY**
velum	**VEE** ləm
velure	və **LUUR**
velveteen	**VEL** və **TEEN**
vena cava	**VEE** nə **KAY** və
venal	**VEEN** əl
venality	vi **NAL** ə tee
venation	vee **NAY** shən
Venda	**VEN** də
vendetta	ven **DET** ə
Vendôme	vahn **DOHM**
vendor	**VEN** dər

ə ago, a at, ah calm, ahr dark, air care, aw saw, ay say, ch church
e bet, ee me, eer beer, hw what, i is, ī my, *n* French final n vin,

vendue	ven **DOO**
veneer	və **NIR**
venerate	**VEN** ə **RAYT**
venereal	və **NIR** ee əl
venery	**VEN** ə ree
Venetian	və **NEE** shən
Veneto	**VEN** ə **TOH**
Venezia	ve **NE** tsyah
Venezuela	**VEN** ə **ZWAY** lə
vengeance	**VEN** jəns
venial	**VEE** nee əl
Venice	**VEN** əs
venipuncture	**VEEN** ə **PUNGK** chər
venire	və **NĪ** ree
venireman	və **NĪ** ree mən
venison	**VEN** ə sən
Venite	və **NEE** tay
veni, vidi, vici	**WAY** nee, **WEE** dee, **WEE** kee
venom	**VEN** əm
venous	**VEE** nəs
Venta	**VEN** tah
ventral	**VEN** trəl
ventricle	**VEN** tri kəl
ventricular	ven **TRIK** yə lər
ventriloquism	ven **TRIL** ə **KWIZ** əm
ventriloquist	ven **TRIL** ə kwəst
Ventspils	**VENTS** peels
venture	**VEN** chər
Venturi	ven **TUUR** ee
venturous	**VEN** chər əs
venue	**VEN** yoo
Venus	**VEE** nəs
veracious	və **RAY** shəs
veracity	və **RAS** ə tee
Veracruz	**VER** ə **KROOZ**
veranda	və **RAN** də
verbal	**VURB** əl
verbatim	vər **BAY** təm
verbena	vər **BEE** nə
verbiage	**VUR** bee ij
verbose	vər **BOHS**
verbosity	vər **BOS** ə tee
verboten	fər **BOHT** ən

o on, oh oat, oi boy, oo soon, oor poor, or for, ow cow, sh shush,
th thin, *th* this, u up, ur spur, uu book, *zh* pleasure

Vercingetorix	VUR sin JET ə riks
verdant	VUR dənt
Verde (cape)	vurd
Verdi	VAIR dee
verdigris	VUR də GREES
Verdun	vər DUN
verdure	VUR jər
Verein	fer IN
verge	vurj
verger	VUR jər
Vergil	VUR jəl
verglas	ver GLAH
verisimilitude	VER ə sə MIL ə TOOD
veritable	VER ə tə bəl
vérité	VAY ree TAY
Verlaine	ver LEN
Vermeer	vər MEER
vermeil	VUR məl
vermicelli	VUR mə CHEL ee
vermicular	vər MIK yə lər
vermiculite	vər MIK yə LĪT
vermiform	VUR mə FORM
vermifuge	VUR mə FYOOJ
vermilion	vər MIL yən
vermin	VUR mən
Vermont	vər MONT
vermouth	vər MOOTH
vernacular	vər NAK yə lər
vernal	VUR nəl
Verne	vurn
Verner	VUR nər
Vernier	VUR nee ər
Vernier-Palliez, Bernard	vair NYAY pahl YAY, bair NAHR
Vernon	VUR nən
Verona	və ROH nə
Veronal	VER ə nəl
Veronese	VER ə NEEZ
Veronese, Paolo	vay roh NAY ze, PAH oh loh
veronica, V-	və RON i kə
Véronique	VAY raw NEEK
Verrazano Bridge	VER ə ZAH noh
Verrocchio	və ROH kee OH

ə ago, a at, ah calm, ahr dark, air care, aw saw, ay say, ch church
e bet, ee me, eer beer, hw what, i is, ī my, n French final n vin,

verruca	və ROO kə
Versailles (France)	ver SĪ
Versailles (US)	vər SAYLZ
versatile	VUR sət əl
version	VUR *zh*ən
vers libre	vair LEEB rə
verso	VUR soh
versus	VUR səs
vertebra	VUR tə brə
vertebral	VUR tə brəl
vertebrate	VUR tə brət
vertiginous	vər TIJ ə nəs
vertigo	VUR tə GOH
Vertumnus	vər TUM nəs
vervain	VUR vayn
Verwoerd, Hendrik	fair FUUT, HEN drik
vesical	VES i kəl
vesicle	VES i kəl
Vespasian	ves PAY *zh*ən
vesper	VES pər
Vespucci, Amerigo	ve SPOO chee, ə MER ə GOH
Vesta	VES tə
vestibule	VES tə BYOOL
vestige	VES tij
vestigial	ves TIJ ee əl
vestment	VEST mənt
vesture	VES chər
Vesuvius	və SOO vee əs
veterinarian	VET ər ə NER ee ən
veterinary	VET ər ə NER ee
via	VĪ ə
viable	VĪ ə bəl
viaduct	VĪ ə DUKT
vial	VĪ əl
viand	VĪ ənd
viaticum	vī AT i kəm
Via Veneto	VEE ə VEN ə TOH
Viborg	VEE bor
vibrant	VĪ brənt
vibrato	vi BRAH toh
viburnum	vī BUR nəm
vicar	VIK ər
vicarious	vī KA ree əs

o on, oh oat, oi boy, oo soon, oor poor, or for, ow cow, sh shush,
th thin, *th* this, u up, ur spur, uu book, *zh* pleasure

vicegerent	vīs **JIR** ənt
vicennial	vī **SEN** ee əl
vice-regent	vīs **REE** jənt
vicereine	**VĪS** rayn
viceroy	**VĪS** roi
vice versa	**VĪ** si **VUR** sə
Vichy	**VEESH** ee
vichyssoise	vee shee **SWAHZ**
Vichy water	**VISH** ee
vicinity	və **SIN** ə tee
vicious	**VISH** əs
vicissitude	və **SIS** ə **TOOD**
Victoria, v-	vik **TOR** ee ə
victual	**VIT** əl
victualler	**VIT** ə lər
vicuña	vī **KOO** nə
Vidal, Gore	vee **DAHL, GOR**
vide	**VEE** day
videlicet	vi **DAY** li **KET**
Vidzeme	**VEED** ze me
vie (French)	vee
vie (strive)	vī
Vienna	vee **EN** ə
Vientiane	vyen **TYAHN**
Vietcong	vyet **KONG**
Vietminh	vyet **MIN**
Viet-Nam, Vietnam	vyet **NAHM**
Vigan	**VEE** gahn
vigesimal	vī **JES** ə məl
vigil	**VIJ** əl
vigilant	**VIJ** ə lənt
vigilante	**VIJ** ə **LAN** tee
vignette	vin **YET**
Vigny	vee **NYEE**
vigor	**VIG** ər
vigoroso	**VIG** ə **ROH** soh
Viipuri	**VEE** puu **REE**
Viking, v-	**VĪ** king
Vila	**VEE** lah
vilify	**VIL** ə **FĪ**
Viljandi	**VIL** yahn dee
Viljoen, Marais	fuul **YOON,** mah **RAY**
villa	**VIL** ə

ə ago, a at, ah calm, ahr dark, air care, aw saw, ay say, ch church
e bet, ee me, eer beer, hw what, i is, ī my, *n* French final n vin,

village	VIL ij
villain	VIL ən
Villa-Lobos, Heitor	VEE lah LOH bohs, AY tuur
villanelle	VIL ə NEL
Villa, Pancho	VEE yah, PAHN choh
Villard	və LAHRD
Villeda Morales, Ramón	vee LYAY *th*ah moh RAH les, rah MOHN
Villiers	VIL ərz
Villon	vee YAWN (YAWN French final *n*)
Vilna	VIL nə
vimpa	VIM pə
vinaigrette	VIN ə GRET
vin blanc	van BLAHN (van and BLAHN French final *n*)
Vincennes (France)	van SEN (van French final *n*)
Vincennes (Indiana)	vin SENZ
Vinci, da	VIN chee, də
Vindhya	VIND yah
vindicatory	VIN di kə TOR ee
vindictive	vin DIK tiv
vineyard	VIN yərd
viniculture	VIN ə KUL chər
vinifera	vī NIF ə rə
vin ordinaire	van or dee NAIR (van French final *n*)
vinous	VĪ nəs
vin rouge	van ROOZH (van French final *n*)
vintage	VIN tij
vinyl	VĪ nəl
viol	VĪ əl
viola (instrument)	vee OH lə
viola (plant)	vī OH lə
violable	VĪ ə lə bəl
viola da gamba	vee OH lə də GOM bə
viola d'amore	vee OH lə dah MOR ay
violate (v)	VĪ ə LAYT
violate (a)	VĪ ə lət
violet, V-	VĪ ə lət
violin	vī ə LIN
violoncello	vī ə lən CHEL oh
virago	və RAH goh
vireo	VIR ee oh
Virgil	VUR jəl

o on, oh oat, oi boy, oo soon, oor poor, or for, ow cow, sh shush,
th thin, *th* this, u up, ur spur, uu book, *zh* pleasure

Virgilian	vər JIL yən
virginal	VUR jə nəl
Virgo	VUR goh
virgule	VUR gyool
viridescent	VIR ə DES ənt
virile	VIR əl
virility	və RIL ə tee
Virtanen, Artturi	VIR tah NEN, AHRT tuu ree
virtu	vur TOO
virtual	VUR choo əl
virtue	VUR choo
virtuosa	VUR choo OH sə
virtuosi	VUR choo OH see
virtuosic	VUR choo OH sik
virtuosity	VUR choo OS ə tee
virtuoso	VUR choo OH soh
virtuous	VUR choo əs
virulent	VIR yə lənt
virus	VĪ rəs
visa	VEE zə
visage	VIZ ij
vis-à-vis	VEE zə VEE
Visayan	və SĪ ən
viscera	VIS ə rə
viscid	VIS əd
viscosity	vis KOS ə tee
viscount	VĪ kownt
viscous	VIS kəs
viscus	VIS kəs
Vishnevskaya, Galina	veesh NYEV SKĪ ə, gah LEE nə
Visigoth	VIZ ə GOTH
vision	VIZH ən
visionary	VIZH ə NER ee
visor	VĪ zər
Vistula	VIS chuu lə
visual	VIZH oo əl
vitamin	VĪ tə min
Vitebsk	VEE tepsk
vitiate	VISH ee AYT
viticulture	VIT ə KUL chər
Viti Levu	VEE tee LE voo
vitreous	VI tree əs
vitrify	VI trə FĪ
vitriol	VIT ree əl

ə ago, a at, ah calm, ahr dark, air care, aw saw, ay say, ch church
e bet, ee me, eer beer, hw what, i is, ī my, *n* French final n vin,

vitriolic	**VIT** ree **OL** ik
Vitti	**VEE** tee
Vittorio	vi **TAW** ree oh
vituperation	vī **TOO** pə **RAY** shən
vituperative	vī **TOO** pə rə tiv
viva	**VEE** və
vivace	vee **VAH** chay
vivacious	və **VAY** shəs
vivacity	və **VAS** ə tee
Vivaldi	vi **VAHL** dee
vivarium	vī **VA** ree əm
viva voce	**VĪ** və **VOH** see
vivax	**VĪ** vaks
vivify	**VIV** ə **FĪ**
viviparous	və **VIP** ə rəs
vivisection	**VIV** ə **SEK** shən
vixen	**VIK** sən
vizier	və **ZEER**
vizsla	**VIZ***H* lə
Vladimir	**VLAD** ə **MIR**
Vladivostok	**VLAD** ə **VOS** tok
vocalic	voh **KAL** ik
vocalize	**VOH** kə **LĪZ**
vocative	**VOK** ə tiv
Vo Chi Cong	vo chee kong (vo as in *hot*)
vociferous	voh **SIF** ər əs
vodka	**VOD** kə
voilà	vwah **LAH**
voile	voil
voir dire	vwahr **DEER**
Volans	**VOH** lanz
volant	**VOH** lənt
Volapuk	**VOH** lə **PUUK**
volatile	**VOL** ə təl
vol-au-vent	vaw loh **VAHN** (**VAHN** French final *n*)
volcanic	vol **KAN** ik
volcanism	**VOL** kə **NIZ** əm
Volcker, Paul	**VOHL** kər
Volga	**VOL** gə
Volgograd	**VOL** gə **GRAD**
Volio Jiménez, Fernando	voh **LEE** oh hee **MAY** nez, fair **NAHN** doh
volition	və **LISH** ən

---

o on, oh oat, oi boy, oo soon, oor poor, or for, ow cow, sh shush, th thin, *th* this, u up, ur spur, uu book, *zh* pleasure

volitive	**VOL** ə tiv
Volk (German)	fawlk
Volkswagen	**VOHKS WAG** ən
Vologda	**VAW** ləg dah
Volpe	**VOHL** pee
volplane	**VOL** playn
Volpone	vol **POH** nee
Volsunga	**VOL** suung gə
Volta, Alessandro	**VOHL** tə, **AH** les **SAHN** draw
voltaic	vol **TAY** ik
Voltaire	vohl **TAIR**
volte-face	vawlt **FAHS**
Volturno	vawl **TUUR** noh
voluble	**VOL** yə bəl
volume	**VOL** yəm
voluminous	və **LOO** mə nəs
voluntarism	**VOL** ən tə **RIZ** əm
voluptuary	və **LUP** choo **ER** ee
voluptuous	və **LUP** choo əs
volute	və **LOOT**
vomitus	**VOM** ə təs
von, V- (German)	fawn
von Hassel, Kai-Uwe	fawn **HAH** səl, kī **OO** və
Vonnegut, Kurt	**VAHN** i gət, **KUURT**
voodoo	**VOO** doo
voracious	vaw **RAY** shəs
voracity	vaw **RAS** ə tee
vorlage	**FOR LAHG** ə
Voronezh	vaw **RAW** nesh
Vorster	**FAWR** stər
vortex	**VOR** teks
Vosges	voh*zh*
votary	**VOH** tə ree
Votyak	vaw **TYAHK**
vouchsafe	vowch **SAYF**
vox populi	**VOKS POP** yə **LĪ**
voyage	**VOI** ij
voyager	**VOI** i jər
voyageur	v**WAH** yah *ZH***UR**
voyeur	vwah **YUR**
voyeurism	vwah **YUR IZ** əm
Voznesensky, Andrei	v**AWZ** nyə **SEN** skee, **AHN** dray
Vraalsen, Tom Eric	**VROL** sən

ə ago, a at, ah calm, ahr dark, air care, aw saw, ay say, ch church
e bet, ee me, eer beer, hw what, i is, ī my, *n* French final n vin,

Vries	vrees
Vrsac	**VUR** shahts
Vuelta Abajo	**VWEL** tə ə **BAH** hoh
Vuillard	vwee **YAHR**
Vulcan	**VUL** kən
vulgar	**VUL** gər
vulgarian	**VUL GA** ree ən
vulgarism	**VUL** gə **RIZ** əm
vulgarity	**VUL GA** rə tee
Vulgate, v-	**VUL** gayt
vulnerable	**VUL** nər ə bəl
Vulpecula	vul **PEK** yə lə
vulpine	**VUL** pīn
vulva	**VUL** və
Vyatka	**VYAHT** kah
Vyazma	**VYAHZ** mah
Vyborg	**VEE** borg
Vychegda	**VICH** ig də

W

Waal	vahl
Waals, Johannes	**WAWLZ**, yoh **HON** əs
Wabash	**WAW** bash
Wabuge, Wafula	wah **BOO** ge, wah **FOO** lah (ge g almost silent)
Waco	**WAY** koh
Wadai	wah **DĪ**
wadi	**WAH** dee
Wafd	wahft
waft	wahft
Wagner (German)	**VAHG** nər
Wagner (US)	**WAG** nər
Wagnerian	vahg **NIR** ee ən
wagoner, W-	**WAG** ə nər
wagon-lit	va gawn **LEE** (gawn French final n)
Wahhabi	wah **HAH** bee
wahine	wah **HEE** nee
waif	wayf
Waikiki	wī kee **KEE**
wainscot	**WAYN** skət

o on, oh oat, oi boy, oo soon, oor poor, or for, ow cow, sh shush,
th thin, *th* this, u up, ur spur, uu book, *zh* pleasure

wainwright, W-	**WAYN** rīt
waistcoat	**WES** kət
Wakashan	waw **KASH** ən
Wakayama	wah kah yah mah
Waksman, Selman	**WAKS** mən, **SEL** mən
Walachia, Wallachia	wah **LAY** kee ə
Walden	**WAWL** dən
Waldenses	wawl **DEN** seez
Waldheim, Kurt	**VAHLT** hīm, **KUURT**
Waldorf	**WAWL** dorf
Walesa, Lech	vah **WEN** sah, lek
Walker, w-	**WAW** kər
Walküre, Die	vahl **KIR** ee, dee
Wallace	**WOL** əs
Wallachia	wah **LAY** kee ə
wallah	**WOL** ə
walleye	**WAWL** ī
Wallhauser	**WAWL** how zər
Wallis	**WOL** əs
Walloon	wol **OON**
Wallops (island)	**WOL** əps
wallow	**WOL** oh
Walpurgis	vahl **PUUR** gəs
Walpurgisnacht	vahl **PUURG** əs **NAHKT**
Walsingham	**WAWL** sing əm
waltz	wawlts
Walvis	**WAWL** vəs
Wampanoag	**WOM** pə **NOH** ag
wampum	**WOM** pəm
wan	wahn
Wanamaker	**WAH** nə **MAY** kər
wander	**WAHN** dər
Wanderjahr	**VAHN** dər **YAHR**
wanderlust	**WAHN** dər **LUST**
wangan	**WAHN** gən
Wang Zhen	wahng jun
wanigan	**WAHN** i gən
Wankel	**VAHN** kəl
Wan Li	wahn lee
Wanne-Eickel	**VAH** nə **ĪK** əl
Wantagh	**WAHN** taw
wanton	**WAHN** tən
wantonness	**WAHNT** ən nəs

ə ago, a at, ah calm, ahr dark, air care, aw saw, ay say, ch church
e bet, ee me, eer beer, hw what, i is, ī my, n French final n vin,

wapentake	**WOP** ən **TAYK**
wapiti	**WOP** ə tee
Warburton	**WOR BUR** tən
warlock	**WOR** lok
Warnke, Paul	**WORN** kee
warrant	**WOR** ənt
warranty	**WOR** ən tee
warrior	**WOR** ee ər
Warsaw	**WOR** saw
Warszawa	vahr **SHAH** vah
Warwick	**WOR** ik
wary	**WAIR** ee
Wasatch	**WAW** sach
Wasell	wah **SEL**
Wasiuddin, Khwaja	**WAH** see yoo **DEEN, KWAH** jah
wassail	**WAH** səl
Wassermann	**WAH** sər mən
wastrel	**WAY** strəl
Watanabe, Kiichi	wah tah nah be, kee eech ee
Waterbury	**WAW** tər **BER** ee
Waterloo	**WAW** tər **LOO**
Watling	**WOT** ling
Watteau	wah **TOH**
Waugh	waw
Waukegan	waw **KEE** gən
waxen	**WAKS** ən
Waziristan	wah **ZIR** i **STAN**
weal	weel
weald, W-	weeld
wean	ween
weaponry	**WEP** ən ree
wear	wair
wearisome	**WIR** ee səm
weary	**WIR** ee
Weber (German)	**VAY** bər
weber (physics)	**WEB** ər
Wechmar, Rudiger von	**VEK** mahr, **RUUD** i gər fawn
Wechsler	**WEKS** lər
Wedgwood	**WEJ** wuud
Wednesday	**WENZ** day
weevil	**WEE** vəl
Weicker, Lowell	**WĪK** ər, **LOH** əl

o on, oh oat, oi boy, oo soon, oor poor, or for, ow cow, sh shush,
th thin, *th* this, u up, ur spur, uu book, *zh* pleasure

Weifang	way fahng
weigela	wī **JEE** lə
Weihai	way hī
Weil, Simone	**VAY**, see **MUN**
Weill, Kurt	vīl, kuurt
Weimar	**VĪ** mahr
Weimaraner	**VĪ** mə **RAH** nər
Weinberger, Caspar	**WĪN BUR** gər, **KAS** pər
Wei Quoqing	way choh ching
weir	wir
weird	wird
Weismann, Weissmann (German)	**VĪS** mahn
Weizmann, Chaim	**VĪTS** mahn, **HĪ** əm
welkin	**WEL** kən
Wellesley	**WELZ** lee
Wellington	**WEL** ing tən
Welsbach	**WELZ** bak
Weltanschauung	**VELT** ahn **SHOW** uung (**SHOW** as in *cow*)
Weltansicht	**VELT AHN** zikt
Weltpolitik	**VELT** pawl i **TEEK**
Weltschmerz	**VELT** shmerts
Welty, Eudora	**WEL** tee, yoo **DOR** ə
Wemys, -s	weemz
Wenceslaus	**WEN** sə **SLAWS**
Wenchow, Wenzhou, Wen-chou	wun joh
Wend, w-	wend
Werther (German)	**VAIR** tər
Weser	**VAY** zər
Wesley	**WES** lee
Wesleyan	**WES** lee ən
Westminster	**WES MIN** stər
Westphalia	wes **FAYL** yə
Wetterhorn	**VET** ər **HORN**
whale	hwayl
wharf	hworf
wharfinger	**HWORF** ən jər
Wharton	**HWORT** ən
what	hwot
whatever	hwot **EV** ər

ə ago, a at, ah calm, ahr dark, air care, aw saw, ay say, ch church
e bet, ee me, eer beer, hw what, i is, ī my, n French final n vin,

wheat	hweet
whelp	hwelp
when	hwen
whence	hwens
whenever	hwen EV ər
where	hwair
whereas	hwair AZ
whereof	hwair UV
wherever	hwair EV ər
wherewithal	HWAIR wi*th* AWL
whether	HWE*TH* ər
whey	hway
which	hwich
whiffletree	HWIF əl TREE
Whig	hwig
while	hwīl
whilom	HWĪ ləm
whimsical	HWIM zi kəl
whimsy	HWIM zee
whine	hwīn
whinny	HWIN ee
whippet	HWIP ət
whippoorwill	HWIP ər WIL
whir	hwur
whirl	hwurl
whisper	HWIS pər
whist	hwist
whistle	HWIS əl
Whistler, w-	HWIS lər
whit	hwit
white	hwīt
whited	HWĪT əd
whither	HWI*TH* ər
Whitsunday	HWIT sən DAY
Whittier	HWIT ee ər
whoa	hwoh
whole	hohl
wholesome	HOHL səm
wholly	HOHL ee
whom	hoom
whoop	hoop
whoosh	hwoosh
whore	hawr

---

o on, oh oat, oi boy, oo soon, oor poor, or for, ow cow, sh shush,
th thin, *th* this, u up, ur spur, uu book, *zh* pleasure

whortleberry	HWUR təl **BER** ee
why	hwī
Wichita	**WICH** ə **TAW**
Wickersham	**WI** kər shəm
wickiup	**WIK** ee **UP**
Wicklow	**WIK** loh
widgeon	**WIJ** ən
widget	**WIJ** ət
wie geht's	vee **GAYTS**
Wien (German)	veen
wiener	**WEE** nər
Wiener, Norbert	**WEE** nər, **NOR** bərt
Wiener schnitzel, w-	**VEE** nər **SHNIT** səl
Wiesbaden	**VEES BAHD** ən
Wiesel, Elie	vee **ZEL**, **EL** ee
Wigglesworth	**WIG** əlz **WURTH**
wight, W-	wīt
wildebeest	**WĪL** də **BEEST**
Wilder	**WĪL** dər
wilderness	**WIL** dər nəs
Wilhelmina	**WIL** hel **MEE** nə
Wilhelm Meister	**VIL** helm **MĪ** stər
Wilhelmshaven	**VIL** helms **HAH** fən
Wilhelmstrasse	**VIL** helm **SHTRAH** sə
Wilkes	wilks
Wilkes-Barre	**WILKS BA** rə
Willamette	wə **LAM** ət
Willard	**WIL** ərd
Willemstad	**WIL** əm **STAHT**
Willesden	**WILZ** dən
Willis	**WIL** əs
Willoch, Kåre	**VIL** ək, **KOR** ə
willowy	**WIL** ə wee
Wiltshire	**WILT** shər
wily	**WĪ** lee
Wimbledon	**WIM** bəl dən
wimple	**WIM** pəl
Winchester	**WIN CHES** tər
windage	**WIN** dij
Windermere	**WIN** dər **MIR**
Windhoek	**VINT** huuk
windlass	**WIND** ləs
Windsor	**WIN** zər

ə ago, a at, ah calm, ahr dark, air care, aw saw, ay say, ch church
e bet, ee me, eer beer, hw what, i is, ī my, n French final n vin,

windward, W-	**WIND** wərd
Winnebago	**WIN** ə **BAY** goh
Winnepesaukee	**WIN** ə pə **SAW** kee
Winnipeg	**WIN** ə **PEG**
Winnipegosis	**WIN** ə pə **GOH** səs
Winona	wə **NOH** nə
Winooski	wə **NOOS** kee
Winslow	**WINZ** loh
winsome	**WIN** səm
Winston-Salem	**WIN** stən **SAY** ləm
Winterthur (Switzerland)	**VINT** ər **TUUR**
Winthrop	**WIN** thrəp
winy	**WĪ** nee
wiry	**WĪR** ee
wisdom	**WIZ** dəm
Wisla	**VEE** slah
wisteria	wis **TIR** ee ə
with	wi*th*
withal	wi*th* **AWL**
withdraw	wi*th* **DRAW**
wither	**WI*TH*** ər
withstand	with **STAND**
Wittenberg	**WIT** ən **BURG**
Witwatersrand	**WIT** **WAWT** ərz **RAND**
wizard	**WIZ** ərd
wizened	**WIZ** ənd
Wodehouse	**WUUD** hows
Woden, Wodan	**WOHD** ən
Wojtyla, Karol	voi **TEE** wah, **KAHR** əl
wolfram	**WUUL** frəm
Wolfram von Eschenbach	**VAWL** frahm fawn **ESH** ən **BAHK**
Wollstonecraft	**WUUL** stən **KRAFT**
Wolseley	**WUULZ** lee
Wolsey	**WUUL** zee
wombat	**WOM** bat
wonder	**WUN** dər
Wonsan	**WUN** sahn
wont	wawnt
won't	wohnt
wonted	**WAWNT** əd
wonton	**WAHN** **TAHN**

o on, oh oat, oi boy, oo soon, oor poor, or for, ow cow, sh shush,
th thin, *th* this, u up, ur spur, uu book, *zh* pleasure

Woodward	**WUUD** wərd
woof	wuuf
woofer	**WUUF** ər
Woolf	wuulf
Woollcott, Alexander	**WUUL** kət
Woolwich	**WUUL** ij
Woolworth	**WUUL** wurth
Woomera	**WUUM** ə rə
Woonsocket	woon **SOK** ət
Woosung	woo suung
Worcester	**WUUS** tər
Worcestershire	**WUUS** tər **SHIR**
Worms	wurmz
worship	**WUR** shəp
worsted (yarn)	**WUUS** təd
Worthington	**WUR** *th*ing tən
worthy	**WUR** *th*ee
Wotan	**VOH** tahn
Wotton	**WUUT** ən
Wouk, Herman	wohk
Wozzeck	**VAW** tsek
wraith	rayth
Wrangel, -l	**RANG** gəl
wrath	rath
wreak	reek
wreath	reeth
wreathe	ree*th*
Wren, w-	ren
wrestle	**RES** əl
wretched	**RECH** əd
writhe	rī*th*
Wroclaw	**VRAWT** slahf
wroth	rawth
wrought	rawt
wry	rī
Wuchang	woo chahng
Wuhan	woo hahn
wunderkind	**VUUN** dər **KINT**
Wuppertal	**VUUP** ər **TAHL**
Württemberg	**WUR** təm **BURG**
Würzburg	**WURTS** burg
Wuzhou	woo joh
Wyandot, -te	**WĪ** ən **DOT**

ə ago, a at, ah calm, ahr dark, air care, aw saw, ay say, ch church
e bet, ee me, eer beer, hw what, i is, ī my, *n* French final n vin,

Wyatt	**WĪ** ət
Wycherley	**WICH** ər lee
Wyclif, -fe	**WIK** lif
Wyeth	**WĪ** əth
Wyndham	**WIN** dəm
Wynyard	**WIN** yərd
Wyoming	wī **OH** ming
Wyszynski, Cardinal Stefan	və **SHIN** skee, **STEF** ahn

X

Xanadu	**ZAN** ə doo
xanthic	**ZAN** thik
Xanthippe, Xantippe	zan **TIP** ee
Xavier	**ZAY** vee ər
Xavier (Spanish)	hah **VYER**
xebec	**ZEE** bek
Xenocrates	zi **NOK** rə ᴛᴇᴇᴢ
xenon	**ZEE** non
xenophobia	ᴢᴇɴ ə **FOH** bee ə
Xenophon	**ZEN** ə fən
Xeres	**SHER** eez
xeric	**ZI** rik
xerography	zə **ROG** rə fee
xerophilous	zə **ROF** ə ləs
xerophthalmia	ᴢɪ ʀᴏꜰ **THAL** mee ə
xerophyte	**ZI** rə ꜰĪᴛ
Xerox	**ZI** roks
Xerxes	**ZURK** seez
Xhosa	**KOH** sah
xi	zī
Xi (river)	shee
Xi'an	shee ahn
Xiang	shee ahng
Xi Chongxun	shee chawng shoon
Xingú	sheeng **GOO**
Xining	shee ning
Xinjiang Uygur	**SHIN** jee ᴀʜɴɢ **WEE** gər
Xinxiang	shin shee ahng
xiphoid	**ZĪ** foid

---

o on, oh oat, oi boy, oo soon, oor poor, or for, ow cow, sh shush,
th thin, *th* this, u up, ur spur, uu book, *zh* pleasure

Xizang	shee zahng
Xi Zhongxun	shee jawng shoon
Xmas	**KRIS** məs
Xochimilco	**SOH** shi **MEEL** koh
Xosa	**KOH** sah
Xuanhua	shoo ahn hwah
Xu Shiyou	shoo shu yoh
Xu Xiangqian	shoo shee ahng chee ahn
Xuzhou	shoo joh
xylem	$\overline{\text{ZI}}$ ləm
xylene	$\overline{\text{ZI}}$ leen
xylography	zī **LOG** rə fee
xylophone	$\overline{\text{ZI}}$ lə **FOHN**
xyster	**ZIS** tər
Xystus	**ZIS** təs

Y

Yablonoi	**YAH** blaw **NOI**
yacht	yot
Yadkin	**YAD** kən
yagi	**YAH** gee
Yahoo	**YAH** hoo
Yahweh	**YAH** we (we as in *wet*)
Yaker, Layachi	**YAH** kah, lī **AH** chee
Yakima	**YAK** ə mə
Yeltsin, Boris	**YEL** tsin, bohr **EES**
Yakut	yah **KOOT**
Yakutsk	yah **KOOTSK**
Yalow, Rosalyn	**YAL** oh
Yalta	**YAWL** tə
Yalu	**YAH** loo
Yalung	yah luung
Yamani, Ahmed Zaki	yah **MEN** ee, **AHK** med **ZEK** ee
Yameogo, Maurice	yah may **OH** goh, maw **REES**
Yang Chen Ning	yahng jun ning
Yang Dezhi	yahng du ju
Yang Shangkun	yahng shahng koon
Yangtze	yang tsee
Yang Yong	yahng yawng
Yanqui, y-	**YAHN** kee
Yaoundé	yah uun **DAY**

ə ago, a at, ah calm, ahr dark, air care, aw saw, ay say, ch church
e bet, ee me, eer beer, hw what, i is, ī my, *n* French final n vin,

Yao Yilin	yow yee leen (yow as in *cow*)
yap	yap
Yap	yop
Yaqui	**YAH** kee
Yarborough	**YAHR** bə roh
yare	yair
Yarmouth	**YAHR** məth
yarmulke	**YAHR** məl kə
Yaroslavl	YAH rə **SLAHV** əl
yaupon	**YAW** pən
Yazoo	ya **ZOO**
yclept	i **KLEPT**
Ydígoras Fuentes	ee **DEE** gaw rahs **FWEN** tes
yea	yay
yearling	**YEER** ling
Yeats	yayts
Ye Jiangying	yu jee ahng yeeng
Yakovlev, Aleksandr	**YAHK** ov lev, AHL ek **SAHN** dər
Yemen	**YEM** ən
Yenisei, Yenisey	YEN ə **SAY**
yeoman	**YOH** mən
Yerba Buena	YAIR bə **BWAY** nə
Yerevan	YER ə **VON**
Yesenin-Volpin	ye **SAY** nyin **VOHL** pin
Yeshiva, y-	yə **SHEE** və
yeti	**YET** ee
Yevtushenko, Yevgeni	YEV tə **SHENG** koh, yev **GAY** nee
yew	yoo
Yggdrasill	**IG** drə SIL
Ymir	**EE** mir
yoga	**YOH** gə
yogi	**YOH** gee
yogurt	**YOH** gərt
Yoknapatawpha	YOK nə pə **TAW** fə
Yokohama	YOH kə **HAH** mə
Yokosuka	yoh **KOH** sə kə
yolk	yohk
Yom Kippur	YOHM **KIP** ər
Yorkshire	**YORK** shir
Yoruba	**YOR** ə bə
Yosemite	yoh **SEM** ə tee
Yoshihito	yoh shee hee toh
Yost	yohst

---

o on, oh oat, oi boy, oo soon, oor poor, or for, ow cow, sh shush,
th thin, *th* this, u up, ur spur, uu book, *zh* pleasure

Youlou, Abbe	**YOO** luu, **AH** be
youth	yooth
youths	yoo*th*z
Ypres	**EE** prə
Ypsilanti	ɪP sə **LAN** tee
Yquem	ee **KEM**
Yser	ee **ZER**
Yseult	i **SOOLT**
ytterbium	i **TUR** bee əm
yttrium	**I** tree əm
Yucatan, Yucatán	YOO kə **TAN**
Yucatec	**YOO** kə TEK
Yucatecan	YOO kə **TEK** ən
yucca	**YUK** ə
Yuen	yoo **EN**
Yuga	**YUUG** ə
Yugoslavia	YOO goh **SLAH** vee ə
Yugov, Anton	**YOO** gawf, **AHN** tohn
Yukon	**YOO** kon
Yuma	**YOO** mə
Yunnan	yoo nahn
Yu Qiuli	yoo chee oo lee
yurt	yuurt

Z

zabaglione	ZAH bəl **YOH** nee
Zabulon	**ZAB** yə lən
Zacatecas	SAH kah TE kahs
Zachariah	ZAK ə RĪ ə
Zacharias	ZAK ə RĪ əs
Zagazig	ZAHG ah **ZEEG**
Zagreb	**ZAHG** reb
zaibatsu	zī **BAHT** soo
Zaire	zah **IR**
Zambezi	zam **BEE** zee
Zambia	**ZAM** bee ə
Zamboanga	ZAM boh **AHN** gə
Zangwill, Israel	**ZANG** wil
Zanzibar	**ZAN** zə BAHR
Zaporozhe	ZAH paw **RAWZ***H* yə

ə ago, a at, ah calm, ahr dark, air care, aw saw, ay say, ch church
e bet, ee me, eer beer, hw what, i is, ī my, *n* French final n vin,

Zapotec	ZAHP ə TEK
Zarathustra	ZA rə THOOS trə
zareba	zə REE bə
Zarif, Mohammad Farid	thə REEF, moh HAM med fe REED
Zarubin	zah ROO bin
Zatec	ZHAH tets
zealot	ZEL ət
zealous	ZEL əs
zebra	ZEE brə
zebu	ZEE byoo
Zebulon	ZEB yə LON
Zebulun	ZEB yə lən
Zeebrugge	ZEE bruug ə
Zeitgeist	TSĪT gīst
Zeitschrift	TSĪT shrift
Zeitung	TSĪ tuung
Zelaya, Jorge Luis	say LĪ ə, HOR gay loo EES
Zellerbach	ZEL ər bak
Zelotes	zi LOH teez
Zemgale	ZEM gah le
Zen	zen
zenana	zə NAH nə
Zend	zend
Zend-Avesta	ZEN də VES tə
zener	ZEE nər
Zenger, John Peter	ZENG ər
zenith	ZEE nəth
Zeno	ZEE noh
zephyr	ZEF ər
Zephyrus	ZEF ər əs
zeppelin, Z-	ZEP ə lən
Zerbo, Sayé	zer BOH, sī YAY
Zermatt	tser MAHT
Zernike, Frits	ZAIR nə kə, FRITS
zero	ZEE roh
Zetterling, Mai	ZE tər LING, MĪ
zeugma	ZOOG mə
Zeus	zoos
Zhang Aiping	jahng ī peeng
Zhang Tingfa	jahng teeng fah
Zhang Wenjin	jahng wun jeen
Zhao Ziyang	jow zee yahng (jow as in *cow*)

---

o on, oh oat, oi boy, oo soon, oor poor, or for, ow cow, sh shush,
th thin, *th* this, u up, ur spur, uu book, *zh* pleasure

Zhejiang	ju jee ahng
Zhivkov, Todor	*ZH*EEV kawf, TOH tawr
Zhulev, Stoyan	*ZH*OO lev, stoh YAHN
Zia ul-Haq, Mohammad	ZEE ah ool HAHK, moh HAH məd
Ziegler, Karl	TSEEG lər
ziggurat	ZIG ə RAT
Zimbabwe	zim BAH bway
Zimyanin, Mikhail	zeem YAH nyin, mee hī YEEL
zinnia	ZIN ee ə
Zinzendorf	TSIN tsən DORF
Zionism	ZĪ ə NIZ əm
Zipangu	zə pang goo
zircon	ZUR kon
zither	ZI*TH* ər
ziti	ZEE tee
zloty	ZLAW tee
zlotys	ZLAW teez
zoanthropy	zoh AN thrə pee
zodiac	ZOH dee AK
zodiacal	zoh DĪ ə kəl
Zoe, Zoë	ZOH ee
Zola, Émile	ZOH lə, ay MEEL
Zollverein	TSAWL fer ĪN
Zomba	ZOM bə
zombie	ZOM bee
Zolotas, Xenophon	zoh LOH tahs, ksen oh FAWN
Zonta	ZON tə
zoolatry	zoh OL ə tree
zoological	ZOH ə LOJ i kəl
zoology	zoh OL ə jee
zoomorphic	ZOH ə MOR fik
zoomorphism	ZOH ə MOR fiz əm
zoophyte	ZOH ə FĪT
Zoppi, Vittorio	DZOH pee, vee TAW ree oh
Zorin, Valerian	ZOR in, vah lair ee AHN
Zorn	sorn
Zoroaster	ZOH roh A stər
zoster	ZOH stər
Zouave	zoo AHV
Zschau	show (as in *cow*)
Zubin	ZUUB ən
zucchetto	zuu KET oh

ə ago, a at, ah calm, ahr dark, air care, aw saw, ay say, ch church
e bet, ee me, eer beer, hw what, i is, ī my, *n* French final n vin,

zucchini	zuu **KEE** nee
Zug	tsook
Zuider Zee	zīd ər **ZEE**
Zumbado-Jimenez, Fernando	suum **BAH** doh hee **MEN** ez, fer **NAN** doh
Zuñi	**ZOO** nee
Zurich	**ZUUR** ik
Zweig	zwīg
zwieback	**ZWĪ** bak
Zwingli	**ZWING** lee
zygote	**ZĪ** goht
zymurgy	**ZĪ** mur jee

o on, oh oat, oi boy, oo soon, oor poor, or for, ow cow, sh shush, th thin, *th* this, u up, ur spur, uu book, *zh* pleasure